DATE DUE

GAYLORD			PRINTED IN U.S.A.

THE DYNAMICS OF BUSINESS

Felix qui potuit rerum cognoscere causas.
—Vergil.

THE DYNAMICS OF BUSINESS

*An Analysis of Trends, Cycles, and Time Relationships
in American Economic Activity Since 1700 and
Their Bearing upon Governmental and
Business Policy*

By

NORMAN J. SILBERLING

*Late Professor of Business Research, Graduate School
of Business, Stanford University; Late President,
Silberling Research Corporation, Ltd.*

FIRST EDITION

McGRAW-HILL BOOK COMPANY, Inc.
NEW YORK AND LONDON
1943

THE MAPLE PRESS COMPANY, YORK, PA.

PREFACE

In offering "The Dynamics of Business" to the business and economic world the late Dr. Norman J. Silberling presents an analysis of the long-term trends of American production, price levels, and income, based upon new measurements, followed by a systematic and graphically illustrated discussion of cyclical movements in agriculture, building, production, trade, finance, and wages, leading to theoretical and practical conclusions for both business and governmental policy.

Economics, according to Dr. Silberling, has been mainly concerned during the past century with theorizing rather than measurement. It consisted primarily of metaphysics rather than science. Its purpose has been to investigate the theoretical laws of price and income distribution on the assumption of free competition in a capitalistic system in which growth tendencies and institutional changes are considered unimportant. Insofar as these artificial assumptions are occasionally approximated in the real world this theorizing may have some value, but as a basis for governmental or management policy it has been found to be of relatively little use. Unfortunately economists have long been captivated by the deductive method rather than interested in the observation of actual conditions, and as a result their discussion of such actual conditions and the practical problems of policy has not until very recently attempted to deal with the distortion of "normal" tendencies and the disturbance of booms and depressions and wars.

The study of business dynamics, as distinct from the foregoing approach, stresses the importance of change insofar as this manifests itself in measurable growth tendencies and in the rhythmic vibrations of the business cycle. It is mainly concerned with the course of general progress and the cyclical tendencies in industry and trade, prices, and income, as represented in a general way through composite index numbers or aggregate experience. Conceived in this way, dynamic measurements record historical sequence as a continuous development, and in the course of this continuity there is opportunity to observe the interaction of forces and the impact of political and other noneconomic tendencies upon economic and business processes. In recent years the amount of quantitative data for the measurement of dynamic tendencies has been rapidly increasing and it is now possible to present a fairly clear picture of the amount of growth and the extent of distortion in the course of that growth resulting from specific events. It has also become possible to distinguish

v

to a considerable extent between external and internal forces producing economic expansion and depression.

To the extent that these measurements are possible there is opened up the further field of statistical forecasting and the use of dynamic measurements by business management in order to protect itself against unfavorable external influences. A further and very important field of usefulness is in the better planning of public policy in order to avoid measures that obstruct progress and growth or produce unnecessary cyclical disturbance. Both business managers and politicians have a tendency to follow precedent rather than to plan for the future intelligently. Through long-term measurements there is thus being developed a new applied science endowed with perspective and the principle of continuity which is capable of throwing a powerful new light on intelligent planning.

It was Dr. Silberling's belief that the subject of the business cycle is but one aspect of dynamics, but that thus far that phase has been given more attention than the study of long-term trends, the interaction of dynamic factors for practical policy designed to facilitate future growth in wealth and production, and the avoidance of booms and depressions. He felt that most books on the subject were merely an extrapolation of traditional economic theory rather than an attempt to formulate new theoretical principles on the basis of actual measurement. Only in more recent years has there been definite progress in combining measurement with careful reasoning in the field of business dynamics and particularly business cycles.

The title, "The Dynamics of Business," was selected to emphasize the fact that attention is given in this volume to the trends and relationships of economic factors as well as business-cycle phenomena as such. The book aims to reach effectively the general reader, the business and financial executive, the governmental administrator, the legislator, and the more advanced students (college juniors and up) in the fields of economics, government, history, sociology, law, engineering, and agriculture. The book begins with the subject of long-term trends, first dealing with population growth from the very beginning of the American people, and then discussing the measurement of the general trend of production and trade which is carried back to 1700 or considerably further than Snyder or other authors have attempted hitherto. This long period of perspective affords an exceptional opportunity to observe the rate of growth and it is possible for the first time to reveal the intermediate trend or long wave of economic progress, as well as the shorter fluctuations of the business cycle through a period of nearly two and one-half centuries. The long wave of trade and production is shown to be closely related to wars and to political events, and the book may be said to make a distinct contribution to the knowledge of the economic and dynamic effects of major wars. This phase of the subject is then further analyzed in terms of price-level changes which are shown to be produced mainly by war conditions. New measures of the relation of money and credit to price level are discussed, and the work of Carl Snyder on this subject is carried back with more refined methods almost to the beginning of the nineteenth century. This is followed by a new theoretical presentation of the relations between money, credit, trade, and prices in which an effort is made to correct prevailing misconceptions of the "equation of exchange" as originally formulated by Irving Fisher.

Having demonstrated the statistical and theoretical forces operating upon the price level, a foundation is laid for a discussion of the value of trade and production, the national income, and the important component of farm income which is highly sympathetic to price movements. The political bearings of farm-income fluctuations are particularly emphasized and this is followed by an entire chapter on the short-term cycles of agriculture. Attention is then given to the cyclical behavior of the building industry and real estate activity. In this connection new and important basic indexes are presented extending back to the beginning of the nineteenth century and revealing for the first time the true significance of the building cycle as a major factor in business cycles generally. This is further amplified by similar long-term indexes of the cycles of transportation construction, which represent an entirely new contribution to the subject. What is usually regarded as the business cycle is shown to have been, in American experience at least, the joint result of several types of construction and land-development speculation.

From the foregoing analysis Dr. Silberling proceeds to draw important conclusions with respect to the kind of credit and capital financing which produce or accentuate cyclical disturbances. Here, as in other parts of the book, the principles are drawn from the facts, reversing the procedure so commonly encountered of selecting certain facts to "prove" a theory. One of the most important conclusions drawn from American economic experience is shown to be the disregard for sound capital use through what is known as excessive trading on the equity, and this is demonstrated in succeeding chapters to illustrate its pervasive importance as a source of economic excesses and breakdowns, including the international depression of the 1930's.

The Great Depression of the 1930's created an urgent need for constructive economic policy, but as generally acceptable principles of dynamic economics had not yet been formulated so that this could be put into practice the New Deal worked out its reconstruction by the use of many odds and ends of panaceas and amateur opportunism, thus complicating many of the problems encountered. Thus, public policy has become in itself unquestionably a source of cyclical instability and illustrations of this are given.   At the same time recent legislation has accomplished many desirable objectives and it has seemed important to present these in some detail so that the reader may form a clearer concept of the kind of world he will live in after a great world upheaval and its aftermath of reform and reconstructive legislation.   Throughout this discussion attention has been given continually to the basic principles to determine the soundness or wisdom of public policy.

The discussion then reverts to the dynamics of the financial markets as they bear upon interest rates, stock prices, and corporate earnings. In connection with the interest rate Dr. Silberling has presented some new measures of the factors which appear to govern changes in interest rates and the high-grade bond market.   The factors influencing the stock market are illustrated and the subject of stock market forecasting is discussed.   Attention is then given to the dynamics of corporate earning power, internal savings, and expenditures for capital equipment, with illustrations drawn from manufacturing and public service corporations. Surprising tendencies are revealed regarding the ability of American corporations to accumulate savings in recent years and in this connection considerable critical analysis of government policy looking toward the expropriation of private capital is included.   It is then shown that consumer earnings, savings, and capital investment, both for individuals and for families, have tendencies essentially similar to those shown by corporations.   A novel presentation is developed of the merchandising cycle, and important dynamic aspects of retail trade and consumer credit are considered.

As retail trade is so closely dependent upon wage income Dr. Silberling has devoted an entire chapter to the dynamics of wages in relation to labor productivity and employment covering a longer period, it is believed, than is presented in any other available book.   Some important conclusions are drawn with respect to the forces which have governed the broad changes in industrial wage rates and policies which are thereby indicated as desirable.   This is followed by a more detailed discussion of the means of introducing more stability in wage income through unemployment compensation or similar devices.   This in turn suggests the place that business management should occupy in better planning of management policies as a means of preventing unemployment crises and improving the return on business capital.   New methods of business forecasting are developed and another whole chapter is devoted to the practical application of statistical forecasting to business policy.   After a further discussion of the merits and defects of rigid and fluctuating prices, insofar as these bear upon both business and governmental policy, the book concludes with a chapter on the future trend of the American economy and the contribution to future capital and income growth which might be made by a better system of taxation and by more general acceptance of the principle of private property and its protection against the encroachments of collectivism.

In order that the technical reader may understand exactly how the basic indexes presented in this book have been developed, a Statistical Appendix has been added summarizing the methods used in these measurements. One of the most important features of "The Dynamics of Business" is the care which has been used in preparing the charts, of which there are 76 in the volume. As many of these exhibits portray the dynamic aspects of American business over long periods of time, Dr. Silberling believed that the book would be of value indefinitely. No other book now available presents anything like the wealth of illustrations to which the reader may turn to obtain a clear idea of what has happened and how various aspects of the economic system are related to other aspects. Most of the exhibits are drawn to ratio scale in order to carry through the idea of proportionality, and the underlying principle is clearly explained in an early chapter so that every reader can understand the meaning of the scales.

"The Dynamics of Business" breaks new ground in the attempt to analyze the causal factors creating business cycles. Dr. Silberling had stated on various occasions that no other book known to him analyzes causation satisfactorily, and that most books have merely been concerned with the manner in which small booms become large booms and small depressions become great depressions. Much attention in the past has been given to prices as the central fact of business dynamics, but it was Dr. Silberling's opinion this has merely led to a superficial kind of study in getting to the root of things. He maintained that it is not until one has grasped the significance of dynamic behavior in terms of production, prices, income, the divergent tendencies of agriculture and manufacturing, the peculiarities of wages, interest, profits, and the outstanding momentum of construction as a dynamic factor that clear and accurate reasoning can proceed.

This book lays the foundation for various further lines of scientific research by revealing the nature of the dynamic behavior of building, real estate, agriculture, merchandising, and manufacturing. A basis is provided for the development of a new science of industry analysis, the need for which is already urgent. In pointing toward certain specific factors as the prime movers in booms and depressions, the book may be instrumental in furthering the formulation of sound governmental policy in the post-war period. And in giving for the first time emphasis to systematic procedure in planning management policy a basis is laid for the development of a technique of management and a wider use by

executives of business statistics for internal control.   In the last analysis
the American people are going to move either in the direction of totalitarian dictatorship, which is another form of feudalism, or they will
reaffirm the value and dignity of business management as a means of providing for expansion of real wealth and a higher standard of living.   If
it can be generally understood that capitalism, fortified by a wise use of
capital and credit, a rational tax system, and a few well selected and
strategic devices to avert booms and depressions, is by no means obsolete,
then it will be easier to understand why collectivism of any kind is a sham
and a delusion.

It is not easy to conclude this preface.   Dr. Silberling had given more
than a decade of painstaking research and careful analysis to all the
factors which he believed essential in developing what he termed a "new
science of industry analysis."   He took nothing for granted.   A most
searching analysis and the most exacting tests were made at every step.
The manuscript had been completed, the charts and Statistical Appendix
finished, and the proofs for more than three-quarters of the book returned
to the publisher.   It was Sunday, October eighteenth.   That afternoon
tragedy struck—Dr. Silberling was seized with a heart attack and died
within a few minutes.   Would that he might have lived to see not only
the completion of "The Dynamics of Business," but its reception by the
thoughtful leaders in education, government, and industry!   It is
probable that no scholar has ever given more unselfishly of himself to
complete his magnum opus than Dr. Silberling gave to this study.

The Preface had not been written.   However, from Dr. Silberling's
notes, his correspondence, and from years of association with him, I have
endeavored to present here something of his aims and methods, his point
of view, and his genuine accomplishment.   Any failure to state his true
point of view must be attributed to one's inability to speak fully and
correctly for another.   To his assistants who had worked with him and
to his colleagues and fellow scientists wherever located, I express in Dr.
Silberling's behalf sincere appreciation and deep gratitude for all assistance given in the preparation of this volume.   In "The Dynamics of
Business," my fellow workers in education and industry, you behold the
mind of a true scientist, the judgment of a mature and practical man, and
the soul of a pioneer—one unafraid to step out ahead of the procession
and point the way to his fellow men to richer and fuller living.   That was
Norman Silberling's mission on earth.

J. Hugh Jackson,

Dean, Graduate School of Business,
Stanford University.

Stanford University, Calif.,
  December, 1942.

CONTENTS

THE DYNAMICS OF BUSINESS

CHAPTER 1

INTRODUCTION

A thoughtful businessman, reminiscing upon his progress through the years, would undoubtedly be impressed by the pervasive element of *change*. He would be inclined to reflect upon the manner in which his enterprise had grown from a modest start; how it had adjusted itself again and again to new conditions in the course of that growth; and how its structure and organization had been subject to repeated revision.

Such a survey of the fortunes of a particular business unit—a manufacturing firm, a store, or a farm—might be developed in voluminous detail. There might be episodes shaped and colored by the personality of a founder or a manager; there would be in the full story many accidental circumstances of fire or flood or failure or fortunate turns of the wheel of chance. To each established enterprise there attaches much specialized history, differentiating that unit from the experiences of other units. We should not be able to derive from such an individual business experience anything in the nature of basic principles capable of general application. We might derive inspiration, suggestion, and frequent glimpses of the more general changes in the economic or political atmosphere; but these impressions would usually be blurred and vague.

We might, of course, derive from an intensive study of the history of a business some fairly clear evidence of the pattern of its growth— the slow, uncertain beginning, the period of assured survival, the more rapid acceleration in importance and prestige. And, finally, toward the later years, we might note a tendency to lose some of the old momentum or even to undergo more or less retrogression.

The life of the average individual firm, in the broad perspective of human affairs, is relatively short. The proportion of failures among new enterprises is known to be astonishingly high. If we were to limit our attention to those who initiate but soon fall by the wayside, we might form an impression of business fortune strongly tinged with the element of hazard and difficulty.   But even the more successful enterprises rarely enjoy long life.   Their periods of growth stand in relation to the more general economic trend of the nation as the growth of trees stands in contrast to the growth of a forest.   And the environment of an individual business unit is usually more or less localized; to a high degree it contains the many peculiarities of geography.   It involves changes in the surrounding forces of competition, both within the industry and without, and the influence of these ever-varying environmental factors will by no means be comparable among the various establishments.

Finally, if we limit our observations to a given concern, we are likely to restrict attention to phases of accomplishment that are expressed in terms of money whereby the individual management largely calculates and measures its performance.   The actual *volume* of wealth or service created, as distinct from the *value* of sales, prices, profits, or payrolls, is not so readily measurable.   It is often exceedingly difficult to discover the reasons for changes in these various results, since the many diverse factors affecting the organization from *outside* tend to be so closely intermingled with changes in *internal* policies reflecting the caliber of management or the terms of ownership and control as they exist from time to time.   Thus, a study of the *dynamics* of the business in terms of an individual enterprise would probably in most instances throw but a dim and flickering light upon the broad changes in the business atmosphere, and exact measurement would prove difficult.

If now we broaden our picture to include an *entire industry* by considering a composite record of the experience of all the units engaged in a given type of business, we find more significant patterns revealed.   We need, of course, a large enough segment of a given field to enable us to ascertain whether among these more or less comparable concerns a certain amount of common experience has stood out against the particular details fashioned by locality, personality, sheer accident, and what not.   If it were possible to hit upon the necessary data whereby we could trace the growth and the ups and downs of a *group* of steel companies, or a group of retail stores, or a considerable number of wheat farms, we might expect to find that the nature of the product in each case would introduce certain elements more or less common to all the individual enterprises making up the group.   Company structures, matters of personality, localization, etc., would continue to color the statistical patterns; but they would tend to be subordinated by the influence of the industry characteristics. These, in turn, originate mainly from the manner in which the product or service sold affects the behavior of prices and costs, the extent and intensity of competition, etc.   We should thus expect the dynamic behavior in each field of business to reveal itself in characteristic patterns over periods of time.

for the products of industry and for the carriage of passengers. Beyond this are large fields of service activity, such as warehousing, insurance, and banking, extending to many forms of professional work, some of which are represented by individuals or firms of small size.

To measure many of the aspects of performance of these groups in the "service industries" is not easy, particularly if we seek to measure changes over the years in physical terms rather than in value terms. From the statistical standpoint, this problem is perhaps more difficult than is the problem of obtaining the corresponding measurements for industry. But from a practical standpoint, it is obvious that most of this service activity is directly or indirectly involved in moving along the products of enterprise toward final consumption. Although measurements of trade and transportation operations might not agree exactly with those found in manufacturing, the degree of correspondence is nonetheless significant. It can be at least tentatively assumed that it is the industrial or manufacturing operations that form the dynamic nucleus of the present-day economic system. In the United States and other advanced industrial countries, most of the new wealth created and added to the current real income of consumers has passed—at some stage, at least—through manufacturing processes.

Another broad and important segment of our economy includes enterprises associated with construction. The erection of buildings is a form of business having many peculiar features and dynamic patterns, more fully described in later chapters. Indeed, the manner in which the various types of building enterprise relate themselves dynamically to the general drift or, indeed, influence that general pattern are worthy of special consideration, and evidence will be presented that this great group of activities probably contributes in a powerful manner to wide rhythmic fluctuations in many industries engaged in manufacturing and extractive operations.

Finally, we may refer briefly to the complex processes and peculiar patterns associated with agriculture and animal husbandry. When we refer casually to "business conditions" or business prosperity, we frequently do so without direct reference to, or consciousness of, the agricultural phase of business enterprise. Much of our discussion of business has a distinctly urban point of view, probably because over the years, that segment of our population engaged in the cultivation of the soil and the raising of animals has been a consistently declining part. From a statistical standpoint, this farm group of industries reveals rather peculiar patterns of production and income change. Whereas the production patterns of many branches of manufacture, as previously stated, develop similar reiterating movements, the changes in agricultural production present many dissimilar patterns rather than a repetition of essentially similar movements. We should expect this, since each branch of agriculture has its peculiar relation to weather and soil conditions, growth processes, and even marketing operations. No two branches of animal husbandry are alike in their operations or the patterns of change that result therefrom. We shall see later that, whereas the contribution of agriculture to the real income or wealth of the entire community may be measured in the drift of aggregate farm production, the farmer's changing results from year to year in well-being or buying power, and also those of his hired workers and the surrounding rural community, do not depend on the volume of product but may actually be inverse to changes in the physical volume of output. This is less true of price changes, but it is an important characteristic of volume.

If these dynamic differences which characterize broad segments of industry are borne in mind, it would appear that an over-all measurement of change, in terms of output, would develop a highly significant picture of the course of the entire nation's flow of "real" income from its resources, labor, skill, and management. Such an over-all measure of physical progress, if compared with the detail, would illuminate at many points the influence exerted by the general movement upon the particular segments of activity. The general pattern of change and fluctuation is thus the immediate controlling force in the flow of income of millions of families. And we may also find it useful to look at the matter the other way around and endeavor to discover how particular industry disturbances transmit themselves to the general pattern; or, to put it in other words, to discover whether some particular segments of industry or trade or finance tend to develop dynamic trends or a rhythm of fluctuation so powerful as to influence the general changes and to reach into the far corners of the economic mechanism.

We must not overlook that part of the business environment which is today so potent in its formative and regulating aspects—governmental activity. As we trace the performance of the entire productive system through time and observe its general trends, fluctuations, and vibrations, we should recognize that this system operates in an environment that itself is not stable but that is subject to forces of political evolution or revolution, political and social experiment, mass hysteria, military policy and wartime turbulence and destruction, and all the legal and judicial innovations arising from the vast complex of social change. We shall have occasion from time to time to discuss political emergencies and breakdowns represented by war and the effect that they have upon the pattern of change in business. We might, indeed, carry our studies far afield into foreign affairs and the occasional impact of political and technological and industrial developments in all those parts of the world that may be considered capable of affecting in some degree the course of our own economy.

We must keep in mind, too, the fact that the system of business operates in the service of *people*. The population is gradually but constantly changing in numbers and conceivably, also, in human type and human quality, a fact that suggests fields of study well beyond the scope of the business analyst. One of the first problems we shall consider is the long-term growth of our own population in order to observe clearly its pattern of change and its relation to economic development.

In all these departments of dynamic study the reader will observe that the environment within which the business process as a whole operates broadens out as we proceed from the individual shop or store or farm to the workings of the economy as measured in its aggregate production or income value. We shall be dealing mainly in this volume with the dynamic characteristics of the economy as a whole rather than with individual industries or particular businesses. We shall have something to say, however, about the dynamic peculiarities of construction, transportation, agriculture, and a few other segments having special importance from one angle or another.

We are dealing with the American business system, which, from its inception, has embodied the elements of private property, a considerable degree of unrestrained competition, an increasingly elaborate mechanism of exchange and division of labor, and the use of vast amounts of credit to facilitate the operations of exchange. We shall therefore examine the dynamic patterns of prices, including subgroups of price movements as well as the general drift. There are particular groups of prices in the service markets that have special interest and importance, such as farm prices, the price of capital, the price of bank credit, and the behavior of wages. This analysis of the pattern of prices may enable us to understand still more clearly the changes in money income or business receipts accruing to the nation as a whole or to important segments of it. We shall find that in some instances the economic welfare of a group depends primarily upon the *volume* of its output but in other cases upon the changes in *value* or the product of output and price. Much popular generalization on these matters overlooks these basic contrasts. But after all, it is the substantive, tangible product—the actual physical units of service that we can use and enjoy—that ultimately justify the efforts and sacrifices of business enterprise. For one reason or another, the prices of those products and services do not remain constant, even over short periods; and over longer periods the variations in the fabric of prices may become so marked and complex that measurements only in terms of *value* would become distorting elements in the effort to measure and interpret the more basic aspects of *real* income and *actual* wealth, which make up the moving standard of human living.

As we proceed with this study, we shall have occasion to analyze the methods whereby capital and credit have been used and misused in financing building, speculation, agriculture, wars, and other activities. Factual evidence will be presented to show how booms and depressions have been generated by wars and by specific factors in the land-using industries involving speculative use of capital and bank credit. It is remarkable how much of our current economic thought regarding the business cycle, unemployment, finance, and political policy has been evolved out of monetary and credit theories, which, in turn, have been translated into income and capital theories, without much regard for the facts of actual economic life. The Great Depression of the 1930's afforded an extraordinary opportunity to experiment with various political "income-creating" schemes evolved from observation of *money circulation* rather than *production processes*. The results, although in some measure helpful, have raised many new and complex questions.

During the 1920's, dynamic policy was being enthusiastically expressed in terms of stability of the *price level*, via central-bank manipulation of the money market. In the 1930's, *gold* was supposed to have become "scarce" and, amidst international currency troubles, we were pushed into a gold-hoarding, cheap-money program. Well before the 1940's, this had gravitated to a philosophy, cherished by many economic theorizers and political leaders who accepted their counsel, that regards *capital* as having become "excessive" as population tapers off, so that saving must now be discouraged rather than encouraged. As much private capital as possible, we are being told, must be expropriated by Government, which alone is supposed to be able to use it wisely and thus to sustain employment. Truly economic theories and the political policies embodying them run in cycles, like fashions and styles, with exaggerated emphasis upon some one idea or assumption which may be far removed from reality.

What is most needed now, in a world at war and amidst turmoil that perils the very survival of economic democracy, is much more adequate measurement of the dynamics of the business process and a broader perspective of the manner in which its moving parts interact. We must clearly understand *why* depressions continually have interrupted progress toward a wider distribution of income and capital before we can formulate sound political and business policy, directed toward preserving progress in living standards and eliminating needless cyclical vibration, and capable of more widely diffusing economic opportunity and security. An industrial society that can achieve *steady growth* in wealth creation can also achieve an equitable distribution of that wealth without resorting to political dictatorship or collectivism.

CHAPTER 2

THE TREND OF POPULATION GROWTH

We have sketched in a preliminary way some of the aspects of business and economic activity upon which our attention will be focused. Our fundamental problem concerns time and change. Let us now distinguish between change that occurs gradually, over extended periods of time, and change that is in the nature of vibration or short-term fluctuation, which, in many aspects of production, distribution, and prices, serves, to make the course of economic progress undulating and irregular. The vibration at times becomes so pronounced that far-reaching social reverberations result. But to measure and distinguish these undulating "cycles," we must first study the *underlying trend*.

We have seen that the long-term development of an economic system, such as that of the United States, has occurred in a social, political, geographical, and international environment. The environmental factors have conditioned to a large degree the pattern of historical development. The expansion of population over a vast continental area, endowed with exceptionally rich resources and a generally satisfactory climate, has served to create a partern of long-term change in the American economy that distinguishes it from the experience of other nations. Our expansion in industry and wealth since the seventeenth century proceeded upon the basis of land, forest, and minerals capable of exploitation for widely diversified production. Natural growth was augmented by heavy migration to our shores from Europe. To a large degree, these continuing additions to our people represented relatively advanced cultures, with backgrounds of industrial skill and economic initiative, traditions of opposition to restrictive forms of government, and aptitudes favoring a pioneering spirit. The spreading of such people over a rich new area and their ability to create one of the world's greatest industrial economies within an astonishingly brief period were facilitated by another important factor, the insulating effect of great oceans that minimized the dangers of international friction. In contrast to the developments of the crowded checkerboard of Europe, our people were long able to develop a coordinated, unified system of economic life with virtually a free flow of trade, population movement, and capital investment, little hampered by nationalistic jealousies, historic antipathies, and the paralyzing influence of armaments, standing armies, huge military debts, and the constant threat of destructive warfare.

9

In introducing our analysis of the economic trend by some discussion of the growth of American population, it is not intended to suggest that expansion in numbers must necessarily have a fixed relationship to growth in wealth or income or living standards. In the early settlement and, indeed, throughout the Colonial period and for some time thereafter, business expansion appears to have proceeded at a rate closely paralleling that of the estimated annual increase in population. In any simple and largely agricultural community, a large proportion of the economic effort is called upon to provide the basic essentials of food, clothing, and shelter. With production mainly the result of manual labor, assisted by tools and animal power not subject to rapid changes in design or efficiency, total productivity per capita could not vary from one decade to the next over a very wide range. The introduction of labor-saving devices and expansion in variety of products and services during the nineteenth century has brought about, as we shall presently indicate in more detail, an important change in the relationship between total population and total production and trade. One of the features of this change has been the declining portion of human effort engaged in the simpler pursuits of agriculture and the rapid expansion of urban and industrial population. During the course of these changes, improvement in technology and the application of power and improved mechanism have extended not only to the industries of the cities but to those of the farms and forests as well. But there have been more recently changes in the population growth itself that have further widened the divergence between population and production in the aggregate, and it is of considerable importance to study the dynamics of the human environment as a factor capable of independently influencing the development of the economic system in various aspects in the future.

The first Census of the people of the United States was taken in 1790, and the population has been enumerated every ten years since that time. During our Colonial period, there were no thorough or uniform attempts to obtain an actual count of the people. There are in existence, however, various estimates that have been carefully fitted together and adjusted by statistical authorities, and from these figures we can derive at least an approximate pattern of growth as far back as the early years of the seventeenth century.

If the reader will refer to Chart 1, he will find the data of the American population depicted in two different ways. Corresponding to the arithmetic vertical scale shown at the right, the total population at decade intervals is represented by the middle line. It is impossible to show on this scale the exceedingly small numbers (less than half a million) during the seventeenth century. From the early part of the eighteenth century the curve rises gradually and then describes a rapidly accelerating and rather smoothly advancing course. This continues until the moderate slackening of increase develops in the last decade, ending at 1940. The lower line on this chart (plotted to the same arithmetic scale) indicates the amount of net increase in total population during each decade.

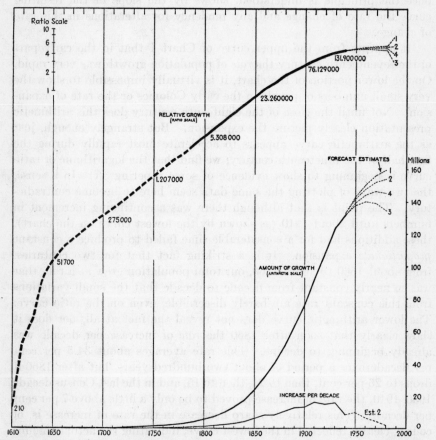

CHART 1.—American population growth. The upper curve shows total population drawn to a ratio scale so that changes in the direction of the curve indicate changes in the *rate* of growth. For the Colonial period estimates only are available. The lower curves are drawn to an arithmetic scale which gives effect to the actual increment per decade.

It should be noted that these are shown as *amounts* of increase. Although the curve describes the growth, it does not necessarily indicate changing *rates* of growth or percentage variation. The upper line in Chart 1 is drawn to what is known as a "ratio" scale, the vertical divisions being logarithmically determined. It is the property of this kind of scale graduation to show a given percentage change, increasing or decreasing, by a designated vertical distance. Thus, if figures plotted in this fashion result in a straight line, inclined steadily upward, it signifies that during each interval of time there is an equal distance gained and hence a *constant rate* of increase. The converse would hold if such a curve formed a straight line steadily declining.[1] Hence this type of graphic illustration, once the principle is understood, shows by the slope of the resulting curve the rate of change and any tendency for alterations in this rate of change.

It appears from the upper curve of Chart 1 that in the early part of the seventeenth century the *rate* of population growth was very rapid. On the lower portion of the chart, it is virtually impossible to show the very small numbers of people in the early Colonies or the rate of expansion. Not until the close of the eighteenth century does this arithmetic presentation clearly picture the expansion. But strangely enough, just as the arithmetic curve appears to accelerate most rapidly during the first half of the nineteenth century, we find that the logarithmic or ratio curve is beginning to show evidence of some tapering off! In a sense, the two ways of plotting the same data seem here to become contradictory. The point is that although there was a continuing increment in numbers until about 1910 (as shown by the lowest curve on the chart), these additions had for a considerable time failed to produce a constant *proportionate* expansion. It is a striking fact that for two centuries, from about 1660 to about 1860, our total population grew at a rate that was so nearly constant from decade to decade that the small variations from this constant rate are barely discernible, even on the ratio curve. The lower arithmetic curve does not reveal the fact at all, nor does it show clearly that soon after 1860 the *rate* of increase per decade was already beginning to decline. This rate averages about 34.5 per cent per decade over a period of about two hundred years, but after 1860 it drops to 26 per cent, then to 21, then to 15, and in the last Census decade 1930–1940, the rate of increase proved to be only a little above 7 per cent per decade. This relatively sharp decrease in the rate of increase is, of course, clearly reflected in the lowest curve, indicating the actual amount of per decade gain. The arithmetic curve of population also begins finally to show the tapering tendency.

[1] According to the logarithmic principle, equal vertical distances may correspond to logarithms of the actual data, or the actual data may be graduated through a range from 1 to 10 (or any multiples thereof) in such fashion that the distances separating the units correspond to the differences between the successive logarithms. As a result, arithmetic progression by equal vertical distances per unit of time is equivalent to progression by equal *multiples* of the actual data. Similarly, equal declines indicate equal *ratios* of decrease. Hence the degree of *slope* of the curve drawn to ratio scale is immediately indicative of the rate of change, and if the scale is known, it is possible to read off approximately the *percentual* change from any point to any other point on the plotted curve.

To examine thoroughly the various factors entering into the relationship of natural resources to number of people would carry us rather far afield; but it is obvious that the problem is one not merely of area and numbers but rather of the kind of people and the kind of technology that motivate the productive processes. This country has never been faced with the kind of problem envisaged by Malthus, the British social philosopher, and his followers in the early years of the last century—the problem of declining sustenance and productivity that might result from exhaustion of resources and particularly of food supply. Part of the reason for this long-continued freedom from any such imagined deficiencies is found in the rapid strides that have been made in applying mechanical devices and improved methods to the land, the forests, and the mineral resources at our disposal and to the transporting of their products. At the same time, it must be remembered that there is under way a counterforce in the nature of deterioration of agricultural land through erosion, improper drainage, and exhaustion of important chemical properties; meanwhile, new mineral and even petroleum output is being obtained from resource discoveries made at longer and longer intervals of time. The physical frontiers have been pushed practically to our geographic boundaries. Henceforth the quality of our technology, productive organization, and utilization of resources must replace the haphazard rough and ready wasteful pioneering of an earlier day if per capita real-income progress is to continue in the future. The possibility of adding to readily available natural resources by appropriation of outlying territory is becoming remote, although trade relations with Latin America may ultimately provide some addition to supplies of various basic materials or advantageous items.

We now come to the human factors—the birth-rate and death-rate trends, the age grouping within the population, and migration tendencies occurring within our boundaries. The slowing down of the rate of population expansion, beginning as early as the decade following the Civil War, is attributable mainly to the fact that the average birth rate per thousand of total population has declined somewhat more rapidly than the average death rate. In 1800, it is roughly estimated, the birth rate might have been as high as 45 or even 50 per thousand of total population. By 1880, the rate appears to have declined to the neighborhood of 35 per thousand; and further gradual decline had brought the figure down to about 24 by 1920. We cannot be entirely sure of these figures, since the official "registration" of births, although undertaken in a few states early in the last century, was not accomplished on a nation-wide basis until 1915, since which year the statistics have become increasingly reliable. This substantial progressive decline in the birth rate has, of course, been a world-wide phenomenon. In many other countries, such statistics have been more carefully recorded, and they leave no doubt that changing ways of life, improving standards of living, and, particularly in recent years, the exercise of voluntary control of family size have been important

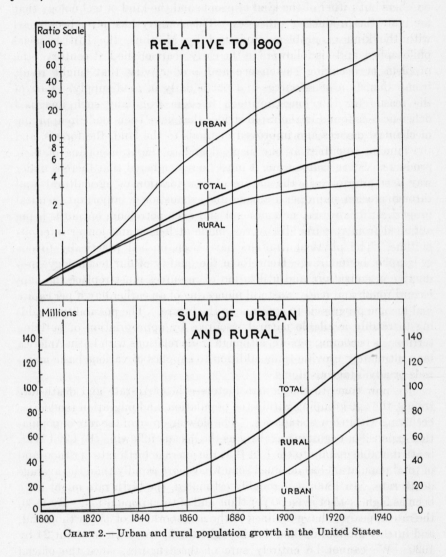

CHART 2.—Urban and rural population growth in the United States.

factors in all advanced countries.   Since 1920, the decline in the American birth rate appears to have accelerated, and this particular change appears clearly to have been due to a spreading knowledge of means of contraception, facilitated by the increasing concentration of population in urban and metropolitan areas.

The birth rate has always been higher in areas having a high proportion of foreign-born persons and in most of the rural areas of the country. The normal trend has been for the cities to absorb the rural surplus. In Chart 2, it will be seen that the population growth in the urban areas for more than a century has been relatively faster than the total growth, whereas the expansion in the rural and farming population has tended to slacken—to such an extent, in fact, that it may be considered now virtually stationary. The rural reservoir of population is thus no longer being steadily increased, and it is quite possible that hereafter the deliberate control of numbers may spread to all sections, along with other evidences of more advanced living standards and the displacement of labor by machines in farming.

Turning now to the essential data of death rates, we again are confronted with the necessity of making rough estimates for earlier years, since the progress of systematic recording for this, as for many other aspects of economic and social change, has been slow. It appears, however, that from a rate probably in the neighborhood of 20 per thousand at the beginning of the last century, there followed a declining tendency sufficient to offset the parallel decline in the birth rate. Hence the excess of births over deaths, along with immigration, sufficed to maintain a fairly steady expansion at the rate of over 34 per cent per decade as far as 1860 or thereabouts. Since then, and particularly since about 1920, the average death rate has not fallen so rapidly. Continuing sharp decline in the death rate of infants has been offset by a less favorable showing in the higher age brackets. To this should be added the fact that the population is gradually growing older. This alone will, of course, contribute to a probable stabilizing of the death rate during the next generation, and beyond that there may even be some rise in this rate. The latest available figures point to a crude birth rate averaging about 17.5 per thousand of total population and a crude death rate of about 10.5 per thousand. Since 1933, both the birth and death rates appear to have increased slightly; the death rate, in fact, appears close to a level that, on the basis of the experience of other countries having relatively low death rates, appears close to the optimum figure not likely to be lowered appreciably in the future. The birth rate may perhaps be expected to decline further, although perhaps not so rapidly as it fell in the decade ending at 1930. There will be a pinching out in future decades of the excess of births over deaths, and the point of equilibrium will mark the time at which further increases in population, apart from migration or, conceivably, enlargement of the national domain or easily available new resources, will be at an end. Although it is so commonly assumed by those who have not examined these facts and tendencies that growth always goes on and on and the trend of population is always pointing upward, there seems no escape from the conclusion that this growth will henceforth taper off rapidly.

If we examine for a moment the internal structure of our population in terms of age groups, as illustrated in Chart 3, it is interesting to see that there has already occurred a slight *decline* in the number of persons under 20 years of age.   There has also been some increase in the number of people aged 65 and over.   In fact, the *proportion* of total population coming within the age group under 20 has been steadily declining for more than a century, and the upper age group, 65 and over, has been relatively gaining.   It is the belief of close students of this subject that in the future the proportion of population above the age that roughly limits the most productive period of human life will increase rapidly, while the number of young persons, below the productive age group, will diminish.   The middle group, aged 20 to 44, has for a long time remained relatively constant; in fact, in the past forty or fifty years, it has slightly increased proportionally.   It is expected that this group will continue without much change for another forty or fifty years.

From what has been said, it might be concluded that, since the middle age group is the productive, or perhaps we should say reproductive, group, its contribution to numbers through natural fertility, apart from other factors, would remain relatively constant.   Such, however, is not necessarily the case, since *within* this segment the "modal" or most typical age will be gradually rising so that a gradually contracting part of that middle group will be capable of making population contributions paralleling those that were made in previous decades.   This intragroup change has not been altogether clear to many people.   The probably gradual shifting in age composition or in the weighting of the average within the middle age group will have its own distinct effect upon the future net fertility rate.   The changes already taking place in the age composition and those that will certainly occur in the future have, of course, some important implications with respect to economic and business affairs.   These matters, along with the significance of the general population trend as it may be projected into the future, will be discussed in later chapters in the light of many other dynamic features and characteristics of our economic system and its political environment.

GEOGRAPHIC SHIFTS IN POPULATION

The shifting of population from the rural areas to the cities is a phase of this subject in which we can observe economic factors and population conditions interacting one upon the other.   As farms become mechanized and as moderate-sized industrial communities establish themselves somewhat apart from the metropolitan concentrations (partly as the result of lessened dependence upon steam motive power), we can expect more of the rural people to be brought within the influences of an essentially urban type of life. This tendency is generally also an influence in the direction of further reducing the natural birth rate. At present there is still a relatively high rate of reproduction in the Southern States. But even in this section the net fertility is already being reduced more rapidly than heretofore by the development of new Southern industries and the decay or transformation of the older forms of Southern plantation agriculture. An excess of births over deaths per thousand of population ranging from 10 to 15 in the Carolinas, Mississippi, Georgia, and Kentucky is not likely to persist indefinitely. In other words, the great reservoir of human resources and labor supply that for so long contributed to metropolitan growth will presently cease to be a source of population for urban expansion.

The movement from farms to cities and from cities back to farms is one upon which fairly good recent statistical estimates exist, at least for the past twenty years or so. From 1920 to 1930, there was a net movement from the farms to cities, but from year to year there was considerable fluctuation in this movement. In 1932, the cityward movement was actually reversed, and although since then there seems to have been a net movement from farm to city, it has been upon a scale much reduced from that which previously prevailed. The Great Depression of the 1930's kept more people on the farms where governmental efforts to restore income achieved a measure of success sooner than was apparent in the industrial urban centers. The urgent call of the national-defense industries for workers, beginning in 1941, however, will again produce some additional rural exodus, possibly of permanent character.

We have noted two "reservoirs" of population from which American industry, and more particularly the urban centers, have recruited population—an alternating and variable flow of people from abroad and a flow from farms to cities. But neither of these is longer capable of contributing to urban growth on the scale witnessed in the past. In fact, some of our largest metropolitan areas have already been shown by the Census of 1940 to be no longer growing or actually to be losing population, probably to the immediate surburban periphery.[1] It does not seem necessary to assume radical future changes in existing immigration restrictions or any such back-to-the-land social movement as is pictured by some observers who believe that our Federal Government policies are pointing the way toward resumption of a rustic static civilization

---

[1] If prevailing birth and death rates at each age level continue unchanged and if no net migration from country to city should occur, the Bureau of the Census estimates that urban population will decline about 24 per cent per generation, whereas farm areas will increase about 36 per cent and rural nonfarm areas will increase about 16 per cent. This is on the basis of preliminary analysis of the 1940 Census data.

comparable to that of the Middle Ages. Hence the rate of natural increase and the death-rate outlook is important. Within our large cities it should not be overlooked that the death rate has not been brought under control to an extent compatible with what we may expect of the progress of medical science. We have successfully lowered the rate of deaths from some diseases, particularly the fevers and tuberculosis; but heart disease, cancer, and deaths from automobile accidents, all of which appear to flourish in crowded cities or to develop from the strain of metropolitan existence, are claiming larger percentages than twenty years ago. On the other hand, infant mortality, which has been cut drastically in the last quarter century, is still twice as high in the United States as in New Zealand. Possibly the further survival gains that can be expected will for a period of time counterbalance the shrinkage in the birth rate itself. One of the important economic factors bearing upon this expectation is, of course, the growing public concern and expanding governmental effort to enlarge the share of national income accruing to the lower income and wage-earner groups. Although we cannot be sure that these measures will be as effective as some have hoped, they will doubtless contribute in some measure to that raising of living standards that appears invariably to result in better medical care of infants and young children, but at the same time the raising of standards of living seems to contribute directly to fewer births per family. To estimate the net results requires, as we shall presently see, careful statistical technique.

There are several additional factors capable of introducing year-to-year changes in population increment in the nature of variations in family status. One of these is the marriage rate. Through the years this rate varies in close response to observed changes in economic prosperity and employment opportunities. Although here again our statistical data are not wholly satisfactory or complete, we can piece together enough of the picture on the basis of selected industrial areas to verify this belief. During a period of depression marriages are deferred until times improve. The number of new families initiated is thus a minor variable and one that is capable of producing some degree of acceleration of the prosperity phase of the business cycle, just as the postponement of marriage tends to contribute to the decline in certain types of business and construction activity. A somewhat similar factor is found in the manner in which "families" live together in larger or smaller groups. During severe depressions there is a greater tendency for both single and married sons and daughters to live with parents or other relatives as a measure of economy. This forms an influence unfavorable to building activity, the furniture industries, and even the sale of automobiles. As the unscrambling process develops with improvement in business conditions, the number of family units increases. The constituent groups separate out into individual places of abode. The reader must therefore observe that what is said about the broad trend of the total population may not be true of the *number of family units*. According to the most recent data, there seems to have been an increase in the number of occupied dwelling units (which may be taken as more or less representative of family units) of over 16 per cent since 1930. This is more than twice the rate of increase in total population. Presumably this increase in family units occurred mainly as a result of the improvement in general conditions following 1933. Since the building of homes, as we shall presently see, is an extremely important and basic segment of American industry, the dependence of this industry upon number of families rather than number of people is a significant economic fact.

Still another aspect of the dynamics of population deserves a brief word. The migration of people in considerable numbers is not, of course, restricted merely to the farm-city movements. Industry today is decidedly in a state of flux, and there are many potent influences that attract workers and their families now to this section, now to that. More than twenty-five million individuals now reside in states other than those in which they were born. The war program of the nation that is being initiated as this is written has already produced significant migrations to new industrial areas and rapid enlargement of some existing centers, especially the smaller communities. The population trend, therefore, in a given area may be widely at variance with the general trend. For a localized area, it may therefore be difficult to project the growth into the future with any degree of accuracy. The most effective approach to this problem probably lies in the careful analysis of the various occupational incentives that are attracting population to the locality and the conditions in other parts of the country that may motivate people to leave those sections.

These problems are of considerable importance to particular states, such as California, where the natural rate of population reproduction is extremely low and where virtually all the increase in population in recent decades has been due to migration into the state. In tracing the origin of these mass movements, there is to be considered, on the one hand, the rise of a succession of major industries on the Pacific Coast—petroleum, fruits, motion pictures, textiles, and, lately, aircraft production. On the other hand, there has been for several decades a substantial westward movement from the Mississippi Valley and, more recently, the Southwest, partly motivated by the desire of the retired farmer to find a pleasant climate for his declining years and, more recently, representing destitute refugees from wind-swept and depleted soil and the swift encroachments of mechanized cotton culture upon helpless workers in the cotton belt. We find evidence also of other recent shifts within the national borders.

There is a tendency toward less than average growth of urban population in the Northeastern and Middle Atlantic sections and a relatively higher rate in the Southern Atlantic and Southwest areas, where industrial development has been accelerating. A solid block of states, North Dakota, South Dakota, Nebraska, Kansas, and Oklahoma, *lost* population from 1930 to 1940.[1] In connection with the growth of individual cities, it is interesting that not only economic conditions but also political factors are potent factors in migration. The Census of 1940 disclosed that rather generally the capital cities of the country revealed considerably faster growth during the decade than cities that did not contain governmental seats. Washington, D.C., and its environs represent a conspicuous example, with the highest rate of growth of any large American city in that period.

ESTIMATING FUTURE POPULATION

Let us return now to the problem of projecting estimates of the total population into the future. This problem might appear to be relatively simple, because the historical trend of population exhibits so consistent a pattern of change, and the variation occurs so gradually. From the curves in Chart 1, the statistician might be tempted to project extensions ten, or twenty, or fifty years in advance merely by the graphic device of sketching out a curve in a direction such as to complete the pattern down to the present. Such a purely graphic method, carefully used, would probably prove superior to an assumption of constant amounts of increase

---

[1] For local areas, it is of some assistance in gauging the population drift and planning adequate regional facilities to be able to estimate the size of the population at annual intervals. It is possible to approximate the population of a county or city by using data of the number of children enrolled in the public schools. This information is collected in many states. From it estimates of the local population can be derived by observing the long-term trend of the ratio of school enrollment to total numbers and converting enrollment into population with a correction for this trend. The *Tax Digest*, a periodical published by the California Taxpayers' Association, presents interesting estimates developed by Paul V. Lane and his associates for the county population figures in California and based upon this method. These project the official Census data to the current year, and some short-range forecasts are also published. Caution must be used, of course, in view of the fact that there is a gradually changing ratio of children to total population in most areas, and allowance for this trend is necessary. But the method is superior to that frequently employed, which averages the results of changes in utility meters, directory counts, and similar correlates of population that individually are less satisfactory than school enrollment. A formula long used by the Bureau of the Census for current population estimates, beyond enumeration years, involved merely short projections of previously observed increments or ratios of change. The results proved to be increasingly inaccurate beyond a few years from the Census count, and the method has therefore been abandoned.

per decade. This certainly is no longer realistic. Extensions from the present time forward would prove accurate if we happened to hit upon just the right amount of decrescent advance followed by stability and in the proper time period.

It might also be assumed that the per decade amount of future population growth would gradually step down in a manner substantially reversing the earlier positive increments, as seen in the lowest curve in Chart 1. Such an assumption is, in fact, made by some statisticians who argue that the increments during a long period tend to develop a certain symmetry. They employ for projection purposes curves developed from mathematical formulas of the so-called "logistic" type. These permit a curve to be fitted to the historically observed data and continued forward in progressively smaller increments of increase that essentially duplicate the decreasing declines toward zero if the observer traces the earlier record *backward* to the beginning. The curve thus undergoes a symmetrical inversion of pattern, approaching a more or less assumed upper limit and with the general form of an elongated "S." Mathematically these curves are equivalent to an integration of the ordinates of a "normal distribution" of growth increments in a symmetrically bell-shaped design, with the highest growth increment at the middle and progressively smaller increments tapering off on either side. This function has been used as a device to express the pattern of multiplication of numbers in any limited environment, by the noted biologists Lowell J. Reed and the late Raymond Pearl.[1]

In their use of this mathematically determined extrapolation, Reed and Pearl have relied very heavily upon evidence drawn from populations of fruit flies raised in bottles and other similarly restricted populations of a very simple biological order. In such instances it is readily assumed that expansion beyond a certain limit becomes impossible in view of the established limitation of space and nutrition. Observations from such cases may be misleading when applied to far more complex human populations living in environments capable of a high degree of voluntary control and even expansion through the exercise of even rudimentary intelligence. Many statisticians who are skeptical of this mechanical principle believe that the equations may be beautifully symmetrical and the future points on the curve of population may issue from a function conforming exactly to the pattern of *past history;* but oddly enough, it is entirely possible to devise for a *given* population record *more than one* plausible equation or logistic curve, with *many* alternative extrapolations! Whether the

---

[1] Another statistical form of the logistic type of equation for the fitting and extrapolating curves of growth assumes that the increments are distributed logarithmically rather than arithmetically.

observer accepts as valid his highest or lowest future estimate then becomes a matter of judgment rather than of mathematical objectivity. Most extrapolations arrived at by this method seem to have reached much *higher* future estimates than have been either reasonable in the light of other evidence or verified by subsequent experience. The Reed-Pearl forecast of the United States population made for the year 1940 was 136 million, but the actual count was less than 132 million. They reached a figure of 175 million for 1980 and an ultimate maximum of 197 million. These figures may be contrasted with the results of other methods that will be outlined below. We need not, however, go quite so far in condemning this general approach as A. B. Wolfe, who has referred to it as "a sort of fatalistic law somehow distilled by the alchemy of mathematics."[1] The curve-fitting method does provide a formal pattern that population movements over centuries of time seem to follow in a general way, and if utilized with discretion in projecting the subgroups of a total so that the total estimate for future years may be derived by summing up the segments in terms of logistic or similar formulas, the results can be at least a useful auxiliary check upon other calculations and a way of setting limits of probable range for very distant future periods.

In contrast to the foregoing more or less *mechanical* projection of population, another type of method has been developed to which we may apply the term "analytical." This is the method that has been skillfully used by the Scripps Foundation for Research in Population Problems, directed by T. K. Whelpton and W. S. Thompson. The essential feature of this analytical approach is the breaking down of the problem into fundamental elements and the making of various detailed estimates that are finally assembled into the aggregate forecast. The population process is visualized as essentially biological, and such aspects as birth rate, death rate, age composition, racial characteristics, and distinction of foreign born from native born are followed out in considerable detail and upon several alternative assumptions covering the less easily predictable conditions, such as net immigration. In extrapolating the course of the birth rate for a given segment of the people, we are, of course, dealing with psychological elements, changing customs, and complex economic and regional shifts affecting living standards and the importance of having or not having children. Death rates, on the other hand, are variables representing primarily the progress of medical science and other surrounding social conditions that may be independent of the decisions or standards of individuals. But if changes in these major elements in the problem are found to be progressing according to definite trends and can each be projected ahead, with recognition given to gradual changes in the age composition for various major groups and types of

[1] *Quarterly Journal of Economics*, August, 1927.

people and reasonable assumptions with respect to future net immigration, the final results are likely to be fairly reliable.[1]

In thus breaking down the problem, it is best to deal, not with the crude birth rates and death rates in terms of the total population but with reference to specific rates, such as births to various groups of women at various ages. Deaths can likewise be analyzed, age group by age group, to throw light on specific past trends. In so doing, it becomes apparent that as a population becomes gradually older this fact in itself will have an effect upon the crude death rate, regardless of changes in the specific death rate for each particular age group. Since the annual figures for births and deaths are now available (and have been available since 1933) for every state, it is possible to obtain detailed survival rates and fertility rates by areas as well as by nativity and racial groups. The Whelpton-Thompson estimates are made up by five-year continuations of the experience observed during 1930–1934. The tendencies of that period were then carried forward in the detailed table by reference to trends found in larger groups of population, extending further back, and, of course, by the use of general observation of current developments and some reference to the conditions obtaining in various foreign countries, the latter to establish extreme limits. These authorities acknowledge that the future estimation of birth rates, either general or specific, involves many difficulties and assumptions requiring judgment. It is not a purely statistical problem. All the more is this true of assumptions regarding future immigration.

As a result of this analytical step-by-step, group-by-group integration of detailed projections, Whelpton and Thompson were able to obtain a variety of future estimates as far ahead as 1980. These are available for the entire country, for each state, and for various age groupings. The results were worked out between 1934 and 1936 and were published in a series of monographs by the National Resources Committee during 1937 and 1938.[2] If we refer again to Chart 1, we shall find several of these estimates drawn to both ratio and arithmetic scales. The projections all extend to the year 1980. The highest estimate at that year represents assumptions of medium birth rate and mortality rate and a net annual immigration of 100,000 persons. The probable 1980 population on these assumptions is 158,967,000. If we estimate in the same manner but allow for no net immigration, the total population of 1980 would probably be no more than 153,628,000. If low average fertility is assumed, with

[1] For a description of the calculations made by Whelpton and Thompson, see the *Journal of the American Statistical Association*, September, 1936, pp. 459*ff.*

[2] See "Problems of a Changing Population," National Resources Committee, Washington, D.C., May, 1938; also, "Population Statistics," by the same Committee, October, 1937.

medium estimates for mortality and no net immigration, the maximum number would be expected about 1960, with a population of approximately 140 million.   An intermediate estimate, if relatively low average fertility and also low mortality are assumed but if an allowance for net immigration of 100,000 a year is included, would date the maximum growth at about 1970, with a population of 146 million.

The Scripps Foundation projections, therefore, as they now stand, based upon assumptions and calculations made about 1935, previous to the actual Census figures of 1940, point definitely to a more rapid tapering tendency for continental United States.   The four estimates that appear to represent the most probable of the various assumptions and expectations range from a low figure of about 134 million to a high figure close to 160 million at 1980.   Estimate 3, resulting in the lowest of these four, as of 1980, is found to coincide almost exactly with the actual Census result for 1940, namely, 131.9 million.[1]   If this particular estimate is carried forward, it indicates that well within a generation the country will reach its maximum population.   It is well within the range of probability that there may be some net immigration during the next twenty to forty years, for the results from 1930 to 1940, during which period there was a net deficit of 200,000, may conceivably have represented exceptionally unfavorable conditions with respect to migration to this country.[2]   But the medium estimate 2, indicating a population of 153,628,000 at 1980, with no allowance for immigration, seems on the whole a fairly safe figure to use for practical projection purposes.

Various other estimates could be cited, some of them reaching a figure close to 200 million of population at 1980 and maximum numbers beyond that date; others result in the expectation of less than 120 million in 1980.   Perhaps the most extreme lower assumption would be arrived at by the crude graphic device of extending through another decade the curve of increments shown in Chart 1.   This is seen to decline sharply at 1940; extending it in a straight line to 1950 would bring us practically to zero.   This would mean that national growth might be already close to its maximum.   It must be remembered that such simple graphic extrapolations may lead us into error, inasmuch as the increment or net addition to the total population each decade has previously pursued a

[1] The actual Census figure is 131.6 million, as of Apr. 1, 1940; but all the data that we have been summarizing express the population as of July 1.   The Bureau of the Census estimates that as of July 1, 1940, the population amounted to 131.9 million.

[2] In addition to the four estimates that were selected for special attention here, there are available twelve other Scripps Foundation estimates, representing various combinations of fertility, mortality, and immigration assumptions.   Some of these are based on an expectation of high fertility and high mortality or other assumptions that do not appear entirely reasonable and, indeed, are not considered by Whelpton and Thompson as sufficiently realistic to deserve much emphasis.

somewhat fluctuating course, and a similar extension of the results in any particular decade would not have produced an accurate figure for the succeeding decade.

As the official Census data of 1940 are analyzed, it is indeed already becoming apparent from samplings that we should expect the future course of our population (barring territorial alterations) to veer toward the more conservative estimates. If present birth and death rates continue, it is the preliminary expectation of Director W. L. Austin[1] that the white population will actually *decline* within a generation by as much as 5 per cent, whereas the nonwhites may *increase* by 7 per cent. The net result would be a failure of the whole population to maintain its numbers to the extent of about 4 per cent per generation. Since 1930, the net reproduction rate declined from 111 to 96, approximately. This would roughly exemplify the Scripps estimates for 1960–1970 maxima between 140 and 146 million.

Before concluding this discussion, it is of interest to notice the forecasts of population by age groupings as they were prepared by the Scripps Foundation for the National Resources Committee. If we refer to Chart 3, these projections will be found condensed into three age classes: persons under 20 years, those aged 20 to 44, and those 45 and over. The projections are shown for assumptions as to natural increase and immigration as already included in Chart 1 and represent the upper and lower range of the assumptions therein included. It will be seen that the group aged under 20, in accordance with the lower of these two sets of assumptions, namely, low fertility, medium mortality, and no net immigration, would steadily decline until by 1980 their numbers would be somewhat less than in 1890. According to the upper estimate, if medium factors of natural increase and net immigration of 100,000 per annum are assumed, the decline in this younger group would be distinctly less rapid, but there would be no tendency to resume the increase that appears definitely to have ceased somewhere between 1920 and 1940. The middle-aged group would be expected to hold its own until about 1950, and in accordance with the lower forecast assumptions, it would then decline almost as rapidly as the numbers of the youngest group. This is shown a little more clearly in the upper section of Chart 3, where the various series have been plotted on ratio scales in two separate sets of curves corresponding with higher and lower assumptions. According to the higher set of assumptions, the middle-aged group would almost hold its own as far as 1980 and in this respect would be expected to describe a *rate* of change corresponding closely to the actual numbers in the lower group.

[1] Census Bureau release, January 31, 1941. See also in this connection the Presidential Address by Raymond Pearl on The Aging of Populations, *Journal of the American Statistical Association*, Centenary Celebration Proceedings, March, 1940.

The numbers in the oldest group would not be expected to reach their peak even by 1980 on either of the assumptions.

The lower section of Chart 3, in which the three classes of the population have been shown superimposed, one upon the other, on an arithmetic scale, vividly demonstrates the relative total size of the oldest age group

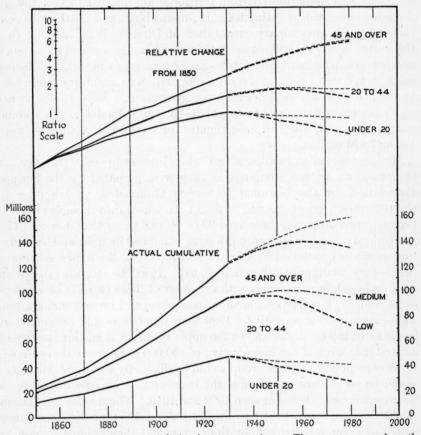

CHART 3.—United States population by age groupings. The upper curves show the growth and projections for each of the age groups relative to 1850. The lower curves, on arithmetic scale, show the age groups superimposed. The medium and low projections correspond to forecast estimates 2 and 3, respectively, as shown in Chart 1.

as it expands through the coming decade and the extraordinary contrast with its numbers as they stood at the middle of the last century. We are truly becoming an "older" country. There is little question that problems relating to the adequate support and care of these large numbers of old persons in our population will bulk large in economic and political affairs in the future. Another interesting and important point that is illustrated in Chart 3 is that the most productive group of the population, aged **20** to **44,** will continue to enlarge the numbers seeking employment probably for at least another decade, and the youngest group, which also includes many who are entering industry and seeking employment, will also continue to be increasing for another decade, anticipating further expansion in the jobs available to the extent of four or five million during the decade. Obviously it is enormously important that industry and trade be in a position to furnish to this still growing segment of our most productive people the full opportunities for work that they have a right to expect.

All the foregoing figures and estimates pertain to the population of continental United States, excluding the people living in the various possessions, such as Alaska, the Philippines, Hawaii, Puerto Rico. As this is written, the world is in a state of unprecedented flux and revolutionary militarism, the results of which during the coming generation are difficult to appraise. From this stupendous turmoil there may well be shifts of peoples and even changes in many political boundaries, which a few years back might have been considered beyond the realm of possibility. Perhaps we have in this global warfare still another reason to lean toward the conservative in estimating population.[1]

[1] See in this connection P. M. Hauser, The Effects of War on Population and Vital Phenomena, *American Journal of Sociology*, November, 1942.

CHAPTER 3

THE GROWTH TREND OF PRODUCTION AND TRADE

The discussion of population trends has developed several significant points. The growth of numbers within the boundaries of the United States has revealed a high degree of continuity, describing a smoothly flowing curve. If the entire record and the most reasonable available estimates of future trend are taken into consideration, the over-all pattern seems more or less typical of the general organic growth process—relatively small increments at first, then rapidly increasing increments to a certain stage, and, finally, *increments* that begin again to slacken and then decline to zero or to negative values.

During the course of national expansion over the centuries, the size of the population and the momentum of its increase have interacted with factors in the economic environment. The progress of science and applied technology have in some measure accounted for the population growth. On the other hand, the number of available workers has contributed to the various incentives bringing about the expansion of productive capacity, industrial diversification, and trade activity. Our fabricating capacity (as distinct from purely extractive production) has tended to be concentrated in urban communities, and these enjoyed a much more rapid rate of increase than the rural areas during the nineteenth century and a portion of the twentieth. In one sense, however, this tendency has met opposing factors with respect to future growth in number of people. Although urban life has contributed to a lower death rate as well as the enhanced productivity capable of supporting a larger population, the birth rate in the cities, almost the world over, has tended to decline, principally as the result of voluntary control of family size. As we turn our attention to an examination of the material and economic phases of national growth, we shall become conscious of continuing developments in the processes of production, sources of motive power, and the facilities for transport, which may tend to modify or even reverse the long-standing social urge toward city life and escape from the open countryside. We shall have occasion to refer to several important aspects of this interrelationship between technology, on the one hand, and population on the other. We shall require some basis for expressing the significance of the broad results of our magnificent technical progress over the years upon productivity per capita. What has the average

30

American gained from secular progress? Has growth in total output of useful wealth kept more or less in step with the growth of population, or to what extent has it been falling behind or advancing more rapidly? These are questions of fundamental importance, and we shall now give our attention to further measurements, again covering the broad aspects of our economy as a whole, to provide factual background for analysis and conclusions.

THE PROBLEM OF MEASUREMENT

To measure the long-term development of the nation's productive power, or, rather, the aggregate creation of useful goods and services, is much more difficult than to depict from Census records the smoothly flowing course of total population. One reason for beginning with the discussion of population trends was to familiarize the reader with the general concept of *trend* as shown by data not expressed in terms of money, extending over an exceptionally long period. We found a high degree of continuity, but in no economic elements do we find such an equally smooth progression within either short or long periods. From year to year the sequence is usually disturbed by abrupt inclines or declines; even over periods of ten or twenty years we find from our best available measures of the volume of aggregate business that there have been periods of rapid acceleration presently followed by intervals during which little or no net progress occurred. If we happen to confine our attention to particular phases or segments of industry and trade rather than attempt to deal with comprehensive composites of performance, we are confronted by the random play of adventitious variability referred to in Chapter 1. We could be led to erroneous conceptions of the aggregate experience if we sought to study only particular and localized facts. The life of one firm tends to be shorter and more subject to disturbing accidents than the industry, and the life of an industry emerges, accelerates, reaches maturity or undergoes decay with more tendency to erratic vibration and frequent interruption than the economic development of the nation.

Recent studies have demonstrated clearly the typical life experience or growth pattern of individual industries.[1] In some branches of manufacturing, mining, forestry, and agriculture, a tendency toward retardation or decline appears already to have set in, following years of growth and maximum output. But meanwhile, new industries and new forms of commerce and of service have been developed. Some of these are in the early stages of what may hereafter be a long and highly creative course of

[1] See, for example, Arthur F. Burns, "Production Trends in the United States since 1870," National Bureau of Economic Research, New York, 1934; also, S. Kuznets, "Secular Movements in Production and Prices," Boston, 1930.

evolution; others are already in the stage of acceleration that eventually will be followed by retardation as they approach full maturity. But for the moment we are less interested in the trees than in the growth tendencies of the entire forest. We must gather together all the segments—or, in a more practical and limited sense—as complete and representative a sampling of them as we can muster, so that the trees already fallen will not obstruct our view of the saplings that presage future growth. Whatever data we use as the basis for measuring the over-all trend of development must therefore not exclude the new, or prematurely discard the old, forms of activity.

Another important feature of our problem is how to secure an aggregation or composite from the numerous individual segments of economic activity. We may happen to have available data for a period of time expressed in money as values and reflecting the convenient manner in which money serves as a common denominator of values in permitting homogeneous *summation* into totals. For some purposes, as we shall later see, such value is in itself significant and important as an economic measure, but it is obvious that time movements thus expressed will give effect not only to the course of the physical volume embodied in the various production or commercial processes but to *prices* as well. And prices may move widely and erratically and thus distort the pattern considerably from what might be expected in terms of quantity alone.

There are several possible solutions of this difficulty, none capable in this finite world of perfectly accurate results but deserving of careful statement to set forth a guiding principle. We may have sufficient pertinent data (even though incomplete) to permit a statement of the relation of the *value* of production (or trade or service) transactions in, let us say, a given year, to what those same activities were worth in money at some previous time. Suppose that in so doing, we make the numerator of the ratio not the actual current values but what this same output or trade *would be* worth if prices since the earlier period had *not* changed. We can, in other words, manipulate our data in such fashion as to show changes in values *at constant prices*, which, of course, means the net over-all changes from one period to another in the volume element, each component being given its due weight in terms of its constant value. If the data should relate to manufacturing output, we could thus trace the course of an index made up by summing each year's output valued over and over again at the unit prices of some previous period serving as the origin or base and dividing each of these sums by an amount equal to what the goods produced in the base year were worth at those same original prices. Of course, there are periods of time in which we must be content with but a meager sample of the data, and all we can attempt is indirect measurement of the whole performance.

A second method of arriving at a volume index of change would start from actual values at actual prices, such as we might find available in records of our foreign trade or some phase of domestic commercial turnover. These data could be "deflated" or divorced from the price element, so to speak, by dividing the items by a separate index of prices (or, rather, of *average* price change) during the period. This method would assume that the prices used in this deflating index matched the prices involved in the actual business figures reasonably well and that in preparing the price index care was used to preserve throughout a fairly representative system of weighting to give each segment its proper degree of importance in the averaging process. Such deflating of actual values would be highly accurate so far as basic principle is concerned if a particular form of price index were used.[1] It is found in actual experience that although different kinds of price indexes built up for the same problem by different formulas may give somewhat divergent results, the degree of correspondence is often sufficiently close to justify the use of much more elementary price deflators if we use the final results merely to piece out difficult periods where more perfect data do not exist and if we do not rest too heavily in our long-term measurements upon data thus computed by deflation.

There is thus some hope of arriving at the determination of the long-term trend of wealth creation in terms of the probably significant, rather than the meticulously accurate, as we move forward to the present time. But we must pause a moment longer in our brief outline of procedure to point out that we have left rather indefinite just what it is that we consider the primary object of measurement. Is it production? Is it trade? Is it both? Here again we must keep historical perspective in mind. In the early Colonial days farming was the principal enterprise; commercial activity was less pervasive than it is now. A great deal of production did not involve sale and purchase; it was self-sufficient. Today farming is a steadily dwindling enterprise, compared to total enterprise, and manufacturing operations have become dominant in their utilizing of resources, human effort, and the facilities of trade and service. If we may refer to the flow of useful goods and services to final users as the national *real income* (as distinct from the flow of money), we can accept the statement of Edmund E. Day that

[1] That is, an index formed by ratios of values for the various time intervals in which numerators were sums of the expression, current price times current quantity, and denominators were sums of the expression, base period prices times current quantities. If the actual values, which would be summations of the expression, current prices times current quantities, were divided by the corresponding price indexes in this form, the results would be expressions of the total of current quantities at base prices or a measure of trade capable of being compared, at any point in the period of time covered, with the base-period trade aggregate.

The most important single barometer of changes in the size of the income is the physical volume of output in manufacture. This follows from the fact that the great bulk of modern articles of consumption pass at one stage or another through factory processes. Even our foodstuffs—our flour, meat, sugar, coffee,—emerge in finished form from industrial plants. Only a few commodities,—fresh vegetables and fruits, milk, household coal,—are not regarded as in any way manufactured. . . . The physical volume of factory output bears a definite relation to the national real income.[1]

What Day says concerning manufacture is more or less true today of most of the other fabricating and service industries, not necessarily because physical materials "flow through" their plants but because the services are rendered so closely in relation to the production and fabricating operations. The engineering, financial, legal, architectural, and numerous other services rendered to and for business reveal an expanding tendency when the production processes themselves are expanding, and vice versa. When industrial production is exceptionally active, the purchasing power of that large segment of the consuming public receiving income in wages, profits, and fees speeds up not only the flow of service facilities and the merchandising and transportation activities but also the personal services of doctors, dentists, cosmeticians, singers, and dancers. In fact, some of this service now utilizes apparatus of considerable complexity, calling for special industrial facilities. Hence it can be stated that if at present the operations of manufacturing so well reveal and represent the dynamic phases of productive enterprise and national real income, then the total amount of service rendered can be expected to vary more or less proportionately with those changes. Each line of industry is, in fact, so related to others that there is a response throughout the system to stimulating or depressing influences; the degree of sympathetic response is indeed remarkable and affords us the opportunity to make statistical measurement on the basis of well-selected samples and representative partial data, even though we cannot make complete enumerations. The accompanying diagram further illustrates the heavy overlapping of production, trade, and service.

We can thus formulate our objective more clearly by saying that the problem is to measure at long range the progress of composite production, considering that in recent years it carries the service and commercial operations along with it and fairly well represents their drift as well, whereas in earlier years, it may be not only necessary but quite representative of the facts to express economic activity by such physical trade

[1] The Measurement of Variations in the National Real Income, *Journal of the American Statistical Association*, March, 1921, p. 554. Dr. Day, now president of Cornell University, made important statistical contribution to the technique of production measurement.

measures as appear to be fairly representative of the underlying productive efforts of the nation.   The details will be discussed later.

We have had occasion to refer to the flow of production and, more
particularly, manufacturing output as a representative measure of the
flow of real income.   It should be pointed out that several qualifying
terms must be added to make this a wholly justifiable statement.   It may
not be precisely true from month to month or even from year to year
that the change in productive operations is proportionate to the flow of
goods and services *to consumers' hands*.   Production in industrial plants
may rise or decline in greater degree than actual use or final purchase
of the products.   This would be true if part of the product were being
added to inventory and stored or if it were contributing to the expansion
of productive apparatus and was thus not in a form directly available
to consumers.   This implies that the "income" concept is associated
with what comes into the hands of individuals for their use and enjoyment.

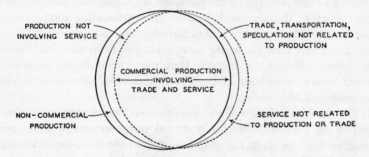

In this sense, we may also limit the term "national income" in the
form of money payments to what is received by individuals in their varied
capacities of wage earners, capitalists, business managers, or landowners.
We might conceive as a special form of national income what business
firms add to their surpluses (or subtract as negative income) after allowing
all necessary expenses; this might be called total "national income" as
distinct from "income payments to individuals."[1]   But we do not ordinarily speak of either national money income or real income as having
anything to do with the payments *to* business units for their materials or
semifabricated products.   In other words, in computing national income,
we eliminate the duplications involved in the passage of materials through
several steps in the process from raw extractive product to finished
product.   That term refers to the value of all raw material plus what is
added in subsequent processes by way of service effort to bring it to the
final stage of usable product.   With the original raw-material values, we

[1] A usage adopted by the U.S. Department of Commerce in its income-statistics
work.

combine the "values added" in the process of fabrication.[1]   To this we may add, of course, further detail to make up the complete income picture, such as the value of transportation service, power service, merchandising service apart from inventory values, and a host of other components, for each of which duplications of material values are eliminated.   But if we are tracing over a long period of time the aggregate of such net values added to raw-material values, the rate of change will probably be found to be much the same as if we have weighted the items by gross values. The discrepancy, if any, would be due to the fact that articles that passed through many stages, each involving a business transaction, might be somewhat overweighted in the final result.   What has been said on this point also indicates that if we wish to secure high accuracy, it is best to use in the weighting of a production index not market prices but, rather, the average "unit values added" in each stage of operations. This is done in some of our modern indexes, but as we go farther back historically in our quest for materials, we must rely on much less precise results.   Finally, it is probably correct to say that the long-term trend of real income will agree with that of industrial output, properly weighted, but to the extent that there are components of service activity or some of the basic extractive industries that have peculiar trend gradients, there will be a modification of the purely industrial over-all trend in the most significant final result.[2]

By the use of the device of an "aggregative" index measure previously mentioned (it matters little for practical purposes whether we use the resulting current totals or ratios to base period totals) or occasionally the deflating of trade values, various types of production or trade data can be translated into a continuous long-term measure of business.   Since we are about to present results extending over a very extended interval of American history, there are naturally limitations in the available data, and we must recognize also the fact that the structure of the economic system itself has been changing through the years.   In Colonial days, over 80 per cent of the population engaged in some form of agriculture or forestry.   The colonists, however, enjoyed fairly active foreign trade, mainly with Great Britain, the West Indies, and some Mediterranean

---

[1] This is done by the Census of Manufactures in computing every two years the sum total of manufacturing net value.

[2] One of the conspicuous cases in which physical volume does not appear to vary consistently with the general average or total of production would be the case of agriculture and animal husbandry.   As will be pointed out in a later chapter, there are special weather factors and other conditions in these fields of industry that cause the annual output in physical units to vary more or less inversely to the money income obtained by the producer.   In most kinds of industry, the reverse is true; the money value of income of the particular group, under conditions of fairly stable prices, will vary directly with the volume of material or service output.

countries. Some of the agriculture of the American colonies represented highly specialized export production, such as tobacco, rice, hemp, and various products of the forest. In such a simple economy, in which the *total* of all production, largely agricultural in nature, and manufacturing was hampered by the simple technology and by restrictive British laws, we should expect the aggregate "real income" of the people to consist largely of food, clothing, and dwelling space, supplemented by those foreign manufactures, luxuries, and semiluxuries, paid for mainly by the great Southern export staples.

As we pass to the nineteenth century, agricultural export as a means of acquiring diversified manufactured products persisted as the predominant pattern of our economy. If we had the complete data of domestic manufacturing output, internal transportation service, etc., these would still not reveal movements as typical of variation in the real income as they would be today. It is apparent, then, that we cannot obtain an entirely homogeneous measure of total production of trade or national real income during a period of time long enough to establish a really long-term trend of aggregate business or income growth. If, however, we can utilize such data for each stage of our national experience as are *most representative* of enterprise at that period, we shall have a tolerably reliable means of extending back even into the eighteenth century the much more complete business measures of the twentieth.

THE INDEX OF PRODUCTION AND TRADE

The details of statistical procedure used in the construction of a long-term index of American production and trade will be found in Appendix 1. The most important feature of this index to be noted here, in carrying forward the summary of procedure and terminology just presented, is that it has been possible to make use of trade figures during the earlier years of national growth and industrial production figures during the later years. If we were to measure the activity of business in the earlier period by using data for production (which unfortunately do not exist), our result would probably be heavily weighted by agricultural output, but since this paid for so much of the manufactures and the services therewith associated, the resulting trend would be in fair agreement with the trend of trade, and both trends would approximate that of population growth. The limited scope of markets and transportation facilities made total farming output the net result of many localized influences, which tended, however, to offset one another, except at times of major disorganization. Standing in contrast to this gradual expansion in extractive output were the occasional abrupt changes in the income accruing of townspeople, merchants, and craftsmen who were directly affected by developments peculiar to foreign-trade conditions. The foreign import trade was paid for by exporting the surpluses of extractive industry, but the flow of trade, particularly the extremely significant inflow of manufactured products from the British Isles, was also subject to the vagaries of speculation, financing, warfare, and the changing laws applying to such commerce.   On the one hand was the mass of extractive producers whose variable individual fortunes merged into a gradually changing aggregate, dominated by farm production, and on the other hand were the much less numerous townsmen, with their merchants, financiers, artisans, and other professional groups deriving income from shipbuilding, construction, foreign commerce, or the rendering of personal services to those whose incomes, in turn, were largely governed by these simple commercial conditions.

Through the years this latter group increased rapidly as manufacturing, transportation, and the growth of cities developed.   We may consider that these groups of merchants, artisans, and manufacturers constituted essentially the "business" group, very minor relative to the total population in Colonial days, distributed along the Atlantic seaboard in the villages and towns but destined to grow into a much more representative group, experiencing simultaneous ups and downs in income through trade booms and depressions.   Apart from the variability and fluctuation in the money and real income of those deriving their living from business operations, there was, of course, a long-term underlying *trend* of development, the pattern of which we desire to translate into figures.   In establishing this long-term trend, the reader should understand that its course would be determined not only by the more or less fluctuating activity or real income of the urban business groups but also by the volume of production by the farmer.   As explained in more detail in Appendix 1, the long-term trend of production and trade shown in Chart 4 involves two component parts: an index of changes in agricultural production, which is represented by population growth during the eighteenth century, and is given a gradually diminishing weight through the years as the estimated value of agricultural production tends to decline relative to total national income and, second, a trade or business index consisting of several segments.   This index refers in earlier years to the estimated changes in physical volume of the most significant part of American import trade and in later years to estimated changes in the physical volume of total industrial output and domestic trade.

Fortunately, we have available excellent foreign-trade statistics extending back to the beginning of the eighteenth century, limited, however, to commerce with Great Britain.   Throughout that century, Britain was the world center of manufacturing, and our imports of British products, paid for with surplus agricultural and forest products, may be assumed to represent faithfully the variations that occurred from

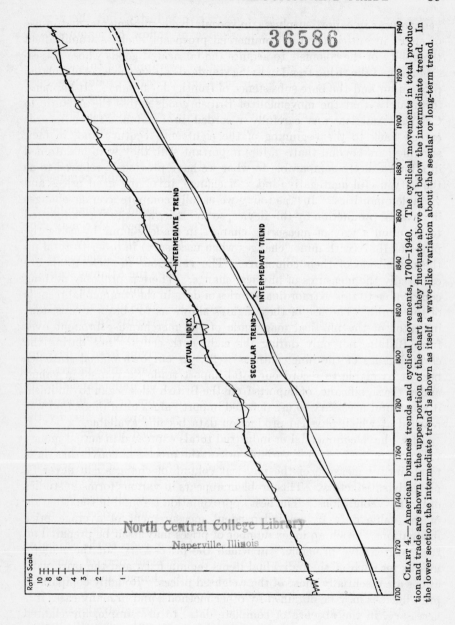

CHART 4.—American business trends and cyclical movements, 1700–1940. The cyclical movements in total production and trade are shown in the upper portion of the chart as they fluctuate above and below the intermediate trend. In the lower section the intermediate trend is shown as itself a wave-like variation about the secular or long-term trend.

year to year in export surpluses, in speculative commitments, and in use of credit in anticipation of commercial prospects, such as would affect the ability of the colonists to acquire the fabricated goods whose possession marked the rising trend in living standards above the level of isolated production and the bare subsistence of frontier husbandry.　It happens, fortunately, that the movement of British goods across the Atlantic to Colonial America was carefully recorded in London.　These records extend back to the beginning of the eighteenth century and, in fact, several years beyond that.　More important still, they were maintained in a form exactly comparable to what we have previously referred to as the very useful aggregative index of change, involving fixed prices and variable quantities.　Just as today we usually compute average changes in physical production by this device, so the British authorities happened to hit upon a way of measuring changes in trade volume by using the prices of 1697 (with minor changes when necessary) in order to total up the magnitude of their commerce.　The variations in these totals are essentially the measures of physical change.　There is probably nothing comparable to this extraordinary series of data in the commercial records of the world.　The use of these figures allows us to obtain a consistent indicator of the physical magnitude of the merchandise brought over from Britain, not only during the eighteenth century but during the early decades of the nineteenth as well.　As our own official statistics became available to record our total import trade (of course, in value) and as the significance of imports from the British Isles began to diminish, it was found necessary to use deflated import values until the period was reached at which physical production data became available.

If we have commercial or industrial totals expressed in actual money value, therefore involving variable prices, the process of converting these totals into a measure of the physical volume of changes can never be perfectly satisfactory.　This problem appears in various forms in studies of business conditions.　The best approximation is found in the deflation of the value data by an independent measurement of average price fluctuations.　Such an index number of prices may itself be prepared on the "aggregative principle," in which the prices vary but the *quantity weights* for each of the individual items remain fixed and the price variations are essentially those of the weighted prices.　Roughly comparable price indexes may be obtained by other methods, and in many cases it is necessary, in the absence of complete data, to use simple, unweighted indexes of price change.　It happens that during the major part of the nineteenth century we have just about enough information concerning commodity prices to be able to deflate United States import statistics with tolerably good results, in order to continue the measure of the physical volume of imported merchandise.　This device has been adopted to obtain that portion of the long-term index that is "spliced" onto the British data early in the nineteenth century and spliced again toward the end of that century to the more completely representative data measuring the changing volume of our industrial production. In referring in this connection to industrial production, the reader should bear in mind that we use the data to gauge not only factory operations but also a wide variety of service activities whose patterns are believed to be essentially similar to those of industrial output.

By a series of splicings of appropriate statistical data, therefore, we obtain a preliminary series that is not, however, the final index of *trend*. The series that we obtain is first smoothed out by means of long-term moving averages, and it appears in Chart 4 as the *intermediate trend*. Not all the data used to determine this intermediate trend are also the best measures of fluctuations in activity from year to year. During most of the period of time covered, special series of data, selected as probably the most indicative of the short-term rhythm of movement, have therefore been superimposed upon the smoother and more gradual undulations of the intermediate trend. In other words, the intermediate trend is the "spinal cord" or central tendency of the index, and the year-to-year index, shown as the upper curve in Chart 4, reveals the degree of minor vibration in general economic activity. This we may refer to as the "cyclical" vibration of boom and depression about the underlying tendency.

LONG-TERM BUSINESS TRENDS

It will be noticed in Chart 4 that there are *long-term* movements, like tidal swells, as well as short-term fluctuations. The existence of these long-term waves has for some time been suspected by economists, and we are now able to carry the necessary observations much further back than they have previously been carried and to express the indexes in terms of physical volume rather than merely in terms of *price* gyrations, as has usually been the case in attempting to illustrate the phenomenon. In the succeeding chapter, further attention will be given to the nature of this tidal action and the apparent reason for its occurrence. For the present, we are concerned with determining a further result. What is the over-all rate of growth *underlying* these wavelike undulations of the intermediate trend?

By methods that need not be described in detail at this point, it is possible to average out these long wavelike movements so that the still longer range pattern of *secular* trend can be observed. Such a secular trend of growth (the word "secular" referring to change "over the centuries," that is, over very long periods) is so fitted mathematically to the wave index as to equalize the deviations above and below the line throughout the entire period of time covered, 1700–1940.   In this sense, it is the average growth slope or gradient, balancing out the extended wavelike tendencies that, in turn, balance out the choppy year-to-year fluctuations.

It should not be thought that this secular growth trend represents anything in the nature of an ideal or "normal" or *inevitable* tendency to which the actual performance of our economic activity necessarily must adjust itself over the decades.   The trend is statistically *derived from* the more or less vibrating pulsations of actual economic life, and it merely expresses the net result of the give and take.   Nor is the trend, as shown in Chart 4, to be regarded as meticulously accurate, for there are obviously many minor deficiencies in the data, and it is therefore presented as a tentative and preliminary result.   But a careful study of the chart will clearly demonstrate that the long-term secular trend, as it has been computed, is a more accurate expression of the long-term average slope than any given segment of the intermediate trend from which it has been derived.   The intermediate trend smooths out the annual fluctuations, but from time to time it alters its own gradient enough to convey a misleading impression for decades at a time of the rate of underlying secular drift.   Had we endeavored, for example, to express the rapidity of growth in the physical volume of business from 1880 to 1920 on the basis of the intermediate trend, the result would have been to establish an excessively high average rate of progress, as tested by later history. For that particular period, the progress, on the whole, was more rapid than could be indefinitely maintained.   On the other hand, from about 1850 to 1870 or from 1800 to 1820, the intermediate index of production and trade would have created an impression of a slower rate of progress than was later found to be attainable.   Thus an approximation to the true rate of national economic progress, in terms of physical creation of wealth or flow of real income, requires a longer *continuity* of pertinent data.   This is why particular pains have been taken to extend the indexes in Chart 4 as far as the eighteenth century.

There is one important precaution to be noted in interpreting the long-term trend of economic growth.   The basic data are obviously drawn from the history of the past.   We do not know what the pattern of the distant future will turn out to be.   Therefore, when these trends, however carefully fitted to conform to the average slope of the data, are extended down to the present time, their position or level is *not yet influenced by those unknown future movements that will later form a continuation of the component data.*   If those future wave movements respond to conditions so that the give and take continues to vibrate around a central tendency of about the same gradient as in the past, we shall assume that the trend position as now shown is tolerably correct.   But if the future brings about a marked and persistent acceleration of the rate of general productive progress or, on the other hand, a continuing tendency toward a faltering of the rising drift, we shall be entirely wrong in assuming that the current position of the secular trend index affords a valid expression of the ultimate level, the ultimately confirmed gradient. If, in the future, declining movements tend to outweigh the effects of periods of temporary business expansion, it will become necessary to introduce more or less curvature into the secular trend, and this will require a relocation of the trend as previously estimated, possibly far back into the earlier years. For this reason the secular trend of growth as shown in Chart 4 has been indicated in a broken line since 1910; the position as shown as of 1940 is entirely provisional and subject to further change in the light of what the future will bring forth. All such trends are, of course, heavily weighted by past experience; and the records of nearly two and one-half centuries may cause the over-all gradient to be a tolerably accurate representation for most of that period. But we should not place too much reliance upon the gradient as shown in the last few decades in view of the unknown future events that will necessarily influence the slope of the trend when it is recalculated in 1980 or 2000.

One of the remarkable features of our economic growth from 1700 to 1940, as indicated in the index of secular trend fitted to trade and production data, is the modest amount of variation in the rate of advance per decade. Since a ratio scale has been used in Chart 4, it is apparent to the eye that the secular trend, being almost a straight line throughout the period, reveals an almost constant *rate* of growth. This rate approximates an annual rise of less than 3 per cent prior to 1750; there is a slowly advancing rate thereafter to about 3.8 per cent per annum in the decades following the Civil War; and since about 1890, we observe a slight tendency toward decline to about a 3.6 or 3.5 per cent rate in recent decades. Even though these surprisingly consistent rates of expansion reflect no inevitable or "normal" law of material progress conforming to the popular notion firmly rooted in human nature that growth is part of the natural order, one may legitimately draw from this record of the past at least one element of assurance and perhaps inspiration. The nation has encountered many intervals of difficulty, crisis, and chaos, but energy, courage, and coordinated effort have overcome them all. Perhaps even in the recent troubled years, during which our complex productive system has been exposed to the shocks of an exceptional depression, followed by unprecedented changes in political structure and administration and, finally, a war of gigantic scope—perhaps even in these days there are constructive influences at work somewhere capable of extending the measures of productivity presently in a direction continuing still upward rather than declining. If such influences are in the making, they are as much concealed from our present view as they were in previous periods of temporary stagnation and crisis.   We shall return to this phase of the subject in Chapter 25.

It has been stated that the indexes in Chart 4 are probably not a perfectly accurate portrayal of the economic progress of the United States.   That progress in all its detail and the psychological aspects of human well-being can probably never be wholly accurately determined or expressed.   Even though we have sought to obtain a reasonably homogeneous index of physical productivity, not distorted by the occasionally wide gyrations in commodity prices, many of the intangibles and the qualitative aspects entirely escape our yardstick.   If the data at our disposal were more complete, making it possible to allow, for instance, for the many changes in the quality of goods and the efficiency of service or transportation activities or the circumstances of health, safety, and comfort in the processes of production, even so there would still be a host of minor intangibles defying measurement.   We should find ourselves ultimately confronted by the necessity of estimating the purely psychological utilities, as distinct from the physical commodity output or the tangible evidences of services performed.   We should be confronted by the subtle gradations of psychic income, enjoyment, sacrifice, personal satisfaction, dissatisfaction.   There are many aspects of human experience and our ways of organizing human life that a prosaic statistical index of business progress fails to record.   But nonetheless, it does record a very substantial portion of those material contributions to physical well-being that, in turn, condition so much of what may be termed individual well-being and cultural amenity.

In order to bring together a measure of change in production and trade with population changes on a reasonably comparable basis, there are shown on Chart 5 (lower section) the decade-to-decade population *increments* and the 10-year increments of the actual measure of business.   In this manner the short fluctuations are smoothed out, and we can compare the behavior of the productive effort at those times when population change introduced variations of increment.   The two lines in Chart 5 have both been drawn on a ratio scale, but the scale for the increase in population per decade represents a range of calibration twice as wide as the scale for the business-index increment.   That is to say, the latter series is shown with one-half the range of variation that it would naturally show, and this is done in order to bring the two curves more closely together for comparison from decade to decade.   It will be noticed that in the decade from 1810 to 1820 a definite retarding tendency appears in both curves.   Then the increases are continued very rapidly until the decade of the Civil War, 1860–1870, when another decided hesitation in both measures of increment is observable.   In the decade 1890–1900, the population increment was again dampened down, but there was in this case less of a corresponding reduction in the momentum of business activity. Further evidence of sympathetic movement thereafter appears in the decade including the great depression, 1930–1940, during which the population increment sharply declines and the per decade net expansion in the volume of business shows a hesitating tendency similar to that in 1860–1870. There appears, therefore, to be some degree of functional relationship between the amount of growth in population and the net accumulated progress *from decade to decade* in general business volume or the real income of the people of the country.

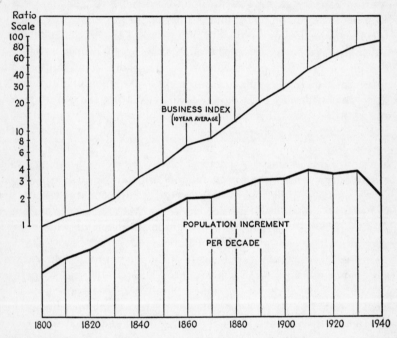

CHART 5.—Population increments and decade averages of general business, 1800–1940.

The causes involved in this interesting relationship might be considered as operating primarily *from* changes in increment of population *to* the business increments or, on the other hand, *from* the state of business conditions *to* the factors giving rise to retarding or accelerating tendencies in population. The truth here is not wholly clear. It will be noticed, however, that three instances of temporarily interrupted increase in the population and business increments occurred during periods of unusual wartime disturbance and postwar readjustment. In the following chapter, we shall examine in greater detail the behavior of the general business index during and following periods of major war disturbances. In the course of this discussion evidence will be presented for the conclusion that in all probability the more or less similar movements of the factors that we have been referring to above may be attributable to a common underlying causal factor.   It is highly significant that whatever relation exists between the business and population increment measures is revealed from decade to decade but not in the long-term drift.   There is little agreement in the general patterns.

CHAPTER 4

BUSINESS ACTIVITY, PRICES, AND WARS

We have seen that the concept of trend as applied to business growth admits of several interpretations. The measurements of such trends that have been presented are of two types, one more flexible than the other. The intermediate trend traces what might be regarded as a moving center of gravity; the secular trend is in a sense a mathematical abstraction or idealization of what the long-term average gradient might have been had there been no alternations of momentum of a wavelike kind. We recognize, then, that there is an apparent tendency over a very long period of time for the volume of general business to expand; but this actual performance proceeds by fits and starts rather than in an even, uninterrupted flow. In this fact there is some degree of analogy to the growth of living organisms. The life process reveals periods of more and less rapid acceleration during the course of growth. But these analogies must not be carried to the point of insisting that there is in economic affairs any necessary or inevitable wavelike tendency, undulating around the secular trend of expansion, or even cyclical oscillation about the wavelike intermediate trend.

Although possibly not intentionally, the impression has been created by some writers who have referred to evidence of these long-term tendencies that there is an *inherent* instability and recurring wave movement involved. In point of fact, however, a study of historical events will disclose that most of the long-term wavelike undulation shown by the intermediate trend seems to have resulted from specific factors in the nature of exceptionally serious breakdowns in business activity and interruption of trade relations. Invariably such unusual interruptions in the progress of economic development have occurred following major wars, that is, wars that have created drastic and far-reaching dislocations not only of the prevailing economic system but of political and social affairs. It is important to consider in more detail the relations between business activity, wars, the course of commodity prices, and the state of the political atmosphere in this country, beginning with the eighteenth century.

Since we now have available an annual index of trade and production reaching back to the beginning of the eighteenth century, it is possible to examine the relationships between political disturbance and economic disturbance and to draw some conclusions such as cannot be derived from

47

a study of relatively short periods in recent history.   The important wars
that have affected the economic conditions of the American Colonies and
the United States have been so spaced in time that we must view the
course of events in broad perspective and with long-term data.   This is

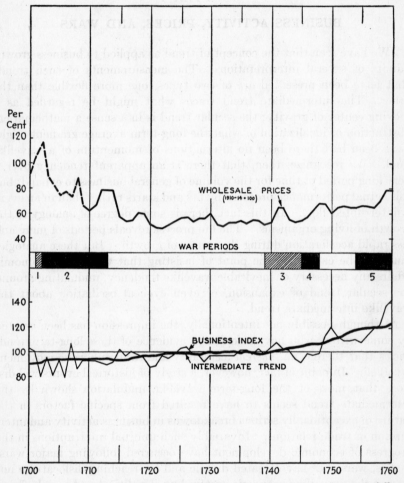

CHART 6a.—Business, prices, and wars, 1700–1760. The war periods are as follows:
(1) Spanish Succession; (2) Queen Anne's War; (3) War between Great Britain and Spain,
and War of the Austrian Succession; (4) King George's War in America; (5) French and
Indian War and (1756–1763) Seven Years' War in Europe and India.

important, too, because the periods of exceptional business breakdown or
prolonged stagnation following great wars have some distinctive characteristics with each successive experience. We would not expect to
find precise repetition of pattern. Of one thing we can be reasonably
certain—major war disturbances are associated with, or followed by,

such relatively violent readjustments in the productive and commercial processes and especially in the prices of commodities, property, and services that even when the year-to-year fluctuations are smoothed out by an intermediate trend (as shown in Chart 4), the course of that trend may

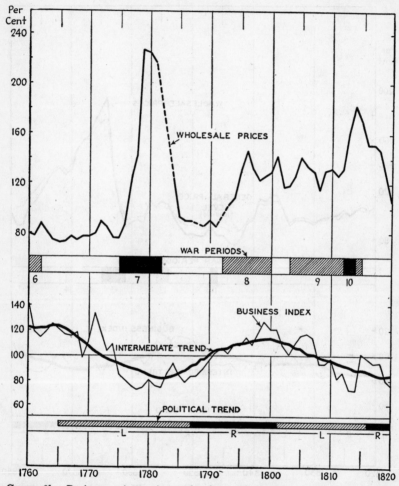

CHART 6b.—Business, prices, wars, and politics, 1760–1820. War periods: (6) Continuation of Seven Years War; (7) War of the American Revolution; (8) First phase of the French and Napoleonic Wars; (9) Continuation of Napoleonic Wars; (10) United States War of 1812 with Great Britain.

be perceptibly diverted temporarily from the generally rising *secular* continuity. At these times hesitation develops. If we study closely these alternating long waves of intermediate trend, it is convenient to express them in terms of their ratios to the underlying estimates of secular growth. The results appear in this form in Charts 6 and 7.

Through these charts there is drawn a horizontal band with lightly shaded or solid black sections. These mark the approximate duration of wars capable of having some bearing upon American economic life. The shaded portions represent wars in which the American people were not

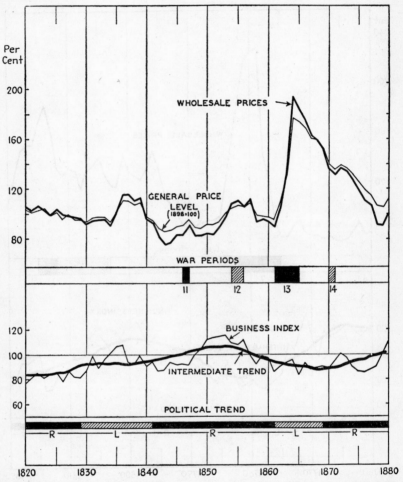

CHART 7a.—Continuation of Chart 6, 1820–1880. War periods: (11) United States War with Mexico; (12) Crimean War; (13) United States Civil War; (14) Franco-German War. The general price level shown here includes wages, security prices, rents, etc., as well as commodities.

directly involved, and the solid black portions refer to war periods that called into action American man power and equipment. The length of these segments naturally does not express the relative importance of these war intervals or the demands upon man power or materials or the general amount of financial sacrifice involved. If, however, we glance at the index of wholesale commodity prices and, after 1820, the general price level directly above the war intervals, we gain a better impression of the impact of these military emergencies upon an important phase of the

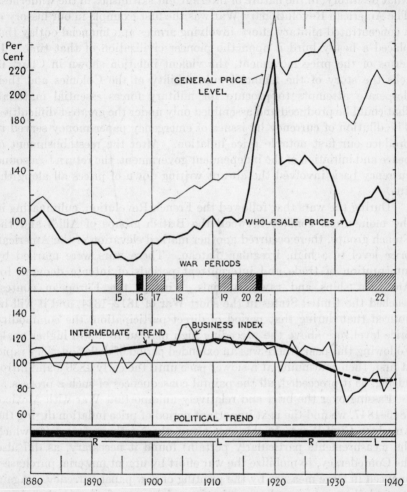

CHART 7b.—Continuation of Chart 6, 1880–1940. War periods: (15) Chinese-Japanese War; (16) United States War with Spain; (17) Boer War; (18) Russo-Japanese War and German-Moroccan War scare; (19) Agadir Incident and Balkan Wars; (20 and 21) World War I; (22) Italian War in Ethoipia, Chinese-Japanese War (1937 ff.), Spanish Civil War, and beginning of World War II.

economic system. It will be noticed that every war that has directly involved American participation has been marked by a more or less violent general rise in prices.[1]

[1] For a description of the data used in the indexes of prices see Appendixes 2 and 3.

WARS AND PRICE LEVEL DISTORTION

Our wars during the first half of the eighteenth century were somewhat desultory, in the nature of intermittent skirmishes in the wilderness. The American Revolutionary War was the first example in our history of a concentrated military effort, involving armies and financial outlay that placed a heavy burden upon the pioneer civilization of that time. In terms of the price movement, the violent inflation shown in Chart 6b tells the story of the financial vulnerability of the Colonies and their desperate attempts to procure for military forces essential materials that could be produced and assembled only under the greatest difficulties. The dilution of currency by issues of emergency paper money served to produce our first notable price inflation. After the reestablishment of peace and initiation of the independent government, the return to a sound currency basis involved the abrupt writing down of prices all along the line.

During the wars that followed the French Revolution, culminating in the momentous conflict between the British groups of Allies and the French groups, there occurred another marked elevation of the American price level to a high, irregular plateau. These wars were marked by interruption of trade and intermittent periods of intense demand for American ships and raw materials. Finally, the European contest reached the United States in the short War of 1812–1814, and it will be noticed that during that period of direct participation, the commodity price level rose above the preceding high plateau to a still higher peak. Following this peak, there was an extended period of deflation, very rapid at first, then continuing at a slower pace until the early 1830's and introducing, as it proceeded, all the painful consequences of such a process.

Passing over the brief and relatively unimportant War with Mexico, 1846–1847, we find the next important period of price inflation during the American Civil War. In this case again, the Northern States (to which the measurements particularly pertain) found it necessary, as did also the Confederacy, to mobilize the war effort by urgent material purchases, financed in large measure by the printing of new paper currency. Again we find the postwar collapse of prices violent at first and then long-continued, the pattern somewhat repeating that following the War of 1812–1814. Deflation of commodity prices was rapid until about 1879; after a brief interruption, it was resumed at a slower pace until about 1897, and in the more comprehensive "general" price-level index, still more gradually. At that point there occurred a significant reversing tendency, probably accelerated in some measure by the Spanish-American War emergency, which was shortly followed by the Boer War in Africa, and later the Russo-Japanese War of 1904. These wars, however, did not produce a movement of basic prices that we could describe as really inflationary, and the gradual rise during the early 1900's probably reflects several special factors. Next we have the period of World War I, which produced a decided rise in prices prior to the entry of the United States into the conflict. After the conclusion of the War, prices continued to soar to another historic peak. This period illustrates characteristic aspects of postwar scarcity of primary commodities, particularly in Europe. The price movement of World War I was accomplished, so far as the United States was concerned, through the medium of credit expansion rather than the issue of inconvertible paper money as such. From the peak of 1920, the first stage of deflation was rapid and brief in this instance, followed by a fairly long table of relatively steady prices that again collapsed during the general depression of the 1930's. The "general" index, however, remained on a much higher level than commodities alone. The rising drift of prices in the latter 1930's, although attributable partly to internal political policies, became part of the momentum created by world-wide preparations for World War II.

If the reader will now again review this remarkable correlation of commodity price inflations and deflations with major war intervals, it will be observed that the business-activity index (shown in Charts 6 and 7 below the war periods) fails to reflect the same pattern of movements. The degree of response of business conditions to wars can be observed in terms not only of the intermediate trend but also in the year-to-year fluctuations. The earliest war period shown at the beginning of the eighteenth century failed to produce any pronounced price inflation, and there is no evidence of a sustained and unusual rise in business (trade) activity. The War of 1745 (King George's War) produced a moderate rise in the price level, but business activity appears to have improved after the War rather than during the conflict, when there was evidence of a rather marked depression. The experience in the French and Indian War is rather different; prices rose somewhat and there was a rather pronounced business boom culminating at the close of the War. The fighting was done principally on land and did not involve the obstructions to foreign commerce that have in many cases characterized major wars. The period of the American Revolution marks a striking instance of directly inverse movements in commodity prices and trade activity. Following a short and violent boom in trade in 1771, there developed a creeping paralysis of all business as the colonists organized opposition to British trade. During the War itself, trade conditions reached an extremely low level of depression, which was sufficient to deflect the intermediate trend into a pronounced trough. Thereafter trade conditions improved and continued a rising drift, even during the first period of the ensuing conflict between the British and the French.

Following a brief respite from 1800 to 1802, the great Napoleonic conflict involved the extension of commercial embargoes, severely restricting the market for American exports and the distribution of the usual imported products. Again we notice an abrupt business depression during the War of 1812, coinciding with the most rapid rise in commodity prices. The intermediate trend of business activity reaches its peak about 1800 and declines until 1819, *despite* the sharp rise in commodity prices between 1811 and 1814. We see that the great waves of price inflation are by no means positively correlated with the underlying cyclical undulations of business activity itself (expressed throughout in terms of volume). The American Civil War was preceded by a period of unusually active business and much reckless capital promotion. From the depression, which began as early as 1853, the Civil War itself did not bring about any significant recovery, and the intermediate trend continued to drift lower until 1869. Business recovery from the Civil War was particularly slow in the Southern States, where industry and trade were demoralized to a far greater degree than in most Northern States. But the recovery that followed the War, although marked by occasional sharp depressions and financial panics, developed a gradual rise in the intermediate trend that persisted into the early part of the twentieth century. As in the previous cases, World War I failed to produce more than a brief interval of productive expansion, prior to the actual involvement of the United States in 1917. Following this, the volume of business activity irregularly deteriorated until after the first collapse in prices in 1921. From what has already happened in World War II, beginning as a gigantic conflict and involving our direct participation as this is written, it appears that another rise in prices is under way, but general production, despite drastic limitations upon many civilian-goods industries, may for a brief period rise to very high levels, since it is destined to be a *war of machines*.

THE KONDRATIEFF LONG-WAVE THEORY

There seems little room for doubt in the light of this historical evidence that major wars have contributed to our most important instances of price inflation; but they have not produced during their occurrence more than fitful and ill-balanced increases in the volume of business activity. Including the war and postwar periods, the intermediate business trend does not form a pattern correlating directly with similar long waves in prices. The wars have a powerful effect on the price level, but in the postwar periods the volume of production and trade is apparently motivated by mixed forces, of which price-level deflation is one. This last point is important because several writers, apparently basing their views on inadequate statistical evidence, have created the impression that long waves in business operations have about the same dynamic pattern as those found in the movement of prices. Thus far the predominant references to these longer waves of activity or major oscillations in the price level have been by European observers. Most important among these, and one of the first to develop the idea, is N. D. Kondratieff, director of the Conjuncture Institute of Moscow.[1] He observed that when various basic production series or price data were smoothed out to eliminate the shorter cyclical fluctuations (including those having periods of as long as nine years), there were observable very long waves that he thought pointed toward a regularly recurring cyclical undulation, with peaks and valleys between forty and sixty years apart. He applied smoothings to a variety of data, most of which, however, consisted of prices or value measurements, but a few fairly long series for coal and

[1] Kondratieff's important article, published as Die langen Wellen der Konjunktur (*Archiv für Sozialwissenschaft und Sozialpolitik*, December, 1926), was translated in summarized form as The Long Waves in Economic Life, *Review of Economic Statistics*, November, 1935. The studies that gave rise to Kondratieff's use of the concept of long waves were undertaken about 1920. Kondratieff was probably preceded in this regard by the Dutch writer Van Gelderen (Springvloed Beschouwingen over Industrielle Ontwikkeling en Prijsbeweging, in *De Nieuwe Tijd*, 1913); *cf.* also S. de Wolff, Prosperitäts- und Depressionsperioden, in "Festschrift für Karl Kautsky", Jena, 1924; W. Woytinsky, Das Rätsel der langen Wellen, *Schmoller's Jahrbuch*, 55th year, 1931; F. Kuczynski, "Das Problem der langen Wellen und die Entwicklung der Industriewärenpreise, 1820–1933," Bale, 1934; F. Simiand, "Les Fluctuations economiques à longues périodes et la crise mondiale," Paris, 1932.

Among American writers there is an interesting discussion, accompanied by statistical measurements relating to the United States and several other countries, in C. A. R. Wardwell, "Investigation of Economic Data for Major Cycles," University of Pennsylvania, 1927. Wardwell used the term "intermediate trend." Another more specialized use of the idea of wavelike movements longer than the usual alternations of the business cycle may be found in the flexible trends fitted by Dr. Simon Kuznets to various price and production series in his book "Secular Movements in Production and Prices," 1930. Professor Schumpeter ("Business Cycles," 1940) appears to accept Kondratieff's evidence that there are long waves in the movements of economic factors, but Schumpeter apparently does not accept Kondratieff's insistence that these waves are necessarily internally generated within the capitalistic system or that they must be considered as periodic.

In a review of Schumpeter's "Business Cycles" (*American Economic Review*, June, 1940, p. 267), Simon Kuznets calls attention to the probability that Kondratieff's conclusions as to the patterns of the long waves in economic data relating principally to European countries were largely dominated by evidence associated with *price* and *value* series. Such data would necessarily have been influenced to a marked degree by great movements in prices throughout the world, and the tendency of these price movements to be probably more nearly the same in pattern from one country to another than would be the movements of production and trade. Kuznets particularly questions the idea that the long waves must be considered necessarily as having periods of fifty years or that they represent any regularly recurring tendency generated within the mechanism of the prevailing economic system.

iron production were also examined.   Most of his data related to England, France, and Germany and little attention was given to statistics for the United States.   In spite of the fact that the various extended waves or cycles that emerged from these series failed to show much agreement in pattern, and without clearly differentiating between *prices* on the one hand and *volume* data on the other, Kondratieff summarized his long-wave patterns as follows:

Wave 1, rising from the late 1780's to about 1810–1817 and declining thereafter to about 1844–1851.   Such a wave does describe more or less the major pattern that can be read into the behavior of commodity prices during that period, but it fails to correspond with the intermediate trend that has been shown on the Chart above for the physical volume of trade in the United States.   According to that index, the business wave extended from about 1782 to 1800 in the rise phase, and the decline extended to about 1819.

Wave 2, indicating a rising tendency from 1844–1851 to roughly 1870–1875, thereafter declining to about 1890–1896.   Again this pattern is much more descriptive of long-term price movements than of the physical volume of business in this country.   Our results show a rising intermediate trend phase from 1820 to about 1852 and thereafter a decline to about 1868.

Wave 3 is incomplete in Kondratieff's scheme, but he conceives it as extending upward to 1914–1920 or thereabouts, and he remarks that probably it would decline to about 1914–1920, an unfortunate error due to the fact that he wrote before this important long wave of decline had actually reached its bottom. According to the writer's measurement, the intermediate trend rose to a peak in the neighborhood of 1910 and has declined until the late 1930's, with a provisionally indicated tendency toward initial upturn about 1939 or 1940.

Kondratieff added a number of other observations concerning the long waves that are interesting and worthy of note.   He called attention to the fact that during the long periods of stagnation marking the receding waves, large numbers of important discoveries and inventions in the technique of production and communication seem to be forthcoming—a surmise that is not yet capable of thorough verification but that deserves further study.   One of the most remarkable features of Kondratieff's views is the contention that all the wavelike action in business activity arises from *within* the economic system, meaning in this connection the capitalistic system of enterprise.   The long waves, he claimed, are "inherent in the essence" of such a system.   According to this remarkable view, wars are not an "external," politically motivated factor impinging upon trade and production from without; instead, wars are believed to arise from the economic conditions associated with periods of exceptionally long-continued acceleration and expansion.   "Wars originate in the acceleration of the pace and the increased tension of economic life."[1] Even the opening of new productive or consuming areas in the world was considered by Kondratieff to be a resultant of the long-continued upswings of production that generate friction, pressures, and the exploitation of new sources of raw materials and establishing of colonies.

Finally, this Russian writer considered that the production of gold, instead of being possibly one of the fundamental factors operating upon the world level of prices and thus having something to do with the long waves of national price movements, is a *resultant* rather than a causal force. We have here, then, an interpretation of this wave phenomena that is very probably associated with a Russian view of the mechanics of capitalism and that attributes to the dynamics of capitalism most of the things that happen in the world, *including the making of wars* and revolutions and the promotion of new colonial areas. We have here a view that insists that these long waves are true "periodic cycles," having a tendency to repeat themselves with a fair degree of regularity through the centuries, so that there are about two to each century. It is the view of the present writer, however, in the light of the fairly definite evidence now available for American experience covering nearly two and a half centuries, that the undulations of the intermediate business trend are probably much more responsive to the play of political disturbances and ambitions and major innovations in the ways of production than are the shorter "business-cycle" vibrations. There is no apparent reason of a conclusive nature, however, why either of these types of business fluctuation should be any more *inherent* in the capitalist economic or social system than are vibrations necessarily *inherent* in a piece of machinery. A high degree of stability in the price level and the absence of important deviations in either direction along the course of the growth trend in production and trade do not seem to be theoretically or basically inconsistent with an essentially capitalist society; and there is certainly no evidence thus far that they would be absent in thoroughly collectivist society.

To eliminate unnecessary and harmful business vibrations requires diagnosis—careful study and measurement of all the possible factors that may contribute to imperfect coordination of a vastly complicated series of parts in motion. There is no conclusive proof that the removal of such sources of disturbance *in* (or impinging *upon*) our economic system would necessarily be either destructive of long-term progress or incompatible with the maintenance of a high degree of individual initiative and a legal framework of private property. But we have yet to advance a long way in our measurements of these dynamic economic forces and their interrelationships and a long way, too, in the art of

[1] Kondratieff, *op. cit.*, p. 115.

political administration before the patterns of disequilibrium and friction give way to the smoothly continuous progress—a continually rising *secular* trend.

GENERAL ECONOMIC EFFECTS OF WARS

Holding to the view that wars have a most important bearing upon distinctive patterns of long waves in prices and in business activity, we may now examine more closely the process whereby a major war brings about inflation of the price level and of money values generally, whereas, on the other hand, it introduces disturbance of varying patterns and proportions in the business system. It is already clear that periods of intense warfare—accelerating some lines of production and trade and discouraging or even destroying others—produce effects upon business that cannot be expressed in a simply defined pattern, repeating itself upon each occasion. What we are now primarily interested in is the question *why* wars are capable of apparently producing such marked aberrations and deviations from the general drift of progress or growth. Before we undertake a study of the minor or year-to-year fluctuations in business, usually referred to today as "business cycles," it is desirable to formulate more definitely some conclusions as to the nature of the forces producing the long-term tidal movements. We shall turn first to the major cycles, because they seem to be associated with political policy under conditions of acute emergency. In fact, it may prove to be essential to divide our study of business dynamics into two distinct phases: wartime conditions and peacetime conditions. This distinction has been inadequately observed in studies of business conditions, doubtless because of the absence of reliable statistics and measurements of trade conditions over periods long enough to reveal the full perspective of relationships.

Probably the most fundamental economic characteristic of a major war emergency is the existence of a sudden, extremely intense, and powerfully mobilized demand on the part of the Government for the materials and equipment needed for the fighting forces (or for actual or potential allies). In our own national experience, this public demand has expressed itself primarily in money payments flowing through commercial channels. The Government has entered the markets as an urgent purchaser, not as an authority exercising the power to commandeer or to operate directly all machinery of production. This aspect of war supply has indeed been changing to a significant degree in recent years; some governments have assumed such sweeping control over production, trade, and finance that the war experience means merely a stepping up and altered character of a regimented production, no important buying of what is needed, and no need for huge issues of new money or credit. But to take the wars that have involved the American people since the beginning of the eighteenth century, the transitions from a peacetime basis to wartime basis, and the diversion of productive activity called for by the emergency have been marked by serious dislocation and extraordinary strain upon the normal mechanism of commerce, finance, and exchange. In none of these wars was there any extended period of previous preparation, gradual and deliberate mobilization of resources or capital or man power. The relatively *sudden* recognition of an inescapable emergency crashed upon an economic system normally functioning with relatively little governmental control over productive, commercial, and financial processes. Under war conditions the fighting personnel is commandeered; but the specialized material requirements, in amounts virtually without limit, are obtained under conditions that very soon cause competition between the Government and civilian consumers for possession of essential goods. The Government enters the markets supplied with virtually unlimited funds and bids against the private consumer or business firm; the result is naturally a swift and more or less cumulative spiral of price advances.

Contrasting with this sweeping intensification of demand and the prospect of enormous spendings of new money, obtained by borrowing or paper issues, to supplement inadequate tax revenue, actual production of the many materials needed can seldom be expanded fast enough. The drafting of men for war service removes labor from farms, factories, mines, and transportation. Women take their places only gradually. The direct allocation of allowable supplies to civilians, although today accepted as a necessary step by all governments, was not so much relied upon in earlier wars. There comes about a substitution of less well-trained, less skillful and efficient workers; a faster depreciation of machinery and transportation equipment and inadequate replacement occur. There may be, depending upon circumstances, an abrupt curtailment of raw materials from foreign countries. This quickly develops into bottlenecks of supply, creating the possibility of further swift advances in prices, in part speculative; at the same time inability to secure strategic materials hampers production of equipment in which those materials are indispensable.

In the case of most agricultural production, expansion of output to serve war needs is a relatively slow process. It requires a year or more to obtain even a modest increase, weather conditions permitting, in the output of field crops, and expansion in production of animal products requires considerably longer periods and tree crops still longer. A similar "inelasticity of supply" characterizes many of the important industrial metals and minerals. Mining operations can be speeded up somewhat if it is essential, but the discovery of new sources that can be economically developed even under the stimulus of intense demand is by no means a

simple routine matter.   Foodstuffs and mineral products invariably are
in urgent demand under wartime conditions, for the fighting forces consume more food per capita than the same number of persons would
require under normal conditions.   Certain metals and minerals, such as
steel, iron ore, copper, lead, tin, zinc, and, more recently, aluminum,
manganese, and nickel, are absolutely indispensable raw materials,
without which a war cannot be effectively carried on.   Likewise, among
chemical products, some are capable of rapid supply expansion, but others
are subject to limitations in technique or to curtailment of imported
ingredients, and the prices of all such things can rise perpendicularly
during a war emergency unless political control is exercised promptly.
As some strategically important articles are observed to rise several
hundred per cent in price, there is an acute psychological effect.   Speculators and individual consumers accumulate supplies in all directions,
and a forward buying and more or less speculative hoarding movement
occur in business firms.   This adds fuel to the inflation flame, and as the
prices mount higher, the Government, in order to continue its purchases
and ensure adequate supplies in the shortest possible time, must either
devise new ways of enlarging its monetary resources, even to the point
of abandoning the principles of sane finance, or impose stringent dictatorial controls over prices and uses.[1]

[1] In January , 1940, for example, the Army and Navy Munitions Board announced
a list of commodities that were considered "strategically important," that is, goods
essential to national defense, for the supply of which, during war conditions, dependence must be placed in whole or in substantial part on sources outside the continental
limits of the United States and for which strict conservation and distribution control
measures were thought necessary.   The following list of these strategic materials is
presented as an illustration of the things that in this particular emergency were in this
classification: *abacá* (Manila fiber), antimony, activated carbon, chrome ore, ferro-
manganese, manganese ore, mercury, mica, nickel, quartz crystals, quinine sulfate,
rubber, silk, tin, tungsten ore.   In addition to these materials, still another list was
announced and designated as containing "critical" materials, those considered essential to defense, involving less difficult procurement problems than the foregoing but
nevertheless some degree of necessity for conservation and distribution control.
These include aluminum, asbestos, cork, graphite, hides and skins, iodine, kapok,
opium, phenol, platinum, tanning extracts, toluol, vanadium ore, and wool.
     It is of interest to note that the prices of the strategic commodities rose, on the
average about 25 per cent from the end of August to the end of September, 1939, after
the outbreak of World War II.   In present-day warfare, in all major countries, a
much more alert attitude on the part of even nondictator governments than ever
before is directed toward accumulation of supplies of scarce materials and the application of equitable rationing or even prohibition of civilian use.   The importance of
exercising drastic control over normal consumption, over prices that are advancing
too fast or under speculative or hoarding pressure, is much better recognized today
by our Federal Government than in past wars.   See the further discussion of this
subject in Chapter 24.

In a simple economy, such as prevailed in eighteenth- and early nineteenth-century America, it was far less easy than today to develop substitute materials to replace those urgently needed for production of arms, explosives, ships, and clothing for the fighting forces. Today the drain upon the strategic commodities is somewhat reduced, although by no means eliminated, through the remarkable developments in the chemical and metallurgical industries capable of providing within a relatively short time alternative or supplementary materials, thus making it less difficult to sustain distribution of consumer goods and preventing skyrocketing prices. Rapid inflation has proved in the past so disastrous in its ultimate results that there is almost universally in a world at war a grim determination to control or avert it, even at the cost of despotic methods. It is by no means beyond question that if ways and means of avoiding the kind of universal conflict now existing are not found and made effective, these elaborate political devices for authoritarian control of war operations will project themselves rather generally into a future pattern of regimented society in which the difference between wartime and peacetime may be rendered permanently inconsequential.

Enough has been said of the economic effect of war to show the difficulty of formulating precise principles capable of application to any and every war period. Generalization is dangerous. But as we look back over the historical record of price behavior and general business changes, not only are the dislocating effects of war clearly evident but the effects appear to follow long after the event. Let us pursue the subject somewhat further. Why does it seem to be true that despite a temporary stimulating effect of war upon some industries, wars are generally associated with a long-term retarding of business growth, as was apparently true following the World War I, which did not fully reveal its distorting effects on the economic system of the world and of the United States until the 1930's?

An adequate answer to such a question cannot be attempted until some further aspects of business dynamics have been more fully analyzed in later chapters. We can, however, supplement the preceding sketch of the fundamental forces of war disturbance by noticing the impact of war demands upon extractive industries, particularly agriculture and mineral production. Again we must emphasize the pronounced inelasticity of supply characteristic of these industries, dramatized by the fierce pressures of military necessity and the accelerated tempo of demand. As prices of the products rise, an enlargement of output does somehow come about. If a war lasts for several years and if it involves the transportation of food, fuel, and metal goods to other countries, there is certain to be a substantial expansion in farm acreage and in the working of mineral deposits. This is usually true also of transportation facilities; there is emergency demand for ships, railroad equipment, and, in recent times, for a tremendous variety of military apparatus moving on wheels or through the air.

This expansion of effort involves the use of capital, which under war conditions has usually been provided under considerable difficulty. The heavy war borrowing by governments, owing to the impracticability of quickly increasing taxes or the reluctance of political leaders to resort to ruthless taxation, depletes the capital market until the Government itself has taken steps to liberalize credit creation by setting aside the usual reserve requirements recognized by sound banking practice or statutory law. Although the issue of private-capital securities is rarely easy under intense war conditions, banking systems come to the rescue of hard-pressed producers and offer loans at longer than usual terms and for essentially capital purposes. In the Civil War period, for example, the commercial banks greatly increased their loans secured by the obligations of manufacturers and farmers. In World War I, with the banking system fortified by the recently established Federal Reserve System, such loans were forthcoming in very substantial sums.

The case of the farmer under these conditions is of special interest and importance because of the temptation to borrow and expand that rapidly ascending prices create in the mind of the average grower of crops or breeder of livestock. It has been consistently true that farm indebtedness tends to multiply fast in periods of wartime inflation, and this means, in turn, that the elevated fixed charges on intermediate and long-term debt remain long after the war is over and the prices of the farmers' products have probably collapsed to much lower levels. Most farmers operate without the refinements of accounting or the principles of sound business judgment. The sudden windfall of high prices and corresponding larger earnings is not seen as the fleeting experience that it is. Land hunger and the speculative urge to secure profit from the appreciation in land values open up the road to financial ruin during the long years of price deflation.[1] When a large productive group is thus caught in the toils of inflation, the ultimate effects upon the total buying power and prosperity of the country should not escape the notice of those who would understand the dynamics of business. The effects have frequently been exaggerated, but there is no denying the fact that such abrupt rise and fall of farm income does serve as one of the many impor-

---

[1] At the beginning of World War II, well-organized farm groups, through powerful representation in Congress, for a time effectively opposed efforts by the Federal Administration to set maximum or "ceiling" levels for basic agricultural prices, even at levels higher (in terms of relative purchasing power) than those prevailing prior to World War I. The "parity-price" philosophy, and other aspects of deliberate price control are further discussed in Chapter 24.

tant distorting influences upon the flow of trade and industry following periods of war.

In the case of mineral products, there are somewhat similar results. Some mineral deposits are controlled by fairly substantial business organizations or interests controlling extensive capital. Expansion in holdings and the working of new or previously uneconomic deposits tend to be a concomitant of war conditions. The effects are broadly similar to those in agriculture, although impinging on a smaller social group. The prices of metals in wartime have been very volatile; demand is insistent, and supply is inelastic over short periods of time. But by the time the emergency is over we face a situation of expanded and excessive mineral production capacity. With war demand ended, huge amounts of scrap metal, war surpluses, or supplies from new foreign sources must be disposed of, and they cannot be fitted into the normal operations of industry fast enough to avert an acute surplus problem and hence a deep, sharp decline in prices. This may also leave behind it, as in agriculture and animal raising, inflated capital structures and fixed charges capable of impairing for a considerable time the solvency of the less conservative units in the industry. This, in turn, restricts their own demand for labor and the products of equipment industries. These are illustrations of but a few of the outstanding sources of price dislocation under wartime conditions and the tendency to expand the scale of extractive operations. These cases serve to depict, in a broad and general way, the manner in which great wars generate not only temporary economic or financial dislocation but disturbance of such magnitude that the broad course of industrial progress may be appreciably modified for several decades. It will be important to keep this in mind throughout the remainder of our analysis of business dynamics.

POSTWAR PROSPERITY AND DEPRESSION

We have not yet considered the experience of the industrial population and the large urban groups whose income is derived from service or finance and is not readily adjustable to the wide swings in the cost of food, clothing, and other essentials that characterize war periods. These groups have become an increasingly large proportion of the total population, and the distortions and strains of war and postwar readjustments have therefore tended to shift their emphasis toward these segments. In a general way, however, it can be said that wage earners in industry seem to have been able to adjust their money earnings to the inflationary price movement created by war conditions. This adjustment has not always been prompt or complete, but the available data on wage rates and prices establish the tendency. When industrial wage rates have been adjusted to the wartime level, they have remained far less sensitive to subsequent deflation than wholesale commodity prices or the retail cost of family essentials. Hence during the postwar period, a dislocating factor introduces itself throughout the field of manufacturing, trade, and transportation. Even before the productive system has completed the transition to normal operating conditions, the higher wage rates in industry have stimulated the demand for goods and houses among wage earners and also the demand among employers for labor-saving equipment as a means of reducing per unit labor costs. Meanwhile,[1] supplies of essential foodstuffs and clothing materials become more abundant and prices decline rapidly. Hence in those industries that are able to continue operations or resume normal production promptly, the working population has the advantage of a higher purchasing power than might have prevailed in the absence of war. The farmers' deflation loss is translated into the industrial workers' gain.[2] Wars are thus a means whereby a pronounced shift in the distribution of real income is brought about, and such far-reaching change in the relative position of important economic groups appears to continue for years after the war emergency itself has passed. Thus the forces created by major wars are of an explosive nature, but the aftermath involves even more basic changes capable of affecting business conditions either directly or indirectly for decades. And as we shall presently see, there are political and social aspects of this aftermath that the student of dynamic processes cannot overlook.

One of the important factors contributing to the recovery of production and trade after the immediate postwar deflationary readjustment is over is found in the necessity of making up for a period of curtailed or wholly suspended production of goods and equipment for civilian use. While prices are rising faster than wages, real income is reduced in many directions. Those living upon incomes that are relatively fixed find their actual purchasing power abruptly curtailed. Government requisitions, the possible shutting off of imported goods, prohibitions upon civilian use of certain articles and services, and the rise in financial payments to Government out of current income and even savings—all these involve the deferring of purchases by individual consumers whose incomes are drawn from industry, service, and finance.

[1] Excluding cases in which the war has directly demoralized productive capacity, as in the Southern States following the Civil War.

[2] The general price-level index in Charts 7*a* and 7*b*, which includes urban wage rates and retail prices, showed little tendency to deviate from the movement of wholesale commodity prices from 1820 to 1880, but thereafter an increasingly wide spread develops. The general price-level index after World War I notably resists deflation and shows a remarkable instance of the effect of maintaining industrial money wages geared to rising war prices after commodities suffer a tremendous deflation. This phenomenon is discussed in more detail in Chapter 20.

This deferment accumulates a potential demand, not only for routine requirements of the family budget but for consumer capital goods, represented by houses, furniture, and other household equipment, and, in recent years, automobiles. We shall further examine in a later chapter the dynamics of durable consumer-goods activity in relation to war periods, but to summarize the principle in a few words here, we can say that a more urgent and effective demand for consumer durable goods, particularly in industrial areas, favored by the revised relation of wage rates to cost of living in the postwar period, tends to revive important branches of industry *despite continuing difficulties in extractive industries.*

The recuperation in urban industry and incomes, partly responding to the accumulated demand for consumer durable goods, can be expected eventually to encounter limiting forces arising from the existence of a continuing unbalance within the economy as a whole. Postwar recovery movements appear to be destined to give way presently to a secondary depression, particularly if the postwar reconstruction is carried on with a reckless and more or less speculative momentum and is amplified by the continued expansion of credit facilities and the ease of capital financing that major wars appear always to have provided as one of their important consequences.[1] Having this train of events in mind, Leonard P. Ayres has formulated it into the generalized observation that after a major war there are two depressions: a primary depression and a secondary depression, the latter following the postwar reconstruction excesses, speculative financing, and overbuilding. This secondary reaction may indeed prove to be more severe and extended than that immediately following cessation of hostilities.[2] Ayres summarizes his conclusions as follows: "Great wars appear to produce regular sequences of economic results which we may identify as (1) commodity price inflation, (2) farm prosperity and farm land speculation, (3) price deflation and short primary post-war depression, (4) a period of city prosperity and widespread speculation, (5) secondary price deflation and a long secondary post-war depression."[3]

The Great Depression of the 1930's, according to this interpretation, was a delayed secondary depression following World War I, complicated not only by the domestic forces of disequilibrium among income and

[1] Disposal by individuals of governmental obligations previously purchased to assist war financing may be a factor contributing to postwar purchasing power and also to the usual tendency for high-grade bond prices to decline sharply in such periods.

[2] This view is developed and illustrated in an interesting way by Ayres' pamphlet, published by the Cleveland Trust Company in 1935, entitled "The Chief Cause of This and Other Depressions." See also his "Economics of Recovery," New York, 1933, especially Chapter 2.

[3] "Chief Causes," p. 50.

industry groups but by the demoralization of international markets and finance traceable to the war. It is doubtful whether Ayres' view is capable of being translated into a hard-and-fast principle, describing a *necessary* sequence of events in every case; but it provides a working hypothesis that is most helpful in interpreting postwar readjustments in the United States after several of our important conflicts. It is rather difficult to discover any substantial verification of Ayres' secondary depression following the American Revolution, since the revival in business activity following the general demoralization attending that conflict was rapid and continuous until the Napoleonic wars again introduced severe disturbance. Nor do we find much evidence of the principle following the War of 1812; there was a brief recession in 1819 and 1820, but the forward sweep of industrial expansion carried the business index upward with but minor variations until the middle 'thirties. Following the Civil War, however, there is some evidence that the delayed readjustments following initial postwar recovery were unusually marked and long-continued. The difficult years of the 'seventies and 'eighties illustrate the final blow suffered by the extractive producers, whose incomes had been particularly deflated by raw-material price collapse. Acute rural distress colored political and social movements and kept alive a spirit of unrest and resentment toward urban industry, capital institutions, and the railroads for many years. The 1930's witnessed a repetition of much the same friction between country and metropolis that strongly colored the reform measures of the New Deal.

TIDAL WAVES OF POLITICS

The impact of postwar economic depressions upon social attitudes and political temper has not escaped the attention of historians and political scientists. One historian who has made notable contributions to the study of economic and political forces during the evolution of the United States is A. M. Schlesinger, who has recently provided a most interesting summarization of political attitudes during nearly two centuries of our history.[1] He finds that there are long-term, alternating, wavelike movements in the general political atmosphere. He is not here concerned with the mere alternation of political parties or formal platforms but rather with the general characteristics of conservatism as distinct from liberalism, or rightism as distinct from leftism, that are revealed in the political policy and expressions of ideas. Beginning at 1765, Schlesinger characterizes each period, as shown in the lower portion of Charts 6 and 7, by the narrow band indicating shifts between leftist and rightist political temper. The first period, 1765–1787, he

[1] Tides of American Politics, *Yale Review*, Winter Issue, 1940.

characterizes as one of dissatisfaction and revolutionary and leftist sentiment directed against the British. It was this feeling, doubtless accentuated by the heavy taxes and debts carried over from the wars against the French, that so rapidly welded the colonists into a unified body of revolutionists. This period was followed by one of contrasting temper, lasting until 1801. There was a conservative backwash during which the new leaders of the successful but still struggling Republic brought to bear upon national policy the talents of business leaders and propertied men of considerable ability as well as public spirit. It will be noted in the chart how well these periods, as designated by Schlesinger, correspond with the phases of the long-term wavelike intermediate business trends, the leftist and liberal intervals more or less coinciding with periods of stagnation and failure to keep pace with the underlying secular growth. Periods of political rightism and conservatism coincide with a contrary pattern.

During the disturbed years of the Napoleonic campaigns there were intervals of war and peace but continuing economic instability, and the broad drift of the business trend again failed to keep pace with the secular growth tendency. This was the period of Thomas Jefferson and the growing influence of the farm groups in national policies, lasting until about 1816. Then followed another rightist movement from 1816 to 1829. This was a period when demands for tariff protection became insistent and large amounts of Federal funds were allocated to the construction of roads and canals and experiments with national banking. The period of the 1830's, until about 1841, was dominated by the spirit of Jacksonian democracy when, as Schlesinger puts it, "the plain people romped into power"—with consequences that will be noted further in later chapters. The party in power abruptly reversed the tendency toward Federal assistance to business and capital promotions all along the line. It cultivated the sentiment that it was "small business" rather than "large business" that should carry the American economy forward. Bankers, in particular, were often denounced in Washington. Although these were years of very rapid national growth, this political temper, especially after 1836, served to incite the popular mind against the financial system and against speculators in land and real property. A period of general economic retrogression lasted until the late 'forties. Between 1841 and 1861, there was again a period characterized as generally conservative and marked about midway by one of the greatest business booms of our history. There was widespread resumption of trading in land values, tolerated by a political temper exemplified by Tyler and not unfriendly to the promoter and speculator. There was even some rather general toleration of the system of slavery until the great crisis of the Civil War broke.

During and following the Civil War, until about 1869, and particularly during the years of collapsing prices, the bitter cries of the farmer were again heard. It was this rural distress that motivated demands for free land for more settlers and a drastic modification of the Federal Government's policy of land distribution. With the doctrine of human freedom and abolishment of servitude, there was a general popular emphasis on the elimination of restrictions upon the access by even the humblest citizen to agricultural acreage. This interval was followed by a long period of relatively conservative political temper, which Schlesinger closes at 1901. With the administration of President Grant, we have a succession of friendly gestures on the part of the Federal Government toward railroads, manipulators, and promotional finance generally. Import tariffs were stepped up, and industry enjoyed one of the greatest periods of stimulation and acceleration that any nation has ever seen. This was our Golden Age of industrial growth, relatively untrammeled by regulation and subsidized in many indirect ways by a sympathetic political attitude. At just what point this attitude, so friendly to enterprise and business promotion, actually gave way to another reformist interval is not wholly clear.   Schlesinger puts it at 1901, with the coming of Theodore Roosevelt's regime of the Big Stick over corporations and the philosophy of more power to the people. Actually, however, this attitude, although dramatic and full of portents of reform, did not produce many far-reaching reforms until after the sharp and sudden business collapse of 1908. This immediately ushered in a wave of insistent and determined reformism, expressed in the adoption of a Federal income tax, various banking and insurance reforms, and particularly the great crusades against the "trusts," resulting in the "dissolution" of the Standard Oil and American Tobacco monopolies amidst a tremendous flourish of animosity toward big business in general. Sometime between 1900 and 1911, there occurred the transition from the remarkably long period of conservatism and political indifference to the *modus operandi* of finance and industry, to an equally extended period of reformism, which the writer is inclined to believe has almost continuously tinged our political atmosphere to the present day. Schlesinger, however, considers the reformist period as lasting from 1901 to 1918, when Woodrow Wilson, according to his view, lost control of his reformist movement and gave way to the opposition forces for more than a decade. And this period of the 1920's was a period of postwar boom, dominated by the activity in construction and the bringing to maturity of great new industries built upon the internal-combustion engine and its material requirements.

These booming years of the 1920's were not of a consistent and uniform political and social temper. All through this period, financial reform was busy, as was also a steady encroachment of paternalistic aid to chronically unprosperous farmers. This was a period of liquor prohibition; the period when political minds were uneasily conscious of the troubles of postwar Europe and when much was heard of ways and means of resolving a mountain of postwar debts and reviving the economic life of conquered nations. It was, therefore, not difficult for American sentiment and political policy to become imbued with an essentially reformist temper as soon as the great secondary depression came after 1929. What has happened in the past decade in the way of reformism is the political counterpart not only of an exceptional economic depression were but of one that was felt the world over. There is thus deep social meaning in the long-term convolutions of the business-activity measurements. In the words of Schlesinger, the rhythmic pattern of our history seems to be "a period of concern for the rights of the few, followed by one of concern for the wrongs of the many."

MOTIVE POWER AND ECONOMIC PROGRESS

Before leaving this subject of the long intermediate waves of economic progress and stagnation in our history, let us hazard a few observations upon some aspects of the technological environment that seem to have a bearing on recuperation following the severe breakdowns. It would, of course, be trite to say that through new discoveries and inventions and the application of new ideas to the acts of production, we are able to progress in an economic sense and can restore prosperity, following even the most demoralizing crises. But we can be somewhat more specific in the matter of the strategically effective innovations and their influence upon reconstruction.

It seems reasonably certain that during the latter half of the eighteenth century the effect of the wars fought in North America was compensated by impelling forces of technological change. As long as the American Colonies were closely dependent upon trade with Britain, the dramatic strides of invention and industrial mechanization occurring in Great Britain formed for us also an economic bulwark against any continued stagnation. The latter half of the eighteenth century was a period of remarkable economic progress in all directions, agriculture, transportation, the introduction of the steam engine as a prime mover, and a long series of inventions revolutionizing the textile industry and creating enormous demands for materials. After the Revolutionary War, this continuing technological and industrial tidal wave continued to provide basic ideas and principles for our own industrial revolution. Among the most potent industrial forces that cushioned the readjustments following our early wars was the vastly improved application of motive power to transportation and manufacturing. The application of steam power to navigation was a means of developing the resources of the cotton states to feed an insatiable mill demand for raw material. The application of steam power in the 1830's to rail transport provided the foundation for thousands of new industries and productive communities. The application of electrical energy in the 1890's served to continue and reinforce that remarkable epoch of industrial expansion. By the time the World War I readjustments were being felt, the application of the internal-combustion motor to individual transportation, as well as to agriculture, formed, certainly, one of the outstanding forces capable of counterbalancing deflationary influences, until unfortunately the economic system of the United States was called upon to bear extraordinary financial shocks emanating from abroad. Even the potency of industrial innovation could not for the time being maintain the pace set by the assembly lines of a motor age.

As this is written, the profound international stresses carried over from World War I have created a still more ominous period of global war with the portent of unprecedented economic, political, and social consequences. But the broad sweep of history strongly suggests that when the readjustments are at length made, we can expect that *new ways of applying power* to *production* and *transportation* will again be the most significant contribution of technology to renewed business progress. Although not making a formal prediction, the writer hazards the opinion that regardless of possible heavy destruction and the interrruption of progress in living standards immediately in store and regardless also of any political aftermath of regimented planning or fatuous panacea, the really dependable sources from which we can expect long-term powers of recuperation to be derived will be found to be these major innovations in terms of power utilization that have been so important in the past. We may not be able for some time to visualize the form or detail or the exact principles of physics or chemistry or astronomy they may involve in their purely scientific aspects. But let no one expect that the mere introduction of *gadgets* or the inception of particular useful *products* will suffice to provide the sustaining stimulus and the new jobs that the next generation of our people will surely need to continue a progressing civilization. We can be tolerably sure that those nations will survive that can achieve the organizing and functioning of their productive resources most efficiently and apply controlled power most effectively to aid the human hand. Continued progress in the general standard of living is not derived from "buying power" fed by doles but from producing power fed by science.

It is conceivable that in the next long cycle of political developments we may see throughout the world another major shift toward placing the *dynamics of production* ahead of the *statics of distribution* and toward recognizing that all progress requires provision for future growth. This means that the perennial need for capital cannot be overlooked nor can the vast importance of a vigorous flow of capital be minimized. Carl Snyder has presented cogent statistical proof that our long-term progress and an increasing use of productive capital have been very closely correlated:

The reason for the growth in output over a century and more must be found in the improvements in the methods of production, the provision of new types of machinery, power, and in the increase in capital available per worker. The evidence for this is remarkably clear. The increase in primary power employed in industry (measured in horsepower) has gone on at practically the same rate as the growth in physical products. The amount of goods produced per horsepower in industry has not materially changed in any decennium of the last century or more.[1]

[1] Carl Snyder, "Capitalism the Creator," p. 48, New York, 1940.

CHAPTER 5

THE DYNAMICS OF THE PRICE LEVEL

We have seen that the intermediate trend of the volume of business describes long-term, wavelike undulations about the secular trend of growth. With the aid of statistical measurement, we can designate the approximate points when these long-term wave movements reach their tops and their bottoms. When we compare this pattern with the corresponding major tops and bottoms in the long-term movements of commodity prices, we find that the patterns do not agree, even though political disturbances and particularly wars seem to have been effective in producing both these types of variation from the respective *secular* trends. In the case of commodity prices, the secular trend, over several hundred years, approaches the horizontal; for the growth in the volume of production and trade the secular trend has continued over a long period to rise at an almost constant rate of change approximating 3.6 to 3.8 per cent per annum, although for recent decades we cannot definitively confirm the persistence of this rate until many years have elapsed.

Since the long-term movements in price level have these peculiarities of pattern when considered from the standpoint of intermediate trend or drift, we shall devote this chapter to an examination of some of the most fundamental factors involved in forming these patterns. We must first, however, give some attention to the more precise definition of what is meant by the level of prices or, more exactly, by measures of average change in prices. We have already illustrated the movements of wholesale commodity prices from 1700 to 1940, based on index numbers of several types spliced together to form a continuous record. Without entering into the technicalities involved in the construction of price index numbers,[1] it will be helpful for the purpose of clarifying the subsequent

[1] On this subject see Irving Fisher, "The Making of Index Numbers," Boston, 1922; W. C. Mitchell, Index Numbers of Wholesale Prices in the United States and Foreign Countries, *U.S. Bureau of Labor Statistics Bulletin* 284, 1921; W. M. Persons, "The Construction of Index Numbers," Boston, 1928; C. M. Walsh, "The Problem of Estimation," London, 1921; The Making and Using of Index Numbers, *U.S. Bureau of Labor Statistics Bulletin* 656, 1938; Carl Snyder, The Measure of the General Price Level, *Review of Economic Statistics*, February, 1928; W. I. King, "Index Numbers Elucidated," New York, 1930; G. F. Warren and F. A. Pearson, A Monthly Index Number of Wholesale Prices in the United States for 135 Years, *Cornell University Agricultural Experiment Station, Memoir* 142, *Part* 1, 1932; Croxton and Cowden, "Applied General Statistics," Chapters 20 and 21, New York, 1940.

discussion to explain briefly the kind of procedure involved in this type of dynamic measurement.

MEASURING CHANGES IN PRICE LEVEL

Perhaps the simplest form of an index number of price change is obtained by averaging the percentage changes for a considerable number of prices, each referring to a previous year or period as its base. The base average will, of course, be 100 per cent. Such an average might be accomplished arithmetically or by geometric or median methods. The resulting average of change might involve no deliberate "weighting" of the various articles and hence the relatives expressing their price variations, although an accidental or haphazard form of weighting of the different components in the index can easily result from careless selection. It is considered preferable, if statistics are available, to introduce deliberately into the construction of a price-index number a weighting or multiple counting to give some of the components more effect on the result in proportion to the commercial significance of the articles and others, less effect. Naturally, in the very early years, we lack sufficient data to establish such weights, and even the price data are incomplete, so that the results are not to be considered of high accuracy. There are difficulties too in interpreting the currency units in which Colonial prices were expressed. Where weights can be assigned the various commodities on an optional basis, either they can be introduced as modifying the relative numbers or they can be used to obtain for each commodity at the base period a value (price times quantity) with which subsequent similar values, preserving the same quantities throughout, may be compared.[1] This is known as an aggregative index of prices. It is of course obvious that if it is desired to measure the course of price changes over a very long period, the selection of weights in an aggregative index number representing quantities produced or sold in a period long past might not accurately represent the relative weights of the different items at present. Hence there is necessary a certain amount of change in the weights from time to time, as well as introduction of new articles as they become important and the dropping of old ones as they become extinct. In the wholesale-price index, which has already been illustrated in Charts 6 and 7, we cannot say that there has been a consistent system of weighting throughout the entire history, but the index is the best picture of wholesale commodity prices that we can present by splicing together a number

[1] An aggregative index number of price changes, in which the values throughout are weighted by quantities relating to the base year, is mathematically equivalent to a weighted average of individual ratios of price change, each of which is weighted according to the value as existing in the base period. For a production index the weights become constant prices or unit values in the aggregative form, and the volume element varies.

of representative series, notwithstanding the fact that these segments are based on somewhat different methods. The curve shown in Charts 6 and 7 represents a weighted form of index beginning at 1849; for the previous years the computations are based on carefully compiled price data, and the absence of weighting is believed not to impair materially the value of the results for the present purpose of broad comparative analysis.

There are, of course, a variety of ways in which subgroups of commodities may be formed to observe average changes in their prices. Over long periods it is possible to obtain significant index numbers for comparing domestic commodities and imported commodities, raw materials and finished goods or even semifinished goods, farm prices and nonfarm prices, manufactured goods and extractive products. When we come to retail prices the material is much less complete, at least for the United States, and measurements of such price changes prior to 1914 must be arrived at by approximation based on other materials. The index numbers of the Bureau of Labor Statistics afford a reliable means of measuring changes in the retail prices of food, clothing, fuel and light, house-furnishing goods, house rent, and certain miscellaneous goods and services. Combination of these groups makes up what is known as the index of the cost of living or, more specifically, the retail cost of a list of items considered essential to an industrial worker's family.[1]

The cost-of-living index number, it will be noted, carries us beyond the range of strictly *commodity* prices, since it contains such items as house rent, electric power, etc. As we move from raw materials to finished manufacturers and then again to the goods on the shelves of merchants ready for purchase by consumers, we find at each stage that there are embodied in the prices a series of labor, capital, and other service costs involved in the processes of production and distribution. As will be shown later, the price behavior of various kinds of services, broadly speaking, differs from that of commodities in the raw state, valued at the farm or mine or at some elementary stage of fabrication. The difference in behavior is in part due to the fact that in many of the fabricating and processing operations it is within the power of producers, within limits, to keep prices under a certain amount of control. In some instances, this control extends to the power of preventing fluctuation over extended periods of time. Such prices are considered in present-day terminology to be "fully administered" prices, but these represent a relatively small part of the value of the finished commodities of commerce.

---

[1] Carl Snyder has computed an annual index of the cost of living as far back as 1860. R. S. Tucker has shown that Snyder's index can be approximated fairly well by combining an index of wholesale prices and an index of industrial wage rates. See *Review of Economic Statistics*, Jan. 15, 1934, p. 8.

The most important single factor, however, that introduces into retail prices the familiar tendency to move more slowly and to drift with an upward bias, as compared with wholesale prices, is the peculiar pattern of industrial wage rates. Because of the influence of labor organization and for other reasons too, it has long been characteristic of industrial wage rates that they rise without marked delay with important advances in commodities, but when commodity prices decline they do not usually decline appreciably. Whereas the long-term pattern of commodity prices shows wide advances followed by violent declines, in a kind of exaggerated saw-tooth pattern, the design of wage rates is rather that of a long stairway, with occasional landings. It is not surprising, therefore, to find that when we average together changes in wholesale prices and wage rates, as in the "general" price-level index, these contrasting patterns merge into a composite having in remarkable degree the pattern of retail prices. It must also be added that other kinds of service charges, such as taxes, interest rates, transportation charges, and all those prices that represent direct payment for service, especially personal service, tend to be less flexible in the major declines than in the wide advances, and these price elements become increasingly important in a complex economy in price measures that are of the cost-of-living type.

THE GENERAL PRICE LEVEL AND RELATED FACTORS

We can now proceed to broaden considerably further the concept of price level. Let us conceive our problem to be one of estimating changes in the prices of *all* the goods and all the services that enter into commercial transactions in terms of money or credit instruments. It might seem at first that such a heroically comprehensive price index would be hopelessly inaccurate and might have no definite meaning. It might be indeed a statistical curiosity. Nevertheless, such a concept does have much theoretical interest and even practical usefulness, even though much of its content would be based on sampling and estimation. What we have in mind in such a comprehensive index of price-level changes is an attempt to separate into two distinct measures the complex aggregate of transactions. Their value must, of course, equal the expenditure of all the money and credit circulated during a given period of time. If such a separation of the two factors—(1) the general price-level factor and (2) the trade-volume factor—can be even approximately accomplished, we have a scientific basis for investigating the relation between changes in the money and credit used for making payments and changes in the volume of production and trade in all markets. The purpose of this becomes a little clearer if we consider that the broad changes in money and credit circulation are measurable to a fair degree, and the volume of production and trade also is measurable in its essential movements.

The general price level would be a resultant of the simultaneous changes in these two magnitudes. By analyzing such measurements we can hope to discover how much our general structure of prices is affected by monetary factors and how much by trade factors.

For the United States, the pioneer effort to construct at least an approximation to an index of changes in the general or over-all price level was made by Carl Snyder, who for many years headed the economic research work at the Federal Reserve Bank of New York and who is widely known as a pioneer in many important statistical studies.[1] In constructing his index (*cf.* Chart 7), Snyder found it naturally impossible to include more than a sampling of the exceedingly voluminous data. He found that price data for many kinds of transactions and markets are unavailable. Nonetheless, a comprehensive index was prepared by averaging separate price series relating to 12 phases of the price system, each of these being regarded as significant of its group and each being assigned a weight. The list is as follows: farm prices at the farm, industrial commodities at wholesale, retail food prices, equipment and machinery prices, hardware prices, automobile prices, urban rentals, other cost-of-living items, transportation rates, realty values, security prices, and several series of wage rates. Snyder carried his computations back to 1860. The resulting index of general price-level changes resembles to some extent the dynamic pattern of the cost-of-living index so far as that is directly measurable. By using this index as a "deflating" series, Snyder was able to express data of bank check transactions, considered as an approximate measure of changes in the *value* of all trade, into a derived index of the *physical volume* of trade, eliminating price change. In other words, the component items and weights were sufficiently well selected that this derived index of "physical" trade movements agrees fairly well with other measures of the physical volume of trade and production independently developed.[2]

[1] For the best description of the index of general price level, see Carl Snyder, *Review of Economic Statistics*, February, 1928, p. 40.

[2] R. S. Tucker, in the reference previously cited, has shown that by carefully selecting the weights in combining index numbers of wholesale prices and wage rates, a composite closely approximating the pattern of the Snyder general price-level index is obtainable. This may be conveniently used to carry back the Snyder index as far as 1791, as Dr. Tucker has done. In the references in the present chapter to the general price level (and in Chart 8), our data have been derived in part from the use of Tucker's series and in part by the use of Snyder's series.

It should be noted that the measure of the general price level in Snyder's sense is associated with a concept of aggregate trade values of the broadest possible sort, in which, of course, there is duplication of raw-material items through the stages of production, processing, and transportation. There is also the presence of a certain volume of speculative turnover. In this sense, the value of trade is to be distinguished sharply from the value of national income (discussed in Chapter 3), a more specialized

It is obvious and has long been accepted as true in principle that the total volume of money and credit mediums that a community is employing to transact its business in any given period must have a definite relation to the total trade and to the prices prevailing. If it were theoretically possible to obtain a statistically perfect index of the changes in the entire price level, such an index, when multiplied by an appropriate and equally comprehensive index measuring changes in the physical volume of all transactions accomplished by monetary means, *would be mathematically equal to an index of change in the aggregate value of all transactions.* In other words, the total expenditure expressed in dollars must equal the sum of all individual transactions, each of which involves a price element and a volume element. At any given moment there is no way to secure a static snapshot encompassing all prices or including the total trade volume. But we can select a *starting point* in time and thereafter observe and record the amount of change occurring in total trade activity (expressed in prices held constant); and by a separate price index of change we can thus measure *change of level.* If we use constant prices (*e.g.*, those prevailing at the origin) in measuring changes in business, there will be a resulting discrepancy between the change in calculated *volume* and the actual change in *value* of transactions. Our general price-level index, however, will measure the extent and direction of this discrepancy. By multiplying the index of average price change by the index of trade volume we *remove the discrepancy.* We shall later[1] return to this formal statement of these relationships, after some observations on the American data over a long period relating to money, credit, price level, and business volume.

In order to obtain a reasonably satisfactory series of dynamic measurements of these basic and interrelated factors, we should have data in fairly continuous form extending over a period of years. Historical information regarding the *prices* of *commodities* is by far the most readily available, and the money and credit measurement is much more difficult. Since each of the American Colonies had its own currency system, the actual course of prices expressed in local currency differed as between one section and another. After the Revolutionary War and the establishment of a national currency system the behavior of prices tended to be much more uniform throughout the country. In fact, this was also true of prices during the Revolutionary War, when currency matters were largely under the management of the Continental Congress. During the eighteenth century and until the Revolutionary War, there were

concept. In casting up the value of national income, the object is not to count all the transactions into which money or credit may have entered but to estimate the net value of each operation in the creation of useful wealth or service.

[1] See Chapter 6.

persistent difficulties in obtaining capital, and, there being very little domestic production of precious metals, the actual money supply was a conglomerate of foreign coins, obtained through export trade, and various kinds of paper money circulated by the Colonial governments (occasionally to considerable excess). There was also a circulation of bank notes, some of them counterfeit and many of them resting upon the ultimate security of land, merchandise, or perhaps nothing at all.

A full discussion of the monetary and banking experiences of the early Colonial pioneers would carry us far afield into analysis of details. That period can perhaps be best summarized by saying that the colonists tended to follow the lead of Massachusetts in the issue of Colonial bills of credit. That Colony and also New Jersey, the Carolinas, Rhode Island, New Hampshire, and Virginia encountered increasing difficulties during the eighteenth century as the result of their public issues of circulating paper. "Sooner or later," says Bullock, "all the plantations were deeply involved in the mazes of a fluctuating currency, for the burdens attending the various wars of the eighteenth century were so great as to induce even the most conservative Colonies to resort to this easy method of meeting public obligations."[1] Even when Great Britain extended to the Colonies in 1741 her own earlier legislation against unrestricted credit issues, she failed to accomplish much control. The movement of wholesale prices, as shown in Chart 6*a*, fails to disclose the whole story of these reckless experiences with Colonial paper money and land-bank credit, since these prices were taken during that period from the records of Philadelphia markets and the currency of Pennsylvania happens to have been one of the more stable and better regulated systems. The chart does show, however, that as a result of the wars, even the price level in the important Philadelphia market registered the existence of inflation.

To finance the American Revolution, vast amounts of paper money were issued, not only by the individual Colonial authorities but also by the Continental Congress. The latter issues alone, under stress of the War, rose from 6 million dollars[2] in 1775 to 140 millions in 1779. With trade conditions demoralized and no possibility of maintaining convertibility of the paper into coin, the result was an enormous rise in prices. In Chart 6*b*, the rise in the index of wholesale prices is shown only approximately as far as 1781 by the use of New York prices, substituted during part of the period for Philadelphia prices. During the years 1782 and 1783, there are no available quotations because of the utter confusion and virtually complete loss of value of this currency. In 1781 the outstanding notes were repudiated as practically worthless,

---

[1] "Monetary History of the United States," p. 33, New York, 1900.

[2] Technically, in terms of Spanish dollars.

but by that time, fortunately, some foreign hard money was again becoming available for use. When the war ended, there was another short period of paper-money excitement in 1785 and 1786 that, as Bullock says, "was most distinctly an agitation carried on by and for the debtor classes of the country, and thoroughly typical of the struggles of the inflationists of the Colonial period."[1] Finally, with the establishment of a new currency system in 1792, clearly defining a uniform metallic standard for the nation, we entered upon a period during which the actual measurement of the elements of money and credit, volume of trade, and general price level becomes increasingly subject to measurement, so that we can study the relationships to advantage.

FACTORS OF CHANGE IN MONEY CIRCULATION

Before further discussing the statistical evidence, let us summarize some of the fundamental characteristics of money and the ways in which various kinds of mediums may be expected to contribute to the total of effective money in use. It will then be easier to understand the influences capable of bringing about changes in the monetary supply and its effective commercial circulation.

Within the jurisdiction of any government are two principal elements composing the total of the monetary mediums used for commercial purposes. First there is the money legally defined as "standard," in terms of which payments and obligations may be finally discharged without qualification. In modern times, such standards have usually been expressed in terms of specific quantities of gold or of silver or of gold and silver indifferently. Whether the standard money actually circulates in trade or not, the law defines the standard as a certain weight (and fineness) of the metal or metals selected. Second, we have the various types of paper money. Such paper may at all times be convertible, upon request of the holder, into the standard metallic unit without qualification; or it may be so convertible but with qualifications; or in still other instances, particularly during wars, it may be inconvertible and circulating by legal fiat.

Under the so-called "bimetallic monetary standard," the law specifies a weight, let us say, of gold and of silver, as the monetary standard; theoretically, the money of the one kind is convertible upon demand into the other. But unlike the case of paper money, gold and silver both have exchange or "market" values arising from their uses as bullion in industry and the arts. If the coinage ratio set by the law differs materially from the market ratio of value, one or the other of the metals as coin will have a higher value outside the money system than inside the system, and it will tend to be withdrawn from circulation. This is

[1] Bullock, *op. cit.*, p. 73.

important from the standpoint of the possible changes in the amount of available money for the use of the public under a bimetallic standard. If, on the other hand, a single metal is selected for the standard, coins of other metals may be kept in circulation by making their metallic content so limited and the amount in circulation so restricted that there is no tendency for these subsidiary coins to seek higher exchange return in the arts. The subsidiary coins then resemble to some extent issues of government paper, since they supplement the relatively limited quantity of standard coin or bullion and yet are kept convertible into definite quantities of the standard.

The quantity of total circulating currency resulting from governmental policies will thus be determined by the amount of the standard metal produced for use in the world, the part of it absorbed by the arts and industry, the part of it entirely withdrawn for hoarding, and the part lost entirely by accident. Of the remainder, a certain amount will be brought into a particular country as the result of international commercial and financial dealings and relationships. To these amounts will be added paper money and subsidiary money, and these will supplement the standard money as long as they are readily convertible into it. If, however, convertibility ceases, the paper money in circulation can theoretically be increased almost without limit; the control exercised by the standard money no longer exists. Under these conditions, two sets of prices may result, one expressed in paper and the other in terms of money metal. If issues of paper become very large within a limited time, prices so expressed will rise, and among these prices will be the price of gold and silver as metal. This creates a situation in which both the gold and silver may become more valuable as metal than as money, and the paper money will force the metals possibly entirely out of circulation.

During a period of war emergency, a government usually decides to limit or discontinue convertibility of its paper into specie in order to prevent the exhaustion of its standard reserves, or their capture by enemy governments. If large payments must be made during a war to foreign countries and large balances of actual cash must be shipped abroad, there will be a further rise in the price of gold and silver expressed in the foreign exchange rates, and the cost of foreign goods will therefore tend to advance even more than domestic products unless proportionate changes occur abroad. The extent of depreciation of the paper money, once it becomes inconvertible, may then be expressed either in terms of the *general level* of domestic prices, which is perhaps the best means of measuring it, or in terms of exchange rates against foreign moneys (if it is assumed that these remain on a metallic standard) or the prices of the precious metals quoted by bullion dealers (if it is assumed that such dealings are permitted).

During periods when inconvertible government paper money must be used, the units in which commercial transactions are expressed tend to be extrapolated by public usage and the need for some medium from the kind of units prevailing prior to inconvertibility. In this sense, the existing *de facto* standard of value becomes a rather subtle entity, although its nature is found in the fact that the public *continues to accept* mere pieces of paper in exchange for various quantities of goods and services. In other words, in actual trade it is ready *acceptability* rather than substance that forms the fundamental characteristic of all money. It is conceivable that people might continue indefinitely to use a paper-money system, if, of course, the quantity of such paper were kept within reasonable bounds by strict and incorruptible governments. So long as people were willing to accept the paper readily in trade, an intricate fabric of price ratios and relationships of one thing to another might be created, and the paper would accomplish the purpose of a medium of exchange, even though the ultimate standard of value would have to be distilled theoretically from the entire mass of goods and services obtainable for the paper money. Since it is this acceptability that gives all money its essential characteristic as money, it follows that the quantity of pieces or specific units of such money in circulation is an important element so far as concerns the making of price levels. Although in most monetary systems of modern times there is, or has been, a specific metallic standard unit, the amount of metal legally designated as a dollar or a pound or a franc has no direct relationship to the number of money pieces actually circulating, once we include all the paper mediums and subsidiary coins as well. To speak historically, the setting of a definite metallic standard money made of metal established in most countries the acceptability of the money and of all the substitutes readily convertible into it. But a money system once established can conceivably perpetuate itself without an effective metallic standard so long as general acceptability continues. If the paper or other forms of money be issued in such quantities that awkward or ridiculous quantities must be used in trade, acceptability rapidly becomes impaired, and if it should fall toward zero the money system collapses. There have been dramatic episodes of such occurrences throughout history, especially following World War I, when Europe experienced extreme and tragic cases of hyperinflation and extreme depreciation.

In substance, then, the metallic standard underlying a money system is principally important as (1) a means of accomplishing and maintaining acceptability, (2) a means of controlling the quantity of paper and subsidiary coin that is kept convertible with the standard, and (3) a means whereby a given money system finds a workable relationship with foreign systems. It should be added that if coinage terms or the definition of a monetary standard consisting of actual metal are varied, more or less extensive changes will be produced in the price system, which will cause an immediate change in the rates of exchange against foreign currencies. This is true regardless of any change in quantity. Under these conditions prices may also rise if there is a general suspicion that further changes will be made and if speculators become active in the commodity, property, and foreign-exchange markets. If such an operation takes the form of reduction in the weight of standard coins, we have what is called "devaluation," which tends to raise the price of imported goods as well as of exported goods. This rise may extend to the entire price system, because under the new conditions either there will be more standard coins made from given quantities of metal or a larger amount of paper and subsidiary pieces will become convertible into a given physical stock of standard money metal. There have been many such devaluations of the coin or money standard throughout history, and in most instances these have represented the desperate measures of bankrupt kings or hard-pressed politicians to obtain additional money to meet emergencies. Our own devaluation of the dollar in 1934 was not exactly of this nature, since it represented rather an attempt to augment the monetary reserve of the country quickly in order to bolster commodity prices faster than could be expected as the result of the natural processes of gold production. This will be further discussed in Chapter 14.

FACTORS OF CHANGE IN BANK CREDIT

What has been said is probably sufficient to impress the reader with the complexity of the various factors involved in the possible variability in effective money supply issued for circulation by government. That supply may vary because of changes in the definition or unit weight of standard money, changes in the amount of standard metal available as the result of its production, use in the arts, and export and import of coin and bullion, changes in the amount of paper money supplementing the standard coin and subsidiary coin, and especially changes resulting from the issue of inconvertible paper money in times of stress. But this is not all. Paralleling and vastly extending the scope of the monetary system is the banking system. Throughout our own history, banks have supplied the circulating medium with a variety of credit instruments. By banks we refer primarily to the "commercial" banks, which are in a position to generate by their own operations and by virtue of their own credit standing what is virtually a paper currency capable of serving most purposes of exchange as effectively as money, so long as it is readily convertible into money. In order to attain this convertibility, banks of the commercial type maintain readily available reserves of standard money to redeem such of their own paper as the public may wish to redeem. The amount of reserves so held either may be a matter of banking judgment or may be dictated by legal regulations. In terms of fundamental principle, what is readily convertible into the standard serves most of the purposes of a medium of exchange. Furthermore, since the prime characteristic of the medium of exchange is acceptability, there ordinarily will be demands for the redemption of bank paper only for purposes of foreign trade, for the use of the standard money metals in the arts, or for reasons of the convenience of individuals.

It follows, therefore, that banks in the course of their operations may introduce into the system of payments a total amount of paper credit that may be five or ten or twenty times as much as the reserve of standard money held in their vaults. This becomes a system of "fractional reserves," the latter being always much less in amount than the super-structure of circulating credit. Should there be doubt as to the possibilities of redemption, those who hold bank paper become fearful of the integrity or reserve position of the banks; there may be sudden demands or "runs" upon the banks for redemption, with the result that more redemption is demanded than the banks can immediately accomplish. Under conditions of widespread hysteria banks close their doors, specie payments are suspended, and trade is abruptly demoralized over a wide area. Thus the system of fractional reserves in a commercial banking system, although it greatly economizes standard money and provides an extremely flexible means of facilitating commercial requirements, has at times become a source of widespread ruin among business-men as well as depositors. This illustrates an economic process subject to violent distortion, because it functions upon a very delicate balance easily disturbed by unusual circumstances. Stated in another way, it is an example of the principle of "trading on the equity." Obviously the commercial bank, as a credit institution, is in a position to make advances to businessmen needing credit or working capital considerably in excess of bank liquid capital plus primary deposits of cash and, like all such pyramiding of obligations upon a narrow base of assets in hand, forces upsetting the delicate balance can create violent and cumulating losses. This has happened many times in American history, and these occasions of breakdown coincide with many of the severe business crises of our past.

Commercial banks sustain obligations to the public in several ways. They may issue promissory notes, supported by convertibility into cash and readily acceptable in payments throughout the community. Actually, bank-note issue has been more and more circumscribed by law, particularly in the United States, and bank notes have in late years become analogous to Government paper money with respect to convertibility and acceptability. Much more important as a factor in augmenting the general circulation is the use of bank credit in another form. Commercial banks may grant to customers who borrow the privilege of drawing checks upon deposits that are created through the borrowing transaction and that can presently be converted into cash. These deposits, originating from the making of bank loans, accomplish their "circulating" function through the checks drawn upon them. Today the use of these checks upon commercial banks has become the predominant element in all modern monetary systems, and in the United States checks probably accomplish over 90 per cent of all the money work.

Governments have been rather slow to regulate the terms upon which commercial banks may expand such credit advances and hence liabilities, since all such deposits are theoretically subject to withdrawal by those receiving checks drawn on them. In the United States particularly, there has long been legal regulation as to minimum bank reserves to be held against such deposit liabilities, but our commercial banks have in the past been permitted to maintain relatively large maximum amounts of deposits in relation to reserves. If national (or historically local) governments maintain or control central banks, the obligations of these banks may also count as assets of the commercial banks available for their reserves. This introduces into the financial system a further degree of pyramiding or flexibility of expansion and contraction.

During our earlier history several of the state governments set up their own public or central banks in order to make possible a further expansibility of "paper reserves" wherewith the individual banks could meet their credit obligations. Today we have an elaborate and powerful Federal Reserve System, which enables the member commercial banks to regard as a part of their effective reserves the amounts that they have on the books of the Federal Reserve Banks as deposits. These deposits in the central banks may themselves be expanded well beyond the actual gold or equivalent reserve held by those banks. This is cited to show the enormous potential flexibility of a banking system that not only pyramids upon fractional reserves but may do this with one potential pyramid resting upon another. So long as demands for actual convertibility of bank credit into money are on the very limited normal scale, there is no difficulty; but let the demand be accelerated by fear or even violent speculative excesses in trade and the smooth functioning of the system may be threatened. An enormous degree of "leverage" may exist in the credit and currency system in the event that a metallic money standard is suspended so that extension of bank credit is based on reserves consisting of inconvertible paper of some kind. Under Government pressure or in a war emergency, the credit *deposits* generated by the central bank in loaning to the Government in turn become available as *reserves* for the commercial banks in making their advances to industry and trade and to individual buyers of the Government bonds. It was this process that proved so inflationary in World War I.

MEASUREMENTS OF CREDIT AND CURRENCY CHANGES

We may turn now to a factual study of the dynamics of the American money and credit system and the relationships that have prevailed between its variations and the volume of business to form the pattern of the general price level. The first problem is to construct an index of changes from year to year in the effective monetary or currency[1] circulation or, rather, that preponderant part of it which may logically be expected to be a reliable gauge of the total means of payment capable of affecting the general level of prices.

From the beginning of the nineteenth century to 1879, the end of the interval of suspended specie payments after the Civil War, the two most important *variables* in our total monetary circulation were (1) issues of inconvertible Government paper money and (2) a very substantial amount of circulating credit arising from the loans and investments made by commercial banks. During much of this period the circulation of actual coin was still important, since the commercial banking system was in process of development and Government inconvertible paper circulated actively only during the War period and a few years beyond. During these years, therefore, beginning at 1811 and ending at 1878, a credit and currency index has been constructed from three elements, Federal Government notes (and equivalent irredeemable notes or certificates), total loans and investments of the banks, and the amount of specie estimated to have been in actual circulation.[2] We shall first consider the circumstances that created marked changes in the amount of effective currency units in use in this period and the relation between the variations in the index of credit and currency to changes in the production and monetary stock of gold and silver in the United States.

Our index begins at a time when Europe was in the throes of the Napoleonic-British Wars, which had alternately stimulating and depressing effects upon American export and import trade and which finally culminated in the involvement of the United States between 1812 and 1814. By this time business conditions had substantially deteriorated. The British had already abandoned the convertibility of Bank of England notes. The strain of the War forced the United States to abandon con-

---

[1] The term "currency" will be used not in a technical banking sense, but to designate in a general way means of payment accomplishing the exchange function.

[2] It is important to note that these elements are selected as being significant indicators, not because they are necessarily the best means of *defining* money or credit. A more detailed explanation of the construction of this credit and currency index will be found in Appendix 3.

vertibility of all paper money and bank notes from 1814 until 1818. Prior to the War of 1812, our banks had considerably expanded their credit circulation, but there was some element of restraint in the existence of the first United States Bank (1791–1811). The removal in 1811 of the restraints exercised over the other banks by this Federal central bank led to reckless expansion of banking operations and bank credit in circulation. United States Treasury notes also circulated during the War. When the time came for resumption of specie payments there was again in existence (beginning operations in 1817) a second national central bank, whose loans and investments are included in our index figures. The return to specie payments took the form of convertibility into standard coin. The United States was operating under a bimetallic standard that happened to be maintaining such a coining ratio that gold did not readily circulate; even the silver money was a mixture of domestic and foreign coins. But the act of reestablishing convertibility with metallic money served to reduce the mass of paper circulation.

We may refer now to Chart 8, at the top of which appears the index of credit and currency. It will be seen that a marked decline in this index occurred after 1817, but at about 1823 there began a gradual rise, considerably accentuated during the early 'thirties and reaching a peak at 1837. During these years the general circulation appears to have adjusted itself with some degree of conformity to the changes in the amount of specie forming the available monetary stock of the country. This is shown in the second curve from the top on Chart 8. Below this is shown also the annual amount of coinage of gold and silver. This remained fairly steady until the 1830's, when a rapid rise occurred to 1836. The metallic resources forming the major part of bank reserves thus expanded rapidly, and bank credit itself appears to have increased steadily and rapidly amidst an era of widespread and reckless speculation. Banks at this time operated under little restriction, save that which from time to time was provided by the United States Bank or some State Banks. The Second Bank of the United States ended its career in 1836, but as early as 1832 circumstances had arisen and abuses had been suspected that led Andrew Jackson in that year to announce his decision not to continue the charter of the Bank beyond its legal expiration. This tended at once to release a considerable amount of luxuriant local bank credit, principally in the interest of land speculators in the far-flung frontier. As a result, the monetary index shows an extraordinary expansion. This occurred under conditions of ineffectual restraints, no standardization of banking practices, and the prevalent Jacksonian idea of *small* banks for *small* business and as many banks as could be organized per square mile. The period was perhaps one of the most extraordinary in our history as to unrestrained banking, much of it directed to questionable uses and all of it accelerated by an adventitious expansion in reserves with enlargement of the stock of specie, mostly silver.

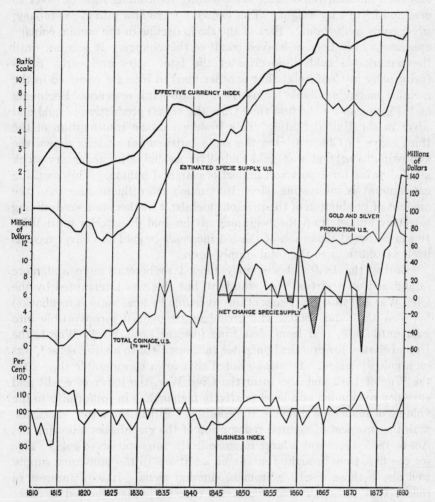

CHART 8.—Supply of metallic-money and effective-currency index, 1810–1880. Statistics relating to coinage, changes in supply of monetary gold and silver, and production of gold and silver are from the reports of the Director of the Mint. The estimates of supply of specie are from reports of the Comptroller of the Currency and the Secretary of the Treasury. The figures are exclusive of Treasury holdings and money held for redemption of United States notes. The curves in the middle section show the principal annual changes contributing to the total stock of circulating metallic money.

At 1836 a dramatic event occurred paralyzing much of this riotous frontier credit manufacture. President Jackson ordered that all payments to the Government for public lands would be demanded *in specie*.

This served to break the land boom and for some years to cause a more moderate temper in the circulation of bank credit. Previously a change had been made in the coinage laws, setting the coining ratio of silver to gold at 15.7 to 1 by weight. This caused gold to flow into use as money, silver coins to flow out. Part of the sharp decline in the annual coinage appears to have been a delayed result of this change. It was not until the remarkable gold discoveries of the late 1840's and early 'fifties (principally in California) that another marked increase occurred in the metallic money available for use in ultimate bank reserves. Beginning at 1845, we can for the first time trace the actual production of gold and silver in the United States. This is shown in the continuation of the third curve in Chart 8. On the same (arithmetic) scale is shown the approximate net value of gold and silver available for monetary stock after allowing for export and import of coin and bullion. This resulting net amount is interesting, since it is much more fluctuating than the amount of production of the precious metals; it further shows a declining tendency almost from the beginning of the gold discoveries until 1872. It will be noted that each of the net increases in gold and silver records itself as additions to the total supply curve.

During the 1850's the country tended to become more and more established on a virtual gold standard, but this was interrupted by the Civil War and the large issues of inconvertible Federal notes (greenbacks) between 1861 and 1865. The greenbacks remained inconvertible into gold until 1879, and from that time forward until World War I, the United States, for practical purposes (although not in a strict sense), was on a gold standard. It will be noted that for a considerable time after the War of 1812 and also after the Civil War, the index of credit and currency remainded at a level relatively higher than in conformity to the volume of monetary specie in the country. But in the latter 'seventies, with the prospect of assured redemption of the greenbacks following the Act of 1875, there was a large increase in the importation of gold. This for the first time brought the annual additions to the monetary supply well above those resulting from production alone. It is of interest to reflect that although the credit and currency index showed a fairly sustained volume of circulation following the Civil War period, both business conditions (lowest curve, Chart 8) and the actual importation of hard money showed a marked expansion as soon as provisions were made to retire the excessive Civil War greenbacks. This involved a somewhat greater dependence of bank reserves upon actual specie and the threat of some contraction in the total amount of bank credit in relation to general business growth. As a result, there was strong agitation from the cheap-money element for more liberal currency issues. But the banking system was now restrained not only by an official policy of sound money, in terms of the gold standard,[1] but also by the rapid development of the National Banking System after 1865. This system introduced the feature of restricting circulating bank notes to those of national banks, secured by Government bonds. There was also more effective supervision of capitalization, reserves, and banking practices generally. But the cheap-money advocates insisted upon restoring monetary abundance and rising prices, through either bimetallism or a single silver standard. This pressure, especially from the rural sections, gave us the ridiculous silver legislation of 1878 and 1890, providing for specified Government purchases of silver, not to establish a costandard with gold, but rather to "limp along" with gold in the hope that the total amount of circulating money and bank credit would expand. The silver, however, accomplished little.

As we turn now to Chart 9 and observe the behavior of the credit and currency index from 1880 to 1890, we find that its general drift more or less paralleled the rate of change in the gold stock.[2] There was a rapid gain in the amount of available gold between 1879 and 1881, but after 1887 the net amount of gold for monetary use (after allowance for export and import), as well as the net amount of gold for the arts, declined, in spite of a larger gold production in the United States. This did not much affect the credit and currency index, which maintained a fairly level position until 1897. The bizarre experiments in the 'eighties and until 1893 for halfway reestablishment of silver actually led to a considerable demoralization of public and private finance in the United States. The system contributed to export of gold and the Treasury was forced to borrow by rather unusual means in order to maintain convertibility of the various Government paper in gold. As soon as these experiments ended at 1893 and the drift toward sound money was again confirmed in the election of 1896, there occurred a remarkable increase in the available gold monetary stock and an almost parallel upward trend in the credit and currency index. The change during this period was a spontaneous response of banking operations to the underlying expansion in available gold reserve. It will be noted that the net annual contribution of gold to the monetary supply was fairly large and in some years exceeded our domestic production. During the period from about 1896 to 1906 there was also a rapid rise in the business-activity index.

Between 1915 and 1920, we enter another period of inflation, which in this case was continued beyond the conclusion of the War. The most

---

[1] This was virtually initiated in 1853, when the silver dollar and other silver coins were reduced in content to keep them in circulation, and in 1873, when Congress dropped the silver dollar entirely from the coinage, although it did not proclaim the gold standard in specific language.

[2] The index after 1878 consists entirely of credit elements. See Appendix 3.

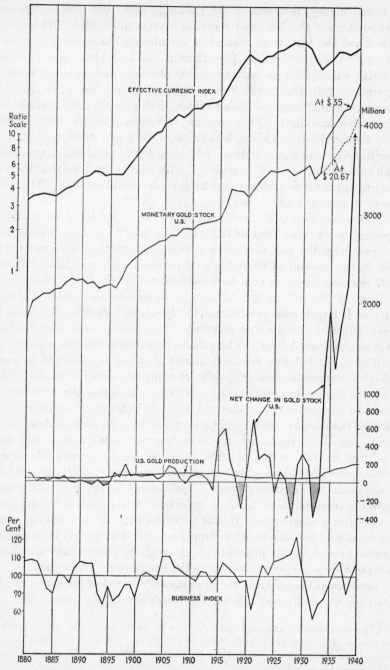

EFFECTIVE CURRENCY INDEX

At $ 35

Ratio
Scale

Millions
4000

MONETARY GOLD STOCK
U.S.

3000

2000

At
$ 20.67

NET CHANGE IN GOLD STOCK
U.S.

1000
800
600
400

U.S. GOLD PRODUCTION

200
0
-200
-400

Per
Cent
120
110
100
90
80

BUSINESS INDEX

1880 1885 1890 1895 1900 1905 1910 1915 1920 1925 1930 1935 1940

CHART 9.—Relation of gold production to monetary gold and effective currency, 1880–1940.
Statistics relating to gold were taken from reports of the Director of the Mint.

remarkable changes were in the net available monetary gold. A change both definite and startling occurred in the financial position of the United States. We shifted from being a predominantly debtor nation to being a nation surfeited with foreign gold. Gold production, somewhat discouraged by the conditions prevailing after 1915, declined moderately, but the annual net additions to our monetary gold stock rose tremendously as the result of the consignments of military supplies and foodstuffs to Europe. We entered upon a period of violent monetary disturbance that has not ended. It has, indeed, brought the country to an entirely new stage of monetary experimentation and control, against a background of world-wide monetary revolution and the possession by the United States of most of the world's gold resources.

EFFECTIVE CURRENCY AND GOLD

As we compare the index of monetary gold stock with the credit and currency index in Chart 9, we are struck by the recent general parallel movement, although in 1920 there was a decline in monetary gold stock due to temporary interruption of gold imports after the Armistice, whereas the credit and currency index rose rapidly to a high peak as the Federal Reserve System assisted the member banks in providing an enormous volume of credit. Remarkable also was the relatively minor decrease in the monetary index in 1921 and 1922; another rise followed to a still higher level in 1928–1930. Large net imports of gold occurred between 1921 and 1924, partly reflecting heavy food and material purchases by Europe. Thereafter, until about 1933, the net flow of gold, as well as domestic production of gold, continued to be relatively limited.

Although from about 1880 to World War I, the credit and currency index very closely paralleled the changes in our gold monetary stock, there was a growing disparity in the succeeding period, especially in the minor fluctuations. At the very end of the period the disparity rapidly increased. During the past quarter century, effective currency in use has adjusted itself less and less to the changes in available gold reserve and more and more to legislative and administrative controls exercised by the Federal Government. World War I brought into existence far wider fluctuations in the annual movement of gold to and from the United States. Gold movements no longer reflected trade conditions but rather reflected the shifting of liquid capital seeking safety from the encroachment of new dictatorships, the renewal of war preparations, and the threat of public seizures of wealth. Finally the gold movement broke away completely from the previous range of fluctuation, the annual increments to our monetary stock soared upward explosively, and the future of the gold standard as a basis for international exchange suddenly became highly uncertain.[1]

It will be noticed that monetary gold stock in the United States rose rapidly in the first years of World War I, but after 1917 there was a decided setback, accompanied by substantial net gold exports. It was in these years that the Federal Reserve System established the new machinery for control of commercial banking reserves and enabled the member banks of the system vastly to augment their lending power. During the War emergency, it was impossible for individuals to obtain gold upon demand, either from the Government or from the banks, unless it was needed for legitimate industrial purposes or international payments. The movement of gold into hoarding or back into banking reserves was thus temporarily checked, although later in the 1930's, hoarding again became a very conspicuous and embarrassing factor. It will be noticed that despite an abrupt slackening in monetary gold supply, the credit and currency index continued to rise very rapidly to a high peak in 1920. This was accomplished not only by lower reserve requirements but especially by the flexibility with which credit could be pyramided within the Reserve System. In fact, there would have been by 1919 a severe credit stringency had it not been for the facilities now available to the member banks for rediscounting approved assets and borrowing at the central banks. Such borrowing augmented member-bank reserve balances, just as a business firm's "cash" balance would be augmented in its bank account as the result of a bank advance. Credit advances by the central banks became a basis for multiplied credit advances by member banks. Thus the gold held by the Reserve Banks served the dual purpose of supporting their outstanding credit in the form of deposit balances and also the credit represented by their note issues. The Federal Reserve issues of circulating notes gradually supplanted the old National Bank notes, although they were not to be used by other banks for reserves. In addition to the creation of credit on behalf of the member banks, the Federal Reserve Banks also contributed directly to the total credit instruments in use by directly purchasing certain approved types of commercial paper (including Federal obligations) in the open market. The Treasury could not sell bonds and notes directly to the Reserve Banks, but indirectly much the same result was accomplished. In view of this, the credit and currency index includes in its composition not only the loans and investments of both member and nonmember

---

[1] A part of this rise was due to the devaluation of the dollar in January, 1934, as indicated on Chart 9. But even at the old rate of $20.67 per fine ounce, there was a tremendous rise in the gold imports. By the end of 1940, the monetary gold stock had reached the enormous total of 22 billion dollars, valuing at the revised rate of $35 per fine ounce. The devaluation is discussed further in Chapter 14.

commercial banks but also these advances made directly by the Federal Reserve Banks themselves through purchases made in the open market from 1915 forward.

It will be noticed that the collapse from 1930 to 1933 in the credit and currency index was much more clear-cut than the irregular and slightly downward movement of the monetary gold stock. The decline in bank loans and investments was primarily a result of the tremendous sweep of the depression, involving liquidation of enormous totals of assets and the impairment of billions of dollars in securities. Federal emergency measures, in addition to the devaluation of the dollar, extended to the removal of all gold from circulation and even from individual bank reserves. The gold was impounded and represented for banking purposes by gold certificates to be held only by the Federal Reserve Banks. Gold today is still available for the needs of industry and the legitimate settlement of foreign financial balances, but credit instruments are no longer internally convertible into gold. This and subsequent monetary policies are fundamentally phases of a world-wide tendency to remove the erratic influence of gold expansion or contraction from the credit system and to place the creation of credit increasingly under political control and manipulation. A mere glance at the great gold explosion shown in Chart 9 is sufficient to demonstrate that some type of control of this nature is inevitable.

It is entirely possible that the gold standard, as it was known prior to World War I, may never be restored. The United States has become more and more an exporter of goods and services to be paid for in gold; and prior to World War II we afforded a financial haven for a world subject to unprecedented fears of war and revolution that forced gold here primarily for safekeeping and only incidentally for use as active balances. Had the gold imports and additions to our monetary stock after 1933 been quickly translated into new circulating credit through the operations of commercial banking, we should have faced inflation possibilities immeasurably more serious than ever before, even apart from the renewed war conditions of the 1940's. This tidal wave of gold reaching our shores has a definite meaning, too, for the monetary and financial systems of other countries. Although world gold production has continued at a somewhat accelerated pace (largely because of political stimuli), most of the commercial countries no longer possess gold reserves capable of sustaining their credit operations unless there is provision for a larger amount of credit circulation per unit of reserve than formerly and unless continuous political control over the monetary and credit system is exercised. There cannot be concentration in the holding of the world's gold on the recent scale if a working international gold standard is to be maintained in the future.

Hence, in summarizing the recent relationships demonstrated in Chart 9 between the credit and currency index and the American holdings of monetary gold, it can be said that all important nations of the world are moving swiftly toward systems of controlled currency and credit, because they have no alternative.   In the United States it is now within the power of the Federal Reserve authorities to vary, within fixed but rather wide limits, the reserve requirements of the member commercial banks. Effective banking reserves can thus be deliberately reduced or expanded overnight.   The Federal Government, as the result of the devaluation of the dollar in 1934, has set up a huge secretly operated "stabilization" fund of several billions, which enables it to accomplish continuous manipulation of foreign-exchange rates, bond prices, or perhaps other financial variables within certain limits.   The Treasury has greatly increased its average working balances and, by shifting these balances geographically from time to time, can directly influence the effective reserve position of the banking system.   This extension of Federal control and manipulation of bank credit is but one example of what is occurring in other major fields of business, which we shall presently have occasion to discuss.   If we are actually moving toward a system approaching collectivism, this control of the central nervous system of finance and credit is surely one of the most potent assurances of progress toward such a possible objective.

THE DYNAMICS OF GOLD SUPPLY

Before concluding the discussion of gold in relation to bank credit and to the perplexing new problems arising from acute concentration of the world's gold store in the United States, something may be said in retrospect of the manner in which gold output has been affected by the price level and hence the cost of its production.   The impression may have been created that additions to the world's gold have come about spasmodically as a result of the purely chance discovery of new sources. The discovery of gold in California in 1848 appears to have been a genuine case of such random discovery having important consequences. The discoveries in Australia in 1851 also appear to have been of a more or less accidental nature.   But although this erratic factor in finding gold deposits capable of being profitably worked has been of prime importance at certain times, such random circumstances by no means account for all variations in gold output in the past century.   An increasing proportion of the world supply has been realized from relatively low grade deposits, whose working has depended in increasing measure upon calculations of profit or loss.   This has been particularly true of the very important production sources within the British Empire, foremost of which has been the Witwatersrand of South Africa, discovered in 1865.   Shortly after this discovery of deposits of vast extent but relatively low grade ore, important advances were made in the technique of refining. The use of cyanide opened up such fields to intensive and systematic exploitation. The cyanide process was also used in the development of the discoveries in the Yukon and Klondike Region, after 1890.

But the profits obtainable from the working of gold deposits have depended not merely upon the technological progress of the industry but upon the purchasing power of gold itself. Obviously gold has been peculiar as a monetary metal in that gold-standard countries, until recently, have paid fixed (or virtually fixed) amounts of coined money for gold bullion of the proper degree of purity. Gold as a commodity, therefore, has had essentially a fixed price in terms of money pieces. But these money pieces have had a purchasing power over other goods and services, depending upon a variety of factors, working out their influence through changes in the total amount of credit currency in actual use. Hence occasional additions to effective bank credit in circulation, although based upon larger gold output and banking reserves, have raised the level of prices and thereby have introduced some advances in material and service prices that constitute costs in gold-producing operations. There is thus a process of action and reaction here. Under certain conditions more gold could spread about among the important commercial countries and increase their bank reserves, thus producing conditions more or less favorable to credit expansion and a rise of prices, but the cost of gold mining in many parts of the world, in particular from the lower grade deposits, would rise, and a lower rate of output, barring fresh discoveries or technical changes, would result. In this sense the gold standard had in it some elements of automatic self-balancing so long as other things remained equal.

We are able to study the effect of the purchasing power of gold for over a century by using the net price of bullion and wholesale prices in the London market, which represents a close approximation to the world market. Great Britain was on a gold standard effectively from 1821 until the autumn of 1914, when the government suspended the convertibility of Bank of England notes into gold. The same gold standard was resumed in 1925, only to be suspended again in September, 1931, perhaps definitively.[1] In Chart 10 is shown the world's production of

---

[1] In the United States the complete effectiveness of the gold standard was frequently in doubt and was not finally confirmed until 1900, although practically it was in effect from 1879 until 1933. Another reason to study the British rather than the American gold market to detect the influence of the purchasing power of gold upon its production is that so much of the world's gold in the last century represented the activity of British enterprises for whose operation the commodity price level, as recorded in London markets, was most representative.

gold (in ounces) and the index of commodity purchasing power of gold in London since 1830.[1]

Let us observe the relationship of the purchasing power of gold as a commodity to world gold production.   It was previously stated that the discoveries of 1848 and 1851 were of the spasmodic nature, but it is interesting to notice that there had been a rising drift in the purchasing

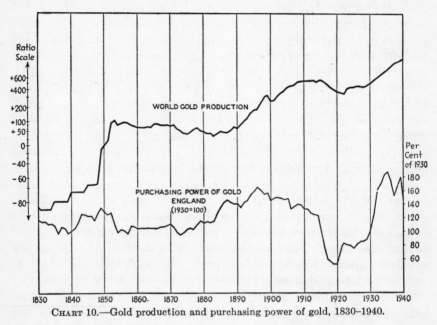

CHART 10.—Gold production and purchasing power of gold, 1830–1940.

power of gold for more than a decade prior to these discoveries.   These discoveries seem to have occurred under conditions growing somewhat more favorable to profits of those who did engage in this glamorous enterprise.   As prices rose in the 1850's, the purchasing power of gold was restrained along a horizontal drift until the middle 'seventies, and gold production not only failed to increase but followed a generally declining trend.   But after its purchasing power again rose between 1874

---

[1] Gold production in the first 15 years of this period is estimated roughly in terms of 5-year averages, but after 1845 the curve represents annual estimates; these become increasingly accurate.   The purchasing power of gold is seen to respond mainly to the changes in the general level of wholesale prices, although there are from time to time very minor changes, prior to World War I, in the precise price given by the Bank of England as the official purchaser of bullion.   Beginning with World War I and the existence of a situation during most of the period since that time in which gold has been relegated to the position of a commodity having its own variable price, the purchasing-power index reflects both the forces operating upon the prices of commodities and those operating upon the price of gold in the London market.

and 1896, there followed about a decade later a significant increase in gold production that may well have been affected by the purchasing-power factor. From 1900 to about the time of World War I, gold production, curiously enough, was being undertaken under conditions of declining purchasing power, but probably this was more than offset by the influence of the cyanide process in rapidly bringing into profitable production some of the low-grade and remote deposits. During the remainder of the period, disturbed by wars and the breakdown of international finance, the relationship between purchasing power and the rate of production nevertheless remains fairly close. Gold has risen in price relatively more than commodities, and in spite of the brief interruption in this tendency in 1938, an upward drift appears still to be in progress. If gold production in the next few decades were to depend primarily upon its purchasing power, we could expect still larger addition to supplies, and these might continue to flow to a considerable degree toward the vaults of the United States, where the yellow metal is again buried to await its ultimate fate as a money metal.[1]

THE RATIO OF EFFECTIVE CURRENCY TO TRADE

We return now to examine the credit and currency index in its relation to changes in the index of business volume and changes in the general price level. These relations are shown in Chart 11. At the top is shown the annual credit and currency index extending from 1811 to 1940. We have seen that the course of this index has been determined by a number of different factors. War financing has produced several bulges in the course of the general upward drift, denoting either large issues of inconvertible Government paper or inconvertible bank credit. Over considerable periods, however, the index has responded to more gradual undulations in the available national stock of specie or, in later years gold, the basic credit reserve. Occasionally there have been outbursts of speculative promotion giving rise to credit excesses. Finally, during the latest years, there has been far more governmental control over commercial credit. This has been stated once again to emphasize the point that fluctuations in the course of the generally upward drift of effective purchasing mediums (mainly consisting of credit in one form

---

[1] The index of the purchasing power of gold in London is based upon an unpublished manuscript, "The Purchasing Power of Gold in England, 1560–1939," by Roy W. Jastram and H. B. Woolley, Stanford University. Production of gold taken from R. S. Tucker, *Review of Economic Statistics*, Feb. 15, 1934, and, since 1909, from Reports of Director of the Mint. Production figures include estimates for Russia. The data from 1830 to 1844 used by Tucker represent estimates of Alexander Del Mar, from his "History of the Precious Metals," 1880. Data from 1845 to 1875 are estimates of Joseph Kitchin.

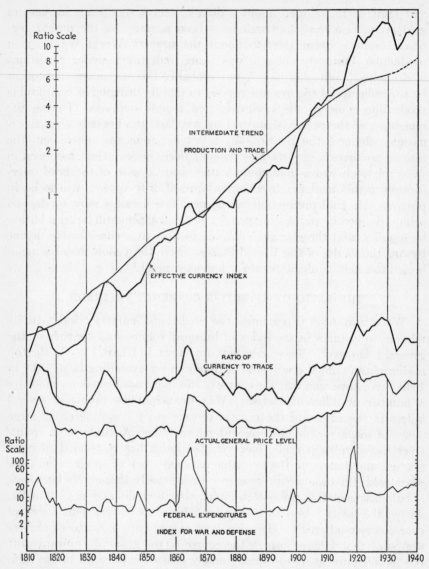

CHART. 11.—Relation of credit-currency to trade, and the general price level in the United States, 1811–1940.   The ratio of the index of effective credit currency to the intermediate trend of production and trade results in a pattern having fluctuations and long-term drift closely paralleling the movements of the general price level.   The description of the various indexes is presented in Appendix 3.

or another) should not be interpreted in terms of a single motivating factor. We must not oversimplify the process. The pattern that finally develops is highly irregular, and it is obvious that it bears little resemblance to the pattern of the business activity index shown in previous charts. In Chart 11, the credit and currency index is so drawn that its average of the entire period is made to coincide with the average of the *intermediate trend* of the business index. Here we bring the monetary and the trade-volume elements in our general equation of exchange into close relationship.

The question immediately arises: What allowance is made in developing this relationship for the factor of the so-called "velocity of circulation" of the effective money and credit? Thus far we have said nothing about velocity or the possibility of a measure of the average rate of monetary or credit turnover. Strictly speaking, the credit and currency index is not complete. It reveals from year to year merely how much money, both coin and Government paper, has been outstanding and available for trade purposes and how much change in bank credit in use may have resulted from variations in the earning assets of commercial banks. Of course, during a given period of time, a given amount of circulating money can accomplish numerous transactions as it passes from hand to hand. Similarly, loans or investments made by banks result in deposit accounts that may be kept in existence or shifted from bank to bank and used to perform numerous exchanges before being liquidated. If we had chosen to express the credit resulting from banking operations in the form of average annual *deposits subject to check* rather than *earning assets* (roughly equivalent magnitudes), we could then say that the velocity of the deposits could be represented by the ratio of total check transactions to the average deposits in banks subject to check. Now it is not to be denied that the velocity of circulation of both legal tender money and credit instruments does vary, the velocity of credit varying probably more than that of money. But it has been clearly demonstrated by Carl Snyder,[1] over periods of time long enough to be significant, that annual variations in the velocity of turnover of bank deposits agree closely with the minor fluctuations of the volume of business about its intermediate trend. Hence if we are developing a ratio of effective credit and currency to trade volume to express the two great variables determining the average amount of money per unit of trade—the general price level—the velocity oscillations in the numerator will tend to offset the cyclical oscillations of limited duration in the denominator. We can then use the ratio in terms of the credit and currency index, excluding velocity changes, against the business index,

---

[1] "Capitalism the Creator," pp. 39 and 428, New York, 1940. See also Turnover of Deposits, *American Bankers' Association Journal*, February, 1924.

excluding the short cycles, or, in other words, its intermediate trend. These are the elements shown in Chart 11.

What is the result, then, when we plot the ratio between the credit and currency index and the intermediate trend of the volume of business? The result is indeed startling when it is brought into comparison with the actual course of the general price level (Snyder's index). We find definite verification of the principle of price-level determination. *The long-term trend movements in the general price index are essentially derivatives of two forces—the wave trend of business volume and the rather irregular variations in the circulation of credit and currency.* Such a degree of covariation between two statistically independent indexes cannot be accidental. To be sure, there are occasional discrepancies that must be set down to the unavoidable minor inaccuracies of the data. This comparison of the two sets of measurements carries the verification of the basic principle involved in the determination of prices far enough back historically to enable us to survey the experience of well over a century. These results also are important in demonstrating the overwhelmingly great importance of the check circulation (checks drawn upon bank accounts) in the make-up of the monetary elements capable of influencing the general price level. Observe also that the patterns of the monetary and trade measures show little tendency to agree. This leads us again to the conclusion, previously expressed in Chapter 4, that to identify the long-term drift of the price level with the "long waves" described by the volume of business activity is an inherent fallacy. Over short periods and in terms of monthly data, prices do reflect the oscillations of the trade cycles, but in the broader perspective we have no such evidence of sympathetic action.

In the lower portion of Chart 11 is shown an index of Federal Government expenditures for war and defense purposes, expressed in relation to the index of business activity in order to eliminate long-term trend. These fluctuations are drawn on a greatly reduced scale. The purpose is to show that the most pronounced cases of inflation in the general price level have been clearly due to war expenditures. The marked rise in prices in 1836–1837 is probably a case of unrestrained speculative activity for which the banking system was exploited. The rise in prices after 1897 and down to the period of World War I was primarily, although not entirely, a matter of gold discoveries and additions to gold stocks and bank reserves. War expenditures incident to the very brief and relatively unimportant clash with Spain in 1899 contributed very little to the price movement. During the 1920's, the secondary period of prosperity following World War I had in it elements of reckless use of credit in speculation in securities and real property rather than in commodities. During the entire period from World War I to 1940, effective credit in circulation has remainded far above the center of gravity of the business volume index, and the general level of prices has consistently remained on a level far above the trough of the middle 1890's.

If we were to compare the pattern of the general price level with that of wholesale prices of commodities, we should find no marked difference in short-term movements; but the latter index would describe a long-term trend gradually diverging from that of the general price level in a downward direction. This growing divergence in long-term drift is to be explained primarily by the inclusion within the general price-level index of elements representing various types of service that, as we have already noted, have tended to move higher or to resist deflation at the same time that prices of many raw materials were drifting irregularly lower. In later chapters, we shall have occasion to return to this interesting phenomenon of the divergent long-term trend within the general price level. It has some important economic implications.

Since the index of the general price level describes a pattern that is inverse to the "purchasing power of money," the view has prevailed in certain quarters that the value of the dollar is essentially highly unstable. Some economists have referred to the never-ending "dance of the dollar." They have admonished the Government to bring this dance to an end and to create a "stable" dollar by keeping the quantity of dollars in sober step with trade requirements. But one conclusion that follows from the foregoing measurements is that the dollar dances about most wildly when the monetary and credit system is subject to the political pressures of war and the makeshift financing methods that always seem to accompany war emergencies, except where dictatorship prevails. *If this one factor had been completely removed from the course of our business history, almost all the instability in the purchasing power of the dollar would have been eliminated!*

To control the value of money and make it stable is doubtless a most commendable objective. To accomplish this end, however, an indispensable requirement would be *avoidance of wartime inflation* and its sequel of *disastrous deflation*. This might be accomplished either by discontinuing wars or by the alternative of introducing in wartime such dictatorial economic policies that war could be conducted with complete control over all production and trade by the State. Since wars seem to have developed to the global scale and make stupendous demands upon industrial output, an ominous path is being marked out toward political regulation of consumption, production, and price systems, along with everything else. If in the future we *must* have wars, far more drastic regimentation may prove inescapable if national security is to be defended. The alternative of uncontrolled distortions of the monetary system and recurrent inflations of price levels by exposing the social

order to chaotic stresses would bring us in the end to a like result.   This
has been the little heeded lesson of Europe after World War I.   If we are
to have a reasonably steady general price level in the United States in
future decades, there must also be reasonable stability in prices in other
great nations, and this means either further extension of controls through
complete economic regimentation to afford military security or the
abandonment of the crude and wasteful device of war as a method of
settling essentially economic problems.   The mere juggling of monetary
systems or money markets is no solution.   We shall return to this
problem again at the end of Chapter 24.

CHAPTER 6

THE INTERACTION OF MONEY, TRADE, AND PRICE LEVEL

The preceding discussion of the relation between money and credit, the volume of trade, and the general price level has been primarily historical and has been illustrated by statistical measurements over a long period. Let us now turn to a brief analysis of the logic underlying these observed relationships.

We can best develop this phase of the subject by means of symbols and simple equations such as have been made familiar to students of the subject in recent years. The writer proposes, however, to state these equations without attempting the excessive degree of refinement that might be appropriate in an extended treatise on the intricate subject of price-level analysis.[1] The method of stating the relationships among the various factors in the general equation of exchange will depart in certain important respects from the form adopted by previous writers, notably Irving Fisher, in his "Purchasing Power of Money" (1911).

The simplest expression of the equation of exchange for a given country and time period might be written as

$$P = \frac{M}{T} \tag{1}$$

Here P stands for a measure of change in the general price level, M for the amount of money used, and T for a measure of the volume of trade accomplished by means of money, but valued in constant prices. We must clearly understand the meanings by explaining that P is strictly an index number of change from a given starting point or base in the general price level; M may be considered as the money that has been spent in all types of purchases during a stated period of time. T is the "value" of the trade accomplished in that period, valued at the prices of the base period and hence expressed independently of any variations in P. The terms M and T can also be considered as index numbers relating to a base period identical with that used for P.[2]

---

[1] See, for example A. W. Marget, "The Theory of Prices," Vol. 1, New York, 1938; Vol. 2, 1942—an extremely detailed analysis.

[2] It can be shown mathematically that in order to be strictly accurate, such an equation requires that the index number for P must be either an aggregative index with the weights taken as the quantities of the *given* year (not the base year) or an index such as the "ideal index" of Irving Fisher, which is a geometric average of

If we should conceive M as referring to the *average stock of money* circulating during a period (let us say a year), then the expression for the money expenditure will become M multiplied by the average rate of circulation, which we may call V, and the equation then becomes as follows:

$$P = \frac{MV}{T} \tag{2}$$

In this form, the equation would read: The price level index varies as the ratio of an index of money in circulation, multiplied by the index of average money velocity, to an index of all trade. Since, as we have previously seen, the short-term or minor cyclical fluctuations in trade activity more or less synchronize with the fluctuations in the velocity of circulation of the mediums serving the purpose of money, it follows that V in equation (2) would tend to fluctuate in accordance with the cyclical fluctuations in the denominator T. If we canceled out this much of the changes, we should come back substantially to equation (1), in which T would be defined as the *trend* of trade activity.[1] Our previous statistical measurements essentially in terms of this interpretation of M and T conform so closely to the pattern of P, as independently measured, that we can consider the importance of V as mainly confined, either causally or a resultant, to the short-term cyclical fluctuations of T. If we could accurately measure V over very long periods, it might be found that the pattern has not exactly paralleled that of T but that the discrepancies apparently were not of great significance.

With equation (2) before us, it is well to turn to some questions that thus far have not been sufficiently considered. These become important when such an equation forms the framework for theoretical analysis, especially for arguments as to causation and the *direction* in which the causal forces operate. There has been long and voluminous controversy on these matters. Our statistical results in themselves do not immediately furnish the answer to questions such as the following: Are price-level changes always the *result* of the factors on the right side of the equation? Does causality run from M/T to P or also from P to M/T? If it is true

---

two aggregative indexes, in one of which *base* year quantities are used and in the other, *given*-year quantities. By using P in either of these forms, it will be theoretically correct to say that the *change* in price level will be in exact proportion to the ratio of the *change* in money circulation to the index of physical trade *change*, if it is assumed, of course, that a *completely representative* measurement is made of all those variables. Actually, our best available measures are but sampling estimates.

[1] See Carl Snyder, The Problem of Monetary and Economic Stability, *Quarterly Journal of Economics*, February, 1935; also, his "Capitalism the Creator," p. 428, note 14 to Chapter 3. Snyder conceives the trend of T as the *secular* trend; the present writer refers to the intermediate trend.

that the price level is invariably *determined by* ratio of money elements to trade elements, is the effectiveness of this influence mainly determined by changes in the numerator or in the denominator of that ratio?

DEFINING TERMS IN THE EQUATION OF EXCHANGE

In order to keep our thinking straight, let us be precise as to the meaning of P. We have defined it as an index number of general price change. But what are "prices"? Are they invariably the prices *paid* in actual transactions? In order to keep the equation always in balance, this might seem to be necessarily true. But are there not many "prices," such as quoted "bids" and "offers," prices that sellers are hoping to get, and prices that buyers would be willing to pay? These may *not* represent any *actual* transactions. These potential prices that at the moment are merely quotations may nevertheless have a causal bearing upon changes in money use and trade activity without appearing directly in the equation. Let us keep clearly in mind, therefore, that while in the equation as stated we refer to transactions that actually occur during a given period of time and all the prices represent actual transactions, it is logically possible for important changes in quoted prices to affect the terms on the right side of the equation referring to money expenditure and trade volume.

Examining more closely the meaning of M, or money, it is obvious that to be wholly realistic we must expand this into its constituent parts and designate them precisely. In a society not using refined systems of banking and credit, M would presumably refer to coins or to paper money circulating as the convenient representation of coin, bullion, or other forms of recognized money. If such paper circulated without convertibility into real wealth (as, for example, the greenbacks), this element in the circulation might be the outstanding factor capable of producing changes in the other variables. Under more normal conditions in a highly developed commercial country, we should need to have represented in the equation in the right-hand numerator *all* the elements entering into what we may call means of payment for goods and services. But there is a further question as to any one of these elements, whether coin, paper money, bank notes, or bank deposits subject to check—do these represent only the *circulating means* of payment as they have appeared in transactions, or are they to be understood to mean the total or average *available amount* of such means of payment, qualified by a turnover factor?

Another way of stating this, if we take account of the velocity of circulation V, is to ask whether this should refer to the *intensity* of turnover of the circulating medium (that is, all money and credit that circulated at least once) or whether velocity refers to the *over-all degree of activity* of an average inventory of M. This is a very basic question.

The equation of exchange has been used as a basis for theoretical argument with the premise that M represents only the *circulating* means of payment, that is, the *flow;* but before the argument is completed, the monetary factors suddenly appear as the average inventory of the means of payment.[1] In order to be entirely definite and consistent on this point, let us consider that each of the monetary factors in the exchange equation refers to the average amount *available for use*, while the velocity factor, if used at all, qualifies these by expressing their average rate of turnover during a period of time. It must be recognized in so doing that "velocity" is capable of a double meaning, just as in the case of the cars of a railroad; we can refer to the average speed of the cars that are moving and again to the average intensity of use of all available cars.

Considering that M will refer to the average stock of all available legal tender money, we can proceed to break this into two parts: that which is held in bank reserves and that part which is in pocket, in safe deposit boxes, in the public treasury and the tills of business firms, that is, in the "hands of the public." There is, of course, a constant give and take as between these holdings, but it is desirable to distinguish the portion of the total money that is in banks, especially in central banks serving the purpose of reserves, from that part which is in the hands of the public and is mainly in the form of smaller denominations of legal tender paper and subsidiary coin. Since the M in bank reserves is so large an amount, we shall use M to designate that segment; the average stock of money that is in the hands of the public may be designated as m and its velocity by v. We then have $MV + mv$.

We must still further expand the numerator of the M/T ratio to include the important element of "checkbook money," that is, bank deposits subject to check and their rate of turnover in making payments. Let us take a snapshot of these deposits at a given instant. We are not interested in bank deposits that are not subject to check, since use of such deposits involves handling of actual funds equivalent to pocket money or till money. Confining our attention to total bank deposits subject to check, which are being continually drawn upon to make payments comprising the bulk of all trade circulation, just what do these

[1] Irving Fisher, whose "Purchasing Power of Money," 1911, has done so much to make the equation of exchange a working tool of economic analysis, seems to have shifted his meanings constantly as between "money in circulation" and "money supply," or average inventory. Thus (p. 24) M is defined as the average amount of money *in circulation* in the community during the year. But at a later point (Chapter III, Sec. 5) M is used as though it referred to the average *stock* of money serving as bank reserves and having some consistent relation to the inventory of bank deposits. At still other points, Fisher speaks of M as though it meant the stock of money as a complete *monetary metal* inventory, which varies as the result of production or net import of gold.

deposits mean?   Obviously they do not physically represent actual money, because banks do not keep available more than a very small fraction of such "demand liabilities" in the form of cash money.   When checks are drawn against deposits, what is it that is turned over or transferred as a means of payment?   The answer is that it is mainly "credit," built up and maintained by the continuing flow of commercial banking operations.   It is a mass of credit whose validity ultimately rests with the assets, such as loans and investments, of the banks.

But we must now be careful not to confuse ourselves by confining attention to an individual bank and its *particular* asset and liability account.   We are here thinking of *all* commercial banks and the substance of what is used in payments, and when we do this the accounting distinction between assets and liabilities disappears.   What we have at any moment is a total that can be broken down into holdings of *money* and holdings of *claims* upon all those who have borrowed from commercial or credit-creating banks.   These banks, in the aggregate, can validate checks drawn upon them to the extent that they hold vault cash, plus the extent that they *are able to liquidate* at once other assets and translate them into actual cash.   The checks drawn on "deposits" in the aggregate accomplish the means of payment so well simply because those who receive these checks for the most part do not question the ability of banks to validate or "redeem" them in money.   Hence this vast magnitude of credit remains suspended in existence as an addition to actual money, performing most of the functions of money, except in times of panic, when there may be acute fear and loss of confidence and an unusual amount of checks is presented suddenly to banks with demand for payment in *actual money*.

The point that is most important here is that when we speak of "deposits subject to check" for all the commercial banks combined, we are dealing fundamentally with two elements—that portion of so-called "deposits" which has come into existence *as the result of banks extending their own credit* in making loans and investments and that part (omitting any earning assets provided by capital and surplus) which has been actually and physically deposited *in money* in checking accounts and which remains at a given time *in* the banks collectively as deposits of money but *physically identical with what appears on the asset side of each individual bank among its cash reserves*.[1]   This point is not entirely easy to grasp, and it has been commonly overlooked in discussions on this

---

[1] This oversimplifies the situation to the extent that commercial banks have most of their reserve on deposit with the Federal Reserve Banks, but in principle we may merely extend the foregoing statement to include the Reserve Banks in the mechanism. To the extent that these banks issued no notes and made no loans, their deposits and reserves would be almost equal, and the deposits would represent deposited cash money.

subject.   In other words, for the purpose of our equation, we can consider that what these checks are drawn against is ultimately the money comprising bank reserve, plus that part of the deposits subject to check that represent merely advances of bank-created credit—a magnitude that we shall refer to as C.   It is difficult to measure this exactly, but it is important to recognize that logically the ability to write checks and make payments with them is, for the community as a whole, the right to turn over certain deposits that physically are actual money, plus deposits that are book items maintained in existence by the flow of banking operations.   If commercial banks are holding large amounts of deposits subject to check in the form appearing on *individual* bank statements in the asset column as reserve but are making small amounts of loans and investments, element C will probably be limited, and the ability of people to write checks in making payments will also be limited, because deposits subject to check vary mainly with lending operations.   In the converse case, when banks are making large advances of their own credit and are also receiving additions to their cash assets by way of cash deposits (insofar as these are subject to check), it will be possible for the community to draw many more checks and the circulation of the means of payment will expand, as we have noted in historical instances.

We may now express this in our equation as

$$P = \frac{(M + C)V + mv}{T} \tag{3}$$

In this form the money in banks is separated from the money in general circulation and nonbanking reserves.   The bank money (apart from what may be a small portion of bank capital and surplus) is both asset and, since it is deposited by customers, liability.   The rest of the deposits are liabilities created in the form of pure credit expansion, and they are represented among the assets by various noncash items, claims upon borrowers.   But for the equation, the deposited cash that is held as reserve against claims of depositors is itself part of what banks call their demand deposits and these deposits $(M + C)$ have an average turnover V during a given period.   The money in outside hands is a smaller segment of total purchasing power and has its specific velocity term v.[1]

---

[1] An interesting verification of the manner in which m is correlated with P in terms of cyclical deviations from long-term or secular trend is to be found in a chart prepared by G. F. Warren and F. A. Pearson, based upon money in circulation outside banks and *commodity* prices, 1830–1931.   See *Hearings before the Subcommittee of the Committee on Banking and Currency*, HR 72d Congress, First Session, Mar. 28 and 29, 1932, p. 25.

Irving Fisher expresses the equation as $P = \dfrac{MV + M'V'}{T}$, referring to M as money, and M' as bank deposits subject to check.   The ambiguous character of both

We have made, in other words, a logical distinction between the *cash* element and the bank-created *credit* element in the checkable deposits, that is, M as distinct from C.   This is desirable because significant relationships exist, as between $(M + C)$ and M and also between M and m, in view of the traditional and legal requirements governing the holding of reserves against deposits.[1]   In other words, C depends partly upon M, when we consider the banks in the aggregate, as common prudence and (in the United States, particularly) the banking laws set certain limits beyond which C cannot be expanded per dollar of M.   Usually this is stated the other way around, in terms of the minimum reserves M, to be held against $(M + C)$.[2]   In our own banking experience, it has already been made clear that $(M + C)$ has varied over a fairly wide range with respect to M, and the complete expression $(M + C)V$, if we could accurately measure it, would probably exhibit a somewhat greater degree of variability.

It is possible that the element M, bank reserves held against deposits in American practice, may expand without affecting C either temporarily or over extended periods.   Also, C may expand and contract independently of M temporarily and within certain limits.   Conceivably M might expand considerably without any expansion in C if there were a situation persistently unfavorable to the enlargement of bank loans *and* investments.   We must avoid falling into the error, which has long been prevalent in monetary thinking in the United States, of assuming that merely an addition to bank reserves (perhaps as the result of large gold imports) *must* automatically increase credit and the means of payment and create immediate inflation.   But actually, if enough time elapses, there will always be at least a partial and perhaps substantial rise in either bank loans (including discounts, acceptances, etc.) or investments in securities, or both, when larger amounts of cash come in from depositors. Naturally some of investments are made with cash and do not involve credit (C) expansion.[3]

---

his M and M' should now be obvious.   See "The Purchasing Power of Money," *passim.*

[1] The term "deposits" here refers, of course, to $(M + C)$, the usual relation of "reserves to deposits" in banking and legal terminology being really the relation of M to $(M + C)$, not M to C.

[2] We are speaking of reserves against *checkable demand* deposits.   Whereas demand deposits of commercial banks are usually subject to check, some time deposits may also be under certain conditions or to a limited extent subject to check, and to that extent M as minimum reserves would have to be redefined.   This, however, is not of much practical consequence, especially since about 1935.

[3] Lauchlin Currie, in his study "The Supply and Control of Money in the United States," *Harvard Economic Studies*, 1935, Chapter 5, carefully states his reasons for approving the practice of monetary theorists in considering bank deposits subject to

We now have the equation so stated that the right-hand numerator breaks down into the turnover of an average supply of potential means of payment.   But we still have made no place here for the possible existence of bank notes.   In some banking systems notes are still an important or even predominant means whereby commercial banks extend their credit. But in our own system bank notes have in recent years become essentially Government paper money, that is, circulating paper backed by gold certificates, which, in turn, are now backed by gold held in the Treasury. Insofar as such notes are legal tender, they would be included partly in M as well as in m.   If such notes are not legally available for use as bank reserves against deposits, the amount in public hands would appear only in m.   To the extent that the notes are specie certificates, the money serving as redemption fund is excluded from M.   This would be true of our present Federal Reserve notes.

Having now clearly in mind that our monetary numerator contains specifically a substantive element of supply that is regarded as "turned over" in actual trade, we must logically develop a *similar* concept for the right-hand denominator, which thus far has been expressed merely as

---

check as the entity whose use by means of checks accomplishes the making of payments.   He then definitely restricts the term "credit" to the deposits and at the same time vigorously denies that bank loans or bank investments can or should be considered as being credit.

His reason is mainly that variations in the earning assets of commercial banks *need not* correlate *exactly* with variations in deposits or, more particularly, demand deposits subject to check.   He cites cases in which earning assets may be increased by enlargement of bank capital, surplus, and undivided profits; or in which banks may borrow from the central banks and thus maintain earning assets constant, even though deposits may be declining.   There may also be changes in earning assets unaccompanied by corresponding variations in "individual" deposits.   Currie also calls attention to the fact that if bank investments were to be included in the concept of effective credit, it would involve attaching to time deposits (which mainly take the form of investments in the asset account) as well as demand deposits a "credit" characteristic.

In the previous chapter, we used, as our measure of the historical changes since 1878 in effective credit and currency in use, banking earning assets rather than deposits, but this is not necessarily inconsistent with Currie's contentions.   Variations in earning assets (loans plus investments) are a sufficiently accurate *indicator* of variations in deposits of *commercial* banks to warrant their use in this fashion.   Even rediscounting operations are not undertaken by such banks unless credit expansion is being effected by loans and corresponding additions to demand deposits.   If deposits are enlarged by holdings of idle cash, indicated by large "excess reserves," the earning assets are a *better* indicator of credit in use than are the total deposits.   Today a fairly large part of demand deposits is certainly not credit, even though those may be withdrawn by the use of checks that are credit instruments.

As for the matter of time deposits and bank investments, it will be noted that in the foregoing we have considered reserve held against time deposits as part of m, and hence

T (trade). This is a point at which in the past much equation making has gone wrong, with unfortunate results. Most equations have presented an inadequate basis for reasoning in the fact that although they may include in the numerator a term referring to monetary *supply* or average amount of deposits, at the same time no attempt is made to factor out the element of *T* or trade into comparable aspects of *supply and rate of flow*. Hence, naturally, the numerator of the equation readily becomes in the argument the powerful and active agent in governing the price level, whereas trade comes to be regarded merely as a kind of *fait accompli*, having no degree of causal potency whatever. We are certain to fall into inconsistencies if we fail to factor out *T* completely.[1]

---

any increase or decrease in time deposits or in the investments corresponding therewith would be mainly allowed for in fluctuations in this reserve element. At the same time it may very well be true in considering the entire banking situation that at any given time among the demand deposits there will be "derived" elements, originating in the making of investments by banks on the basis of increases in their time deposits. These funds, resulting from security purchases and probably mainly in the form of credit, as they circulate through the system of business, take the form of demand deposits in banks and may for a considerable period remain suspended in the total of bank credit, the element *C*. It will be shown in later sections that on several occasions a much better measure of the effect of bank credit upon the general price level could be obtained through observation of loans and investments rather than deposits subject to check because the changes in loans particularly correlated more closely with the total *turnover* of deposits than with the average *amount* of deposits.

This seems to have been true, for example, in the period from 1926 to 1929. When Currie says (p. 54) "Loans and investments . . . grossly exaggerate the rate of expansion of the money supply up to 1929 . . . " the writer believes that he is definitely in error if he means by money supply the total effective credit and monetary contributions to changes in over-all trade values. This is confirmed by the measurement already presented in the preceding chapter. It is a fundamental principle of commercial banking that it is the loans (and investments in some measure also) that mainly *create* the demand deposits, not vice versa.

Another point at which Currie appears to the writer to have made unnecessary and not altogether constructive criticisms of central bank policy in the United States is his insistence that the Federal Reserve authorities in the 1920's were too much concerned with the "qualitative" aspects of bank credit, that is, the composition of the earning assets of member banks and the nature of rediscounted collateral, whereas inadequate attention was paid to the "quantitative" elements that have to do with the general price level or level of total trade values. Currie's criticism fails to take into account that there may be qualitative aspects of the manner in which banks circulate their credit and make advances to business or speculation that in the long run *do* have very potent effect upon their ability to continue to serve the community and effects, also upon the extent to which the banking system may become oversensitized to disturbing factors. This is further discussed in Chapter 11. Currie's concept of qualitative credit policy and control, like much of the rest of his analysis, is decidedly narrow.

[1] The failure to factor *T* into its separate aspects is a notable defect in Irving Fisher's theory of the relations between money, trade, and prices.

To illustrate, let us go back to equation (1) in its simple form. *P* will be expected to rise if *M* remains constant and *T* declines. This might actually be true, perhaps in terms of a long-term change in conditions, but it would be untrue of changes occurring in the course of a typical business cycle. A pronounced and general cyclical *decline* in trade is very seldom correlated with *rising* prices except under war conditions. Conversely, the price level does not ordinarily *fall* when trade is *increasing* during the prosperity phase of a typical cyclical movement. Thus the use of trade in this form as an element in the equation that supports causal reasoning leads to irrational results. The reason lies in the fact that *T*, in the sense of a measure of the over-all physical turnover of business, represents trade *performance*, in which prices and money and credit have done their work. As such, it is logically *necessary* to consider it as a passive *resultant*. It is passive virtually by definition. This explains why Irving Fisher so frequently in his discussions of his equation of exchange ($P = MV/T$) was able to refer to trade as of little if any dynamic effect in the mechanism, something restricted in its changes to the limits of *productive* capacities and techniques. Thus his denominator of the equation ratio plays a role of an idler pulley, and the numerator represents the prime mover. Here we are bound to recognize the necessity of careful statement of monetary principles. The excessive emphasis that much accepted doctrine places upon the effectiveness of the monetary and credit factors (and hence monetary and credit *policy*) through the use of imperfectly factored equations and elliptical reasoning may not be valid for all circumstances and conditions, even though it may occasionally apply to cases in which there happens to exist a relatively violent change in the money-credit variables. We have seen that these are almost entirely wartime contingencies.

Can we factor this *T* or total trade activity into its component elements for logical purposes? Let us first divide the measure of total trade into two parts, one consisting of the movement of physical goods, materials, and property (even though represented by paper claims), the other consisting of all the intangible services. One important distinction between the two arises from the fact that for physical trade there is always likely to be a related element of physical *inventory* that is distinct from current *production* and distinct again from the *flow* or movement of the goods. For services, there is only in a more remote sense an inventory, in the existence of *potential capacity* to render service; but the service that forms a part of the concept of trade, involving circulation of money and credit, is something that exists only during the rendering of the service, and we cannot always think of this as being the "turnover" of a capacity.

Let us now consider the cases of tangible goods and property and negotiable claims thereto. For the purpose of the equation, we could express such trade in terms of initial inventory, plus production during a period of time. This would represent the available average *supply*, which is then further qualified by a rate of turnover R. For the sake of consistency with our numerator, expressed in averages, it is best to regard these supply terms as averages of a number of observations during a time period. For each interval of observation we have supply composed of (1) inventory carried over and (2) new output added during the interval. The average of the physical inventory terms plus the average of the production terms times the average percentage of $R = T$, trade. The supply $(I + O)$ "turns over" in the sense of moving along the line toward final possession and utilization. The concept T may, however, include many circular transactions affecting the same item, especially in speculative markets.

We may now write the equation as follows:

$$P = \frac{(M + C)V + mv}{(I + O)R + S} = \frac{\text{monetary turnover}}{\text{trade turnover}} \tag{4}$$

I is the inventory component, O is the current output component, so that $(I + O)$ becomes all available average supply during the entire period. The rate of movement of this total available supply into the hands of purchasers is expressed in the average rate of turnover R. This is a percentage of supply actually disposed of in trade. This brings into the denominator of our equation a substantive magnitude of supply that is coordinate with M or C or m. Observe that $(I + O)$ may vary directly or inversely with T according to conditions. The term I may vary independently through production, being carried beyond the rate of current requirements, without regard to price. *Hence I can affect P directly*, especially in periods of excessive output of basic raw materials, excessive construction activity, or speculative inventory accumulation by merchants. *P* can then in some degree *affect M, C, and V*.

We may also extend the denominator by including the element of service as an index of that part of T which involves no physical inventory. We may simply write S to represent this factor, being careful to remember it refers to units of service activity valued at *constant* prices or rates.[1]

[1] If we wish to take into account the element of service capacity, we may use equation (5)

$$P = \frac{(M + C)V + mv}{(I + O)R + (Sc)r} \tag{5}$$

S is the result of the average rate of utilization r of the average potential capacity Sc to render services during the time period. Thus, for example, if we are considering those aspects of total trade having to do with the labor market, we can consider all potential man-hours available on the average during a given period, modifying this by the average rate of utilization r, which would give us the man-hours actually worked and paid for (at constant wages). This form of expression, however, is not

In using the equation as a logical tool, we must remember that P is an index number of change in general price level—including commodities, property, services—in other words, a comprehensive entity involving all prices whatsoever but *not* including rates of interest or the prices of bonds or other debt claims.   The P of the equation of exchange excludes prices, representing merely the exchange of present money for future money.   These are transactions *within* the numerator of the M/T ratio and do not in themselves introduce changes in the value of the ratio. Prices that represent what is paid as *rental* for the use of property refer to that part of T classified as service, since there is no exchange of property against money or credit, but the price involved in such transactions is analogous to other service prices.   Of course, the P index could be broken down into many types of goods and service markets.   But statistically, this would involve a separation of the monetary, supply, and trade-turnover terms into corresponding detailed classifications, and from a statistical standpoint this would involve great difficulties.   Nevertheless, it is frequently useful as a way of keeping our thinking straight to segregate some particular markets of exceptional importance and trace their probable relationships to the exchange process as a whole.

On the right-hand side of the equation, the term expressing velocity does not represent quite the same thing as that expressing rate of use, although the meanings are analogous.   Money and credit have an essentially "circular" velocity, since they are continually turning over in making exchanges without ever reaching what may be called a final destination.   In the denominators R and r refer to turnover as used in the merchandising sense—the average extent to which existing goods, tools, property, and labor available for sale are actually moved along in the direction of the final buyer.   Purely speculative transactions, however, have a circular and often very rapid rate of velocity.   The element that expresses the rate of utilization of service facilities or potential capacity r expresses a different kind of turnover in the sense of intensity of utilization.   But all these various terms have the common property of expressing the degree to which certain average amounts of money, credit, goods, or property and human capacity are being moved during a given time period or utilized in particular channels of activity and involve money and credit payments at each turn.   In both numerator and denominator of our equation we distinguish the factor of activity from the factor of average available supply or quantity.

---

easily applicable to all phases of service, since it is not always possible to express potential capacity in a definite way or in terms of statistically measurable units.   Theoretically, however, it is desirable, as far as possible, to make a definite place in the equation for the element of supply as distinct from the element of turnover or utilization.

POSSIBLE CAUSAL RELATIONSHIPS

We are now in a position to visualize the mechanism through which the forces operating upon the general level of prices exert their influence. It has been persistently contended by adherents to the so-called "quantity theory" of money and credit that the general price level usually varies as the monetary factors vary. According to the more extreme statements of this view, it is the *numerator* of the fraction, not the denominator, that does the work of moving the price level up or down. From this dogma naturally flow plausible plans concentrated upon *monetary* policy and *credit* control and fiscal administration designed to rectify the influences bearing upon *prices*, under any and all conditions. But let us examine some of the logical possibilities, to see if such interpretations are sound. Let us first study the denominator of the right side of the equation. To what extent, if at all, are the expressions $(I + O)$ and Sc, which we may call "supply," related to the price level? The reader undoubtedly is familiar with the fact that in the usual demand-and-supply analysis of *particular* commodity markets, it is rate of *supply* changes, not trade or production, that is considered to be the variable coordinate with the influence of demand. We have brought this element of supply, in an aggregate sense, explicitly within the framework of the general equation of exchange. What takes place in the entire economy within a year's time is the establishment more or less simultaneously of many prices. All these prices are established as the result of human desires, of the changes in availability of money and credit, the rise or fall of the supply of goods, and the varying forces contributing to that supply, among which international forces, political pressures, technological factors, and the willingness of those who control goods, property, or service to sell or rent them.[1]

---

[1] It has been claimed by Irving Fisher that what takes place in the equation of exchange is essentially different from what takes place in an individual market. It has been elaborately argued, and strangely enough has been little questioned, that in an individual market both demand and supply factors operate *within a price level*, which is determined by the equation for all markets and apart from mere demand-and-supply mechanics. In other words, it is claimed that we cannot explain what takes place *in* the equation and at the same time *assume* that equation in our analysis. Fisher, for example, ("Purchasing Power of Money," pp. 176–181) says that the price level so transcends all individual supply-and-demand situations that the general level cannot be explained by observation of these individual situations. He illustrates this by reference to the price of sugar; an increase in the price of sugar would not represent a rise in the "demand" if the entire price level also were rising. This is really intended to mean apparently that we cannot draw conclusions as to *changes in the consumer marginal utility* of sugar under conditions of a rising price unless we know how that price stands against the general level of prices. This much is true, but the

The supply factors we are using in the denominator are theoretically just as potent with respect to the price level as the monetary or credit supply or the velocity factors in the numerator. Supply of goods, of labor power, of property, taken in conjunction with their rates of turnover or utilization, cannot simply be thrown aside into a passive "trade" element and regarded as of no dynamic consequence. In fact, there are important possible relationships between supply and prices. Consider the case of raw-material prices such as wheat, copper, livestock during limited periods of time. Why is it that these markets are repeatedly subject to such violent price disturbances? Is it merely the variation in money or credit that causes these wide advances and declines in basic raw-material markets and their effect on the entire level of prices? Decidedly not! Money and credit factors do exert great influence upon occasion, especially in war periods, but this is not the whole story. Changes in supply, because of conditions peculiar to those industries as well as the human equation, actually explain many of these cyclical fluctuations in prices. In inelastic markets it requires but minor shifts in supply to cause wide variations in price.

It is true, of course, that disturbances in the credit system or difficulties relating to money supply may accentuate a weakening of demand schedules pertaining to such raw materials, while production (O) continues its routine way, and inventory piles up. Output may continue unadjusted to demand because of the pressure of debt burdens or the competition coming from virgin areas of high yield or areas previously without transport facilities.[1] But this piling up of inventory (I) that

---

fact remains that *this utility, or psychological aspect,* is extraneous to the main problem. A given quantity of sugar in the market selling at a higher price means a shifted position of the schedule of demand. It is one thing to say that demand, as actually expressed in money or credit, is strengthening or weakening but quite another thing to say that these changes *signify something in the psychology of the buyers.* Fisher here confuses a *demand situation* and a *utility schedule.* Actually there is no sound reason to believe that what takes place in the equation of exchange, if it is properly stated, is not exactly the same as what takes place in individual markets when we consider them functioning simultaneously and do not insist that every variation that occurs measures something psychological.

[1] Some writers have expressed the exchange equation as merely $P = MV$. J. S. Mill's statement, as expressed by J. L. Laughlin ("The Value of Money") is equivalent to $P = MV$, with no place for T, on the amazing assumption that this was fixed or its variations unimportant. Such assumptions have usually been associated with the belief, long cherished by economists of the "static" school, that there can be no *general* overproduction (or underproduction) of goods. This dogma applies to the metaphysical "long-run," not the actual business world, and these hazy generalizations fail to provide for the very realistic possibility that excesses or deficiencies in important, basic, *particular* markets may have far-reaching effects in the *general* trade and price situation for months or even years.

Another line of thought that denies T or supply any effective causal influence in

tends to produce a decline in price is not necessarily explained by monetary and credit conditions. In fact, it may *affect* these, either directly or via *P*. If the supply factors alone rise or fall in such a manner as to influence price level, these price changes, in turn, can transmit influences upon *offers to purchase and "bid" prices* and therefore *upon* the rate of use of the existing supply of money and creation and use of circulating credit. We have included in *P*, price level, only those prices actually representing transactions, but when inventory begins to accumulate and trade activity does not absorb it, the factor *R* declines, and as nominal prices quoted decline, actual prices paid also tend to be weakened. This may even cause some reduction in *T*, which can decline at the very same time that inventory in certain strategically important markets is increasing and total supply $(I + O)$ is temporarily becoming larger than what can be sold at the former price level, unless there happens to be an independent expansion in *M* or *C* or *m*. Under these conditions this would be unlikely; the monetary velocities would decline in sympathy with the decline in *R*. When supply in important segments of trade abnormally increases in this fashion, it tends to influence prices in the sense of "bids and offers." We see this constantly in the commodity markets, in the stock market, the labor market, and the real-estate market. The importance of this is simply that *quoted prices* are one of the hidden and usually overlooked *connecting links* between supply

---

the equation is Fisher's insistence that over short periods (the "business cycles") *T* is motivated by *P*. He has sought to demonstrate statistically that the variations of trade identified with the business cycle are merely complex resultants of *changes in the rate of change* in the price level. By expressing this as a rate of change and "distributing" the results according to a complicated weighting system, Fisher obtains cyclical curves that closely parallel the price-index movements in cyclical pattern, even though the *actual* cycles of prices tend to *follow* rather than to *lead* the pattern of trade activity. These demonstrations, however, are not conclusive nor are they a basis for considering the rate of change in the price level as having any *causal* effect, inasmuch as there are several other similar lagging factors with respect to physical trade or production. Probably much the same effect could be obtained, if we manipulated our figures sufficiently, with industrial wages or interest rates or commercial failures or the cost of living—any of which might be made to show an artificial time lead, in terms of rate of change.

There is lacking a thoroughly empirical basis explaining *why* this should be true and why it may not be equally true that prices merely adjust themselves to certain phases of the business cycle so that peaks of booms cause the most rapid rate of change in prices while the bottoms of depressions happen to be productive of the fastest rate of decline in prices. To the extent that the latter might be found true, it would doubtless hold much more for commodities or for other items subject to speculative influences than for the price level as a whole. This theorizing is merely one phase of the general argument, which the present writer is disposed to question as a general proposition, that all the disturbances in the economic system are created through *price* disturbances, rather than through financial and trade maladjustments.

$(I + O)$ and price level and possibly both prices and credit (C). The effect of prices on M or m is usually not so important as its effect (particularly when declining) upon the more flexible factors C and V. There may also be shifts from M to m if hoarding occurs; or shifts from m to M or enlargement of m by Government paper issues if $(I + O)$ is relatively low and a national emergency such as war brings terrific pressure of demand on scant supply.

We have now brought into the equation all the factors that appear to be potent and capable of causal effectiveness. The forces do not work in simply one direction, but within limits they operate in either direction. The bearing upon monetary and credit policy is obvious, and we shall refer to it again in later chapters after examining first some of the concrete dynamic behavior of a number of key phases of industry. Those who have been enthusiastic in proposing monetary remedies as panaceas for stabilizing the price system or the business cycle have principally built up their case around an imperfectly formulated equation. Hence they invariably fail to concentrate upon particular *phases* or markets that may originate far-reaching maladjustments. Instead of shooting with a well-aimed rifle they use buckshot and trust that it will do some good. Such an attitude also conduces to unwillingness to anticipate disturbances and vibration through *selective* policy and preventive action aimed at averting the use of "checkbook money" (C) in ways that are dangerously topheavy and recklessly speculative. The result is that when such credit collapses and a void has been created in the total currency circulation the void must be filled by some kind of new credit capable of even more dangerous potentialities. Thus we need no longer pay for our financial mistakes and never learn to avoid them.

In our previous discussion and statistical illustrations of the relation between credit currency and the long intermediate trend of trade, we found that it was possible to explain almost all the fluctuations in the price level as to both trend and cyclical movements in the United States through a long period. How does this demonstration fit into the theoretical principles just stated? From a statistical standpoint anything like a complete demonstration of the equation of exchange is, of course, impossible. We can attempt only approximations, and even these do not throw light on the direction in which the causes work and on which elements are dynamic, which passive. We expressed the terms of the equation incompletely, showing merely variations in $(M + C)$ as measured indirectly and for part of the period in m, and the denominator appears merely as T, insofar as industrial activity reflects it. The data previously presented do not enable us to examine the movements of V, v, I, O, R, Sc, or r. The results indicate that $P = (M + C)/T$, so that the omitted variables at best are relatively minor or offset each other.

Particularly, the nature of total output, inventory, and supply cannot be detected and their relationships observed.   During intervals of prolonged hesitation in business activity, the index of trade as we have used it may represent changes that are not necessarily uniform throughout the business system and that do not indicate the behavior of raw-material supply or inventory.   In other words, prices may be declining over a wide front, as they did in the 1870's or in the 1930's, and declines of such unusual intensity and duration may be at least in part traceable to raw-material-supply maladjustments rather than to changes in the circulation of money or credit.   At such times T may indicate a slackening, but some markets are being weakened by a *rise* in $(I + O)$ that is offset and concealed by a decline in R but is at the same time pulling down prices. There are occasionally such hidden factors buried in the measurements, but if brought to the surface they would disclose expanding unsold stocks, accumulation of foreclosed property, or idle labor—a drastic fall in R and r, paralleling and probably causing a fall in V.   Thus, although our statistical representation definitely establishes a dynamic relationship among the three main factors, it does not tell the whole story of causal influences or the factors contributing them.   The influences within the exchange system are therefore complex and capable of action in several possible directions.

It follows, as a broad principle, that derangements in the price system as a whole may arise from monetary or from supply conditions.   In wartime the former factors always predominate, but in normal times and particularly over shorter periods the price variations are capable of being initiated by production and inventory factors in the raw-material and land-using industries.   This means that there is no single formula or remedy for price-level stabilization.   There is no merit in the proposition, so commonly urged during the past generation, that the general price level is merely a resultant of monetary conditions and must therefore be stabilized only by schemes of a monetary nature.   This is a dangerous fallacy, notwithstanding the fact that in wartime it points to the factors that require very special control.

There is still another phase of the equation of exchange that calls for brief comment.   Some economists in recent years have sought to develop subequations in order to concentrate the analysis upon those prices or those classes of goods or services that they consider of exceptional importance or that they imagine relate particularly to the interest of labor or consumer or political objectives.   This has been a favorite device among leading British writers upon the subject, such as Keynes, Robertson, Hawtrey, and others.[1]   The attempt is most commonly made

[1] J. M. Keynes, for example, has factored what roughly corresponds to an equation numerator into means of payment, pertaining specifically to individuals, to business

to link the monetary and credit mechanism with analysis of those forces
having to do with wages or national income.   If, however, we attempt to
explore this new tangent of theorizing, we find the results disappointing.
Intricate complexities of shifting meanings and abstruse overrefinement
serve as barriers to clear-cut and significant results.   The equations so
specialized tend to give the same excessive emphasis to the monetary
factors that we have noted in Fisher's form of the general equation.   This
involves the possibility that one may overlook disturbances in some
omitted sector of the price system that may bear *indirectly* upon the prices
or values under special consideration.   Breaking down the equation is
legitimate and can be useful if the various parts are not considered to
be independent of each other.   It was just this tendency to depart-
mentalize and pigeonhole the workings of the credit system and the price
system of the United States during the 1920's that brought such confusion
of policy and lack of efficiency in the control of one of our worst inflations.
It is most important at this juncture that the reader have a firm grip
upon the basic mechanics of the exchange system as a whole and then
make his particular analyses without the preconceived idea that an equation of exchange is the correct or invariable framework for that specific
study.

One further point is important.   The mechanics of the equation of
exchange in the general form developed above must be understood to
pertain not merely to definite time periods but also to a given commercial
area.   Influences may be transmitted from prices, monetary factors,
foreign-exchange rates, production, inventory, turnover, etc., in a given
area to price conditions outside the area.   If we took the entire world
and its commerce as the area and made suitable adjustments for the
diversity of money, credit systems, price quotations, etc., the problem
of intersystem relations and many minor indirect influences would be

---

firms, and to other groups, and the equivalent terms in the denominator become the
correlated specific transactions representing labor, transfer of goods, transfer of
property, etc.   But the meanings are subject to various interpretations, and there
are many highly artificial assumptions not capable of verification.   The separation
of the exchange mechanism into watertight compartments also involves the logical
difficulty that causation may not run in the same direction or in the same manner as
it does in the *general* equation.   Hence conclusions based on general equation causal
relationships may be carried over into the departmentalized equations, with erroneous
results.   By substituting such partial equations, all in a form that exaggerates the
monetary and credit factors, for straightforward demand-and-supply analysis, conclusions can be derived that appear to support the thesis that industrial wages or the
national income can be raised by money juggling.   This has become a favorite past-
time with economic thinkers who do not carry their analysis beyond money prices
and money values into the realities of actual wealth, real income, and the *physical*
aspects of their enhancement.   See J. M. Keynes "General Theory of Employment,
Interest, and Money," London, 1936.

eliminated. Actually, however, we should find this global analysis of baffling difficulty statistically. If the price system or equation of exchange only for the United States is considered, it must be remembered that our level of prices may be affected by the occurrence of numerous minor changes, such as the change in definition of money in a foreign nation, tariff laws abroad, etc. Or we may redefine our monetary unit, as was actually done in 1934, and thus directly by legal act influence the rates of foreign exchange and thereby also prices of commodities exported and imported. The price system of a given area, in other words, includes elements that involve trade with outside areas and that reflect the influence of possible changes in translating dollars into other currencies, and vice versa. The extent to which the rest of the world is doing business on a gold standard or a paper standard thus has a direct bearing upon our price level. It may have indirect effects through gold movements or even changes in the supply of basic commodities. The definition of what a dollar *is* naturally is a legal matter; what it may mean in terms of price level can be interpreted by correct use of the equation of exchange.

SUMMARY OF PRICE LEVEL DYNAMICS

In conclusion, let us summarize the discussion of the dynamics of money, credit, trade, and prices in the following propositions:

1. The equation of exchange expresses algebraically the factors in a ratio whose changing value is associated with change in the general level of prices in a given area and unit of time.

2. The familiar "quantity theory of money" is not a satisfactory designation of the general price-making process, because it insists that the price level varies proportionally with changes in the "quantity" (often ambiguous) of legal tender money, without necessarily including credit circulation or velocities. Furthermore, by stressing quantity of money or even the quantity of money and credit, there is inadequate attention to other factors, such as changes in trade and the component factors of supply and turnover that affect prices directly and may also affect money and credit circulation.

3. Bank-reserve money has a relation to the credit circulation created by bank loans, but the relationship is not rigidly fixed or constant. In general, so long as bank-created credit C is convertible into cash, the expansion and contraction of bank credit depends upon expansion and contraction in reserves, but in short periods this may not necessarily be true.

4. Money in the hands of the public usually varies in accordance with the changes in price level and trade; it is not a major causal element. Its velocity of circulation v tends to be lower than the velocity of bank

demand deposits V.   Government paper money issues not convertible into specie may cause m to vary considerably more than $M + C$, and in periods of extreme inflation there may be a fantastic expansion of m and an exceedingly rapid turnover v.   Inflation can also develop through the exploiting of a banking system by governments seeking to issue evidences of debt without limit and thus virtually monetizing the public debt to finance war or other emergencies.

5. The velocities associated with money means of payment or credit vary more or less directly and proportionally with the rates of turnover R and r of supply entering into trade T.   The intermediate trend of trade, therefore, indicates the path that total means of payment should follow in order to keep the general price level stable.   Any temporary excess or deficiency in the means of payment about this trend affords a practical means of formulating public policy to correct the variance, but such policies must also give attention to unnecessary variations in trade activity, possibly arising from supply and production abnormalities.

6. The general price level does not necessarily move, either during short periods or long periods, in exact conformity with the changes in *commodity* prices or other specific price groups.   In order to examine the forces pertaining to changes in these segments within the price system, we may form subsidiary equations, but it is probably better practice to analyze the dynamic factors involved in each phase with attention to detail and not merely in terms of an exchange equation assumed to be similar in its mechanics to the general equation.

7. Although price level is primarily the resultant of changes in the money/trade ratio, a change in the numerator or some part of it may transmit effects *through* price level to the denominator and vice versa Such causal influences may also pass through *quoted* prices that are not included in P.   The changes in the ratio affecting P may arise in either the numerator or the denominator or both, and attention exclusively to the monetary factors is inadequate analysis.

8. It frequently happens that supply in the basic raw-material markets or in property development, productive equipment, or mercantile inventory becomes excessive in the sense that financial involvement of the holders and forced liquidation occurs.   In these cases, there is a rise in I, producing a fall in related prices (particularly in quoted prices), and a shrinkage in bank credit may *result* from the combined effect of price decline, excessive supply, and impaired trade conditions for a period of time.   Conversely, a shortage in supply may raise prices and stimulate activity, with the result of enlarging credit and *spreading the price rise* over many markets.

9. It is possible for deficient supply and urgent need, as in time of war, to affect prices overnight and to force the Government in making

purchases to expand the means of payment through issues of inconvertible paper money.

10. The relations existing between M and C, or M and $(M + C)$, are substantially those that govern the short-term rate of interest in the money market. These rates are not part of the price level, but they are *derivatives from* factors in the equation to a very important extent. Changes in the money market rates may affect long-term interest rates and hence have a bearing upon the return on investments, the tempo of business activity and even employment generally, although here again we do not have unilateral causation. The rate of interest or discount may also be affected by relations existing between M and m. Although through the rate of interest, some factors in the equation may operate upon other factors, the extent to which the rate of interest is itself a factor capable of effecting major changes in P has probably been greatly exaggerated in theoretical discussion (see Chapter 16).

11. There has long been an excessive degree of importance attached to changes in the price level as a basis for Government policy in controlling the business cycle. As will be demonstrated in later chapters, the business cycle is not primarily a *function* of price-level movements. In most cases, cyclical movements in industry and trade originate in financing practices and promotional activities at levels in the business system, where changes in prices capable of being attributed to monetary influences are of relatively minor importance.

12. Although the long-term trend of gold production in the past has conformed to the broad trend of physical trade reasonably well— being stimulated in periods of falling general prices and curtailed in periods of rising prices—the more recent concentration of the world's gold in the United States raises disturbing questions as to whether a stable currency system can still be based upon a gold-reserve foundation without the addition of continuous political manipulation and adjustment.

13. If gold is abandoned as a more or less self-balancing and yet flexible medium for ultimate bank reserves, the alternative appears to be the use of Government paper or paper representing the public debt or some combination of selected bank assets as equivalent to the basic reserve against deposits subject to check. A combination of basic commodities might take the place of gold as an ultimate standard, but convertibility problems are then rendered complex.

CHAPTER 7

THE VALUE OF TRADE, NATIONAL INCOME, AND FARM INCOME

Since we have at least a fairly reliable measure of changes in the general level of prices and also an index of changes in production and trade, it would seem logical that the product of these two indexes would measure changes in the total value of all business transactions. Theoretically, this is an entirely logical assumption.[1] If our index of the general price level were meticulously accurate, as well as comprehensive, and if our index of the physical volume of trade included not only commodities but also personal and other services, we should be able to secure a very reliable index of change in the value of all business transactions accomplished.[2] This result would be influenced by the fact that during the course of time a great many kinds of goods are exchanged over and over in speculative "futures" markets; securities are turned over in similar fashion, and even in production operations the original raw materials are handled again and again in the successive operations. Hence it follows that a measure of changes in the value of "all transactions" contains much haphazard and probably meaningless weighting.

The actual aggregate value of the annual turnover of goods, property, and services in the United States would reach astonishingly high figures, possibly approaching 1,000 billion dollars in recent prosperous years. Although the annual value of all transactions would trace the course and the continual fluctuation in the nation's economic activities, the result would not be adaptable to certain purposes that are important. It might not be an accurate measure of change in the value of national income. When the term "income" is used, attention is primarily focused upon the useful end products of these multifarious business processes. It is necessary then to exclude the repetitive turnover of all the speculative markets. It is also necessary to extract from the aggre-

---

[1] Subject only to minor discrepancies if the index numbers are not precisely weighted.

[2] This result would not, of course, include numerous kinds of direct service rendered gratis or the personal enjoyment of the utilities derived from sources or objects not requiring compensation; nor would it take account of direct exchange by way of barter. But as the use of money and credit enters into such an overwhelmingly large part of all the activity having to do with the creation and transfer of wealth and service, the omission of these items would be of no consequence.

gate value of trade the duplications resulting from valuing materials over and over as they move through the stages of production. The income concept, therefore, is associated with calculations of what might be called the "net," rather than the "gross," value of the products, if final form within a given period of time is assumed. For manufacturing operations, the total values that would be pertinent would be a sum of the net values added by all the processes of manufacture to the value of the original materials. If we could total the net values in this sense all along the line, not only in manufacturing but in construction and transportation and service and industries, the final aggregate value would represent a highly significant figure—the net value of business performance.

Such a total of the *net* value of production and service would be considerably smaller than the over-all value of gross transactions. And the average change in prices in referring to national income might be somewhat different in pattern from that exhibited by the general price level, although marked discrepancy is unlikely. Unfortunately there is no long-term measure of changes in this subgroup of net prices or net unit values. Obviously the prices would be mainly those pertaining to raw materials and service, and the latter element would be of considerable importance. Each price element would be associated with a particular value representing payment accruing to economic function, not necessarily business units. The difference between the net values or value added in productive operations, as computed by the Census of Manufactures, and the value of income payments would be mainly in the fact that the former may include a sum of value retained by business units as addition to surplus (that is, not disbursed). A further minor difference arises from the fact that there may be income payments representing not current production but the use of facilities or properties created in the past. Approximately, however, the flow of payments as income to people closely parallels the net value of the nation's economic effort currently. But for the appropriate price index corresponding thereto, we have at present no satisfactory independently constructed series; we must fall back upon such rough approximations as measures of the general price level or perhaps the cost of living.

VARIOUS MEANINGS OF NATIONAL INCOME

It is not necessary, however, that we restrict ourselves to the foregoing method in measuring changes in aggregate personal income by the net value of production and service minus surplus of business units. The aggregate values can be approximated by adding up payments (or estimates thereof) during a given period of time to the various groups of recipients of business, property, and governmental income. To these totals various adjustments can finally be made to allow for business savings and capital formation. Estimates of the national income, in the sense of aggregate payments to individuals, have been prepared by Robert F. Martin, reaching as far back as 1799, although from that point until 1899 the available estimates provide a figure only at 10-year intervals, thereafter annually.[1] For the National Bureau of Economic Research, Simon Kuznets has also prepared very careful estimates of national income, beginning at 1919 and continuing earlier and less complete estimates of W. I. King and others. A third source of income data is the U.S. Department of Commerce, which has drawn upon the methods of the two foregoing agencies in making estimates beginning at 1929 and extending in monthly form currently. Prior to 1900 the best we can do is to carry backward Martin's figures, after making some minor adjustments in the totals, using our annual index numbers of physical trade adjusted by a general price-level index as the basis for this annual extension.[2]

Another way of expressing national values of the flow of useful wealth might begin, not with payments to all individuals but with the outlays made by consumers. Adding to such outlays for goods and services the capital expenditures, such as for housing, durable household

---

[1] This series of income payments for the United States was prepared by the National Industrial Conference Board under the direction of Robert F. Martin. The results are contained in "National Income in the United States, 1799–1938," New York, 1939. In this volume will be found totals of national income, private-production income, income from government and miscellaneous sources, and also data classified according to industrial and functional groups.

[2] Our index of national income extends back the total national-income estimate from the 1900 figure obtained by Martin, after an alternative segment for Martin's agricultural income has been substituted. From 1900 to 1928 the adjusted figures of Martin are used and from 1929 to the latest available date, the figures of the U.S. Department of Commerce for income payments to individuals without the detailed adjustments for pensions, benefits, or relief payments. It is surprising to find that the adjusted figures of the Conference Board, when compared with the estimates arrived at in the latter fashion, agree very closely for the years in common. Further details are given in Appendix 4.

The brilliant work of Simon Kuznets in connection with the National Bureau of Economic Research investigations in national income is embodied in a number of detailed volumes, and his discussion of concepts and description of methods may be found in "National Income and Capital Formation, 1919–1935," New York, 1937, and in the more recent and complete study "National Income and Its Composition, 1919–1938," 2 vols., New York, 1942. For a description of the U.S. Department of Commerce figures on national income, mainly prepared under the direction of Robert R. Nathan, Frederick M. Cone, and E. A. Tupper, see the pamphlet "Monthly Income Payments in the United States, 1929–1940," U.S. Department of Commerce, and the pamphlet "Income in the United States, 1929–1937," published by the U.S. Department of Commerce, November, 1938; also, occasional issues of the *Survey of Current Business*. Revisions of these figures are made from time to time, and the user of such statistics must keep in touch with these changes.

equipment, etc., the results would be roughly equivalent to those arrived at by the preceding method. Both methods might afford national-income results equivalent to the adjusted net value of current production and service. In other words, national income can be conceived either in terms of the adjusted net value of production and service or from the standpoint of the outlays made by, or payments made to, individuals. Perhaps the clearest way to summarize the ideas involved would be to say that totaling the payments made by all business to all individuals (including those who work for themselves) constitutes a highly significant, statistically practicable way of conceiving and estimating the national income. A broader concept would be arrived at by allowing for the undistributed savings made by business units and by governmental bodies; and if we allow for such savings (considering them as plus or minus, as the case may be), our totals would be equivalent to the "net value" of all economic or commercial production. This latter total would include the net value of all consumable finished goods produced plus additions to inventories of goods and exports of goods and services, the latter items being, perhaps, a form of capital formation or saving. In the statistical results of the National Bureau of Economic Research and the U.S. Department of Commerce will be found estimates conforming to both these ways of conceiving national income.

A marked advantage of a measure of national income in any of the foregoing senses is that we can make some comparisons among the various economic segments for which data may be available. This cannot always be done with significant results in terms of physical volume of production or trade. It must be remembered that although physical magnitudes are our only reliable measures of change in total *real* income, the investigation of dynamic changes in the distribution of real income are best arrived at by the use of money values. And for some special purposes of importance, the physical product alone tells us very little with respect to either the money income or the real income of a particular group. One of the most important of such cases is that of *agricultural* income.

AGRICULTURAL OPERATIONS AND FARM INCOME

Although the farm population of the United States is now barely one-fourth of the total population, the opinion is still frequently expressed that the gross income accruing to farmers or the degree of pecuniary prosperity among the rural population has a very considerable influence upon the soundness and vitality of the entire business system. Of course, it is obvious that agriculture is not in fact a single and homogeneous industry. The term "agriculture" is applied loosely to what is really a conglomerate of many distinct occupations, which differ one from another in many important respects. They differ to a certain extent for reasons of geographical location and concentration. But in spite of these diversities there are certain more or less common characteristics involved in the raising of crops from the soil and the breeding of animals. This justifies the attempt to measure the movement of prices, production, and income for the "aggregate farm enterprise" as well as for particular subgroups of farmers.

Before discussing these measurements and their relationship to the general long-term drift of national income, it is well to remind ourselves of some of the peculiarities of most farming operations. Agriculture is in some respects a type of "business." Yet in other respects it is, in the common phrase, a "way of life." Most farmers live *with* their work, and the business aspects of their operations are peculiarly intermingled with the maintenance of household and family. To take farmers generally, they represent the survival of small individualistic enterprise, despite the fact that there has been a fair development of large-scale and even incorporated farming enterprise. In certain localities of the South and the Pacific Coast, these are mainly adaptations of "plantation" systems. There has been a gradual drift toward a larger proportion of tenants and a declining proportion of cultivators who own and operate their properties. But despite all this, the farmer remains the outstanding type of medium and small-scale entrepreneur. He typically operates in a highly competitive market, which, despite tariffs, is affected by world-wide conditions of agriculture, prices, warfare, and prosperity. In recent years the stark results of competitive forces upon American basic agriculture have been tempered by governmental farm-aid policies and the development of a greater degree of coordinated and cooperative effort among farmers in production, marketing, and finance. If we take a long view of the fortunes of agriculture in this country since the beginning of the nineteenth century, there is revealed the drama of hundreds of thousands of producers alternately prospering and suffering from the results of their individual miscalculations and the impact of varying demand for their products throughout a virtually world-wide market. The individual by his own plans and efforts has no effect upon the general market forces controlling the value of wheat, cotton, and similar basic products.

Farming has been a relatively easy industry to enter. Even today it is still true in many rural sections that the farm unit is essentially a household, all of whose members contribute to the enterprise. Farms pass from one generation to members of the next. Once established, however, a farm of even modest proportions tends to be continuously worked, to the point of complete erosion of soil or radical population shift. Farm production from year to year, particularly field-crop production, is geared to weather conditions that are not yet capable of long-range prediction. The raising of crops requires a large expanse of area to provide exposure to sunlight and other atmospheric and chemical factors. The acquisition of land requires capital, and the young farmer more often than not begins his career in debt, even if he carries on the family enterprise. The equipment, the structures, and the drainage system, however limited in scale, represent financial commitments and obligations that tend to hold the farmer to his land, unless extraordinary circumstances tempt him or force him off. As long as he continues to produce (and it is estimated that it requires seven or eight years before the typical farmer begins to earn anything on his investment), the processes tend to be continuous. The farmer essentially produces ahead of demand. A given crop, once planted, is not likely to be abandoned regardless of market conditions. In times of depressed prices, there may be a tendency to introduce some diversification, if that is possible, or to vary proportions as among several possible crops. But these responses to market conditions are slow and irregular.

American agriculture has long been characterized by a high degree of specialization with respect to important products. Although this condition is now in process of gradual change toward greater diversification, in past decades the concentration in such products as corn and hogs, cotton, wheat, and even some fruits has been a typical and important characteristic of our agricultural system. In these more specialized segments, such as cotton in the Old South—perpetuating a plantation system—the response of plantings to previous market conditions has been notably imperfect. Occasionally, exceptionally favorable market situations will lead cultivators to expand their acreage recklessly and even to migrate to new areas to take advantage of boom conditions, and production consequently expands. Curiously enough, although such occasional exceptional price stimulation to production has usually resulted in some additional output, the reverse conditions of very low prices and low money returns have not tended to *decrease* the incentive to produce, either promptly or in degree. In fact, there is reason to believe that when markets are very unprofitable, the typical farmer still continues the routine of seeding and cultivating and harvesting, and in highly specialized agriculture there is really no alternative. The reason lies in part in the overhead charges, which are relatively high in agriculture; a small crop or none at all provides no answer to the *individual* farmer's financial problem. As previously stated, and the point is worth repeating, agricultural production tends to vary from year to year in close correspondence with the yield per acre, which is a function of the weather primarily, while the acreage responds irregularly and usually slowly to market factors. The production of animals represents somewhat different types of routine revealing curious examples of cyclical pattern and responses to internally generated relations between prices of products and cost of feed.

To measure annual changes in agricultural income, our index will be built up from the value of the products rather than the payments to those participating in farming. These values will be *gross* rather than *net*, because we are dealing with extractive activity and raw materials, priced at the source of operations. This gross income will not be precisely comparable with that developed for national-income payments as a whole, but significant comparisons will be possible. Let it be recalled once again that total national income, as we are conceiving it, represents all payments to individuals corresponding to the value of their participation in production, as measured by wages, salaries, the receipts of those operating their own enterprises, interest, rent, dividends, etc. But in the case of farmers and also miners, lumbermen, fishermen, etc., the income is considered to represent the *value* of what is *produced* (with minor adjustments). We must be careful not to interpret such income (or, for that matter, national income) as implying anything in the nature of net *profits*.

The gross value of the products of agriculture, then, represent the money values of the crops on either a calendar- or crop-year basis, at prices received by farmers. There are fairly reliable official figures available for these "farm values," beginning in the 1870's. Prior to that period we must carry back the record by data approximating such values, as explained in Appendix 5.[1]

Let us now turn for a moment to physical production. Since the various types of agriculture have their own peculiar relationships to weather conditions or, in the case of animals, to the production cycles and since there are many hundreds of farm products, an index of *physical* production, representing average changes in the grand total, has an important characteristic that distinguishes it from total industrial output. An annual production index for agriculture would accomplish the smoothing out of many *diverse output patterns*. If we take, let us say, a number of series of field-crop production and combine them in an annual index, with appropriate weights expressing the relative importance of the products, the index would describe a succession of elevations and recessions. But this pattern would not closely correspond to the production patterns of the individual crops, unless a group happened to be very heavily weighted by a crop having a distinctive production pattern.

---

[1] From the total farm values, a deduction of roughly 12 per cent would allow for the value of seed and fertilizer and depreciation of equipment. Duplication is avoided by interpreting "production" as that portion of total output which is either marketed or used for consumption by the farm family but excluding that portion which is fed to animals or used in further production, whose final values alone are counted.

The more items we include in such an index of agricultural production the more weather and other erratic factors tend to offset each other in their effect on particular products, and the line is thus *smoothed out* to a remarkable degree.

Chart 12 (upper curve) shows this principle very clearly in terms of a comprehensive farm-products index. From year to year the changes in aggregate volume are relatively small. Compared, however, with the pattern of agricultural *price* changes, prepared on an equally com-

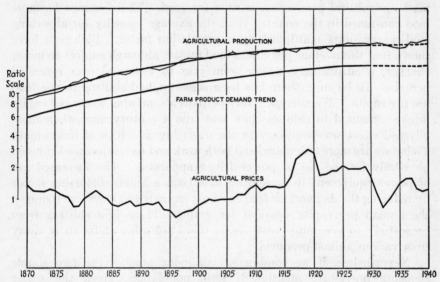

CHART 12.—Total agricultural production, trend of demand for farm products, and agricultural prices. The trend of agricultural production in the United States precisely parallels the trend of demand for farm products expressed in an index combining total population and the physical volume of agricultural exports (U. S. Department of Agriculture data), the latter weighted proportionally to the ratio of farm export values to national income.

prehensive basis and plotted on the same ratio sale, the production variations fade into insignificance. Here we are dealing with a field of operations in which *prices* happen to be predominantly important, not only in themselves and in their relation to the prices that farmers pay for what they buy *but as contributing to fluctuations in the value of the output.* Market prices, as they vary, generate most of the variability in values, and output enters in mainly in terms of its long-term growth trend.

In Chart 12 there will be noticed another striking characteristic of agricultural production in the aggregate. Through the variations in the production index a trend has been drawn. Just below this is seen another trend of almost exactly the same gradient but entirely independent.

This is an estimate of the *trend of demand* for total farm output.   It is based upon the hypothesis that the drift from year to year in aggregate demand for farm products is determined by two factors—the domestic market and the foreign market.   For the foreign market we have export figures (in the form of a volume index) to trace the course of that phase of total demand.   For the domestic market we use (as a preliminary hypothesis) an index of *total population*.   The justification is obviously that apart from a few items such as textile materials, hides, feed, etc., most agricultural production is used for food.   There cannot be more food consumed in the country than the average capacity for absorbing food-energy units multiplied by a population factor.   Biologists have shown that this average per capita food intake, although subject to minor changes, is surprisingly steady from year to year and over extended periods.   To be sure, there has been some gradual shifting in the food use per capita.   We average today perhaps a somewhat lower per capita intake measured in calories than was true a century ago, when more physical effort was necessary in the everyday activities of individuals. Today we are more sedentary, and both work and recreation are lightened physically by the use of power-driven apparatus.   The increased use of power equipment in agriculture has been a minor distorting factor by reducing the demand for feed for draft animals and therefore reducing the human per capita demand for grains.   There is a shifting from breadstuffs to vegetables and sugar; there are other shifts to or away from various animal products.

Nevertheless, if we combine in an index number the two simple elements previously mentioned, total population (given the major weight) and the index of volume of farm exports (the latter smoothed out), we obtain a composite demand trend *that so closely parallels the trend of agricultural production that for all practical purposes the one curve is indistinguishable from the other*.   It is on the basis of this principle that we can work backward historically to periods where actual production data do not exist to obtain a reasonably close *approximation* to farm production as one factor in farm income.   The population index, establishing for practical purposes the drift of total farm production, adjusted by an index of average change in the price of many agricultural products (these figures being now readily available) provides an approximate index of the value of farm production capable of being carried back to the beginning of the nineteenth century.[1]   By keying these index numbers into the gross income values, as computed in more recent

[1] It should be added, as explained in Appendix 5, that in the case of cotton it was found possible to estimate the annual value of the crop, and these estimates of value were added to estimates derived by the foregoing method of value approximation, excluding cotton.

years, we can extrapolate backward to obtain an extended continuous series of estimates capable of being compared with the estimates of total national income or other value data. By having long series, we may be able to draw conclusions that would not be possible from the study of a few decades only.

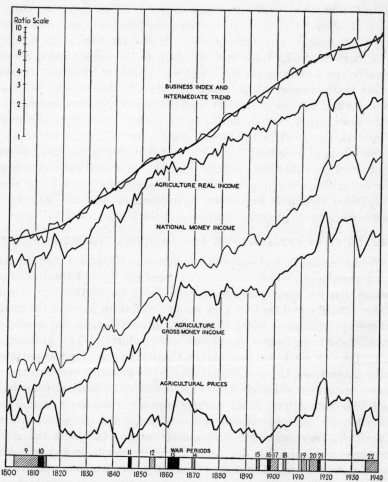

CHART 13.—Agricultural and business indexes, 1800–1940. For description of the data see Appendix 5. For identification of war periods see Note to Chart 7.

In saying that agriculture is a type of enterprise in which (gross) income is peculiarly affected by price movements, it is necessary to formulate the principle a little more carefully. We must distinguish between long-run and short-run observations. *From year to year* it can be said with a fair degree of precision that the income of farmers (and those directly dependent upon farm revenue) will vary almost in unison with the average change in farm prices. Over periods of some length, such as several decades, this would not be perfectly true, because of a trend that might exist in the aggregate production. So long as this trend rises, the pattern of income accruing to agriculture will approximate that of the farm-price index *tilted upward* at the angle or gradient equivalent to the production trend. This appears clearly in Chart 13, upon which have been drawn the indexes of national income, total farm income, and farm prices.[1] If the farm-price index, shown at the bottom of Chart 13, were tilted up to the proper slope, it would virtually synchronize with the index of agricultural income. In view of this vastly important influence of prices in determining the value of income and in view of the fact that the year-to-year farm price movements have such a close similarity to the broad variations in the general price level, discussed in Chapter 5, what conclusions can be drawn as to the effect of monetary inflation and deflation upon *farm income?* What effect does that income have, in turn, upon total national income? In investigating these important relationships as we proceed, the reader is reminded that it is important to distinguish carefully between the short-term, year-to-year fluctuations and the longer trend movements.

THE DRIFT OF FARM INCOME AND NATIONAL INCOME COMPARED

We have already had occasion to observe in Chapter 2 that the trend of our population, which so closely governs the drift of total farm production, has for many years been rising more slowly than the trend of total production and trade. This would account for much of the gradual divergence between an index of national income (income payments) and that of total farm income (farm value of products). This growing disparity became marked following the Civil War. As for the pattern of major *fluctuations*, there is a high degree of similarity between the two income measures, although it was somewhat more marked prior to the Civil War than after. Since national income is made up of unit-price elements and physical-volume elements and since the price elements, as a whole, vary more or less in unison with variations in the general price level (and to a fair degree, also, the farm-price index), we should expect to find a certain degree of similarity between the fluctuations in the income patterns. But a close inspection of Chart 13 reveals that the farm income has experienced more violent changes during major price fluctuation than did total national income. This is seen, for example, in the movements culminating in 1821, when farm income declined much farther proportionately than did national income, and it continued,

[1] The price index shown in Chart 13 represents the *wholesale* prices of agricultural products rather than prices paid to farmers *at the farm*. In terms of index numbers, there is no appreciable disparity in these patterns on an annual basis.

in fact, to decline for a year beyond the bottom established by the general index. In the succeeding pronounced rise in farm income, culminating in 1839, the momentum was somewhat more pronounced than in national income. It is interesting again to observe that farm income reached its peak slightly later than national income. The ensuing decline in farm income was much more pronounced than in the case of national income as a whole. The next period of pronounced general expansion was one of roughly parallel movements, interrupted by some irregularities prior to the Civil War. Following the income peak during the Civil War, when the greenback inflation was such a pronounced factor in the price level, we again see the tendency for farm income to shrink more violently than national income, which, in this case, moves along a more or less horizontal drift for more than fifteen years. And during the 1880's and far into the 1890's, farm income tends to be maintained on a fairly steady level, while national income describes a decided rising trend.

The entire period following the Civil War reveals an interesting divergence between the broad movements of farm income and those of total national income. During this long interval prices of farm products were drifting along a definitely downward trend, which reached its bottom in 1896, about the same time that the general price level reached its lowest point. Thenceforward, farm income rose, probably as the result of infusion of new gold into the credit system and also as the result of the favorable market for agricultural products abroad and in the fast growing industrial centers of the country. But its rate of increase was not quite as marked, down to World War I, as was that of total national income. World War I brought a pronounced inflation of farm income, very closely approximating the pattern of farm prices. National income also spurted to a new high point, culminating in 1920, as the prices of many nonagricultural products, finished goods, and services reached very high prices in 1920. The reaction in national income in 1921 was again distinctinctly minor in comparison to the deep decline in farm income and farm prices. It will be noted, however, that farm income reached its peak in 1919, and there were then two years of decline, whereas there was but brief interruption of a generally rising drift in national income in the year 1921. Farm income then recovered for a few years, tabled off, and relapsed into the deep depression of 1932, once more far exceeding the rate of decline in national income as a whole.

It will also be noted that with the tendency for total farm production to drift sidewise in recent years, the income pattern for agriculture more and more closely approximates that of farm prices shown at the bottom of the chart. For some of the individual components of farm production, the correlation between prices from year to year and income is remarkably close, and in some cases this is even maintained over periods as long as several decades.   More and more, therefore, American agriculture will be dependent upon prices for changes in revenue accruing to the farming segment of the population.   This clearly explains the emphasis insistently placed by agricultural politicians and organized farm pressure groups upon *prices*, price relationships, and the monetary circulation.   This is why inflationary "riders" are attached to appropriation bills in Congress. This emphasis is no mere accident or idiosyncrasy; it emanates from an inherent characteristic of this industry and an awareness of the manner in which income can be manipulated by exerting the proper degree of pressure on the monetary and fiscal policies of Federal administrations incapable of resisting such group pressures.

In the comparisons made possible by the indexes shown in Chart 13, one of our objects is to determine to what extent, if at all, the major fluctuations in agricultural prices and income have contributed to the long-term wave movements in general industry and trade.   These wave movements appear at the top of the chart in the intermediate trend that runs through the general index of business.   The second curve from the top is another agricultural measure, in the form of annual estimates of the "purchasing power" of agricultural income.   We are interested now in two relationships.   First, we wish to observe the extent to which the pattern of the intermediate business trend may be accounted for by the major price and income changes emanating from agriculture. Second, we are interested in comparing the actual business index with the nearest available approach to an equivalent measure of *real* income for agriculture.

From the evidence presented in Chart 13, the conclusion may be drawn that whenever farm money income has suffered an unusually marked depression for an extended period, the intermediate trend of general business seems to have reflected this situation by moving through a *trough* rather than a period of unusual acceleration.   This may be noted in the early 1820's and to a certain degree in the early 1840's and in the years immediately following the peak of Civil War inflation, although the succeeding flattening out of agricultural income fails to correspond to the pattern shown by the underlying drift of general production and trade.   Following the downward inflection of the intermediate trend of business in the 1920's and through the 1930's, the index of farm income, although vibrating violently, pursues a definitely downward course, in contrast to the steadier behavior of total national income.   These cases are not entirely clear-cut, but they tend to substantiate the view that unusually severe and prolonged agricultural depressions may be a contributing factor in restraining the progress of total production and trade to the extent that the intermediate trend of this activity is depressed. In the case of periods of unusual and relatively rapid expansion in farm income (still referring to dollar values), the principle is much less clear, and, indeed, it is doubtful that the available factual evidence would support the proposition that rapid acceleration in the intermediate trend of business volume is essentially dependent upon the behavior of farm income.

Turning now to the relationships expressed in a different form, let us explain further the meaning of the second curve from the top in Chart 13, showing an index of agricultural buying power. It is obvious that there are peculiar difficulties confronting the attempt to construct a *physical* index of the degree of farm "prosperity." This follows directly from the fact that fluctuations in total agricultural production, although they contribute to the shaping of the trend of farm money income, do not have much to do with the *short-term* variations in that income. This is even true in terms of changes in *real* income or purchasing power of the farmer's dollars over nonagricultural goods and services. In years of relatively large production, farm prices fall, and total farm income usually declines unless, at the same time, there are opposing forces in the *general* price level of overwhelming importance. In other words, year-to-year changes in farm production as such do not establish corresponding variations in farm real income comparable to those measured in the index of national real income as this responds to variations in general production. The real income of the entire nation does consist primarily of the current flow of product, of goods and services, and, of course, these include the products of agriculture. But the farmers' aggregate claim upon all these goods and services is expressed in the market by the amount of money the farmer is able to offer in exchange, and this, by and large, is not a variable corresponding over limited periods to his total output. In order to compare *annual* changes in farm real income with change in total real income, as measured by the course of general production and trade, it is necessary to resort to an index of farm "purchasing power." This expresses the changing value of farm products "deflated" by an index of the cost to farmers of things they *typically* purchase *as a group*. It might, of course, be argued that a close comparison of farm income with general income in dollars would of itself allow for this price element, to the extent that its pattern happened to be similar for farmers and for the total population. But insofar as the farmer's typical outlays represent types of goods or equipment differing in some measure from those associated with the outlays of the much larger urban groups, comparisons by way of money income alone are probably not completely satisfactory.[1]

[1] Several types of index numbers of farm living and production costs have been prepared, notably by the U.S. Department of Agriculture. A careful comparison of the annual data from 1910 to 1940 discloses that it makes no great difference whether one uses indexes of the cost of commodities, used typically on farms, or more compre-

The annual index of farm purchasing power shown in Chart 13 is based upon the principle that a ratio between changes in farm money income and prices of commodities that farmers buy approximately reflects the broad movements in the purchasing power or real income of the *farm population*. This is not the same as a measure of net profits of farm operators. As shown in Chart 13 this index, in comparison with the general business index in terms of intermediate trend, points to conclusions similar to those pertaining to income values. Again we find it true that extensive periods of depression in farm real income also mark long periods of hesitation or stagnation in general production and trade. It appears again that in periods of rapid acceleration in the trend of farm real income, there have been similar movements in the intermediate trend of general business. In this respect the comparison points in fact to a somewhat more positive result than in the case of the money-income data. During the long interval between the Civil War and World War I, the real income of agriculture tended to rise with less hesitation and cyclical irregularity than was noted in the drift of money income. But the trend is notably more restrained than the rapidly accelerated trend of general business during those years. In the period since World War I, about the same conclusions would follow as in the case of money-income comparison.

DOES THE DRIFT OF FARM INCOME INFLUENCE THAT OF GENERAL BUSINESS?

To be sure, it can be argued that in these periods of major depression, as well as in long periods of general business acceleration, the causal influences may have run mainly *from* industrial *to* agricultural conditions. The writer is disposed to believe, however, that this is not the proper way to state the case as to the longer term variations. The changing phases of farm income during what may be termed the *major* cycles appear, on the whole, to have contributed more to determine the pattern of general business than the reverse. Farmers have invariably increased their indebtedness during periods of exceptionally high prices, thus making the initial years of price-deflation periods of exceptional hardship and abrupt curtailment of expenditures in many directions. Furthermore, it must be remembered that major difficulties in agriculture are transmitted throughout the business system in several ways. They

hensive measures, including also such cost items as interest, taxes, wages, and depreciation. In order to work with long-term data, it seems best to deflate farm gross income by as homogeneous a *commodity-cost* index as possible. It is not wholly clear that even were the more complete cost measures available prior to 1910, they would reflect changes which are as typical of *general* farm experience in making expenditures as is the case with well-selected and weighted commodity data. See Appendix 5 for the method of deriving the real farm-income (or purchasing-power) index.

exercise an influence through the effects created on the credit structure—through the long-drawn-out processes of liquidation, foreclosure, and credit destruction—which leaves its trail of ruined rural banks and the effect of this ruin, in turn, on other banks.

Periods of extended agricultural depression have always generated powerful social pressures and political movements capable of disturbing confidence and seeking in one way or another to raise or "reflate" the price level and restore the good old days of farm prosperity and solvency. Unfortunately, these organized pressures have been capable of slowing the wheels of industrial progress by creating apprehension and uncertainty, discouraging capital investment and new enterprise. We shall defer to a later chapter some more detailed discussion of the acute difficulties arising mainly from agricultural maladjustment on a world-wide rather than merely national scale during the late 1920's and early 1930's, a remarkable period of agrarian protest translated into far-reaching changes in the popular attitude toward finance, capital, industry, and productive progress.

Before concluding, we may refer to still a third reason for considering that agriculture has primarily transmitted its influences to the "waves" of business conditions. As already stated, agriculture cannot readily readjust itself. The production routine permits but slow and gradual revision in the case of most of our basic products. A manufacturer can usually alter his procedures, his location, his business structure, even to the extent of introducing new types of products. For agriculture the problems of diversification or of shifting from one major product to another are tremendous problems. The rigidity and the force of custom are primarily rooted in the fact of direct concern with natural processes. Over periods of five or ten or fifteen years, possibly even longer, there may be persistent excesses of production, particularly during periods of major war and following cessation of emergency demands or readjustments of foreign markets, the term "excess" referring to such supply as creates pressure upon prices relative to other goods.

The retail prices of farm products are less sensitive and volatile than are farm or wholesale prices. Consumers of farm products in the cities, therefore, do not find prices that they pay reduced during periods of such surplus production as much or as rapidly as one might suspect. The distributive system seeks to dispose of a larger total supply of food than can all be sold at the resistant prices prevailing in city markets. As a result, part of the raw-material supply accumulates as carry-over. Eventually a still more severe decline in prices is likely to occur unless export demand happens to expand. Although some urban living costs are cut, industrial employment may be reduced also if impairment of demand or political agitation arising from rural discontent and protest act as restraints upon the aggregate demand for industrial products. Thus, in the farm production system, there seem to be potential forces capable of providing distinctive and potent influence upon the entire economy, not only through sustained aberrations in purchasing power but through the efforts of a large social group to regain lost purchasing power by political maneuvering that for years can effectively retard enterprise in other fields, where steady progress depends much upon confidence in the stability of the financial mechanism.

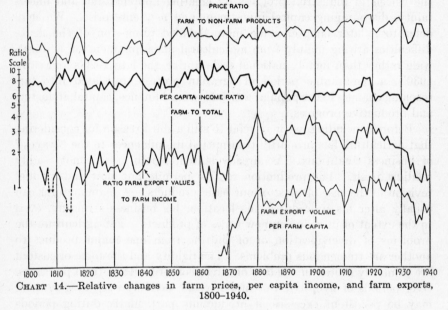

CHART 14.—Relative changes in farm prices, per capita income, and farm exports, 1800–1940.

It has been suggested that declining farm prices are an advantage to industrial development because food and clothing are among the important costs in supporting the families of industrial workers, accounting for roughly one-half of the total annual expenditures of urban wage earners. A reduction in such prices does not ordinarily increase the amount of consumption, although probably clothing purchases may be somewhat expanded. Lower food and textile prices at retail, although not immediately responding to the sensitive wholesale or farm markets, eventually follow their course, and the result is no doubt a saving to the urban population. This saving presumably can be applied in other directions, to the purchase of houses, of automobiles, and of other equipment of a durable nature. This would increase the demand for many products of urban industry and for transportation and other services. We have already presented reasons, however, for believing that this process alone would not immediately serve to lift the general level of production and trade out of a long major depression. But if one will again observe the curve of the prices at the bottom of Chart 13, he will note an occasional contrast between unusual declines in farm prices *in their later stages, as they approach bottom, with a volume of general business* again beginning to accelerate enough to affect the intermediate wave trend. Notice, for example, the situation from about 1826 to 1830 and from 1880 to about 1892. Perhaps we may say, as a tentative hypothesis, that long-continued declines in farm prices in their later stages do not seem to correspond closely to the pattern of general industry, and the reduction in living costs for maintenance of the urban population, after it has continued a long time, may contribute sufficiently to industrial acceleration to create something of a rebound effect still later to agriculture itself.

In concluding this discussion, it may be helpful to state these relationships in a somewhat different form. In Chart 14, farm income, relative to estimated farm population, is expressed as a ratio to per capita national income. In neither case were the income data adjusted to a real income basis. In this chart are also shown the annual ratios of farm-product prices to wholesale prices of nonagricultural products and two ratio series relating to agricultural exports.

WAR EFFECTS UPON FARM EXPORT, FINANCE, AND INCOME

Let us refer first to the index of relative per capita farm income. This index clearly reflects the war periods of price inflation and the long-continued postwar deflation. In this form the data indicate that the *relative* position of agricultural income for many years following major wars is even more unfavorable than was suggested by Chart 13. It is evident also that following the major wars, the immediate decline in the relative income of agriculture is followed by several years of a sustained higher level, although following World War I this was much less marked than in previous cases. Another interesting feature is that there was a rising ratio of farm income to total income *prior* to each of the important wars, the War of 1812–1814, the Civil War, and World War I. The war-prosperity periods have the appearance of climaxes, topping off the rising drift of the preceding periods. When the index of relative farm income is compared with that of the ratio of agricultural to nonagricultural prices, there is more or less similarity of movement, but it is curious that the broad secular trend of this ratio is upward, whereas the broad trend of the relative income, at least since the Civil War, has been definitely downward. Not only are the trends in contrast but the year-to-year changes also do not correlate in their movements in anything like the degree that one would imagine who may have done his thinking about agricultural problems under the influence of current political emphasis upon "price parities" and price ratios. Despite all that may be said of the very important part that prices do play in farm income, the *relative* position of the farmer is not *perfectly* measured by this yardstick.

Following World War I, the relative position of agricultural income was sustained for a brief period. Then came an abrupt collapse, followed by but feeble recovery. From this level a further decline brings the index to the lowest level of the entire period, and this is again followed by a relatively feeble recovery, then by relapse. The American farmer appears since 1920 to have been in a much less favorable position than is commonly supposed. While we are discussing these broad tendencies, let us seek the causes underlying this extraordinary sagging tendency in relative income. One of the underlying factors seems to have been the less rapid rate of growth of the general population, coupled with declining per capita consumption tendencies for several important staples produced on farms. Probably more important has been a progressive deterioration of the farmers' export market. The failure to maintain even a reasonably satisfactory per capita relative-income position can be attributed largely to a substantial weakening of foreign demand that was actually beginning even prior to World War I and that, following the brief artificial stimulus of that period, has been intensified in recent years.

Fortunately, we have good statistical data to demonstrate this tendency. Chart 14 shows an index of the ratio of the value of agricultural exports to farm income and also, beginning at 1866, an index of the physical volume of farm exports per capita of farm population.[1] It was customary in the early years of the nineteenth century to think of farm exports as an outstandingly important phase not only of agriculture but of our foreign trade as a whole. From the beginning of the century until as late as about 1890, farm products constituted close to 80 per cent of the value of all domestic merchandise exports. After about 1890, because of the extraordinary acceleration in manufacturing enterprise, farm exports began relatively to shrink, until in recent years, prior to World War II, they were barely one-fifth of all export trade. When farm exports are expressed as a ratio to estimated total farm income, the long-term pattern is somewhat different. Apart from occasional war

[1] Since the official data of exports relate to fiscal years, ending June 30, the ratio shown in Chart 14 was worked out for export values on the basis of fiscal year exports set against farm income of the preceding calendar year (*e.g.*, calendar-year income of 1900 against fiscal-year exports of 1900–1901). The data of volume of farm exports per capita of farm population relate to fiscal years and are plotted to correspond with the foregoing data. Farm population prior to 1850 was estimated on the basis of recent data of the U.S. Department of Agriculture, extrapolated backward proportionately to the Census data of *rural* population, calibrated to annual form.

years, when exports were sharply curtailed, the proportion of total farm income represented by sales abroad rose during the nineteenth century from around 10 per cent to as high as 34 per cent in 1880. This was the historic peak from which there ensued a gradually declining tendency, intensified after the brief export recovery during and just after World War I. Prior to World War II we were again back to less than 10 per cent.

If we express export of farm products by an index measuring relative changes in the physical *volume* of a broadly representative list of items and express it in terms of per capita of farm population, we find that the export movement has indeed described a steeply downward trend, which World War II had not, at the time of this writing, reversed in the slightest degree (see the lower curve of Chart 14). When we realize that our total export trade has seldom reached much beyond 10 per cent of the estimated value of all American production, this shrinkage in farm-product exports assumes considerable significance. If we examine a number of leading products, the tendency becomes even more impressive.[1] Through most of the nineteenth century and until World War I, cotton exports contributed nearly 70 per cent, one year with another, to the total gross farm income from cotton. By 1940, cotton exports had shrunk to little more than a million bales—probably an abnormal wartime condition. Exports of wheat have usually accounted for a much more variable proportion of the total farm income from that crop, ranging from 10 to 50 per cent; but since 1920, when Europe was restoring wheat reserves from our production, the wheat farmer has obtained less and less of his income from exports. Much the same is true of pork products, which have shrunk from a 30 per cent contribution in 1919 to farm income in that division of agriculture to about 2 or 3 per cent in 1940. These are instances of major farm products, concerning which it had become customary to suppose that they would always be on an export basis and that occasional surpluses could thus be disposed of, at low prices if necessary. But the world that followed World War I became a different world, striving for self-sufficiency within national boundaries and requiring less and less from the United States. Financial derangements, new tariffs, quotas all have done their work. The foods led this decline. Cotton was successful in more or less holding its own until the last few years. This was true also of tobacco. Some specialties among the fruits and the more concentrated dairy products have continued to find the foreign market important, although these

[1] Interesting computations, with the use of a slightly different method from that employed in the foregoing, supplemented by materials on individual products, will be found in Frederick Strauss, "The Composition of Gross Farm Income Since the Civil War," *Bulletin* 78, National Bureau of Economic Research, Apr. 28, 1940.

account for a relatively small proportion of total farm income. There seems, then, good reason to believe that the exceptional violence of price collapse that marked the Great Depression and the curious difficulty encountered in reviving agricultural prices, despite the deliberately

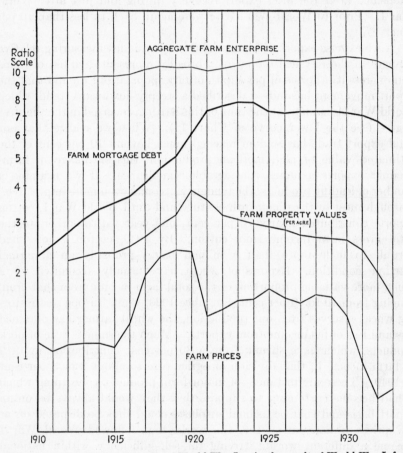

CHART 15.—Agricultural results of World War I. As the result of World War I, farm-mortgage debt was vastly inflated out of all proportion to the very moderate expansion in the aggregate physical aspects of production facilities. The decline in farm property values after 1920 was much more rapid than reduction in farm-mortgage indebtedness.

inflationary measures and political subsidization of the 1930's, are traceable to this ebb tide of farm export, which individual producers were powerless to control. It goes far to explain the movements of relative farm income in Chart 14.[1]

[1] Regarding the policies that have been adopted to deal with this persistent problem and the expressions of resentment and protest from farming sections, more will be said in later chapters.

We may obtain a clearer picture of the recent unsatisfactory position of American agriculture if attention is given to the expansion of our production facilities during World War I and the way in which this period affected farm finance. The War and immediate postwar years provided extraordinary export opportunities to farmers. The accompanying dramatic upward sweep of prices stimulated farmers to expansion that later brought many of them to grief. Although the experiences of that period cannot be generalized into principles that will invariably apply, the facts do afford an excellent example of the manner in which inflation of the sensitive prices of farm products may extend its influence to the value of farm property, thus encouraging tremendous speculative activity, not so much in the actual equipment of farm enterprise but in financial commitments and obligations with which agriculture is left to struggle for decades. In Chart 15 some of the essential facts are presented from just before World War I to the postwar depression bottom of 1933. Statistical data are available to illustrate clearly what happened during this period, but we cannot readily measure these particular factors for earlier war periods.[1]

It appears in Chart 15 that the per acre estimated value of farm land throughout the United States responded definitely, even though somewhat tardily, to the wartime rise in farm-product prices. This farm-property-value index is an average representing many types of farm production. In some of the areas whose products were most affected by temporarily expanded demand, the index rose considerably higher than for the country as a whole. The rise in values was particularly pronounced in the South Central, North Central, and Great Plains areas. Thousands of people, many without previous farming

---

[1] The data in Chart 15 were taken from the following sources. Indexes of estimated per acre value of farm real estate from the *U.S. Department of Agriculture Yearbooks of Agricultural Statistics;* total farm mortgage indebtedness from the same sources, expressed in terms of farm population. Indexes of the size of the farm enterprise were taken from Size and Production of the Aggregate Farm Enterprise, 1909–1936, *Works Progress Administration National Research Project Report A-6,* prepared by R. G. Bressler, Jr., and J. A. Hopkins, 1938, p. 19. These indexes include acreage of crops and numbers of livestock on farms. The combination involves a weighting of the individual series in proportion not to values or income but to the estimated labor requirements of the various items. Despite this peculiarity of weighting, the index is a valuable measure of the physical variations in farm enterprise. The indexes were reduced to per capita basis by the writer. In connection with the trend of mortgage indebtedness, tentative and preliminary figures are available to show the amount of involuntary transfer of farm properties in selected areas. These will be found in *The Agricultural Situation,* February, 1940, p. 18. The figures are given for five-year periods, beginning at 1910, and show the following results for each five-year period ending at 1934: 100 (base), 148, 287, 465, 581. Similar indexes for voluntary transfers are 100, 108, 79, 73, 52.

experience, were induced by promise of high returns to expand wheat, cotton, and animal production in areas that had previously been undeveloped. A new migration of pioneers spreading over the plains resulted in removal of the original soil-binding grasses and conversion of what should have remained grazing land into grain acreage. By 1924 the Great Plains were growing some seventeen million more acres of wheat than in 1909. In Chart 15 is also shown the general expansion in American agricultural enterprise in physical terms. The upper index curve on the chart combines a considerable number of products and types of farming and shows the average change in acreage cultivated and in number of animals raised. This is perhaps the best measure now available of the over-all physical response to the price and income stimulus. Probably the most striking increase occasioned by the War was in acreage devoted to small grains, particularly wheat. The small-grains index rose nearly 30 per cent between 1912 and 1919, the peak year.

DEFECTS OF FARM MORTGAGE FINANCING

It is also interesting to observe that although the aggregate farm enterprise expanded during the War period, this, after all, was a relatively moderate expansion compared with the rise in land values and with the most interesting of all these measures, the expansion in long-term farm-mortgage indebtedness. The War boom was predominantly a *financial* boom, an orgy of reckless borrowing to speculate in farm-land values. The addition to mortgage debt is seen to have been out of all proportion to the effect of expansion in the physical status of crop and livestock development. Many farmers who were successful and prosperous, instead of reducing their debt, could not resist the temptation to borrow more in order to expand operations.   Lenders were glad to lend and threw conservatism to the winds in the way in which they appraised land values and solicited loans from farmers at interest rates of 6 to 8 per cent or more.   With the dazzling prospect of almost overnight gains in values and income, the farm-mortgage indebtedness reached a peak considerably later than the peak in prices or farm income.   For the country as a whole, the mortage peak was reached about 1924, but in the South Atlantic region it was not reached until 1927, followed by the East South Central in 1928, the West South Central in 1930, and the Pacific States in 1932.

At the beginning of this borrowing movement, individual lenders provided the largest contribution to farm capital. The commercial banks were the most important of the institutional lenders, followed closely by life-insurance companies. In addition to mortgage loans, there was a large amount of lending at shorter term. Producers of animal products were accommodated by cattle-loan companies and commission lenders, whose advances were enormously stimulated by the high prices of livestock. The continued rise, after the peak in prices in 1919, in the long-term debt represented by mortgages on farm property is explained by the fact that loans previously made at high prices on a medium-term or unsecured basis were refinanced into mortgage loans. Lessors now desired additional real-estate security. Many farm owners who previously had no mortgage indebtedness financed operating losses after 1920 by taking out new mortgages. There was thus a continuing expansion in mortgage debt due to the very reversal in the situation and superimposed upon that created directly as a result of the inflation. This is rather typical of debt creation during prosperity and through the immediate succeeding phase of reaction, financial reverses, and distress. We find it in commercial borrowing as well as in long-term borrowing operations.

By the middle 1920's, commercial banks had been able to turn over a part of their farm loans and mortgages to the life-insurance companies, which then continued for nearly a decade to carry the largest part of the institutional mortgage burden. Somewhat prior to that time, however, with growing distress among farmers who had overextended themselves during the inflation, the Federal Government had created the Federal Land Banks, supplemented by the less important Joint Stock Land Banks as institutions for direct long-term loans to agriculture. The Federal Land Banks, during the 1930's, under the pressure of new difficulties partly stemming from the shrinkage in export demand, were forced to "bail out" part of the insurance-company and bank loans, and today the Federal Banks are carrying the preponderant portion of all farm mortgages. The present loans of the Federal Land Banks (the Joint Stock Land Banks having been virtually liquidated) plus a large volume of emergency loans made in the early 1930's by the Land Bank Commissioners to meet cases of unusual distress now amount to about 40 per cent of the outstanding farm-mortgage debt. The proportion carried by individuals and loan companies is about the same. Starting from an inflationary debt expansion, it has thus been necessary to erect new institutions and to accomplish several emergency blood transfusions in the system of farm financing.

We can now discern several general characteristics of agricultural finance in the United States. One is the absence in our earlier history of adequately developed and specially organized mortgage-credit institutions for agriculture, adapted to the slowly liquidating operations of that branch of production. Until very recently we have not had a system of long-term mortgage credit for farmers (or, in fact, for anyone else) distinct from demand-deposit banking institutions, equipped with facilities for the rehypothecation of mortgages, and providing ready emergency rediscount of sound obligations of farmers. This defect in our financial institutions created terrible weakness among the rural commercial banks, which failed by the hundreds through the 1920's and 1930's. As for the life-insurance companies, most of them were vastly stronger than the rural banks, but the financial emergencies of the 1920's and, again, of the 1930's forced these companies to foreclose and reacquire an enormous amount of rural property.[1] These acquisitions of farm real estate by the larger life-insurance companies have indeed shown surprising persistence. In 1929 they amounted to properties valued at 88 million dollars, which had become 465 million dollars by 1934. At this writing it is in the neighborhood of 700 million dollars.[2] These holdings are far larger than the combined holdings of farm real estate in the hands of other lenders.

The second feature of special importance in farming finance, emphasized by war-inflation experience, is the fact that loans were made to farmers to finance long-term operations but with relatively short maturities *and, in many cases, inadequate provision for regular amortization.* This has been a common feature of mortgage financing in general in the United States. It has bearings, as we shall see, in many directions. This defect cannot be too strongly emphasized, because it has been strangely overlooked as a factor in generating economic disturbance and maladjustment. It underlies the failure of the capitalistic system to operate efficiently and its tendency to break down under the unusual stress occasioned by great political emergencies. The practice of creating 25- or 30-year loans on a 5-year basis, throwing all the risks of nonextension upon the borrowers and making no provision for systematic repayment of principal, has been particularly flagrant among the commercial banks, but other sources of long-term (or what should properly have been long-term) financing were also at fault in this regard. One close observer of farm finance states the matter clearly by saying: "The banker, of course, had overlooked the desirability of long-time credits because they did not 'square' with his idea of liquidity. Too few banks had ever made the requirement of any periodical principal payments. A five-year maturity made his farm mortgage liquid, in his judgment."[3]

In this manner, under the spell of the deceptive principle of "liquidity," an excessive temptation was spread before our farmers to "trade upon their equity"; only interest payments seemed important. Here

---

[1] Early in 1940 the five principal mortgage-lending insurance institutions were estimated by the U.S. Department of Agriculture to own not less than 28 million acres of farm land. This does not include the holdings of commercial banks, mortgage companies, and other similar groups that also held substantial acreage.

[2] Statistics presented by Norman J. Wall, U.S. Bureau of Agricultural Economics, at hearings before the Temporary National Economic Committee, Feb. 14, 1940.

[3] A. G. Brown, Land Values and Commercial Bank Policy, *Journal of Farm Economics*, February, 1939, p. 268.

we deal with a phase of human nature that comes close to the problem of business disturbances and business cycles—the temptation to trade upon the equity through unamortized borrowing and to forget the cardinal fact that merely paying 7 per cent interest on long-term loans does not liquidate the loans or enable the borrower to remain solvent. The anxiety of the lenders in many instances to preserve their "liquidity" by reducing the period and yet participate in the lucrative long-term interest rate amidst the mirage of a great inflation could result only in the ultimate freezing of those loans and the collapse of the entire system of private agricultural finance. It goes almost without saying that with the less favorable turn *in farm exports* following 1929 and a shrinkage in domestic demand for farm products, the weight of this accumulating and more or less frozen farm debt became acutely embarrassing. Its effect became apparent far beyond the rural sections.

When we examine these problems of long-term financing and the reckless use of long-term borrowing, there are, of course, marked differences between one farmer and another. The shrewd and thrifty farmer, who resisted the temptation to overexpand his obligations during and after World War I, was able to salt away the handsome profits of a few good years; he was then in a position to purchase new equipment, to improve his methods of cultivation, and to avail himself of new developments in soil technology, seed selection, etc. It was he who supplied urban industry with effective demand for its products. The period that we have considered divided farm operators into two broad groups: one very large segment pushed by foreclosure farther down the scale to struggle for mere subsistence and the other a relatively prosperous minority, continuing to produce economically and to benefit from improvements in equipment and methods. This segment has been able thus to defy the decline of prices by being able to produce more per acre at less cost per unit.

As the farm situation presented itself to our legislators in 1933, after the second great deflation had brought some farming areas to the point of revolution, it was the hapless majority rather than the efficient and sober minority that exerted the pressure for the subsidization and paternalism that we shall consider further later. Agriculture, prior to the occurrence of World War II, was faced by the problem of persistent surplus, and after this present War has been concluded, surpluses may be even more embarrassing. Rapid improvement in cultivation methods and expansion on the part of the minority plus the persistent addition to supply made by the majority of more or less unprosperous farmers who will not shift to other occupations readily but who keep on adding to supplies will probably continue to afford a powerfully organized "vested interest," demanding doles and subsidies for years to come, while at the same time the urban population pays excessive prices to keep inefficiency intact.

There are many observers who hope that technological progress may eventually greatly expand the utilization of farm products in industry. Possibly we are already in the early stage of a further technical or "chemurgic" revolution, the outcome of which cannot as yet be accurately appraised. We read of the use of cotton in the making of roads, the insulation of houses, or in the production of certain types of cellulose products and plastics. The soybean is replacing wheat in certain areas, and plastics possibly suitable even for automobile bodies and similar products may be made from them. Thousands of acres of land may yet be cultivated to crops capable of yielding substitutes for *hevea latex* rubber. In many areas, particularly the South, where cotton as king may soon be dethroned, forestry and diversified agriculture are encroaching on what has been this country's most unfortunate plantation institution. Doubtless World War II will hasten these tendencies and stimulate research anew. But all these developments may not suffice to give to the rural or farm population the full employment or return needed to establish this entire group upon a more satisfactory and stable income level.

There is now a surplus acreage of perhaps as much as 30 to 45 million acres. Agricultural experts claim that 50 per cent of the farm population produces 85 per cent of the products. This means that 50 per cent of the farmers are responsible for only 15 per cent of the production, and their average income must therefore be extremely low. Why should this be necessary? There has been a large potential reserve of unemployed and semiemployed labor, much of it representing the younger age group, on American farms. This reserve has been pressing upon the labor supply in the cities and upon the wage level. It is not remarkable, therefore, that prior to 1941 we had such unwieldy unemployed surplus in our industrial areas, threatening a chronic situation. If the agricultural labor surplus should be actually further enlarged by the progress of technology and by further marked shifts from old products to new, after World War II, and if this labor supply presses upon the cities as the result of the re-establishment of a more nearly normal migration flow from country to city (which was interrupted for a good part of the previous decade), there will be repercussions throughout the field of industry.

We shall conclude this chapter on the general dynamics of agriculture by quoting from an experienced observer of the dynamics of farm enterprise, Alonzo E. Taylor, writing shortly before the beginning of World War II.

We have in this country a farm population of about 32 million, including gainful workers approaching 11 million in number, operating not much below 7 million farms, containing about 1,050 million acres. Available to this farm population on this area of land in farms is a constantly improving and expanding technique in the positive sense, with a continuously improving protection against deteriorating influence on crops. This is entirely too large a farm area and farm population for a total population of 130 million, living a highly mechanized life and having the international purchasing power necessary to draw from all parts of the world desired foodstuffs not produced in the United States. The agriculture of the white world is geared to an output of agricultural staples which is potentially in excess of the demand of the white world, and the actual output tends more and more to approach the potential. Agriculture thus faces technological unemployment and externally has the prospect of an unexpanding, or even contracting, need for staples which are naturally in relatively inelastic demand.[1]

This should be kept in mind in connection with our previous discussion of the importance of physical supply factors as well as industry factors in the general price level. It is also of prime importance in developing sound postwar policy in the years to come.

[1] "Why Agricultural Gluts Develop," p. 28, University of Minnesota Press, January, 1939.

CHAPTER 8

FURTHER CYCLICAL ASPECTS OF AGRICULTURE

In the foregoing discussion, attention was given to the dynamics of agriculture viewed from the standpoint of the major fluctuations extending over decades rather than in terms of years or months. It remains to examine the patterns of the shorter intervals and what may be termed the minor cycles of change in prices, production, and income.

One feature of Chart 14 provides a convenient point of departure for this analysis. Observe that in years of rising relative farm income, there has usually been a declining tendency in the export ratio. At first glance this seems rather curious. It is particularly evident in the shorter movements, from year to year. In Chart 16 there will be found a more detailed analysis of this relationship in terms of monthly prices and monthly export volume. It appears from Chart 16 that despite a number of exceptions, a rising tendency in the ratio of agricultural prices to nonagricultural prices is accompanied by a decline in the volume of agricultural exports, whereas a decline in the price ratio is accompanied by a rise in the export movement. It should be kept in mind that the reference is to the physical volume of exports, not to the value. Although this interesting inverse tendency is not perfect, we can conclude that it is low prices that primarily attract export and high prices that discourage export of American farm surpluses. Export has perhaps repeatedly assisted in absorbing some surplus, but its influence is tardy and is exerted only after markets and income have suffered. The foreign buyers of American farm products, by and large, have come into the market when the farmer had larger surpluses than usual and except in cases of extreme emergency demand, such as during wartime, these foreign buyers have shopped elsewhere when our prices seemed relatively high or out of line with those in other surplus markets.

The question now arises, do the *short* (year-to-year) cyclical variations in farm prices, values, or income tend to precede and perhaps contribute to those of the typical minor business fluctuations, or is the converse predominantly the best description of the situation? This is a matter that has been long debated, and opposing views have been illustrated with more or less pertinent data, not always, however, preserving a careful distinction between short and long periods. We shall utilize annual data extending back to 1800 but for the most part shall eliminate

152

those fluctuations clearly attributable to war conditions, since we have
already seen that the peculiar influences associated with currency infla-

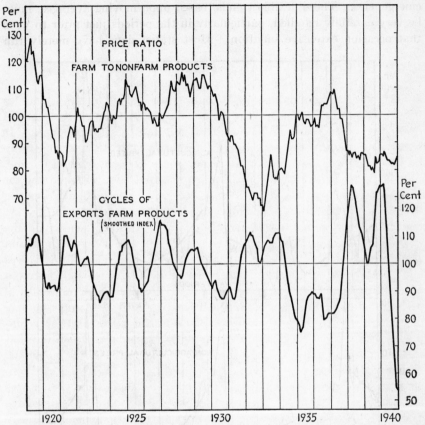

CHART 16.—Cyclical movements of relative farm-product prices and volume of farm
exports, 1919–1940. The farm-product export index, in terms of physical volume, as
prepared by the U. S. Department of Agriculture, has been smoothed by a 12-month moving
average. The above index represents the deviations from the long-term trend. The purpose of the chart is to show the degree of inverse movement in relative farm prices and
volume of exports, apart from long-term trend.

tion and postwar deflation are primarily transmitted from agriculture
to other phases of the economy.

FARM AND NONFARM PRICE CYCLES COMPARED

Let us examine first the short-term fluctuations in agricultural prices
relative to price changes in nonagricultural products.   Chart 17 shows
the annual data of these two groups, the upper portion being the index
of agricultural and lower nonagricultural price movements.[1]   It will

[1] Data taken from Demand, Credit, and Prices, 1941, *U.S. Department of Agriculture Agricultural Outlook Charts*, p. 12.   The prices are at wholesale.

be seen that the estimated trends trace the underlying drift preceding and following the exceptional price explosions attributable to the war emergencies.   These flexible trends, based upon moving averages, must be very carefully handled, particularly in the periods just prior to wars that occasion extensive inflation.   Most statisticians have merely run

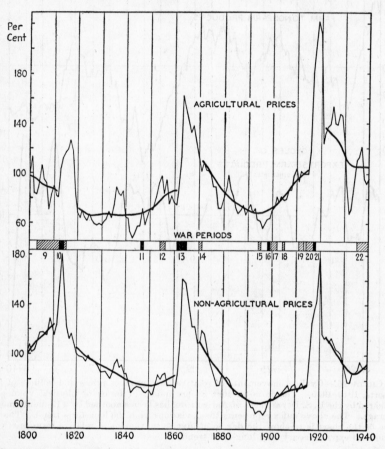

CHART 17.—Agricultural and nonagricultural prices, showing inflation periods and intermediate trends, 1800–1940.   For description of data see Appendix 5, Sec. 3.   For identification of the war periods see Charts 6 and 7.

their moving averages through the entire series, regardless of the fact that wartime inflation so greatly distorts price movements that there ceases to be a homogeneous concept of drift through conditions of peacetime and conditions of wartime.   If moving averages are used to express these broad trends, the usual result is to show a considerable rise in the trend possibly ten or fifteen or twenty years *prior* to a war, simply because as the average mechanically begins to pick up the inflation years (if it is assumed that average is centered), there is a decided rise in the trend, and the *actual* price level appears then to be depressed far below the "trend." This is illusory. The actual level of prices just prior to an inflationary explosion must be shown relative to the trend as it was determined prior to that inflation and on the assumption of a nonwar give and take. After war inflation has begun to reverse itself, some years elapse before it is possible to ascertain just where the broad drift of prices marks out its path and forms a new moving center of gravity balancing out the year-to-year fluctuations that we seek particularly to emphasize for our present purpose. In Chart 17, the estimates of trend position have been carefully made with this specific purpose in mind.[1]

In Charts 18a and 18b, the cyclical price movements, *apart* from the war-inflation periods, are shown separately for the nonagricultural and agricultural price groups. These are brought into close comparison with the corresponding cyclical changes in the general index of business, these fluctuations being the ratios of the actual annual index to the flexible intermediate trend. We are interested for the moment in observing the relation of the two groups of price movements to each other and their relation also to the general business cycles. It is at once evident that there are many minor divergences in the price cycles. In some instances one group will reach a peak or trough ahead of the other, and in other cases the reverse will be true. There is no consistent lead or lag either between the two sets of price cycles movements or between these and the business index. Broadly, it is true that when business conditions have been temporarily above the trend, the price cycles have also shown more or less clearly a similar position, and vice versa. But there is no possibility of drawing a definite conclusion as to leads and lags or of detecting the direction in which causation may run.

On the whole, there seems to be a tendency for the nonagricultural prices more often to lag somewhat in their declines from high peaks, but their upturns from depression levels appear to be almost as sensitive and prompt as is the case with the farm prices. If we compare the agricultural price cycles with the cycles in the business index, the conclusion again, although not clear-cut, seems to be that the swings in business

---

[1] When the price movements during the war-inflation years are examined, it is clear that prices of nonagricultural products have actually reached somewhat higher inflation peaks on two occasions. In World War I, however, the agricultural groups moved somewhat higher in relation to the other group. When we confine our attention to the shorter, year-to-year cyclical fluctuation, we see that the farm products display a much greater sensitivity and amplitude of fluctuations. This does not mean that in every single instance of upswing and downswing we can expect this to be true, but it would be true in the majority of cases.

volume are just about as sensitive as those in farm price vibrations. In a number of instances there is a slight tendency for the business index to move a little ahead, as in 1836–1837, 1853, and 1882. On recovery turning points, business activity recorded a prior upturn in 1830 and in

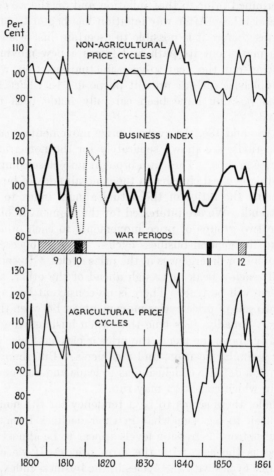

CHART 18a.—Relation of agricultural and nonagricultural price cycles to business cycles, 1800–1861. The cyclical comparisons omit periods of war inflation.

1895 and a more vigorous upswing after 1921 than in the case of agricultural prices.

CYCLES OF FARM AND NONFARM INCOME

Turning now to Charts 19a and 19b, we can examine similar cyclical changes in several ratios, particularly from the agricultural standpoint. The cyclical pattern at the top is that of the ratio of agricultural prices

to nonagricultural prices, the ratio rather than the individual series being
adjusted for trend.   In these charts all series are carried through the war
periods to show the complete picture.   The second series in the chart is
the ratio of our index of real farm income to its long-term trend.   When

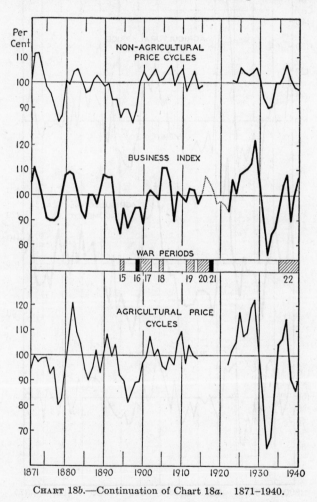

CHART 18*b*.—Continuation of Chart 18*a*.   1871–1940.

the comparison is made between these two sets of cyclical patterns, it is
apparent how important the relative price position seems to be as it
bears upon the cyclical pattern of real farm income or purchasing power.
It can almost be said that if we omit consideration of production trends
(which, of course, enter into the calculation of actual farm income)
and confine our attention to the cyclical deviations from the trend,
relative prices tell the story about as well as relative real income.

When the agricultural real-income cycles are now compared with the business index, the result is again to leave in doubt the matter of consist-

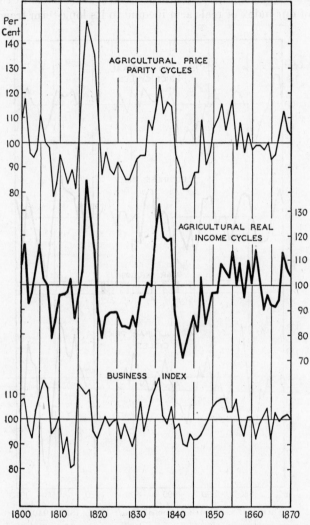

CHART 19a.—Relation of agricultural price-parity and real-income cycles to business cycles, 1800–1870. The agricultural price-parity cycles are deviations from long-term trend. The real-income cycles are deviations also from long-term trend, the real-income index being based upon farm gross income deflated by nonagricultural prices. See also Appendix 5, Sec. 2.

ent lead and lag relationships. There are about as many cases in which one of the indexes leads as the other. In some instances the turns are simultaneous. Broadly speaking, the business index has shown some of its most emphatic cyclical gyrations when agricultural real income has behaved likewise. Notice, for example, the extremely violent change in both indexes since World War I. A careful examination of the chart

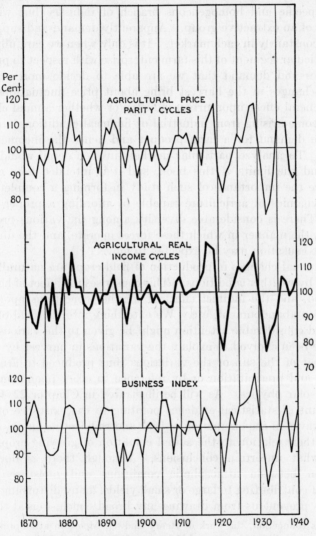

CHART 19b.—Continuation of Chart 19a. 1870–1940.

suggests that in somewhat more cases than not, the downturns from peaks have come *first* in the business index, whereas in several cases the agricultural index has shown the first indication of recovery from depression. Probably business conditions can transmit short-term reactions to agricultural income, but the longer term depression forces, as we have clearly observed, seem to be mainly in the reverse direction.

The somewhat inconclusive deductions that have just been drawn are, after all, entirely natural when we realize that we are dealing not with a specific and homogeneous branch of industry but with many branches of an extractive group. Apparently demand-and-supply forces interact constantly in each market. It is only when we carefully analyze each particular segment of this farm enterprise with respect to production and prices and demand that we are able to decide more specifically whether changes in the harvest bring about price fluctuations capable of any general effect upon urban industry or whether annual changes in urban income arising from industrial or financial conditions can sharply affect the demand for a farm product and hence the income from its disposal. To analyze particular markets in such detail would carry us far beyond the limits of this book, and it is intended here merely to emphasize the importance of such study in forming a complete picture of the dynamics of agriculture capable of affording a proper basis for policy. There is considerable diversity among the various products of the farm, the manner in which these forces operate, and the direction in which the causation may be expected to move.

The annual changes in production of field crops are naturally closely governed by weather conditions. This comprises the effect of heat, moisture, wind, and the indirect effect of weather conditions upon insects, blight, crop abandonment, etc. We enter here into the field of meteorology, and considerable attention might be given to the various theories that have been evolved to explain the variations in harvest by reference to the heat of the sun or the variations thus produced in atmospheric pressures and precipitation or by reference to other phenomena in the realm of solar physics. As will be illustrated in Chapter 22, there is a fair amount of statistical evidence pointing to the existence of definite cyclical waves in the emanation of heat and radioactive energy from the sun, but their relation to the actual condition of growing crops has led to somewhat uncertain conclusions. Although there is doubtless a connection between atmospheric conditions and moisture elements capable of contributing to large or small yields, many disturbing counter-influences prevent us from drawing any broad conclusions at this time.[1]

---

[1] In this connection, the work of Henry Ludwell Moore in attempting to trace statistically the relations between planetary conditions and rainfall, on the one hand, and production and prices of several crops, on the other, is of particular importance. See, for example, "Economic Cycles, Their Law and Cause," New York, 1915; "Generating Economic Cycles," New York, 1923; also, P. G. Wright, Review of Moore's Investigations, *Quarterly Journal of Economics*, May, 1915. Among the British writers on the subject, see particularly W. S. Jevons, "Investigations into Currency and Finance," London, 1884, and Sir William Beveridge, Weather and Harvest

It will suffice for our present purpose to say that for any given crop, the annual fluctuations in yield per acre are more or less irregular in their occurrence and show no conclusive tendency to coincide with any regular periodic function, such as is defined by a sine curve. Since it is claimed by meteorologists that the alternations in solar radiation conform more or less closely to a regularly recurring rhythm, it is obvious that various extraneous influences serve to bring about the erratic year-to-year fluctuations in actual crop yields. For most of the important field crops, the total production in the United States is much more closely related to the yield per acre than to changes in acreage planted or harvested. The amount of acreage utilized will itself respond in a slow, uncertain, and irregular fashion to the degree of farm prosperity or depression and the principal inflationary and deflationary movements in price of a particular crop. But it is the changes in yield per acre that are most pronounced and that dominate the annual fluctuations in production and hence in relative prices.

As the production cycles are studied in relation to the price of a particular crop, such as potatoes, wheat, or cotton, it is usually found that the closest (inverse) relation between production and price is in terms, not of actual prices but of *relative* prices. This naturally follows from the fact that the broader price movements, in which monetary and war finance factors exert the major influence, tend to form tidal-wave patterns quite independent of the short-term changes in production and supply. Hence if the prices of potatoes or corn are analyzed as ratios to general wholesale prices, the specific influence of the supply factor becomes more readily apparent. It is also desirable to express the final relationship in terms not of *production* but of *available* supply from year to year. This involves the amount of carry-over or surplus that at any time expresses the result of a previous lack of perfect market clearance or equilibrium. The production of a given year affects the relative price to the extent that it alters the position of the available supply known to exist. In some cases, such as in the case of wheat and cotton, the commodities are bought and sold on organized speculative exchanges, and the "futures" quotations express the aggregate opinion of the buyers and sellers as to the position of supply and demand several months ahead. These prices in the futures markets are highly sensitive and are con-

Cycles, *Economic Journal*, December, 1921. See also C. G. Abbot, "Solar Radiation and Weather Studies," Smithsonian Institution, Washington, D.C., 1935; C. G. Abbot, assisted by Gladys T. Bond, "Periodicity in Solar Variation," May, 1932; Hannay and Lacy, Influence of Weather on Crops, selected bibliography, *U.S. Department of Agriculture, Miscellaneous Publication* 118, 1931; V. P. Timoshenko, Variability in Wheat Yields and Outputs, *Stanford Food Research Institute Wheat Studies*, April, 1942.

stantly vibrating. The price in what is termed the "cash" or "spot" market will usually be influenced by what the futures markets are doing. Because of the difficulty of keeping supply in perfect adjustment to total demand, the price responds more to supply than to demand variations.

At a given time or over very short periods, a relatively small variation in available supply of a field crop is likely to have a relatively large effect upon price. Conversely, a shifting of demand one way or the other will cause any existing supply to vary much more than proportionally in price and in value. Individual products, of course, differ materially in this respect. The degree of "elasticity" in the market, in the sense of the willingness of buyers to accept or their ability to utilize larger quantities or to forego purchase if quantities are reduced, would be very low for such a commodity as potatoes, fairly low for wheat, slightly higher for cotton. The degree of elasticity depends mainly upon the variety of uses to which the commodity may be put and the extent to which it serves a vital human need, having relatively inflexible per capita limits. When business conditions are prosperous and national income is rising, the demand for cotton will accelerate, and supplies will be more widely used for a time in the manufacture of textiles, tire fabrics, and numerous industrial products for which cotton is adapted. This expansion, however, would be much more limited in the case of per capita consumption of wheat or potatoes. The foods as a group are mainly of the inelastic demand type, and changes in production from season to season tend to create more than proportionate inverse changes in price (relative to the general price level).

It should be kept clearly in mind that this tendency holds from year to year but is not necessarily true over long periods of years. Hence it is not in itself an adequate basis for artificial or arbitrary administration of agricultural output designed to raise the values or gross income accruing to crop farmers. This is important, because artificial scarcities, having the objective of increasing farm values, and therefore gross incomes, if continued mechanically over a period of years, will probably have a tendency gradually to discourage consumer use and to encourage the use of alternative products. Such a policy (unless world-wide in scope) will also have the effect of encouraging sooner or later large additional production in outside areas beyond the range of the control measures, and hence ultimately there will be a larger world supply that directly or indirectly will affect particular markets. This has been the usual result of restrictive measures and may be the ultimate result of our own policies of agricultural adjustment if they do not take into account the possibility of lowering costs by greater efficiency as a factor in farm earnings.

The varying relations between annual production, total supply, and relative price, in the case of wheat in the world market, are shown in Chart

20.   Since this chart is drawn on a uniform ratio scale, it can readily be seen that the response of price (that is, relative price) to a given change in the supply is volatile, indicating an inelastic demand.   It is also apparent that although available world supply conforms generally to the changes in production, this is not invariably true.   The available supply has a slightly less variable tendency than production itself.   If we were to observe the relation between supply and relative price of a certain

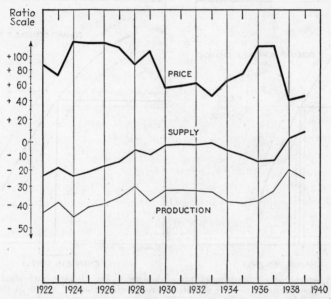

CHART 20.—Production, supply, and deflated British price of wheat, 1922–1939.   Production and supply exclude Soviet Russia and China.   Price of British parcels is deflated by the *Statist* index of wholesale prices and converted to American currency at par exchange. This is roughly indicative of the world basic price relative to other commodities.   The years are crop years, beginning July.   (*Data from U. S. Department of Agriculture.*)

variety of potato raised in a given area, it would be found that relative price is even more sensitive to the changes in supply, and the supply will vary almost exactly with seasonal production because of the fact that the carry-overs of a highly perishable crop tend to be much smaller than for products that can be safely stored.   If the cotton market were to be examined in similar fashion, it would be found that the American crop, plus carry-over, is usually the most important single factor in relative price change.   Other factors entering into the price position (in the world market as it functioned prior to World War II) would be changes in the production and carry-over of Indian and other types of cotton and in the demand for cotton as affected by the general industrial cycle and consumer income variation.   The fluctuations in mill consumption of raw cotton are relatively wide in amplitude, but the timing is closely geared to the minor fluctuations of the general business cycle.[1]

EFFECT OF MARKET ELASTICITY ON PRICE BEHAVIOR

These illustrations will perhaps suffice to demonstrate the important characteristics of price behavior of most field crops. The potential behavior of these markets may be illustrated in simplified fashion by the

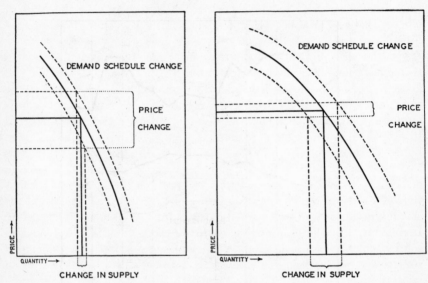

CHART 21.—Graphic comparison of price changes under inelastic and elastic market conditions. Inelastic conditions are shown at the left, elastic at the right.

diagram in Chart 21. This is designed to emphasize the contrast between a typical field-crop market and the market for a typical manufactured commodity. At the left are a number of diagonals, rather steeply inclined from left to right, indicating the successive possible positions of the demand situation. On each of these curves, any given point would indicate at what price (vertical scale) the supply (measured horizontally) would be wholly absorbed within the normal marketing period or season, with a normal working surplus. Alternatively, any point would also indicate how much would be taken by all cash buyers at that price.

These "schedules" of the various possible relationships of supply and price (always in terms of relative price) shift to the right or the left, depending upon the strength or weakness of demand as it may be affected by the varying incomes of consumers, the nature of the speculative interest, consuming habits, or the breadth of the market in terms of population. Under any given conditions of general business, national income, popula-

[1] This matter is further developed in Chapter 19.

tion, customary use, proportion of waste, etc., the pattern of demand relationships represents the play of a single factor—the *utility* of the commodity to the typical potential buyer. It shows what would happen to price offers if there were sudden changes in supply impinging upon this sense of the importance of having more or less to use. When consumer willingness to purchase is affected by a *new* set of conditions altering their purchasing power, the variety of uses the commodity may serve, or their familiarity with it, the schedule will shift bodily to the right or left, as the case may be, and a new set of prices will then measure the utility variable.

In the case of field crops, these shifts are, of course, transmitted through various intermediary markets until they reach the farmer and are expressed in price at the farm. The amount of demand shift to the right or left will roughly express the extent to which changes in general economic or technological conditions induce ultimate users of these crops to extend or contract the amount that they are willing to buy at given prices (adjusted to price level), or, conversely, the (adjusted) prices that they are willing to give for additional specific amounts. This shifting of position tends to be narrow, relative to the shifts in economic conditions, for most of the typical farm field crops. In the case of cotton, the shifting occurs over a wider possible range for the reasons already given. In general, a market will absorb readily a given quantity; an increased supply quickly becomes excess and encourages waste, and a sudden contraction of supply produces lively bidding and an abrupt rise in relative price.

Contrast the mechanics of these farm markets with the situation shown at the right, again simplified to bring out essential features. Here we have a typical widely used fabricated product but selling in a market not yet wholly saturated and subject to the familiar industrial conditions of relatively flexible adjustment in the rate of production. The commodity is offered by manufacturers in quantities more or less promptly adjusted to the demand conditions existing in the market from time to time. The pattern of demand at any given time is elastic in the sense that it expresses the willingness of purchasers, under any given set of economic conditions, to acquire more at lower prices but unwillingness to purchase as prices rise. These schedules or patterns of demand also shift back and forth according to the changing conditions supporting purchasing power and utilization. There is considerable elasticity, therefore, in this sense, too.

In the case of a semiluxury product, the shifting of demand to right or left may at times occur over a wide range. But the *slope* of the lines, expressing mainly the utility pattern, graduates gently toward the right, and as the schedules shift back and forth, *they tend to produce a less than proportionate alteration in the price of any given supply.* The more nearly elastic are the utility patterns the more this will be true. In other words, the supply can vary during moderate periods without having the effect of violently changing price, as it does in the case of the typical field crop. Furthermore, producers of fabricated articles usually are able readily to control the rate of additions to supply, and they aim to stabilize the price by varying the volume offered to the market in some rough relation to what they observe to be the shifting of the demand schedules.

As the result of these dynamic differences in the two types of market, we find most of the explanation of the much wider range of fluctuation in farm prices and the source of the complaint of the farmer that he purchases what he needs in the cities at prices that are rigid and inflexible, whereas he sells his own commodities always at wholesale and in the rough at prices that soar and collapse with astonishing volatility. This is further discussed in Chapter 24, since the point has obvious political implications.[1]

THE DYNAMICS OF THE HOG MARKET

Before concluding, let us observe some further illustrations of the dynamics of farm prices taken from the markets for animal products. In these cases we have interesting patterns of *price cycles*, that is, rhythmic variation, internally motivated. Let us observe first the hog market. It is a familiar fact that most of the corn crop is fed to hogs and marketed in this form. There is, therefore, a close functional relationship between the price of corn and the price of hogs. Corn makes up over two-thirds of the feed used in pork production. It has become customary, therefore, to express the advantage of raising hogs by the ratio of hog prices to corn prices or the "hog-corn ratio." As usually stated, this expresses the number of bushels of corn equivalent in current farm value to 100 pounds of live hogs. Throughout a long period of time this ratio has varied above and below an average of about 11.6 bushels. A rise in the ratio indicates that corn is cheap relative to hog values and that hogs can be fed cheaply; a decline in the ratio means that corn is increasing in its purchasing power over hogs and that hog raising is discouraged. It must be kept in mind that the variations in the ratio come about in response to change in both the price of hogs and the price of corn.

---

[1] In recent discussions of the apparently inflexible prices of many manufactured goods, it has been incorrectly assumed that elasticity of demand is relatively high, and therefore a larger quantity can be sold at little concession in price, but much of this reasoning confuses the elasticity in the sense of a broad shift in consumption, as the market is widened by mass-production techniques, with elasticity in the usual sense of the immediate responses resulting from utility calculus. Actually the differences in elasticity in this sense, as between one commodity and another, are not so great as is commonly assumed.

The actual price of hogs is shown in the lower curve of Chart 22. Apart from the inflation period of World War I, hog prices have been high when the marketing of finished hogs to the packing plants (second curve from the bottom) was relatively low, and vice versa.[1] But the hog-corn ratio also expresses the effect of the size of the corn crop, plotted as the second curve from the top. When the crop is large, the ratio of corn to hogs tends to rise. The fact that hog marketings (monthly data smoothed) appear to move in cyclical waves, about two years later than the corresponding changes in the hog-corn ratio, is explained not merely by the production incentive arising from the hog market but by price spreads influenced by the corn crop. When there is a relatively large supply of corn there will be smaller marketings of the available hog supply than otherwise, because animals will be withheld from market for breeding and feeding purposes, with the use of cheap corn. This automatically *reduces* the meat supply and brings the price of pork products to a higher level than might otherwise exist. In other words, this causes the spread expressed by the hog-corn ratio to rise abruptly, and this, in turn, adds more stimulus to hog raising, which appears as larger marketings within a year or two. The marketing of these hogs lowers pork and lard prices, but the marketings will be affected *also* by the extent to which corn supplies may be reduced through smaller production and through the greater utilization of the existing corn supply in the previous period of enlarged breeding and feeding.

Along with these factors there must also be considered the influence of consumer demand, which, through most of the period covered in Chart 22, includes an export element. In good business years and with large export demand, pork prices will be higher than otherwise, and vice versa. But pork products are to such a large extent a staple commodity that the shifting of the demand patterns back and forth along with corresponding changes in general prosperity and income is less pronounced than it is in the case of beef, lamb, poultry, or specialized dairy products. A more or less downward trend of hog marketings, as well as hog prices, from World War I to the beginning of World War II represents progressive shrinkage of the export market more than it does impairment of domestic demand.

The hog market thus represents to an unusual degree a tendency toward repetition of cyclical movements in production and prices. The variation in the corn crop is probably at the basis of these variations, but the influences resulting from the price of corn are greatly amplified as they affect incentives to raise hogs by the intermediary effect upon the marketing of available live animals. The resulting swings in building up and

[1] Other disturbing factors are seen in 1934 and 1936, when extreme drought conditions affecting the corn crop led to heavy slaughter of pigs.

reducing the total supply of hogs are wider in amplitude than would be accounted for by the variations in the corn crop alone or by variations in the price of hogs alone.   Putting all these together, we obtain a more or less self-generating series of variations *that tend to be carried through regardless of intervening minor changes in prices or business conditions.*

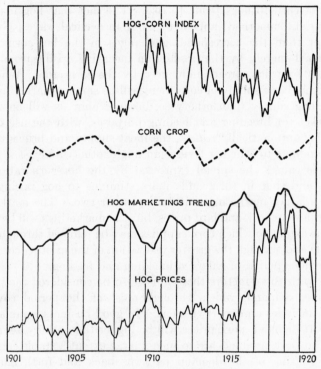

CHART 22a.—Factors affecting hog prices, 1901–1920.   The trend of hog marketings is a smoothing of the actual monthly data.

The resulting swings in hog prices do not repeat themselves with exact periodicity, but there is a rough approach to a five-year cyclical movement.

By taking into account all the related variables, including, of course, the influence of demand conditions, it is statistically possible to arrive at a fairly accurate forecast of the hog market more than a year in advance.[1] But the raising of hogs represents a branch of farm production less motivated by forecast than by *existing* market conditions and income

[1] See Haas and Ezekiel, Factors Affecting the Price of Hogs, *U.S. Department of Agriculture Bulletin* 1440; C. F. Sarle, Forecasting the Price of Hogs, *American Economic Review*, September, 1925; and O. V. Wells, Farmers' Response to Price in Hog Production and Marketing, *U.S. Department of Agriculture Technical Bulletin* 359.

possibilities. As the result of this, hog raisers do most of their marketing at the lowest prices, and their sales of hogs to the packing plants are lowest when prices are high. Their incomes tend to be higher when prices are high than when they are low. Hence there is the possibility of persistent complaints that the packer exploits the producers. The repeated investigations of the meat packing industry by the Federal

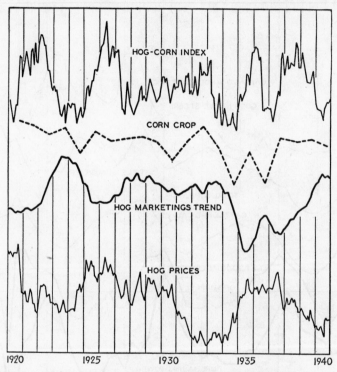

CHART 22b.—Continuation of Chart 22a, 1920–1940.

Trade Commission are primarily the result of the mechanics of the industry. A further result has been to make the packing industry extremely efficient, with exceedingly close profit margins.

THE DYNAMICS OF THE CATTLE MARKET

Another interesting example of a more or less self-propelled price-production cycle in agriculture is found in the case of beef cattle. In this case, the production period is considerably longer than in raising hogs. Preparations for raising large herds of cattle constitute a substantial undertaking, requiring a fair amount of capital. If the cattle-price situation becomes increasingly favorable, some time will necessarily elapse before those connected with, or interested in, this industry begin

operations.   *The relatively slow response of supply* to price movements is
an important feature of the dynamics of this market.   But once the cycle
of cattle breeding and feeding is well under way, it continues, almost
regardless of external conditions, until the herds of cattle and calves have
attained a size representing very considerable expansion from the original
level.

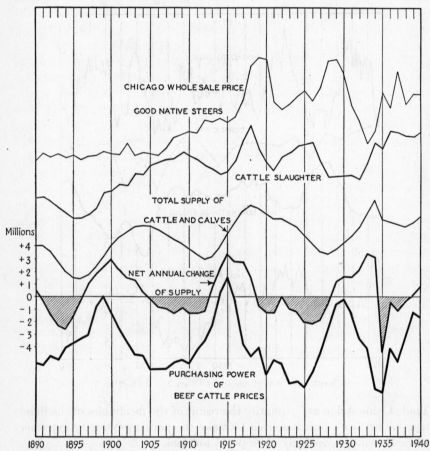

CHART 23.—Factors affecting cattle supplies and prices, 1890–1940. The chart is
drawn to arithmetic scales, but the scale figures, except for net annual changes in supply,
are omitted in order to simplify the chart, as the cyclical movements are of primary interest.
The figures of total cattle slaughter include calves.

The operations of the industry are shown in Chart 23.[1]   At the bottom
appears the *relative* price of beef cattle, expressed in terms of general

[1] Data for this chart were obtained from *Farm Economics* (Cornell), June, 1941;
U.S. Department of Agriculture Technical Bulletin 703, pp. 112–114; Livestock, *U.S.
Department of Agriculture Outlook Charts*, 1941; and *U.S. Bureau of Labor Statistics
Wholesale Price Bulletins*.

wholesale prices, since the direct costs in cattle raising involve a wider range of commodity elements than in the case of hogs. As the cycle of relative cattle prices ascends, the next curve above, indicating the *annual change* in herd numbers, also rises. This denotes, first, that year by year there are *smaller reductions* in herds and, later, that there are *increasing additions* to herds. As this index of changes crosses zero upward, it marks the point at which the existing herds of beef cattle and calves are at a minimum. As herds are built up, actual numbers rise to a peak when the index of changes has again declined through zero. There is thus a lagging cycle of the actual number of cattle on farms, the peaks and troughs appearing from about four to six years after those in the relative price movements.[1] As cattle numbers increase, there is a *still later* tendency to expand the marketing and slaughter activity, but this does not usually begin until the index of relative price has reached a high peak. Thereafter the marketing expands, and the meat packers prepare and dispose of increasing quantities of beef and veal. The cyclical movements in this phase of the industry tend to be somewhat irregular because of occasional factors entering the market from the standpoint of general consumer demand, which has somewhat greater influence here than in the case of the pork market, and also weather conditions affecting the forage and feed supplies. Drought in the corn belt may force the cattle feeders to sell to packers prematurely, as was the case in the unusual years 1934 and 1936. When herds are being built up from a relatively low level, several years elapse during which the amount of finished beef and veal output declines as more cows and heifers are withheld for breeding purposes.

The peaks in meat packing and marketing tend to occur considerably later than the peaks in numbers of beef cattle on farms. An interesting instance is seen in 1909. In 1918 there was a high point in meat production, coinciding with a peak in the number of cattle on farms, but this was followed by a decline and a second top in 1927, the decline having been due to the ending of the War and the brief depression of 1921. But thereafter there was still a liquidating tendency that, with improving business conditions, forced a large amount of beef into final feeding and into the packing plants, so that herds reached a minimum again in 1928. In the past few years herds have been built up rather rapidly under the stimulus of a rising relative price, and probably large supplies of beef and veal will have been prepared for market for a number of years after 1940. The wholesale price of finished beef at Chicago is shown as the top curve in the chart. There is some tendency for slaughter and meat prices to move inversely. If this relationship is examined in the light

[1] This is another example of the relation between an *increment* variable and a *total inventory*.

of general business and income changes, it will be found that large slaughter in good years does not lower prices so much as in poor years and that low periods of slaughter do not raise prices so much in poor years as in good years. Note particularly the situation in the 1890's and also during the period of World War I.

Usually, it will be noted, changes in the amount of beef cattle reaching the packing houses move inversely to the relative price of cattle, and hence there emerges a recurring cyclical tendency, expressing itself in a rising and falling index of change in numbers of cattle, or what might be termed the expansion and liquidation phases of the industry. As in the case of hogs, by the time the livestock farmer comes to do most of his selling, he does so at the lowest relative prices and frequently at low actual prices. The length of the cycles that emerge from this process are much longer in duration than the average hog cycles. From peak to peak and trough to trough of relative price movements and supplies of cattle, the period varies from about fourteen to sixteen years.[1]

We have now seen that it is inadequate to discuss agriculture and its dynamics merely from a generalized standpoint, since farming abounds with great diversity in detail. But having pointed out some of the interesting and useful features of this detail, we may close the discussion by referring once more to comparative changes in farm income in recent years as shown in several important segments. Chart 24 brings out the fact that since the boom conditions of World War I, total farm income has maintained itself much better than has the total income derived from wheat, cotton, and hogs, all of which have encountered not only the marked irregularity in domestic demand, particularly after 1929, but also

---

[1] The long-term trend of per capita beef consumption in the United States is gradually declining, but the trend of veal consumption has been rising. Since World War I, United States exports of beef have become of little importance. There is a gradual tendency to increase herds of dairy cattle more rapidly than those of beef cattle, partly as a result of the foregoing conditions. The occasional incentive to market cattle quickly has the effect of increasing the proportion of calves and yearlings sold to the packers. There are also constant interactions as between beef-cattle and dairy-cattle operations.

Good current discussions of the livestock situation as to both beef and hogs are to be found in publications of the U.S. Department of Agriculture, particularly the monthly issues of *The Livestock Situation*. A part of the exhibit in Chart 23 is based upon discussions of livestock conditions contained in *Farm Economics*, issued by the Department of Agricultural Economics and Farm Management, Cornell University. See also Alonzo E. Taylor, "The Corn and Hog Surplus of the Corn Belt," Food Research Institute, Stanford University, 1932. On the economic phases of the beef-cattle industry, see also, Beef Cattle Production in the Range Area, 1937, *U.S. Department of Agriculture Farmers' Bulletin* 1395. Also *U.S. Department of Agriculture Technical Bulletin* 764. It may be added that other examples of delayed long-term responses to price incentive can be found among the vine and tree crops. Space, however, does not permit further multiplication of illustrations.

the undertow of a shrinking export market. Farm income from wheat, cotton, and hogs is shown separately at the bottom of the chart. It will be noticed that wheat particularly has suffered much more heavily in the shrinkage of gross farm value than has total farm income. The latter

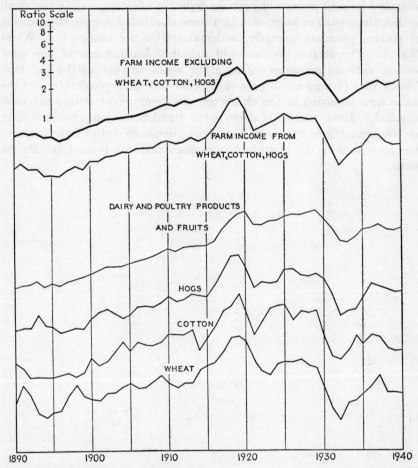

CHART 24.—Components of contrasting trend in gross farm income, 1890–1940. While farm income from wheat, cotton, and hog products has shown a declining trend since 1919, the income excluding these items has been well sustained, particularly as a result of such items as fruits, dairy, and poultry products.

has been sustained by the fact that the demand, particularly in the domestic market, for dairy products, poultry products, and fruits has continued to be vigorous and has forged ahead in spite of depressions as severe as those of 1932 and 1938. The combined income from these three most prosperous major groups of farm products is shown in the middle part of Chart 24. It stands in marked contrast to the situation revealed by the major divisions, which seem to be broadly in retreat. When, therefore, we refer to the agricultural trend, we must keep in mind these diversities.

The principal difficulties of agriculture in recent years represent a slow and painful process of postwar deflation affecting mainly the small grains, the raising of hogs, and, to a somewhat lesser degree, the growing of cotton, products urgently in demand after the outbreak of World War I. The cotton problem will probably become one of our most serious national problems within a few years, in view of the fact that World War II may accentuate the decline of export possibilities, at the same time resulting in the shrinkage of a temporarily strong domestic demand. Along with this there is the trend toward mechanization in cotton production, which will mean large displacement of labor, such as has been seen in the migration from the Southeast toward the Pacific Coast.

CHAPTER 9

THE DYNAMICS OF BUILDING AND REAL ESTATE

From the preceding analysis of the dynamics of agriculture, we have seen that variations in total farm income tend to be much more closely geared to changes in *prices* than to changes in *production*. We found reason to believe that conditions accompanying major wars encourage moderate expansion in the physical aspects of agricultural enterprise but very large additions to long-term financing and mortgage indebtedness. Price inflation appears to be responsible for excessive speculation in farm land and wide variations in farm-property values. We found also, in the case of animal products, that cyclical movements in production of rather extended duration exist, probably as the result of the relatively long periods required by production and the tardy adjustment of supply to changes in demand. A number of these points were emphasized, not merely because they round out the discussion of agricultural cycles and trends but because they will be found repeated with minor peculiarities in other important phases of economic activity.

The use of large amounts of borrowed capital to invest (or speculate) in land is by no means limited to agriculture. Urban and suburban real-estate development represents an even more important cyclical element capable of contributing to general economic instability. It forms the intensely variable atmosphere within which one of the most important of all our industries has functioned—the building industry. The heart and core of the construction industry is residential building. This phase of activity is characterized by long-term cyclical movements having some degree of resemblance to the long livestock cycles.

There are some characteristics of speculative promotion in the creation of housing facilities that do not apply to other types of construction enterprise. Nonresidential building, however, is indirectly affected by the sweeping dynamic forces involved in the activities of land subdividers and speculative home builders, particularly in urban and suburban areas. These activities, as in agriculture, involve the use of considerable quantities of borrowed capital. For many years—in fact, until recent financial reforms modified the process—they have been productive of far more general financial abuse and instability than anything that has occurred in the field of agriculture. These powerful *tidal waves* of construction activity, followed by prolonged periods of decline and inactivity, stamp their pattern upon a broad segment of our manufacturing and fabricating industries and hence the income of their personnel. These lines of production tend to be caught in the same wide swings of feast and famine as the result of circumstances over which they have no direct control. If we wish to understand why industrial production and trade vibrate constantly in a cyclical pattern, it is necessary to understand the dynamics of urban real estate. Following our analysis of this field, we shall give attention to the somewhat similar gyrations to be found in transportation development.

THE DEMAND FOR URBAN RESIDENTIAL PROPERTY

Since houses are built on land and since the cost of land is a considerable component in the final cost of building, land suitable for urban housing development has long been a very important object of investment, speculation, and promotional manipulation. We can go back in the historical records virtually to the beginning of the American Colonies and observe how important a place dealings in land formed in the activities of prominent men. Underlying these activities is the familiar factor of the growth of population and changes in the rate of this growth in particular areas. The development of villages into towns, towns into cities, and cities into great metropolitan areas has come about as the result of three distinct tendencies: (1) the natural increase in population in a given area, (2) the migration of families and individuals from one part of the country to another, and (3) migration from the Old World and the tendency of many of these immigrants to concentrate by national groups in particular sections. Probably most important is the internal migration. It has been stimulated by developments in transportation, the opening up of new territories through national acquisition, and the adoption of legislation tending to stimulate the agricultural development of new areas, with resulting development of urban commercial and transportation centers, sometimes with astonishing rapidity. While, as we have already seen, the growth of our total population has proceeded along a very regular course, with a minimum of intermediate fluctuations, the expansion of individual communities, especially along the frontier as it has shifted from east to west, has been marked by pronounced variations in rate of growth and in many cases by long-term wavelike tendencies. To these marked variations in growth, immigration from abroad has, until recent decades, contributed conspicuously, although it is difficult to obtain exact detailed statistical evidence to illustrate this for particular urban areas. The growth rate of a typical city may also be affected, occasionally to a marked extent, by the location in or near the community of industries capable of affording a strong inducement to workers drawn from surrounding rural areas or even from foreign countries.   Each new industry as it developed has fostered such concentration of people.

From the standpoint of demand for housing accommodations, two relatively minor factors also contribute some influence. First, some acceleration of a rising rate of growth, especially in urban communities, may result from the fact that component parts of families separate into distinct household units rather than living together. Thus the number of family units increases when employment in industry is high. Second, there may be variation in the marriage rate, which also tends to fluctuate rather closely in harmony with general business activity, with the result that under favorable conditions the number of families tends to increase. Opposite tendencies might under certain circumstances reinforce declining rates of local growth produced by emigration.

The major fluctuations in the residential building industry and in related real-estate development have been associated with waves of migration and settlement, which from time to time have been accelerated by major improvements in transportation, opening up new areas of virgin territory in one of the most richly endowed continental areas of the earth's surface. It was not long after the United States became an independent nation that great highway enterprises, such as the Cumberland Road, were undertaken, and steamboats began to carry people along the rivers into the new West. Then followed the era of canal enterprises, particularly the very successful Erie Canal and the state-financed waterway systems of Pennsylvania, which by the 1820's were vastly stimulating the Western movement. In 1820 the inducements to settle new land was heightened by lowering the cash price of public land to settlers and reducing the minimum size of tracts available to individual purchasers. Again, in 1830, the general preemption land law further enhanced these movements by giving settlers priority rights. Although much of this land settlement was in agricultural sections, the development of new commercial centers was also exceedingly rapid. With the coming of the railroad in the early 'thirties, such centers developed with astonishing rapidity. The political principles of Andrew Jackson, who entered the Presidency in 1829, proved more favorable than otherwise to the opening up of limitless opportunities for individual enterprise, promotion, and speculation but tended toward discouragement of financial, transportation, and business enterprise being conducted in large units or along lines of well-planned and orderly development. The country was suddenly thrown wide open to reckless banking, conducted by small and ill-equipped individuals, many of them essentially land speculators. Railway building from its very inception was colored by the excessively reckless competitive atmosphere of Jacksonian democracy. By 1837 there came the first harvest of ruined banks and financial involvement of the army of promotional speculators that the political system had unwittingly encouraged. But the Cumberland Road was being extended as far west as Illinois, and steamships were beginning to bring droves of immigrants from Europe. Then, in the 'forties, more large areas of land were added to the national domain; a gold rush to the West Coast followed, and there came the enormously important expansion of the railroad network, aided by newly developed Bessemer steel rails and a fast-growing export market for farm products. To all these forces of continental expansion the building industry responded with all the intensity of its own speculative characteristics.

SPECULATIVE PROMOTION IN REAL ESTATE

Early in the nineteenth century, towns and cities at strategic commercial and industrial crossroads were being actively developed by promoters whose interest was primarily in acquiring profit through enhancement of land values as expanding numbers were attracted to these communities. Many of these new communities were poorly planned; others failed to develop, since the promoters paid more attention to quick profit than to matters of wise location or the planning of urban facilities and lots on a sound long-term basis. As population moved west of the Alleghenies, town jobbing became one of the great preoccupations of individual capitalists. At this point, the emphasis upon individuals is important, because both real-estate development and urban housing represent fields of activity quite unlike those organized enterprises that take the form of farms, factories, mercantile establishments, or transportation enterprises. The subdividing of rural acreage into suburban lots, the disposing of these lots to those who make up an urban community, and the building of the houses by speculative or semi-speculative enterprises all represent a field of small-unit business. Here are represented constantly shifting groups, the participation as a side venture by persons engaged in some trade or profession, and, on the whole, a high degree of reckless competition among many thousands of amateur entrepreneurs, seeking the profits of turnover, primarily motivated by the profit opportunities in the purchase of cheap land to be sold at higher prices.

The activities of the typical speculative builder occupy an important place in the field of venture capital, which we call "real-estate development." Naturally, the speculative builder has not been responsible for more than a part of all housing construction. Many home builders use their own capital and engage builders to do the work according to plans and specifications. Such properties are usually to be found in the higher value range. But in the construction of the lower priced small properties destined for urban wage earners and clerical workers, the general American tendency has been to provide ready-made housing in connection with promotional development of new subdivisions. The builders undertaking such ventures have rarely been organized as large units; in most cases they have been individual contractors, hiring a few laborers in good times and none at all in poor times, working usually on one plot of land at a time and turning the property as fast as possible but operating frequently in conjunction with land syndicates and subdividing organizations.

These land-subdividing groups have characteristically consisted of men of substantial capital, often working with banking groups and real-estate brokerage enterprises. The subdividing groups have usually grown in size and number while the boom periods lasted and have quickly melted away or shifted to other areas after a given expansion reached its limits. The activities of the subdividers, creating building lots from farm land and endowing them with glamor and more or less of the community facilities, such as streets, water and sewer connections, have again and again assumed spectacular momentum. They thereby contributed to the incentive motivating thousands of speculative ready-made builders and to the tenuous financing devices whereby prospective home owners were able, at least temporarily, to possess a home. Prior to the organization of the National Banking System, a good deal of the activity of banks and bankers originated in the flamboyant operations of land development, both rural and urban. Even the Second Bank of the United States "did a large business in granting loans secured by mortgages on land. At one time it had under pledge almost all the area of Cincinnati. In 1823 defaulted real estate loans in that city alone exceeded two million and a half dollars."[1]

Even foreign capitalists, particularly in England, maintained close relations with the activities of those in this country who participated in systematic operations in real estate. Wealthy merchants in the larger, rapidly growing cities of the United States found boundless opportunity for the investment of their surplus wealth in land. Much of this represented shrewd, long-term investment in commercial property capable of enhancement in value with the growth of an urban center, but a substantial part of the wealth overflowed into the suburban ventures of subdividing and speculative building. The building of the railroads represented much the same motive to gain from appreciation in the value of urban land adjacent to or served by the new transport facilities. Large landowners were intimately associated with railroad projects.

[1] A. M. Sakolski, "The Great American Land Bubble," New York, 1932. This book contains well-documented information and many interesting ancedotes concerning the various forms of land speculation throughout a long period of American history. This is a field of activity that has largely escaped the notice of economists who have persistently sought the reasons for economic instability in the wrong places.

As land speculation was repeatedly and vastly overdone, so too was the building of railroads, undertaken by bold and vigorous promoters, with results that will appear statistically in a later chapter.

We do not have more than a sketchy factual record of urban real-estate activity during most of the nineteenth century, but recent investigations have pieced together the broad outlines of the process whereby suburban and even rural land was usually brought to the stage of sub-divided units. The county records of many localities have afforded amazing statistical pictures of the cyclical gyrations of subdividing operations. Measured in the terms of the number of lots subdivided per capita of local population, these numbers in repeated cases have risen to peaks 50, 150, 200, or 300 per cent above the long-time trends of urban growth. After reaching these dizzy peaks, when the number of lots might be sufficient to care for population growth perhaps fifty or a hundred years ahead, the additions have quickly ceased, and the number of lots for many years thereafter has declined until it became a small fraction of the trend. A few of these records go back to the middle of the nineteenth century or even beyond. As between one community and another, the major peaks and troughs of these great cycles in land development rarely coincide exactly, but nevertheless there is a *tendency* toward a rough sort of synchronization. The duration of the long cycles is between fifteen and twenty years from peak to peak and trough to trough.

During the past century the most important operations have been in the undeveloped areas just beyond the settled section of established communities. Relatively little promotional enterprise of this sort has taken the form of developing entire communities *de novo* from the wilderness, although this formed occasionally a rather important type of project in the preceding century. Activity in converting acreage to building lots has ordinarily not been the forerunner of a major expansion in building itself; usually the fundamental population and other demand influences have first indicated a rising market for housing accommodations before systematic enterprise in subdividing occurred. But once the latter was under way, it tended to reinforce very powerfully all those types of ready-made buildings that travel upon the momentum of optimistic interpretation of future prospects for demand and for property values.[1] Frequently the actual subdividing of suburban plots has been undertaken by individuals and groups after the land had been acquired or controlled in substantial parcels by land syndicates, or even a series of syndicates. There has thus been a cumulation of turnover profits even before the land has reached the subdividers or final owners. The activity of land

[1] This is the interpretation arrived at by Homer Hoyt in his valuable study "One Hundred Years of Land Values in Chicago," University of Chicago Press, 1933.

syndicates in disposing of properties has usually been most evident as the realty boom reached close to its extreme height. The price of land has been known in some cases to advance on a single turnover as much as 100 per cent.[1]

A considerable amount of this turnover in land has been financed with borrowed capital, some of it by short-term credit extension. Since sooner or later the more speculative types of subdividing activity resulted in lots being laid out far beyond what the local population increment could possibly absorb, taxes would accumulate rapidly, and delinquency in tax and capital payments would ensue. The commercial banks, which frequently financed the larger syndicates and subdividers, found the recoil of these speculative adventures falling upon themselves and their depositors. Since the country has not had until very recently a strong specialized financing system, operated under careful regulation and devoted to real-estate and property-mortgage financing, the banks (as in the case of farm loans) have from time to time been involved to a dangerous extent in operations where commercial banking has no proper place. Herbert D. Simpson goes so far as to say in retrospect that

. . . real estate interests dominated the policies of many banks, and thousands of new banks were organized and chartered for the specific purpose of providing the credit facilities for proposed real estate promotions. The greater proportion of these were state banks and trust companies, many of them located in the outlying sections of the larger cities or in suburban regions not fully occupied by older and more established banking institutions. In the extent to which their deposits and resources were devoted to the exploitation of real estate promotions being carried on by controlling or associated interests, these banks commonly stopped short of nothing but the criminal law—and sometimes not short of that.[2]

During the course of typical real-estate booms, some of which have lasted for a full decade, the activity of property turnover is also evident

[1] Ernest M. Fisher, Speculation in Suburban Land, *American Economic Review*, Supplement, March, 1933, p. 154. This article is an excellent summary of the speculative and cyclical aspects of urban land speculation in the United States. See also E. M. Fisher, Real Estate Subdividing Activity and Population Growth in Nine Urban Areas, *Michigan Business Studies*, Vol. I, No. 9, July, 1928, and E. M. Fisher and R. F. Smith, Land Subdividing and the Rate of Utilization, *Michigan Business Studies*, Vol. IV, No. 5, 1932. See the statistical studies of land subdivision and real-estate cycles in several California metropolitan communities by Lewis Maverick, *Journal of Land and Public Utility Economics*, May, 1932, and February, 1933; also, Helen Monchow, "Seventy Years of Real Estate Subdividing in the Region of Chicago," Evanston, 1939. One of the most interesting measures of fluctuation in the number of lots subdivided per capita pertains to Allegheny County, Pennsylvania, beginning in 1830; see reproduction of a chart prepared by S. Keyes, in Warren and Pearson, "World Prices and the Building Industry," p. 107, New York, 1937.

[2] Real Estate Speculation and the Depression, *American Economic Review Supplement*, March, 1933, p. 164. Further comment on the banking phases of speculative activity will be found in Chapter 11.

in the number of deeds recorded or the number and value of mortgages executed. Naturally, many of the transfers recorded with county clerks involve not merely land but improvements, and some of the activity in transfer of real estate has to do with older properties that begin to change hands more readily in the very early stage of an incipient rising cycle. Increasing local population, in terms of family units, first brings about a stiffening of rentals and a rise in the prices of existing improved properties. Then new building gets under way, and the enthusiasm to participate in the rising values spreads throughout the field of land development. It is an interesting fact that for many communities whose records have been examined, the broad swings in the activity of property transfers, recordings of mortgages or of deeds, despite the inclusion of some irrelevant entries, correlate very closely with the changes in subdividing activity, as measured by number of lots per capita. The great waves of these real-estate movements have local peculiarities in pattern and timing, but the major cyclical swings show up in many communities at about the same time, although conspicuous departures will be found.[1]

THE GREAT CYCLES OF REAL-ESTATE ACTIVITY

Two interesting examples of urban realty cycles in comparison with construction activity are shown in Charts 25 and 26. The first relates to the number of lots subdivided annually in Cook County (Chicago area), Illinois, from 1875 to 1940, and the number of buildings constructed over the same period in Chicago. Observe the remarkable amplitude of variation as well as the degree of similarity in pattern of these data. Hoyt says:

Recurring land booms in Chicago . . . have generally been sustained and carried to their peaks partly by a sudden and extraordinary rate of increase in actual population growth which persisted for a few years, helped to foment speculative excitement, and led to even more extravagant hopes for future population increase. This increase in the rate of population growth was one of the factors that led to an increase in rents, building activity, and subdivision activity, each of which in turn was carried to speculative excess, and each of which interacted upon the other and upon land values to generate and maintain the boom psychology. There is thus a chain of events communicating with each

[1] Chart entitled "One Hundred Fifty Years of Real Estate Experience," published by Roy Wenzlick, Real Estate Analysts, Inc., St. Louis, 1939. Mr. Wenzlick and his associates have gathered together property-turnover records of numerous cities, some of these records extending back to 1870. See also files of the *Real Estate Analyst*, a service devoted to real-estate economics and forecasts, prepared by this organization. Recent study of the recording of deeds in various localities has been undertaken by the Division of Economics and Statistics, Federal Housing Administration, Washington, D.C. The results show instances of astonishingly wide swings, rising far above the trend and falling to extremely low levels, approaching close to zero in some cases.

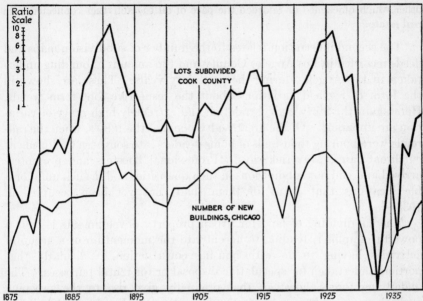

CHART 25.—Building and subdivision activity in the Chicago area, 1875–1940. Subdivision activity has experienced extraordinarily violent fluctuations during the course of the major building cycle.

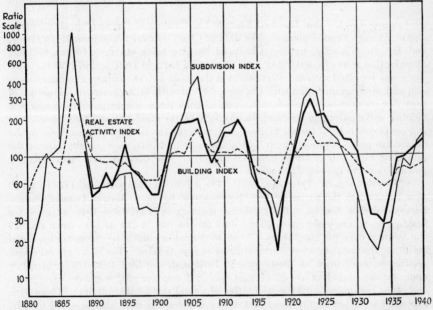

CHART 26.—Building and real-estate activity in the Los Angeles area, 1880–1940. The above measures are in the form of deviations from long-term trends in order to show clearly the nature of the major cyclical movements and the fairly close similarity in the cycles of the three phases of activity.

other which quickened or retarded the pace of all the activities connected with real estate.[1]

The second illustration relates to the number of subdivision maps and deeds recorded in Los Angeles County and the amount of building undertaken in Los Angeles during the past sixty years. These are shown in the form of cyclical variations about the respective long-term trends. Here again the fairly high correlation and extremely high range of variation are apparent. Of the great realty boom of the 1880's, when the railroads were pouring thousands of homesteaders into southern California at cutthroat fares, Maverick says, "Professional boosters and promoters arrived and laid out subdivisions in such quantities and in such unfavorable locations that many of them (had) not yet been occupied in 1933."[2]

The subdividing of land for urban property developments is thus a powerful amplifier, tending to accentuate the momentum of a group of activities having to do with housing construction, particularly that portion undertaken for speculative disposal or for rental purposes. The underlying forces, however, that originally give rise to the sweeping cyclical movements in real-estate transactions and residential building alike are found in population changes. This is shown in a comparison of building activity and the estimated *annual* rate of growth in population

[1] Homer Hoyt, "One Hundred Years of Land Values in Chicago," p. 369, University of Chicago Press, Chicago. The data of Chart 26 were taken from Hoyt's book, and Mr. Hoyt kindly supplied additional data to bring the record down to 1940. Hoyt further states (p. 391): "In 1836, in 1856, in 1872, in 1890, and in 1925 the same story was repeated with some variations in the mode of transportation to the subdivision and of communication with the prospect but with little change in the nature of the sales arguments. The assumption at all such times is that population and new building will continue to grow indefinitely at the same rapid rate and that vacant land will continue to be absorbed at least as rapidly in the future as it has been in the immediate past. Close or careful calculations are not even made on the basis of the prevailing rapid rate of absorption, and the territory subdivided into lots exceeds any possible demand for years to come."

[2] Maverick, *op. cit.*, February, 1933. The subdivision map data used for Chart 26 were supplied to the writer by Dr. Maverick and by H. A. Harris, Deputy County Surveyor of Los Angeles. The cycles for building activity, 1889–1940, adjusted for building costs, are based upon permit data for the city of Los Angeles down to 1928 and county data for later years. They were made available to the writer by Elden Smith, of the Security First National Bank of Los Angeles. The index of real-estate activity is based upon all deeds (except Torrens deeds) filed 1880–1927; thereafter upon totals, excluding deeds of partition and conveyance, road, cemetery, tax, and other instruments not representative of actual real-estate activity. These data expressed on a per family basis and adjusted for trend were also supplied by Mr. Smith, whose work on this subject, as manager of the research department of his institution, has done much to illuminate the workings of the property cycle in southern California.

in 17 cities in Chart 27, based on the work of William H. Newman.[1] It will be seen that the broad variations of the two series describe similar patterns, whereas the index of population changes tends to *precede* that of building activity.

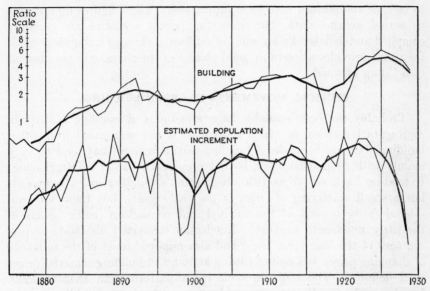

CHART 27.—Urban building activity and population increments, 1875–1929. The building data represent permits, in a considerable number of cities, while population increment estimates represent a limited number of large cities. The relationship throughout the period between the smoothed trends is highly significant. (*Data prepared by William H. Newman, "The Building Industry and Building Cycles," 1935.*)

The problem of securing a reasonably accurate general measure of the fluctuations in residential building throughout the United States is a difficult one. Building, like real estate, represents one of those fields of enterprise about which statistical data have accumulated more or less by accident rather than by deliberate interest and design. For recent years we have good records of building contracts and awards for many parts of the country (east of the Rocky Mountains), prepared by the F. W. Dodge Corporation as a part of their statistical services on behalf

[1] "The Building Industry and Business Cycles," University of Chicago, 1935. The estimates of annual growth in the population of these cities was derived by Newman from data relating to school enrollment, which tends to respond to movements resulting from migration during short periods of time. The building figures used by Newman represent building permits which although largely responsive to activity in residential construction, contain other elements as well and may, therefore, slightly distort the degree of correlation with population change.

of those interested in building plans and construction.[1]   These contract statistics on building activity extend back, however, only a few decades. As we go back into the nineteenth century reliance must be placed upon the records of city-building inspectors, and these are principally in the form of the recorded value of permits granted for construction in order to enforce compliance with local ordinances.   These figures do not give us actual volume data, but when the permit statistics are carefully compiled and deflated by an index of estimated changes in building costs, the result provides a tolerably good picture of the changes in the amount of building planned.

CYCLICAL MOVEMENTS IN URBAN BUILDING

Probably the best available long-term index of building activity in representative cities, in which residential is not segregated from other building, but use is made of building-permit figures that tend to vary mainly with residential work, is that prepared by John R. Riggleman.[2] Extending back as far as 1830, Riggleman's building index represents but a small scattering of cities in the early years, but these are considered fairly typical of the spirited and contagious realty booms of the early nineteenth century.   Riggleman converted his index to percentages of the long-term trend and also removed most of the influence of changing prices and costs by using an index of building-material prices as a deflator.   The building cycle index pattern from 1845 to 1940, based mainly on Riggleman, is shown in Chart 28 (middle curve).[3] Observe particularly the intensity of the cyclical movements and the tendency of building to describe cyclical waves widely separated in time.   The average period of these major cyclical movements is between 17 and 20 years.   The relation of these cycles to the very much shorter minor business cycles will be considered at a later point.[4]

---

[1] The complete F. W. Dodge figures are prepared as a subscription service rather than in readily available published form, although summary data may be found in the *Survey of Current Business* of the U.S. Department of Commerce, the *Statistical Abstract of the United States*, and in various investment service publications.

[2] In its preliminary form, extending back to 1875, Riggleman's index is illustrated in the *Journal of the American Statistical Association*, June, 1933, p. 181.   Since then the index has been revised and extended backward to 1830, and the writer has been given permission, through the courtesy of Mr. Riggleman, to utilize his revised data extending to recent years.   See Appendix 6 for the use made of these data.

[3] Riggleman index 1845–1920, spliced to the writer's deflated permits index 1921–1940.   See Appendix 6 for further details.

[4] Another series of American building indexes has been developed by Clarence D. Long, Jr.   See "Building Cycles and the Theory of Investment," Princeton University Press, 1940.   Long, like Riggleman, utilized building-permit figures for a varying number of cities, but he segregated residential from other types so far as number of structures is concerned.   There are two indexes of value of building permits, one

In Chart 28 the building index is shown in comparison with two other series, the lowest curve being a smoothing of the ratio of immigration to annual population.[1] It is obvious that there is a striking degree of relationship between the waves of immigration and the waves of urban building activity. Throughout the period there is also a tendency for the waves of immigration to *anticipate* the turning points in the building index. During the period following 1920, with a marked falling off in immigration due mainly to the legal restrictions already considered in Chapter 2, the degree of correlation between the two series becomes much less marked. It must be kept in mind, however, that during the 1920's and the major building cycle that came to a peak at about 1925, there was a considerable amount of internal migration produced by the shifting of industrial operations. Much of this was connected with the rate of development of automobile transportation, which rapidly created and expanded manufacturing centers about the Great Lakes. It also promoted the shifting of American families from crowded metropolitan areas into suburbs and stimulated suburban property development. The striking degree of relationship shown between immigration and building tends to support the evidence of Chart 27 in suggesting that the *movement of people* is a primary factor in generating the major building cycles.[2]

The relation between mortgage solvency (measured by inverting an index of foreclosure rate) and the volume of residential building has been

---

extending from 1868 to 1935 for a group of cities ultimately 14 in number, and the other with a somewhat different classification of building type covering ultimately 27 cities for the same period. Long also has an index of the number of buildings with three comprehensive classifications, extending from 1856 to 1936, and an index of the number of families accommodated in 16 localities from 1871 to 1935. The index most closely corresponding to the Riggleman series shows no marked deviations from that index, and it was decided to use Riggleman's series for the period prior to 1921.

[1] Figures for *gross* immigration were used, inasmuch as there is no good reason to believe that the net immigration, even if the figures were available during the entire period, would correlate any closer than gross immigration with building activity. The gross immigration ratio in annual form was smoothed by a five-year moving average centered at the middle of each period.

[2] Some careful study has been made of international migration as related to business cycles in the United States and to business and social conditions in Europe. See, for example, Harry Jerome, "Migration and Business Cycles," National Bureau of Economic Research, New York, 1926. In this study it was found that the minor cyclical fluctuations of migration into the United States and domestic business conditions were very closely related. But although this suggests that the immigration movement was at least in large measure responsive to the minor changes in industrial conditions and employment opportunities in the United States, the broad, major wave-like movements, with which Jerome was not concerned but which are shown in Chart 28, primarily represent the influence of conditions in foreign countries and constitute movements that clearly precede the building cycles. They appear to be in large measure *originating forces* in the strict sense.

determined with considerable accuracy for St. Louis as the result of the combined studies of Roy Wenzlick and Charles F. Roos.   In Chart 29 the building curve is shown in terms of the number of housing units added each year; the broad cyclical movements are preceded in each instance by the mortgage-solvency index.   The latter has both a more

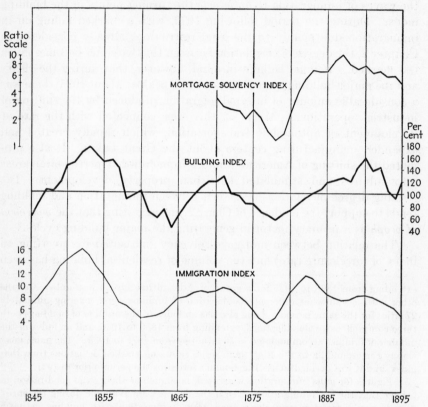

CHART 28a.—Building, immigration, and mortgage solvency, 1845–1895.   A significant similarity in broad cyclical movement exists among these factors.   The index of mortgage solvency represents the reciprocals of per capita urban foreclosures; the immigration index is the five-year smoothing of the ratio of gross immigration to estimated annual total population.

sensitive relation to building construction and a more similar pattern of amplitude than are reflected in either of the supplementary indexes, rental-cost ratio or local housing rental rates adjusted for occupancy rates and for tax payments.[1]

Let us turn now to an examination of the building cycle in terms of the various motivating forces and financial processes involved in this

[1] See Charles F. Roos, "Dynamic Economics," Chapter 4, Bloomington, Ind., 1934.

field of activity. When we speak of the building industry in this connection, we have in mind primarily the operations of speculative house builders and also of builders erecting houses to order on a contract basis. We are not directly concerned with the many phases of the building materials or equipment industries, although our conclusions will have important bearings upon these lines and their cyclical instability.

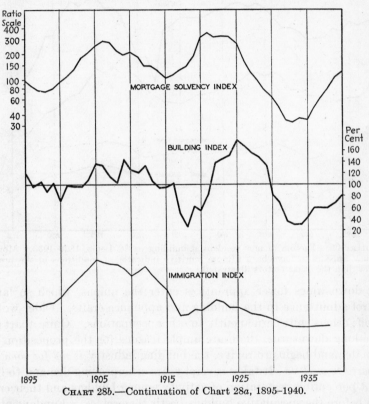

CHART 28b.—Continuation of Chart 28a, 1895–1940.

As a surging wave of demand for housing accommodations begins to develop, it follows a relatively long period of decline, the nature of which we shall discuss presently. During this long period of inactivity and declining real-estate values, the excessive supply of housing accommodation carried over from the preceding boom continues to weigh upon the market. Population factors do not for some time resume a tendency favorable to revival of operations.[1] Since the building industry is

[1] The values of both vacant land readily available for building and the existing structures tend to move through cycles essentially similar to those described by the number of transfers and the subdivision activities. Although property does not change hands frequently and the records of transfers are not easy to obtain in many

primarily one of very small operating units consisting of entrepreneurs, subcontractors, and varying numbers of hired craftsmen, these organizations mushroom and then fade away.   There is not the enduring structure of a factory, plant, or merchandising establishment.   During the

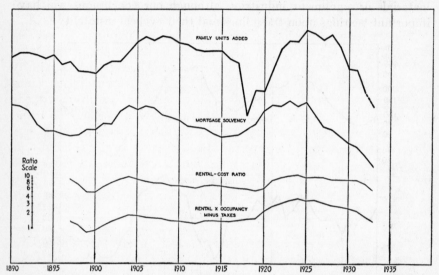

CHART 29.—Factors in new residential building in St. Louis, 1890–1933.   Mortgage solvency appears to have been a more sensitive indicator of conditions in the property market than the other factors illustrated.

long downswings fewer apprentices enter the unions, which so largely control admittance to the building and appliance crafts.   Older workers die off; others shift permanently to other occupations.   Quite apart from these long downturns, there are ample reasons for the proposition that when demand begins to revive, the building industry *is not for some time prepared to meet it*.   It takes several years of improving demand to bring about perceptible restoration of activity among builders and their crews, even before the speculative builders bestir themselves.   Fundamentally,

cities, we know that there tends to be a tremendous range of fluctuation in these values.   This can be illustrated from Hoyt's study of Chicago, in which he speaks of the value of land within the 1933 limits of Chicago at selected years of peaks and troughs.   In 1833 these values were $168,000; 3 years later they were $10,000,000; in 1842 they had fallen to $1,400,000; after 14 years of appreciation, in 1856, they became $125,000,000; 5 years later they had been reduced one-half; by 1873 they had again risen to $575,000,000; but in 1879 were $250,000,000; by 1892, however, there was a sixfold increase to $1,500,000,000.   This promptly shrank in 1897 to an even billion dollars; then, after a long period of 29 years of appreciation, the values rose to $5,000,-000,000 in 1926, which was cut in half in 1933.   Despite rapid growth in the aggregate size of the city, it can be seen that these values fluctuate around the growth trend with extraordinary violence.   Data from Hoyt, *op. cit.*

buildings are among the most durable products of human industry. Existing structures can be made to serve with a little crowding, a little patching here and renovation there, for a considerable period of time before the need for new houses becomes sufficiently acute to push rental values sharply higher and definitely to stimulate the slow-moving, cumbersome, scattered operators into more systematic action.

Here we have a sequence essentially similar to what we have observed in the livestock industry. The response to the initial stimulus tends to be slow, because the period during which materials will not be produced in adequate quantity is rather long. During inactivity material plants are shut down, or nearly so, and distribution facilities have disintegrated; it requires time to resume operations and reassemble personnel. Numerous bottlenecks result, retarding the smooth flow of construction. Once there is an awareness of a reversal in the cycle of demand, usually in response to some basic shifting in the number of people or number of families, the rental values of existing property and the values of new property and of land ready for use tend to rise, but the rise continues for years before the expansion in construction has reached a satiation point. Since the building industry, when at full steam, can provide employment, directly or indirectly, for between 7 and 10 million workers in over 60 industries, the rising cycle of activity creates a parallel major expansion in employment and earnings. This *in itself* is a basis for a part of the improving demand for housing. Families "unscramble" and establish separate households, and from many other reinforcing tendencies within the business system additional demand is created for housing facilities. Thus the cycle pushes itself along by its own momentum. The original stimulus multiplies itself before the top of the major cycle is reached. The accelerating rise in activity not only is accompanied by higher land values and property values, reflecting the higher rentals, but is projected by the optimistic far into the future. According to Hoyt, "Land values are capitalized not merely on the new basis, but even on the assumption that the profit margin of landlords will continue to increase. Taxes are levied, bank loans are made, and long-time commitments are entered into on this new basis, until the whole financial structure of society is involved in the support of the newly created land values."[1]

Let us review the course of a typical major cycle in housing construction, beginning in the trough of depression. For a number of years there has been a pronounced shrinkage, not only of new construction of houses but of other phases that so largely depend on the residential work. Overbuilding during the previous boom has resulted in distressed properties

[1] Hoyt, *op. cit.*, p. 233.

being held by financial institutions. Many of these are vacant but are grimly held at prices still far out of line with existing conditions. The average vacancy in residential property is perhaps between 7 and 12 per cent of the total existing capacity. Families have doubled up, but many are not yet beginning to feel acutely the need for better accommodations. Some natural or migration growth has taken place in the community, and one by one the better vacant properties are taken over by families with higher than average income. Presently vacancies are reduced to the point at which a few new houses are again being planned, especially in the higher value groups. Meanwhile, some families have left the crowded sections of the community and sought cheap land in the suburban fringe, where a little activity in lower priced housing begins as a means of affording these families an opportunity to reduce housing costs in view of the slow reduction in rentals in the more congested districts. A little stir of activity is seen among contractors, who add a man here and there and create new orders for lumber, plumbing supplies, glass, and other essentials. For some little time, however, possibly for a few years, the shifting about of families to absorb the vacant dwellings, apartments, and flats prevents any considerable amount of new construction. But little by little there is a tapering off in the decline in rental rates, and a gradual upward turn can be detected by the expert.

The more alert and enterprising owners of rental property now begin to hire workmen to paint and renovate. As the number of independent family units increases and perhaps long-deferred movement of people into the community revives, there begins to be a more active interest in new construction on the part of those contemplating investment in rental properties. Meantime, industrial activity is feeling some beneficial effect of the initial orders for materials. When the rental rates, after taxes and other necessary costs of construction and maintenance are allowed for, multiplied by occupancy rates, begin to reveal an upward tendency, the signal is given for cautious but vigorous casting about for options on parcels of land suitable for the erection of new income property. Along with this stirring of activity, the shrewd and relatively prosperous families are taking advantage of the existing moderate price of materials to build new houses, although for a time the old ones vacated fill much of the demand on the part of new families in the lower income groups coming into the community. As the movement develops there are families in the middle income group and just below it who have felt for a long time the need for better accommodations to provide for growing families. There is by now enough enhancement of employment and income in the community (barring offsetting persistent depression factors that might, of course, exist in a given area), to make possible more comfortable provision for those parts of families that have been living under a single roof. By the time the new building, which has been done mainly by those interested in rental properties and those having houses built to their specifications and financed largely by equity capital, shows a definite upward movement for several years, the speculative contractors and the real-estate firms interested in multifamily projects begin to be more active in planning the subdividing of suburban plots, laying out of streets, and sale of these lots to prospective home owners who can be induced to build homes, provided that the financing terms are attractive.

In the process of creating new areas of land, partially improved and ready for building operations, there are to be considered the local vacancy rate, the rise in rentals, and the tendencies affecting the general cost of living. If rentals begin to rise rapidly, if the vacancy rate descends below 5 per cent of capacity, and if the cost of living in terms of food and clothing and other such immediate essentials is not unduly high, the processes of real-estate development have an open road for rapid expansion. This expansion has usually been attended by more or less fanfare and promotional effort, and in what follows we shall describe tendencies that are not likely to be repeated in detail in the future. In order to sell lots, it is necessary to offer practical financing terms to prospective buyers. Until very recently, this was characteristically accomplished by arranging loans from banks, building-loan associations, life-insurance companies,[1] mutual savings banks, trust companies, or private individuals, the terms of each class of lender being somewhat at variance with another. Since financing arrangements for residential properties comprise many types of borrowers, some building for personal use, others for income property, and still others for quick turnover as "building merchants," it follows that no generalizations on this subject will be perfectly accurate. There is unfortunately a remarkable dearth of precise information, inasmuch as the building industry has been one of the notorious blind spots in our economic history. In fact, the significance of the building industry in economic affairs and in the dynamics of industrial fluctuations has been recognized only within the last few decades.[2]

EFFECTS OF UNSOUND MORTGAGE FINANCE

So long as the number of families in the community is increasing and there is an active interest supported by rising income, employment, and general prospects, the opportunity for financing lot sales and home build-

[1] Only during the last twenty years or so have life-insurance companies taken a substantial interest in this field.

[2] When George H. Hull wrote his book on "Industrial Depressions" shortly before World War I and stated categorically that "what we call booms result almost entirely from the great periodic increases in the volume of construction, and what we call industrial depressions result almost entirely from the great falling off in the volume of construction," his was a lone voice, virtually ignored by the economists of his day.

ing for the middle and part of the lower income group can expand. It must be recognized, of course, that in the United States families in the lower income group (let us say, roughly below income levels of $2,000 a year) have been accommodated mainly by rental property or by purchase of property at third or fourth hand. A much larger part of the new building than proportionate to the size of the group has for many years been done to accommodate the upper middle and higher income groups.[1] In order to make it possible for the middle and lower income groups to participate at all in the ownership of homes, in view of the relatively small equity available to these families, the promotional activity has relied (until recent reforms served to restrict the practice) upon the use of mortgages requiring no regular annual payments of principal and, in fact, no outlay for several years on capital account. Here we come back to the deeply rooted evil which has lurked more or less unnoticed in so much of our long-term financing—*the unamortized capital loan.*

From one point of view the use of such a device is readily explained by the historical background of a new country chronically short of long-term capital and hence accustomed to interest rates well above 5 per cent. It is obvious that if a five, ten, or fifteen-year property loan is systematically amortized so that it is paid up at the end of the period, the regular payments by way of amortization of the principal, added to the interest payment on a flat basis, appreciably raise the actual annual outlay for financing to the borrower. If he wishes to "trade" heavily on his equity, as most property buyers and farmers have done, the financing naturally gravitates toward a flat loan payable in its entirety at the end of the period, at which time the borrower takes his chances upon being able to accumulate the principal or relies upon his efforts to secure a renewal of the loan for at least one more joy ride. From the standpoint of the subdivider offering parcels of semiimproved property, the financing problem has historically been met in part by the all too familiar device of dividing the land into very small lots, crowding the neighborhood unduly, and creating a neighborhood subject to obsolescence and depreciation risks, of which the borrowing home builder has rarely been conscious. He weighed merely the rentals or the conditions of his existing accommodations against the interest cost of "his" new property. And he seldom allowed for depreciation as one of the treacherous hidden costs that the future would bring to light.[2]

[1] See the evidence of Dr. Isador Lubin, Commissioner of Labor Statistics, before the Temporary National Economic Committee, June, 1939, *Report*, Part II, pp. 4943*ff.*

[2] George L. Bliss, President of the Federal Home Loan Bank of New York, in his *Seventh Annual Report*, 1940, states rather pointedly: "It might not be amiss to draw attention to the curious psychology of the average property owner, who refuses to make allowances for ordinary depreciation and obsolescence in valuing his own prop-

As the building cycle in a typical large community characteristically reached the upper third of its course or thereabouts, it became relatively easy for the promoters of subdivisions and the professional builders of jerry-made houses to dispose of their properties by means of the existing mortgage system. The lenders, although representing mainly highly reputable and established institutions, usually recognized that loans made under these promotional conditions represented unusual risks. Hence they sought (like the lenders to agriculture) to protect themselves by relying upon the curious fiction of "liquidity" of their loans and stubborn refusal to make commitments beyond relatively short periods, even though the properties upon which the loans were made were likely to be in existence for many years and the individual borrowers (apart from the purely speculative and turnover enterprises) were expected to hold the property for relatively long periods.

First, then, was the figment or fetish of liquidity, expressed in the usual practice of not extending maturities on residential mortgages beyond about ten years. A considerable proportion of such loans were, in fact, restricted to five years, and commercial banks in some communities rarely made realty loans beyond three-year terms. A second means whereby the lenders sought to protect their depositors and their capital was by restricting the amount of first-mortgage loans to amounts not over 50 per cent of the appraised value of each property. This restriction was easily overcome, however, by means of the second-mortgage lender. Since a large proportion of the families seeking homes to whom the subdivision operations catered could not afford more capital outlay than was enough to purchase the land or a part of it, the balance of the capital was raised by a first mortgage plus a second and even a third. The first carried a rate from 6 to 8 per cent, and the second cost from 10 to 15 per cent. In most instances the rate of interest on the total capital borrowed seems to have been in the neighborhood of 7 per cent, since the second mortgage was usually a smaller part (and this also was frequently amortized).

---

erty, insisting instead that it is always worth what he paid for it, and that an inability to sell it at the original purchase price is an indication of economic maladjustment. . . The competent appraiser recognizes that there is little other than sentimental value remaining in the average forty or fifty year old house. A person who buys a home for five thousand dollars, with one thousand dollars representing the value of the land, and four thousand dollars the value of the property, should recognize that at the end of ten years a depreciation of, say, twenty-five per cent has taken place in the value of the improvement and that its aggregate value has then been reduced to about four thousand dollars. Twenty years after its purchase, in the ordinary case, about fifty per cent depreciation has taken place. There would be less wailing and complaints about economic injustice, if such a home owner recognized that his property is half worn out."

Observe now the effect of this financing system upon the building industry when it reached the top level of a major cycle of expansion. As it entered this range there was in evidence the full swing of real-estate activity, a very active sale of lots, busy speculative builders competing more or less blindly with each other and having no accurate estimates of the future trend of population upon which actual demand would largely depend. Some part of the financing operations was undertaken directly by the speculative and rental builders and their clients who acquired the properties, and this part of the mortgage lending became increasingly fraught with risks and dangers. The more cautious savings-banks and building-and-loan operators became less inclined to make new loans, and, what is most important, they tended to frown increasingly upon the extension of loans that had been made a few years before and that were coming up for renewal, which might or might not be granted, depending on conditions *at that date*.

In the course of the expansion a point was eventually reached at which it became apparent that the speculative building and financing had been overdone. Some subdividers of land actually found themselves in financial difficulties, unable to pay taxes or to repay loans that had been taken out to provide for operations during the unsound stage of the boom. This immediately threw some land upon the market through distress sales. There followed a few cases here and there of foreclosure of loans representing the thinnest equities or the most reckless borrowers. The excesses of the boom began to show themselves in a shifting of families out of rental properties, thus bringing about enough wavering and hesitation in the movement of rental rates to affect the earning power of a few speculative multifamily structures and therefore the loans upon these properties.

From this point forward a process of disintegration set in. It tended to travel a cumulative course, marked out by the blind character of the competitive overexpansion during the upswing and the unsound financing machinery, which resulted in many thin-equity loans at or near the peak of overbuilding. As the values began to suffer as the result of additional distress sales, the financing agencies became ultraconservative; they refused renewals, stepped up the cost of new loans (if granted at all), and new building began to feel the competition of the existing properties thrown on the market. Employment among the building workers and the producers of building materials began to feel the initial effect of what would prove a tragically prolonged deterioration of activity. This process again proceeded on its own momentum. More properties became involved in the snares of the flat loan and the remorseless, routine operations of financial repossession. The number of foreclosures then began to rise rapidly, even before building operations had actually turned the corner downward.

THE SIGNIFICANCE OF FORECLOSURES

This acceleration in housing foreclosures may be considered, in the light of statistical evidence, to be probably the best single indication that a change in the tide is at hand. Referring again to Chart 28, observe the upper curve, which shows, in inverted form and thus as an *index of mortgage solvency*, an index of property foreclosures (per capita) in a number of American cities.[1] The chart clearly reveals how well the index of mortgage solvency has preceded the broad swings of the building cycle itself. It summarizes, in effect, all the complex factors that make up that cycle. In the rising phase of realty development, we find declining difficulty in financing; in the declining phase there are increasing involvement, distress selling, and addition to the ownership of property by financing institutions. Most important, from our present standpoint, has been the *cumulative* effect of this shrinkage upon employment in the building trades and in that vast group of durable-goods industries that is mainly dependent upon the construction market. As employment and wage income and entrepreneur income drawn from these sources have moved downward, the income factor entering into demand for housing itself has shrunk and produced additional foreclosures, lower values, lower rentals, more vacancies, etc., down the years to the bitter end in a long, deep trough of building (and general business) prostration.[2]

During the course of this contraction there naturally occurred a folding up of speculative operations, and the number of acres of land subdivided in a community might actually decline to zero. During this period there was a tendency to shift loans and refinance. Three- and five-year loans made by commercial banks were taken over by building-and-loan associations; others, by life-insurance companies, which became active in this field after World War I. It is difficult to say just what has been the typical maturity of loans that were finally kept outstanding during the storm, but the evidence appears to suggest that an average or

[1] The data of mortgage foreclosures were kindly supplied by Roy Wenzlick, who has probably done more than any other research worker in the statistical investigation of this phase of the American economy. Beginning at 1938 Wenzlick's series was spliced to similar data which have become available through the studies of the Home Loan Bank Board and published in their monthly *Review*.

[2] Charles F. Roos has also noted the importance of foreclosures as a sensitive barometer of the realty situation. He finds a threefold significance in them. "First, foreclosed houses are additions to the supply, so that prospective buyers may purchase a foreclosed house instead of building. Second, foreclosures affect the general value of buildings in the community in which they take place, and impair the equities and mortgages. Third, foreclosures are a measure of the state of the investment market, of the willingness of bankers to loan or to refrain from pressing debtors, of the very availability of credit itself from either banks or long-term investors. This line has a distinct forecasting quality." From "Dynamic Economics," p. 78, Bloomington, Ind., 1934.

modal maturity of about ten years was the common practice.   This would suggest that about ten years from the bottom of a building cycle a fairly large fraction of mortgage loans reaching maturity date either failed to pay out or were refinanced under conditions that made the terms more onerous and created further obstacles to paying out some years later.

The entire process strongly suggests, as previously stated, the historic background of capital scarcity, the impracticability of housing ventures for families of modest income that could pay interest but not principal. Mortgage loans were made on what seemed to the individual lender to be a safe proportion of the value of a property and for what seemed at the time to be conservative maturity, insuring, so it was thought, the liquidity of the loan.   *But as in so many cases where the general is confused with the particular*, the over-all result of all this narrowly conceived caution was unfortunate for the entire system and for many banks that dabbled in it.

The large insurance companies in the last great depression carrying only a part of their investments in urban mortgages, strong enough to weather the storm of deflation, were holding billions of foreclosed property, patiently waiting to dispose of it in a better period.   In contrast, the commercial banks in some areas of excessive promotion, as in parts of Michigan, in Cleveland, and in other areas of very rapid growth, did not fare so well.[1]   The mutual savings banks appear, as a whole, to have been sufficiently conservative in their loans and sagacious in the selection of their risks to come through these difficult periods with fair success.   The building-and-loan associations had varying results; many of them were outstandingly conservative and successful, and they avoided the unsound features of unamortized loans and encouraged payment loans long before other financial institutions had adopted them.   But in some localities, particularly on the Pacific Coast, some building-and-loan associations became involved in speculative building and apartment construction at the top of the last cycle of building in 1923 to 1926 and

[1] Robert G. Rodkey has shown in his study, State Bank Failures in Michigan, *Michigan Business Studies*, Vol. VII, No. 2, University of Michigan, 1935, that "little attention has been given to the ability of the borrower to meet his interest payments and to amortize the principal periodically."   He points out that the failed State Banks in the great banking crisis of 1933 had invested 37.5 per cent of their savings deposits directly in loans secured by real estate; they had also invested heavily in real-estate bonds, representing larger structures, such as apartments, hotels, and office buildings, which for the first time were financed to an important extent through bond issues following World War I.   The real-estate loans of these banks were almost twice as large as those of all country National Banks.   These loans were badly frozen when values began to collapse.   The banks were unable to meet demands for withdrawal of deposits readily, and the demand for such withdrawals accumulated as depositors recognized these difficulties.   This was the immediate background of the banking crisis of 1933, which spread like wildfire from Michigan to other metropolitan centers and forced the Federal Government to close all banks.

placed themselves and their communities in serious difficulty as the cycle collapsed. The banking crisis of 1933 is no mystery to those acquainted with the building cycle and the old system of financing that that crisis served finally to abolish.

During the trough of a major depression the financial institutions were holding large amounts of foreclosed property, which was offered on the market only as fast as local conditions warranted. The property was usually placed at rental, and this action held down rental rates for a while. As this overhang of foreclosed property, some of it of high quality, continued, there was a tendency for gradual shrinkage in prices. The important point is that this distressed property was sufficient in the aggregate to take care of a large part of the incipient demand for housing as the continued revival of replacement demand for various products began to form the basis for recovery in general trade conditions.

Thus in the early phase of recovery the response of actual construction tended to be slow and uncertain, and considerable time was required to get the ponderous building industry once more under way. The overhang of foreclosed property may be considered, therefore, to have been one of the most important factors in this slow response. As in the case of the livestock cycle, the stimulating influences do not seem to have sufficed at the beginning to call forth enlargement of actual supply. But when the productive operations began to add to the inventory, those additions developed a reinforcing momentum continuing well beyond the period of strong demand stimulus. Sales of property occurred under distress at the top of the cycle, just as in the livestock industry herds will be offered for sale when conditions become less favorable, because of either higher costs of maintaining the herds or acceleration of falling prices as overstocked areas begin to unload and market their cattle.

From these considerations there develops a rather fundamental principle to which attention has not hitherto been sufficiently directed. *In any industry whose products are capable of extended life, in which production activity responds slowly following the initial stimulus of demand and in which supplies resulting from previous production continue to be marketed long after the peak of output has passed, conditions are created favorable to cyclical movements of relatively long average period.*

The building industry in the past has described just such cyclical movements. Over a long period of history and in all countries where the data have been examined, the major peaks and valleys of house-building activity are separated by long intervals. The periods are not exactly regular, but the tendency toward cyclical movements so much longer than the typical "minor" business cycles, yet so much shorter than the long-term "wave" movements that we examined in Chapter 4, suggest that population movement plus mechanical forces within the construction process and the miscalculations attending a bad system of speculative finance afford a large part of the explanation. Without ignoring the occasional effects upon the pattern of building activity of cyclical variation in business conditions, there is nevertheless to be observed a distinctive long-cycle tendency here that far transcends the minor trade oscillations; in fact, it exerts a powerful influence over a large segment of employment and industry and logically becomes one of the originating or causal factors in the vibrations of the typical business cycle. We shall return to this phase of the matter more specifically in the following chapters.

THE RÔLE OF LABOR AND CAPITAL COSTS

Among the forces tending to give rise to the characteristic building cycle, the element of labor costs must not be overlooked. It is a familiar fact that the wages of the highly organized building crafts tend to be relatively high. That is, they tend to be "high" in terms of daily or weekly rates, compared with the pay of other skilled workers in industry. Building workers have organized themselves, at least in the larger cities, into strong union organizations, partly from the powerful motive of ensuring these high rates of pay while they are working. This motive stems at bottom from the very existence of the widely varying and long-period building cycle. On the other hand, it tends to perpetuate these great cycles. Since building workers are fully employed only about once every fifteen or twenty years, those who remain in the industry as carpenters, masons, plumbers, plasterers, and painters must carry themselves and their families through long periods of underemployment as well as through seasons of the year when building activity is naturally restricted. But it is the high cost, in terms of wages per unit of construction, that directly presents itself to the home builder or the speculative operator.

There has, of course, been technological progress in supplying these workers with better equipment to economize time, although this holds much less true of the so-called "wet processes," such as plastering and bricklaying. Carpenters are today equipped with many timesaving devices, and much of the work on a dwelling is prefabricated or partially fabricated in industrial establishments. But union rules have generally been in the direction of restricting the day's output of each worker. As for the general layout of work, building jobs cannot be easily centralized unless operations are carried on on a large scale by well-financed operators on a broad, continuing basis. But the provision of dwellings of medium or low price by large-scale, well-equipped enterprise seeking continuity by careful planning has made but slow progress. Operations have remained essentially a small-scale, scattered, and ill-coordinated type of enterprise so far as the actual construction work on the site is concerned.[1]

Since even the speculative building has been commonly undertaken by relatively small-scale operators, it has meant that the labor employed on the job has represented essentially the belated survival of simple handicraft processes only partially subject to the cost-reducing features that might be associated with expertly planned community or neighborhood-scale property development. Thus the high cost of labor, in terms of units of construction work performed per man-day, has operated as a limiting factor in those periods when values and net rental rates have been at low ebb. Not until the cycle has carried these considerably higher, to what might be termed the "flash point," above which this high cost of construction readily could be absorbed, was new building undertaken on a rapidly expanding scale.

The high labor costs have in a sense tended to create vacuums, followed by eventual excessive acceleration. During the accelerating period, as the top level of the cycle was approached, wage rates were usually raised from a high level to even higher levels, along with parallel movements in the prices of materials of many types. Throughout the material industries there has been fairly generally a long-standing tendency to charge what the traffic will bear when times were good in order to make up for the long periods of inactivity. Thus a kind of vicious circle has been created. The high average cost of labor and material, arising in part from the very existence of the major cycle, has tended to create an excessive momentum after pressure of demand has finally shot values and rental returns above the temporary barrier of production cost. This, in turn, has produced a pinching-out effect as costs rise higher, but the overbuilding in relation to existing demand has trimmed down rentals, values, and, after a long delay, incentive.

The circular effect of relatively high labor cost can also be seen in the past in the effect of interest rates. The interest rate on mortgages over a long period of years has shown until very recently surprisingly little flexibility. Different levels of rates on housing mortgages have prevailed in various sections of the country, usually somewhat lower in the older sections and much higher in the frontier and newly settled sections. As estimated by David L. Wickens[2] in the Middle Atlantic region,

[1] Out of a total of 144,396 contracting establishments enumerated in the Census of Construction in 1929, no less than 113,799 represented small contractors whose average annual volume of business was nine thousand dollars. "The Construction Industry," *U.S. Department of Commerce Market Research Series* Vol. I, No. 10, April, 1936, p. 28.

[2] Developments in Home Financing, *Annals of the American Academy of Political and Social Science*, March, 1937, p. 77.

78 per cent of the building loans as late as the early 1930's were straight, unamortized loans, whereas in the East North Central area only about one-fourth of the loans were of this type, and a considerable proportion had amortization provisions.

Thus the amortization features also have varied geographically, and the actual capital cost per annum to the borrower has varied from section to section to a greater extent because of the amortization features and risk elements than because of the differences in the interest rate itself. But in any event, the building-mortgage rate has averaged relatively high when it is considered that over the country as a whole second mortgages were widely used, especially during the boom of the 1920's, and the combined rates paid by borrowers on unamortized realty loans represented much higher rates than those associated with corporation bonds, municipal bonds, or even the average rate of return on common stocks. Thus the lenders sought to protect themselves in part by liberal allowances for risk, but this in itself contributed directly to the risks of instability, involvement, and foreclosure.

As of 1934,[1] commercial banks and building-loan associations held about 30 per cent of all the mortgage loans on real estate in 61 representative cities. It is important to observe that both these groups of institutions, particularly the commercial banks, sought deposits upon which interest was paid but which, although earmarked as term or time deposits requiring notice for withdrawal, were actually and for all practical purposes on a *demand* basis. Hence these suppliers of a large part of the urban mortgage money were all the more driven to seek an illusory liquidity and paradoxically a relatively high rate of return on what was essentially long-term investment. Capital was extended to long-term ventures on the assumption that they could be considered short-term risks, but when depositors requested withdrawals, usually at awkward times, the result was difficulty all along the line, particularly to the thin-equity borrowers who, in many cases, were still struggling with interest on their second mortgages. Too much reliance was placed upon asset security by lenders and not enough upon scrutiny of the borrower and his particular income prospects. This, in fact, has been an important characteristic of both bank credit and capital finance in this country. The writer has received from a Los Angeles banker interesting comment on the lending practices that prevailed in southern California:

The straight loans . . . were almost invariably of three to five years' duration. That was true in all of the Los Angeles banks which contributed much of the real estate credit of the period. Moreover . . . as late as 1929 and 1930

[1] David L. Wickens, "Residential Real Estate," National Bureau of Economic Research, p. 9, New York, 1941.

lenders were commonly resisting the efforts of borrowers to reduce the principal of their loans. The urge to keep the money at work at 7 % was much greater in the mind of the lender than was the desire to see the principal reduced as time passed. One reason for this was the absence of any fear of a collapse in land values. . . . Not until lenders became frightened regarding the trend of land values did pressure for amortization develop.

As the result of foreclosures made by life-insurance companies on their real-estate mortgages, the amount of property coming into possession of 110 of the largest companies in the United States during the early 1930's is of definite significance. During the middle 1920's the value of real estate owned averaged about 300 million dollars and was still less than half a billion as late as 1930, but these values rose rapidly as the amount of new mortgages declined. By 1936 they amounted to more than two billion dollars. During the rapid increase in foreclosures in 1932, they were occurring at the rate of 1,000 a day. In that year the emergency facilities of the Home Owners' Loan Corporation probably served to avert a still greater avalanche of redistribution of property, but the large lending institutions, particularly the life-insurance companies, had by that time begun to adopt policies of extension and other easement in the interest of avoiding further acquisition of properties. When it is recognized that foreclosures in urban property began to rise as early as 1926 or 1927, it can be seen how belated this policy was.

In 1934, the Government's Survey of Urban Housing disclosed that somewhat over 20 per cent of the residential mortgage debt represented loans by individuals. In view of this rather persistently large group of individual lenders, it is not surprising that institutional financing has so long held to the practice of making unamortized loans on an excessively short-term basis. The individual lender usually does not wish his capital to be constantly returning by way of principal payments. To the institutional lender this is acceptable, but in meeting the competition of individual lenders, it has been difficult to avoid the immediate competitive advantage that the small individual local lender ostensibly provided to the unthinking borrower—a somewhat higher average appraisal rate and higher proportion of loan to appraised value. It is probable that rates charged by individual lenders were somewhat lower in many cases, but these advantages were deceptive in view of the fact that individuals as lenders usually preferred not to amortize.

Those who have imagined that the cyclical movements in residential construction have somehow resulted from *variations* in the so-called "general rate of interest" (if this is intended to be distinct from entrepreneurial *profits* on invested capital) must not expect to find much factual evidence supporting their view so far, at least, as American experience goes. This, indeed, seriously qualifies the interest-rate theory that of late has been popular as a factor alleged to be a causal element in generating business cycles. The recent vogue of that body of theoretical doctrine seems to have been based more upon plausible argument than upon careful examination of the facts. But if we look at the interest rate in terms of the secular trend and recognize the marked decline that this trend has undergone in the past decade, one corresponding effect upon building finance seems important. This is the possibility of lengthening the term of systematically amortized realty mortgages. At a low rate, if it is assumed that it can be continued, amortization is much more practicable and capable of wide extension than at relatively high rates. In this sense the level of the rate, not its long-term cyclical gyrations, have an undeniable importance in this connection and also for all other forms of long-term property financing.

It should also be emphasized that it is in residential building that we find this cyclical mechanism most pronounced and characteristic. Industrial building tends to move closely with the minor cycles of business activity to which further consideration will be given presently. The erection of social-utility structures, such as hotels, large apartment buildings, etc., and also of substantial commercial structures consisting mainly of offices, has usually represented a kind of fantastic excrescence, pyramided on the crest of the residential cycle and deriving much of its motivation from the general expansion usually occurring at that stage. Since these elaborate structures require several years to plan and get under way, it has usually happened that by the time they were completed the housing cycle had already begun to reverse, and as the decline continued, with its usual destructive effect upon general business and financial conditions, these ambitious properties became involved in financial embarrassment. Many of them were built in the later 1920's and were financed by bond issues. The impaired status of realty bonds of this type in the years following 1929 has been excellent evidence of the manner in which the incentive to build does not actually produce results until the conditions creating that incentive have already begun to disappear.[1]

As for public building, this depends on a variety of factors, having to do with the financial condition and temper of local government bodies and the changing policies of the Federal Government. Further features of this phase of building construction and the general question of utilizing public-building programs as a means of offsetting the influence of the building cycle or the business cycle generally, will be given attention in a later chapter. We may add at this point, however, that in the past the

[1] See the interesting chart in Warren and Pearson, "World Prices and the Building Industry," pp. 111 and 112, showing the dates at which various metropolitan skyscrapers and other large buildings were built during the past hundred years. Very few of them were constructed below the top third of the major building cycle.

reckless pace of subdivision and speculative house-building activity has produced a prompt counterpart in local government extravagance in providing supplementary facilities and installations. Much of the municipal debt and subsequent heavy local tax burdens can be directly traced to the developing of utilities to serve new subdivisions, usually far in advance of actual demand. Mr. Hoyt, on the basis of his Chicago observations, states that during the typical boom

. . . there are lavish expenditures for public improvements in some localities. The cost of these is financed either by bond issues, which are readily passed by popular vote at such times, or by special assessments payable in five or ten annual installments, which are likewise cheerfully assumed by landowners in the belief that it will enhance the value of their land still more. Consequently, new bridges are built or streets are widened in old neighborhoods, and miles of pavements, sidewalks, and sewers are constructed in outlying subdivisions. Thus the public authorities not only do not limit the output of subdivided lots, but they encourage the rapid increase in their supply by enabling sewers, sidewalks, and pavements to be installed on vacant prairies without cost to the subdivider. The sight of newly installed sidewalks in a tract that would otherwise be only a farm or cow pasture gives the misleading impression that it is the first step in the growth of a new community, the other steps of which are to follow shortly.[1]

In the broad major movements of the building cycle, important wars naturally have important effects, since, as we have already indicated, wartime price inflation and the violent distortion of living costs tend to be disturbing factors rather than stimulating factors in construction work. We shall defer consideration of the manner in which wars have affected building until a later chapter, wherein the building cycle will be related to other major movements in the durable-goods industries and the relation of construction to war, price level, and the business cycle will be specifically analyzed.

SUMMARY

Let us now summarize briefly the essential features of the great cycles of urban real estate and housing construction. Changes in the number of families to be provided for appear to be the underlying causal factors in realty developments. Since houses are very durable it is the *change* in families not the number of families itself that produces building demand, and this goes far to explain why that demand can vary so widely. Once the construction industry has overcome its inertia and acceleration is fostered by speculative subdivision activity, expansion in residential building can be carried much further than the demand on the basis of

[1] Hoyt, *op. cit.*, p. 392. See also the interesting data presented in "Fluctuations in Capital Outlays of Municipalities," U.S. Department of Commerce, 1941.

added family units and the replacements warrants. The succeeding long decline carries new construction well below the level represented by the measure of family or population change but, of course, not below zero.

Although each community represents special factors and influences on the realty cycle, there is, nevertheless, a remarkable tendency for the movements to occur with a rough degree of concentration in timing in the important cities. The extent of the cyclical movements, however, will differ from locality to locality. In a few extreme cases, such as Miami, Fla., in the early 'twenties, there will be very extreme movements followed by spectacular collapse. The housing boom appears to have reached its last major peak on the Pacific Coast in 1923; in New England, the South Atlantic, and the East North Central sections, in 1925; and in the Middle Atlantic States, in 1928. During these great swings, broad movement of the index of mortgage solvency appears to have preceded the corresponding phases of the building cycles. Population increment and the status of the realty loan market thus appear to have varied consistently ahead of actual construction by several years. Following these more sensitive indicators, there were usually changes in the rental and vacancy indexes, the one being practically inverse with respect to the other.

Building costs have tended to lag in their response to the cyclical movement and have appeared to be of critical importance only after the cycle itself extended over a long period of years and into very high ground. Changes in interest rates appear to have been of no important effect, but the willingness of lenders to make loans in consideration of the general solvency and foreclosure situation has been much more important. Exceptional activity in the subdividing of suburban land and in the turn-over of land and real property appear to have been characteristic of the realty cycle in its later phases rather than in the initial phases of recovery. With the tendency toward a vicious circle created by relatively high and rigid building costs, particularly for labor and interest charges and with the relatively tardy response to demand changes, the cycle has tended to be pushed to levels far beyond the effective demand that was capable of validating the expanded volume of debt, and this has brought the collapse of the overexpanded situations in a cumulative spiral of deflations and contraction, affecting broad segments of national income. Thus the cycle has tended to generate its own spectacular unbalance and volatility. But, as we shall presently see, it has been externally affected by other important factors, such as those emanating occasionally from war conditions or the disturbing effect of wide fluctuations in other segments of promotional capital-goods industries. Like the cycle in the livestock production, we have a prime mover, with internally propelling mechanism, but it is also subject from time to time to impulses and cycles of solvency in other departments of the economy.[1]

[1] The factors that operate to form building and real-estate cycles will be found further illustrated in the following publications: Charles F. Roos, "Dynamic Economics," Chapter 4, 1934; Lowell J. Chawner, "Residential Building," *Housing Monograph Series* 1, National Resources Committee, Washington, D.C., 1939; Clarence D. Long, Jr., "Building Cycles," Princeton University Press, 1940; William H. Newman, "The Building Industry and Business Cycles," University of Chicago, 1935; Homer Hoyt, "One Hundred Years of Land Values in Chicago," 1933; Helen C. Monchow, "Seventy Years of Real Estate Subdividing in the Region of Chicago," Chicago, 1939; and Arthur F. Burns, Long Cycles in Residential Construction, in "Economic Essays in Honor of Wesley Clair Mitchell," New York, 1935.

CHAPTER 10

TRANSPORTATION DEVELOPMENT AS A CYCLICAL FACTOR

The foregoing discussion of building and property financing revealed a distinct source of industrial and financial instability in the movements of large numbers of people as they affect changes in urban growth and generate more or less speculative and promotional development of housing facilities, forming patterns of long and violent cyclical oscillation in construction and land turnover. This necessarily affects a large number of other industries.

In examining the nature of these building cycles, our object has been not merely to present their characteristics as an interesting and important feature of business dynamics but to establish the thesis that such extended and violent fluctuations form one of the basic originating and causal factors in the cyclical instability of industry and trade and income generally. We do not find here the *sole* explanation or perhaps even the most important causal factor in propagating the typical minor cycles of business conditions. The building cycles are much longer in period than the minor cycles of general business, whose average period has usually been between three and five years. But it is obvious that the general course of trade and industrial production and the flow of national income cannot be expected to remain stable or to pursue a smoothly ascending trend of growth when there are occurring within the business system such pronounced oscillations capable of affecting so large a segment of the working population and having such violent effects upon financial solvency and the entire credit system. Before we compare the building cycles with business cycles closely, it is well to examine some other phases of capital formation and durable-goods creation to discover if there may be disturbing elements of similar potency, although perhaps different time patterns, which, when considered *in combination* with the building cycles, may throw additional light upon the initiation of those persistent fluctuations known as "business cycles."

BUSINESS CONDITIONS MOTIVATE INDUSTRIAL CONSTRUCTION

It has already been pointed out that *industrial* construction, having to do with manufacturing plant, docks, warehouses, storage tanks, blast furnaces, and the like, also displays the wide amplitude of fluctuation that was found typical of the building industry. But the time pattern of industrial construction is not identical with that of residential building; it rather parallels closely the shorter movements of the general business cycle. It would not be difficult to show that a very substantial part of the additions made to factories, stores, and other business facilities arise from the undulating current of trade activity itself. The more active the flow of trade and the placing of orders for goods the more necessary becomes expansion and improvement of the structural facilities for production and distribution of these products.

It has been demonstrated by J. M. Clark and others[1] that a given demand for final products tends to give rise to much more violent changes in the increment of productive equipment used by the industry, the assumption being made, of course, that no usable excess capacity exists prior to the increase in demand. A tapering off in the rise of demand

[1] See J. M. Clark, Business Acceleration and the Law of Demand, *Journal of Political Economy*, March, 1917; "Economics of Overhead Costs," Chapter 19, University of Chicago Press, 1925; "Strategic Factors in Business Cycles," pp. 33–34, National Bureau of Economic Research, New York, 1934. See also the critical article by Simon Kuznets, Relation between Capital Goods and Finished Products in the Business Cycle, in "Economic Essays in Honor of Wesley Clair Mitchell," New York, 1935.

Kuznets shows that the extent of the fluctuations in production of durable equipment or construction resulting from changes in the demand for products made therewith depends partly upon the amount of the stock of these capital goods per unit of the finished product, the extent to which this ratio is maintained throughout the subsequent changes in demand for finished goods, and the assumptions made as to replacement of the durable capital goods in any given situation.

If capital goods are infinitely durable and no replacement is necessary and if there is a one-to-one ratio as between the current demand for finished products and stock of capital goods and building facilities, then changes in the demand for finished products will exactly match changes in the new capital facilities needed (if no idle capacity exists). The relation between the demand for finished products and the changes in demand for capital goods and building for their production will therefore represent merely the relation between changes in a total flow and changes in the increment of that flow. In any such relationship of aggregate change and differential change, we come upon the familiar principle of larger percentual changes in the differences than in the aggregates and the further principle that the former changes will tend to precede in their turning points and directions the changes in the aggregates.

There is nothing mysterious about these statistical characteristics, but a good deal of difficulty has surrounded the presentation of these principles through certain more or less hidden assumptions as to the ratio of the stock of capital goods to the demand for their products, the necessity for replacement, and intermediate changes that may occur in these elements. In actual cases, there are so many irregularities and psychological, financial, and other peculiarities entering into the relationship that it is dangerous to generalize these principles into any proposition capable of being used to explain the variations in the business cycle as a whole. In fact, statistical evidence indicates that even in particular industries the expected behavior of production of capital goods and structures in the face of changes in the demand for their products does not often verify the assumed hypotheses.

for a product tends to bring about not merely a tapering off in the production of the capital goods and plants associated with that article but an actual *reduction* in the creation of *new* plant. Hence the cyclical movements are not only more violent but tend to be more sensitive in changing direction than in the case of the pattern of ultimate demand itself. In view of the relationship thus existing (at least in theory) between demand for product and demand for capital equipment, it cannot be safely argued that the ups and downs in the creation of equipment of this type serve primarily to *explain* the changes in demand for consumer goods and other finished products. To be sure, they may serve to explain why a movement in the business cycle may accelerate cumulatively for a time and generate *still further* changes in some given direction. In this special sense the use of complicated mechanism and elaborate industrial plant in making fabricated goods probably contributes occasionally to more instability in the flow of industrial activity as a whole than might otherwise be the case. It serves as an amplifier and spreader of such changes in general buying power as are somehow already being produced *by other primary forces*.

We are now in search of these other "independent" forces. One of them obviously is found in the swings of residential building, depending upon the movement of people and major changes in rate of growth of population and occurring in several large areas at about the same time and in the same direction. It is important to distinguish between the long cycles of residential building and urban land development, on the one hand, and fluctuations in the creation of industrial plant and equipment, on the other. There is always the temptation, repeatedly seen in recent economic and political literature, to place most of the blame for business and industrial instability upon the *manufacturing* industries, especially in the capital-goods field. Here, to be sure, we do find wide variations from year to year in output and employment. The tendency is natural to associate these broad swings of activity, translating themselves into wide variations in the buying power of wage earners, with the failure of management in these industries to adopt a more stable course in their plans and operations. Unfortunately, most of these segments of industry are *unable* to adjust themselves to a stable course for the very reason that the things that they produce are made to order and cannot be made to stock; orders come to the makers of capital goods in a highly irregular cyclical pattern that exposes these industries to conditions exceedingly difficult to control. It is literally a feast one year and a famine the next.

Much misunderstanding has been created through the tendency to argue about this type of industrial production as though it were concerned with the making of staple materials or identical units of things. But most complex production material or mechanism is made to order, to fit into certain particular uses, and until these are defined and specifications drawn up in detail, few manufacturers of capital equipment dare to produce for stock and thus attempt to stabilize their production. If they make machine tools, they must await exact specifications. Even if we are considering the simpler tools or materials, such as the metals, there is no way of knowing the proportions in which they are to be produced to serve future requirements in production or construction.

In the case of the industrial plant, it is impossible for such construction to be made speculatively very far ahead of actual need, and the usual tendency of business concerns is to add a little here and a little there as the need requires. There is, of course, always a speculative fringe of enterprise stumbling into difficulties through blind enthusiasm, taking long chances with structural expansion, but the activities of the urban land speculator and the speculative house builder have no real counterpart in the industrial field. These specialized characteristics may be seen even among the raw and semifabricated industrial materials. Steel, for example, is not just steel; the popular term applies to a wide variety of highly technical combinations of iron, carbon, and numerous possible alloys, designed for particular uses in particular places. And when steel is formed into semifabricated shapes, these are primarily "tailor-made" products incapable of being made to stock. The demand for them is variable, for reasons lying entirely outside of the steel-making industry.

In order, therefore, to discover the ultimate reasons for relatively wide variation in the flow of demand that impinges not only upon makers of building material (including industrial and commercial buildings) and almost all the durable goods utilized in manufacturing, we must endeavor to locate the moving forces of an originating character—those that are not primarily merely resultants of changes in the industrial cycle, magnified through the magic glass of "rates of change."

TECHNOLOGICAL INNOVATIONS AND PLANT CREATION

Where shall we find other types of economic activity capable of exercising a disturbing influence upon demand and production, which are not merely resultants of their vagaries? It might be suggested that invention, innovation, technological change might point the way to what we are seeking. Consider the infinite number of improvements resulting from the discovery of new methods of making things that have crowded one upon another in the past century of dramatic economic progress. It would appear almost commonplace that technological advances tend to be unsettling, since they involve the scrapping of old processes and familiar materials as new ones capture the field.

Joseph A. Schumpeter has developed in interesting fashion the thought that these production innovations constitute the most important source of those "external" forces that impinge upon business system and bring about dislocations, waves of promotion, economic excess, human failings, and hence an essentially irregular course in general business growth over the years.   This seems plausible as well as fascinating as we review the colorful succession of these new contributions, new methods, new industries arising from patient experiment or adventitious discovery by someone impatient with old ways.   But as we carefully analyze these innovations, we fail to see conclusive reasons why most of these technical changes that are important from a scientific and technological point of view should necessarily generate broad *simultaneous* cyclical disturbance in the entire industrial system.   That system, as it has evolved in American experience, or, for that matter, the experience of any other advanced nation, is a sturdy fabric, highly resistant to disturbances that originate here or there within its own expanse.   It requires very considerable impetus *along a wide front* to distort that general dynamic pattern.   It requires the existence of changes somehow affecting the financial filaments in the fabric, whose strength and soundness largely condition the strength and evenness of the whole.

Technical innovations appear, in fact, to be in most cases localized and specialized as they affect a product or a process.   As improved machinery, for example, becomes available for the making of shoes, the shoe industry feels the effects, and they are transmitted throughout the economy, but with net results that are so diffused as to be almost imperceptible, even though in one or two localities, where shoemaking happens to be concentrated, there may be appreciable and long-continued effects of such an innovation.   Occasionally an invention, such as the electric light, provides a basis for an important new industry whose development sustains and even accelerates for a time the general drift of all industry because of a cluster of related electrical developments associated with this one far-reaching improvement.   Frequently such innovations stimulate activity that, however, is canceled by the decay of obsolescent product or method.   We notice the rise of the new in its engaging and spectacular aspects, but we forget the old and fail to take account of its fading from the picture.   Let it be granted that occasionally an innovator, as Schumpeter has persuasively argued, may develop some new product or device capable of accelerating a boom already in progress or hastening cyclical collapse in the early stage of a topheavy situation existing through a broad segment of industry.[1]

[1] See his "Business Cycles: A Theoretical, Historical, and Statistical Analysis of the Capitalist Process," New York, 1939.   Schumpeter has taken pains to explain that "innovation" is a much broader term than "invention" and has to do with the

Schumpeter's hypotheses emphasize the manner in which "innovations" in industry broaden themselves by the tendency of many minds to copy and then rapidly exploit an original innovation, once its practical potentialities are apparent. Important innovations "tend to cluster, to come about in bunches, simply because first some, and then most, firms follow in the wake of successful innovation."[1] Schumpeter further states: "Innovations are not at any time distributed over the whole economic system at random, but tend to concentrate in certain sectors and their surroundings."[2] He recognizes the possibility that some innovations, particularly in the basic and durable-goods industries, may occasionally bring about changes of exceptional consequence by propagating a cumulative series of new developments and adaptations all along the line, but the hypothesis lacks the support of convincing detail.

THE OUTSTANDING POTENCY OF TRANSPORTATION DEVELOPMENT

It is at this point that the writer believes it desirable to venture more specific propositions to differentiate the really *important* innovations from those that remain localized and of no *general* significance as disturbing factors or generators of far-reaching cyclical movements in production and trade. *The thesis is that of all the innovations bearing upon durable capital equipment, those tend to be outstandingly important in their effect upon general economic stability and pervasive in geographic scope that have to do with methods of transportation.*

Keeping in mind that construction of transportation facilities differs in the matter of degree rather than in kind from other durable capital, let us proceed to examine why major innovations in this particular field of enterprise have been so important as an originating factor in general industrial fluctuations. Let us fully recognize at the start that there may be self-reinforcing tendencies in the process; that is, the impulses may react upon themselves and reinforce each other rather than operating

---

actual development and incorporation into the economic system of new ways of doing things, not merely with the incident of discovery or the determination that a new device is workable. He shows also (*op. cit.*, p. 85) that inventions and innovations, too, may at times result from an economic situation that creates an immediate need for some new material or process or product. Schumpeter also regards innovation, in the broad sense in which he uses the term, as an *internal* economic factor, mainly operating in conjunction with existing factors of production, rather than an *external* factor impinging *upon* economic dynamics. In other words, innovations are part of the fabric and are integrally involved in the evolution of capitalistic processes. They express the way in which evolution involves the combining of various factors in new ways. They are the elements that defy the ever-potential tendency toward diminishing returns from enterprise.

[1] *Ibid.*, p. 100.
[2] *Ibid.*, p. 101.

unilaterally. To some extent, and at various times, creation of new transportation equipment may be directly a function of, or resultant from, the oscillations of the minor business cycle itself. But there are good reasons for believing that *basic* improvements in transportation apparatus are likely to stand apart in their power at certain stages and under certain conditions to affect the course of production, trade, speculation, and finance in unmistakable and characteristic fashion.

The wide use of mechanism to enable industry to provide an infinite variety and expanding quantity of useful goods is but an example of the intricate division of labor, clearly set forth by Adam Smith in his "Wealth of Nations." Adam Smith pointed out that the division of labor is always limited by the extent of the market, which, in turn, involves the extent and efficiency of the means of transport. Manufacture exists by virtue of the transport system that connects its manifold units. Economic progress is inconceivable without parallel improvement in means of communication. Since transportation is fundamental in expanding the scope of trade and the efficiency of all production, a major innovation likely to prove successful in a practical way has far-reaching effects and can produce profound and violent expansion if developed under the stimulus of unrestrained speculative promotion.

It should be kept in mind that we are primarily concerned with the initial phases of structural development, that is, with the production of transportation equipment marking various stages of technical innovation. The ups and downs in demand for units of such equipment, once the general structure embodies the results of improvement or has adapted itself to the population throughout a newly settled area, will obviously result mainly from changes in conditions originating from many conceivable minor causes. We shall have occasion presently to examine fluctuations in what may be called the "replacement demand" for transport equipment, which have interesting characteristics but are not pertinent to this discussion. During most of the nineteenth century the outstanding phase of transportation development was clearly the application of steam power to the railway and the construction of a vast railway network over an expanding domain. These occurred in response to waves of growth and movement in population and the local concentration of population that we have already seen to have been such potent factors in originating major building cycles. We shall presently illustrate the interrelation between the major cycles of building construction and those associated historically with the developments in transport construction.

Using the railroad as the basis of our analysis, let us first consider some of the peculiarities of this type of transport that appear capable of making the construction phase, in conjunction with the very similar, *although not identical*, major waves in building activity, so potent in generating cyclical movements in industrial production generally. In its physical aspects a railroad system, representing the application of steam power to land movement of commodities and passengers, involves massive units of structures and equipment. Unlike water transport, an elaborate, specially prepared roadbed is necessary. Canals, supplementing rivers and lakes, whose development marked the decade prior to the first successful steam locomotives, were construction projects of a relatively simple type, involving no such complex fabricating operations and facilities as were needed for metal tracks. They were limited, too, with respect to the size of the carrying unit, the small canal boat. The use of steam locomotives afforded transportation plus speed, and speed required a roadbed that early took the form of iron rails laid upon stone and later upon ties and ballast. With increasing size of locomotives generating tremendous power, not only speed but tremendous carrying capacity per train marked a clear departure from any previous form of transportation. This is extremely important and has not been enough emphasized in connection with the railroad as a peculiar contribution to transportation technique. As locomotives were made more powerful, cars became larger, and tracks became heavier and were made of steel; the bridges, terminal facilities, and, of course, the engines themselves required new production techniques.

These features of the railroad meant a hundred years ago that the capital necessary for a railroad company was destined to be of an order quite out of focus with the normal capital needs of early American business, although naturally this was not clearly recognized at the beginning of the development. It is not sufficient to say that railroads require large capital because of the massive nature of their plant requirements. Many industries share this feature. The precise point that is important is that the capital necessary to accomplish *a minimum* of railroad service, under the control of a given management, is probably larger than for any other type of economic effort. There is, in fact, a minimum size of railroad unit that conditions the success of any given segment in the network. In fact, a railroad network is composed of segments that in themselves are units of considerable dimensions.

In the case of large manufacturing industries there are many cases in which the industrial plant may be of relatively modest size. Transportation necessarily involves space and extent, and if the roadbed supporting the movement of heavy equipment must be carried over a broad expanse of territory, over bridges, through cuts and tunnels, the material needed cannot be less than is sufficient to bring the line all the way from point of origin to point of destination. It cannot operate in small pieces. Nor is that all. It is necessary to develop service to adjacent "feeder" areas, and there is the constant temptation to expand the area served too rapidly. From a somewhat different point of view, this matter of area is of primary importance. Railroad networks were developed in many parts of this country more or less simultaneously as various sections attracted new people, and improvements in methods and design involved a wide extent of activity with sweeping effect upon the building industry and all the numerous material and equipment industries. Thus enormous capital requirements went hand in hand with far-flung structural promotion. This is merely another way of saying that the coming of the railroad was not merely the beginning of a major industry; it was a superindustry and was capable of stamping its own pattern of violently irregular growth upon the whole economy.

The railroad and, indeed, other forms of transportation as well have another important characteristic. Flexibility is lacking. The railroad tends toward rigidity from the standpoint of diversion of plant to alternative uses. A railroad line, once established, may readily equip itself to serve a developing community with varying proportions of freight and passenger transport and varying proportions among the different types of freight, express, etc. But it is limited in its structural facilities to the work of transportation. If adequate traffic does not develop, it is exceedingly difficult to adapt the plant to other profitable uses. If a railroad is successful and has been well planned and soundly financed, it is likely to be *exceedingly* successful.

In fabricating industries and in commercial operations, there is usually a wide range of potential adaptation of equipment to alternative uses or products, but this is not true of transportation. Ships and aircraft admit of considerably greater flexibility than railroads, for ships and planes can be moved about, and even their terminals are not difficult to construct or relocate. Railroads have terminals that are more elaborate than those of ship lines or air lines. A railroad, therefore, is in a material sense a massive unit, spreading its plant over a wide geographic area, and its initial development naturally has simultaneous effect upon many places and many industries. The effect can be astonishingly constructive or, again, disastrous, since a road has little chance of success if it fails to tap an adequate amount of traffic within a reasonable period after its construction.

PROMOTIONAL FINANCING OF THE RAILROADS

The foregoing peculiarities of the railroad have not been given adequate consideration in economic discussions, and we are therefore emphasizing them.[1] In addition to these basic and inescapable characteristics

[1] Most economic treatises on railroads are essentially discussions of *rate* problems and theories—a natural result of the preoccupation of traditional static economics with *prices* as the central topic.

of railroads, there are some incidental features of the development of the railroad network in this country. The difficulties of securing sufficient capital for projects of such enormous magnitude appeared at an early date, and they have stamped themselves upon the railroad enterprise ever since. These difficulties had already been experienced in the case of the canals, whose development was active following the conclusion of the War of 1812–1814. Our early corporations received charters to build turn-pikes and bridges and to improve roads, but the canals represented a larger order of enterprise that did not prove too successful under private control and promotion. Hence we find that the successful canals of any importance were those constructed by the States of New York, Pennsylvania, Virginia, and Maryland. The Erie Canal, completed according to initial plans in 1825, was so successful that it quickly stimulated other State Governments to emulate it, and several ambitious state enterprises continued to flourish or flounder during the next two decades.

The States played an important part in financing or subsidizing these forms of transportation development, because British capital could be readily obtained through investment in the obligations of the State Governments, even though most private projects were not then attractive to British investors.[1] The marked success of the Erie Canal and the apparent soundness of state finances, at least as far as the 1830's, finally induced some investment of British capital directly in railroad building. During the 1840's, State activity in developing public works was carried to excess, particularly among the Southern States. This marked virtually the end of public enthusiasm for comprehensive transportation development under State Government authority. It also tended to shift foreign-capital investment from state obligations to the securities of the new railroads.

The Federal Government, as early as 1806, had begun to carry out the policies of Jefferson and Gallatin in undertaking such projects as the Cumberland Road, for which large amounts of money were spent in 1819 and in the middle 'thirties. But it is a curious fact that just as the vast new development of railway building was getting under way, political considerations in the sense of the shifting toward reformism (*cf.* Chapter 3) forced the Federal Government to stand aside. Andrew Jackson, as early as 1829, his first year as President, expressed an almost fanatical determination to hold the Federal Government aloof from any public works at the very time when wise and far-seeing policies for the super-

---

[1] In addition, the states received from the Federal Government a percentage of the receipts from sale of national land and used this income for their internal improvements. Thus public land booms directly helped to finance local government construction booms. See J. B. Sanborn, *Congressional Grants of Land in Aid of Railways, Wisconsin University Bulletin, Economic Series*, Vol. II, No. 3, 1899.

vision and coordination of the complex financial problem of railroad building might have averted serious difficulties. Jackson feared, and there was doubtless some reason for his fear, that the National Government might become the unwitting source of huge subsidies and contributions to salvage the results of reckless promotion; he was determined to reduce and, if possible, extinguish the national debt rather than expand it for such purposes. It was his conviction that if the Government was to be helpful along economic and financial lines its aid should be to small businessmen engaged in "healthy competition," and particularly to the farmers, whose problems he thought that he especially understood. There was too a Constitutional aspect. Jackson was disposed to interpret the principle of "States' rights" literally and narrowly.

In 1835, therefore, at the very time that the Federal Government debt was being practically paid off, the States were beginning to enter upon a course of extravagant financial aid to all types of transportation projects, but in the following decade there came a shocking repudiation of State debt and several years of utter financial demoralization. Thereafter the field was wide open to private enterprise and private capital, much of it obtained from abroad. During the succeeding years the course of railroad development in the United States followed a course somewhat analogous to the development of the British railways, in considerable contrast to the more restrained and politically determined course on the Continent of Europe.

With the field thrown open to individual promoters, it is important to recognize the peculiar nature of the incentive that prompted the venturesome to undertake railroad projects. The men who built the railroads were not primarily transportation experts. They represented in the main aggressive individuals who had amassed some wealth in shipping, stock speculation, or merchandising. They were men who shrewdly sensed the inherent characteristics of railroad transportation as a source of enormous gain. Steam transport over rails was soon accepted as sound in principle and likely in the long run to be economically successful. The early roads were short lines serving limited areas, but each little road, as it connected rapidly growing towns and cities, opened up brilliant and limitless prospects such as no other type of enterprise could possibly have done.

The basic element in this bonanza was land—superlative opportunities for speculation in land values certain to be created by new lines of communication not only in the terminal areas but along the lines themselves. Those who had some experience in property dealing and who keenly envisaged the probable course of trade, industrial, and agricultural expansion found it attractive to enter the ranks of the railroad builders, even though they may have been unfamiliar with the first principles of transportation engineering, economics, or even finance. Merchants in thriving cities who had been using their accumulating capital in real-estate ventures, town-lot subdivisions, and the like were instantly attracted to this new means of exploiting potential land values. The promoters of the Illinois Central, in the 1850's, "placed lands which were likely to increase in value with the building of the railroad in their own name or in that of their Illinois Land Association. Station sites were kept secret until the Association had bought the land."[1] It was entirely natural that British investors looked upon this project as a "land company" rather than a railroad. Even after the Civil War, Jay Cooke was fully as much interested in capitalizing upon property values in Duluth as in the success of the Northern Pacific. Many other instances of the sort could be cited.

The early railroads were financed by small groups that were able with much effort to attract local capital and foreign capital only after the roads had been put into what appeared to be successful operation. Since the stakes were high, in view of the auxiliary attractions of land-value enhancement, it was natural that many more short lines would be built than could be financially solvent. This opened up a new field for those who found that they could derive advantage by purchasing small roads and selling them to the larger roads at a profit. Abundant opportunity was presented to put a struggling railroad venture in a difficult position, then purchase it cheaply, and finally sell it to another line. Selling property of all kinds to railroads became one of the great sources of promotional wealth. Even the builders of some of the railroads, including the Union Pacific, formed auxiliary companies, known as "construction" companies, which nominally sold construction to the railroad—that is, to the stockholders—at inflated prices. Throughout the railroad-development period such methods continued virtually unchecked and unsupervised and were clouded in secrecy, since most of the promoters took the view that roads were not primarily built to serve the public.[2]

[1] K. T. Healy, "The Economics of Transportation in America," p. 101, New York, 1940.

[2] "From the moment a railroad company was formed, it fought for its existence in a world characteristized by anarchy and chaos. Despite the fact that transportation companies invited public subscriptions to their securities and were of a quasi-public nature, the only inviolable law was that of self-preservation. Common concepts of everyday honesty and fairness were ignored. Most of the great systems had been built by fraudulent construction companies, and if perchance a road had been honestly built, there was always an opportunity to correct this oversight by disreputable, but highly profitable, manipulation of its securities. Often railway companies were managed, or rather mismanaged, not with an eye to fulfilling their functions as transportation facilities, but solely with a view to making money from speculations in

As the railroads developed into distinct systems and their access to capital funds was widened, they were able to undertake bolder steps in constructing track far ahead of population movement or traffic requirements. Unlike most ventures in merchandising or manufacturing, the railroad builders in the decades following the Civil War were captivated by the very long-term outlook for their projected lines, and plans were made for distinct objectives and vast growth. The tendency was to jump over thousands of miles, whereas the pioneers of the 'forties and 'fifties had proceeded by hundreds. This tendency to overcapitalize the distant future and to invest enormous sums in the hope of remote return has probably been characteristic of all private railroad enterprise the world over.

These tendencies toward overbuilding were accentuated by a change in policy of the Federal Government during the Civil War. Congress, beginning in 1862, approved a number of land grants to assist construction of the Union Pacific, the Central Pacific, and several other roads. This tended to overstimulate these undertakings still more, although adequate financing might otherwise have been difficult at the time. Thus, when the Federal Government did step obliquely into the picture, it contributed essentially nothing to eliminate excesses and financial abuses that flourished in most of these projects on a scale probably not to be found in any other segment of our industry and trade.

The cycles of urban real-estate promotion and the cycles of railroad building, as well as all transportation development, have been closely interrelated in that both have responded to the underlying changes in population growth and investment. New communication facilities stimulated movement and the growth of new cities; the prospect of this growth, in turn, afforded the primary incentive for new transportation service and its elaborate physical equipment. The two phases of development are, indeed, of a single pattern.[1] In this pattern we discern the simple truth that shelter and transport are equally basic and ele-

---

their securities." (E. G. Campbell, "The Reorganization of the American Railroad System, 1893–1900," p. 15, New York, 1938.

[1] "The chief ultimate importance of the canal, the lake traffic, and the plank roads was that they gave Chicago sufficient advantages to attract the railroads, whose importance in making Chicago a great wholesale and manufacturing center and in causing a tremendous rise in its land values far transcended any other single factor. . . . From 1852 to 1853 the population of Chicago increased from 38,754 to 60,666 and half the population in the latter year was foreign born. Most of this increased population was poured into the city by the railroads. . . . As a result of the heavy volume of European immigrants and homeseekers from the East coming West on the railroads to Chicago, the city grew rapidly in population to 80,000 in 1855, a seven-fold increase in the decade since 1845." (Homer Hoyt, "One Hundred Years of Land Values in Chicago," pp. 54, 62.)

mental human needs. The promotional instability of house building and real-estate development superimposed on the high leverage arising from variable rates of change has in the past stemmed from the speculative motives and limited competence of small local enterprise. The equally pronounced cyclical vagaries of *transportation* construction have stemmed from the extraordinary opportunities for direct and indirect profit motivating pioneer capitalists and ultimately huge corporations whose financial structures, as the result of their historical development, have peculiar elements of weakness and instability. But so fundamental is the demand for better and faster means of transport that it is not surprising to find innovation in transportation exerting such a profound effect upon manufacture of equipment and hence (as in building generally) upon the conditions in a wide range of manufacturing and fabricating industries.[1]

A MEASURE OF BUILDING AND TRANSPORT CYCLES

Having in mind the characteristics of transportation construction, we are now prepared to examine the results of these alternating waves of boom and collapse in terms of statistical measurements extending over a long period of years and including several other transportation elements. In Chart 30, we bring together a pattern of the annual fluctuation in building construction, transportation construction, and the index of general business activity from 1800 to 1940. This affords an opportunity to compare these measurements with the movements of commodity prices and to observe the various relationships during war periods. The solid black curve in the lower portion of the chart displays primarily the cycles of building construction, but during the early decades, beginning at 1800, the index is based upon transactions in land only, representing the cyclical fluctuations in the acreage sales of the public lands until 1832, when these are averaged with the cycles of building as measured in the Riggleman index down to 1839.

Thereafter the index represents urban building in terms of computed volume, adjusted for the long-term trend. The dashed curve is an index of transportation construction, including the major types of equipment. It is intended to measure the annual fluctuation about the growth trend of railroad building throughout the course of that experience and, in

---

[1] It is an interesting fact that of the enterprises incorporated between 1783 and 1800, two-thirds represented some type of transportation facility. (Joseph S. Davis, "Essays in the Earlier History of American Corporations," *Harvard Economic Studies* 16, Cambridge, 1917, Vol. II, p. 22.) Of all the special charters for business corporations in Pennsylvania from 1800 to 1860, 64 per cent represented charters for transportation enterprises. (William Miller, A Note on the History of Business Corporations in Pennsylvania, 1800–1860, *Quarterly Journal of Economics*, November, 1940.)

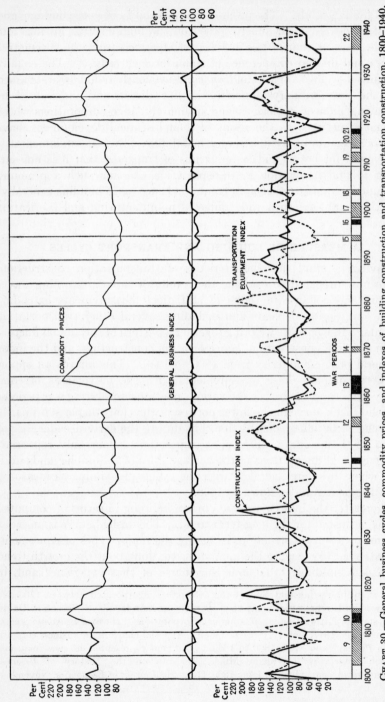

CHART 30.—General business cycles, commodity prices, and indexes of building construction and transportation construction, 1800–1940. All curves are drawn to uniform arithmetic scales to permit comparison of the cyclical fluctuations. For description of data see Appendix 6. For identification of war periods see Note 2, Chart 7.

addition, to show the cyclical movements in production of other types of transportation facility, in terms of equipment, prior to the railroad era, and to include the development of the automobile industry after 1900. From 1800 to 1831, the transportation index measures the cyclical movements in shipbuilding only. Beginning with the railroad era, the shipbuilding cycles and changes in miles of railroad track laid down are merged together as far as 1839. During the succeeding period, until 1899, the index traces the course of railroad development only, in terms of track built and new equipment ordered. From 1900 to 1940, railroad equipment and automobile production are combined with appropriate weights. Thus the index, throughout its course, portrays the history of transportation-development fluctuations in terms of the three most important types for a century and a half.[1]

In the early years of the nineteenth century, there was much road-work, and manufacture of wagons was an important enterprise. But statistical facts relating to these aspects of transportation are very scanty. As for early navigation of the rivers and carriage of merchandise by ships along the coast or abroad, shipbuilding was the dominating form of enterprise all along the Atlantic seaboard. Since the available data include canal boats, the ups and downs in activity reflect all phases of transportation equipment having to do with water.

For years prior to the nineteenth century, the building of ships had been a leading industry in the American Colonies. "The coast from New York harbor to Eastport, Maine, was one long row of shipyards."[2] Shipbuilding was encouraged in Colonial days by British law, which long penalized the carrying of British trade in vessels constructed outside of the British Isles or the Colonies. Shipbuilding has always been peculiarly subject to the fortunes and exigencies of war. This is easily seen in the behavior of the transport index during the first decades of the nineteenth century, when foreign trade was subject to alternating intervals of peace and war and embargoes arising from the long campaign of the British allies against the French. The index reflects the brief foreign-trade revival of 1805 and the drastic embargoes against European commerce in 1807, 1808, and 1809. A sudden boom in 1810–1811 was followed by a deep depression in shipbuilding during our own conflict with Great Britain from 1812 to 1814. Following the return of peace in Europe in 1815, trade immediately became intensely active. American ships were in urgent demand to make up the heavy losses suffered during the war. "Everybody began to think of ships, and in less than a week

---

[1] See Appendix 6 for more detailed explanation of the methods used in preparing these indexes.

[2] Henry Hall, United States Census of 1880, Vol. VIII, p. 63.

after receipt of the news shipbuilding sprang into activity and every part of the coast engaged in the industry."[1]

Meanwhile, there was a burst of activity in the construction of canals, which had been held back by the long war and its uncertainties. By 1823, steamboats were beginning to multiply fast on the Mississippi River, and were ready for Atlantic crossings. This was a great industry, mainly dominated by small builders, some of whom appear to have been speculators constructing ships for future demand.[2] Many of the substantial merchants of the day were shipowners; Cornelius Vanderbilt and Daniel Drew, who played such an important part in later railroad ventures, built up their initial fortunes as shipowners. What is of particular interest is the violent gyration of shipbuilding from year to year and the suggestion of a speculative enterprise pecularily subject to fitful impulses created by war conditions. Following the great shipbuilding boom of 1815, there was a substantial decline, even though prior to 1820 there was a significant boom in land promotion. Conversely, in 1825 and 1826, with the completion of the Erie Canal and a vast boom in foreign trade following the opening up of Latin America upon gaining freedom from Spain, there was a pronounced boom in shipbuilding, and land speculation and, presumably, building activity were depressed. The astonishing height of the booms and depths of the depressions challenges attention. Compared with the very modest range of fluctuations in the index of general industry and trade, which is drawn on the same scale, transportation and building cycles are of a distinctive amplitude.

More important still is the relationship of the general business index to the transport and construction indexes from the standpoint of cycle patterns. An examination of Chart 30 discloses that after making due allowance for the wide difference in amplitude, the business-index fluctuations, in the main, indicate *the combined effect* of the somewhat *dissimilar* cyclical movements of the transport and building indexes.[3]

RELATION OF BUILDING-TRANSPORT CYCLES TO GENERAL BUSINESS CYCLES

The preceding analysis and that which immediately follows serve to support the basic proposition that the causal influences in the cyclical

[1] Hall, *op. cit.*, p. 62.

[2] See R. G. Albion, Early Nineteenth Century Shipowning, *Journal of Economic History*, May, 1941.

[3] We refer to the building index in the earlier period, measuring speculation in land, as a rough gauge of the related (but not measurable) activities in urban real estate and building construction. A comparison of the cycles of public land sales with the transportation of lumber or expenditure of the Federal Government for various types of public buildings and with the first few decades of Riggleman's building index all serve to support this interpretation.

variation run predominantly *from* the transport and property cycles *to* the cyclical movements of industry and trade. This does not, however, exclude the possibility that there is some interaction among the factors and that certain phases of transportation development particularly have occasionally been given impetus, upward or downward, by fluctuations in general business conditions or circumstances in the credit system at home or abroad closely associated therewith. Another important point that may be drawn from this chart is that during periods of war, particularly when a major war has directly affected the United States, the foregoing relationships are less clearly defined. There enter into the situation complex political factors and the play of price inflation, which independently affect all the indexes and at times produce divergent patterns.

The effect of war disturbances in delaying plans for important structural undertakings has a direct bearing upon the cyclical pattern. As has already been set forth in preceding chapters, wars of any magnitude or duration have always meant inflationary price trends that militate against long-term investment in fixed capital projects associated with land transportation or urban property, even though these movements at the same time have had a stimulating effect upon land speculation in agriculture. The forces that lead farmers to expand their debt during these wartime inflation periods usually have a diametrically opposite effect on other forms of land and property speculation. Conversely, when wars end and prices begin to decline there tends to be a sudden dramatic release of pent-up, accumulated demand for these building and transportation facilities. This is capable of initiating a strong postwar boom in these directions, *despite* declining commodity prices or more probably *because* of a broad shifting of purchasing power toward the cities and a dilution of available capital funds carried over from the usually extravagant public financing accompanying any major war.[1]

[1] Joseph S. Davis, in his "Essays in the Earlier History of American Corporations," Vol. II, p. 7, has the following interesting remarks concerning the situation at the close of the eighteenth century, following the Revolutionary War. "Capital, accumulated during the War by many members of the community, was available for investment; fortunes in property other than real estate were undoubtedly larger than before the War. The disbanding of the army set free a labor supply, and throngs of immigrants rapidly added largely to it. The War had done much to bring into mutual acquaintance men of business acumen and property, had forced some experience in cooperative activity, and had necessitated the exercise of ingenuity in a thousand directions." Another striking instance of financial resources accelerating postwar activities in construction was the accumulation of British capital after the Napoleonic Wars had been concluded and the search for investment opportunities in all directions. The fall of interest rates following the tight money market so characteristic of most wars in the past took the form in this case of conversion by the British Government of 5 per cent obligations into 4 per cents and then into 3½ per cents, so that capital was

Still another aspect of war conditions, looked at particularly from the standpoint of Europe, is the evidence that following major wars there has been an accentuated tendency for Europeans to emigrate to the New World. A considerable part of the immigration from Europe in the 1830's, the 1850's, and the 1880's resulted from political factors reflecting the effect of war conditions. The close relation between land booms and the major waves of immigration has already been illustrated.

We may now return to Chart 30 and trace in more detail the course of the transport-construction indexes, beginning with the 1830's. The great boom, culminating in 1836, can be understood only in terms of the vast movements of population from the Eastern section over the Alleghenies into the rich new areas opened up by the Erie Canal and the improved roads and turnpikes to the West. Immigration was a minor stimulating factor during this period. After the postwar depression of the 1820's had run its course, the movement of people accelerated. "There began to be a serious exodus to the western country. The roads were filled with moving families and almost entire neighborhoods moved west. Fertile land at low prices[1] was abundant, and speculators were numerous. Under this credit system men became loaded with large land purchases, expecting to make sale of a portion at an early date to incoming immigrants at an advance, and to hold the remainder for themselves."[2]

Andrew Jackson's evident intention to discontinue the Second United States Bank was known as early as 1830, and the prospective disappearance of this moderating influence in pioneer shoestring banking created a most extraordinary profusion of banks, bank notes, and bank credit, which assisted the land promoters to capitalize upon the movement of people between 1830 and 1836. But in July of that year President Jackson dashed cold water upon the speculative orgy by suddenly demanding that Federal lands would henceforth be paid for only in hard coin. The boom immediately collapsed. But while it lasted it was sufficiently vigorous to have a pronounced effect upon commodity prices, an effect, indeed, that has never been witnessed before or since, save in wartime. As this boom broke it carried with it the price of cotton and a serious demoralization of income in the Southern States, leading, as we have seen, to a repudiation of state debt. This tended to obstruct the

---

all the more eager to flow across the Atlantic to engage in our ventures at a much higher rate.

[1] After 1820, public land was sold at auction or on a cash basis at low prices. The Federal Government accepted the notes of the State Banks, and in return the latter freely accepted United States Treasury notes. War veterans were given scrip that was transferable and greatly assisted not only land ownership but land speculation.

[2] *U.S. Executive Documents*, 46th Congress, Third Session, p. 202.

willingness of both domestic and British capital to supply funds for the new railway ventures. London became skeptical of American finance, but nevertheless railroad building continued to be much more active than property development or building as far as 1841. Between 1842 and 1845 every phase of American business was in deep depression.

By this time, however, a new wave of European immigration had begun. This was perhaps the most pronounced of all the mass movements from Europe during the century. Beginning shortly after 1845, the movement lasted until 1854, forming the underlying influence for a new major cycle of expansion in real-estate operations and building activity as well as construction of the railroad network.[1] During the 1850's railway construction was resumed in earnest in the Southern States, following Federal Government aid in the form of direct land grants to the Illinois Central. Meanwhile, the Pennsylvania Railroad had received important assistance from the State and by 1852 had reached Pittsburgh. By 1853 there was railroad connection from Buffalo to Chicago. The discovery of gold on the Pacific Coast in 1848 was a contributing factor to the general boom atmosphere. The brief War with Mexico caused but slight temporary interruption. Paralleling these expansive conditions here was a condition of easy credit and rapid financial expansion in Great Britain. By 1853 a great wave of real-estate and building promotions swept the Midwest. "In the cities," says Hickernell, "speculators built large numbers of dwelling houses with borrowed money and were generally able to resell quickly at a handsome profit."[2]

Finally came the Crimean War (1854–1855), creating a temporary tightening of finance and signs of apprehension in the British financial market. There was revelation of unsavory practices in the management of the railroads that affected confidence. But the real collapse of the boom did not come until 1857, when it was accentuated by the greatly overextended condition of the Eastern banks and obviously excessive property development and railroad construction that had created many unsound, inflated, manipulated, and otherwise vulnerable situations. Each of the great booms in the basic transport-building factors has had this effect. Some of these ventures were soundly conceived, even including railroad companies, but each boom carried with it many unsound, dishonest, and visionary projects, and the higher it soared the more the imminent difficulties facing these marginal projects served as a menace to the rest. Each boom, in other words, tended to reach a level where

---

[1] The principal European factors accounting for this extraordinary wave of migration were the crop failures in Ireland and the revolutionary disturbances in many parts of Europe.

[2] W. F. Hickernell, "Financial and Business Forecasting," Vol. I, p. 248, New York, 1928.

qualitative as well as *quantitative* aspects became important.   At the top level the dissolution of these booms seems to have been brought about by the more topheavy ventures, which only boom impetus and atmosphere can generate and finance.

Conversely, in the trough of the great depressions following the boom, it has been the shrewd activity of the most conservative and the more solidly financed capitalists and promoters that came into play.   They absorbed the properties in liquidation at absurdly low prices and initiated the foundations for a new wave of expansion.   In the case of the railroads, this process is clearly evident in each of the major depressions of the last century.   Railway properties were put together in a way that represented in many instances sound physical assets but highly unsound capitalization.   Those who commanded adequate funds of their own had extraordinary opportunities for acquiring distressed properties at a profit when their nominal values shrunk amazingly during the periods of foreclosure and receivership.   And in these periods, such was the strain on general confidence, credit, and trade that impairment of a far-reaching character was inevitable.

Following a secondary peak in railroad expansion in 1856, there occurred a general deterioration in capital enterprise, lasting throughout the Civil War period.   With the exception of work done on the Union Pacific, the major cycle of property and railroad development remained at a very low ebb.   General industrial conditions, however, as is to be expected in some war years, responded to the demands of the military forces.   So far as building was concerned, the Civil War had the effect of deferring expansion and improvements.   Both in this instance and later, during World War I, the military emergency occurred after the major cycle of building had already been reversing for several years. It is therefore not easy on the available evidence to generalize concerning the probable effect of a major war upon building and real-estate development.   In view, however, of the swift recuperation in this field as soon as peace was restored, both in the case of the Civil War and after World War I, there is reason to believe that war uncertainties, the high urban cost of living, and the siphoning of available capital into Government securities all had the effect of postponing or deferring structural activity. But by the same token the subsequent recuperation developed a much more powerful and extended momentum than would otherwise have existed.

Following the Civil War, conditions in the South remained desperately bad for decades, and recuperation throughout the country was not particularly rapid.   The Civil War left a heritage of dubious political experimentations and meddling with the financial machinery, which delayed the recovery of long-term enterprise.   Therefore the cycles in building and railroad construction that developed after 1865 were of relatively modest proportions. It was in this interval that the so-called "Granger" railroad lines were projected and the transcontinental network was extended to the Pacific Coast. In 1862 the settlement of the remaining Federal lands was facilitated by the Homestead Act, but this, in turn, delayed the sales of the railroad land that had been obtained by Federal or State grants and thus somewhat slowed down the progress of railway expansion.

During these years the smaller roads were incorporated into larger systems, usually with an ample amount of manipulation and financial sleight of hand, hidden from the public gaze by the absence of effective requirements as to corporate publicity. The activities of the larger promoters now shifted to efforts to control systems of considerable size. The builders of the Union Pacific were reaping a harvest of profits from the Crédit Mobilier, a cleverly conceived "construction" company designed for easy and certain profits to the directors. But this period of unwholesome, even though impressive, formation of railroad systems was interrupted by the Franco-German War, which temporarily restricted British participation in financing. There were also the impairment of many insurance companies by the Chicago fire of 1871 and the exposure, with ill effects upon the financial community, of glaring corruption and manipulation of railroad enterprises by such adventurers as Jay Cooke, James Fiske, Daniel Drew, and Jay Gould.[1]

As a result of so much railway construction far ahead of the traffic and absorption of short segments into integrated systems, with consequent overexpansion of capitalization, some roads were beginning to pay their interest by new borrowings. Financial structures became decidedly vulnerable. With banking reserves rather short and credits inadequate to handle a crisis, the scene was set for the memorable panic of 1873, and the long-ensuing depression, especially marked in the farming areas, naturally extended to all industry. During the uncertain years of the middle 1870's British capital was frightened away from American investments, since it was not known whether the farmer-greenback-inflation element was to dominate the money system or whether the Civil War paper would actually be redeemed in gold. But the Resumption Act of 1875 inspired more confidence, and a successful issue of government bonds in London led the way to resumption of railroad building at a terrific pace. This was indeed one of the most spectacular of all the railroad booms. It culminated with the construction of 11,000 odd miles of track in the single year 1882. In this case the railroad

[1] A very readable and substantially accurate account of railroad finance and its relation to our ramshackle banking system will be found in W. F. Hickernell's "Financial and Business Forecasting," Vol. I.

boom was not closely followed in its pattern by recuperation in building operations, which appeared to be awaiting the stimulating effect of larger immigration from abroad. In due course this developed between 1878 and 1882.

In the meantime, railroad capital was again at work, and the developers were active, seeking control of larger and larger systems to satisfy more and more grandiose ambitions. Huge stock dividends appeared in the early 1880's, but at the same time savage rate wars were springing up between competing systems. The more reckless promoters were busy with all manner of schemes contributing to the overcapitalization of railway lines. Hence the financial strain of 1883 and 1884, rather acute in London, found numerous weak spots here. Meanwhile, however, in spite of the setbacks in 1884 and 1885, urban building conditions were improving, and this phase of expansion appears to have been sufficiently powerful and widespread to serve as a sustaining factor permitting a secondary railroad boom to occur in 1887, when the first Federal regulatory efforts began in the establishment of the Interstate Commerce Commission.

Building development reached its peak in 1890 or shortly thereafter, and the inevitable liquidation of overdeveloped properties pursued its dismal course for a full decade. During most of this time the depressing general economic effect of the construction collapse made railroad development exceedingly difficult, and the index reached a low point at 1894. We now enter the period when the railroad network was becoming substantially complete and when all the excesses of previous speculative activity and efforts toward personal aggrandizement from railway land speculation were bearing fruit in the badly financed and poorly managed major roads. Railroad failures were exceedingly heavy in the early 'nineties, and no less than 29,000 miles went into receivership in 1893, involving a capitalization of nearly two billion dollars. More than half of the capital of the important railroads at that time represented funded debt and a growing practice of trading heavily upon the equity by railroad owners and boards of directors. The high cost of construction and the inflated property values, layer upon layer, were mainly perpetuated in capitalization. Against this excessive capitalization, competitive pressures and agricultural demands for lower rates, as grain prices reached new lows, created a menacing situation. In addition, there occurred in 1890, with an impact that continued to be felt for years in Great Britain, the repudiation of debt by Argentina after a decade of flamboyant railroad and property development in that country, mainly with British capital. This left all financial markets highly vulnerable. Our own banking was vulnerable because the banks had begun to make heavy advances on the security of railroad collateral, and the community of interest between bank and railroad ownership had already involved large infusions of stopgap or floating bank credits.

THE FADING OF RAILROAD MOMENTUM WITH CONTINUANCE OF RIGID OVERCAPITALIZATION

We now approach the end of the period of railroad development. What follows is much less important in terms of the *prime movers* in the cycles of business. More and more the railroad system becomes an example of a mature industry past the stage of promotion, but with the marks of past promotion clearly upon it. More and more the fortunes of the railroads came to depend *upon* business conditions made favorable or unfavorable by more fundamental and primary forces. But in this period of transition, just before one of the new prime movers—the automobile and its satellites—becomes important, it is interesting to observe a further change in the railroad financial picture brought about as a direct result of the reorganization of the bankrupt roads during the early 'nineties.[1]

The reorganizations between 1893 and 1900 are of outstanding importance in giving to the railroad system its characteristic topheavy and oversensitized capital condition as we see it today. In other words, although railroads after 1890 became largely *transmitters* and *amplifiers* of business disturbance, they assumed this capacity by virtue of the excessive leverage created by their capital structures. There is no inherent necessity for this leverage. Had there been better control and a more competent type of pioneering, especially more honesty and moral fiber among the initial promoters, our railroads today might be of such sound and strong financial caliber that they would not be among the important transmitting and amplifying forces in the business cycle.

What happened in the early 'nineties? Essentially there was a transition from the promotional period of reckless "trading on the equity" to one of banker control, in which the effort was to place as large a debt upon the railroad as the traffic would bear and to keep it there forever. The interests of stockholders became permanently subordinated to the interests of bondholders. This change came about

[1] A further point may be noted here to clarify the distinction between the construction of the railroad plant, in terms of roadbed, trackage, yards, and other terminal facilities, and construction of engines, rolling stock, and other equipment. The latter branch of fabricating industry now receives orders from the roads mainly representing replacement needs, rather than phases of original promotion. It seems legitimate for practical purposes to regard the making of equipment for the railroad as a phase of promotional enterprise until about 1890; thereafter the railroads were reaching a mature stage with little further expansion of basic structural features and an actual reduction in new trackage. After about 1900 the combined index represents the gradual fading out of the railroad factor, contrasting with the rapidly expanding and temporarily dominant motor-industry element.

through the fact that J. P. Morgan, who assumed the role of leading reorganizer of the bankrupt roads, was also a commanding personal influence in developing the principle of railroad community of interest and coordination of management policy, replacing the old cutthroat competition and reckless mismanagement.

But the price exacted for this excellent service was high. The financial principle underlying the major reorganizations, such as the Southern, the Erie, and the Baltimore and Ohio, was to revise the debt structures moderately and yet retain a very substantial portion of the watered capital resulting from all previous excesses and manipulations. By giving creditors of the roads in receivership new bonds carrying lower coupons, but mainly of very long-term maturity and in most cases non-callable, the effect was to render capital charges rigid, representing too large a part of the value of the properties. In addition, it became the practice, not only of the Morgan group but of other financing houses engaging in rail reorganizations, to perpetuate their control over the roads at the expense of the stockholders by means of voting trusts and other devices.[1]

The result of this process was twofold. In the first place, railroad financial structures, particularly those that had been reorganized, were made unduly sensitive to the effects of the business cycle and variations in traffic volume. In the second place, it was devised that the investment houses would continue to handle future security issues in the form of bonds, and as the equity shrunk to smaller and smaller proportions the roads were presently driven to new borrowings for extensions and improvements. In other words, the investment bankers took advantage of the desperate condition of the railroad systems after the crash of 1893 to fasten upon them a virtually perpetual debt in whose profitable distribution they hoped to participate forever. This goes a long way to explain the more recent status of our railroad system and the inability of the railroads, with only a few exceptions, to weather the storms of severe depressions.[2]

[1] The manner in which these reorganizations contributed to maintenance of fixed charges and overcapitalization is well described in the study of E. G. Campbell, "The Reorganization of the American Railroad System, 1893–1900," New York, 1938.

[2] The Interstate Commerce Commission stated in its study of "Railroad Sinking Funds and Funded Debt," 1939, p. 98: " . . . railroad policies both of indefinite expansion and the nonrepayment of funded debt are largely obsolete. Both have been founded upon assumptions as to the permanency of the plant investment and the future expansion of traffic and revenue which now appear to be erroneous. For example, the almost unprecedented declines in business and revenues during the depression as well as the comparatively low recovery since indicate little that is favorable to the future growth and increase of railroad traffic. The competitive and other developments of the last decade by undermining the foundations of theories of a permanent and increasing railroad debt point to the necessity of a change of policy."

The riotous gambling of the nineteenth century, through the necromancy of investment banking, has finally left us a heritage of financial unsoundness which now defies rectification. We thus have a fairly considerable segment of our industrial system highly sensitized to every wind that blows. The exaggerations of fluctuations in railroad revenue, when translated into net profits or into purchases of equipment, become tremendous gyrations. This became apparent in the decade from 1900 to 1910, which happened to be a generally prosperous period, although largely for reasons outside the railroad sphere. During this period railroad dividend payments were vastly increased, but the total debt was also increased, at a time when it could have been and should have been, by all standards of financial judgment, considerably reduced. The railroad owners continued to "trade on their equity" and expand their indebtedness by mortgages built, layer upon layer, over existing debts. At the same time a great boom in railway stocks was occurring on the New York Exchange, and presumably many of the original promoters were thereby able to step out of the picture and pass over their vulnerable equity holdings to the man in the street, to great advantage. It was the last decade in which the turnover of railroad stocks was the dominating component of the total transactions on that Exchange.

It is not surprising, therefore, that in 1905 there was one last fair-sized boom in railroad-equipment activity, largely, however, the *result* of the high degree of earnings leverage and the extravagant earnings of the period that permitted a few further extensions and improvements. The Interstate Commerce Commission was now beginning to acquire increasing regulating power over rates, but the quality of service rendered ceased to be developed on a par with progress in other directions of American industry. The railroads, once so powerful a factor in progress and in dynamics, found themselves more and more in a straitjacket from which they have not thus far escaped. New ideas, research in new types of equipment, ways of meeting the coming competition with motor vehicles all tended to lapse into a routine rather than an aggressive, adaptable, forward-looking segment of American business enterprise.

The building boom that culminated in the period 1905–1909 was much more potent as an original industrial stimulant than anything in the railroad industry. It was supported once more by an influx of immigration from abroad that reached a crest in 1906–1907. This was the last great wave of migration to this country. Just as the preceding major building cycle went into a decline prolonged by the disturbed international situation of the late 1890's and punctuated by our brief War with Spain, so the decline from 1909 to 1918 was intensified by war and preparation for war. Ominous storm clouds appeared on the European horizon as early as 1911, followed by the Balkan Wars and, finally, by the outbreak of World War I in 1914. While the War lasted there was a brief, although sharp, recovery in the production of railway equipment to serve national defense, but the urban real-estate promotions and building operations were suspended.[1]

Again we find, as in previous major was periods, a discrepancy between the behavior of the general business index and the *combined* patterns of the transport and building indexes. World War I was instrumental in hastening the development of a new major factor in the transportation field—the internal-combustion motor. Ever since the beginning of the century there had been quietly developing a momentous new industry. It was indeed a combination of industries, clustering about the manufacture and use of the automobile for individual and commercial transportation. The culmination of this development came soon after the close of World War I, and the major peak was reached in 1929. The broad, irregular crest of the transport production cycle of the 1920's was accompanied by an equally spectacular major boom in urban real estate and building. Demand for accommodations was stimulated this time, not by immigration but by the restless shifting about of mechanics toward and among the new industrial centers, many of them already enlarged by war production, others by the swift development of the motor industry itself.

THE MOTOR TRANSPORT BOOM

With the coming of the automobile and the many new industries that it brought into being, a new major form of transportation innovation passed in an astonishingly short time from its experimental stage to that of full development. Since automobiles have mainly been produced for individual ownership and operation, the making of the vehicles has developed as an industry distinct from that of the preparation of the roadbed. The latter has been undertaken at State or Federal expense, and a large part of the financial outlays to accommodate automobile transportation have been provided by Government in marked contrast to the railroad history.

Automobile development (apart from trucks) has essentially represented durable consumer goods, financed by methods as distinctively new as the vehicle itself. In marked contrast to the financing of the railroads or the manufacture of their equipment and in contrast also to the typical financing of urban housing, the automobile has been distributed to the

---

[1] During the War a Federal *Priorities Circular* was issued ordering that except by special permit no new nonwar building construction was to be undertaken involving an expenditure of more than five thousand dollars and no extensions costing over twenty-five hundred dollars.

public by relatively short-term loans. These have represented essentially sound, self-liquidating capital financing. The manufacture of automobiles became rapidly concentrated in a few large corporations whose financial policies have contributed to ample resources and equity, with a minimum of long-term indebtedness. The result has been a high degree of efficiency, flexibility, and very rapid progress in development of the potentialities of the internal-combustion motor.

Although all this is in marked contrast to what has happened in rail transport development or the creation of urban housing, we may properly consider the development of the automobile one more example of the powerful accelerating effect upon all industry for a decade by a major change in the transportation field. The motor vehicle between 1910 and 1930 rounded out a major cycle of development to the point of virtual maturity, traversing this sweep in a far shorter period of time than was required for the full development of our railroads. In the course of this short but momentous evolution there occurred a more or less parallel development in production of new fuels, production of innumerable public and private garages, service stations, and salesrooms, and a great expansion in industries producing glass, aluminum, tires, and accessories, all of which contributed to the population movement.

Even more important was the contribution of this swift evolution of motor transport upon the building industry in suburban areas of our cities. The motorcar brought with it a powerful decentralizing force, which is still in progress. This, in turn, meant more mobility of people and new demands for housing, which would not have existed without the automobile. Lacking many of the financial excrescences and promotional peculiarities of the railroad and lacking also the peculiarities of shipbuilding, the automobile-development period can be considered a prime factor in the business system, at least during the 1920's, and its attainment of maturity status at the end of that decade doubtless also contributed to the deceleration in many capital lines that deprived the lean years of the early 'thirties of a supporting cushion. Already the motor industry, like the railroads, has yielded its previous position as a prime mover and has entered the era of replacement cycles.

It may be added that a secondary promotional capital factor also contributed to the expansion phase of the late 1920's. This was the development of the electric-power industry and its involved corporate structures. In the 1920's this industry came into the hands of promotional groups that sought concentrated control over widely expanded properties through the device of the holding company. They followed much the same financial procedure that had fastened excessive rigid debt upon the railroads. The great *financial* promotions of the 1920's were therefore in real estate and in the electric-power industry, the latter not reaching its major peak until 1930.[1]   In order to get the complete picture of the financial momentum of these years of tremendous stock-market speculation, the existence of this third factor, representing the kind of large-scale innovation capital essentially similar to the railroad system, should be kept in mind.   The electrical-industry promotions were the essential basis of the great 1929 stock-market boom.

If we go one step further, we come to the latest phase of basic transport enterprise—aircraft.   We cannot consider air transport and its fabricating phases without being struck by some analogies to shipbuilding, especially in the adaptability of aircraft to war purposes.   (For that matter, the gasoline-motor vehicle is also developing swiftly as a device for conveying troops and as the basis of tank warfare.)   But in spite of this close association with warfare, air-transportation development will probably carry forward the primary thesis that movement of goods and people is an outstanding phase of new capital promotions.   Numerous industries the world over are deriving their market from the expenditures of governments upon motorized war equipment and military and naval aircraft.   This has many distinctive features contrasting with the promotional extravagance that built our railroads, but in terms of the probable impact upon capital goods manufactured for a long time to come it is highly significant.   Although up to 1940 the aviation industry was not yet sufficiently developed to warrant the inclusion of its production data in the transport index, this will certainly be appropriate in future years.

The building boom of the 1920's culminated about 1925–1926, although there was divergence in timing in various localities.   This boom had all the earmarks of financial unsoundness that had marked such booms in previous eras.   The starting of subdivisions, the movement of population into suburbs, facilitated by the automobile, the growth of automobile centers attracting new people all contributed to make new suburbs and home-building enterprises urgently needed.   The mortgage system made possible easy initial ownership and difficult ultimate payment of debt.   But once the downward slide of building began to accelerate, it marked the doom of any long-continued survival of capital-goods promotion in other directions.   There was the familiar snowball effect of declining mortgage solvency and a steady contraction in building and in the building-material industries.   While the stocks of chain merchandising companies, railroads, and particularly electric-power enterprises and their related "investment" trusts were being shot higher on the New York Exchange by manipulators, surfeited with the easy credit of an indulgent banking system, the underpinnings of a great prosperity

---

[1] The indexes shown in Chart 30 do not include electric power, but its inclusion would alter the patterns very little.

period were being eaten away as in previous times by the reversal of the primary forces.

But there was a deeper significance in the stock-market boom of the late 1920's. So long as billions of credit could be mobilized to distribute common stocks among small investors and speculators, those familiar

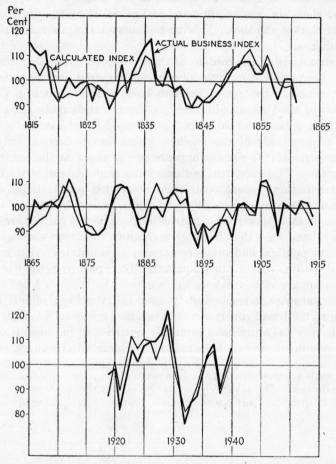

CHART 31.—Actual and calculated business indexes (excluding war periods), 1815–1940. The curve in light line indicates how closely the actual index of business cycles is approximated by a weighted combination of the building and the transportation-construction indexes, apart from war periods.

with the workings of the business system were well aware that they probably were being favored by an exceptional opportunity to separate themselves permanently from positions of ownership, not only in railroads but in manufacturing enterprise, where the future trend was already implying replacement demand rather than vast new market potentials.

In an intoxicating atmosphere of speculative frenzy, in which millions participated, many local governments repeated the performance of the 1830's in the handling of their finances. It was little wonder that the acute depression of the early 1930's equaled in extent the depression of the 1830's. In a later chapter we shall attempt to show how the vulnerable condition of American business, in the course of a major deflation of basic elements, was complicated and menaced by the financial breakdown of Europe and the underlying weakness of the raw-material producing countries.

In summarizing the content of this chapter, we may illustrate statistically the consistent response of general industrial and trade conditions to the combined pattern of the two basic indexes shown in Chart 30. In Chart 31 the two basic indexes have been translated by the technique of multiple regression into a single computed index having the average range of amplitude of the business index and pertaining only to the nonwar periods. The result appears in the chart as the lighter of the two curves. This computed business index represents what the business-cycle fluctuations would be if they responded solely to the impulses impinging upon manufacturing and trade activity from the cycles of building and transportation construction.[1] The war periods are omitted, since we have seen that business conditions in major wars tend to be subject to political and other emergency circumstances that cannot be brought within any statistical formula. But apart from the war periods, the exceedingly close relationship between the combined basic indexes and the business index definitely establish the logic of our analysis, leading to the broad conclusion that business cycles in the United States for well over a century have primarily represented impulses transmitted to manufacturing and trade from land speculation in its various forms.

[1] There is a high correlation also between the computed index and the cycles of steel production. This is entirely natural in view of the importance of steel as a material for structural purposes and the manufacture of transport equipment.

CHAPTER 11

COMMERCIAL BANKS AND CAPITAL FINANCING

In our discussion thus far, we have examined cyclical instability as it has manifested itself in fluctuations of commodity prices, in the volume of production, income, trade, and the major fluctuations of building and transport construction. We have seen that the patterns of the price level and of the money income of agriculture have been determined mainly by the effects and after-effects of war finance. The inevitable deflation of wartime monetary and credit circulation and reestablishment of the metallic money standard have contributed to prolonged periods of falling prices. We have found that the intermediate wavelike undulations in general production also appear to have their origin in political and economic disturbances accompanying and following major wars. As for the minor cyclical oscillations of business activity, we have reason to regard them as to a large extent the joint result of violent and long-extended gyrations associated with building construction and the initial construction phases of transportation plant and equipment. These waves of innovation and expansion in durable plant both have their roots in the changing growth rate and the movement of population. They have involved the utilization of capital and credit resources in ways that have not been consistent with continuous and orderly expansion.

Capital in the form of accumulated savings, expressed in terms of money, has from time to time been mobilized and directed by promotional zeal and optimistic enthusiasm toward developments involving land and the exploiting of potential appreciation in land values. This has brought about again and again the phenomenon of badly misdirected investment, and the aftermath has forced the entire economy to proceed for long intervals at greatly reduced momentum and through troughs of depression during which the relations of debtors and creditors could be painfully readjusted to conform to sober reality.

These prime movers in creating economic instability have involved the use (and misuse) of capital funds—representing the accumulated savings mobilized in a form available for use in costly structural enterprise —and also the additional purchasing power that hitherto has been referred to as bank credit. Wars have been financed by the hasty mobilization of savings into governmental obligations and through appropriation of both income and capital by taxation. Railway building and real-estate development required vast amounts of capital, mobilized

239

from scattered sources by the skill and persistence of enterprisers and financial middlemen. We probably should have experienced fairly extended cyclical movements in the total amount of capital used for projects relating to such basic construction, *even though there were no contributions of bank credit.* The difficulties resulting from the use of capital savings in these developments looking toward the distant future have represented the repeated tendency to overcapitalize future earning power, the squandering of resources in blindly competitive duplication of durable facilities, and the waste of considerable sums through pure chicanery. Following each major boom there has been for a time a scattering or demobilizing of these sums of capital, and this has made necessary the slow, paralyzing processes of liquidation and reorganization requiring years before the financial markets were prepared once again to support the next wave of expansion or major technological innovation.

We have seen that the tendency of promotion has usually been one of extensive "trading on the equity," with the absence of sound practice that would have required, in the case of borrowed capital, that repayments be made at scheduled periods to ensure amortization and to discourage the reckless. There has been a remarkable absence of legal safeguard to prevent the exploitation of the co-owners of structural wealth from being the victims of manipulation and secrecy on the part of the controlling interests and the mortgagees. These defects, which have been glaringly demonstrated by the use of savings in construction and transportation development, have their roots deeply embedded in the legal and political structure of our society. Since laws are made by men and since the men framing laws have at times been associated in some measure with promotional enterprise or personally dependent upon it, it follows that the legal framework itself that formed the typical procedures in using capital funds has been strangely negligent in the matter of safety factors and sound standards. It has already been suggested that these difficulties in the case of capital used in promotional structural development are partly due to the fact that in our earlier history and, in fact, well into the nineteenth century, much capital has been contributed by individuals rather than through the intermediary of financial middlemen. Hence the relations between the capitalist and the promoter have been so direct and so little affected by a public interest or a sense of fiduciary responsibility that even legislation has been slow to extend its regulatory influence into dealings that seemed to have so personal a nature. The supervision of such matters by State Governments, following no uniform standard and lacking full disciplinary power, has gone far to delay the full recognition of the problem.

In fact, the Federal Government itself has not generally established precedents in the use of capital that are beyond criticism. When governments enter the capital markets under the exigencies of war emergency or with the object of assisting in the development of building or transportation projects of any magnitude, they have been negligent, reckless, and unobservant of the most elementary necessity of keeping the flow of capital moving through provisions for the regular amortization of borrowed money.   Governments have used capital very much as speculative individuals have used it—without due allowance for the long-term consequences that inevitably follow when a debt burden is inadequately supported by current productive income capable of retiring the obligation. This was precisely the situation in the 1840's, when most of the Southern States and some Western States were so recklessly subsidizing road and canal projects and heading for the repudiation cataclysm that followed. National governments seek to escape these consequences through the various devices open to them, such as taxation, manipulation of money, etc.   But it can be said with emphasis that governmental finance the world over, so far as *borrowed* capital is concerned, has not contributed in any material degree to setting up *sound standards of self-liquidating debt in either public or private finance.*   Hence it is not surprising that American legal codes and traditional practice, as applied to the great promotional projects considered in previous chapters, have been so ineffective in protecting both the projectors and the providers of resources from their miscalculations.

THE USE OF BANK CREDIT FOR LONG-TERM AND NONLIQUID FINANCING

Thus far we have been speaking mainly of *capital* in the form of savings, but we have had occasion from time to time to refer to the part that commercial *bank credit* has played, not only as a factor in the price level but also in contributing to building and transportation development. Our banking system has been related to these phases of major expansions and contractions of activity in interesting and complex ways that call for some further analysis.   It will be assumed that the reader is already more or less familiar with the fundamental characteristics of banking institutions and the manner in which credit is made available through this mechanism.   It will not be necessary to review the history of American banking in detail or to explain all the devices whereby banks facilitate the financing of trade and production.   We shall rather examine some of the ways in which the so-called "commercial" (or demand-deposit) banks, as distinct from purely savings (or loaning) institutions, have managed to supplement financial resources by making available the equivalent of long-term capital for construction and plant development. We shall examine also the manner in which the deposit banks of the United States have been in a position to transmit and amplify both the rising and the declining phases of the business cycle, occasionally to the point of creating panic and trade paralysis. At many points our banking system has evolved from conditions quite unlike those that have prevailed in other leading commercial countries. It is well to remind ourselves of these peculiarities and characteristics, since banking reform, coming tardily and being not yet complete, has not always been attentive to the peculiarities and characteristics of our industrial structure and the nature of our production problems; it has derived perhaps too much from foreign models and hence has failed to produce the best results.

During most of the Colonial period, banks served mainly as facilities for the current deposit of funds and for making advances required by merchants. Foreign trade was an important part of Colonial and early United States business. The banks patterned themselves largely on the models of English commercial institutions. This was particularly true of banks in the port cities of New Orleans, Philadelphia, and Boston. The Bank of North America, organized in Philadelphia in 1782, was a good illustration of the larger commercial banks of the latter eighteenth century, making advances based on the goods bought and sold by merchants. It made no loans on mortgages and did not participate in the financing of agricultural operations other than those of a commercial nature.[1]

In a society where mobilized capital was scant and the individual businessman desired to invest as much of his surplus as possible in land or expansion of his own durable equipment, the commercial banks were relied upon to finance the seasonal trade requirements and occasional temporary personal or special purposes. There are many instances of early banks established with inadequate cash capital, revealing no little irregularity in the granting of credit, but by and large it appears that the banks of deposit limited their operations to commercial advances. In this sense they conformed rather closely to the contemporary standards of commercial banking as set sorth (perhaps somewhat idealistically) by Adam Smith in his "Wealth of Nations":

A bank cannot consistently with its own interest, advance to a trader the whole or even the greater part of the circulating capital with which he trades. . . . Still less could a bank afford to advance him any considerable part of his fixed capital; of the capital which the undertaker of an iron forge, for example, employs in erecting his forge and smelting-house, his workhouses and warehouses, the dwelling-houses of his workmen, etc.; of the capital which the undertaker of a mine employs in sinking his shafts, in erecting engines for drawing out the water, in making roads and waggon-ways, etc.; of the capital which the person who undertakes to improve land employs in clearing, draining, enclosing, manuring,

---

[1] Bray Hammond, Long and Short-term Credit in Early American Banking, *Quarterly Journal of Economics*, November, 1934.

and ploughing waste and uncultivated fields, in building farm-houses with all their necessary appendages of stables, granaries, etc.[1]

He goes on to say that those who undertake fixed capital projects should, in justice to their creditors, make their own personal capital a sufficient part of their total resources, and the part that is borrowed "ought to be borrowed upon bond or mortgage of such private people as propose to live upon the interest of their money without taking the trouble themselves to employ the capital, and who are upon that account willing to lend that capital to such people of good credit as are likely to keep it for several years." What Smith had basically in mind was the remarkable success of the Scottish banks in confining themselves to commercial credit *of a strictly amortized character;* and he was also concerned to point out that unless banks functioned in this manner in serving trade and industry and prudently confined their advances to relatively short credits, they would essentially be making available to the community funds that in the aggregate would be larger than the total of actual available money. The banks, in other words, would be adding to the total circulation of purchasing power and might thus tend to raise general prices and create conditions inconsistent with the maintenance of solvency.

In these trenchant opinions of Adam Smith there are two essential points: commercial banks should restrict themselves to mercantile loans and grant their credit with careful attention to the qualitative aspect of each advance; they should not inflate the total national currency as the result of their lending operations. The one is a qualitative standard, and the other is quantitative. The quantitative aspect is important in view of the fact that banks of the commercial type have virtually the power of creating the immediate equivalent of money through the issue of their circulating promissory notes. But as we have previously explained, this is not the only way in which the commercial bank may extend credit considerably beyond the total cash funds deposited by savers. Such banks began at an early period to extend their credit to borrowers rather than extending cash. Advances were made that took the form of authorization of the borrower to draw checks upon new deposits created *ad hoc* and representing nothing more than the obligation of the bank to honor these checks. The essential difference between the extension of bank credit through note issue and through the creation of these credit deposits lay in the fact that the notes circulated a considerable time, sometimes far distant from the point of issue, and they formed a part of the circulating money used by all classes.

[1] "Wealth of Nations," Book 2, Chapter 2, 1776.

On the other hand, the checkbook money (to use the convenient phrase of Irving Fisher) generally circulated for a much shorter period and mainly accomplished, at least in earlier days, transactions of large denomination among businessmen. From the standpoint of purchasing power over goods, property, or service, there is no essential difference between bank operations resulting in (credit) deposits or those resulting in the issue of notes. But there has long been a curious tendency of the law in most countries to fasten attention upon the note issues and to draw rather arbitrary lines of distinction between the two classes of bank credit. It was long considered important to regulate bank-note issue because of its obvious monetary significance. Hence, in our Colonial period and until the first decade of the nineteenth century, we find that bank charters were difficult to obtain; it was considered a high legal privilege to operate a bank and circulate credit by means of notes. Banks were recognized as essentially public utilities. Although individuals might engage in banking, both British law and American procedure for many years permitted nonchartered groups to exercise banking functions only by special sanction. As pointed out by Shaw Livermore; "The long tradition of central government control over currency as an earmark of sovereignty made the states particularly jealous of letting banking corporations assume powers that were not carefully restricted. Charters were to be given only after inquiry, and were given in the spirit of delegating a sovereign power to a special group in the community."[1] In the early decades of the nineteenth century, after it had been recognized that corporations for ordinary business purposes might be formed under a general law, there persisted powerful pressure to continue special restrictions for corporate banking charters.

In view of the monetary function of commercial banks, the restriction of their operations by law, and the circumscribed range of their lending activities, there early developed a struggle to supplement these banks with institutions specially organized to make long-term agricultural and real-property loans and to do away with the almost monopolistic privileges of strictly commercial banking and the limited range of its accommodation. In Massachusetts, for instance, there were attempts to set up banks under state authority, capable of issuing notes secured by real estate with the specific purpose of accommodating property development. We have already referred in a previous chapter to the issue of bills of credit in the various Colonies to finance governmental projects and extend capital loans to enterprisers. Most of the "public-loan offices" that functioned in the Colonies met with unfortunate results;

[1] "Early American Land Companies," p. 246, New York, 1939.

there were inadequate sound precedents to guide their operations.   During the War of the Revolution and the years immediately following, the Bank of North America and similar chartered banks in New York and Massachusetts made loans to the Federal and State Governments and even to some favored business enterprises, although at the time these were regarded as rather exceptional deviations from accepted banking practice. But after the turn of the nineteenth century the need for much larger amounts of agricultural and construction capital developed growing pressure to break down the legalistic restrictions upon banking organization and banking practice.   Since banks had already begun to purchase long-term public securities and had made loans to Government agencies on noncommercial principles, the demand emanating from agriculture and property development, as well as the growing need for industrial long-term financing, had the effect of opening the field of banking under provisions of general corporation law rather than special charter.   This made rapid progress in the 1830's, both in the United States and in England.

As banking became a field easier to enter the "commercial" standards cherished by Adam Smith soon ceased to limit the operations of bankers. The neat distinction between mercantile credit and long-term capital financing became increasingly blurred.   While the metropolitan banks continued to be relatively conservative in providing commercial credit, the making of bank loans on security collateral and the purchase by banks of corporate securities developed rapidly, and in the smaller communities and the frontier areas banking developed into a free-for all, opportunistic game for the financing of land speculation and rural capital requirements generally.   It was this insatiable demand for agricultural, structural, and promotional capital that made it impossible to continue the early Federal banking institutions, the First and Second Banks of the United States. The antagonism arising, particularly in the rural sections, against any form of restrictive "monopoly" privilege was clearly evident long before Andrew Jackson finally and permanently destroyed effective central banking and removed at least one restraining and coordinating influence over credit deposits and note issues.

From the ending of the Second Bank of the United States in 1836 to the establishment of the National Banking System during the Civil War, the distinction between commercial banking and capital banking was almost entirely obliterated.   Banks made heavy loans to the State Governments; many states contributed to the capital of banks in order to obtain these loans, many of which financed permanent improvements; and the land subdividers, railroad promoters, and building speculators generally found ways of establishing "banks" as an adjunct to their promotions.[1] It was thus possible to monetize the estimated value of a new private-capital promotion and to proceed without recourse to savings. Although in some states, notably New York and Massachusetts, there continued to be relatively conservative bank operation under state supervision, this was in general a "wildcat" period. Much of the bank-note circulation represented long-term and more or less speculative assets that caused bank notes to circulate at varying rates of discount and to be extensively counterfeited. It was this wretched condition of the note circulation, as well as the necessity of widening the market for Federal bonds, which prompted the banking reforms of 1864. But in so intently concentrating upon the note-issue problem and its monetary aspects, legislators failed to include in the new system the credit operations of the deposit banks. The importance of the monetary aspect of bank-note issue was held to justify the exercise

---

[1] There was ample precedent for this, as may be seen from the following cases cited by Cleveland and Powell:

"As early as 1814 Maryland chartered the Susquehanna Bank and Bridge Company, with power to employ half its funds in the banking business. In an amendment to the charter of the Delaware and Hudson canal granted by New York in 1824, the company was given the right to exercise banking powers during a period of twenty years. New Jersey, the same year, granted a charter to the 'Morris Canal and Banking company' which gave the enjoyment of banking functions through a term of thirty-one years. Maine, which in 1823 had authorized a lottery for the benefit of the Cumberland and Oxford canal, chartered 'the Canal bank' in 1825, with authority to invest one-fourth of its paid subscriptions in the stock of the canal company. The directors of the Blackstone canal announced in 1831 that they had received a charter for a bank to be operated for the benefit of the company. Shareholders were privileged to duplicate their holdings of canal stock with shares in the bank; and three-fifths of the funds thus raised by the bank were to be exchanged for stock of the parent company. The same year, the 'New Orleans Canal and Banking company' was chartered by Louisiana to construct a waterway from Lake Ponchartrain to the Mississippi at New Orleans. . . .

"The bank of Macomb county at Mount Clemens made no attempt to build the Macomb and Saginaw railroad, and in order to preserve its charter it obtained legislative permission in 1840 to build a turnpike instead of a railroad. The bank failed in 1858. The Ohio railroad charter of 1835 contained a provision that the funds of said company shall be paid out in orders drawn on the treasurer, in such manner as shall be pointed out by the by-laws of the company; and 'that all such orders for the payment of money so drawn shall, when presented to the treasurer, be by him paid and redeemed.' Without collecting a dollar from the stockholders, and with an empty treasury, the company under authority of this clause began banking operations, and successfully maintained a large circulation. Laborers and contractors were paid in notes, and from the proceeds of the bonds of the state received as a subsidy, some of these notes were redeemed. When the company suspended, there had been no work of permanent character done on the road, and there were outstanding several hundred thousand dollars in worthless currency." Frederick A. Cleveland and Fred W. Powell, "Railroad Promotion and Capitalization in the United States," pp. 167–171, New York, 1909.

of Federal power, but it was held that under the Constitution the Federal Government could not extend its regulatory power to lending operations, and this was left to "state" banks under state authority.   Thus arose our dual system of banking.   There developed rapidly after the Civil War indifferently supervised state institutions and trust companies, unable (after 1869) to issue notes but able to engage in what was accepted to be commercial banking and the extension of credit through creation of deposits.[1]

A DIVIDED AND INADEQUATE BANKING SYSTEM

Within the space of a generation the commercial banks operating under state authority actually became more numerous than National Banks, and by 1920 their total resources exceeded those of the National Banks.   Meanwhile, bank notes had become little more than money certificates (representing the holding by National Banks of Federal bonds), and since these issues did not vary with the needs of trade or even the seasonal requirements of agriculture and merchandising, the variable elements in bank credit were almost entirely represented by the lending that generated demand deposits.   As time passed, circulating bank notes became a less and less important phase of the financing of business.   The issuing of notes became subject to peculiar technical conditions relating to the outstanding Federal debt and the return available from Federal obligations.   For all practical purposes the National Banking System accomplished little more than to render the circulating notes uniform and relatively safe and to submit at least a part of the banking system to regular examination and uniform supervision by public authority.   This tended gradually and indirectly to improve the regulation of banking by the states, and to eliminate some of the more flagrant abuses of bank management in the matter of capitalization, reserves, and exploitation of banks to further promotional enterprises of directors or favored customers.   But unfortunately, this dividing of commercial banking supervision into political groupings permitted much unsound banking to continue and flourish beyond the

[1] The National Bank legislation contemplated bringing all commercial banks into a Federally supervised system by placing a prohibitive tax upon the circulating notes of State Banks.   This was a futile expectation, since it overlooked entirely the growing importance of deposit credit and checkbook money.   Had Congress fully and accurately recognized the essentially monetary characteristics of bank deposits subject to check, it is doubtful whether sound constitutional objections could have been raised against extension of Federal regulatory powers over all banking institutions.   The extension of Federal power over the functions of note issue, previously exercised under state authority, was fully recognized by the Supreme Court in 1869.   See Bray Hammond, The Banks, the States, and the Federal Government, *American Economic Review*, December, 1933.

range of any effective control. It is this characteristic of American banking in the expansive pioneering decades that warrants our special attention.

Although the National Banking Act, until 1913, did not authorize National Banks to make loans secured by real estate, they were empowered to make collateral loans with very minor restrictions, and there was no effective way of preventing them from making short-term loans for ostensibly commercial purposes but nevertheless renewable to the extent that they often virtually represented advances of long-term working capital or even fixed capital. This fact has been commonly overlooked, but it is important in fully appreciating the tendency of even that part of our system functioning under the National Banking law to become repeatedly embarrassed by the freezing of what seem on the surface to be "liquid" assets. Furthermore, the state-supervised banks, operating under much less effective and by no means uniform regulation, were able in most agricultural regions to extend loans liberally on agricultural property and intermediate-term loans on security of agricultural products. Thus a fairly considerable proportion of total bank lending represented advances well beyond the range of strictly self-liquidating commercial paper or the discounting of merchants' notes and drafts.

The United States has never utilized an appreciable part of its resources in foreign trade, and hence the kind of purely mercantile credit that so long prevailed and gave undoubtedly a high degree of liquidity to the British banking system has not been available to our banks, even in New York. A relatively large segment of our economy has been engaged in *extractive industries*, catering to construction and agriculture, with all their vagaries, special hazards, and wide fluctuations. These users of credit have infused into banking operations a conspicuous element of nonliquidity in the loans that in itself would have militated against any attempt to restrict deposit banking to purely commercial standards, such as those entertained by Adam Smith.[1]

[1] American practice and regulation have leaned strongly toward emphasis on the currency creating and formally "secured" loan in contrast to the principle of what has come to be called the "banking principle"—emphasizing the importance of making sound loans as a means of avoiding banking difficulties. This distinction between the "currency" principle and the "banking" principle really developed out of British experience, when, during the Wars with Napoleon, the Bank of England was criticized by certain groups, hostile to its prerogatives and power, for overissuing its notes and thus inflating the currency circulation. In Parliamentary investigations, which finally led in 1844 to legislation restricting Bank of England note issue, it was repeatedly asserted by leading bankers that so long as each advance to businessmen was made on conservative lines with thorough knowledge of the purpose of the loan there could be no abuse of credit or inflation.

Actually, these seemingly opposing principles are aspects of diverse problems. The currency principle is valid and of practical bearing if the banking system is placed

From still another point of view, as a result of our banking experience and the sectional bias in legislation regulating it, there has been a pronounced tendency to bring essentially capital loans more or less consciously within the province of commercial banking, but at the expense of providing deliberately for the establishment of institutions specially adapted to making long-term loans for capital purposes. It is an astonishing fact that almost every country of importance has made far more progress than the United States in the development of mortgage banks, agricultural-loan banks, industrial-credit agencies, and savings-and-loan associations for capital and structural financing. What actually happened here was a merging under the guise of commercial banking of functions that actually represented substantial indirect accommodation to capital finance. After 1913 the National Banks were permitted to make loans secured by real estate up to 25 per cent of their capital and surplus and one-third of their time deposits, but even this concession (primarily to the farmers) was not in the direction of sound property financing, inasmuch as such loans were limited to five years and hence represented the typically American banking straddle—capital loans at short term. The financing of property, in other words, was made to appear as "liquid" financing by limiting the period, but by this very device the mortgages and collateral upon which much of this credit was extended were inherently unsound, because the many borrowers could not in the very nature of things liquidate the loans within the period. This also contributed to perpetuate the emphasis on asset security as distinct from the careful analysis of the personal elements in each case and the ultimate purpose served by each loan made.

As for bank loans upon security collateral, these have been important in the larger financial centers, particularly New York. Loans of this type have been made by banks in the United States for at least a century. They represent a type of advance principally employed in speculative

---

in the position of financing war and creating either notes or deposit credits for Government account. But under *normal* conditions, with respect to standards of business financing, the banking principle is important as emphasizing the *qualitative* aspects of the lending operations as these bear upon avoidance of *cyclical* overexpansion and the amplifying of depression. Much debate on this subject has confused the issue by implying that note circulation *alone* has a currency aspect or that deposit credit has *no* currency aspect, both of which contentions are fallacious. If reasonably formulated, there is something of value in the proposition that banks can dilute the circulation of means of payment by public and war loans (or excessive private loans not consistent with sound banking standards) and also in the proposition that sound banking practice in meeting business demands can go a long way (if bankers can be made to adopt such practice uniformly and consistently) to minimize *both* inflation of price level and encouragement to speculative promotion of capital projects, which, in turn generates most cyclical instability in production and trade.

operations on the stock exchanges and to some extent the need for advances in distributing bond issues. These loans are either on a "demand" basis, subject to overnight recall of the funds, or on a "time" basis, but both classes may be subject to indefinite renewal, and hence the loans are not inherently self-liquidating. A considerable proportion of such collateral lending has been done on a time basis in the financial centers and has thus represented a peculiar type of bank lending from the standpoint of liquidity and the standard of self-liquidation. Such loans may be considered a means whereby a commercial bank, not itself engaged in the purchase of common stocks or corporate capital financing, makes funds available to those who purchase corporate shares or bonds, usually on a margin. In the aggregate, such purchasers, even if mainly with merely speculative intent, may make up a fairly substantial volume of supply of industrial and mercantile or construction *capital*, despite the fact that the individual traders or speculative investors operate on a conditional or short-swing basis.

There is clear evidence that the vast expansion in this kind of bank lending, which occurred after World War I and culminated in the great market inflation of 1929, was preceded in the late 1890's and almost down to the beginning of that War by an almost equally conspicuous contribution of such bank credit to the speculative market in railroad shares accompanying the railroad reorganizations of that period. In this sense the commercial banking system for a long time was frankly exploited to serve the needs of security "distribution." One may go further and observe the manner in which many banks and trust companies in the 1920's went far beyond strictly banking functions in forming or acquiring "affiliates," engaged directly in the distribution of securities and mortgages. Through these affiliates these banks found a convenient means of keeping a substantial volume of *essentially capital loans* well out of sight. In the hectic speculation of the late twenties some of these banking affiliates even engaged indirectly in stock speculation. By 1930 bank affiliates were actually sponsoring nearly 55 per cent of all new corporate issues.[1]

---

[1] A. M. Allen, and others, "Commercial Banking Legislation and Control," p. 427, London, 1938. While we are considering the manner in which banks of the commercial type actually made a large part of their loans essentially capital advances, the remarks of B. M. Anderson, Jr., are of interest, inasmuch as he was one of the first American economists to emphasize this tendency. In the *Chase Economic Bulletin*, Nov. 6, 1928, he wrote: "I would still maintain that the growth during the past three or four years in bank investments and in bank loans against stock and bond collateral has been unduly rapid, and that a period of pause in this matter, with stock-taking and with a waiting for investors' demand to take up some of the current supply of securities carried with bank money, is distinctly in order." It is unfortunate that this warning was not widely heeded.

The business of making loans of the installment type to facilitate purchase by consumers of durable equipment has been of relatively recent importance so far as the banks are concerned. This type of lending was first developed outside the banking system, but the rapid recent growth has been associated with a considerable volume of bank loans when we include those made to finance companies or others making advances to dealers. Such loans, although of longer term than the familiar discount of commercial paper, should be placed in that general category of primarily self-liquidating or systematically amortized credit of an essentially sound type, even though there have been abuses in matters of detail and unreasonably high total interest charges. But with the minor defects and abuses being brought under control and regulation, it seems clear that the principle of installment credit is thoroughly in accord with sound financial practice and with the operations of commercial banks, and we shall have occasion to comment later upon its growing significance as a phase of durable capital expansion in the future.

It will have been noted in our summary of banking operations that American banks as a general tendency have stood ready to pay virtually on demand the sums owing to depositors. This includes even a substantial fraction of what were ostensibly labeled "time" deposits. In the case of distinctly savings banks, with which we are not here concerned, the feature of deposits being subject to immediate payment has not been of primary importance in generating weaknesses, although in certain cases, particularly among some types of building-loan organizations, the attempt to combine essentially demand deposits with long-term loans has been known to occur. In the face of potential deposit withdrawals and the many circumstances that might produce an abnormal rate of withdrawal, it has been the tendency of American banks, over and above regulation and legislation, to stress the element of liquidity among their earning assets. But this so-called "liquidity" has been in large measure an illusion. The illusory element arises from the fact that merely because in a *particular instance* a security seems to be readily salable, it does not follow that the total of all securities held by all the banks would be salable without heavy losses in values and the unfortunate effect on those values of a simultaneous calling of collateral loans which would become necessary. A given flat real-estate loan, made for a limited period, is not necessarily solvent if the loan is made with the tacit expectation on the part of both banker and borrower that it may be renewed several times. In that event the loan is virtually a gamble on the part of the borrower that he can secure a renewal and that conditions will be favorable for the bank to grant a renewal. The same thing holds true of all capital (or working-capital) loans, or secured loans that are incapable of being amortized and therefore are not self-liquidating.

In fact, our commercial banks have actually been in the service of capital finance to a surprising degree, but on a *contingent and conditional basis.* Many of the "liquid" commercial loans made ostensibly for a year have been carried along with the knowledge and assent of the examining authorities to five or ten or twenty years and have thus been of virtually the same status as long-term capital obligations of the borrowers. Despite surface appearance of liquidity in the earning assets, if the combined statements of all the so-called "commercial" banks were analyzed, it would disclose possession by the banks of much formal security against loans, which is actually merely a long-term unsecured debenture.

Another distinctive feature of American banking has been the preoccupation of rigid legal provisions as to reserves and the setting up of specific statutory requirements that minimum cash reserves be held by a commercial bank against its deposit liabilities. To be sure, such regulations were not of much consequence prior to the establishment of the National Banking System,[1] but with the coming of the National System, legal reserves were prescribed against both deposits and outstanding notes, although the latter was soon eliminated in view of the strong Federal-bond-security setup for National Bank notes. In the laws of the various states, which more or less patterned themselves after the National Banking laws, it became a common practice to require state commercial banks to maintain minimum reserves as specified in legislation. This matter of "required reserves" against deposits is related closely to another peculiarity of American banking that legislation until very recently did little to alter—the almost complete limitation of banking to unit control and the persistent restrictions upon large banks operating through branch offices. This has clearly been a result of the antimonopoly prejudice often revealing itself in the attitude of Congress, particularly the large segment of the Senate representing agricultural sections, where fear and distrust of moneylenders is (for reasons that we have already noted) proverbial. This limitation of banking to the unit principle has been accompanied by a tendency in Federal and state legislation to permit banks of the commercial type to be organized with relatively small capital. Capital requirements indeed have been largely based upon the size of the *particular community* served

---

[1] In the wildcat days of the 1840's and 1850's, reserves were in many instances nonexistent. There are amusing ancedotes describing the manner in which a single box of coin circulated among the banks of a remote community and served to satisfy the examining authorities that each bank in turn had something in the nature of a cash reserve.

by a bank. It has therefore been possible to organize small banks, and the United States has been a country of very numerous independent banks and all the resulting competitive tendencies and the inherent weaknesses due to inadequately trained personnel and local hazards.

While banks in the larger cities grew into powerful and well-equipped institutions, the size of the average bank in the interior, or what we may call the typical country bank, has been found weaker in times of stress than would be true in Canada, the British Isles, or most of Europe. This has been an important source of instability, because so much of our production has been agricultural and extractive. Many banks have been unable to diversify their loans beyond the risks attaching to a particular crop, lumber area, mining operation, or industrial town, dependent for its prosperity upon relatively volatile conditions. In marked contrast to the experience of most other countries, the opposition in the United States to large banking companies operating through branches is explained historically by the unfortunate results of the various State Banks in the 1830's and the 1840's, and back of this were the personal bias and obstinacy of Andrew Jackson. Although failures among such institutions can be mainly explained by their loans to land speculators and the reckless State Governments of those days, there developed among the agricultural states and among the rural lawyers who dominate Congress a persistent animosity against branching systems. This animosity, it will be recalled, opposed the existence of any further Federal banking after the demise of the Second Bank of the United States in 1836. Thus, until the establishment of the compromise Federal Reserve System in 1915, the individual banks were deprived of the services that might have been rendered by a special institution serving as a bankers' bank and capable of affording emergency assistance when necessary by rediscounting earning assets of the individual banks.[1]

THE ABSENCE OF RESERVE LENDING POWER

The essential feature of a central bank, whether it is set up as a publicly controlled institution or, like the Bank of England, as a private institution with public functions and responsibilities rooted in tradition,

---

[1] A certain amount of local branching had occurred among the National Banks, but no important expansion along these lines was possible, because many state laws prohibited branch banks. The National Banking law was relaxed in some measure after 1927, permitting National Banks to maintain branches where state laws did not forbid them, but branching developments were still somewhat restricted. As late as 1920 there were only 56 National Bank branches and 996 State Bank branches. Much of this expansion, such as it was, occurred within New York City and a number of other cities where the branching was localized in the metropolitan area rather than extending over a considerable territory. See J. M. Chapman and R. B. Westerfield, "Branch Banking," New York, 1941.

is to hold a major part of the actual reserves of the commercial banks and, *by virtue of this command of reserves,* to hold always a substantial potential lending power *inactive* to be brought into use when the individual banks face extraordinary demands and find it necessary to supplement their own lending power. The central bank stands in relation to the other banks somewhat as the individual bank stands to a customer. The merchant who has received a shipment of goods from a manufacturer and who "accepts" a draft or has given to the latter a promissory note for subsequent payment provides the manufacturer with the means of monetizing, so to speak, the goods by discounting the draft or note at his bank. But the banks of this country have lacked a means of thus quickly monetizing the advances that appear on their books as discounted commercial paper. One reason why it has been difficult for the banks to realize upon such assets and to turn them back into "cash" to support new advances has been the character of the so-called commercial paper itself. Most of this paper, with the exception of that originating in the transactions of fairly large corporations, was not of the type that could be resold or used for rediscounting outside the locality in which the bank was situated.

The country, in other words, lacked a broad acceptance market, for many notes and drafts represented firms not widely known and the paper lacked sufficient endorsement to render it readily acceptable to banks outside the particular locality. There was, of course, a certain amount of resort by country banks to city correspondents, but it was never developed as a systematic practice and had nothing in common with the kind of bill market found in London, where the specialists dealing in short-term paper (known as "discount houses" or "bill brokers") have long maintained a liquid market for commercial paper, relying upon the Bank of England for working capital and upon the large metropolitan commercial banks as ultimate purchasers of these instruments. The lack of a broad discount or acceptance market here, therefore, served to reinforce the characteristics of unit banking, excessively localized with regard to advances and to risks. The absence, during the period of rapid promotional development, of any kind of central bank capable of affording rediscount facilities in times of stress greatly reinforced this rigid localization and the inability of the banks to obtain access to reserve lending power deliberately conserved for emergency conditions. Thus, when periods of liquidation and insolvency came, they brought with them again and again banking collapse.

The large banks of New York and, to a certain degree, other metropolitan centers naturally developed correspondent relations with interior banks which were to a certain extent in the nature of central-bank functions. Balances were kept by country banks in New York as part of the routine of carrying on remittance and exchange operations. But over and above this routine reason for some reserve to be maintained in New York, there were factors that created a most unusual and dangerous concentration of bank reserves in New York without formal or adequate responsibility for their use or provision for their immediate availability when interior pressures developed. It is at this point that we can readily see the shortcomings of the legalistic philosophy of "required reserves," as developed in American legislation and practice.

The widespread banking difficulties of the 1840's had already produced state laws establishing the principle of cash reserves to be held as minima against liabilities (in the early days, mainly notes). The National Banking System developed this further and more systematically in the form of statutory reserve minimum requirements for National Banks. These were finally worked out to provide for three distinct types of banks: the smaller country banks, the banks in so-called "reserve cities," and, finally, those in New York and several other metropolitan areas. The principle was to require a 25 per cent minimum reserve against all deposits[1] in the central reserve city and reserve city banks, but the latter might hold half of the reserves in the former banks as deposits, and the country banks were permitted to keep as much as three-fifths in other banks. Thus the minimum cash *actually on hand* in the vaults of those banks might legally be no more than perhaps 6 per cent of their total deposits. This system represented in part the acceptance of what was already banking practice. It also represented the idea that the essential reponsibility of a banker was to his depositors and those who might present checks drawn upon depositors demanding payment. What the law virtually said with respect to banking reserves might be stated in terms of reservoirs. Every detached and possibly flimsy house was required to keep a reservoir of water in case of fire, but the little houses might have a large part of their water supply in the possession of very remote but larger structures! Instead of maintaining a *single adequate reservoir*, capable of being quickly drawn upon at strategic points in case of emergency, the water supply was scattered about, and when emergencies occurred the small local reservoirs proved utterly inadequate. The law failed to recognize that a credit system operates as a functional unit and that weaknesses in one part of the structure quickly spread to all other parts.

Our curious old reserve system, sanctioned by law rather than common sense, was rendered even more ineffective in practice because the banks in New York City found it very profitable to pay interest on

[1] The Comptroller of the Currency at an early date permitted banks to deduct from deposits owing to other banks to the extent that these amounts were covered by amounts due from other banks.

bankers' balances and thus competed with each other for these interior funds. They accumulated in their vaults much larger amounts of funds than the legal provisions contemplated. The surplus resources of the interior banks, therefore, tended to be pushed toward the metropolis where the banks could make profitable use of this additional lending power but in *highly unliquid* extensions of credit. We say this because of the fact that most of these funds served as the basis for expansion of collateral loans to stock speculators and dealers in securities. Trusting again the treacherous illusion of liquidity, the New York banks were misled into considering that the salability of securities in the individual case meant also the ready salability in general; they considered their collateral loans essentially liquid, whereas in fact they were anything but liquid. The attempt to call back or refuse renewal of collateral loans inevitably meant severe pressure upon the Stock Exchange and perhaps also upon the bond market, and these pressures were capable at times of turning unfavorable developments into real panic situations.[1]

When these characteristics of American banking, including the practices under the National Banking System, are considered in relation to one another, it is clear that the system was full of destructive and dangerous illusions as to the strength of our banking mechanism. The *character* of the loans and investments, as distinct from their *amounts*, were not of primary interest to the legislators who concentrated their attention first upon *notes* and later upon minimum reserves against deposits. It is not surprising that lending practices and investment procedure among commercial banks early developed unfortunate qualitative tendencies. *The banks essentially attempted to straddle two quite distinct fields—capital financing and commercial credit.* The banks were always aware of the possibility of withdrawals and hence tended to place funds of an essentially nondeposit or savings character in capital loans but security lending and investment on a peculiar contingent or conditional basis. These advances had strings tied to them and were thus not really true investments or capital loans in the sense that the lender

---

[1] The Comptrollers of the Currency were not unaware of these evils. John Jay Knox, in his Report for 1877, made some very pointed remarks concerning this system of scattered reserves tending to pyramid in the hands of New York banks. He suspected that funds were sent to New York mainly because the interior banks, limited in the scope of their lending, frequently could not utilize to advantage all their resources in commercial credit. He therefore suggested that some type of Federal obligation should be made available to them as a means of investing surplus funds and obtaining a return of perhaps 4 per cent on them. He particularly suggested that these be in small denominations to freely enable the banks to dispose of them to the public, and vice versa. "This policy," he claimed, "would . . . have the effect . . . of retaining in their hands a considerable portion of those idle funds which are now sent to their correspondents in the central cities, and are loaned by the latter, upon call, to dealers in speculative securities." (P. xxi.)

was able and willing to maintain a position until the user of the capital had been able to recoup from his own activity the funds for repayment over a period long enough to permit or encourage amortization.

As for the banks generally, the practice of making short-term loans that really were or soon became long-term loans through renewal tended to hold back the development of true capital-investment institutions, particularly those capable of serving the needs of the smaller business firms and new enterprises as distinct from large and established corporations. This, in turn, was one factor contributing to the growth of very large business units, and this trend in the 1920's was paralleled by the use of the security market as an important source of industrial capital financing.

RECURRENCE OF FINANCIAL PANICS

Once the banking system (particularly in the period prior to World War I) was subjected to shock, it converted minor vibrations into panics. It became impossible for many businessmen to secure additional credit or even to maintain lines of credit already outstanding. When conditions reached the point of panic, the sudden failure of the weakest banks simultaneously swept away not only the savings of the poor but the working funds of business houses and monies to be used for payrolls. The tendency of the old banking system to accentuate and spread the vibration emanating from such basic factors as we have considered resulted to a large extent from overexpansion of speculative advances in New York and the difficulty of obtaining reserve funds placed in New York quickly enough to provide additional credit for business in the interior.

In order to show more specifically the functioning of our banking system, as it operated prior to the establishment of the Federal Reserve System, Chart 32 will be helpful. In the chart can be seen the relation between bank loans and the fluctuations of the business cycle and the cyclical movements of commodity prices relative to their underlying trend. The expansion in bank loans between 1904 and 1907 more or less paralleled the expansion of business activity, and the rates charged by the banks for discounting commercial paper (and presumably the rates on most other short-term loans) also rose. In general, prior to World War I and during the long period when the United States was primarily in a debtor position on international account, the variations in bank-discount rates reflected the cyclical movements in loans rather than independent changes in reserves. Occasionally there were demands upon the New York banks for funds to settle foreign balances, but withdrawals of gold in most instances were not of themselves a major cause of credit stringency.

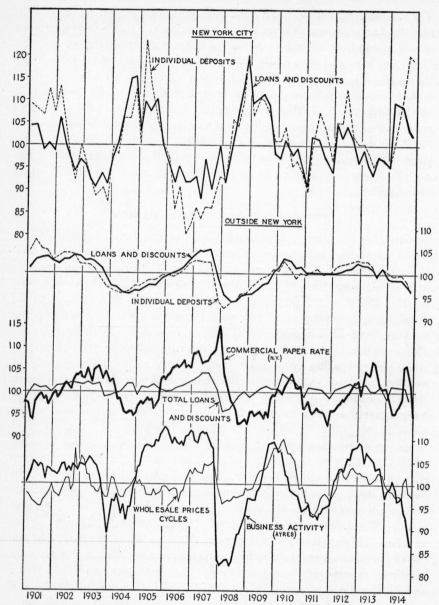

CHART 32.—Credit conditions, business activity, and wholesale price cycles, 1901–1914. All of these measures are shown in the form of indexes relative to long-term trend in order to portray clearly the cylical movements. The scales are uniform throughout.

A careful study of the gold movement by months between 1880 and 1910 would reveal that in almost all cases during those years, gold entered the United States when money rates were *rising* rather than falling, and gold moved out of the country when low rates here coincided with higher rates in European centers.   At the top of Chart 32 is shown the cyclical course of deposits in the National Banks of New York City and those outside New York.   If it is kept in mind that the loans and discount of the New York banks closely paralleled their own deposits (reflecting the tendency there to use balances from the interior in advances to the stock market), it will be seen that New York deposits moved *inversely* to *outside* deposits.   It was the shifting of funds to meet interior developments and, of course, the seasonal requirements of agriculture, that mainly affected the reserves as such.   In addition, however, it must be remembered that not only were reserve funds shifted about between interior and metropolis but cash funds were also shifted, as between the banks as a whole and the general public.[1]

During the early stages of a business boom the banks generally would continue expanding loans and discounts freely, but as business activity increased and the tempo of trade tended to affect commodity prices also, there began to be a demand on the part of the public for more pocket cash. This outflow of cash from banks to people became more rapid as the cyclical tendency expanded, and presently it served to a perceptible degree to check further liberal credit advances.   In conjunction with the faltering of business and some early insolvencies in trade or promotional construction, this served as the first notice of a coming storm.   Loans began to be refused; rates rose swiftly; the New York banks called in speculative advances.   Security prices began to decline.   Merchants feared that credit was becoming tighter and stopped adding to inventories.   Failures in industry began to multiply.   Those endeavoring to stave off insolvency or embarrassment eagerly sought additional personal loans.   Finally there came frantic calls from interior banks for return of reserve balances held in New York, with the natural result of bringing about grave embarrassment in New York, beset by its own difficulties. Time and again during these periods of acute emergency it was necessary for banks to close, and this naturally produced a spiral of panic conditions throughout the country.   These panic phenomena were, therefore, definitely associated with the weaknesses of our banking system and should not be regarded as a necessary concomitant to business reversals or depressions as such.

Chart 32 also reveals that in the particular case of the business reversal leading to the panic of 1907–1908, the expansion in the loans and discounts of the National Banks outside New York City, which began in

[1] We may omit for the present consideration of funds held in the national Treasury.

1904, coincided with a *declining* tendency in these items in New York City. The New York banks were beginning to reduce accommodation to the stock market, and perhaps also to merchants, a considerable time before there was any evidence of general strain or even a significant rise in short-term money rates. By 1906 the outside banks had withdrawn considerable funds from the metropolis, and money rates began to be decidedly firm. Shortly thereafter stock prices began to wilt in the face of higher cost of speculative credit and an even faster rise in the collateral loan rates than in the commercial paper market. The critical point of strain came at the end of 1907, intensified by a rapidly collapsing stock market, selling of investment securities by all banks, with an accompanying decline in bond prices and demands for emergency loans by businessmen.[1]

As the data used in Chart 32 relate only to National Banks, it must be added that in the period that we are now discussing there were further elements of vulnerability in New York City because of the rapid growth of trust companies and the shifting of loans from the banks to these even less conservatively managed institutions. This tended to sustain the loans destined for use in stock-market speculation somewhat longer than the data indicate. As these loans during the acute stage of the crisis were in part shifted back to the commercial banks and particularly to the metropolitan National Banks, it was necessary for these institutions to face a local strain in New York and also the emergency withdrawals of reserve balances by interior banks. The acute phase of the crisis of 1907 revealed, as similar phases many times previously had done, the close association of certain banks and trust companies with those interested in basic capital promotion. In this instance there was promotion of copper-mining properties by a group whose activities had begun to create suspicion, and from this developed the first important runs on banks, a long-familiar sign of approaching strain and panic. Depositors began to withdraw money from savings banks, and business firms reduced deposits in commercial banks throughout the country. Under these conditions the banks in the large financial centers found themselves greatly handicapped by the rigid character of the legal reserve requirements that served as a barrier to the extension of emergency credit, where

---

[1] For further statistical details relating to the behavior of the assets and liabilities of banks during the period 1901 to 1914 see the excellent analysis by Allyn A. Young, "An Analysis of Bank Statistics for the United States," Harvard University Press, 1928, particularly Chapter 1, from which the banking data shown in Chart 32 were obtained.

See also the detailed historical study of panics and crises during the existence of the National Banking System down to 1908, prepared by O. M. W. Sprague for the National Monetary Commission under the title "History of Crises under the National Banking System," Washington, D.C., 1910.

it would do most good to restore confidence and allay panic. According to Sprague, "It was restriction in New York that inevitably precipitated more or less complete suspension throughout the entire country."[1]

The desperate situation in New York was finally relieved by resort to a makeshift device somewhat similar to one that had previously been found effective in such emergencies. This was temporary support to bank-lending power by the use of the local Clearing House as a source of temporary advances of credit. But for two months the banks of New York could not function on a normal basis, and money was bought and sold at a premium. The crisis of 1907 essentially repeated what had been seen in 1873 and again in 1893. In the country at large, many banks were forced to suspend, and there was everywhere uncertainty, confusion, and embarrassment to business. As in previous emergencies, manufacturers found it difficult to obtain funds to meet payroll, and many industries closed down, and their workers were idle for weeks or months.

The rate of mortality in our old banking system (exclusive of savings banks) as the result of acute strain and panic in 1907 is revealed in the Reports of the Comptroller of the Currency. In the year ending June 30, 1908, 153 National, state, and private banks were forced to suspend, representing a total of nearly a quarter of a billion dollars of deposits. This was by far the largest impairment of deposit liabilities thus far experienced in the United States. In the 1893 fiscal year, the number of failures had been 291, representing 55 millions of deposits. In 1884, 60 banks failed, with about 21 millions of deposits. The severe impairment of business conditions in 1873 and ensuing financial difficulties stretched along for several years, and the largest number of bank failures was not reached until 1878, when 80 banks failed, with total deposits of 32 millions. Having in mind the close dependence of merchants and manufacturers upon the solvency of the banking system and their ability to secure accommodation continuously and readily, these failure figures are highly significant and are indeed a shameful aspect of our financial history.

Chart 33 displays an index of business insolvency, including failures of banks, mercantile and manufacturing companies, and the estimated annual totals of fixed-charge obligations of railroads placed in receiver-

---

[1] Sprague, op. cit., p. 261. Sprague further says (p. 269), "Banks with relatively large New York trust company deposits or numerous correspondents in the West and South were subject to the greatest demands for cash and for the liquidation of loans. When the outside banks and the trust companies called their loans, brokers, to whom call loans are principally made, immediately resorted to the banks carrying their regular accounts, and the banks felt under obligation to afford them accommodation so far at least as it could be shown to be absolutely necessary."

ship. A separate curve at the top of the chart shows the insolvency record in terms of real-estate mortgage foreclosures.[1] The interesting features of this exhibit are the marked degree of volatility in financial impairment, the rather distinctive pattern of the cyclical movement in real-estate foreclosures, and (referring to the lowest curve) the evidence

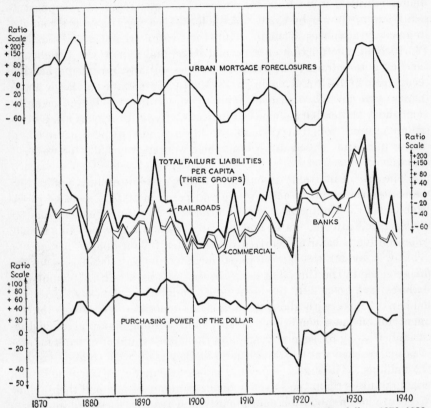

CHART 33.—Business mortality and the purchasing power of the dollar, 1870–1939. As the failure liabilities (partly estimated, and expressed on a per capita basis) are plotted to a ratio scale, the component parts of the totals should be interpreted as proportions rather than cumulated amounts. The purchasing power of the dollar has no very consistent relationship to business failures. See also Appendix 12, Section 1.

that although significant increases in the purchasing power of the dollar were frequently related to a rise of failures, this was not uniformly true. This is what we expect from our previous analysis of the vital part played by transportation and building construction in producing industrial cycles and depressions, which were intensified by the additional stresses arising from a vulnerable, poorly integrated banking system.[2]

[1] Based upon the same data shown in Chart 28.

[2] The failure experiences in the later years shown in Chart 33 will be further commented upon in Chapter 14.

Returning now to Chart 32, we can briefly summarize the financial sequel to the panic of 1907. It will be noted that toward the end of that year there was a prompt return flow of funds to New York. This was in some measure due to the effect of high money rates in encouraging imports of gold from Europe. Gold imports in November, 1907, reached the highest point that had been attained in a single month for many years. But it cannot be claimed that the banking crisis was in any measure *due* to an *outflow* of gold during the business boom, for the years 1906 and 1907 had also been years of rather large net gold imports. Conversely, the net outflow of gold in 1909 and 1910 did not visibly impair the recuperation of the banking system. During these years, when the country was still not definitely in a creditor position internationally (save for very short periods of time), the tightening of money rates was almost entirely a matter of *internal* banking strain produced, first, by the rise in business and speculative loans and, later, by the acute pressure of emergency loans and shifting of loans from bank to bank. Again with reference to Chart 32, we see that as soon as some measure of ease was reestablished in the banking situation and funds again began to flow back to New York, with trade conditions stagnant, money rates immediately responded. The short-term discount rate and the call rate on collateral loans in New York rapidly declined throughout 1908.

This sensitive responsiveness of the short-term money rates in the financial center to the business cycle and occasional panic phenomena was for many years of practical importance. It made it possible for financial observers, businessmen, and security investors to determine the approximate time at which tension was definitely being relieved. A careful study of money rates revealed the approach of periods of strain, and thus it became a well-accepted business principle in that the state of the banking position in the country's financial nerve center, New York, was the most reliable advance indicator of general business conditions. Whereas money rates always reached their highest peak *during* the strain that followed a business reversal, the peaks almost always *preceded* by a significant interval the turn toward recovery of manufacturing industry and trade activity. In other words, the basic factors tending toward recurring overcapitalization of long-term investment projects and impairment of mortgage solvency first registered their effects upon the banking mechanism, and this a little later transmitted and amplified the impulses as they appeared in manufacturing and merchandising. Industries producing raw materials and capital goods used in construction not only entered a period of dwindling orders as the excessive momentum in promotion passed its crest, but also suffered the further embarrassing effects of an acute impairment or shutting off of their credit facilities. A further extension of inactivity, closed-down factories, destruction of general buying power, and, what is also very important, the shattering of investment confidence all contributed to carry the industrial recession even farther than its intrinsic volatility alone would have warranted.

It is well to state this matter with care, because the writer has observed many cases in which economists and statisticians have seized upon the working of the New York money market and the peculiar sensitiveness of its lending rates as being virtually the motivating forces producing business collapse and later engineering recovery. Although undoubtedly money market conditions were long a useful forecasting factor (if we restrict ourselves to short-term cyclical forecasting), it by no means follows that we find in the banking system of those days more than a transmitting instrument or amplifier of more fundamental prime movers, such as our previous analysis has revealed.

Somewhat the same comment may be made concerning the well-established tendency—at any rate, until recent years—for stock prices also to describe a cyclical turn somewhat in advance of those in the index of general business conditions. More will be said of this in a later chapter, but while we are speaking of the banking system and money rates we may conveniently record the fact that this sensitive property in the stock market was a mere reflection of the variations in money rates.

CHAPTER 12

THE FEDERAL RESERVE AND CREDIT CONTROL EXPERIMENTS

Our banking system prior to World War I proved to be so important an amplifier of the stresses contributing to business instability that it is worth while to carry forward the analysis of subsequent changes in the structure and in banking policy.

The panic of 1907 generated keen public interest in banking reform and considerable study of the problem, out of which emerged the Federal Reserve System to supplement and coordinate the operations of the commercial banks.[1] The most important objectives of the Federal Reserve organization were, first, to introduce more flexibility into the bank-note circulation by permitting the central banks (operating as 12 regional units but with policy determined in large measure by a governing board) to issue Federal Reserve notes against earning assets held in the form of gold or commercial paper of approved character; and, second and most important, to provide a kind of safety factor by making available the rediscount of approved member bank assets in times of emergency credit demand. Membership was obligatory to National Banks but open to other commercial banks meeting specified qualifications. This supplementary lending power through rediscounting short-term notes and mercantile drafts arising from business rather than speculative transactions contemplated the establishment of a broad and fluid commercial paper or "bill" market, based upon trade instruments several times endorsed and thus made readily merchantable throughout the financial centers of the nation and widening the access of businessmen to credit resources.

This was essentially an attempt to transplant from London and Continental Europe to the United States the kind of commercial-paper rediscount machinery that previously had existed here to a very limited extent. But circumstances failed to confirm the hope of Paul M.

---

[1] Actually, the new system was not quite in working order when the War broke out in 1914, but previous legislation had provided the organization capable of affording a temporary device for pooling the lending power of the commercial banks, or at least a substantial number of them. This was developed in outline by the Aldrich-Vreeland Act. The banks were able under the provisions of this Act to meet the temporary strain occasioned by the outbreak of war, and highly disturbed foreign-exchange market at that juncture, and an orderly transition was facilitated to the new system in 1915.

Warburg, Carter Glass, and other founders of the new system that American businessmen would alter their commercial practices and readily adopt the type of credit instruments and the dependence upon short-term trade credit that had been so long familiar to businessmen in Europe. Our business transactions continued to be mainly of domestic character, and the amount of accepted drafts arising from foreign-trade transactions was never developed to anything like the importance that had been attained, for example, in the London money market. Hence, at the very start, the system whereby "emergency credit" was to be available to the member banks not only was of foreign origin but represented a narrow segment of the total earning assets of a majority of our commercial banks. Therefore, the plan to base the new form of note issue mainly upon rediscounted mercantile and industrial notes and drafts rather than upon gold soon encountered obstacles.

In order to provide the Federal Reserve bankers' banks with real banking prerequisites, they were to hold in their vaults *all the legally recognized reserves* of the member banks. This was mobilization of reserve power. When this transfer of gold from members to Federal Reserve was completed in 1917, the Reserve Banks were able to extend credit to members within such limits as were set up by law. The gold reserves now supported two types of liability: the Reserve notes and the Federal Reserve deposits, which represented primarily deposits to the credit of member banks. These credits, in turn, constituted the recognized or legal reserve of those banks, and any additions to them created by rediscounting operations were therefore additions to their working reserves. A new concept of bank reserves was thus introduced into American practice. Every dollar of deposits that a member bank had to its credit on the books of the Federal Reserve Bank of its district represented available reserve. Fresh reserve could be expanded by the rediscount of approved paper if member banks happened to have assets in that form. Thus it was possible for the total reserve available to the member banks to be greater than all the gold held in all the Reserve Banks. We added a flexible expansion joint to our bank reserves but curiously enough at a time when inadequate gold reserve was just beginning to disappear as a key problem in our credit system.[1]

THE FEDERAL RESERVE AND WAR FINANCING

The exigencies of World War I not only gave this new system a severe test but soon necessitated changes in the relationship of member

---

[1] Naturally, there was a penalty attached to rediscounting. This was available at rates that usually would not make the practice profitable and would restrict it to emergency conditions as a means of avoiding the panic phase of financial stringency and the cumulative freezing of assets.

banks to the central banks. The first phase was one of marked advance in commodity prices as we undertook to supply the Allies with urgently needed armaments and food. The member banks rediscounted commercial paper in large amounts during the first few years of the War. This process, however, may have introduced an additional inflationary element and even speculative element in the commodity markets, since the Reserve Banks could not legitimately deny rediscounts of commercial paper, even though that paper might actually have represented a tendency on the part of businessmen to increase inventories unduly or even to speculate in commodities.

Soon after our entry into the War, enormous new Federal financial requirements had to be met. Therefore, in the autumn of 1916, the Reserve Act was amended to permit Reserve Banks to make advances directly to member banks if the latter presented promissory notes secured by collateral of United States Government securities. This vastly extended the "reserve-creating" power from trade paper to Federal bonds. Although this provision contemplated only short-maturity advances of this type, the member banks found it possible and expedient to renew them. They were thus in a position to assist the Government very materially in carrying through its various war-loan drives but by an essentially inflationary operation, since many individuals and business firms purchasing war bonds borrowed at their banks to provide the money, and these banks, in turn, borrowed on the very same collateral from the Federal Reserve. The Federal Government virtually monetized its own credit in the form of circulating purchasing power. Whether the easy availability of credit under this new system, both for private business and for the War effort, had any influence in encouraging borrowing as against taxation is difficult to say, but the presumption is that had these highly flexible and expansible facilities been absent the country would not have endeavored, as it did, to maintain the gold standard, either at home or abroad. There might easily have been a repetition of the greenback experience in some type of outright fiat currency. At any rate, the advances made to the member banks on Government collateral formed the most important part of central-bank assistance to the commercial institutions during the War period.

In addition to these tremendous bond collateral advances by the Federal Reserve, their rediscounting of commercial paper temporarily also assumed large proportions. With the Reserve Banks carrying so large a part of the credit load to finance the War, the member banks were in a position to contribute in still another direction to the mounting spiral of credit inflation by direct investment in Government obligations. Their holding of Federal securities almost quadrupled after our entry into the War. This momentous transition to central reserve banking under the abnormal and distorted conditions of war actually produced a threefold expansibility of total bank credit (primarily, of course, within the total membership of the system) by (1) concentrating reserves and reducing normal reserve requirements against deposits, (2) providing for essentially "paper" or credit reserves by regarding member bank deposits with the Federal Reserve Banks as legal reserves,[1] and (3) the fortuitous circumstance (not anticipated in the initial legislation) of a substantial net inflow of gold during most of the War period and, indeed, for some time thereafter. Although the new system was intended to stabilize credit conditions and eliminate panic stringency, all these factors were, in fact, contributing toward overexpansion, and the very ease of this emergency expansion undoubtedly created serious obstacles to inflation control and financing the War by a more adequate measure of taxation.

Referring back to Chart 9, showing the net gold movement during the period that we are considering, we can say that the World War definitely marked a transition not only as to banking organization but from an era of recurring inadequacy (or perhaps unavailability) of reserves to a tendency for large, even though irregular, receipts of gold capable of expanding the available reserves of the banking system. The Federal Reserve System had been predicated upon the presumption that our gold position would not be radically altered by international developments, whereas, in fact, there soon appeared a tendency toward serious disturbance in the equilibrium of international settlements. The new system constituted a mechanism capable of infusing a permanently larger credit superstructure per dollar of reserve on a gold foundation that itself was destined to expand tremendously. As events worked out, the end of the War did not bring about an immediate credit deflation here, for Europe remained in dire need of essential materials and particularly food. The sudden release of this additional foreign demand produced a considerable further enlargement of bank credit and rediscounting of commercial paper with the Federal Reserve Banks in 1919 and well into 1920.

This is clearly seen in Chart 34, which illustrates the rapid rise in commercial money rates and commodity prices to a peak in the late spring of 1920. This sharp and short-lived postwar inflation was easily financed despite some temporary loss of gold in 1919.[2] In other words, the new system was so flexible that minor oscillations in net gold movement were no longer of consequence in their effect upon credit availability.

---

[1] Average reserve requirements against deposits of the commercial banks prior to the organization of the Federal Reserve System were about 21 per cent. By the summer of 1917 these became less than 10 per cent. (Phillips, McManus, and Nelson, "Banking and the Business Cycle," New York, 1937.)

[2] Nearly half a billion was shipped to South America and the Orient following the release of the embargo on foreign gold that had prevailed during the War.

It is true the credit expansion just after the War did subject the system to some temporary strain, for the Reserve Banks by 1920 had expanded their note and deposit liabilities to a point beyond which their existing gold reserves would have proved inadequate according to the minimum legal level. Had further Federal Reserve credit been extended, it would

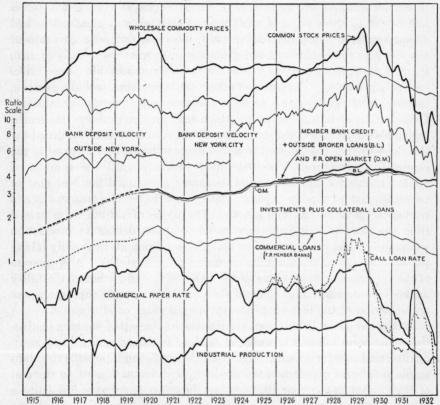

CHART 34.—Commodity and stock-market inflation in relation to credit conditions, 1915–1932. The commodity price inflation of 1916–1920 and the stock-market inflation of 1926–1929, were both correlated with cyclical changes in credit circulation, but with differences in the character of the credit factors in the two cases. All curves in the chart are drawn to uniform ratio scale, permitting comparison of proportional fluctuations.

have been necessary to do so under emergency conditions provided for in the Reserve Act, involving payment of a penalty tax. But the Reserve authorities, late in 1919, began to apply the brakes by raising the rate at which they would discount commercial paper. Since the rediscount rate had been below the rate prevailing in the money market, this step was not fully effective but did suffice as warning that credit for speculative operations was to become less readily available. The rediscount rate was finally raised to 7 per cent in the middle of 1920 and remained at that level through the spring of 1921.

BANKING ASPECTS OF POSTWAR DEFLATION

But months before this point of apparent credit strain and these steps to curtail needless credit extension, the structure of commodity prices had begun to show signs of weakness. Livestock and meat prices had already suffered sharp declines in 1919, reflecting excessive government supplies and the beginnings of liquidation in farm areas. Early in 1920 there came signs of distress in the silk industry as raw-silk prices broke violently in Japan. The prices of other textile products, including cotton, followed in the early spring as buyers refused to pay current quotations. Cancellation of orders, many of which had previously been duplicated through fear that delayed deliveries would result from the railroad-car shortage, further contributed to an ominous faltering and reversal of the commodity structure. Prices declined violently until the summer of 1921. Industrial and mercantile demand for commodities had now to be readjusted to a peace basis. The United States Government began to dispose of huge material stocks. The needs of Europe soon passed from the state of acute shortage to one of more deliberate production recuperation and more normal trade. As in all periods of rapidly falling prices, business failures rapidly mounted (*cf.* Chart 33). And in spite of the supposed strengthening of the banking system, a heavy mortality among commercial banks marked the year 1921, even though there was no repetition of the historic tendency toward panic conditions.

What happened in this instance was the folding up of banking institutions that were inherently unsound because of frozen agricultural, commodity, and collateral loans. The sound banks found it possible to obtain ample relief and supplementary credit by rediscount almost to the end of 1920. But in the year 1921 (ending June 30), there were 357 failures among National, state, and private commercial banks, involving 161 millions of deposits. Failures were most prevalent among the smaller state banks outside the Reserve System and particularly in the agricultural areas. The collapse of wartime inflation, as we have seen, usually exerts its most acute pressure upon farm-product prices, but the Federal Reserve System really did very little to attack this problem. There remained in existence an excessive number of small banks, facing high credit risks and exceedingly vulnerable to a swift deflation of commodity values. Nor did the Federal Reserve System eliminate the risk of the shrinkage in investment values that forced numerous banks to suspend as their assets shrank in value and loans based upon collateral of securities became impaired or frozen. And the Reserve Banks themselves, enlisted almost from the outset in the financing of the War, continued to maintain an easier and more lenient rediscount policy in 1919 and 1920 than an inflationary price tendency demanded, and they helped to build up a larger extension of credit—albeit "secured" by evidences of "legitimate" commodity transactions—than was consistent with a sound general banking condition.

In retrospect we see clearly the weaknesses inherent in the very nature of our banking structure and in the processes involved in creating earning assets, which the Reserve System, as primarily an emergency-device safety valve (and mechanism for war financing) utterly failed to reach. The old emphasis upon the crying need for emergency credit had finally found an answer; but in adapting to that problem the pattern of banking controls, the traditional disregard of the *qualitative character* of banking assets was perpetuated by formal discounting devices that did not serve adequately to prevent inflation; at the same time the ensuing enlargement of credit on Federal war loan collateral nullified any effective quantitative controls as they had to do with the monetary circulation aspects of banking.

This price inflation and the sharp deflation generated a decade of rather confused discussion and controversy concerning central-banking policy with respect to the stabilizing of prices and thereby the stabilization of business operations. Prices became the key to all policy. As business recuperation asserted itself under the compelling influence of the basic construction factors that we have previously considered, the participation of the commercial banks in building up a new mass of "capital credit" was given scant attention, with results that ultimately proved disastrous. By this intense preoccupation among economists and politicians with the Reserve Banks as supreme controllers of the *money supply* and providers of apparently liquid short-term credits to business and Government, the necessity for adequate liquidity of sound assets among the commercial banks, inside or outside the Reserve System, was almost completely ignored. Attention has fastened more and more upon the manipulation of money rates and the investment portfolios of the Reserve Banks as devices for attempting price-level stabilization or, perhaps, price reinflation following the 1921 collapse. It came to be rather generally believed that by controlling the price level we should attain the millenium of economic stability and never-ending prosperity. Meanwhile, the member banks of the Reserve System, relieved of the old worries over stringencies and panics and conscious of the unprecedented inflow of gold, proceeded to load up their assets with paper that represented less and less rediscounting potentiality. This meant that the Reserve authorities had to resort more and more to the manipulation of the investment portfolios of the central banks as a means of keeping the system at least under nominal discipline and the *monetary* aspect of credit circulation reasonably under restraint.

By 1923 it was already becoming evident that this country might never be able to develop a substantial commercial-discount market built upon readily marketable drafts and bills of exchange, capable, as in Europe, of affording delicate control by the central bank over commercial credit and presumably trade conditions. One further reason was that industry in this country chose to finance itself through nonbanking channels to an increasing extent. This led to the beginning of what is now referred to as the "open-market" policy of the Federal Reserve Banks. Begun experimentally in 1922, this was to become a major part of the mechanism of credit control. By making purchases of the highest grade acceptances or drafts, the Reserve Banks released funds to the money markets and the banks serving commerce; by reducing these securities funds could be taken out of the market and credit conditions tightened. This technique could readily be extended to purchase or sale of short-term government securities of the type that the Federal Government had begun to issue during the War. In fact, even long-term Federal securities could be used as part of this open-market regulating system. Further encouraging the use of this new control technique was, of course, the change in the gold movement. We were being surfeited with gold, and control of credit in view of this change, although at first not clearly recognized, ultimately became an explicit responsibility on the part of the Reserve Board. This responsibility extended beyond the borders of the United States through attempts at collaboration with the central banks of other countries, particularly Great Britain. The postwar decade was one of general chaos in international exchange, following price inflations that in some countries had reached fantastic levels. The Federal Reserve System thus became involved in international financial diplomacy, which presently began to exert a perceptible influence upon internal credit and a course of action not well adapted to the circumstances developing in the domestic economic situation.

DOMESTIC AND INTERNATIONAL FINANCIAL POLICY

The 1920's were a period of great prosperity in the United States for fundamental reasons that have already been discussed. Meanwhile, Europe struggled with the problem of internal rebuilding, restoring international trade relations and stabilizing currencies and exchange rates. By and large, the world feared deflation of prices. The raw-material countries, including parts of the Orient and most of Latin America, had enjoyed tremendous prosperity during the War, but the postwar collapse introduced grave difficulties and delicate problems of readjustment. Few countries shared the fortune of the United States in having ready at hand a new apparatus fortuitously designed to make deflations relatively painless and neatly cushioned affairs.   For countries whose currencies had been divorced from gold and whose price levels had soared far higher than ours, the problems of returning to normality and stability were indeed complex and difficult.

When the Swedish economist Gustav Cassel, whose writings commanded wide attention in the early 1920's, came forward with persuasive pleas that the deflation process be made as easy as possible, his words found broadly sympathetic response.   Cassel accurately diagnosed the price inflation of most countries as immediately based upon expansion of war credits, and he saw no reason why a substantial part of this redundant credit should not remain permanently in existence.   Cassel was inclined to be critical of our own deflationary experiences in 1920–1921 and insisted that our collapse of commodity prices had been harmful to the world.   Further violent deflation, he insisted, would bring about a vast amount of frozen credit and liquidation throughout the world. The scramble to return to the gold standard as it had existed in 1914 would be disastrous.   It would be desirable, he thought, for the United States to refrain from attracting additional gold, but he doubted that even with our assistance few countries outside Britain would be in a position to return to anything like the prewar gold standard.[1]

Aggravating the international problem of currency rationalization were the particular problem of Germany and the payment of reparations, which could not be successful under general conditions of falling world prices.   In such an atmosphere, reasoned words of caution against deflation served to cultivate a new philosophy, known as "reflation." During the 1920's many American economists came forth in defense of measures for credit and monetary "control," not primarily designed to minimize the impact of business cycles or to prevent panics or to maintain a steady national income, but rather to provide a means for *sustaining prices*, averting further deflation, and incidentally providing what positive support could be mobilized for the prices of the products of agriculture and the mineral industries.   To all such objectives the Federal Reserve System offered a most strategic instrument, to which various circumstances contributed additional reflationary and expansionist elements.

Following the brief commodity deflation of 1921, attention continued to be devoted throughout that decade to the distressed condition of agriculture.   It is indeed remarkable that American agricultural prices were supported to the extent that they were during the 1920's.   Among the sustaining factors was further legislation adapting the banking system more particularly to the service of agriculture.   The Federal Reserve Banks, even during the War and the crisis of 1921, served rural credit

[1] Cassel, "The World's Monetary Problems," London, 1921.

needs through the fact that nonmember banks in the smaller rural communities leaned upon correspondents in the larger centers who were members of the Reserve System and who were able to discount short-term farm notes with the Reserve Banks.

In 1923 further steps were taken to recognize the normally longer term of agricultural marketing paper, and the Federal Reserve Banks were authorized to rediscount agricultural notes and drafts having maturities as long as nine months. In addition, there was set up a system of intermediate-credit institutions, particularly for the financing of the still longer term working capital needs of the livestock industry. Beyond this the Federal Land Banks came into the picture in the middle 'twenties as a further step toward developing a type of cooperative long-term agricultural financing at reasonable interest rates, such as had already long been in existence in northern Europe. These steps were all indications of the previous ineffectiveness and unsoundness of the "renewable" short loans to agriculture made by local banks for what were actually capital purposes. The United States was at last beginning to recognize that *long-term and intermediate productive credit was not a kind of financing that could be combined indiscriminately and safely with short-notice deposit banking.*

In addition to these financial steps, there came later in this decade the ambitious but ill-starred experiments of the Federal Farm Board to support the price of wheat by trying to conceal the wheat surplus and the forming of an articulate farm bloc in Congress dedicated to the proposition that agriculture was fundamentally in distress and should be granted exceptional assistance along financial lines. One of these, incidentally, was permission to National Banks to make loans (within limits) on property mortgages. Since these loans were limited to five-year maturity, the plan was inherently unsound, and it would have been very much better to have avoided this further potential freezing of bank assets by setting up distinctive institutions for long-term property financing, as we have previously stated. This provision for limited property loans by National Banks was further liberalized in 1927. In addition to specific measures such as these, some supporting influence in the domestic market for agricultural products came from the building boom and continuance of a high rate of industrial activity generally. But in spite of this, agricultural prosperity was never fully restored in the 'twenties; failures were heavy among farmers, and few farming groups were able to share the rise in income of metropolitan areas that enjoyed for their land and security speculations the full benefit of credit largesse provided by new-era banking.

As we follow the course of events through this momentous decade and reflect upon the significance of the large gold imports during most of that period, it is difficult to avoid a feeling of astonishment at the attitude taken by the politicians of European countries toward resumption of the gold standard. Germany was experiencing fantastic inflation in the early 'twenties. Then came France, with almost as spectacular an episode of paper-money expansion. Great Britain, meanwhile, soberly planned resumption of the former gold standard to take effect in 1925. The British economist J. M. Keynes was as deeply skeptical of the possibility of resuming gold on the old basis as he had been of the success of the Versailles Treaty. From a baffling demoralization of currencies Germany finally emerged with a staggering war debt that remained a menace to international stability, despite all the whittling-down "plans" and repeated modifications of transfer procedure. France emerged with a sharply devaluated franc, and so did Italy and most of the smaller nations of Europe.

All this confused financial revolution contributed to two important tendencies in our monetary and banking policy. First, there was a tendency on the part of many countries, including Latin America, to base their currencies more or less directly upon the dollar and to use dollar exchange or funds deposited in New York for the redemption of their revised monetary standards. Foreign funds arriving in New York included these public deposits of gold and foreign exchange. From time to time there developed sizable imports of essentially "refugee funds" sent to the United States for safe deposit while foreign governments were wrestling with the problem of just how to attain some kind of workable gold standard. The important point is that this gold did not represent trade balance or permanent deposit here, but essentially temporary and conditional demand deposits. Furthermore, Federal Reserve policy was constrained to assist the British effort to resume gold at a price that now represented a higher value of the pound than in the immediate postwar period. This assistance was rendered by maintaining money rates in this country as low as possible after 1924 in order that gold should not be unduly drawn from London by higher short-term rates in New York. There was already a superabundance of gold here that in itself made it difficult for the Reserve authorities to enforce such a policy through either the rediscount rate or the open-market policy. Such control devices, as they were operated for many years by the Bank of England in a more suitable environment, presume a situation of relatively limited gold movements that can be delicately manipulated by credit policy to prevent any marked increase in or withdrawal of gold from the banking system. As the decade moved on, there was additional evidence that the Treasury was endeavoring to augment its authority over the operations of the Federal Reserve Board, the Secretary of the Treasury being ex officio a member of the Board.

THE CONGEALING OF BANKING ASSETS

Although the rising momentum of the residential building cycle culminated as early as 1926, general industrial activity continued to be well sustained for several years. Underlying this condition of remarkably persistent prosperity there were a number of outstanding factors. The building boom and its atmosphere of speculative promotion overflowed from the purely residential field into the building of metropolitan commercial structures, hotels, and large apartments, many of which came to be financed along new lines by the use of mortgage bonds. These securities were purchased by banks, and even trust departments of banking institutions invested part of their portfolios in obligations representing structural enterprises of this type. If we leave out of account the industrial building that naturally became necessary to provide for this, as well as the transportation and electric-power developments of those years, the over-all building boom was continued well into 1929. Building was also proceeding apace in Europe and Latin America. Germany, despite the onerous burden of reparations, found in the United States a ready source of capital that was liberally utilized for the construction of all manner of public works, bridges, docks, and housing projects, and a part of the borrowed sums also served conveniently for indemnity payments. During the 1920's large loans were floated in the United States to serve the needs of Bolivia, Brazil, Chile, Colombia, Peru, and others. Such of these sums as were not squandered in mere political extravagance and attempts to support tottering currency structures or raw-material prices went into railroad and building projects. It was essentially a repetition of what had happened in Argentina during the heyday of the British lending from 1880 to 1890. This was a part of our transition from a debtor position to a creditor position. In the five years from 1924 to 1928, nearly a billion and a quarter dollars a year was invested abroad. By the end of 1930, the total foreign investments of this country, excluding the nominal amounts of the inter-Allied debts, exceeded fifteen billion dollars. "What England had slowly accumulated in a century of saving and foreign investment America achieved in a decade and a half."[1]

It was this flood of foreign investment, much of it ill-considered and augmented by the mildly inflationary implications of the new credit system, that gave a semblance of reality to the inter-Allied debt claims and the possibility of enormous indemnity payments being wrung from Germany for many years. But the United States chose to adopt trade policies and tariff measures that made it increasingly difficult for these debtor governments to discharge their obligations in goods and services.

[1] Alvin H. Hansen, "Economic Stabilization in an Unbalanced World," p. 70, New York, 1932.

The debtors merely borrowed for a while to pay interest, and it is strange that our bankers and investors were so easily deceived. Long-term financing extended to countries fighting against the tide of postwar dislocations and readjustments could not be expected to remain solvent. These foreign credits could not be promptly tested by the salutory provision of amortization. This was but a part of an astonishing combination of factors temporarily supporting high business activity and creating a psychological attitude of supreme confidence in the long-term future. This, in turn, supported the extravagant issues of new securities and startling stock-market manipulations to promote their distribution.

The feverish prosperity of the late 1920's reflected itself in the earnings of industrial corporations and the ability of well-managed companies to accumulate comfortable surpluses. The war years had been profitable to some major industries and, despite the short setback of 1921, war profits served as a backlog upon which the systematic plowing back of earnings marked a new phase of corporate financial policy. The course of events strongly favored a policy of retiring outstanding industrial debt. This was rendered all the more practicable because so many of the outstanding obligations of *industrial* companies (as distinct from railroads, for example) was in a form permitting the calling in of the securities. Despite the urge to expand plant and the temptation to undertake mergers and combinations, not always warranted by the facts, corporations did not follow the stupid policy of the railroad reorganizers in piling new debt on existing stale debt. The tendency rather went in the direction of increasing equity capital by the flotation of stock, and this became progressively easier as the public, already rendered familiar with security ownership through purchase of the war loans, found it increasingly attractive to purchase equities with the assistance of the lush facilities of the banking system for making collateral loans. But the readiness with which the banks developed their collateral loans was itself furthered by the very increase in corporate solvency and financial solidity that pointed to a future of rising values of many shares. The making of commercial loans became less and less important; many large manufacturers were perfectly able to extend credit rather than to borrow in the money market. As transportation facilities improved it took less time to obtain inventory goods from sources of supply. Merchants who had gone through a trying period of price collapse and inventory liquidation in 1921 had learned a lesson that stood them in good stead now, and they bought from hand to mouth rather than far ahead. Even working-capital loans, which had previously been negotiated with commercial banks by manufacturing and mercantile enterprises, became less and less important as funds could be so readily secured by floating securities in a market that seemed insatiable.

Although banks could not themselves own common stocks they were induced by the decline of commercial and working-capital loans to place their earning assets in the form of investment in promotional and vulnerable bonds and the obligations of electric-power holding companies, loaded with leverage; at the same time their advances increasingly took the form of collateral loans, particularly in the metropolitan centers. Such extension of "capital credit" proceeded under the illusion that so long as the securities were "marketable" they were essentially liquid in the aggregate; and as for the loans to the stock market, were these not amply secured by certificates that could be sold on a moment's notice?[1]

As a matter of fact, there was little possibility of converting bank investments and collateral loans against stocks and bonds into cash without bringing about simultaneous liquidation capable of decimating the value of billions of securities—railroad bonds, "guaranteed" mortgage bonds on skyscrapers in New York and hotels in Chicago, municipal bonds representing extravagant outlays of local governments for roads and schools and parks. Add to this the even more volatile common stocks that were beginning to reflect the high leverage of holding companies as well as the untested securities of merged enterprises and the various and sundry foreign bonds floated to provide new housing projects in Berlin or attempts to bolster the price of coffee in São Paolo. There was absolutely no direct possibility of rediscounting bank assets resting on such enterprise with the Federal Reserve, and reserve banking through rediscount died a quiet death.[2]

[1] Even so acute an observer as B. M. Anderson, Jr., was prone to exaggerate the liquidity of stock-market collateral in these years, although he recognized that the banks were actually becoming involved in a type of credit extension serving purposes that in themselves were not in the nature of commercial credit. "The development of the modern stock market has changed the facts and provided a safe machinery for using the funds of commercial banks directly or indirectly for many capital purposes, still keeping them liquid. No commercial bank would lend directly on the road-bed, terminals, and bridges of a railroad. If the loan were not paid and the bank was obliged to foreclose, it would have a white elephant on its hands. No ready market exists for a railroad as an aggregate, or in fragments. But the bank may with entire safety lend money against the $100 shares or the $1,000 bonds representing the road-bed, terminals, and bridges of the railway, because for these bonds and shares a wide and active market exists. . . . When bank investments are bought at proper prices and are of proper quality and marketability, when collateral loans against securities are limited to well margined loans against readily marketable securities, and when growth in bank investments and in stock and bond collateral loans is moderate and kept reasonably in line with the growth of commercial loans, there is no occasion for concern about the development." (*Chase Economic Bulletin*, Nov. 8, 1926, p. 26.)

[2] At this point the Federal Reserve machinery differed from some other important central-bank systems. The Bank of England, for example, had been accustomed on occasion to extend credit to the joint-stock banks on various types of collateral, including even common stock, and this gave these central banks much more direct

Strongly contributing to this transition from commercial banking to "capital" banking was the tendency of corporations to maintain larger cash balances in the banks. This was partly a result of experience following the War, when adequate cash resources were found immensely helpful in preserving solvency and competitive position. But there were features of the banking system that encouraged the piling up of these balances. The Federal Reserve Act permitted member banks to accept time deposits and pay interest on them. Although corporate balances were divided between demand and time deposits, a tendency developed in the later 'twenties to take advantage of the higher rates paid on time balances, but nevertheless many banks granted depositors a presumptive right to withdraw funds practically on demand. Here lies one of the basic difficulties of banking in this period, although, as we have already seen, it was not really new.

Following the War, time deposits in trust companies multiplied fourfold and in National Banks almost as much. Between 1924 and 1928, the reporting member banks of the Reserve System added two billions to their time deposits, while their net demand deposits remained almost stationary. In New York City, the reporting member banks increased their time deposits in the same period by nearly 50 per cent, while net demand deposits declined slightly. To the member banks there was a great advantage in time deposits, because reserve requirements for these were but 3 per cent as compared with a range from 7 to 13 per cent against demand deposits. Thus the shift from demand to time deposits meant a further reduction in required reserve ratios beyond all the other means whereby the Federal Reserve System provided for more credit per dollar of reserves. But it was not so much the fact of this shift as the interpretation placed by banking practice upon the legitimacy of using such balances that became the principal evil in the situation. As the Federal Reserve Board itself pointed out in 1926:

Member banks were able to comply with legal reserve requirements with a considerably smaller amount of reserve than would have been necessary had the proportion of time and demand deposits remained unchanged, or, to put it another way, to add a larger amount to their loans and investments without a corresponding increase in their reserves. As a matter of fact, reserve balances of member banks have not increased since the end of 1924, while there has been since that time a growth of about $2,900,000,000 in the total amount of credit extended by these banks.

By the middle of 1929, loans and investments of reporting member banks had expanded by $3,700,000,000 against an actual slight decline

---

control over the situation and widened the range of possible assistance in case of emergency.

in reserves.   Considering the National Banks alone (for which statistics are more complete), there was an increase of about 100 per cent between 1922 and 1928 in noncommercial loans, a like amount in investments other than Federal obligations, and an expansion of about 300 per cent in real-estate loans.   We shall later examine more closely the relationship between money-market conditions and the issue of new corporate securities, confining attention now to the failure of the Federal Reserve System to control in any effective way the mushrooming of capital expansion as it is clearly depicted on Chart 34.[1]

THE IMPOTENCE OF THE FEDERAL RESERVE AUTHORITIES

Under financial conditions such as we are now considering, the Federal Reserve Board, quite apart from its general attitude of timidity and subservience to the Treasury, found itself without adequate power to keep bank credit within channels assuring the true liquidity of earning assets.   The swollen investment portfolios of the banks provided, along with collateral loans, adequate means of meeting periods of at least

---

[1] Broadly speaking, the expansion of bank investment in securities was most pronounced among the country banks in this period.   On the other hand, the rise of collateral loans was naturally much more pronounced in New York City.   The former tendency was not wholly unconnected with rediscounting operations, inasmuch as the smaller banks found it advantageous to rediscount such short-term paper as came into their hands, but the proceeds of these rediscounts were not used to expand credits to agriculture in view of the new Federally sponsored facilities for agricultural financing and the lack of strength in farm prices.   Hence these banks purchased securities, frequently on the advice of their correspondents in the larger centers.   As for the New York banks, their active participation in collateral loans was considerably accelerated by the creation of "affiliates" directly engaged in distributing securities and by the extension of interlocking directorates, forming virtually giant pools of banking power and giving the larger investment banking firms control over an enormous amount of banking capital in the metropolis.

According to George W. Edwards, the commercial banks generally, through their bond departments or affiliates, accounted for 22 per cent of the long-term capital issues in 1927, and by 1930 the portion rose to nearly 45 per cent.   Some bank affiliates even resorted to speculation in the stock of the parent bank.   (George W. Edwards, "The Evolution of Finance Capitalism," p. 226, New York, 1938.)   Mr. Edwards goes on to show that although this large indirect contribution of banking resources to industrial capital was occurring, it did not give the banks either individually or en masse any degree of control over the enterprises whose securities were involved.   This was in marked contrast to the practice of banks in Germany, which for many years had made even heavier advances directly to industrial and utility enterprises but frequently gained control of these organizations and even domination over an entire industry. The growth of American investment trusts in the later years of the decade was also a means whereby banking and investment-distributing groups obtained very liberal advances of bank credit in order to accomplish the distribution of millions of shares of stock to the public through a process that represented little more than high-priced brokerage.

moderate cyclical expansion in business requirements. Instead of resorting to the Reserve Banks for supplementary reserve, the member commercial banks merely called a few outstanding demand loans from the brokers or from their own customers and perhaps sold some bonds.[1] If the Reserve Banks resorted to their open-market policy and liquidated part of their investment portfolio, the member banks might counter by rediscounting some paper, so that the total of bank credit was little changed. So long as the money market remained easy, primarily in response to the comfortable gold position, the Federal Reserve authorities seemed reluctant to bring about too much liquidation. They kept rediscount rates and rates for purchase of short-term acceptances in the open market more or less in line with the prevailing market level.

All along there was a tendency on the part of Federal Reserve management to pay undue attention to the minor month-to-month fluctuations in commodity prices and business activity and to endeavor to counterbalance these minor movements in their rate and open-market policies. Little effort was made to understand or get at the reasons for these fluctuations. Attention was also given to the inflow and outflow of gold, and the authorities appeared to be committed to a policy of "neutralizing" these movements in order to sustain a perpetual surplus of reserve power rather than to permit international net payments or receipts to have their usual or natural effect upon the size of the reserve surplus. This was merely another way of maintaining indefinitely a security market and "capital-credit" inflation. In pursuing these policies on the pattern of the long-established compensating steps taken by the Bank of England to maintain the gold reserve on fairly even keel, it was entirely overlooked that London accomplished its financing operations on a mere handful of gold that the Bank carefully husbanded, at the same time preventing it from becoming an avalanche.

In this country we were beginning to encounter the deep-seated problem of a permanent surplus of gold, far in excess of reasonable requirements. The superficial effort to compensate gold movement naturally led to cross purposes, since the domestic business situation clearly dictated the opposite policy. As early as 1927 it was clearly essential to have begun to apply effective brakes to the rampant security speculation before it assumed dangerous proportions. There was already beginning to be a moderate outflow of gold that the Federal Reserve authorities promptly endeavored to counteract by the easy-money policy. This was dictated only in part by the fact that in the latter part of that year there was a minor business recession; it was probably mainly explained by the desire of the Federal Reserve Bank of New York to play

[1] See Winfield Riefler, "Money Rates and Money Markets in the United States," p. 31, New York, 1930.

a directive role in helping London to retain gold after restoration of the gold standard under conditions that made the retention of gold uncertain and difficult unless (so it was thought) New York money rates were kept well below those of London.   Thus, instead of proving an effective aid in restraining our own financial excesses and unwise use of credit, the Federal Reserve Board merely introduced spasmodic cross currents of influence that were confusing and contradictory in their effect and on the whole proved of no material consequence as stabilizing factors.

One development in particular toward the end of the decade defied the efforts of the Reserve Board to deflect the roaring current of bank credit from these security and capital channels.   This was the practice whereby metropolitan banks made loans on stock-market collateral with funds representing mainly cash balances of large corporations that were loaned by the banks *as agents* for the owners of the funds, these appearing in the statements as "brokers' loans for the account of others."   This was an extraordinary development that had unfortunate consequences. These were essentially capital loans and not bank credit, save in the sense that some portion of the balances thus loaned might have been indirectly derived from prior expansion of credit through various channels.

Bank credit once set afloat is difficult to hold in watertight compartments, and what appears at a particular point as cash may have been created, at least in part, at some previous point through a credit deposit. These brokers' loans for account of others rose from not much over half a billion dollars in the spring of 1926 to a billion at the end of 1927, under the very nose of the Federal Reserve Board.   The stock market was moving substantially higher.   Mr. Mellon, Secretary of the Treasury and ex officio member of the Federal Reserve Board, appeared very reluctant indeed to raise Federal Reserve rediscount rates after the turn of the year.   He was willing to cooperate with London and the New York Reserve Banks as to easy-money rates here but was especially interested in easy money to facilitate retirement of Federal debt by refunding on an advantageous basis.   In 1928 tardy action was taken to raise the official rates somewhat, but this merely provided an incentive to move another billion and a half dollars of outside funds into brokers' loans.   It was in 1928 that the volume of trading on the New York Stock Exchange for the first time assumed really feverish and abnormal proportions and the basis was laid for an inflationary advance of equity prices.

In the face of all this, the Federal Reserve Board, more interested in following foreign precedents than in averting an American inflation, expressed mild warnings but did nothing to alter the intimate relations of banks to security speculation.   The higher went the rates the more the brokers obtained outside funds.   At the peak of stock prices in 1929 these outside balances alone reached close to four billion dollars!   Meanwhile, it still seemed important that movement of gold to the United States be kept at a minimum in order to permit not only Great Britain but France and various other countries to reestablish their currencies on a gold standard of some sort. Temporarily, however, *even foreign funds* were attracted to New York under the stimulus of the higher rates for short-time balances. These actually rose rapidly during the latter months of 1928 and until February of 1929. This situation led to a larger use of the "gold-exchange standard" in Europe, a device that pegged currency to gold and at the same time provided high interest return on the gold balances. In a few years the sudden withdrawal of these balances was destined to come at a most inopportune time.

When we add up all the contributions of credit and foreign and corporate balances and top the structure with the stock-market loans "for account of others" (as seen on Chart 34), the general result in creating inflation was fully comparable to that which was permitted to occur during the period following the Armistice.[1]

THE CHIMERA OF AUTOMATIC PRICE-LEVEL CONTROL

It may be well to interject at this point some comment with respect to the efforts of certain economists and legislators to force the Federal Reserve to adopt a mechanical procedure designed primarily to stabilize the price level. As was previously pointed out, this was essentially a carryover from the deflation days after the War. It represented basically the firm opposition of the farm groups and other inflationists to any material lowering of prices. This insistent clamor for some kind of automatic push-button banking device that would hold prices constant, regardless of international conditions or any changes in production technique, appeared in many forms. Most of them had their origin or received much of their publicity in the writings and statements of Irving Fisher. He proclaimed a plan for "stabilizing the dollar" in

---

[1] At the peak of the stock market in 1929, there were in existence not only collateral loans for account of other lenders than banks, in the neighborhood of four billion dollars, but over one and three-quarters billions placed in the collateral market by banks for the account of interior banks and nearly another billion of loans made on collateral by the New York banks for their own account. Thus the total represented some seven billion dollars of essentially speculative credit, without which the stock-market inflationary boom never could have been carried to such absurd heights. And curiously enough, during 1928, the total amount of Reserve Bank credit in use reached the highest level that it had attained since 1920. On the whole, we can say that far from introducing a helpful influence into the difficult problem of reestablishing European currencies, the failure of credit control here, in some *direct manner affecting the earning assets and lending practices* of banks rather than tinkering with holdings of Government paper and rediscount rates, seriously impaired the efforts in European capitals to accumulate adequate gold reserves.

the first instance through manipulating the weight of the gold dollar and later by compensatory variations in the specie backing of a paper circulation. As discussion on this subject proceeded it took the form of an organized agitation to make Federal Reserve credit a mechanically compensating influence over the entire credit-currency system. It expressed itself in several bills before Congressional committees. The reflationist gospel also appeared in England in the writings of J. M. Keynes, who contributed the idea that the Bank of England should vary the price that it paid for gold from time to time and should utilize the rediscount rate to control and stabilize foreign exchange and thus, presumably, the price level. It came to be an accepted dogma in certain influential circles here and abroad that the central banks really possessed effective powers over the "price level" that was imagined, without much actual study of the matter, to be the leading causal factor in all industrial and trade cycles.[1]

Among the attempts to put this control philosophy into practice was the Goldsborough Bill (introduced as HR 11788 late in 1922), which proposed formal stabilizing of the purchasing power of money. This was to be accomplished primarily by varying the quantity of gold in the dollar in accordance with an index of price changes. As an adjunct to this mechanical device, Irving Fisher suggested that the Federal Reserve Board should be given authority to maintain total bank deposits in some stable relation to monetary reserves, which, in turn, would be ultimately controlled by the variations in the weight of the gold dollar.

The recognition that credit control would be indispensable in any compensatory plan gradually brought crystallization of numerous proposals to that end, and these regulating credit devices eventually became the most important feature of this stabilization agenda. An example was the so-called Strong Amendment to the Federal Reserve Act (offered in 1926), proposing to force the Board to manage discount policy with the object in particular of "promoting a stable price level for commodities in general. All the powers of the Federal Reserve System shall be used for promoting stability in the price level." Elaborate hearings were held, and the views of the proponents were thus given wide circulation. During the hearings, Adolph C. Miller, of the Federal Reserve Board, stated that the Board actually did not attempt to pursue any mechanical procedure in these matters; he was frankly doubtful that any such schemes for automatic stabilization would be successful in the face of continually changing situations that required a flexible attitude and the

---

[1] See Irving Fisher, "Stabilizing the Dollar," New York, 1920; J. M. Keynes, "Monetary Reform," New York, 1924; J. S. Lawrence, "Stabilization of Prices," New York, 1928; and Irving Fisher, "The Money Illusion," New York, 1928, especially Chapter 4.

exercise of judgment.[1] It is fair to say that the Reserve Board had not actually worked out a thoroughgoing philosophy of economic control and was frankly feeling its way along, constantly hampered by difficulties inherited from the War, and defects historically imbedded in our banking organization and never reached by the Federal Reserve Act in any effective manner.

Apparently, there was a rather general acceptance by the Board of Dr. Miller's viewpoint and, whenever challenged, the Board expressed no desire for powers and responsibilities such as were entertained by the mechanical stabilizing enthusiasts. But these discussions nevertheless did keep alive and before the public a type of thinking that continued to emphasize the monetary aspects of bank credit rather than getting to the root of banking problems, that is, to the manner in which banks were permitted to straddle the short-term and long-term money markets and to finance unbridled security market inflation. It is remarkable that so little attention was given to the existing inflation of *security* prices as distinct from *commodity* prices. On the whole, there seemed to be a much more realistic recognition of the complexity of the processes underlying the business cycle and the movements of commodity and other kinds of prices on the part of Federal Reserve technical experts than on the part of the economic theorizers.[2] The proponents of automatic

---

[1] This was well expressed in a later discussion of the objectives of monetary policy by the Board of Governors in 1937, in the light of further experience. "The Board is convinced, however, that the broader objective of maximum sustainable utilization of the Nation's resources cannot be achieved by attempting to maintain a fixed level of prices, and that, therefore, price stability should not be the sole or principal objective of monetary policy. . . .

"No matter what price index may be adopted as a guide, unstable economic conditions may develop, as they did in the 1920's, while the price level remains stable; business activity can change in one direction or the other and acquire considerable momentum before the changes are reflected in the index of prices. There are situations in which changes in the price level would work toward maintenance of stability; declining prices resulting from technological improvements, for example, may contribute to stability by increasing consumption. There are other situations when the restoration and maintenance of relatively full employment may be possible only with an advance in prices. Correspondence between price stability and economic stability is not sufficiently close, therefore, to make it desirable to restrict the objective of monetary policy to price stability." (*Federal Reserve Bulletin*, September, 1937, p. 827.)

[2] E. A. Goldenweiser, of the Federal Reserve research staff, patiently explained to the House Committee on Banking and Currency, during discussion of the Strong Bill, that so far as the wide swings in commodity prices were concerned they were historically attributable (as we have already seen) to war financing. He frankly confessed doubt that any formal money-regulating statutes would cope with such emergencies or could even be maintained in effect during a major war. He also showed that the long-term and more gradual (secular) changes in the price level involved causes that were by no means simple or even thoroughly understood. As for

credit control for over-all stabilization via the price level seem to have been misled by the fact that during the 1920's the general level of commodity prices was relatively steady, and they attributed this unconsciously to what they imagined was a systematic regulatory policy of the Federal Reserve. They overlooked entirely the fact that this stability was the result of opposing forces—a *downward* pressure, in a sense completing the postwar commodity deflation, opposed by an *upward* pressure, developing out of the speculative uses of credit and capital and surging upward almost throughout the period.

It was at the Federal Reserve Bank of New York, where naturally the inflow and outflow of gold has its most immediate and pronounced effect upon the reserve position, that the doctrine of far-reaching credit control over prices and hence all business seems to have had its most vigorous adherents among the official personnel of the Reserve System. Benjamin Strong, Governor of that Bank until his death in 1928, admitted that there was no magic formula for the automatic control of prices, but he nevertheless lent his support to, and placed a measure of confidence in, manipulation of Federal Reserve control devices to stabilize the gold movement. He also insisted that sweeping powers to regulate prices as such were not wholly feasible or within the province of Federal Reserve management, and hence its policies could best be directed toward exercising control within acknowledged limits and with clear recognition that within the general price structure there were always likely to be divergent forces requiring a selective regulatory policy. But far less modest in this regard was W. Randolph Burgess of the same bank, who repeatedly and confidently claimed that the country had already gone a long way in the technique of preventing the gold movement from being a source of disturbance in the financial system.[1]

---

the ability of the Federal Reserve to neutralize the gold inflow during the 1920's, Dr. Goldenweiser insisted that despite all the attempts at control, there was actually a marked expansion in bank reserves that led to a rapid increase in credit during this period. He then went on to display a chart of wholesale prices and called attention to the very diverse group movements during the years 1924–1927, particularly among the agricultural commodities such as cotton, livestock, and grain. He showed that credit controls might well have the effect of intensifying the dispersion among price changes, and this was an aspect that the Congressional and theoretical discussion of the subject usually ignored.

See the statement of E. A. Goldenweiser, Director of Research and Statistics, Federal Reserve Board, before the Committee on Banking and Currency, House of Representatives, 70th Congress, First Session, on HR 11806, Mar. 19, 1928, pp. 23*ff.*

[1] "It may safely be asserted that the Reserve System has been a powerful force toward business stability and toward the stability of employment. The Reserve System has been lauded for its aid in the return of Europe to the gold standard and monetary stability. It has been lauded for its prevention of money panics [*sic*]. But over a long term of years it seems reasonable to expect that more important than

Still another of this New York group was Carl Snyder, who developed several interesting suggestions, first offered in 1923, toward a deliberate and statistically controlled central-bank policy. His principal objective, however, was to counteract an excessive inflow of gold whose potentialities as to economic stability in the United States he clearly envisaged. Snyder's plan contemplated the segregation or sterilization of all imported gold above an amount likely to serve legitimate business purposes. He proposed to prevent this from affecting bank reserves in either direction as the measurement of various sectors of economic activity might require. The manipulation of discount rates and open-market security transactions by the Federal Reserve formed a part of his scheme, but he saw these mainly as incidental adjuncts to an attempt to deal effectively with a new international financial situation. Although Snyder recognized the underlying fundamental factors in the business situation such as the building boom, foreign lending, etc., he did not develop detailed banking methods to extend stabilizing influence in those directions. Had the problem of gold been intensively studied and measures adapted to deal specifically with it, as Snyder urged, the results might have proved of definite value.

But the enthusiasm that was currently being reflected at the time over what seemed to be successful Federal Reserve regulation of the minor financial fluctuations was entirely unjustified; it served to create an illusory faith in the underlying stability of a situation that by 1928 had already entered the acute inflationary stage. In contrast to the cautious attitude of Governor Strong and the long-range suggestions of Carl Snyder as to the gold-redundancy problem, a complacent optimism regarding business stabilization was much more typical of the general feeling. It was comforting to have the assurances of the proselytizers that depressions could be ended quickly, surely, painlessly. It was this state of mind that led speculators in stocks, commodities, real estate, and foreign bonds into reckless adventure.

SOUNDNESS OF BANK ASSETS VS. THE SIZE OF BANK DEPOSITS

When a stock-market situation such as existed in 1928 and 1929 once develops, merely quantitative manipulation of the credit supply is wholly inadequate; it cannot readily be mobilized to bear upon this particular segment of credit circulation and speculative turnover. As H. L. Reed has stated it:

---

either of these may be its influence toward leveling out the booms and depressions which in past times have brought with them so much of human unhappiness and distress." (W. R. Burgess, A Balance Wheel of Gold, *Survey Graphic*, April, 1929.) See also his "Reserve Banks and the Money Market," Chapter 14, New York, 1927.

The old guides to reserve credit policies did not seem to meet the demands of the situation. . . . Moderate rate increases did little to test out the market thoroughly, that is to shake out purchasers who depend too largely upon borrowed funds; and thus the market became gradually educated to paying higher rates. With the failure to test out the market thoroughly in early 1928, a further speculative advance developed which rendered higher money rates ineffective in discouraging the security market demands for credit.[1]

In the words of B. H. Beckhart:

It is this emphasis on the liability side of bank statements by the quantitative school that has precluded interest in commercial banking theory. One may search in vain in many of the recent works on monetary policy and theory for any discussion of the economic functions of commercial banks, or of the effect on economic fluctuations of changes in the character and composition of commercial bank assets, or of the need to relate commercial bank assets to types of deposit liability. This very general disregard of changes in the character and composition of commercial bank assets is further evidence of the attitude of this school of thought that credit is a homogeneous quantity. This assumption is implicit in the attempt to measure the credit volume by bank deposit liabilities.[2]

[1] H. L. Reed, "Federal Reserve Policy, 1921–1930," pp. 139, 141, New York, 1930.

[2] Monetary Policy and Commercial Bank Portfolios, *American Economic Review*, March, 1940, Supplement, p. 21. This opinion is directly contrary to that maintained by Lauchlin Currie. In his study "The Supply and Control of Money," (Chapters 4 and 5) referred to in Chapter 5, he sought to establish the proposition that the *currency* phase is the paramount consideration and was inclined to ridicule the allegations of those who support the "banking" principle, without noting that the two schools are arguing at cross purposes. But his contention that the policy of the Federal Reserve authorities has been too much identified with assets rather than liabilities (that is, the banking or loan aspect) seems superficial and inaccurate. Actually, the mistakes of the Reserve authorities in the 1920's were due fully as much to their inadequate emphasis upon, and inquiry into, *how* the member banks were making advances and to whom and for what purpose as they were to any undue concern about the *magnitude* of the demand deposits or their relation to the trend of total production and trade. In order formally to establish his main thesis that control of "money," that is, checkbook money or demand deposits, is the primary problem of central-bank policy, Currie erroneously minimizes the importance of the existence of uniform and sound standards governing extension of credit and investment of savings in the first instance. This is, of course, directly a result of his narrow interpretation of bank "credit" as being solely associated with demand deposits and having nothing to do with the banking operations that mainly generate such deposits, an interpretation that seems thoroughly unsound.

The Federal Reserve management did make an effort, although a feeble one, to compensate for gold movements by their open-market operations. In this sense they were motivated essentially by the very objective that Currie considers commendable, "to achieve stable commodity prices, stable monetary incomes or stable business conditions." They were indeed watching index numbers of commodity prices and index numbers of business conditions, but they were apparently *not* watching the real-estate cycle and its fateful disintegration in the late 1920's or the giddy spiral of

It was very largely for reasons springing from the underlying weakness in farm prices and overexpansion in various extractive industries that the 1920's decade was actually a period of unprecedented banking failures in the United States, in spite of the glamorous prosperity in the large cities. And even in the cities, we have previously seen that there could be detected under the surface, well before 1929, a stealthy rise in real-estate foreclosures, particularly in centers where property development had been most rapid during the first part of the decade. As the end of the decade approached, banks were also beginning to feel acutely the deflationary effect of tighter money rates upon their bond portfolios. Bank investments in foreign bonds, many overrated municipals, and the lush real-estate mortgage securities were depreciating, and this intensified the difficulties lurking in too large an element of illiquidity among the loans. To take the total of reported actual failures of National Banks and all state banks (including savings banks and trust companies), there were 357 failures in 1921 and 915 in 1924. In the immediately succeeding years, the numbers were 542, 573, 831, 484, 549, and 640. The total of liabilities associated with all bank failures between 1924 and 1929 amounted to no less than a billion and a quarter dollars. This compares with but 140 millions in the War period 1914–1919.[1]

Among commercial firms generally, as reported by Dun's credit agency, the mortality remained fairly steady, but for the decade as a whole it stood at a higher level than in the prewar period or during the war years. When reduced to the form of percentages of the estimated number

stock price movements. We may therefore summarize the point by saying that such qualitative aspects of banking as were given attention by the Federal Reserve were not the ones that counted most; in the meantime, the attention given to index numbers measuring merely surface phenomena did not extend to the very measures of inflation that were important. Had the Federal Reserve authorities and bankers been more familiar with the views of Adam Smith and had they not been confused by the theories of the price-level manipulators, the general economic results would have been very much more satisfactory. It does not necessarily follow that either the level of prices or the level of general trade and national real income would have suffered in any material respect had commercial banks confined themselves to commercial loans and consumer installment loans. It is entirely probable that banks organized along different lines, as to the nature of their deposit liabilities or their facilities to meet obligations to the public, might have been the logical supplement to the purely commercial banks during this period. In other words, what our banking system needed during the 1920's was a qualitative segregation of functions with more specialized responsibility.

[1] W. E. Spahr, Bank Failures in the United States, *American Economic Review*, March, 1932, Supplement, p. 235. The detailed figures show that failures among the state banks were very much more numerous than among the National Banks, and this applies also to the difference in liabilities. If we take the period 1921–1930, 60 per cent of the total suspensions of banks (which includes temporary as well as permanent closings) occurred in places with a population of less than a thousand people.

of active business firms, the failure figures show but a slight rise toward the end of the 'twenties. From 1924 to 1929, the percentage of total bank failures to all banks ran from two to three times as high as the percentage of commercial failures to the number of concerns in business. This was a relationship very different from that which had prevailed in previous years, when the percentage of bank failures was much lower than the percentage of mercantile failures. With respect to the earnings of banks, Spahr's study showed that: "A large proportion of the banks outside of metropolitan centers were not earning enough to justify their existence. This was true even in such relatively prosperous years as 1925, 1926, and 1927. In 1927, nearly 966 National Banks were operating at a loss, and an additional two thousand were earning less than 5 per cent. This constituted about 38 per cent of all the National Banks in the United States. The situation among the state banks was even worse."[1]

It is abundantly clear, then, that while commercial banks in the large cities were helping to pump up a prodigious inflation in common stocks and fancy real estate, the position of many country banks was being undermined to the extent of causing actual stringency in the meeting of legitimate agricultural requirements and bringing about loss of capital and savings to thousands through failures and suspensions that can only be described as shameful.

[1] *Op. cit.*, p. 219.

CHAPTER 13

THE GATHERING INTERNATIONAL STORM, 1928–1931

Federal Reserve stabilization policy might have met with some success had more attention been given to the proper use of credit and capital and if the distribution of gold among the financial centers of the world had continued to function as in the past. But with gold surging about and intensifying currency crises in so many parts of the world, our Reserve System was placed in a paradoxical position. A control policy primarily for neutralizing surplus gold might have done little to avert reckless use of speculative credit, but a total disregard of the gold problem and the use of stern measures merely to restrict speculative credit expansion might have been regarded as implying that direct and effective responsibility over bank reserves was not officially recognized. The basic difficulty of weak banks and unconservative banking practice was aggravated by the fact that world forces threatening monetary chaos were at work, in the face of which superficial money-market manipulations could not be expected to be effective.

In order to understand more fully the background of this dynamic situation and the still more sweeping changes yet to come, we must survey international forces as they affected price levels, debts, international transfers, and gold.

A striking feature of the American scene during the 'twenties was the brilliant performance of industrial corporations in freeing themselves from debt, providing ample capital resources through plowing back earnings and by equity financing, in perfecting the powerful technique of the assembly line and the automatic machine tool, in efficient use of labor and large-scale operations. The aggressive business corporation came into its own in American economic life. The earning power of leading corporations, particularly in manufacturing and merchandising, expanded sufficiently to justify a rising level of stock prices, at least until about 1927 or possibly early in 1928.[1] Because of the accepted practice of permitting the commercial banks to be "department stores of finance," with security affiliates and close relationship with the investment bankers

---

[1] This is not intended to imply that the prices of stocks that were particularly subject to reckless manipulation or that represented new mergers, tenuous holding companies, or other high-leverage situations were necessarily in line with either actual or prospective earning power.

of New York, adequate facilities were not available for financing the legitimate working capital or plant requirements by small industrial businesses. The typical modest-sized or newly formed corporation or partnership, not having access to the stock market through public flotation of securities and unable to do business with banks that preferred "liquidity" of assets to the financing of industry and exacted rates inflated by the credit requirements of Wall Street, found itself handicapped in securing capital funds. Concentration of industrial power into gigantic units was thus accelerated by the banking practices and policies of this period, with the result of greater efficiency of production, no doubt, but also a thwarting of investment in desirable new ventures having promise. In the electric-power field, integrated control was being achieved by the device of holding-company structures and the interconnection of generating facilities. Between 1919 and 1927, the gross assets of 72 of the largest American corporations increased 46.7 per cent, and those of 36 public utilities of comparable importance increased 157 per cent.[1]

ECONOMIC DEVELOPMENTS IN EUROPE

It happens that this impressive expansion in size and producing power of industrial companies in the United States was also more or less paralleled in Europe. By the middle 'twenties, Germany had passed through her experience with extreme currency inflation. Despite the handicap of the reparation demands, she was engaged in earnest in stabilizing her money and planning a far-reaching policy of industrial expansion and "rationalization." In terms of the size and integration of control of industrial units, the Germans went far beyond any other country during the succeeding decade. This program of industrial rehabilitation was stimulated by the fact that Germany, as the result of the Versailles Treaty, lost 13 per cent of her area; she lost control of 16 per cent of prewar coal output, 48 per cent of her iron ore, 60 per cent of her zinc ore, and 26 per cent of her lead ore. It became necessary to import across national barriers set up by the Peace Treaty many essential raw materials and foodstuffs, the supply of which had been impaired by loss of the Eastern provinces.[2]

Following the collapse of the mark and acute disorganization and depression in 1923, recovery of industrial operations developed rapidly in 1924–1925, assisted by the availability of American loans. Cost of production was lowered by concentrating industrial production in the

[1] Gardiner C. Means, The Large Corporation in American Economic Life, *American Economic Review*, March, 1931, p. 24.

[2] Carl T. Schmidt, "German Business Cycles, 1924–1933," pp. 5–6, National Bureau of Economic Research, New York, 1934.

most suitable and efficient plants, which operated at high capacity under systematic quota arrangements. Less efficient, obsolete plants were scrapped on a scale unprecedented in industrial history. A vast program of simplification and standardization of products was worked out.[1] It was perhaps only by such sweeping measures, with close governmental cooperation, that the staggering payments on reparations account could be begun. After 1929, for the first time, their requirements had to be paid out of the current output of German industry without further resort to foreign credits.

American lending abroad began to be restricted as early as 1928, and in 1929 a scaling down of the German debt payments, as previously stipulated under the Dawes plan, was permitted under provisions of the Young plan. There was then some hope, particularly after the Geneva Conference of 1927, that the nations would rationalize their tariff policies and that a broader flow of international trade might facilitate the payment of at least a substantial part of the German war debt, which, in turn, would permit the British, the French, and other war debtors to pay what they nominally owed to the United States without unduly burdening their own industry to provide the means of remittance. This was part of the illusory and ill-informed wishful thinking of that period. The expectations of international-trade revival were thwarted by the unfortunate passage by the United States in 1930 of the Hawley-Smoot Tariff Act. This raised rates and further penalized the importation of European products. Other countries retaliated, and a tariff war, leading ultimately to extreme and fantastic restriction of world trade and demoralization of the foreign exchanges, was the outcome.

The economic position of Great Britain in these years was less reassuring. Despite recuperation, there were a persistent drag in British industry following the War and failure to modernize industrial organization and plant equipment to keep step with progress abroad. Instead of rationalizing by concentration of authority, as in Germany, or accelerating the development of transport and power, as in the United States, the British relied upon a policy of cost reduction principally through control of the prices of raw materials, since a large part of British industry depends upon imported basic commodities. The decision of the British Government to return to a gold standard was made as early as 1920 under the influence of generally high world prices (even as expressed in gold). The reasons for this decision are complex and not wholly clear, but apart from the maintenance of national honor and prestige, it was doubtless designed to avert the danger of further price inflation such as would militate against revival of British export trade.

---

[1] The industrial rehabilitation of Central Europe had some degree of parallel also in Japan, in spite of the disastrous consequences of the 1923 earthquake.

By 1925, when restoration of the pound at the old parity of $4.86+ to the dollar was achieved, world prices had already fallen far enough below the British level that some further price deflation in England was necessary if the new arrangement was to hold. By making the pound dear, that is, adjusted to relatively high British price level, the British manufacturer paid fewer pounds sterling for his imported raw materials than he had paid when the pound was at the depreciated level below $4.50 early in 1924. The currencies of Argentina, Canada, and some other raw-material countries were stabilized at levels more or less corresponding to the British pound, but the French franc after 1926 was stabilized at a much lower relative level, so low, in fact, that it was economical for other countries to purchase French goods, and France therefore attracted gold. Great Britain, on the other hand, was unable to develop export trade to the extent that had been hoped. In contrast to Germany's rapid expansion of foreign exports, the British situation grew distinctly unfavorable. It had frankly been the expectation in British financial circles during the early 1920's that prices in the United States would continue high or that depreciation of the dollar would continue to the extent that the pound, even at the rate of $4.86, would be in world sense relatively "cheap" and Great Britain would be able to expand her export trade with the United States and other nations without undue difficulty. But the greatest disappointment, so far as Britain was concerned, came about as the result of a persistent over-expansion in world production of foodstuffs and some other raw materials.

The dynamic contrasts between manufacturing industry and agriculture, which we have already discussed in the case of the United States, were now evident in the world as a whole. Quite apart from currency policies, gold production, or any other monetary factors, the evidence clearly points to a tendency of agricultural production on a scale naturally involving declining prices of commodities important in world trade. This was indeed a twofold problem. In the old consuming areas of Europe, the postwar period was one of deliberate encouragement of domestic agricultural production as part of political rehabilitation programs. This was true of most of Europe. Russia, which had ceased to be a wheat exporter during the War and for a decade thereafter, again became interested in the European market in 1930, when she shipped large quantities of wheat to Central Europe and even Great Britain. Central Europe being chronically forced to economize foreign exchange, allocated its foreign buying power to essential industrial commodities and strove to reduce imported food to a minimum. This was true also of Italy and Hungary. France encouraged agricultural production even though able to support her population by domestic food. Such policies tended to restrict the export market for the newer countries that before the War had made a specialty of food production for export. These areas included Latin America, Australia, and New Zealand, and in this group we must also include American farmers. It is unwise to generalize too far on this situation, since there are many peculiarities of detail, but as a general trend it is fair to say that the international price position of the staple raw materials of agriculture and in some measure also of the basic minerals was deteriorating in the later 1920's.

RAW MATERIAL SURPLUSES AND INTERNATIONAL SOLVENCY

The large borrowings from the United States by many of these raw-material producers had not in all cases been wisely used or employed in effective diversification of products. The tendency was to continue along old lines and to seek again the old markets, which unfortunately were gradually closing. This was already evident in the raising of tariff rates against wheat by Germany after 1925 and the very stiff increases by Italy during the same period. The countries of Europe began to introduce all manner of minor restrictions: milling quotas, quality regulations, etc., as obstacles to the free movement of crop surpluses upon which some countries depended to maintain payments on their foreign borrowings. Much of the foreign-debt claim held in the United States during the 1920's rested for its validation upon a reasonable relation of the production of these raw-material countries to world demand or, in other words, maintenance of stable prices in terms of gold.

As these problems of disappointing export demand and raw-material surpluses grew ominous late in the 1920's, there were signs of a distinct tendency on the part of the governments concerned to subsidize their producers of export raw materials. This deserves careful attention in the light of subsequent developments. In some cases this took the form of export bounties or what was virtually a double-price system. Producers were able to cut under the market in another part of the world by recouping export losses from governmental bounty payments. Another device was purchase of a part of the crop by a government agency, which then disposed of its holdings through competitive prices made possible by foreign-exchange manipulation. Exchange manip-ulation became a fine art, and its complex ramifications have developed continuously ever since. The world was beginning to learn how to give government agencies the power to focus trade along particular channels by devices that went far to destroy the functions of international money and the international system of prices. When loans were no longer easily forthcoming from the United States in 1928 and 1929, many of these forced-export countries soon found themselves in a des-

perate situation. There began to be resort to even more ruthless measures, such as deliberate devaluation of currencies, to gain evanescent
trade advantages. One by one the nations of Latin America resorted
to currency manipulation and devaluation. This meant abandonment
of the gold standard or the use of gold-exchange redemption of paper
money.

Once started, this course easily becomes a desperate race. The only
advantage of debasing a money system, so far as exports are concerned,
lies in making products cheaper to foreign buyers than similar products
from competing sources. All such devaluation measures serve more or
less to raise domestic prices and thus support *internal* debt structures,
but they have a disastrous effect upon the service of foreign debt. In
this case not only was it impossible to import foreign capital, even for
such dubious uses as to pay interest, but the import of foreign goods
had to be drastically curtailed to conserve dwindling exchange balances
available in New York or London. Each rise in the rate of foreign
exchange in a country depreciating its own currency meant that service
on the foreign (gold) debt became more expensive, and when balances
were finanlly exhausted repudiation of the debt became inescapable.
Although this disintegration had gone but little way prior to 1929, it
was moving in this direction perceptibly and ominously. As the heavy
food and raw-material importing countries of Europe found their international trade position less favorable and reparation requirements more
and more pressing, they raised their barriers against foreign imports
and encouraged substitution of domestic products, including synthetics.
Thus the world was headed for an impasse and a breakdown of trade and
international debt service. It was this underlying economic deterioration in the raw-material areas, associated with the fantastic artificial
debts imposed upon Central Europe, that presently contributed to a
world-wide tidal wave of liquidation, depreciation of values, and destruction of income on a scale never before seen and utterly beyond the range
of the kind of money-market tinkering in which we entertained such
misplaced confidence. The world wheat market, not the New York
money market, should have been the critical subject for study at that
time.

The heavy loans that we had made to the raw-material countries
(paralleling the further expansion of farm debt within the United States)
were predicated upon the supposition that there would be a continually
expanding export outlet for all these extractive production areas. This
is a fundamentally important point in understanding what follows.
The industrial countries divided into two groups: the creditor nations,
foremost of which, as the chief (nominal) beneficiary of the War, being
the United States, with Britain and France in intermediate position as

both debtor to the United States and creditor on war claims against Germany. Even after the drastic scaling down of the original reparation schedule, Germany was in a position in which the only possible solution was in developing an enormously increased export of manufactures. Such exports could be successfully attempted only by developing new markets in the raw-material areas. But Germany had been preceded in this exploitation through the fact that vast American capital and capital-goods exports had already been under way in those directions, and the Germans were entering too late in this race for manufactured-goods markets. If we turn to Britain and France, overlooking the minor countries, we find a large expansion occurring in internal debts, particularly in France, where financial extravagance of the most fantastic sort was evident even after stabilization of the franc had been accomplished in 1928. All this expansion of debt rested upon the premise that Germany would pay the reparations and thus permit Allied settlements with the United States, with something over to provide maintenance of adequate gold reserves and command of working capital to promote the recovery of home industry and public-works progress. The basic fact was that the burden of the debt created during these years rested ultimately upon the ability of the raw-material countries to find markets, to maintain prices and income levels, and to validate their foreign and domestic debts. *It was the breakdown of this phase of world economy that mainly precipitated the ensuing catastrophic difficulties.*

FROZEN EXPORTS AND FALLING PRICES

The impending deterioration in the relative position of raw material countries could not fail to affect the debt situation *within* the United States also. Not only the fast-growing mortgage debt on American agriculture but an equally important local-government debt in the rural section rested upon the solvency of agriculture and its world-price position. It rested, too, upon the ability of the American farmers to continue substantial exports to world markets, which, we have seen, did not materialize. Even the building debt in many of our urban areas rested finally upon the solvency of our agriculture, because so much of this construction had been done in the newer cities. Automobile manufacture was important. The sale of cars does not depend preponderantly upon the farm market, but disposal of used cars, which is essential to make way for new models, has depended to a large extent upon the purchasing power of farmers. Anything that brought about a material decline in farm income would certainly have its effect not only upon the automobile industry but upon employment opportunities and wage incomes in the great motor-production area about the Great Lakes and thus, in turn, upon the maintenance of the local housing-mortgage debt and the financing institutions there. It is in this manner that world-wide conditions intruded themselves into the internal-debt structure at a time when, as we have seen, there existed no facilities for effective rehypothecation of urban mortgages. In one way or another the rapidly increasing stresses and derangements in the world's financial system brought about such internal maladjustments in almost every country.

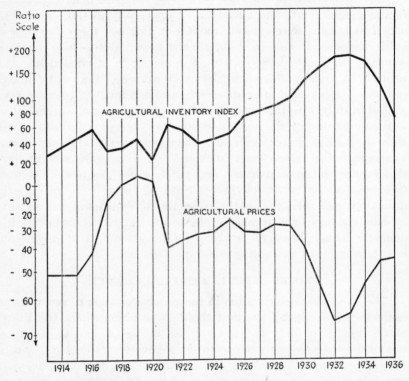

CHART 35a.—Agricultural prices and inventory index for agricultural products, 1913–1936. The inventory index is a weighted average of changes in the physical inventories of wheat (United States and Canada), corn, cotton (United States), coffee (world visible), raw sugar (United States and Cuba), dairy cows on farms, and hides (United States). The result is expressed as a ratio to United States population calibrated to annual data.

The first incentives to solve the international problems of insolvency seem to have come about as the result of *internal* pressures from harassed or hopeless debtors carrying larger obligations than could be met out of current or prospective income. The steps taken with ever-increasing desperation by one country after another during the early 1930's were primarily designed not so much to secure minor advantages in the way of foreign trade or to lighten external obligations but rather to prevent internal financial prostration or outright revolution. It was natural that many of those who gave attention to the raw-material markets and the problems of agriculture tended to associate the difficulties of declining prices and accumulating surpluses with *monetary* causes. Falling prices of commodities implied rising value of *money*, and this was interpreted by some influential observers as meaning that something was wrong with *gold*. Thus arose a new faction among the protagonists of money

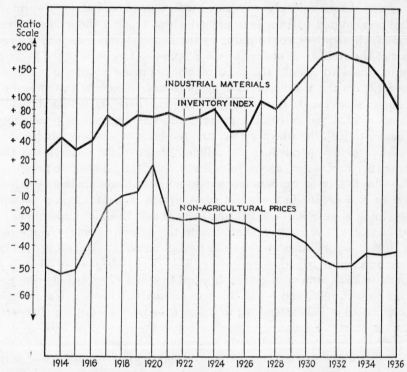

CHART 35b.—Nonagricultural prices and inventory index for industrial raw materials, 1913–1936. The inventory index is a weighted average of changes in the stocks of silk (at United States warehouses), bituminous coal, crude petroleum, refined lead, refined copper, refined zinc, tin (world visible), silver (United States and Canada), finished cement, newsprint paper (United States), and crude rubber (United States). The result is expressed as a ratio to the intermediate trend of general production.

juggling, and we shall presently observe how the "gold doctors" wrote their prescription for American monetary reflation in 1934.

We have already observed the characteristic postwar difficulties of agriculture in Chapter 7, but let us pause to comment further upon the remarkable situation prevailing at this juncture in the markets for some of the great international agricultural staples.[1] In the case of wheat,

[1] See V. P. Timoshenko, "World Agriculture and the Depression," *Michigan Business Studies*, Vol. V, No. 5, 1933; "Monetary Influences on Postwar Wheat Prices," *Wheat Studies*, Food Research Institute, Stanford University, April, 1938;

world production rose very rapidly between 1925 and 1929, far in advance of the rate of increase in population. Wheat prices made their postwar peak in the United States in 1925, and the trend was then distinctly downward, inverse to world production. Although wheat stocks did not rise rapidly, there was nevertheless some increase between 1926 and 1929. In 1930 there came a huge increase in world wheat acreage and production, and Russia suddenly reappeared with 100 million bushels of surplus. This precipitated a scramble to unload wheat supplies and a demoralization of wheat prices, contributing to the financial impairment of a large part of the grain areas of the British Empire. The efforts of the Federal Farm Board to sustain the price of wheat proved disastrously unsuccessful.[1] In the middle of 1931 all pegs were removed, and the price collapse accelerated, Russia again exporting over 60 million bushels. Even in 1929 the Australian government was engaged in price-fixing schemes to help the wheat grower and methods to *stimulate* production!

More or less paralleling the collapse of the wheat market was the experience in rice, tea, cocoa, jute, hemp, flax, and other basic products. The situation in cotton was one not so much of overstimulated production as of a decline in the world consumption of United States cotton. Beginning in 1928 and accelerating in 1929 and 1930, an impairment of cotton export was partly connected with the difficulty being encountered in British export industry to retain foreign markets. British buying of American cotton fell off sharply after 1925. From the peak of 35 cents a pound in 1923, American cotton dropped to about 12 cents following the large crop of 1926, and by 1932 it was selling for 5 cents. The Federal Farm Board in 1929 attempted to support the price of cotton at 16 cents, but the market continued to decline below the loan value fixed by the Board—an interesting and costly lesson in elementary economics.

There was a marked international trend toward self-sufficiency with respect to sugar in the postwar period. A sharp rise in world sugar production and in stocks available occurred throughout the 1920's,

---

M. T. Copeland, Raw Material Prices and Business Conditions, *Business Research Study* 2, Harvard Graduate School of Business Administration, May, 1933; by the same writer "The Raw Commodity Revolution," *Business Research Study* 19, March, 1938; R. F. Martin, "International Raw Commodity Price Control," National Industrial Conference Board, New York, 1937. See also the series *Foreign Agriculture*, published by the U.S. Department of Agriculture, dealing with government policies with respect to agricultural prices and trade during the late 1920's and the early 1930's.

[1] In Canada, also, a bolstering agency, known as the "Wheat Pool," had been formed. In 1928, the Pool began for the first time to support the market by buying up surplus. As these stocks became unwieldy the following year, the Pool became insolvent, and it was necessary to obtain the assistance of the Provincial Governments of the wheat-growing Provinces.

accelerating rapidly between 1929 and 1931. Europe heavily subsidized sugar-beet growing. Even in Great Britain there were schemes
to develop beet-sugar production. Cuba's cane sugar found itself in
competitive difficulty vitally affecting her delicate financial position.
Various attempts at "sugar-stabilization" plans here and there proved
ineffective in preventing a severe decline in prices. The case of coffee
in Brazil is well known, but it is not generally recognized that stocks of
coffee in Brazil more than doubled between 1926 and 1928 and nearly
doubled again in the *next two years*. From 23 cents a pound early in 1925,
Brazilian coffee fell to less than 14 cents in 1927 and after a brief respite
declined below 6 cents in 1931. According to Timoshenko's figures, the
leading agricultural commodities in the United States declined in price
roughly 30 per cent between 1925 and the middle of 1929, and the
available supplies increased by nearly two-thirds. It is very significant
that this increase in unmarketed surpluses of agricultural staples was
under way well *in advance of the financial crisis of the autumn of* 1929.
Chart 35 summarizes the situation as to farm and industrial raw-
material inventory and prices according to the writer's index numbers.

A COMMERCIAL AND MONETARY BREAKDOWN

In the system of world trade, as it was conducted prior to the World
War I, it appears that interchange of the manufactures of industrial
countries for the raw materials of less developed areas was fundamental.
For many years this was represented by the give and take between the
great British manufacturing centers and much of the rest of the world,
colonial and otherwise, which contributed food and raw material. It
was this exchange that made for the smooth working of the gold standard.
It was a standard peculiar to that system, in view of the fact that so much
of the gold originated within the system and merely passed from its mines
through the delicately adjusted valves of the London banks. Now, however, the world was entering upon a new phase in which the solvency of
the raw-material areas was being rapidly impaired because the prime
motivating system of British manufacturing was falling somewhat
behind, while the rest of the industrial world was failing to generate a
corresponding demand capable of absorbing the surpluses from the
hinterland. Without a continuing exchange capable of sustaining the
debt load, gold tended to lose its money function. Already there was
appearing in dim outline a reorganization of world economic structures in
terms, not of the traditional, self-liquidating trade between complemen-
tary areas within a great political orbit but of increasingly ruthless and
aggressive competition between one great *industrialized* area and another
on a basis becoming more and more subject to the insistent political

demands for military self-sufficiency.   This was the beginning of nationalism, of autarchy, expressing itself in economic warfare.   This economic
war was fought for several years with the weapons of currency depreciation and artificial allocation of trade resulting in virtually a barter basis.
This commercial revolution was accomplished at first by imperceptible
skirmishes, but its unfolding on the world scene in later years was an
event stemming directly from the maladjustments that we have been
examining.[1]

Even as early as 1928, the agricultural countries heavily indebted
to other nations were able to service these debts to the extent of only
about one-half by their export surpluses, and the balance represented continued borrowing under more and more unfavorable conditions.   The net
balance of merchandise trade of Canada, Australia, India, Argentina, the
Union of South Africa, and New Zealand combined declined from a
credit of 261 million dollars in 1928–1929 to a debit of 482 millions in the
following fiscal year.   The net fixed charges for interest on external
debt alone amounted to $772 millions!   This was a very sudden shift,
capable of violent and far-reaching repercussions.   In an international
capital market already under strain, the situation became distinctly
dangerous.[2]   But the flow of loans, particularly toward Latin America,
instead of being able to stem the situation was already contracting,
because of the very impairment of financial prospects in those countries.
There was more internal short-term emergency credit expansion in these
raw-material countries, and this contributed to the credit inflation that
shortly followed.   After the middle of 1929, the Argentine peso, which
had previously been maintained in close parity with the pound sterling,
began to depreciate rapidly.   Australia had begun even earlier to lose
gold, and after August, 1929, these exports rose swiftly.   Canada began
to lose gold in 1928, and in 1929 her exchange market came under pressure.   Argentina and Australia were forced to abandon the gold standard
before the spring of 1930.   This marked the first significant impairment
of the gold standard, a few short years after the world had so painfully
struggled to revive it.

[1] Of the total world imports of manufactured goods, according to Timoshenko,
63 per cent in 1913 and 66 per cent in 1929 represented purchases by agricultural
countries.   Even the United States sold nearly three-fourths of its exports of finished
manufactured goods in 1929 to agricultural and raw-material-producing countries,
mostly outside Europe.   ("World Agriculture and the Depression," p. 575.)   Timoshenko also points out, and it has an interesting bearing upon the foregoing discussion,
that in the latter 1920's, the volume, as well as the value, of exports by industrial
countries was increasing much more rapidly than the total exports from the raw-
material countries.   The latter apparently were unable to service their foreign debt
adequately from sales of their staple products.

[2] Timoshenko, *op. cit.*, pp. 612–613.

The darkening prospect of acute difficulty in maintaining currency stabilization and international solvency was now being reflected in the world's security markets. A growing banking stringency had already depressed the trend of the American bond market since the spring of 1928. In varying degrees, this signal of tighter money manifested itself throughout the financial capitals of the world. In fact, in every major financial center except New York, the stock markets had reached their major tops either in 1928 or very early in 1929. The peak in London came in April, 1928; in Brussels, in May, 1928; in Tokyo, in midsummer, 1928. The Swiss market reached its top in September, 1928; Paris and Amsterdam saw their highest prices early in 1929. In Germany stock prices had reached the major top long before, in the spring of 1927, and ever since the spring of 1928 prices on the Berlin Bourse had slipped considerably lower. New York alone of all these centers was in an almost continuous whirl of bullish excitement through the spring, summer, and early fall of 1929. But clearly the world setting, industrially and financially, was entirely unfavorable to the indefinite maintenance of a rising stock market in New York. With monetary tension and after ineffective warnings by the Federal Reserve authorities, the first shakedown of prices began early in September. Once it became apparent to the speculative public that thinly margined holdings for the rise could not be maintained, there came in October a staggering avalanche of liquidation quite without precedent. This great collapse inevitably accelerated the already declining values in foreign centers, and the autumn of 1929 witnessed a world-wide liquidation of securities and a colossal wiping out of fictitious values.

So tremendous a financial loss meant more bank failures and the insolvency of brokers and investment houses around the world. From the highest prices of September to the lowest in November, industrial shares on the New York Stock Exchange lost nearly half their value, but even at the lowest they had barely readjusted themselves to a sane level.

The terrific rise of stock prices in the United States in 1928 and 1929 had all the earmarks of a manipulated inflationary phenomenon. The public bought shares today with the expectation that they would rise tomorrow, and when tomorrow came skilled professional manipulation saw to it that they soared considerably higher. The longer those who had surplus funds waited for opportunity to invest the more they seemed to be wrong, even by the words of noted economists. Even in November, 1929, Stuart Chase was saying: "We probably have three more years of prosperity ahead of us before we enter the cyclic tailspin which has occurred in the eleventh year of each of the four great previous periods of commercial prosperity." Almost every day reassuring statements were issued from high places in Washington. Businessmen who heard the confident comments of Secretary of Commerce Lamont saw no reason to change their plans, predicated upon an endless rise of purchasing power and continuance of prosperity. Charles M. Schwab, one of the greatest optimists of all time, stated in October: "In my long association with the steel industry, I have never known it to enjoy a greater stability or more promising outlook than it does today." In December Mr. Schwab continued to be highly hopeful, stating: "Never before has American business been as firmly entrenched for prosperity as it is today." Irving Fisher contributed to this state of mind by venturing the thought in October: "Stock prices have reached what looks like a permanently high plateau. . . . I expect to see the stock market a good deal higher than it is today within a few months." There was, in general, a tendency to dilate upon the truly remarkable performance of American corporate enterprise without recognizing that this could not escape when the very foundations of the international credit structure and the capital mechanism itself were being undermined by the deflation of income in the raw-material-producing areas of the world and the beginnings of that shifting of world competitive forces from individual to Government sponsorship.

The year 1930 began with a subdued revival in the financial markets of the United States, but by summer it became clear that industrial conditions were not really improving, and deterioration was evident in the mortgage and banking structures. Apart from a stir of belated distribution of electric-power securities, capital issues were small. Abroad there were a generally lower trend in stock quotations and a creeping shrinkage in industrial production. Industrial activity in Great Britain had held up surprisingly well throughout 1929, but in the late spring of 1930 a sharp decline in business occurred, probably reflecting new crises in the raw-material countries and new steps threatening the maintenance of the gold standard generally. Conditions in Germany, Belgium, Italy, and Japan steadily deteriorated. Not only American agricultural products but also manufactured goods were finding the going more difficult in foreign markets, and after the Hawley-Smoot tariff export resistance was abruptly accentuated.

From the very beginning of 1930, farm-product prices in the United States weakened and continued in a state of collapse for two to three years. Merchants and manufacturers found themselves confronted by shrinking inventory values, and bank loans were required to stave off insolvency. Fortunately, 1930 was a year of continuing inflow of gold, not a healthy movement, as we shall soon see, but along with Federal Reserve purchases of securities in the open market and a conscientious effort to help by rediscounts, the gold position was temporarily beneficial. Meanwhile, however, the steady deterioration in both urban and rural mortgage solvency made it almost impossible to secure long-term capital for builders or farmers. The reduction in the official discount rates from 4½ to 2 per cent during the year really had little significance other than to show that gold was plentiful but trade was stagnating. More than 760 banks failed during 1930, and the deposits of impaired banks reached the unprecedented figure of over 300 million dollars.

In the semisolvent railway system of the United States, the growing traffic impairment brought net operating incomes dangerously close to fixed charges, and by the end of 1930, in some instances, fixed charges were not being earned. The New York Central, the Chicago and North Western, Wabash, Chicago, Milwaukee and St. Paul, Atlantic Coast Line, and Northern Pacific had all reached the point by the end of 1930 where net operating income barely covered fixed charges. The Erie had characteristically increased its fixed charges during 1930 and along with the New York, Chicago and St. Louis, and St. Louis Southwestern roads already found net operating income below fixed charges. In the case of the Chicago and Eastern Illinois, there was actually an *operating deficit* by the end of 1930. Almost all roads sharply curtailed maintenance outlays, thousands of employees were dismissed and joined the ranks of workers in the building and building-material industries who were beginning to walk the streets. They were soon to be joined by millions thrown out of work in the automotive and other industries, and thus the crisis gathered momentum.

FUTILE BOLSTERING OF DEBTS AND PRICES

Let us turn again to the international situation. The year 1930 brought internal political disturbances in many raw-material countries where prices were declining: Brazil, Cuba, Argentina, Peru, India, Egypt. Desperate efforts were made to bolster these prices by every device that political ingenuity could invent, but stopgap measures merely served to create new maladjustments. The political expedients to bolster collapsing markets were primarily designed by and for creditors who saw the interest and principal on contractual obligations gravely menaced. It is most unfortunate (but usually overlooked) that rigid contractual debt obligations rested to an excessive degree upon those very branches of production having little flexibility or ready resort to other means of securing capital. In other words, the debt was built up during the war and the postwar period of financial extravagance and the false confidence that inflation invariably generates. What could not now be accomplished by a frontal attack in adjusting debts to a new level of income and values (which might, indeed, have been a way of undermining all contractual obligations) was attempted by opportunistic indirection and subterfuge. The ultimate results, however, did not protect the structure of private capital investment from a world-wide intrusion of Government efforts to reflate prices and underwrite values, to manipulate currencies, to assume responsibility for production, and, in short, to build a new order of dictatorial paternalism.

Out of this welter of expediency arose two kinds of economic sophistry. One was the challenging thought that debt burdens, after all, were inconsequential, because it was so simple to manipulate currency and prices to accommodate the debt, whether it was initially sound or unsound. The second, in various forms, asserted the nominal validity of all outstanding debt to the extent of transforming old debt into new debt, either by mortgaging the future still more heavily or by bringing the *combined resources of the nation,* openly or by subterfuge, to guarantee the validity of particular frozen debts for which the whole people were not responsible. In the great world revolution of the past few years, these ideas have developed into an articulate new economic code. They furnish the basis for much of the political action that economic exigency has called into being, not only in the United States, but in virtually every country.

Let us observe a few further details. In 1930 there was rapid depreciation in the currencies of the periphery of the food-supplying hinterland—Australia, New Zealand, and the Argentine. This accentuated the competitive effort of the major wheat-growing countries to market their mounting surpluses, but these efforts were obstructed by the industrial importing countries of Europe in the interest of protecting their own subsidized agriculturists from still more ruinous prices. As export grain from the surplus countries faced increasing resistance, these countries determined to combine the inflation of their paper currency with measures calculated to *stimulate* rather than contract wheat production. Australia, after finding loans from London unavailable, began to ration her supply of foreign exchange (that is, funds abroad available to Australians) as a means of restricting imports. The fall of wheat prices in terms of gold was severely felt in Canada, although the currency system was not yet affected. Germany resorted to stiff increases in the wheat tariffs, and France and Italy took similar measures. A wide disparity was developing between wheat-export income and the gold prices of industrial products in gold-standard countries, particularly England, where prices and costs since 1925 had held their level. The astonishing rise in physical inventories of selected agricultural products, mainly in the United States, on a per capita basis, appears in Chart 35. On such a basis there should have been but little rise in an index of available surpluses, but the actual rise, accelerating during the early 1930's, is shown to be definitely correlated with rapidly shrinking prices (in gold).

There was an almost equally marked expansion in aggregate physical inventory of industrial raw materials (expressed in this case as ratios of the index to the trend of industrial production generally), although price movements in this group of materials were less uniform and differed somewhat as to timing, when compared with the agricultural prices. Most of the artificial control and rationalizing measures that had been taken during the decade of the 1920's to raise the price of rubber, tin, copper, etc., had broken down by the spring of 1930. Some of these efforts had already begun to give way to spontaneous enlargement of production before the 1929 crisis was precipitated in the United States.[1]

In the case of American copper, the industry's export control, which had held the price unduly high during 1929, collapsed early in 1930, largely as the result of clear evidence of demand curtailment that was making copper unsalable at 18 cents a pound. The sudden readjustment of such prices one after another created a series of shocks and stresses that might have been avoided had these schemes been more flexibly and reasonably adjusted to demand conditions. But it was in the grain-producing countries and especially those having close relations to the great British market that this commodity crisis had its primary significance; the currency depreciation within the British group of countries was the first indication of inability to maintain the gold standard that had been so laboriously restored between 1925 and 1927.

The situation in Great Britain itself was anything but reassuring in 1930. The traditionally important industries, such as coal mining, textile manufacturing, and shipbuilding, were all suffering acutely from postwar changes. Coal mining was affected by the wider use of oil for fuel. Textiles were meeting strong competition in the Orient, especially in the Indian markets, where Japan had been carefully cultivating trade while other nations were fighting. Shipbuilding was depressed as hundreds of merchant ships were tied up following the war boom in construction. British labor was expressing its growing power in the ability to hold wages steady and to incorporate unemployment insurance into legislation—a worthy objective, so long as it could be paralleled by increased production. British export trade was slipping ominously. Unfortunately, by 1931, the unemployment-insurance fund was found to be insolvent. The British had made a serious effort to promote economic and financial reconstruction in Europe, but too much reliance

[1] The Stevenson plan for the restriction of rubber exports from the British East Indies was an outrageous example of an attempt to elevate prices. The temporary success of this regulation through application of variable export quotas appears to have been highly profitable to the British and doubtless assisted in the restoration of the gold standard in 1925. In that year crude-rubber prices in New York were raised from about 20 cents to over a dollar a pound!

was placed upon intermediate-term and short-term loans whose uses were not followed through. The European debtor countries faced an acute scarcity of working capital, since foreign long-term capital was no longer obtainable.

This tightening of the international-capital market contrasted strangely with the easing of short-term money in London and New York and Paris. The latter phenomenon, long regarded as the harbinger of better industrial conditions, was now a symptom of a creeping trade paralysis and shrinking demand for commercial credit. The fresh collapse of stocks in most centers had materially lightened the demand for collateral lending, and hence there was a plethora of "liquid" capital that by 1930 and 1931 was restlessly searching out some of the distressed industrial areas of Continental Europe, where interest rates remained high. London served as the funnel through which large amounts of French, Swiss, Belgian, and Dutch funds sought the remunerative rates prevailing in the rest of Europe. London banks made short-term working-capital loans designed to stave off acute industrial difficulties in Austria, Hungary, Germany, Poland, and the Balkans, but in view of the less favorable export and therefore industrial conditions, the loans quickly became frozen. Thus a situation was being created on a broad scale essentially similar to that which had prevailed here prior to the crash in New York—advances of bank credit for working capital and even permanent capital purposes but on a *contingent* basis, with funds that were essentially short-notice deposits and with inadequate attention to the means whereby such loans could be repaid. It was another case in which the attraction of interest-rate differentials proved a snare and a delusion to lenders who failed to carry their thinking far enough to examine the reasons for these differentials and the intricate tangle of political factors thereby involved. It was the money market and not production conditions that received all the attention.

One reason for this growing accumulation of liquid funds or demand deposits was the fact that the French, in returning to the gold standard in 1928, had devalued the franc 80 per cent, creating a situation that attracted gold to Paris.[1] France received large amounts of reconstruction material and equipment from Germany by way of war indemnity and was regaining a fair degree of industrial activity. By the end of

---

[1] When a country's financial structure has been subject to paper-money or credit inflation but no action has been taken with regard to a change in the metallic standard, speculators tend to accumulate gold (if that is the standard metal of the currency system) or acquire gold exchange in foreign centers and retain these balances pending the time when they believe there will be an opportunity to re-exchange these gold holdings for new currency following devaluation. This usually takes the form of increasing the number of money units per unit of standard metal. This operation may be enormously profitable, as, indeed, it proved to be in the case of France.

1930 short-term credits extended by Paris and other centers of the French gold standard to London were being recalled because of apprehension over the future of British conditions. The French also began to withdraw large balances that had been maintained for some years in New York, since New York money rates were now less attractive and a general movement toward liquidity made itself felt among the financial institutions of the gold group. One of the most important factors in accentuating this tendency in 1931 was a growing feeling that Germany would find ways of evading payment on reparations account, as laid down in the Young plan of June, 1929. Germany had done fairly well industrially through 1929 and even part of 1930, largely through the drastic curtailment of imports, which helped to balance the nation's finances, even though it was harmful to the British. But the collapse of prices (in terms of gold) was affecting German industry and agriculture, and, in fact, the farm situation throughout Europe was bringing acute pressure upon the institutions that had made loans on farm and building mortgages.

It must be kept in mind that by 1931 European agriculture had made enormous strides in the direction of self-sufficiency in food. This was particularly true of Germany, which had been able to curtail import of grain from 7.5 million tons in 1927 to 1.8 million tons in 1931. Net import of cattle and beef practically disappeared. Behind this tendency were also such factors as the curtailment of emigration from Europe to the United States, making it necessary to find agricultural work for many laborers and, perhaps still more important, an exacting and unintelligent carving up of European states into small political units insulated by tariff boundaries, unable to maintain their usual industrial exports and forced to reduce their standards of living by becoming agricultural and self-sustaining. This was a far worse result of the Versailles Treaty than the provision for reparation payment. It arose primarily from the desire of the French to reduce Europe to a mass of small, weak states in order to preserve the security of France.

THE CRISIS IN CENTRAL EUROPE AND COLLAPSE OF GOLD

One of the most flagrant cases of atomizing Europe was the division of Austria-Hungary into a number of smaller states without visible means of support. The situation in Austria by 1931 had become particularly acute. This remnant of a formerly prosperous, industrial nation had been living on short-term loans ever since the late 1920's, and the efforts of the Austrian Government to obtain a substantial capital loan in world financial centers had failed. Many small industrial enterprises that had been started during the later 1920's in such portions of formerly prosperous nations could not avoid disaster as the agricultural population found its ability to purchase even local products fast shrinking.   In the face of these growing difficulties, foreign credits were being nervously withdrawn, and a flow of badly frightened capital away from Austria-Hungary, Rumania, Yugoslavia, and similar areas began in the spring of 1931.   By summer large increases in the gold reserves in creditor Switzerland, Belgium, and Holland were evident.   German gold reserves had followed the downward path already marked out by the gold holdings of the agricultural periphery in the Southern Hemisphere.   Gold withdrawals from the United States did not become important until the end of 1931.

The financial weakness in Austria had become quite apparent by 1930, when it became necessary to merge two of the largest industrial and agricultural banks.   The Kreditanstalt was left in a weakened condition, unable to withstand the gradual spreading world depression.   In May, 1931, the Austrian Government was forced to guarantee all deposits of the banks.   Emergency advances were somehow obtained from the Bank of England.   The Bank for International Settlements,[1] which advanced 100 million schillings to the National Bank of Austria.   There was a somewhat similar crisis in Hungary, temporarily alleviated by similar means.   Germany meanwhile had sought to make capital of the strained situation by proposing a Customs Union with Austria, but the French objected.   This matter contributed to further distrust of affairs in Germany, whose financial institutions were more or less involved with those of Austria and Hungary.   The Reichsbank had by this time used up a large part of its reserves and was receiving emergency help from various central banks and Bank for International Settlements.   But heavy withdrawals from the Reichsbank were taking place, and in July serious commercial failures induced bank runs, and cash payments were restricted in mid-July.   It was evident that a very serious financial crisis was in the making.

President Hoover was aware of the increasingly serious situation and saw the grave consequences that it portended.   He therefore proposed in June that a moratorium be arranged on all intergovernmental debts arising from the War, predicated upon the willingness of the Allied governments to accept a moratorium for one year on German payments of reparations.   His proposal was acceptable in principle; but as usual the French raised objections, and their bickering led to a delay in the moratorium plan, although it did become effective in August.   Unfor-

[1] This had been organized as a means of superintending the transfer of German reparations in accordance with the Young Plan of 1929 and for a limited period performed useful services as a central bank for the various European countries involved in the reparations problem.

tunately, this very fact of a moratorium proposal led to swift aggravation of the fears of financial collapse in Central Europe.

It was instantly realized that, not only other banks in Austria and foreign countries, but virtually the whole industrial structure of Austria, and other Eastern European countries, would be involved. It was equally evident that neighbouring debtor States, and particularly Germany, would be at once exposed to the danger of panic withdrawals of capital. A crack had developed in the carefully constructed and patched facade of international finance and, through that crack, already timid investors and depositors caught glimpses of a weak and overburdened structure. It was not only a bank which threatened to collapse, but the whole system of over-extended financial commitments which was the worst legacy of the war and of subsequent credit expansion.[1]

Despite the moratorium, runs on banks continued to create havoc throughout Europe. The French seized the opportunity to demand return from London of the short-term credits previously advanced, but London could not extract more than a part of her advances from the nearly frozen mass of European obligations. The Bank of England, as had been customary in such cases, took vigorous action to raise its discount rate from $2\frac{1}{2}$ to $4\frac{1}{2}$ per cent; but it proved impossible to retain gold, and the balances available were smaller than usual since Great Britain had not been able to build up adequate reserves under the international trade conditions previously existing. London was in much the same position that the banks of New York City had frequently experienced in critical times, when their unwisely selected earning assets were freezing and the interior banks were demanding gold. London frantically secured some short advances from Paris and New York early in August and again at the end of August. But the drain continued. Over 200 million pounds sterling were taken out of the London money market in two months prior to Sept. 20. On the next day the momentous decision was at length announced that the government had permitted the Bank of England to suspend the obligation to sell gold upon demand in exchange for paper currency. England had abandoned her effort to retain the gold standard.

In this step, the British were essentially recognizing the fact that parts of the Empire and countries close to the British economic system had already permitted their currencies to depart from the gold basis, and she was taking steps to close the widening gap between her price level and those price levels prevailing in the colonial periphery. Further large movements of gold toward France, Switzerland, Belgium, and Holland occurred, and Germany, the United States, and Japan lost considerable amounts of gold. The departure from gold abruptly intensified the rate

[1] "World Economic Survey, 1931–1932," pp. 72, 73, League of Nations.

of decline in American industry, construction work, commodity and security prices, and the issues of new corporate capital. Had it not been for this blow to confidence, a turn for the better would probably have been negotiated early in 1932. Although there was no indication as yet that liquidation of urban mortgages or the impairment of activity in some industries had run their course, this additional shock, transmitting its effects immediately to the capital market and all other markets, introduced into the business situation literally a *doubling* of the intensity of the depression.

Previous to the British suspension of gold currency, depreciation had already occurred in Argentina, Australia, New Zealand and Uruguay, Brazil, Chile, Venezuela, Paraguay, Peru, and Mexico. Following the British suspension, other countries joined the list: Bolivia, Denmark, Canada, Egypt, India, Norway, Sweden, Finland, Portugal, Colombia, and Japan.[1] In the countries that abandoned gold, the course of prices in domestic currency tended thereafter to be fairly well sustained. In the case of British prices, there was a mild recovery, followed by a relapse early in 1932 and then a fairly steady level. In the remaining gold countries—the United States, France, Belgium, Holland, Italy, and Germany—prices continued to decline. The decline of prices in terms of gold, due primarily to commodity factors, was accentuated by falling rates of exchange on the various centers which had left gold. That is, no country attempting to preserve a gold standard was able to resist the external factors whittling down its internal level of prices, whereas countries off gold could with some effort avoid an inflationary rise in internal prices, since the underlying price trend in gold was still declining. This was the case in Great Britain. In 1932 the British took steps through their Exchange Equalization Account (operated by the government jointly with the Bank of England) to keep sterling as depressed as possible through manipulative purchases of foreign exchange and other devices, which proved measurably successful.

Continued pressure on (gold) prices, particularly in the United States, was beginning to create a very acute situation in our farm areas and in our extractive industries generally. This became a matter of interest to speculators in Paris and other gold money centers. They sensed that the United States might soon be constrained to follow Britain in bringing the dollar to a readjusted level. Speculators in New York also were becoming apprehensive of the same thing and were beginning to purchase

---

[1] J. P. Day, "An Introduction to World Economic History since the Great War," p. 114, London, 1939. This book contains an excellent brief account of the circumstances and events of this period. See also Lawrence Smith, Suspension of the Gold Standard in Raw Material Exporting Countries, *American Economic Review*, September, 1934.

balances in Paris and Amsterdam, feeling that this was a way of hedging against devaluation and probably inflation. Thus a torrent of gold started to flow from New York (see again Chart 9). The Federal Reserve Banks early in 1932 began large open-market purchases of Government securities, which by the end of the year reached 1,855 million dollars. The effect of this export of gold upon money rates and bond prices will be examined in a later chapter, but it can be said that the Reserve policy did alleviate the situation to some extent, and the worst of the gold loss was over by spring of 1932.[1]

This evidence of a tendency to lose large amounts of gold, contrasting with the very comfortable gold position of the middle 'twenties, served curiously enough to extend the influence of that type of economic thinking that fastens upon gold as the root of all financial difficulties. Gold, it was contended, was gradually becoming "scarce" as the result of the effort of the various nations to reaccumulate gold reserves (efforts that had really not proved very successful except in the case of France and her satellites) and the activities of gold hoarders in increasing the "demand" for gold. During 1932 and especially 1933, this view attained wide circulation and was usually phrased in the proposition that the falling trend of world commodity prices *was due* to an "increased demand" for gold. Therefore, by *cheapening* gold the United States could likewise accomplish in one step the stabilizing of prices. This meant, of course, devaluing the dollar or making smaller the gold content of what was called a dollar, a step that would retain the gold standard, but on a basis of lower purchasing power of each dollar over other goods. This was the manner in which that device of cheapening the money by debasement, for so many centuries the last resort of bankrupt kings, became theoretically justified. We shall return to this again presently.

---

[1] In addition to loss of gold by shipment to Europe, an even larger amount appears to have been withdrawn from the banks for personal hoarding, a further example of the double drain on reserve that always accompanies financial strain.

CHAPTER 14

INTERNATIONAL FACTORS IN MONETARY POLICY, 1931-1938

The abandonment of the gold standard by Great Britain and many other countries had wide political repercussions as well as economic results. There were now unmistakable signs that a new alignment of national interests, new kinds of competition, and new forms of protection against international competition were in the making. The policies that had been adopted in 1929 and earlier by the raw-material-producing countries to force outlets for their accumulating and depreciating surpluses represented forces too powerful to be resisted, now that currency chaos and a baffling confusion of price levels confronted business enterprise everywhere. Resort to a new kind of refuge was therefore inevitable by the alignment of national interest in new groupings. One such group aligned itself with the pound sterling and included, in addition to most of the British Colonies, such countries as Argentina, the Scandinavian countries, and Egypt.[1] France, Switzerland, Holland, Belgium, Poland, and Czechoslovakia constituted a gold bloc, with Germany and Italy following somewhat similar monetary policies but not coordinating economic or political affairs so closely with the other countries as was the case within what came to be known as Sterlingaria.[2]

Japan, meanwhile, was taking advantage of the disturbed conditions and the bickering among the European powers to launch her ambitious designs for a New Asia under her control. Late in 1931 she formally abandoned the gold standard and launched upon a military career tinged with inflation. The previous collapse of silk prices had hit the Japanese economy disastrously. Population and employment problems were becoming acute, and the invasion of Manchuria was in part a result of this situation. Although conquest of the area that came to be known as Manchukuo was ostensibly territorial aggrandizement, it was primarily designed to bring pressure on the Chinese to relax their "popular boycott" of Japanese manufactures. The Japanese had already made serious inroads in India in competition with the British

[1] Canada was somewhat apart, although commercially closely related.

[2] The Union of South Africa continued substantially on its former gold basis until the beginning of 1933 but may be considered in a political sense as one of the Sterlingaria units.

314

textiles, and they were desirous of making inroads in Chinese trade with the same successful results.

But from the standpoint of our present interest, these developments in the Orient have their place as revealing the beginning of a rising tide of nationalistic political policy, the beginnings of the new groupings of national power to which the demoralization of the gold standard and of international trade conditions and the world price system directly contributed. By the summer of 1932, there were signs that political power in Germany was moving toward a strong nationalist direction of the country's affairs. The Hitler-fascist party was forging ahead in the elections.

FACTORS INTENSIFYING THE AMERICAN DEPRESSION

In the summer of 1932 a conference at Lausanne resulted in agreement among the Allied nations to reduce very materially the obligations of Germany on reparations account and to make more flexible the means whereby payments would be made. This was done by the Allied countries as a way of hedging themselves against the ominous possibility that Germany might soon undergo a revolution and become a collectivist state like Russia, whose five-year plan of industrial promotion was already commanding world attention, particularly since it appeared to involve distinct militaristic as well as proselytizing aspects. If the United States could be convinced of the merits of the proposal, it was expected that American claims upon the Allies for war-debt payments might be scaled down, since they had all along been delicately linked by implication with the reparations. But the United States, not yet fully aware of what was going on in the world outside, was in no political frame of mind to accept this proposition. The Presidential election campaign was a complicating factor. The Democratic platform proclaimed that the United States would make no concessions with respect to the Allied debt, inasmuch as we had consistently ignored (or had professed to ignore) the existence of any relation between the Allied debt to this country and German reparation payments. Since the conferees at Lausanne had made a *secret* agreement among themselves not to ratify *until* the United States should declare itself satisfied to make a war-debt settlement of a compensating character, the net result of it all was that an opportunity was given Germany to repudiate the entire reparations matter. By the same token our Allies relieved themselves after December, 1932, from making further debt payments other than a few token payments that were entirely suspended (except for Finland) in 1934.

This had the immediate effect of lending support to the Hitler movement in Germany, and Hitler was able to capitalize upon his apparent success in defying powerful nations whose claims had been an obstacle to any political party that had professed willingness to accede to the demands of foreign creditors rather than to the immediate needs of the German people. Here is the crux of the political situation that has since developed throughout the world. It was the common people—farmers, artisans, the unemployed, in all countries—who were forcing their governments into radical policies directed primarily toward internal solvency, reemployment, industrial and structural revival—the direction of all political policy toward these ends, with no regard to foreign creditors, foreign competitors, or any combinations of foreign interests. Lausanne gave Germany this opportunity to declare a new position and to organize the planning of a new order, the results of which have since become abundantly clear. In January, 1933, Hitler became Chancellor. Later in the year, Germany stepped out of the League of Nations and began preparations for the use of force to restore Germany's position in Europe. This implied a ruthless program of combining the needed industrial and raw-material areas of Europe under a dominant political leadership, probably through the use of force.[1]

Meanwhile the British bloc was taking shape. The British broke with many precedents. They began to levy emergency tariffs on a wide range of imports. In July, 1932, an embargo was placed on loans to foreign countries. The emphasis henceforth was to be placed upon restoration of employment and the forced lowering of interest rates to enable reduction of excessive accumulations of internal debt by refunding.[2] With definite abandonment of the policy of free trade, a new schedule of duties was imposed, covering a large proportion of the total imports into Great Britain. This policy toward economic protectionism and political nationalism was further extended as the result of the 1932 conferences at Ottawa, whose objective was the lowering of tariffs within the Empire but whose final result was rather to raise the duties of countries in the Empire orbit against nations outside Sterlingaria. Mean-

---

[1] The leaders of the new German totalitarian regime appear to have proceeded on the assumption that Germany as a nation could be preserved only by a ruthlessly independent course, harshly contemptuous of financially embarrassed Britain and America and their economic traditions, covertly hostile toward Moscow and its mendacious Internationale, whose alleged subtle, well-financed secret machinations throughout all Europe might perhaps have been given exaggerated import. On the whole, Hitler's fear of the growing power of the Soviets seems to have goaded him to developing the internal resources and economic activity of Germany, by self-worship and a fanatical rejuvenation, into a military state, half capitalist, half collectivist, designed ultimately to contest the swelling tide of armed communism. Hitler overlooked the fact that had Germany followed a less provocative program, Russia, despite its dictatorship, might also have been content to develop its socialist experiments along nonaggressive and peaceful lines.

[2] The British successfully converted two billion pounds sterling of War Loan in 1932 from a 5 to a 3½ per cent basis.

while Russia was fast developing her intensive program of collectivization and forming a more or less self-contained and insulated unit of vast geographic proportions.

During 1932 the United States began to feel rather unfavorably the effect of these gradually crystallizing new aggregations of political and economic interest. There was a further decline in prices, and the Ottawa agreement served materially to reduce our already shrinking exports to countries included in that understanding, particularly the British Isles. The effort within Sterlingaria to resort to various devices, such as export bounties, government purchase of surpluses, government guarantees of farm prices, served to confirm a world-wide trend toward agricultural excess and intensified pressure on prices. Evidence of the existence of international competition cutting across old alignments appeared in the difficulty of obtaining agreement upon some limitation of world crop production and the failure of the London Economic Conference in 1933. A new order of international competition by currency juggling, competitive inflation, competitive regimentation, and ultimately war, was launched. In the United States it came to be called the New Deal, ostensibly for internal reconstruction but in fact part of the new world complex of political turbulence and reorientation.

During President Hoover's final year in office and under the most trying conditions, legislative steps were taken to cope with a desperate situation not amenable to the usual palliatives. The decline in bond prices and the continuing wave of property foreclosures during 1931 and 1932 had brought unprecedented strain upon the banking structure. In 1932 the wave of failures was becoming a tidal wave (see again Charts 33 and 34). There were in that fiscal year almost 2,400 closings of banks having 1.7 billions in deposits. This situation was increasing the deliberate hoarding of gold. Had the banks during this period been forced to contend merely with the problem of writing off impaired agricultural and urban mortgage loans and the usual emergency demand for solvency credit, it is entirely possible that with the help of the Federal Reserve and a fairly comfortable gold position, the strain might have been surmounted. But in the face of this tremendous wave of suspensions and the beginning of nation-wide runs and gold hoarding, the banks, as we have seen, were loaded up with investments that were rapidly shrinking in value and had little that was available for rediscount. Open-market purchases by the Federal Reserve merely offset fresh gold withdrawal.

Intense pressure upon the banks occurred in the Great Lakes section, where the building boom had been greatly overdone and where unemployment in the newly developed transportation-equipment industries was making impossible the validation of mushroom real-estate obligations. Various emergency measures were hastily devised by the Federal

Government[1] late in 1931 to bolster weak institutions and prevent the spread of panic and embarrassment of insurance companies and savings banks.

EMERGENCY RELIEF MEASURES IN THE UNITED STATES

In January, 1932, there came into being a new type of financial institution known as the Reconstruction Finance Corporation.   It was designed to afford immediate emergency assistance to banks that were finding it necessary to write off so much of the stated value of their outstanding loans that they not only had erased what surplus they had but were trenching upon capital and found it impossible to raise additional capital. According to the old-fashioned and long-since-forgotten theory of strictly "commercial" practices, banks would have found it easily possible to avoid marked depreciation of assets, since these would have consisted primarily of self-liquidating, short-term advances, and by rotation of maturities and caution in making new loans, serious depreciation would have been averted.   Actually, however, the banks were unable to reduce a large mass of frozen "capital-loan" assets.   Loans on real estate had been reduced since the end of 1929 only by an insignificant amount; collateral loans had been reduced during the two years ending December, 1931, by only about 25 per cent.

With ample financial resources, the RFC was empowered, among other things, to make direct loans to solvent banks and financial institutions.   It was also in a position to aid many railroads in view of the rapid disintegration of their solvency.[2]   Because of the wave of mortgage

---

[1] In connection with the heavy withdrawal of deposits from banks between 1930 and the spring of 1933, when the entire banking system had to be suspended, it is interesting to observe that a much larger percentage of reduction occurred in large deposits than in small deposits.   A 70 per cent reduction took place in demand deposits amounting to $100,000 and over, and a 6 per cent reduction occurred in the case of balances amounting to less than $500.   (*Federal Reserve Bulletin*, March, 1939.)   The reduction in interbank deposits was extremely drastic; but as might have been expected in view of the structure of the banking system, there was a large withdrawal of time deposits, only moderately exceeded by the rate of reduction in demand deposits.   It can readily be seen that the sudden withdrawal of funds by large corporations or their local branch plants and offices from unit banks in cities and towns of moderate size could quickly place these banks in an extremely vulnerable position in view of the fact that many of them had so little in their earning assets that could be used as the basis of assistance from the Federal Reserve.

[2] As first set up, the RFC had a capital of 500 million dollars extended by the United States Treasury and was authorized to issue notes, debentures, or bonds up to 1.5 billions.

It was also empowered to make available emergency funds to be administered by the Secretary of Agriculture.   The RFC was essentially an outgrowth of two previous Federally sponsored financing institutions, the War Finance Corporation, which assisted in the financing of industries during the World War, and the National Credit

foreclosures, the RFC was given authority also to assist building-loan associations, savings banks, insurance companies, farm-mortgage associations, and livestock-finance companies. It was believed the RFC could thus allay panic hoarding and withdrawals of bank deposits; by restoring confidence the banks would be able to extend loans on property and working-capital advances to industry, and thus the process of readjustment would not become an endless cumulating spiral.[1]

Thus the RFC attempted to sustain, at least for the time being, the existing credit and capital structure by virtual blood transfusions from the Treasury to private financial institutions. Thereby it pointed incidentally to the previous lack of development in the United States of institutions specifically organized for long-term capital advance, either by loans or equity finance, to the extractive and structural industries. By first bringing financial succor to banks and railroads, the Government was led to explore this underdeveloped phase of our financial structure and to recognize that what private financing had not been able to do (outside the insurance companies, a few of the so-called "investment trusts," and the surplus investment of corporations) might perhaps be developed through the direct or indirect lending of Government-controlled capital.

The RFC, however, in its early phase and apart from the railroads, did not make direct loans to industry but sought to provide emergency credit to support banking structures. In July, 1932, however, the RFC was given additional resources nearly doubling its potential loan fund and was authorized to advance emergency funds to states and municipalities to be used for direct relief or work relief to the needy and unemployed, to provide for local construction projects of a self-liquidating type, to finance sales of agricultural surpluses abroad (an indication of our entry into the international economic war), and, finally, the making of advances to regional credit corporations for agriculture.

At about the same time the Federal Government had also created a new system of Home Loan Banks in view of the intensified and threatening nature of the mortgage insolvency crisis.[2] These regional Banks

---

Corporation, incorporated in October, 1931, as a means of relieving banks in the more distressed agricultural areas. The latter institution was organized upon too restricted a basis and was not much of a success, but the RFC expanded its scope and general purpose with much larger resources and broader powers.

[1] The RFC at the close of 1934 held 426 millions of the capital notes and debentures of 2,781 banks and 776 millions of preferred stock, representing 3,913 banks.

[2] The Home Loan Banks were set up by requiring the RFC to allocate to the Secretary of the Treasury 125 million dollars to purchase the stock of 12 regional Banks somewhat paralleling the Federal Reserve Banks in the commercial banking field. (J. Franklin Ebersole, "Current Economic Policies," pp. 116–117, edited by J. B. Hubbard, New York, 1934.)

were designed to afford relief to home owners who were in danger of mort-gage foreclosure. Receivers of closed National Banks were instructed to suspend foreclosure on first mortgages on sound properties until these Home Loan Banks could be set up. Although this was merely an emergency stopgap to hold back the tidal wave of foreclosures and to deal with the generally critical financial situation in Chicago, Cleveland, Detroit, and the surrounding areas, it was also clear evidence of the abominable shortcomings of the housing-mortgage system as it had existed. The Home Loan Bank Board, supervising general policy, was able to extend significant help and ultimately had about two billion dollars outstanding as the result of its mortgage-rescue operations. It marked a first step in the direction of much more fundamental reforms that will shortly be discussed.

In addition to setting up the RFC, the Hoover Administration per-mitted the Reserve Banks, through the Glass-Steagall Banking Act, to issue notes on the basis of long-term Federal Government bonds, sup-plementing the usual backing of gold plus commercial paper. The Federal Reserve Banks thereupon began large purchases of United States Government securities, and by the end of 1932 they had increased holdings by nearly one and three-quarter billion dollars and had made their notes available to member banks as a means of meeting currency needs. This was a move designed to attack the second great problem— that of deposit withdrawals. But again it was in the nature of an emergency stopgap that did not reach the cause of the difficulty. Despite the easing of credit conditions after the middle of 1932 there continued to be a widespread uneasiness and suspicion as to frozen assets. Even a sharp recovery in the prices of bonds[1] and common stocks in the early autumn failed to restore confidence in the banking system. The very fact of resort to Federal financial pulmotors tended to create the impres-sion that the rescue work was not over.[2] When the Ottawa Conference

---

[1] A 100-million-dollar bond-supporting pool was formed in Wall Street in June and may have been responsible for part of the temporary rally in security values.

[2] In November, 1932, Frank A. Vanderlip, formerly president of the National City Bank of New York, wrote for *The Saturday Evening Post* a pertinent and very candid article on the banking problem and the steps being taken to deal with it. Referring to failures, he wrote: "A great proportion of these insolvent banks had been constant borrowers from other banks over a period of years. Many of them had been heavy borrowers even at the height of the New Era of prosperity, when depressions were supposed to have been permanently banished. Many had invested too heavily in new and too elegant bank buildings. Many had boards of directors who had been inactive and negligent. There were a considerable number of dishonest officers. Local enterprises had been given capital financing which should have been assumed by permanent investors, instead of permitting demand deposits to be frozen in loans that had no true due date on which payment might reasonably have been expected. There were hundreds of cases in which the bonds of small local corporations having

adjourned in August, there were those who foresaw abrupt curtailment of our already shrunken wheat and cotton exports to countries of the British Empire.   In December bank suspensions, after having declined temporarily, again began to increase.   In the first six weeks of 1933, a new wave of failures became apparent, and these involved a number of metropolitan banks of considerable importance.   "The volume of deposits of the suspended banks was particularly large in southern New Jersey, District of Columbia, Tennessee, Illinois, Iowa, Missouri, Nevada, and California.   Finally, renewed banking difficulties in February, 1933, led to the temporary closing of all banks by official action, first in the State of Michigan, then in other States, and finally by Presidential proclamation throughout the country."[1]

The closing of all banks by the declaration of a banking holiday on Mar. 6, 1933, gave the new Administration an opportunity to devise emergency measures of far-reaching character.   The panic had to be

---

no general market were carried in the investment accounts in a manner which led depositors to assume that they were readily marketable securities.   Competition led to paying unsafely high interest rates on deposits.   Larger loans were made than were permitted by legal limitations.

"In a word, it was unsound banking that caused the bank failures, and not a depression which engulfed well-managed banks. . . .

"Why did not bank examiners stop practices of which they were aware and concerning which they wrote constant criticisms?

"The reason why bank examiners do not close banks before the depositors' money is lost, even though they know the banks are not well run, is easily understood by anyone who has ever had the responsibility of deciding whether or not to close a bank which is nearing, but has not reached, a critical danger point.

"Closing a bank is capital punishment for the bank.   Every jury hesitates before pronouncing a death sentence.   The evidence must be 'beyond a reasonable doubt.' There is much the same sort of hesitancy when considering a life or death sentence for a bank."

Turning back a century and a half, let us add, for contrast, the words of Adam Smith: "The banking companies of Scotland . . . were for a long time very careful to require frequent and regular repayments from all their customers, and did not care to deal with any person, whatever might be his fortune or credit, who did not make, what they called, frequent and regular operations with them.   By this attention, besides saving almost entirely the extraordinary expense of replenishing their coffers, they gained two other very considerable advantages. . . .

"First, by this attention they were enabled to make some tolerable judgment concerning the thriving or declining circumstances of their debtors, without being obliged to look out for any other evidence besides what their own books afforded them. . . .

"Secondly, by this attention they secured themselves from the possibility of issuing more paper money than what the circulation of the country could easily absorb and employ."   ("Wealth of Nations," Book 2, Chapter 2.)

[1] J. D. Paris, "Monetary Policies of the United States, 1932–1938," p. 5, New York, 1938.

stopped once and for all.   The most direct way to accomplish this quickly was to take drastic action with respect to gold.   The President, as the result of emergency legislation, was empowered to prohibit all transactions in gold, and the Secretary of the Treasury was authorized to mobilize all gold coin and bullion in the United States in the Treasury vaults.   Banks were forbidden to pay out gold, and gold exports were prohibited except on license.   This meant that the United States had abandoned the gold standard and circulation for *internal* commerce, although not for foreign intercourse.   On Apr. 5, the President "nationalized" all gold coin, bullion, and gold certificates by requiring delivery to the Federal Reserve Banks.   Permission to secure gold was given to those requiring gold for industrial use or operations not interpreted as hoarding.

While these measures were being taken, there was a decided impetus to inflationary sentiment in Congress by recognition of the wide latitude now afforded by modification of the gold standard for internal credit expansion or even paper-money inflation or "reflation."   The prices of raw materials had declined from the temporary rally in the fall of 1932 to a very deep new bottom in January, 1933, but thereafter the expectation of some inflationary measures continued to be a stimulating speculative factor.

Broadly speaking, the modification of the former gold standard of the United States resembled what followed the complete suspension of gold by Great Britain.   Prices of commodities and securities rose very rapidly, and a burst of speculative activity affected even commodity prices in British sterling.   In other words, enough psychological stimulus was given by the inflationary implications of the gold policy to bring about a rise in the world price of basic commodities, particularly agricultural products.

Early in May the President gave a radio address in which the determination to raise prices of basic commodities was thus expressed: "The Administration has the definite objective of raising commodity prices to such an extent that those who have borrowed money will, on the average, be able to repay that money in the same kind of dollar which they borrowed."   This pronouncement recognized the existence of a large and more or less distressed commodity debt and conditions in some agricultural areas that from time to time had verged upon revolution. Fulfilling these expectations, there came into existence the Agricultural Adjustment Act, the main purpose of which was to accomplish what agricultural experts were by this time fairly well convinced was the major problem—surpluses.   Contraction of excessive acreage and production of a few key products seemed to be called for.   This Act, however, contained a potentially inflationary amendment (the Thomas Amendment), authorizing the President at his discretion (1) to purchase through the

Federal Reserve Board Government bonds in the open market to the extent of three billion dollars; (2) to issue United States notes up to a maximum of two billions; (3) to reduce the weight of the gold dollar to the extent of 50 per cent; (4) to fix the weight of the gold and silver dollar at such a ratio as the President might find necessary and provide for unlimited coinage of gold and silver at that ratio; and (5) to accept silver at 50 cents an ounce to the amount of 200 million dollars from foreign governments in payment of indebtedness.[1]

In order further to implement his monetary revolution, the President in June signed a joint resolution that formally invalidated clauses in contracts calling for payment in gold coin. Also, Federal Reserve notes and National Bank notes were for the first time made legal tender. The important point in these radical changes is that the United States avowed a new form of gold standard, subject to modification at any time as a means of maintaining a money of "constant purchasing power" over debts, this being primarily understood to be the debts of those producing *commodities*, whose debt-paying power can be roughly measured by an index of commodity prices. The intrusion of the familiar potent agricultural influence in Congress in the early 1930's kept in the background the very much more important mass of debt, much of it frozen or insolvent, representing urban mortgages, railroads, and other public utilities that did not derive any power of validation from commodity prices as such. The Administration was content for the moment to leave these matters in the hands of the RFC, which, by the end of 1933, had managed to extend a helping hand to the extent of some 4 billion dollars, of which 1.4 billions served the purpose of resuscitating embarrassed banks, 400 millions went to shore up railroad companies, while about 200 millions served directly the purpose of assisting mortgage companies (mainly in agriculture).

In June, 1933, there was, however, a significant effort to extend the capital salvaging process by setting up a special organization within the Federal Home Loan Bank System, known as the Home Owners' Loan Corporation, to furnish emergency relief to distressed homeowners who were faced with the loss of their homes through imminent foreclosure or tax sale. This was accomplished by refinancing the mortgages on more favorable terms. This was a temporary arrangement, the operations not extending beyond June, 1936. Through the combined efforts of the RFC and this HOLC, an enormous amount of impaired mortgage capital was

[1] As a safeguard against excessive inflation, the Federal Reserve Board was authorized, with the approval of the Secretary of the Treasury, to take appropriate steps to prevent undue credit expansion and to increase or decrease under certain restrictions and with the approval of the President reserve balances against demand or time deposits of member banks.

at least temporarily held in suspense or refinanced. In order to carry the program still further, it was desirable that broad leeway be used to permit Federally sponsored agencies to convert old debt into new debt. This required, in short, that *interest rates be kept as low as possible* and that no limiting restrictions be placed upon the expansion of such short credit as might be necessary in achieving this general purpose. This meant that rigid adherence to a definitely fixed gold standard or any system of rigidly determined minimum banking reserves—implying frequent or spasmodic limitation upon the credit-extending power of the Reserve System—had to be scrapped. Old debt was to be, in other words, translated into new debt, carrying much lower fixed charges, but in order to accomplish this an atmosphere of *expansive, yet regulated,* monetary, credit, and capital facilities had to be developed. Toward this general purpose the measures taken with respect to gold and the monetary standards were of prime importance. We shall now trace the further expansion of these policies in succeeding years.

The experiments in the direction of what has come to be called in Government circles "the New Finance" explain the negative attitude taken by President Roosevelt in July, 1933, toward the proposed London Economic Conference. There were some indications that the British, French, and other representatives preparing to discuss ways of stabilizing world economy again were building their agenda around a program contemplating the reestablishment of some form of fixed gold standard. Mr. Roosevelt apparently felt that this matter might so confine or limit his New Finance within the economy that he suddenly took action that virtually blocked the proceedings. In this he was also strongly pressured by inflationist organizations and money theorists. A great opportunity to rectify international economic relations along fundamental lines was lost, perhaps for many years to come. The die was cast in the direction of rebuilding the economy of the United States to the already vaguely delineated plans of regionalized hegemony conforming to the pattern of change in the basic philosophy of all the great nations. This momentous shift, briefly, looked toward rebuilding and fortifying internal financial structures after the great storm by governmental agencies using flexible instruments, armed with vastly magnified administrative powers and discretionary authority. The year 1933 marked a great turning point in American affairs, as it did in world affairs.

During the balance of 1933, gold was bought with paper money or credits by the United States from domestic mines at prices fixed by the Secretary of the Treasury and more or less comforming to the existing foreign-exchange valuations of the dollar.[1] The price at the end of the

[1] The RFC, financial handy tool, was pressed into service in the closing months of the year as the agency to handle gold purchases.

year stood at about \$34 per fine ounce. This rise in price naturally meant that the gold now held by the Treasury had risen in "dollar" value, automatically expanding the dollar's worth of potential credit that might be created on this base. But as we shall see presently, this structure was not built on the old model, making large credit resources available to private speculation or semi-investment processes. The foundations were enlarged to *provide for a new superstructure of Federally dominated credit for capital and quasi-capital purposes.*[1]

THE REVALUING OF GOLD

Thus far the Government had merely suspended the circulation of gold as money and the circulation of paper backed by gold but had not formally revalued its gold. This step was taken by the Gold Reserve Act of January, 1934. The Treasury was now to be the exclusive holder of all (nonindustrial) gold; even the Federal Reserve Banks were to be permitted to hold "reserves" only in gold certificates or credits on the books of the Treasury, not in actual gold in their own vaults. International transactions could be settled only by gold released through central banks. The President was given power to set the nominal standard weight of the gold dollar between 12.9 and 15.48 grains of gold, nine-tenths fine, as compared with the old dollar of 25.8 grains. Mr. Roosevelt actually set the dollar at $15\frac{5}{21}$ grains of gold, nine-tenths fine. This represented a devaluation of 41 per cent or, in other words, a 59-cent dollar. Expressed in terms of the new price of gold, this meant \$35 an ounce, as against the old price of \$20.67 a fine ounce, an increase of close to 70 per cent.[2] Chart 36 illustrates the results, in comparison with the experience in Great Britain.

One important fact in this connection is that the nominal profit of about 2.8 billions was not all added to the reserve potentially available for sustaining credit expansion. An amount close to 2 billion was set aside as a special Stabilization Fund, somewhat similar to the Equalization Account used by the British Government and designed to be used as a secret means of stabilizing international-exchange rates, snubbing speculative movements in these rates, and, in the event of unusual

[1] In the references to gold and monetary policy immediately following in the text, the writer has drawn material from the convenient summary presented by J. D. Paris in Chapter 2 of the work previously cited.

[2] A short time before the new policy became effective, the price of gold in the United States was about 60 per cent above the old parity, and the price of gold in London was about 50 per cent above the presuspension level. The Canadian price was about even with that of the United States; South Africa was lower, but Australia and New Zealand considerably higher—about 90 per cent above the old parity. In other countries the price varied as high as about 100 per cent above 1929 levels in Argentina and 150 per cent in Japan.

difficulties, stabilizing Government security values. The new gold price of $35 an ounce proved, on the whole, to represent an undervaluing of the dollar (that is, too high a price) in considering the average of

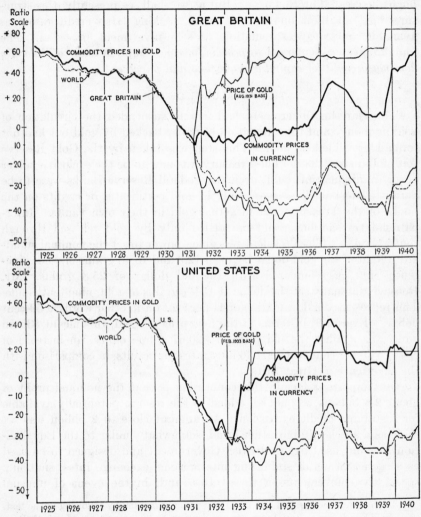

CHART 36.—Commodity prices in gold and currency and the price of gold, 1925–1940. The price of gold in Great Britain is shown as an index number with base at August, 1931, to enable comparison of relative movements. The price of gold in the United States is shown as an index number with base at February, 1933. The price index numbers are those of F. A. Pearson, Cornell University.

relationships between typical basic prices expressed in the currencies of many foreign countries and the same articles or forms of wealth stated in dollars but translated into the various foreign currencies through

New York exchange rates.   This was one factor among others that soon caused a heavy inflow of gold from foreign countries, a flow that, as we have already noted on Chart 9, ultimately became an avalanche.   It is inaccurate to say that our buying price alone caused this movement as more powerful factors were at work.   There was the return flow of American capital which had been hastily sent abroad in cash in 1932 and 1933; more important was the growing flight to the United States of foreign capital (largely in the form of actual gold) seeking a haven of refuge from the growing danger of serious international friction. Although giving the country only a slightly enlarged base for its credit banking or even for emergency Federal financing, the new dollar plus other factors drained into the United States in the next few years a preponderance of the world's stock of gold, enlarging reserves beyond all reason and requiring new steps for control.   Thus one step in the direction of flexible or opportunistic financial manipulation produced the need for many more.[1]

The political forces of the world after 1934 rapidly shifted toward a grim competitive struggle among more or less clearly defined groupings and alliances of powers, leading to the final dénouement of a new World

[1] We may note in passing the somewhat parallel policy, and a strange one indeed, with respect to silver.   A Silver Purchase Act was approved in the summer of 1934, providing that the Treasury purchase silver at home or abroad, issuing legal-tender silver certificates therefor, with an upper limit that would maintain a silver reserve not over one-third of the gold reserve.   In fact, the President had previously, in December, 1933, authorized the mint to accept all domestically produced silver at a price nearly 20 cents above the prevailing market.   This silver, however, has not actually been considered as an addition to the monetary reserve in the credit system, and such mild and indirect inflationary effects as the policy may have had have resulted from the placing in circulation of more silver certificates.   Of course, one ulterior object in this silver legislation was to raise the value of the money in which Chinese trade with the world was supposed to be paid and thus, by helping the allegedly "oppressed" domestic silver miners, the Chinese were also to be assisted to a higher standard of living.   In actual fact, the raising of the world value of silver *depressed* Chinese prices quoted in silver, and soon forced China off the silver standard and into monetary chaos, followed by war inflation.

One other effect of the policy of purchasing silver was to keep in existence a flow of foreign remittances to buy silver, thus preventing any marked rise in the value of the dollar in the foreign-exchange markets.   In any event, a great hoard of silver was accumulated, the ultimate use of which (apart from some wartime uses) remains a mystery.   Basically, the curious silver episode illustrates the powerful effect of a small sectional group upon legislative policy.   The growth of such articulate blocs has directly contributed to the formation of powerful central governments.   Today governmental authority is greater in all countries, partly for the reason that highly organized group pressures are immensely greater and national governments cannot function if they do not by compromise or force make terms with these mobilized factions pressuring for special favors, special legislation, and all manner of economic benefits.   This, in turn, is a phase of the breakdown of trade and industry after 1929.

War in September, 1939.   By early 1936, after localized conflicts in Spain, Africa, and China, international financial and price developments clearly reflected a new and grandiose pattern of aggression and accelerated planning of armaments in all directions.   The United States, after adopting a revised form of the gold standard serving internal trade by paper and credit proxies and foreign transactions by carefully supervised actual use, relinquished formal adherence to even a fixed international gold standard when it appeared to be expedient in the autumn of 1936 to participate with Great Britain and France in a three-way "exchange-stabilization" plan.   This aimed to support sterling, because the British were so heavily engaged in the purchase of materials and reserve stocks of foods in preparation for the coming crisis that the pound was under persistent pressure.

At the same time, the United States desired not to permit the dollar to *appreciate* with reference to either sterling or the franc.   The year 1936 was one of rising social tension in France, which had insisted upon retaining a fixed gold standard as set up in 1928, despite the terrific decline since that time in world prices in terms of gold.   The devaluation of the dollar had further intensified this strain on the French price level, and thus there were two factors threatening to raise the relative value of the dollar and depress prices after several years of rise.[1]   The Popular Front administration that came into power in France in 1936 was following a generally inflationary course in public finance, and this led finally to suspension of the gold standard by decree in the autumn.

In October, France formally devalued the franc more or less in line with the reduced purchasing power of French paper money, and, the smaller gold powers having already devalued or abandoned gold, the record was complete.   Further devaluations then occurred in Italy and various other minor countries.   Our agreement with Britain and France to participate in stabilizing the rates of exchange, now moored to nothing very substantial, was part of the operation whereby France belatedly joined the procession of managed currencies divorced from a fixed gold basis, without internal circulation of gold coins.   In connection with these arrangements, it was found necessary even to restrict gold shipments for settlement of international balances to such operations as would contribute to the purpose of this agreement.   The dollar and the pound were maintained for several years in a fairly stable relation, but the French, even before the outbreak of the new war in September, 1939, found it impossible to maintain the value of the franc as contemplated

[1] As early as the spring of 1934, Czechoslovakia had been forced to devalue its gold unit.   Belgium followed in April, 1935, by a 28 per cent devaluation; Poland resorted at the same time to exchange control.   The end of the gold bloc came when Holland limited export of gold and Switzerland virtually revalued her franc by 30 per cent.

by the tripartite agreement.   As the war crisis approached, the British also found it difficult to prevent some further depreciation in sterling due to the mounting import balances.

In the meantime, Germany had gone a long way to develop an unprecedented technique of foreign-exchange manipulation and export price control.   The need for conserving gold and deliberately rationing foreign exchange already existing in 1931 was exploited to capture foreign materials needed for war.   With the coming of Hitler and the activities of Dr. Schacht as head of the Reichsbank in the spring of 1933, the government, in the words of Douglas Miller,[1] "had made a virtue of necessity" and begun to use the "totalitarian control of foreign commerce transactions as an offensive as well as a defensive weapon."   From that time forward an intricate series of "allocated" exchange drawn on foreign financial centers, multiple prices on export goods, direct barter deals, etc., all represented a policy converging toward a single purpose—the placing of foreign trade and finance and, incidentally, all production of goods entering into foreign trade, in the control of the central government.   This meant that the traditional system of free exchange and international trade *among individuals* was ended.   Efforts were made, temporarily with some success, to place the import and export affairs of Germany on a unilateral barter basis, with the government setting the price of export goods and regulating or allocating all imports according to domestic policy and, of course, with an eye to restricting imports to those things most likely to develop the armament program.   Thus came about the formation of a Central European money bloc, the widening of the gulf between the group in which the United States was financially an active participant, and the militant, increasingly self-contained, war power centered in Berlin.

As Europe stepped up its preparations for the new conflict and as the United States remained the great source of needed materials, gold continued to flow to our shores so rapidly that it appeared for a time in 1936 that the offer to purchase gold from all and sundry at $35 an ounce might have to be discontinued.   No change was made in the price, but an important new departure was begun in order to prevent the avalanche of gold from raising reserves in the banking system above deposit requirements by too fantastic an amount.   It harks back to the suggestions of Carl Snyder years before as to direct reserve control.

In December, 1936, the Treasury began to sterilize gold by acquiring with notes most of the receipts and impounding them in an inactive account, really a very simple and effective device.   This was important in that it has since continued to form part of the evolving technique of reserve and credit control.   With an abrupt rise of commodity prices

[1] "You Can't Do Business with Hitler," p. 64, Boston, 1941.

stimulated by war-material buying in many parts of the world and a growing atmosphere of speculative enthusiasm, rising stock prices, and accumulation of industrial inventories, it was felt by the Federal Reserve that some further action was necessary, not to prevent further increase in member-banks excess reserves but actually to reduce the unwieldy volume of excess reserves.   Therefore, in January, 1937, the Board of Governors, by legislative authority, announced that minimum reserves required against member-bank deposits would be raised 100 per cent,[1] one-half taking effect in March and the balance in May.   Such a broad, direct power to vary the previously fixed minimum ratios of reserves to deposits was a far-reaching step in credit-control authority and technique. Its unfortunate aspect was that it proved to be exceedingly strong medicine that injured the patient rather than helping to attain his equilibrium. The action contributed to the drastic reversal of general business conditions in the latter part of 1937, and it was therefore necessary to reverse the policy in some degree in the spring of 1938.   At that time the Treasury also released the impounded gold that had accumulated up to that time in the inactive fund, but all this was done months after the country had begun to suffer from a severe intermediate depression.

The net effect of the gold policy, together with the insistent flight of liquid capital back from Europe, plus the use of new gold mined in the British Empire and Russia to make war-preparation purchases in the United States, combined by the end of 1940 to bring the gold stock of the United States (valued at $35 an ounce) to 22 billions of dollars.

The foregoing discussion has given special emphasis to the manner in which the world-wide financial chaos, coupled with the inherent weaknesses in our own methods of handling credit and capital, led to drastic political action.   Our devaluation of the dollar is a prime example of emergency policy.   The action of our Government was conceived in an atmosphere that made it natural for us to go along with monetary and financial expedients rapidly circling around the globe.   Following this emergency stage there came various plans and revised structures that were conceived in calmer deliberation and were, on the whole, salutary steps, as we shall see in Chapter 15.   As the Government proceeded along a course of experiment, reform, and managed recovery, it became evident that finance was to occupy an important place in all public policy.   Accompanying these novel measures, sometimes by way of rationalizing indiscretion, there naturally evolved theories—expressions of principle and formulas to justify practical action.   Although the economic philosophy of the New Deal is still in a formative process and will no doubt be further modified by the emergencies of World War II,

[1] By law the Reserve Board might not make adjustments below the former requirements or beyond 100 per cent above them.

it seems important, before we proceed further, to summarize and to evaluate, at least tentatively, several of the more articulate expressions of monetary thought that appear to have been woven into the fabric of the New Finance.

THE THEORY UNDERLYING DEVALUATION

Let us first consider the ideas that seem to have led to the devaluation of the dollar. This grew principally from the ideas of the late George F. Warren and of F. A. Pearson at Cornell University. Warren was an agricultural economist who had been greatly impressed by the farmers' difficulties throughout the 1920's and whose conclusions regarding the monetary means of creating farm solvency by raising prices were presented in a book entitled "Prices" in January, 1933. The principles developed in this book formed the framework for Mr. Roosevelt's emergency monetary policy as Warren, along with James H. Rogers and Irving Fisher, conferred with the President on this subject. Unfortunately the principles are not so clearly formulated as one might wish. They include stray bits of very old ideas on altering the coins of the realm, convictions popular in the 1920's on "managing" the currency, but withal, strangely enough, a skepticism as to the effectiveness of *credit* policy or the management of *banking* operations as a means of accomplishing price recovery. The basis of the ideology is *gold*, not credit.[1]

With regard to gold and prices, the doctrine of Warren does not run along the lines of the traditional "quantity theory" of the money and the price level.[2] In one sense Warren agreed with the quantity theorists in believing that "for an explanation of the price changes, we must look outside the commodities themselves. The logical place to look is at the other side of the price equation—the supply of and demand for money."[3] This was, in fact, a *demand-quantity* theory rather than a

---

[1] Warren looked upon all credit and paper currency as similar to warehouse receipts for wheat. Their value is established *by* the "value" of gold, just as the value of a wheat receipt is established by the value of wheat. This is indeed a crude and extraordinary theory, denying to gold any value by virtue of its properties as a circulating medium and reserve for the credit and paper-money superstructure. This forms a substitute for gold in a very different way from the sense in which a warehouse certificate is a "substitute" for the commodity in storage. Flour is not made with warehouse receipts.

[2] By this we refer to that body of doctrine that regards the price level as incapable of influencing money or trade and general price-level changes as the proportional result of changes in the combined amount of velocity of money and credit in use—changes in the physical aspects of supply and trade being considered relatively unimportant. Irving Fisher has referred to the advice given the President by Henry Wallace as representing the "overproduction" school, a very different doctrine.

[3] "Prices," p. 56.

quantity theory of money. The crux of Warren's thinking lies in the peculiar concept that money is primarily gold (at least, in the world as a whole prior to 1930), whereas the circulating bank credit generated by drawing checks upon demand deposits is merely a resultant, subservient to trade *and prices*. In another of his writings, Warren went so far as to say "rising prices and increased business result in extensive use of credit. The rising prices are a cause of the expansion of credit rather than that the expanding credit is a cause of rising prices."[1] And further, "banks are more influenced by business than business is influenced by banks."[2]

Because of this peculiar view of the unimportance of bank credit among the forces operating to form the pattern of the price level, Warren paid little or no attention to the fact that a given amount of gold, serving either as circulating money or as reserve for the credit system, may support a total of circulating credit of widely varying magnitude as the gold reserve may or may not be effectively economized. Warren seemed to regard changes in the "value" of gold as due to variation in the demand for and supply of *the metal*, and these value changes somehow *caused* changes in the level of prices. The usual doctrine holds that the price-level change and change in value of gold (under a gold standard) are aspects of the same thing. The supply of gold available to "support" the price system seemed a matter of acute concern to Warren. He did his principal thinking about these matters in a period of declining prices, particularly farm-product prices. As we have seen, the war price level was not favorable to gold production, and it was some time before the postwar slump in gold output was reversed, particularly by the rising trend in the Transvaal, Russia, and Canada.

The idea of a "gold shortage" had been a source of concern to many influential financial writers. Gustav Cassel, in Stockholm, had for years been endeavoring to persuade the world that gold scarcity was a desperate threat to monetary stability.[3] Warren seems to have considered the alleged scarcity value of gold after 1930 as due not merely to several years of subnormal output but to the existence of a *hoarding demand*

[1] Warren and Pearson, "World Prices and the Building Industry," note, p. 94. New York and London, 1937.

[2] *Ibid.*, p. 144.

[3] See, for example, Cassel, "The Crisis in the World's Monetary System," Rhodes Memorial Lectures, Oxford, 1932. "If gold production had continued normal . . . the present scarcity of gold would have been far less intense and the Central Banks would certainly not have been so eager in their competition for the gold coming on the market. Thus a more liberal discount policy would have been possible, and the extraordinary pressure to which the general price levels throughout the world have been exposed during the last few years would have been at least very much relieved." (P. 20.)

for gold. He was aware that various countries in the late 1920's had attempted to revert to the gold standard and in so doing had apparently created a strong "demand" for the metal for their reserves. When, however, the world crisis became serious, there was not only a continued race among the leading nations to secure what gold they could but a general hoarding demand due to distrust of economic conditions and of the banks. This seems to have impressed Warren as a very significant element in making the "value" of gold so high *and therefore* prices so low. In order to remedy this unnatural demand for gold, it was first necessary to restore the solvency of basic industry and particularly of farming so that the farmers could pay debts contracted *at a higher price level*. Obviously, according to his philosophy, this meant cutting gold pieces into smaller units. By thus assisting hard-pressed debtors, harassed by falling prices and further exposed to price decline insofar as important countries insisted on standards of fixed gold pieces, the hoarding could at once be checked, the "value" of gold lowered, and prices *therefore* raised.

Warren considered that during major wars the value of gold always declines because the *demand* for it declines. Instead of saying, what we can prove to be correct, that wars lead to enormous use of paper and credit currency, at a time when physical supplies of goods are inadequate to meet emergency needs, he chose to view everything in the light of gold. Because gold declines in value, prices rise; hence if gold pieces are made smaller, prices will rise. Without much regard for consistency, he also argued that when prices were rising, the demand for gold in the arts usually *rose* considerably. He did not stop to consider also that during major wars governments usually seek in every possible way to conserve their gold resources in war chests, thus *raising* the demand for gold.[1] The reader can easily perceive by this time the tenuous and devious reasoning pervading the Warren philosophy of money.

It was repeatedly made clear by Warren that he was not interested in the "general price level" but rather in particular groups of commodity prices, especially of the basic raw materials. He ignored entirely and specifically repudiated the possibility that any changes taking place in physical supply in relation to market requirements might have anything to do with their price movements. Everything centered upon gold. The solution of the current difficulties was, after all, so simple. Could not every country create its own price level and validate its debt

[1] Warren said, "The great rise in prices in the United States was due to the fact that most of the gold-using world ceased to use gold and ceased to bid for it. This reduced the demand and the value of gold, and commodity prices rose. When the whole world began to bid frantically for gold, its value rose and commodity prices collapsed." ("Prices," p. 90.)

structure merely by revising the terms of its gold standard? Since everything depended upon the "value" of gold in the accepted money unit, a larger or smaller amount of gold defining that unit *immediately* changed the basic prices and hence the general commodity level. As simple as pushing a button.

In this one respect Warren's thinking was typical of that of many managed-currency enthusiasts. Their efforts cannot, of course, be brushed aside as unintelligent, in view of the known vagaries of gold supply, changes in commodity supply, expansion and contraction in credit, and many other sources of instability and disequilibrium that call for something better if it will work. But the suspicious feature about these panaceas is their stress upon simplicity and the ease with which complicating factors can be ignored, calmly brushed aside, as it were, so that emphasis can center upon discount rates, the juggling of security holdings of central banks, the manipulation of gold money, and what not. So far as the latter is concerned, it is the ancient device of *debasing the coin to make it cheap.*

MONETARY DEBASEMENT AS ECONOMIC WARFARE

All this dubious and vaguely defined theorizing is quite unnecessary in explaining why creating a lighter or adding to a heavier dollar, if carried far enough, must produce certain effects on the price level *and on some other things, also.* What it all reduces to is the willingness of a country faced by falling prices and distressed debtors *to declare economic and financial war on the rest of the world.* It devalues its money and by parting from the rest of the world's monetary structure determines its own price level. Or it may, as in the British instance, keep a manipulated price level without any metallic standard. (All things bought and sold become the "standard.") As Warren correctly held, a country can have whatever price level it chooses, so long as it makes its money changes *while other countries do not.* This is equivalent to the proposition that a country can obtain as much of raw materials, land, and industrial plants as it deserves, *provided* that other countries remain inactive and do not defend their property against conquest. We enter here the realm of moral questions rather than purely economic questions. The basic question is: Should all countries engage in an endless devaluation race by continually readjusting their money units to gain advantages over each other? Does this in the end solve anything? Or does it raise innumerable new problems that defy solution?

It was perhaps one of the merits of the old gold standard—crude, unstable it undoubtedly was—that it introduced at least a kind of moral code applying to international economic affairs and exchange relations. It tended to restrain an important country from going permanently off at a tangent to seek advantages in export trade by selling its product for momentarily cheap exchange. Under the gold standard there was not (so long as the rules were generally respected) a strong temptation for a government to scale down its internal debts by currency debasement, at the same time stealthily pursuing a trade war by cheapening its export products against its rivals. Instead of having the terms of foreign trade rest upon relative advantages in quality and efficiency of production, this insidious new philosophy implies, in what Mr. Warren personally advised Mr. Roosevelt to do, an endless juggling of money and prices, irrespective of relative efficiencies, for purposes not confined to economic stabilization. The result is likely to be in the long run exactly the kind of economic warfare leading to the utter destruction of external trade that the world is now beginning to face.

This aspect of the matter does not, of course, dispose entirely of the question as to the wisdom or unwisdom of devaluing the dollar in 1934. Probably some devaluation then was politically inevitable. The United States had extensive extractive industries that were in acute distress. By cutting down the content of the gold unit, the prices of the basic international commodities exported did rise in price, more or less proportionately to the rise in the paper price of gold, as we have seen. The cost in dollars of imported commodities rose and contributed another factor to the general rise in commodity levels. The *general* level of prices was elevated to an intermediate degree only. But the moral aspect is seen in the fact that no serious effort was made by major governments of the world to stabilize their cheaper gold (or paper) moneys by some firm understanding or agreement so that international relations and peaceful trade might once again be restored. There was in the Warren philosophy no such thing as *willingness to discuss*. Warren unfortunately seemed quite unconscious of the fact that he was urging the nation to engage in economic warfare much more certainly than he was urging it to reestablish a defective mechanism. In fact, so long as the United States retains its present anomalous kind of partial gold standard (with Presidential authority to vary it still further at his discretion), other countries can, and probably will, remain upon variable metallic or nonmetallic "standards," and when the time comes someday to develop American export markets, the present amorphous international currency situation may well produce a great devaluation race plus the logical concomitant—unilateral barter dealings forcing still further devaluations.

We may, therefore, pay heavily in the end for our artificial price support, which very probably could have been achieved through the various agricultural control measures developed under the AAA, and the revival of general income and buying power through expeditious housecleaning in capital finance and broad rehabilitation of the construction industry.

In point of fact, all this furore regarding gold and devaluation and price reflation seems actually to have delayed by several years the sound recovery of the heavy industries, whose prosperity does not primarily rest upon a rising price level in the commodity markets. It is significant that the U.S. Department of Commerce estimated, at about the time the gold manipulation matter was being discussed, that of a total of nearly 120 billions of long-term debt in the United States, *the farm mortgage debt was only about 9 billions; most of the balance was not the kind of indebtedness that juggling of commodity prices could directly alleviate.* The rescue of marginal farmers was an urgent problem, and we cannot deny that devaluing the dollar did contribute something to inflate farm income and that this assistance extended to other industries by diffusion; nevertheless, as a solution of the general debt phases of this great depression, devaluation of the dollar cannot be rated very highly.[1]

[1] The Warren-Pearson doctrine emphasizing the possibility of price adjustment through gold devaluation was given enormous circulation through the formation of what was known as the Committee for the Nation to Rebuild Prices and Purchasing Power. Although neither Warren nor Pearson was a member of this Committee, which was headed by a group of businessmen under the leadership of J. H. Rand, Jr., there was a close liaison between these parties. In May, 1933, the Committee began a public campaign of wide scope demanding that the dollar be revalued to reestablish the 1926 price level and that the price of gold in the future *be changed* in such manner as to maintain "a dollar of stable purchasing power that will protect us from future disruption of our price level." It seems typical of the proponents of monetary, as well as credit, manipulation that they are all excellent propagandists.

This Committee seems to have had considerable influence upon the Roosevelt Administration in urging that the United States refrain from entering into definite commitment regarding international stabilization, it being feared that this would prevent an adequate revaluation of the dollar and the price level, in view of the fact that so many other countries had already revised their currency basis drastically. In these efforts the Committee found support in a similar hostile attitude toward gold "deflationism" and stabilization attempts expressed by J. M. Keynes, who desired a British-American plan of "managed" paper money. Aristide Briand, in France, meanwhile was urging Britain to join the Continental gold bloc in the interest of developing his favorite proposed project, a United States of Europe.

CHAPTER 15

FINANCIAL RECONSTRUCTION

Let us turn briefly to several other important changes in banking policy and structure. These are important in view of the fact that 22 billion dollars of bank reserves, or potential reserves, even in a banking system having some degree of direct control over reserve requirements, is certainly an impressive base for credit inflation. It is remarkable how persistently since 1933 has been the opinion of financial authorities and writers on investment problems that inflation was inevitable and would be of tremendous proportions. What these analysts omitted to consider was the powerful combination of banking regulations and reforms that came into existence as the gold hoard was built up. It will be remembered that following the banking crisis in the spring of 1933, the Reconstruction Finance Corporation promptly stepped in to revamp the weaker banks and to assist in reopening suspended banks by loans to the receivers. The banks were reopened only after giving evidence of their ability to maintain solvency. After thus clearing the ground of banking wreckage, a new structure and a greatly modified type of banking practice developed. Before summarizing the outstanding points of banking reform, we may add that after 1933 banking failures dropped abruptly and have since remained insignificant, after having reached the unprecedented total of about 4,000 suspensions during 1933.

BELATED STEPS IN BANKING REFORM

By the Banking Act of 1933, a number of basic and long-deferred changes were made, some of them hitting directly at the weaknesses and deficiencies that we have repeatedly noted as among the factors contributing to amplify cyclical business instability. The functions of investment banking and commercial banking were divorced insofar as concerns participation by commercial banks in the flotation or sponsoring of security issues, and even the private banks had now to decide whether to be bankers or issuers of securities. No longer were there to be interlocking directorates between security houses and commercial banks (after June, 1934), and the latter might no longer participate in underwriting operations. Nor could banks act as agents for outside parties wishing to make loans to the security market, a wise provision, ten years too late. Federal Reserve authorities were now to scrutinize the loans on collateral made by the member banks, and there is not likely to be repeated in the future the kind of credit orgy in the interest of security speculation (at least, as to private securities) witnessed in the late 1920's.

At this time, also, a new principle of deposit guarantee, or insurance, was introduced through the creation of the Federal Deposit Insurance Corporation, a step in the direction of insurance of financial and economic risks. The Roosevelt Administration carried forward such insurance principles in many other directions and, indeed, made them a basic feature of governmental policy intended to stabilize conditions and to mobilize the resources of the entire people against specific risks that in the past, particularly in the case of banking operations, have been of vast consequence. Some rather feeble encouragement to branch banking within state boundaries was provided. Finally, commercial banks were prohibited from paying interest on demand deposits, and the Federal Reserve was given authority to regulate the rates of interest paid by these banks on time deposits, the latter features being important in view of the misuse of deposits during the 1920's and failure to distinguish clearly between the two types of deposits.[1]

In 1935 there was still further banking legislation that removed certain doubtful features of the deposit insurance system and placed the guarantee of bank deposits up to five thousand dollars maximum per deposit on a practical and probably enduring foundation. This Act also gave the Federal Reserve Board authority to continue the policy of varying reserve requirements within prescribed limits, as already explained in connection with the procedure in 1937–1938. Most important among the features of the 1935 legislation was the crystallization of a banking philosophy along broad and flexible lines. A new Com-

---

[1] As a result of the lowering of interest paid by banks on time deposits, there occurred a shifting of large corporation and individual balances from time to demand accounts. At the same time the various Federal policies for strengthening the financial machinery serving the mortgage market served to define more clearly the character and proper handling of essentially *savings capital* destined for long-term investment. If we take these various reforms together, an excellent beginning, at least, was made in reducing the previous tendency of banks endeavoring to utilize time deposits in a tentative and "straddling" fashion through mortgage and capital loans of inadequate maturity and deficient amortization provisions. It has been evident in recent years that corporations have continued to maintain fairly large cash balances, despite the restricted opportunity to accumulate additional surpluses during the years of the great depression. As will be emphasized in a later section, however, the reader must not be confused in believing that the enormous growth in total bank deposits since 1933 has represented merely idle balances of domestic corporations and individuals arising from their productive earning power; the vast preponderance of this increase in bank deposits has represented the combined effect of the devaluation of the dollar and the inflow of gold.

mittee was formed within the Reserve System to coordinate and administer the open-market control policy. This is important in view of the continuing trend in the banking system toward assets representing security investments rather than loans and discounts. More and more these securities, as will be seen in Chart 37, have emphasized United

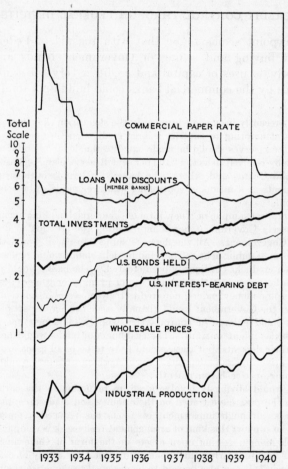

CHART 37.—Credit conditions, prices, and production, 1933–1940.

States Government obligations. Increasing importance was attached by Marriner Eccles (Governor of the Reserve Board since 1934) and others to the Open Market Committee and a variable Reserve security portfolio to absorb any shocks which might be transmitted to the bond market through commercial banks disposing of Government securities. We have here a mechanism somewhat similar to the various international stabilization funds, in the sense that a Government agency is specifically designed as a shock absorber, in the one case, for foreign-exchange rates and their constant artificial manipulation and in the other case, in connection with the rate of interest and Government bonds, coming rapidly to be the medium of capital investment in the United States.[1]

CREDIT CONTROL THROUGH FEDERAL DEFICITS

This viewpoint seems to be that with the aid of Federal Reserve open-market buying and selling of Government bonds and effective brakes on private uses of capital and credit, a very substantial holding of such bonds by the commercial banks could build up a total of deposits

---

[1] There has recently been some interest in the suggestion that instead of the commercial banks attempting to support a large credit structure on a fractional cash-reserve base, the reserves should be made equal to the deposit liabilities at all times. This is commonly referred to as the "100 per cent Reserve plan," sponsored by Irving Fisher, Lauchlin Currie, and others, who have considerable faith in monetary and credit instruments as a means of controlling whatever needs to be controlled in the business system.

There might, for example, be a new form of commercial banking agency that would hold in its assets Government bonds representing the creation of deposits to the credit of the Government. All the deposits subject to check would thus represent assets in the form of public debt. These public-debt claims would replace all the other assets on which credit has ordinarily been created. The banks would not be able to make loans as before except through the use of primary or time deposits, and they would thus become moneylenders, not credit creators, *except* in relation to the State. In this manner the Government would virtually issue the major part of the means of payment and could enlarge or contract the "supply of money" as conditions or political exigencies might warrant. The customers of banks would be able to draw checks upon their deposits, but these would have to be in all cases primary deposits and not derivative or credit deposits. Such checking accounts would be merely a means of turning over cash conveniently.

This plan would obviously involve a severe reduction in the earning power of banks that in the past have traded on their equity and made exceptional profits in many instances, although impairment of assets has reduced average net profits. What those who support this kind of arrangement really seek is complete control over the checkbook money, resting upon assets in the form of Government securities. According to Lauchlin Currie, this scheme "divorces the supply of money from the loaning of money"; it can also be said to be designed to monetize the national debt. It would accomplish essentially the same purpose as the issue of greenbacks, although being somewhat camouflaged, it escapes the immediate implication.

This plan would naturally appeal to those who feel that unlimited Government spending and a one-way system of accumulating deficits is excellent economic policy. On the other hand, it should always be considered that the gold standard, as it formerly functioned, is probably obsolete, and a camouflaged system of Government-regulated checkbook money is not inherently absurd. It is merely open to suspicion in a country that contains explosive pressure groups having a traditionally inflationist philosophy, and being strongly entrenched in Congress. If the banking system

credited in the first instance to the Federal Government and not subject to the erratic and disastrous depreciation such as occurred in past periods of crisis and liquidation. Whether such a volume of deposit or checkbook money brought into existence by continuous enlargement of Federal borrowing is equally likely to forestall periods of relatively excessive bank credit actually in use cannot be summarily disposed of. At any rate, machinery has been set up that, by implication and intent, gives the Federal Reserve heavy responsibility through open-market operations (rather than rediscount policy) for the maintenance of satisfactory general credit conditions and stable accommodation to commerce and industry but apparently on the tacit assumption that *private-loan* capital and credit will gradually be displaced by *Government* financing.

---

pursues its present course, it is by no means inconceivable that 100 per cent reserves in the form of Government obligations held against a variable liability of checkable deposits circulated through governmental activities may come. How such a monetary circulation could be kept closely adjusted to the trend of trade when we already have evidence that Government deficits appear to be spirals rather than incidents remains to be demonstrated. Bills have already appeared in Congress toward setting up such a proposal, and Irving Fisher has written a book entitled "One Hundred Per Cent Money" (New York, 1937), that promises to be just as effective propaganda as that which in previous years supported other schemes of monetary manipulation at the expense of detailed analysis of specific economic maladjustments.

There is evidence that Mr. Eccles, Chairman of the Board of Governors of the Federal Reserve System, is, or has been, sympathetic to this philosophy. In his earlier speeches and writings, which preceded the passage of the Banking Act of 1935, he warmly endorsed the idea of Government bond sales to banks and continued deficits to restore the supply of checkbook money. Irving Fisher wrote articles for the newspapers in the fall of 1935 calling attention to the support that he had obtained for his ideas in Washington. In this way the principle of open-market policies has mushroomed into a principle of governmental domination of checkbook money. Fisher, in releases to the press (see *San Francisco News*, Sept. 16, 1935), actually stated, "When it is the Federal Reserve Banks which buy the bonds, the Government debt is in effect reduced. This is because, under the new law, the Federal Reserve Banks are practically an arm of the United States Government," a clear indication of the greenbackism underlying this entire philosophy. The Federal Reserve Banks presumably would purchase and hold Government securities and thus keep checkbook money in circulation, even though it might be necessary to reduce these holdings in the member banks. Thus we could have our cake and eat it too, each time moving a little closer toward an outright paper standard of money.

It is true that Fisher, Currie, and others supporting this movement recognize that as banks have operated in the past, there has been much overexpansion, followed by reversal in lending policies that have brought hardship to bank customers, but somehow an attitude of fatalism or mysticism seems to prevent a square facing of the problems involved in rectifying these particular defects instead of burying them under a fresh avalanche of Government paper. The writer has endeavored in these chapters to indicate, on the basis of historical and statistical evidence, what some of these important defects have been, and he insists that these be given more study before the country is permanently committed to sheer greenbackism in sugar-coated form.

That is, credit control will work if the nerve center of *all* finance becomes located in Washington rather than New York.[1]

With a revamped, more solvent, banking system and a broad policy of reducing interest rates to permit unscrambling of old debt and larger Federal bond issues, the Federal Administration secured a considerable advantage in attacking the difficult problems involved in the mortgage system. We shall defer comment upon the regulatory policies affecting the security exchanges and the issue of corporate capital and confine the present summary to those features of the mortgage mechanism that, as we have seen, had been so important a factor in land speculation, the excesses of the building cycle, and, indeed, cyclical disturbance in all business and banking. We have already noted that the original plan of the Home Loan Bank System proved inadequate and that legislation of 1933 setting up the Home Owners' Loan Corporation and expanding Home Loan Bank facilities represented salvage operations to rescue urban mortgagors. This resulted incidentally in a genteel liquidation of many building-loan associations that joined the 9,500 banks that had disappeared since 1929.

BASIC CHANGES IN MORTGAGE FINANCE

The new and important principle in the insuring of deposits in home financing institutions was accomplished in 1934 through the Federal

---

[1] The Act of 1935 introduced a new and more flexible interpretation of what constituted a banking asset acceptable at the Federal Reserve Banks. Instead of restricting acceptable paper by specific definition, the new provision merely stated that *any* asset considered sound by the Federal Reserve Board would be suitable for rediscounting. This represented a shifting of emphasis from formal liquidity of an asset to the ultimate soundness of the loan represented by the asset. It also contemplated the extension of Federal Reserve credit through rediscount, with less concern as to the time of maturity represented by the member bank advance. All this, however, is important by way of principle rather than from a practical standpoint, inasmuch as there has been in recent years very little rediscounting, and the open-market operations have been the principal manner in which the Federal Reserve has operated to stabilize or unstabilize the money market.

It is significant that the Banking Act of 1933, providing several fundamental reforms in the commercial-banking and central-banking practice, was not primarily a product of the New Deal; the Act was largely an embodiment of the views of Senator Carter Glass and was a belated formulation of convictions and observations of banking malpractice that had accumulated for more than a decade. The Act of 1935, on the other hand, represented, in its emphasis upon the guarantee of bank deposits and their insurance by the Federal Deposit Insurance Corporation and the emphasis on the open-market operations as part of a broad philosophy of Federal control over *investment* machinery, very distinctly a New Deal viewpoint, and in particular the personal views of Mr. Marriner Eccles, whose suggestions for legislation as embodied in the House bill were considerably more radical than those actually embodied in the legislation.

Savings and Loan Insurance Corporation. Under jurisdiction of the HLB Board, this corporation insures against loss each savings account (below a maximum limit) in building-loan and similar savings institutions capable of meeting the necessary standards for a Federally insured association. We are not concerned with the details of the new form of deposit insurance, but the underlying principle is important. First, it provides adequate publicity and information as to the operations of construction finance and thus remedies one of the serious defects previously existing in this field. Second, and even more important, is the manner in which these insuring operations (usually providing for exchange of specified Federal bonds for frozen deposits) afford an opportunity by the Federal agency to supervise and regulate *lending practices* and to enforce better standards of financing and accounting. Savings and loan associations, as in the case of banks coming within the supervision of the FDIC, can take advantage of the insurance feature and offer this additional protection to depositors only insofar as they agree to conduct their operations in conformity with standards that have been vastly improved as the result of the various measures that we are discussing. Since 1934 the Federal Savings Associations have assumed the dominant position in this field.

The principle of insuring deposits in mortgage-loan institutions was greatly extended in a related direction by creation of the Federal Housing Administration in 1934. Here the principle of insurance was applied to Federal underwriting (not actual financing) of home-building mortgages. In its initial form, the arrangement extended such guarantee to approved mortgages to an upper limit of 80 per cent of appraised valuation, with maximum maturities on urban properties at 20 years. This gave the Housing Administration authority to revise the traditional practice in making mortgage loans on urban residential property in very fundamental ways. The insurance technique involves a commitment on the part of a Federal agency to substitute its obligations for FHA mortgages that might become impaired in spite of their being made in accordance, in the first instance, with the regulations for FHA mortgage loans.

To summarize the new features and omit many details, the essentials are (1) elimination of the multiple mortgage, accomplished by restricting insurance to first mortgages only and making the first mortgage on housing property of such character that the borrower can be expected to validate his loan successfully, (2) eliminating the short-term contingent and renewable (or supposedly renewable) loan, and recognizing that the average home owner will and must spread his repayments of principal over an extended period, (3) *requiring the regular amortization of all loans* as a prerequisite, so that the borrower is *accumulating his equity as the loan is being paid off, rather than merely gambling on the future,* (4) setting interest rates at more moderate levels approaching 5 per cent,[1] and (5) exercising close supervision of the plans and construction work as to technical standards, requiring careful study of each mortgaged property with regard to potential "neighborhood risks," probabilities of obsolescence and depreciation, and the personal status and character of the individual borrower.

There has probably never been any reform more needed than this. Had mortgage lending in the past been carried on essentially along such lines, it is certain the more violent swings in the building cycle and outrageous gyrations of real-estate speculation would have been avoided. Put another way, the long-term amortized mortgage simply means that if capital is soundly invested by careful attention at the outset to *all* aspects of the loan, and the rate of interest is such as to enable borrowers to meet both interest and amortization payment *from income*, it enables lenders to be thinking less of the "liquidity" of their loans and to be less nervously on the jump to be free of them if passing events prompt them to protect that precious liquidity. In the making of loans of this type, savings and loan associations and commercial banks have played the leading role, with insurance companies a poor third.

In the future, it is probable that with the further development of the Home Loan Banks to fulfill their functions as rehypothecation agencies (similar, in a sense, to the Federal Reserve Banks), the entire system will be so thoroughly protected from at least economic and financial hazards that we shall have brought mortgage-lending practice at least on a par with time-tested systems of the Scandinavian countries and other parts of Europe where sound principles have prevailed.[2] Since creation of

---

[1] This was accomplished not only by the contemporary monetary factors tending toward lower interest rates but by eliminating a major part of the moral and economic *risk* element that had contributed in the past to relatively high mortgage-loan rates.

As of July, 1940, the maximum interest rate on FHA insured mortages was 4.5 per cent, plus a mortgage insurance premium of 0.5 per cent on the decreasing balance. For loans up to six thousand dollars, a mortgage might be approved to the extent of .90 per cent of appraised value. For larger loans, the maximum was 80 per cent. Twenty years was the maximum maturity. It was thus not necessary, as in many cases in the past, for loans to be continually refinanced or renewed, with attending expenses and uncertainties. Although there has been criticism directed toward these apparently very liberal features of FHA financing, most of this criticism entirely ignores the superlative importance of amortizing long-term debt in some regular prearranged fashion and the great advantage of *accumulating* the borrower's equity rather than *deferring* it to some distant period.

[2] It is impossible here to discuss the important related problems of large-scale low-cost housing for those in the lowest income group, which is provided for by more recent legislation permitting direct and indirect Federal financial assistance and also the expansion of life-insurance investments directly in substantial rental projects of somewhat the same general type. These represent efforts in the direction of rehabilitation, relief, and conservation of human assets to which the Government has devoted

FHA, over three hundred enabling laws have been passed by various states permitting investing organizations to participate in the program. Among these are laws extending the FHA mortgage in the life-insurance field and enabling banks to participate in it. The Federal Banking Act of 1935 also permitted National Banks to liberalize their real-estate lending *if loans were amortized*, especially if they were of the FHA standard.

The revival of home building in the 1930's (see again Chart 30) developed somewhat tardily, probably because of the serious general financial deterioration in 1931 and 1932 at the bottom of a "double depression." The preoccupation of Congress with superficial inflationary panaceas and of the Administration with social emergency problems in 1933 retarded spontaneous termination of the spiral of foreclosure. Raising farm prices was no logical remedy for the urban mortgage chaos. The new system of financing did, however, contribute to consistent and healthy recovery in private residential building after 1934 and until war again complicated matters late in 1939. There is now a broad recognition of the soundness of these changes, since not only have they stimulated home building in the medium and lower cost range, where the need is greatest, but also they will restrict the ruthless necessity in the future for waves of foreclosure and will thus limit the extremes of the building cycle so far as the financial factors are concerned.[1]

---

much attention. We are here emphasizing those changes in general financial structure and procedure that have a direct bearing upon the soundness of the banking and capital structures as a whole and that form an important part of the bulwark against needless violent disturbance of industrial equilibrium and alternating periods of rapidly rising and rapidly falling employment and income.

[1] Paralleling basic improvement in lending standards in the mortgage field has been the activity of the FDIC in developing better standards for commercial banking. Two of the matters that have especially engaged the attention of that agency in strengthening banks are the expansion of banking capital to an adequate proportion of liabilities or earning assets and development of the principle of *amortized* term loans made by commercial banks to industries. Leo T. Crowley, while Chairman of the FDIC, repeatedly stressed in his reports the fact that many banks were inadequately capitalized. There had been a downward trend for many years in the ratio of capital to liabilities. The tendency to "trade on the equity" has always been strong in our commercial banking. As to term loans, Mr. Crowley stated in a speech in 1938: "I think it likely that a properly written term loan, carrying provisions for serial repayment, is superior as a bank asset to the continually renewed short-term instrument, the familiar 'sleeper' loans, with which banks heretofore have engaged in capital financing" (*Wall Street Journal*, New York, Oct. 26, 1938).

Mr. Crowley went on to say, and to confirm what has been emphasized in our previous chapters, that banks in past years had provided a great deal of "capital" but did so without admitting it. Recognizing the need for loans of intermediate or fairly long term for working-capital purposes for the smaller businesses and commercial firms as a form of credit advance coming within the province of commercial banks, if it is explicitly recognized and surrounded with proper safeguards, Mr. Crowley

In the case of the great mass of insolvent and semisolvent railroad-mortgage indebtedness, the Federal Administration thus far has been able (or willing) to accomplish little, probably because of the focusing of interest upon the problems of the individual citizen, the farmer, small business—the "wrongs of the many." Most of the emergency help made available to railroads was rendered early in the 1930's through the RFC. The total bonded indebtedness of the railroads in 1933 was about twelve billion dollars. We have already seen how it came about that the railroad system was saddled with this mass of rigid, unamortized, and virtually perpetual indebtedness. There was without question an utter disregard of the fact that times change and obsolescence and competitive forces are potential threats to the validity of heavy fixed charges.

Reorganization of roads in an insolvent condition has been an intolerably slow process, complicated by inept legislation in 1933 and, again, in 1935 to bring railway reorganization under the general bankruptcy procedure, as distinct from equity receivership, but this retarded rather than expedited matters. In order to keep the railroads running, the best thing emergency measures could accomplish was to provide weak roads with temporary financing, obtained by pledge of their last bits of assets, through the RFC. This agency, from its inception to the end of 1934, disbursed nearly half a billion in rescue loans to railroads and railroad receivers, and by 1940 the advances were still above the half-billion mark. Although some loans have been paid off, others have been made necessary by the continuing wretched condition of railroad credit, the heritage of the fatal financial blunders made toward the end of the last century. This problem is probably much more difficult than the

---

was disposed to regard such advances as by no means inconsistent with the objectives of sound commercial banking or the requirements of the Federal Deposit Insurance System.

In the matter of improving standards of bank investment in securities, the problem has been more complex and up to this time perhaps less satisfactorily solved. It may be stated, however, that since the middle of 1938 some progress has been made in formulating new classifications to designate the quality and valuation of investments. Bonds held by banks are now grouped in four categories, for each of which an approved method of valuation is set up to guide general practice. These regulations tend to protect banks that purchase relatively sound securities from fluctuations in market values and give them time to charge off losses on securities of the middle grade. But as to securities that are in default and of speculative character, banks are brought to accept losses more promptly. There are still unsolved problems in improving the technique of investment policy to guard against long-term, gradual shrinkage in the caliber of the securities in a portfolio, even though the "conventional" valuations may prevent the necessity for needless liquidation or impairment of nominal asset valuation over short periods. See W. A. Morton, Liquidity and Solvency, *American Economic Review*, June, 1939.

other financial problems that we are considering. Its proper solution lies in the lap of the future, and the willingness of a Federal Administration to meet the problem squarely is perhaps a fair indication of whether it proposes deliberately to leave the railroads in a financially precarious position to facilitate Federal acquisition and operation, perhaps along with electric power and communications. Much will depend also upon how far the railroad managements can utilize the lush earnings resulting temporarily from World War II in eliminating their excessive long-term debts.

REHABILITATION OF FARM FINANCING

We come now to the steps taken to rescue farmers from their financial difficulties. In 1933 these were unquestionably of a socially menacing character. The disappearance of many rural banks was in itself a major disaster, and the RFC had early stepped into the breach to provide emergency credit for areas whose banking facilities had been swept away. Through loans on commodities and advances to agricultural lending institutions, the RFC by the end of 1934 had disbursed nearly a billion dollars. There now followed a series of measures more or less paralleling the reforms made in the urban mortgage and the banking fields. These were supplemented by efforts toward curtailment of basic crop production, which we shall not discuss in detail here.

In 1933 a Farm Credit Administration was organized under Federal auspices as a means of refinancing farm mortgages. While Senator Frazier and Representative Lemke of North Dakota were still vociferously agitating for the issue of billions of greenback paper money to "redeem" farm mortgages, the Government adopted a saner procedure. The Federal Land Banks, already in existence, were given authority to refinance existing farm mortgages on favorable terms, and many creditors accepted a substantial scaling down of their claims. In addition to the extension of credit by the Land Banks, the so-called Land Bank Commissioners made emergency loans to farmers, especially in the Great Plains area. The combined amount of financing by these agencies served in an important way to relieve the life-insurance companies of their most serious problem, as they were at that time the largest interest in the rural mortgage field. Altogether, these two agencies expanded outstanding advances by over one and three-quarter billions from 1933 to the peak level in 1936.[1]

[1] An interesting feature of this refinancing was the attempt to extend maturities and enlarge the percentage of value of the underlying securities, which was accomplished in part by deliberately appraising the property on a level of "normal value," presumably representing what might be considered probable over a stretch of years, in contrast with the existing property values based upon low prices and incomes. See

In spite of this assistance, the problem was so desperate that by 1937 the Federal Land Banks, the Joint Stock Land Banks, and the life-insurance companies acquired over 28 million acres through foreclosure, representing nearly a billion dollars in farm property. The Joint Stock Land Banks were not a success and had to be placed in voluntary liquidation. The Federal Government became the prime factor in supporting and refinancing the farm-mortgage debt, which in 1935 stood close to eight billions of dollars. Of course, one reason for the acuteness of the problem presented by this debt was the high price level at which so much of it had been created and the slipshod, reckless manner in which a large fraction of the debt had been originally created.

Another interesting feature was the extension to farmers of debt-relief measures under state authority. By the end of 1934 every state in the Union had passed laws easing the terms of foreclosure and providing moratoria of various kinds on foreclosure procedings. In general, such easements gave mortgagors the privilege of remaining on the property if they maintained specified payments. In addition to state legislation, Messrs. Frazier and Lemke proceeded in Congress toward the same objective. The first Act (1934) was invalidated by the Supreme Court, but a second Act, passed in 1935, correcting the defects, was upheld. This Act provided a three-year period of stay of the mortgagor's right of possession, provided that he paid a reasonable rental and met certain other limited requirements, the whole matter being subject to the discretion of the local courts.

In addition to easement and rehabilitation of mortgage debts on farms, the organization of farmers' cooperatives was given considerable encouragement. The so-called Farm Credit Administration built up new facilities for short-term and intermediate-term farm loans to the cooperatives, which served as channels for advances to individual members. This was rendered important by the decimation of banking facilities in some rural areas. The Federal Intermediate Credit Banks now provide discounting facilities somewhat parallel to those of the Federal Reserve Banks. In addition to the cooperative associations, there are also organizations known as Production Credit Corporations, originally set up with Federal capital and operating in 12 districts as sources of short-term and working capital financing. A very large part of this lending is done on an amortized basis, with installments of repayment timed to coincide with crop-sale periods and livestock shipments. This is another cogent illustration of the shift from unamortized to amortized lending, even in the

---

N. J. Wall, and E. J. Engquist, Jr., "A Graphic Summary of Agricultural Credit," *U.S. Department of Agriculture Miscellaneous Publication* 268, September, 1938.

shorter term field. In recent years interest rates charged by the intermediate credit or rediscounting institutions have fallen from over 5 per cent to less than 2 per cent per annum.[1]

As the result of these changes, bringing the facilities of Federally sponsored agencies into the agricultural field, a large proportion of all the farm-mortgage debt, as well as the shorter term debt, has been placed upon a systematic amortization basis. Loans that were tentatively refinanced on a 12- or 13-year basis in the period of emergency have since been extended to terms of 20 years or more. Much of this financing, therefore, has been permanently taken away from the commercial banks, mortgage companies, and insurance companies, and it seems likely that the Federal agencies, together with the capital provided by individuals through the growing cooperative associations (very much as in the European farmer cooperatives), will continue to dominate the agricultural credit field hereafter. It is highly probable that despite a repetition of the inflationary tendencies in World War II, there will not be after that conflict the degree of agricultural distressed indebtedness that followed World War I.

Looking back over these extensive reforms of the credit mechanism and in the field of mortgage financing, one cannot avoid being struck by a curious underlying inconsistency. If a large amount of Federal debt is to be kept in existence as a means of supporting a credit currency based on debt claims (and in lieu of the older short-term trade debts), it is to be presumed that little effort will be made to keep this total of governmental debt within any set limits. The prevailing official view is that such debt is inherently sound and inherently desirable; it serves to stabilize finance, to maintain the money and price structure, and to build the "national income" (in dollars) higher and higher. Since the public debt is owed by Americans to Americans, it really is innocuous. There is no assurance whatever, official or implied, that any steps will be taken to amortize or retire this mounting debt, presently to become of stupendous size as a result of World War II. There is a glaring inconsistency, therefore, between a credit mechanism based on permanent and ever-increasing *public* borrowing and a beautifully amortized system of private long-term

---

[1] As in the case of the Land Banks, the Intermediate Credit Banks issue obligations in which various financial institutions may invest. In addition to the normal short-term farm credit facilities of the type described above, farmers may also secure emergency loans in various ways. In recent years an additional source of crop loans has been made available through the Commodity Credit Corporation, whose advances on a limited number of basic crops are designed to stabilize marketing conditions and to remove from the market, at least temporarily, supplies likely to depress prices below the average seasonal level.

borrowing. The Government, like many of the states a century ago, sets up one standard of financial procedure for its citizens but an entirely different standard for itself.[1]

In still another sense, we find Federal policy in the trying period of the 1930's revealing an inconsistency or, rather, a tendency to neutralize a sound reconstruction policy by a dubious or unsound one. We find evidence of this contradictory tendency in that phase of the New Deal program concerned with the flow of *income*. It was not enough to give extractive producers higher prices or to create a renovated mortgage system. It was feared apparently that revamping of solvency was not enough; there had to be a surge of purchasing power poured like irrigation water along the channels of trade and industry to create activity again. Or, to use the favorite phrase, the pump had to be primed to restore its operation. To a degree, this pump-priming operation and its financial devices have a rational aspect, once depression has been permitted to reach exceptional depth. Money and credit made unavailable by bank suspensions or income wiped out by wholesale insolvency *can* be recreated by governmental action through doles or through the hiring of labor temporarily on various types of public projects. We shall defer until later discussion of the actual state of unemployment in this crisis and emphasize here merely the plain fact that money somehow restored to millions of people and spent for goods *can* serve as a stimulant to trade and production. If doles are distributed, it is, of course, difficult to allocate such funds so that they prevent hardship among industrial workers while serving as easy windfalls to the idle and shiftless. Usually these dispensations are made after depression has run its course and the collapse is not prevented; there is no long-term and well-planned program for releasing the relief funds and later recouping the disbursements. This aspect of systematic compensation for the major breakdowns in production and income continuity will receive more attention in Chapter 21. We are here concerned with the emergency policy of making up lost or impounded money income quickly and getting trade again under way.

If such emergency relief is to be paid as a kind of Government wage to people put temporarily to work on public projects, there is supposed to be some gain in maintaining morale; but there are new problems, among

[1] In 1942, under the stress of new war-financing problems involving the sale of billions of war bonds to the commercial banks, the official views as to the desirability of always maintaining an adequate ratio of banking capital to total assets were already being modified. It was now the *quality* of bank assets, in the form of Aaa Federal bonds, that really made capital ratios secondary. Thus, governmental opinion seems to veer toward the "banking principle" when it is a matter of urgent war finance, while in normal times that opinion tends to be critical of the absence of banking moderation in creating excessive *magnitude* of earning assets, a phase of the "currency principle."

them the danger of creating an inducement for the shiftless to remain so indefinitely and the technical difficulty that projects of real social importance, such as public buildings, require a considerable time to plan and get under way. As a matter of fact, both straight doles and work relief were employed as income creators in this period, but on a scale and with ultimate consequences that deserve some attention. What began as a hastily adopted means of limiting the social impact of an unusual depression presently became something quite different, and to see how this happened we need to discern the circumstances under which it was thought necessary to embark on these methods when so many other recovery stimulants were being quickly mobilized.

PUBLIC WORKS AS AN IMPERATIVE RECOVERY MEASURE

The alleged urgent necessity for Government pumping more "national income" into circulation was developed mainly by British thinkers, particularly J. M. Keynes and his numerous followers. It was essential, they contended (presumably having British conditions in mind), that prosperity be restored by injecting into the economic system an amount of monetized debt claims and especially *public-capital* investment to provide more employment. This could be done with best results, it was claimed, by extensive programs of public works. It was more or less tacitly assumed that business enterprise everywhere was defeated and impotent. Keynes was frankly skeptical of mere price raising as a satisfactory solution to the problem of restoring prosperity, and he placed all overt price-reflation measures well down in his list of remedial policies:

Competitive currency depreciations and competitive tariffs, and more artificial means of improving an individual country's foreign balance such as exchange restrictions, import prohibitions, and quotas help no one and injure each, if they are applied all around. . . . We are left, therefore, with the broad conclusion that there is no effective means of raising world prices except by increasing loan-expenditure throughout the world. It was, indeed, the collapse of expenditure financed out of loans advanced by the United States, for use both at home and abroad, which was the chief agency in starting the slump.[1]

This is a very revealing statement. It expresses the thought that the world really needed the revivifying influence of new "investment," but this was to be primarily *loan investment* or the revival of debt. One might well agree that the situation did call for a broad expansion of *capital flow* into business, but the emphasis on borrowing appears to imply that *Government* was somehow to sponsor this new debt creation and that the real objective was to expand bank deposits to sustain the general circulation. In an open letter to President Roosevelt, dated

[1] J. M. Keynes, "The Means to Prosperity," p. 19, London, 1933.

Dec. 30, 1933, Keynes asserted that in his opinion the United States could gain little by further attempting to raise prices according to the Warren doctrines. He urged the President to launch a bold and comprehensive program of Federal spending based upon borrowing, not on taxation, the proceeds of which would be used for huge capital expenditures upon various kinds of public works. This would therefore be not merely a new diversion of use for available credit balances but the infusion into the economy of a vast amount of *new credit* money capable of raising what we have termed "element C" in the general equation of exchange. This clearly recognized that insofar as the national income is a flow expressed in money or in terms of money values, the kind of credit system that we have floats upon a mass of indebtedness that essentially is monetized. Keynes, being a financial theorist rather than a student of industrial processes, saw in the millions of unemployed in Britain and the United States a failure of "circulation," expressed in deficient money income. His proposal, therefore, amounted to substituting (temporarily?) Government debt, already held in large measure by the banks, for those defunct debt claims of private origin that no longer sufficed to sustain the flow of checkbook money. "I lay overwhelming emphasis on the increase of national purchasing power resulting from governmental expenditure which is financed by loans and is not merely a transfer through taxation from existing income. Nothing else counts in comparison with this."[1] Keynes has not, so far as the writer is aware, examined the reasons for the alleged "propensity to hoard" purchasing power or retarded investment of available balances, but he undoubtedly made a momentous suggestion, since, in substance, it was followed by the Roosevelt Administration.

In developing this idea of brushing aside private industry and initiative and having Government take over the problem of putting money and credit to work, Keynes frankly implied that a part of his objective was to restore the faith of the people in the *wisdom* and *power* of Government. It is not wholly clear how far this type of program appealed to him as merely an *emergency* or cycle compensating program and how far it was something to be pursued *indefinitely*. Lest there might be doubt that the contemplated spendings *would* be quickly productive of "prosperity," Keynes made much use of theories worked out by R. F. Kahn,[2] who "demonstrated mathematically" that all initial investment in capital projects serves ultimately to create a volume of employment larger than that provided by the specific projects. The employment ultimately extends to the material industries, transportation, service, etc.,

---

[1] Letter to Mr. Roosevelt.

[2] R. F. Kahn, The Relation of Home Investment to Unemployment, *Economic Journal*, June, 1931.

and there is a further business stimulus as the original work groups spend their wages on consumer goods. Keynes variously estimated this so-called "multiplier" of the original outlays at from one and one-half to two times. By thus increasing the national income eventually by a larger amount than the initial spendings (or "investments"), even the National Treasury could save money by reducing or eliminating the relief doles and could even tax additional income in the bargain.

Neither Keynes nor Kahn appears to have recognized that a deliberate and comprehensive plan virtually to put the Government in business as a great employer of labor naturally would affect the state of mind and confidence of private capital and private industry and hence retard the revival of privately compensated employment. It is one thing to argue theoretically and mathematically about the net result of an abstract new Government "investment" of money in a given project with respect to materials and labor and income; it is quite another matter to proclaim a remedy that implies that things are so bad that the Government must go much further than mere reforms in capital and credit machinery. It must expand deficit financing for a program of indefinite duration as an unavoidable alternative to the stubborn fear or greed that "holds back" the flow of private capital in some mysterious manner. Private capital goes "on strike"; hence public capital moves in. When private initiative is thus rebuked and in a sense repudiated, even by implication, it is not unintelligent to assume that such initiative and enterprise *will* shrink back and in so doing *may entirely neutralize* all of this overrefined analysis of multipliers and amplifiers of lush public spending. The idea of accelerating or timing public building projects to offset depression was, of course, nothing essentially new; its merits had been debated in Congress for years, and President Hoover had frequently urged that more of such sensible planning of buildings, roads, river, and harbor work be done. But Keynes translated the idea into a novel scientific jargon and greatly extended its scope as an integral feature of what was already being attempted in rebuilding the national income.

Keynes warned the President against rigid stabilization of the American money system to assure availability of ample funds free of such restricting influences as the old gold standard, whose elimination from the British monetary system Keynes strongly approved. "I see no reason why you should not reduce the rate of interest on your long-term government bonds to $2\frac{1}{2}$ per cent or less . . . if only the Federal Reserve System would replace present holdings of short-dated Treasury issues by purchasing long-dated issues in exchange." A few years later the Treasury *was* borrowing at long term at $2\frac{1}{2}$ per cent.[1]

[1] At about the same time Keynes was urging the United States to launch a public-works program to rebuild circulating income and employment, the British economic

The NRA experiment of 1933 already provided for a program directly along the line of these public-works suggestions. It set up a Public Works Administration with an initial appropriation of 3 billion dollars. Projects were divided into two types, Federal and non-Federal, the latter comprising those toward which the Federal Government made grants and loans to local public bodies for a wide variety of undertakings. The PWA outlays were highest in 1934 and were rather steadily maintained during the succeeding years. Down to June, 1940, total allotments for 17,818 Federal projects had been made, representing expenditures of 1.8 billion dollars.[1] By the same date 16,648 non-Federal projects had been approved, costing 4.2 billion.[2]

Meanwhile, under the pressure of various groups insisting that public construction work was not enough, there were supplementary agencies, one after another. A Civil Works Administration, formed in late 1933 to take care of urgent cases of indigence, gave way in the late spring of 1934 to the Federal Emergency Relief Administration. Its plan was one of cooperation with local government bodies by way of grants and loans. Still the depression persisted, and relief was being demanded on all sides. In spite of an expenditure of about four billion dollars by the close of 1935, the FERA had not been able to do much more than provide occasional jobs for white-collar workers and some others in miscellaneous

---

system was already well on the way toward recovery, principally through the expansion of the building industry with private capital. Following the War, building had made rather slow progress, but after 1931 when mild inflation, without a radical rise in the cost of food and imported raw materials, served as a stimulating factor in the building industry, a substantial revival occurred. By 1937 this reached the proportions of a construction boom. Three and one-third million houses were built in England and Wales between 1918 and March, 1937, two million of which were built without any kind of government subsidy whatever. The rapid development of building-and-loan associations and the existence of declining interest rates made it unnecessary for the British Government to undertake the kind of program that Keynes was advocating for the United States. See Harold Bellman, Business Recovery and the Housing Program in Great Britain, *Journal of Land and Public Utility Economics*, May, 1938.

[1] About half a billion of this was spent on streets and highways, 34 million on utilities, 300 million on buildings, 262 million on flood control, water power, and reclamation, 257 million on water-navigation aids, 23 million on engineering structures, 45 million on aviation, 270 million on vessels.

[2] Of this amount nearly two billion were supplied by the local governments, 800 million of loans and 1.5 billion allotted as grants by PWA. Streets and highways accounted for about 450 million of total estimated cost; sewers, waterworks, power, and other facilities close to 1 billion, buildings 1.8 billion, flood control, water power, and reclamation 179 million, aids to navigation 19.7 million, aviation 3.2 million, railroads 201 million, engineering structures 469 million. "Federal Aids to Local Planning," p. 117, National Resources Planning Board, June, 1940.

"make work." The contributions of local government bodies upon which reliance had been placed proved utterly inadequate.[1]

Hence there followed the WPA (later known as the Work Projects Administration), which began in 1935 to hire workers on a vast jumble of projects, most of which represented no permanent additions to the nation's durable capital wealth. Apparently a considerable amount of waste occurred.[2] One supposed advantage of the WPA was that it seemed to avoid the *appearance* of an outright mendicant dole, since the money paid out purported to represent payment for work which a self-respecting person could consider employment. It should in fairness be added that a good deal of this work, although not of permanent value, was productive of contributions to statistical data, to the production of some things that might be termed works of art, and to a good deal of miscellaneous civic improvement and renovation that otherwise might never have been attempted. From the summer of 1935 to the middle of 1940, over eight billion dollars had been spent on programs operated under the WPA. This included road building, completion of bridges, laying of culverts, building of airplane landing fields. There were three million persons employed at the peak of WPA activities in February, 1936, which represented assistance to probably ten or twelve million individuals.

The WPA program[3] was sharply curtailed during 1937 in view of a considerable improvement during 1936 in the general business situation, mainly a result of new war preparations rather than of the complete restoration of American capital finance. The Federal Government, now fearing there might be unnecessary stimulation to a boom already indicated in the speculative advances in commodity prices and much inventory accumulation, took steps to reduce its "net contributions" to the flow of income. It also took action, as we have already noted in the preceding chapter, to tighten credit by drastically increasing member bank-reserve requirements. The combination of these two policies

[1] Throughout the depression there were a number of supplementary agencies, such as the Civilian Conservation Corps of young men, working mainly in the public parks and national forests, the National Youth Administration, affording subsidies to students for miscellaneous services, and the Resettlement Administration program to assist farmers in relocating on better land.

[2] The following are random excerpts taken from the Working Procedure File of WPA in 1935: construction of rural recreation center, jack-rabbit control, translating foreign scientific writing, story telling and reading service to handicapped persons, public forum service, making rayon and cotton underwear, making and canning sauerkraut, repairing shoes for the needy, making rag dolls from scrap material, canning soup, broth, stew, and hamburger, making Ping-pong and game tables, etc.

[3] See "Economoc Effects of the Federal Public Works Expenditures, 1933–38," Report of the National Resources Planning Board, November, 1940, and later numbers.

produced an almost overnight shrinkage in business activity, one of the sharpest, most violent recessions in our history. By the middle of 1938 almost all the gain achieved by the enormous public outlays and the dazzling variety of sociological expedients had been lost. But this merely meant that spending had to go on! From the beginning of 1938 WPA outlays again mushroomed, and PWA contruction projects were pushed ahead. In terms of Lauchlin Currie's estimates of income-creating Federal expenditures, these served to raise national money income from a low point of about 1 billion in 1937 to 3.6 billion in 1939. In this way the Federal Government was learning the art of "controlling" the business cycle by *direct manipulation* of total *income*. It was illustrating what Walter Lippmann had previously proclaimed: "The business cycle has been placed within the orbit of government, and for laissez faire and individual adjustment and liquidation there has been substituted conscious management by the political State."[1] But his trust in public spending as a cyclical stabilizer was not confirmed by results. Actually the public spending program merely delayed national recovery through private construction and capital flow, and the correctives suddenly injected in 1937 to stem a commodity inflation were excessively violent, poorly timed, and created widespread, wholly unnecessary mischief. It appeared to some observers in 1938 that the crackdown was deliberately engineered to create the basis for new Federal experiments.

[1] The Permanent New Deal, *Yale Review*, June, 1935. Among those who laid the groundwork for the application of Keynes' doctrine to American experience along the line of public-works spending was J. M. Clark, who prepared a study, "Economics of Planning Public Works," for the National Planning Board in 1935. Clark took cognizance of the fact that one of the central causes of depression was a shrinkage in construction activity. Hence a public-works program "fits into this picture" by substituting a public demand for the shrinking private demand. He emphasized the peculiar factors associated with international financial and commercial disturbance and contraction that seemed to make it doubtful whether full employment in American industry could be achieved unless the Federal Government undertook some special means of creating demand for durable capital goods and, in general, followed, with rather elaborate illustrations, the principles already summarized by Keynes.

In the matter of financing, Clark was considerably more explicit and conservative than Keynes. He expressed the undesirability of creating a *continuing* public deficit. He believed that although the Government should borrow *during depressions* for public-works purposes, it should also endeavor in every way to balance its budget *during good years* to avoid an indefinite increase in indebtedness. "An indefinite progressive increase in the public debt is precisely the thing which must be avoided if we are to be prepared to meet difficulties of this sort in the future. If there is any temptation toward borrowing during emergencies and then neglecting to pay off the loans during subsequent periods of prosperity, then the program must be so drawn up as to call attention to that danger and provide against it as, for instance, by requiring amortization of the emergency loans over an unusually short term of years." (*Op. cit.*, p. 120.)

PUBLIC WORKS NOT MERELY A BUSINESS STABILIZER

Although Keynes' public-works philosophy superficially suggested throwing fresh borrowed funds into the business stream and injecting new purchasing power into a depressed economy to lift it out of depression, there began to be doubts in serious minds as to just how far it is possible for these ventures to remain *merely* cycle-compensating devices. There had been a curious official reluctance to dig down into the facts and operations of the business system to find out just *why and how* severe depressions are brought about. The more we study these pump-priming schemes, the more we see underlying them a tendency to regard business boom and slump as a *mysterious visitation*, a strange malady of impaired circulation. Blood infusion is the one sure cure. But once these infusions have been administered, one might fear, from the reading of history and from knowledge of the human nature of politicians, that they may become not only a stimulant but perhaps a new kind of sustenance. The Government planner, however sincere his purpose and judicial his temperament, tends to form a low opinion of the helter skelter of profit-seeking businessmen. The private builder, industrialist, banker, or capitalist, being well aware of the power that lies in the hands of Government, fears its intrusion in production activities. Keynes may very well have considered his 1933 proposals not merely as depression stimulants *but as a phase of the long-term substitution of Government construction* in fields where private undertakings had not shown themselves particularly successful. This brings us to consider the public-works idea from two further points of view: (1) as a way of *building* where private initiative is inadequate, (2) as a way of gradually enlarging the role of the State in *all* production.[1]

Once Government establishes itself as an agency hiring millions to do constructive work, even in those fields that we should consider on the border line of legitimate private participation, various relationships and patterns establish themselves in the channels of trade and production that make a *continuing* public demand important. Should Government, having once originated this demand, decide to withdraw in part or altogether, the results are likely to be temporarily upsetting or even demoralizing. The violent setback in business in 1937–1938 is a clear example. Thus the "legitimate" works activities are constrained by a powerful social

[1] In his pamphlet "Laissez Faire and Communism" New York, 1926, Keynes significantly said, "The most important *Agenda* of the State relate not to those activities which private individuals are already fulfilling, but to those functions which fall outside the sphere of the individual, to those decisions which are made by *no one* if the State does not make them. The important thing for Government is not to do things which individuals are doing already, and to do them a little better or a little worse; but to do those things which at present are not done at all." (P. 67.)

pressure toward something much broader and more permanent.   A point is reached where they cease to be cycle stabilizers and become a "recognized" and indispensable function of Government.

This leads us to consider the matter of financial provision for works programs.   If, along with J. M. Clark, we think of these devices strictly as balance wheels to operate against business-cycle vibration, the borrowing of enormous funds by the State creates deficits to be absorbed *during prosperity* by heavier taxes.   But there has developed a new financial theory that argues that these *are not deficits at all; they are investments*. The accounts of the Treasury should therefore be set up (and President Roosevelt has been sympathetic to this view) in such fashion as to show that these spendings are really investments in plant and equipment, water power, national integrity, human security, and the enrichment of social living.   Of course, not all the money spent on mere doles for raking leaves and patching clothes should technically be counted as investment, but it is not easy to draw the line, and even much of the WPA outlay might conceivably be accounted for as an investment in social morale or the salvage of family life.   Why, then, should not this constructive investment build-up be continuous?   What limits are there to such beneficence?   Since a little welfare is good, a great deal of welfare is better.   The "investment" is accordingly to be appraised in proportion to its *size and its ability to grow, not merely to vary* with the rhythm of that banal cycle in private trade.   Since so much investment as created in the past has gone astray, is it not better to rebuild the structure of investment by something durable, planned, and guaranteed by Government?   Can we not assure (or insure) general stability by replacing unstable and *shrinking* investment by stable and *accelerating* investment without being too particular as to what specific material assets are created thereby?   In fact, why should not "investment" extend to human as well as physical resources?   The former are just as real as the "good will and patent rights" that appear on corporation statements.

We may go even further than this.   Why should we not consider these growing "deficits" in Federal finances merely aspects of an outworn illusion?   Is not all this debt owed by Americans to Americans? The borrowing and spending can be accomplished by the New Finance at such low rates of interest that the *annual charge* is after all but little. Just as we have first the suggestion that taxes should be heavy in prosperity and light in depression, we now find the sentiment veering toward a continuous heavy tax on large income and a continuous subsidization of small income.   The policy evolves into a *social trend*, not a *business stabilizer*.   And is there not a further advantage in planned investment? The flow of income can readily be focused toward those areas of the economy that encompass large bodies of wage earners.   We can prevent excessive accumulation of income and idle surplus in the hands of investors who refuse to invest. We can create capital directly from wage income. Private capital worked well in an economy of scarcity when interest rates were high and investment incentive was high, but as initiative wanes and interest rates fall, there is a cumulative force toward the "propensity" to save and hoard. So runs the train of thought, in its more elaborate form, of which this innocent device of "public works for depression stimulus" is but a sparkling facet. Thus we can proceed to rationalize a strong pressure to project the principle of public works far beyond its original limited scope as a kind of business balance wheel and to implant it solidly and permanently in the economic system as an independent, never-failing, and ever-expanding source of income and a fairer distribution of income.

In 1937 all the Federal housing and slum-rehabilitation projects were transferred to an ambitious new bureau known as the U.S. Housing Authority, but subsequently this was incorporated with the general works program under the Federal Works Agency. The Housing Authority was designed primarily to assist local communities to eliminate substandard housing areas and develop new low-rent housing projects.[1] This, of course, is a field in which private enterprise has without question failed to produce more than a vast social problem. But this merely means that the rapidly evolving theory of unlimited Government spending on a permanent basis, has that much more justification. In stepping into this field with a philosophy of permanently running at a deficit in order to put people to work, the Government has no clearly delimited field. Here we are dealing with forms of "investment" from which the ultimate return, so far as it goes, will be derived from the lowest income strata. Very possibly the hopes of *any* net return will not materialize. But, so it is said, if the whole people, through their Government, should provide more decent homes, why should there be any return at all? Says David Cushman Coyle:

Time was required before the idea became widely understood that housing cannot be fully self-liquidating. Government housing, if it is to avoid causing uncomfortable capital losses and yet stay within the reach of the poor, has to be subsidized. The Government should not only tear down old houses, it should write off the cost. Each new house should be matched by the demolition of one old tenement. . . . The Government will have to charge only what the traffic will bear, and absorb the rest in its own budget. As a matter of fact, housing under private auspices has usually been heavily subsidized through lost invest-

---

[1] The formal definition of a "slum" is difficult, because the attempt to define substandard housing involves a standard, and this, of course, will vary subjectively, like all intangibles. What may be thought a slum today may not have appeared so to the social conscience of a generation ago.

ments.   In real estate development the swamps are filled with dead investors. Voluntary subsidy is better than forced subsidy. . . . Housing, insofar as it is not self-liquidating, is Government spending, and if the money comes in the long run out of income taxes, this Government spending is a direct addition to our national income.[1]

The Housing Authority was set up to make loans to local public-housing agencies in order to develop, acquire, and administer the projects.   These local operating units are established under State Enabling Acts.   In addition to loans, the USHA also makes annual contributions by way of subsidy in order to permit the local authorities to keep rentals within the financial reach of families in the lowest income groups.[2]   As of June, 1940, USHA had made total commitments of only 638 million dollars, but this is a good example of the gradual shifting of public-relief emphasis.   We move from work relief to compensatory timing of public construction and, finally, to a permanent program of building for the underprivileged with *no limit* to what is meant by that term. Catherine Bauer, a leading figure in this movement, significantly pointed out as soon as the USHA legislation was passed: "It represents not merely a political victory, but a reasonable basis for the initial step in a long-term housing program.   The solid foundation is definitely intact. With a few minor changes here and there in the superstructure, this bill *only needs continuing and larger appropriations and bond issues in order to meet the requirements of an almost infinitely expansible program.*"[3]

But if Government were actually to follow out this philosophy to the limit and to mark out for its own *all* the fields of construction, transportation, and basic enterprise that in the past have yielded handsome rents, unearned increments, profits, and interest to individuals, it follows that these sources of private income must shrink or disappear.   This would mean that the private income that will have to pay the interest charge on the Federal borrowing and the losses on "charity investment" in the future will be more and more restricted to return from direct investment in the manufacturing and commercial industries.   If the latter are then more and more heavily taxed to provide for public adventures in structural enterprise, the *central framework of our industrial economy* will be impaired and perhaps be in line for unlimited political exploitation.

No fair-minded person will challenge the inherent soundness of an effective movement for ridding the country of slums and writing down

[1] "Brass Tacks," pp. 74–75, Washington, D.C., 1936.

[2] These contributions are contracted for over long periods, now 60 years.   With regard to loans, the USHA is authorized to loan up to 90 per cent of the development cost of projects.   Loans bear interest at the going rate on long-term Federal obligations plus $\frac{1}{2}$ per cent, which at present works out at about 3 per cent.

[3] *The New Republic*, Sept. 8, 1937.   Italics are by the writer.

the cost of crime that is largely created by slums. But we must avoid the persistent error of assuming that slum areas, like business depressions, come about as mysterious visitations that cannot be directly attacked by intelligent diagnosis and manifold attack on poverty and depression. If we float ever-expanding programs of public construction *merely* on the hypothesis that slum dwellers just happen, and must necessarily always exist, without studying *all* the underlying causes of these substandard incomes, we may merely be trying to lift ourselves by our bootstraps and eventually complicating the very problem that we seek to solve. It seems most important to attempt a clearer demarcation of capital and structural enterprise that is logically, in a broad dynamic view, well *within* the province of Government, needing large amounts of capital for very long-range general purposes that can contribute with little question to preservation of national physical assets, to national defense, and to adequate communication, power, and land qualities. On the other side of the line is the great field of private initiative that can direct capital toward useful innovation in the fields of manufacture, mining, construction, and trade. So long as the dividing line shifts with the winds of social pressures and the aims of equalitarian reforms, the use of capital instead of aiding production could be made, as it has been in many parts of the world already, merely a lever to accomplish a *redistribution of less production and less wealth*. There remains the stubborn question: who pays for the *permanent* deficit?

PUBLIC SERVICE PLANNING VS. MERE PUBLIC SPENDING

Since 1939 all the Federal Works activities have been assembled under a single head in the Federal Works Agency. This may yet become one of the most important of all Government agencies having to do with the spending of funds. At the same time there is being developed, under the National Resources Planning Board, a vast network of relationships with local boards, organized in states and cities and having this same objective of developing land resources, water resources, transportation integration—covering, indeed, the entire field of enterprise, which as we have seen has been so thorny a problem to private capital and therefore so large a factor in the repeated breakdowns in our financial system. With the country covered by local planning agencies whose activities are stimuated and assisted by the technical consultants and research activities of the Central Board, there is under way a comprehensive program of research, of fact finding, of mapping out basic coordination, rehabilitation, and reorganization of national and local resources. These include land, power, fuel, and transportation. On the analogy to USHA, one can already visualize a vast network of public activity not only in housing but in strategic phases of social capital resources and one, unlike mere public-works spending, capable of sound results. These phases of activity were those that a century ago were so vigorously obstructed by Andrew Jackson. There are real and legitimate phases that Government can and should claim as its field if it will define them so that all can understand. The nation undoubtedly lost precious opportunities in the last century to rationalize the broad underpinning of its industrial and commercial processes, which we may call the social-utility framework and its facilities. Fortunes were built up from the unearned increment of rent and the speculation in land appreciation that, by being capitalized, restricted the opportunity of the common man to acquire durable capital without running the risk of bankruptcy. Better use of land, of transport, of water, and of power must develop to aid the progress of private industry and open new opportunity for its working forces and the capital that vitalizes it.

The National Resources Planning Board has already under way studies of land classifications and land acquisitions in the interest of conservation, removal of cultivation from unsuitable areas, reforestation, and the acquiring of land for clearly essential public projects. "Plans are being developed," says the Board, "for a study of the complex land use problems of the rural-urban fringe areas, which lie at the outskirts of cities, between city and country. These areas of extensive premature subdivision and of shifting commercial and residential land usage, are, in many cases, severe problem areas vitally affecting local planning. The Land Committee is seeking to outline studies which will develop findings and recommendations for the better control and development of rural-urban fringe-land use."[1]

In the field of transportation, plans are being worked out to formulate the broad outline of a permanent and efficient over-all transportation system, particularly with regard to the complex problems of railroad rates and the badly needed physical rehabilitation of the entire railway network. Water resources are being given special attention, and this ties in with the work of the Energy Resources Committee in developing a coordinated national policy for the conservation of coal, petroleum, natural gas, and all water power. The Tennessee Valley Project and the great electrical developments in the Northwest are examples of only a few segments of the general program that is implied. The War will extend all this activity far beyond its original scope. But if the reader will perceive the distinction between such planning and the financing that it will involve and the mere exploiting of construction and fiscal deficits to redistribute wealth, he can view much of this planning as constructive and not necessarily a prelude to collectivism.

[1] "Federal Aids to Local Planning," National Resources Planning Board, June, 1940, p. 3.

In summary, we have found governmental effort in financial reorganization carrying far beyond the mere revamping of capital and credit mechanism. The idea of bolstering income by public construction in depression is not wholly devoid of merit, but in practice it is difficult to apply without actually retarding the recuperation of private construction and opens the way to a spiral of unlimited public activity of a quasi-philanthropic type whose true costs are disregarded and whose effects on fiscal integrity can be disastrous. There is much public building, however, that Government can and should undertake. There are many lines of research and planning to strengthen and render more efficient that great interlocking system of public-service facilities, all of which Government can and should carry forward as a means of making *private industry* more productive and less subject to boom and depression. Either Government may proceed on the assumption that depressions are mysteriously created by inexorable forces and exploit them for every last ounce of political advantage, ultimately at the expense of all private enterprise; or, on the other hand, Government can lend a helping hand to industry and commerce by providing research effort, sound finance *everywhere*, a sound money, and a continuing effort to eliminate from the economic system the basic causes of cyclical instability. From this standpoint Federal and regional planning of public-service facilities is potentially sound; make-work development, although having some worth-while and socially important aspects, *as a cyclical stabilizer* is an illusion and a subterfuge.

CHAPTER 16

INTEREST RATES AND CORPORATE BOND ISSUES

Thus far we have not had occasion to consider interest rates apart from references to the discount rate as a phase of banking operations and central banking policy and to some of the factors that have influenced the interest rate on mortgages. In the various markets for loan capital and credit there is, of course, no uniform level of interest rates at any given time. Competition among borrowers and lenders is very keen and exerts a leveling influence in the metropolitan money market for short-term and collateral loans. But the rates prevailing there will not be the same as in other localities, where special factors of risk, character of collateral, or of business operations are important in setting actual rates. So, again, in the field of long-term loans, the mortgage rates pertaining to farm loans have varied widely in different sections and have not been identical with rates on urban mortgages. In the case of corporate and Government securities, the yield rates tend to converge to a more uniform level if risk and local elements are allowed for. Competition in the highly organized security markets is very effective, and the pure rate of interest expressed in yields on the highest grade long-term bonds may be considered the most reliable indicator of the position of the capital market, having a bearing upon corporation financing and the cost of Government borrowing. It is this particular phase of the general capital market, a phase, as we shall see, closely allied to banking operations and control policies, that we shall examine in this chapter.

There is marked disagreement among economists as to the dynamic importance of the rate of interest, some observers holding that the terms upon which loan capital may be obtained are of dominating importance in shaping the pattern of the business cycle and even the broad direction of the general level of prices; others believe that the significance of changes in interest rates depends upon the kind of economic, financial, or political background that happens to exist at a given time. Obviously it is pertinent to determine whether the investment of capital by and large is at all affected, from the side of either demand or supply, by changes in the level of the rate of interest; whether rising rates of interest tend to exert any limiting effect capable of terminating a business boom; whether low rates are capable of reviving industrial activity following a recession; or, again, whether the value of productive property as represented by the prices of common stocks or the prices of such capital goods as machinery and plant are in any way affected by the rise or fall in interest rates. Are interest rates a part of the motive forces in business, or are they for the most part reflections of primary forces without special potency in themselves?

Satisfactory statistical data covering a significant historical period do not exist for many of the segments of the capital market. It happens that we have excellent data for the highly organized short-term money markets extending over a long period. We also have fairly satisfactory long-term data pertaining to the prices of marketable securities representing borrowed funds, particularly those that have represented a wide participation by those having capital through the existence of organized security markets and the services of the middlemen who mobilize savings into effective capital. But beyond these highly organized and continuous markets a vast amount of borrowing and lending takes place that does not involve bank credit or publicly offered securities. This finds its counterpart in the case of labor performed in remote and isolated enterprises or under conditions that remove the work from the competitive influence of the general labor market, leaving prices to be set by local bargaining, with results that may be widely at variance with scales of pay determined by the leveling action of broad and fluid markets.

If we consistently confine the meaning of interest to the payment made by borrowers to lenders for the use of loan capital and do not confuse it with other forms of return or income, it follows that interest payments are made possible primarily by the productive use of capital. This means in plain language that by using borrowed funds in ways that ultimately increase salable wealth or service, there remains in the hands of the borrower over and above necessary outlays for labor, materials, sales costs, management, etc., a net operating income that may finally be divided with the lender in accordance with some prearranged contractual understanding.[1] If we consistently maintain that these are *borrowing* operations, it logically follows that the contractual understanding provides also for return of principal. Either this may be a return in full at some future period or it may provide for the gradual repayment by sinking funds or by systematic amortization, which, in the opinion of the writer and in the light of historical experience, is the only sound way of negotiat-

---

[1] In the case of rented property, there is a somewhat similar bargain between owner and user, the latter paying from net operating income such portion in rental as the competition for the use of the property will permit the owner to exact. Rental contracts differ from loan contracts in the fact that they are usually of shorter term; they may provide for variable payments corresponding to variations in gross profit, and they do not involve the problem of currently accumulating funds to discharge a principal payment except in cases where the rental agreement is a form of purchase of the property or assets by installment payments.

ing long-term loans. If this view is accepted, a borrower must take into consideration in planning his use of loan capital and the terms of his contract with the lenders not only the payment of *interest* but the payment of *installments of principal*. He must calculate as carefully as possible whether the net operating income accruing from his operations or from other sources is likely to permit carrying out the contract and also to leave a final net income that justifies the undertaking. This applies to a firm or corporation just as it applies to individuals.

BORROWING OPERATIONS AND LEVERAGE

Since, in case of the borrower's failure to validate the contract, a lender may exercise the right to sue or foreclose upon collateral or mortgaged assets, it follows that the current charges for interest, or interest plus capital repayments, are *fixed* charges. If the net operating income of a business is variable, then the final net income remaining after these fixed charges may be subject to much greater fluctuation. This introduces us to the concept of *leverage*, which is of basic importance in the study of business dynamics. To the extent that borrowed capital is large in proportion to equity capital or the resources under the immediate ownership of the borrowing enterprise, the fixed-capital charge will be relatively large as compared to the average size of the net operating income prior to interest (and any amortization) payments. Whenever a large and fixed component is deducted from a variable revenue, the degree of variability in the residual (in this case, final net income) will depend upon the relative magnitude of the fixed outlays. If variations in the net operating income are of minor proportions but the size of the fixed charge is great, variability in net income will be considerable. If the fixed charge is relatively large compared with the average amount of net income but the latter varies over a wide range, then the result will be an extreme degree of variability in net income, with the probability of net losses from time to time. Since borrowers of capital are usually optimistic and their borrowings are based upon anticipated return rather than demonstrated fact, it follows that many borrowings are undertaken under the incentive of large eventual profits *arising from leverage*. Stated in another way, there is a temptation for those who have a modest capital equity to *control* a much larger amount of resources through borrowed funds, so that net income may be expanded to a very high proportion, or even multiple, of the original capital fund. *This temptation to "trade on the equity" will obviously be much stronger if the loan contract does not provide for amortization of principal.* This point must be repeatedly emphasized, because in spite of historical evidence of its importance economists have usually overlooked it.

Put in another way, the absence of any plan for amortizing long-term debt is in itself one of the major incentives to the use of borrowed money in reckless and speculative ways and one of the surest avenues leading to the overdevelopment of important lines of enterprise, and sooner or later to reorganization, impairment of production, and depression. It is the avenue, also, that leads politicians to equally reckless use of their borrowing propensities, with results we have considered in previous chapters. There has long been inadequate attention to the economics of *amortization,* and a lax attitude has prevailed toward repayment of loan capital that has characterized most descriptions of the capital mechanism. Amortization is important because if it is provided for between the parties, it is an effective deterrent to excessive optimism and reckless exaggeration of future profit possibilities through the effect of leverage. At the same time, it forms one means of directing capital, *at reasonable cost,* into sound projects and uses since wasteful and reckless uses are discouraged. It is also a way of protecting both borrowers and lenders from the calamity of insolvency because of the too common tendency to consider in the fixed charge for the borrowed portion of their capital the current interest charge only, with no provision for a schedule of repayments.

From the point of view of the prospective revenue from which the borrower hopes to be able to repay the loan with interest, we may distinguish several types of cases. In the first instance, the borrower has in hand a productive enterprise, providing salable goods or services. Repayment prospects depend upon a more or less continuous flow of operating income, and through repayment capital is kept circulating and does not become frozen. Since for present purposes the various borrowers of this type are assumed to be in competition with each other, there will naturally be some powerful tendency toward setting a rate (excluding risk factors) not in terms of the most productive uses of capital but in terms of the least productive, or marginal, uses that still leave something above direct costs for capital purposes. In the second group of cases the borrower uses capital in ways that permit him, if fortunate, to secure a capital gain through the purchase of commodities, securities, or property and their sale at a higher price. Such undertakings may be completed within a very short period, as in the stock market; they may be undertaken in the property market through the speculation in land; or they may be the familiar operations of businessmen in seeking gain through speculation in raw materials or merchandise or what is known as "inventory write-up." There is still a third case, in which the funds for validating the debt are in the form of what we may call "derived" income, accruing (or expected to accrue) to nonproductive or consumer borrowers. In this class we have as outstanding examples much of the borrowing by governments and by wage earners or "consumers."

When governments borrow, they anticipate future income to be obtained by exercise of the taxing power or, in extreme cases, the exercise of the power to expropriate the wealth of citizens, the power to acquire new territory or valuable assets by military conquest or diplomatic skill, and in certain instances the ability to obtain revenue accruing from such productive operations as governments may own and manage. Apart from the latter case, these possible prospective sources of revenue to permit repayment of borrowings are all derived from the *productive operations* of individuals or their accumulated surplus. In societies not dominated by government through the ownership of production facilities, government borrowing implies a subsequent levy upon the value of the products of private enterprise.

In the case of individual consumer loans, we have an important example of borrowing undertaken on the assumption and with the anticipation of a continuing flow of income, mainly from productive employment or from investment income, not directly resulting from the use of the borrowed funds. These sources may be supplemented by auxiliary income, such as occasional windfalls, gifts, capital gains, inheritances, etc. Loans of this sort are further classified in several ways. First we have loans for acquisition of durable consumer goods by a gradual process of saving and amortized repayments. These are a means by which those with slender resources may ultimately enlarge their equity in durable wealth, such as furniture, automobiles, and houses, by a program of saving that is turned over at regular intervals to the supplier of the capital.[1] Second, there are advances made to necessitous borrowers for the purposes of maintaining existence in the absence of *any* current income but with the hope of future income, provided that life and family existence can be maintained and starvation averted. These necessitous loans are really in a class by themselves, because they involve sordid, harsh, or usurious exploitation at the hands of grasping moneylenders whose operations have not yet been brought under regulative control, even in the United States.[2]

[1] See Chapter 19 for further illustrations of installment credit.

[2] It would be easy to enumerate still further special types of so-called "consumer" loans, such, for example, as those that have as their objective the education or training of individuals to enhance their future earning power or the consolidation of various small loans into a larger loan, with the object of making the repayment easier, etc. The exploiting of the individual borrower by exorbitant interest is an important phase of lending for the world as a whole. It is probable that the retarded development of such countries as India and China has been largely due to the prevalence of the most flagrant practice of usury, combined with an equally harsh system of land rental.

There is, therefore, no necessary correlation between the amount of productive *enterprise* being undertaken and the amount of *loan capital* in use. Practically every productive enterprise actually represents some equity before borrowed funds are added. The size of this equity ownership varies over a wide range, and some considerable part of the borrowing operations results from the fact that adequate surplus funds must in some manner be brought into the hands of those who own and operate productive enterprise but do not control enough capital to assure satisfactory efficiency, productivity, and net return. An increase in total borrowing may represent factors associated with the distribution of wealth between those having surplus and those not having enough of it, as well as changes occurring in the volume of production itself. If all productive capital represented ownership shares and if this ownership coincided with willingness among the owners to undertake management responsibility, it is conceivable that there would be no borrowing at all for these purposes. Although it is desirable for many reasons that resort to borrowed capital in productive operations be held to a minimum, there is no reason why borrowing is likely to produce major economic difficulties if it is associated with systematic amortization, and this has indeed been increasingly recognized in very recent years. "Consumer" borrowing especially develops tremendous difficulties if it is not amortized, and we have already considered instances of the serious consequences of failure to amortize consumptive debt in American experience. But it is probably the governmental form of consumptive borrowing that does most to keep unamortized, virtually *permanent debt* in existence on a grand scale. It is war finance that lies at the basis of this tendency, since all governments *could* manage to secure the necessary funds for current and for capital purposes through taxation alone, were it not for the recurring emergencies of costly wars. National governments, however, do more than borrow savings; they have the power to print money and to exploit and inflate credit by forcing the banking system to accommodate fiscal policy. Thus government policy can expand both demand and supply simultaneously, creating an influence over rates that affects all capital.

Let us now consider the manner in which available surplus funds are mobilized for capital uses. We have, first, the individual capitalist, who may or may not supplement his own capital with borrowed funds or with equity capital obtained from others in the form of shares in the ownership of a productive property or organization. If an enterprise is owned by capitalists who are able to plow back earnings sufficient to develop the full potentialities of their enterprise, no resort to borrowed funds is necessary, although short-term bank loans may occasionally be a consequence. Capitalists ranging from very large to very small savers, who wish to make indirect rather than direct investment, place their funds in the hands of middlemen, who can be classified in two general groups. First are those who use funds to make long-term loans to enterprise. In this group are included life-insurance companies, most savings banks, the building-loan associations, mortgage companies, estate trustees, and investment trusts. The second major group consists of the commercial banks.

The most important distinction between these two groups lies in the fact that the first group represents essentially the mobilizers of savings that find their way into extended loans—predominantly for productive purposes for government and for property development.

COMMERCIAL BANKS AS LENDERS AND INVESTORS

Let us now confine our attention to the capital market in terms of corporate and governmental bonds and to the banking influences that appear to be of special importance in determining that segment of the basic interest rate expressed in the average yield on high-grade bonds. Let us consider the function of the commercial banks as mobilizers of savings and as lenders. The commercial banks are receivers of deposits, payable either upon demand or at relatively short notice. This dictates certain peculiarities and limitations in their advances of credit and capital. Here we begin to approach close to the forces that bring about fluctuations in interest rates. Since every commercial bank is constantly endeavoring to put its time deposits to profitable use and to extend its own credit as far as the limits of legal reserves or banking prudence will permit, the result is to make loans not with the object of keeping funds invested in productive or other long-term commitments but to consider the loans either very liquid, that is, maturing quickly, or in a form providing the bank with collateral that is readily salable (at least, in the individual case) or to make investments in securities that are regarded as readily salable. Commercial bankers thus participate in such lending operations and such investment operations as are calculated to emphasize liquidity of loans and shiftability of investment assets. To the extent that bankers are confident of this ability to sell assets quickly in a highly fluid market and let others carry the securities, these securities are regarded as a "secondary reserve." Supplementing the primary reserve of cash (in the United States) is cash held by the central banks.[1]

The ability of a bank to sell quickly to avert asset depreciation in value or to provide additional means of meeting liabilities or demand for loans may involve an illusion, because what is true of an *individual* bank in relation to the securities market is not necessarily true of *all*

---

[1] See Chapter 14 for further details on reserves.

the banks simultaneously in relation to that market. It is precisely in shifting of commercial bank assets from cash (derived mainly from primary deposits) into the form of loans and into investments and back again from investments and into cash that the most significant changes in the going rate of interest in the bond market takes place.

Let us assume a rising phase of the business cycle, characterized by expansion of industrial production, enlargement of construction activity, perhaps some advances in commodity prices, etc. Under these conditions banks are called upon to make more loans for a variety of purposes. Some of these are directly associated with the flow of trade to finance the shipment and warehousing of goods. As we shall indicate presently with measurements, the average variation of trade activity during the phases of the general business cycle has a relatively moderate amplitude. The movement of goods to consumers, the flow from manufacturers to retailers, and the marketing of agricultural produce all represent operations that in the aggregate do not develop violent cyclical gyrations. Hence the amount of bank lending necessary to accommodate the rising phase of the business cycle, insofar as "commercial" loans were concerned, would not ordinarily expand lending operations materially. But what the banks have usually done under these conditions was to expand short loans heavily to those who wish to realize short-term and more or less speculative gains through the operation of the "leverage" principle.

In view of the fact that so much of the business process has a substantial fixed charge, there is always a much more rapid rise in the net profits of companies and hence in the value of the equity represented by their shares of stock than in the volume of production or trade. There is thus a great demand for loans by those who wish to speculate in stocks, and these are the "collateral" loans whose wild expansion in years like 1928 and 1929 was fantastically overdone, although in late years this has been no longer important. It may therefore be said that the bank-loan expansion that has usually characterized a period of rising business activity throws upon the banks a demand for essentially *speculative credit* that is not essential to actual productive or mercantile operations. Such loans may, however, have a decided effect on commodity prices if they are for the purpose of permitting individuals, business firms, and processors of farm or mineral products to acquire large inventories with a speculative objective. The desire to accumulate inventory and to undertake speculative forward buying and the outright commodity speculation on the Board of Trade, the Cotton Exchange, etc., all contribute through bank credit to the rising course of business by contributing to price advances and hence to an unsound or illusory stimulus to trade activity that may become cumulative and dangerous.

As this expansion in bank lending takes place, it presently reaches a point (unless it is controlled by political action or the effect of control policy) at which banks must seriously consider their reserves, particularly in view of the legal minimum requirements. Changes may occur that force the banks to modify loans and investments in ways that are not at all analogous to what direct capitalist investors, such as insurance companies, are likely to do. During the rising phases of general business activity, there tends to be a shifting from bank reserves to money in circulation (M to m). Conditions arising in international trade and, indeed, a wide variety of other contingencies may accelerate this movement of cash from the banks to the public or to foreign banks or even to the public treasury, as tax payments may also be a factor. Thus there are many special factors in the case of the commercial banks that make it necessary to fortify reserves. Additional reserves may be obtained, of course, by the rediscount of suitable collateral with the Reserve Banks, but this is restricted to commercial paper and Government securities and may not suffice. As the cost of obtaining added resources in this way is also a consideration, bankers undertake it only when a state approaching emergency impends. As a result, the fortifying of reserves involves the liquidating of some of the "secondary-reserve" investments. In the converse case of general business recession, after the temporary strain has completely passed, the banks again obtain cash deposits from the hands of the public, gold may flow in from abroad, and so long as demand for both business and speculative short-term credit is slack the banks seek what return they can get by investing the otherwise idle resources in bonds.

We actually find evidence over a long period that as the demand for bank loans increases during the expansion of business, the holding of securities by the banks has tended to be either retarded or actually reduced. This reduction in bank-security holdings involves an interruption of the investment flow through the fact that the bond sales made by the commercial banks (unless offset by heavy Federal Reserve buying of prime securities in the open market) devolves upon other capitalist or middlemen groups that had not expected to be faced by these additional floating supplies of securities at the very time that new security issues for expansion of corporate operations are making their appearance in the market. We thus have the makings of the oft-repeated situation of "undigested securities." As the banks sell, the price of high-grade bonds falls, and the interest yield on such securities rises. It does not take much selling to affect prices sharply. The rise in the interest rate in this sense correlates usually with a more emphatic rise in the short-term rate for bank loans and discounts. What cannot any longer be obtained in the form of long-term capital by the sale of bonds must now be obtained in part by additional credits that the banks can make only by selling *still more* of their investments; thus a spiral of financial liquidation may begin. Further expansion, insofar as it is conditioned upon ability to secure *loan* capital by the sale of bonds, may be quickly impaired. If a generally overextended condition has previously developed in important directions, a sharp recession or depression may thus be precipitated. The depressions of 1907 and 1937–1938 are illustrations of this.

We must be on our guard, however, against theories that tie all changes in the interest rate and bond market with what goes on in *productive operations* or that assume that these conditions in themselves bring about a change in the *willingness* or "propensity" (as J. M. Keynes says) to use capital in production or commerce. Although expansion in industry does initiate the loan expansion and bank-investment contraction, it is the latter concomitant of the rise that contributes not only accentuation and a spiral action but also the excessive severity of the compensating reaction. The bond market and related interest rates move much more in response to the phases of banking policy (as banks move from one side to the other of their "straddling" position) than to the underlying capital demand and supply forces. In retracting from their *characteristically tentative* investment positions, commercial banks initiate a train of events making it more and more difficult for investment bankers to induce savers to engage in long-term investment in the face of falling values. As the decline extends to stocks and many other sensitive prices, it tends to create apprehension and impair financial confidence. It is an old saying that "you can't finance on a falling market." Thus, while what may be termed the excrescences of commercial banking are being readjusted to the tune of high short-term rates, the productive system itself, insofar as it may be seeking new capital resources, must enter a period of retrenchment capable of producing unemployment, reduction of incomes, collapse of prices, and all the familiar consequences that mark a recession in the business cycle. This process may at times follow a condition of unsound physical expansion, but it is temporary weakening of capital flow by security liquidation that accentuates the interruption of business and employment. This, of course, is not true of *all* depressions, but it has been at least an important phase of most.

We have seen that it is a familiar banking practice to use the lending rate as a medium of control in adjusting earning assets of commercial banks to the loan demand. The operations of the speculators and semi-investors who trade heavily on their equity by borrowing a substantial fraction of their requirements from brokers while the brokers, in turn, borrow from the banks have until recently represented a demand that

is substantial and insistent.   If and when banks find that the latter type
of credit demand is increasing, they first discourage the use of credit
in collateral loans by raising short rates.   They may even refuse to make
such loans, and in this event collateral loans, subject to overnight call,
may be terminated by some banks or, indeed, by many of the banks,
and the banks willing to expand such business are able to secure a very
high rate.   The demand for such credit is highly inelastic.   Historically,
the range of fluctuation in the rate on call money has been tremendous,
from almost nothing up to 50 or even 100 per cent per annum for short
periods of exceptional strain.[1]

FLUCTUATIONS IN COMMERCIAL PAPER RATES

It must be remembered that we are speaking of tendencies over an
extended historical period; in recent years of very subdued speculative

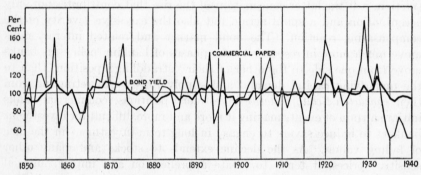

CHART 38.—Commercial paper rates and high-grade bond yields, relative to trend,
1850–1940.   In terms of cyclical fluctuation, money rates and bond yields have had a high
degree of sympathetic variation, the range being much wider for commercial paper rates
than for bond yields.

activity and enormous excess reserves, the range of fluctuation has been
very much reduced, and the rates themselves have been exceedingly low.
The rates that commercial banks have charged on advances to merchants and to industry generally are reflected in what is known as the
"commercial paper" or "acceptance" rates.   The rates on "line of
credit" or unsecured loans are more stable and are not readily measurable.
Despite the declining importance of the commercial loan, the elasticity of
demand for such credit is also inelastic, for businessmen count upon
the availability of credit, and at certain periods of the year it is essential
for many kinds of business, especially for the agricultural processing
industries, to obtain temporary financing from the commercial banks.
Should there be a condition of strain either through declining reserves

[1] Time loans, which also represent collateral credit, are almost as vulnerable as
the call-loan rates.

or exceptional over-all demand for bank credit, the rates on commercial paper tend to be volatile, and they decline quickly under the reverse conditions. Ordinarily the very sensitive rates on collateral loans have shown the first tendency to change, a change followed shortly by the commercial paper rate. The range of fluctuation of the commercial paper rate has, in general, been considerably less than that of the rates pertaining to collateral loans, but at times in the past the commercial rate has risen to very high levels.

Let us now examine the cyclical pattern of the New York commercial-paper rate, in terms of annual data, to eliminate the insignificant vibrations, expressed as ratios to the longer term trend. The results appear in Chart 38 for the period since 1850. The variations in commercial rates may be compared with a similar series derived from average yields on a group of high-grade corporate bonds.[1] The reader is undoubtedly aware that changing conditions in the bond markets express themselves simultaneously in the yield basis of both new and outstanding issues. A decline in bond prices is always associated with a rise in the yield rate, which may be expressed either as the current rate of return, regardless of maturity, or as the rate of return to maturity taking account of amortization of premium or discount. Bonds of very long term or without definite maturity (such as British Consols) would vary as to computed yield almost exactly proportionately to the reciprocals of their prices. Thus, when banks are disposing of bonds in order to accommodate loan demand or to offset gold withdrawals, it is natural that they dispose of their high-grade rather than other bonds, since the former are considered almost the equivalent of cash. Bonds of inferior caliber naturally are affected by the special elements of risk or salability, and their prices and yields reflect what is known as the "solvency" or "income" element rather than the strictly "credit" element that dominates the pure interest rate and the prices of "credit bonds."[2]

---

[1] The actual data for commercial paper are those given by Leonard P. Ayres, relating to his long-term Chart of American Business Conditions. The average yields on high-grade, long-term bonds represent the index of F. R. Macaulay ("Bond Yields, Interest Rates, and Stock Prices," National Bureau of Economic Research, 1938, Appendix, Table 10). These figures run back to 1857, at which point they are carried back to 1850 by splicing to a series of yields computed from the index of prices of municipal bonds prepared by L. P. Ayres. The high-grade bonds used by Macaulay are railroad bonds, and Macaulay has carefully adjusted the indexes to allow for elements of drift in the changing solvency of individual companies so that the bond yields primarily reflect the equivalent of the highest grade bonds. See also Appendix 7.

[2] The term "pure interest" has a double meaning. In one sense, it is a rate expressing the result of the psychological attitude of lenders, as they weigh future income and surplus against present or immediate spending, and of the attitude of borrowers, as they weigh the prospective advantages of having command over such

Let us now bring together the cyclical pattern of bond yields reflecting primarily changes in interest rates not involving solvency factors and short-term credit rates.   In Chart 38 it is strikingly apparent that whereas the amplitude of cyclical movement in bond yield is much lower than that of the commercial paper rate (both series expressed as percentage deviations from long-term drift), nevertheless the movements have many points of similarity.   At some points there is lack of agreement that may be in part explained by the fact that we are using money-rate data pertaining to the New York market, whereas the yields on high-grade bonds are of less localized significance.   A careful study of Chart 38 reveals that every important rise and fall in the commercial paper rate during this long period has coincided with a similar movement in the yield on high-grade bonds.   In more cases than not, changes in commercial paper appear to have *preceded* the related movements in bond yields.   Thus there is statistical as well as logical ground for the proposition that the cyclical movements in the interest rate derived from bond prices have been closely associated with and, in part, considerably affected by conditions in the banking system.[1]

---

facilities as will augment future income or command of resources.   In this sense the pure rate might be thought of as meaning the degree of impatience of income receivers to spend as against the ability of honest and competent borrowers to use immediate funds to advantage.

The second possible meaning of "pure interest" refers to the computed yield upon those securities or obligations with respect to which there is a minimum of solvency risk and whose yields vary primarily with forces of an essentially mechanical character taking place principally within the banking system, the gold or reserve situation, and whatever productive or wholly unproductive sources of capital or credit demand may exist.

This distinction is important because there is a tendency on the part of some theorists to argue that even the intermediate-term changes in interest rates (bond yields) necessarily express the first group of factors, that is, the psychological calculus of lenders and the expected productivity or capital use in the minds of borrowers. Actually, the yield on capital used with the minimum of solvency risk is determined by the psychological calculus working through an institutional funnel that serves not only to magnify the fluctuations (barring compensating control policy) but to introduce influences such as bank reserve position that need not reflect anything as to the calculus of saving versus investing.   Interest rates or yields are usually much higher than the pure rate because of risk factors and inadequate provision for amortization.

[1] It must be kept in mind that if the banks are confronted by a situation that involves the sale of assets held as secondary reserve, the first securities sold will probably be not long-term bonds but various short-term notes, particularly Treasury notes and bonds of short maturity.   These are prime secondary reserves, since the shorter the term of a high-grade obligation (the period prior to maturity) the less fluctuation in value will ordinarily occur, since payment at maturity will presumably be at par.   But to the extent that banks hold a large part of their secondary reserves in longer term securities, the sales of these, perhaps first appearing in the metropolitan banks and later spreading about the system generally, will effect important changes

Let us now consider the characteristics of the interest rate on high-grade bonds as it has expressed itself in the actual data over a long period of years, with no correction for trend. We can state the facts either in terms of the computed yield, or in terms of the prices of the best corporate bonds. In this case we shall choose to work out our statistical illustrations in terms of bond prices, but using prices derived from the same type of bonds as those referred to in Chart 38. The prices of bonds that are sufficiently sound and marketable to be held in large amounts by banks will be accumulated during periods when the demand for loans is relatively weak or when the position of reserves in relation to loans is comfortable. The banks wish to utilize their nonearning assets in order to put them to work as far as is possible and reasonably safe, and the funds are therefore placed in various types of securities, but always with the thought of selling at some later time if necessary. Hence it follows that some form of *ratio between reserves and loans* may be expected to furnish a clue to the empirical determination of the variations of the high-grade bond market. Annual data of this character were, therefore, assembled from the Reports of the Comptroller of the Currency. It was not found possible to obtain satisfactory data between 1863 and 1875 because of incomplete records, but for the banking system as a whole, tolerably good statistics were obtainable from 1836 to 1863 and again from 1875 to date. These are described in Appendix 7, and we shall comment here only upon the significant results obtained by computing and adjusting the ratios of the cash reserves of the entire banking system[1] to the loans and discounts, excluding investment.

Such a ratio is, of course, subject to variation either in reserves or in the amount of loans outstanding. It would be expected that a rise in such a ratio would imply conditions favorable to relatively large bank holdings of securities, especially high-grade bonds. A relatively low ratio would imply that demand for loans was heavy and that banks were reducing their portfolios of bonds. Hence the movement of this ratio will be expected to correspond with the movement of bond prices, if it is

---

in the bond market. As for bonds of inferior caliber, the results cannot be stated categorically. If a business boom is under way, credit is becoming somewhat more difficult to obtain, and high-grade bonds are tending to decline, it may still be true that the recovery movement may be favorable to the prices of the more speculative bonds, which, to the extent that they involve a solvency element, tend to move with the stock market rather than with the so-called "money-rate" obligations. This differentiation between high-grade and lower grade bonds is important in view of the fact that there may actually be diametrically opposite price and yield movements temporarily, depending on the phases of the business cycle.

[1] Noncommercial banks were also included for reasons of statistical convenience, although the results are primarily a reflection of the mechanics of the commercial banking system.

true that these changes in the bond market with which we are now concerned are an expression of what happens in the banking system and only in a derived and partial sense an expression of what happens in the pure rate of interest in the savings-investment sense. It was found that the changes in the ratio do have some similarity to the observed movements of high-grade bond prices, but a much more satisfactory result was obtained by expressing the ratio, not in actual terms but on an accumulative basis. In order to obtain this cumulative derivative of the ratio, the two periods stated were considered separately, and the average of the ratio over the period 1835 to 1863 and again during the period from 1875 to 1932 were computed as the basis for a "normal" level, the deviations from which were cumulated.

The final cumulated index is shown in Charts 39*a* and 39*b*. It will be found to have a more perfect correlation with the pattern of high-grade bond prices than any other variable that has thus far been discovered. The result can be expressed by saying that so long as the ratio of reserves to loans is relatively above the normal average of banking procedure and traditional practice, the bond market, *apart from minor fluctuation, will continue to rise;* but if the ratio runs below that normal average, the bond market not only will tend to decline *but will continue to do so*

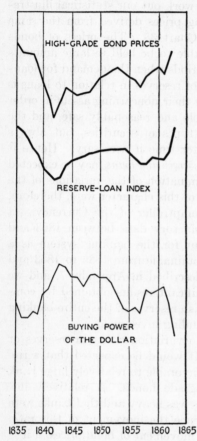

CHART 39*a*.—Factors determining high-grade bond prices, 1835–1863. For description of the reserve loan index see Appendix 7, Sec. 1.

as long as this condition exists. This may be considered from the statistical evidence to be a fundamental law of bond prices. Furthermore, it confirms in still another respect the findings of our previous test, which identifies the proximate forces at work with the mechanics of the banking system.[1]

[1] During the period from the beginning of the National Banking System, the computation of effective reserve presented difficult problems. The operations of the Federal Reserve System were fully taken into account as they affected the "banking

In Charts 39a and 39b the cumulated ratio may be compared not only with the actual course of average bond prices but also with the purchasing power of the dollar over commodities at wholesale (lower curve). This is added because for many years economists have noted some degree

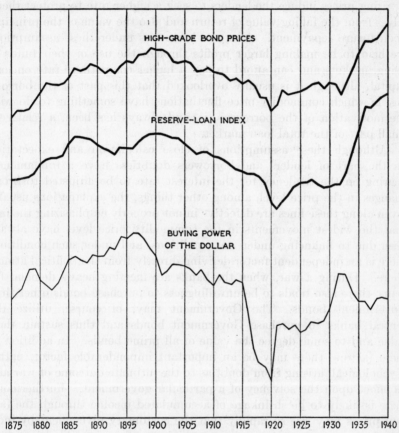

HIGH-GRADE BOND PRICES

RESERVE-LOAN INDEX

BUYING POWER
OF THE DOLLAR

1875 1880 1885 1890 1895 1900 1905 1910 1915 1920 1925 1930 1935 1940

CHART 39b.—Continuation of Chart 39a, 1875–1940. For description of reserve loan index see Appendix 7, Sec. 1.

of correlation between the bond market and the purchasing power of the dollar or, inversely, between the changes in rate of interest and the movements of commodity prices.   This not only has been evident in American experience but can be shown in the experience of Great Britain, France,

value" or, as we have termed it, "valency" of a dollar of reserve in view of the numerous changes in reserve requirements against deposits.   In the latter years account was also taken of the fact that whereas the traditional legal limitation upon potential bank expansion imposed by reserves became almost nominal, the important, but usually inoperative, limitation represented by existing bank capital and surplus had to be introduced into the computation as a modifier.

and other countries.   This relationship between the interest rate and commodity prices (and perhaps, also, the general price level) has usually been explained through reasoning that emphasizes the pure rate of interest as something determined by the psychological calculus.   That is, rising prices induce the lenders to seek a higher rate to protect themselves from the falling value of return and also the value of the principal upon future repayment.   Also, the borrowers under these assumptions are held to be making larger profits through the use of their funds in rising markets and can afford to pay a higher competitive rate on loan capital, although it is usually overlooked that this part of the borrowing, in which commodity-price fluctuations have something to do with the motivation of the borrowers, is, and always has been, a relatively small part of the total loan market.

Although these assumptions of close calculation and expectation on the part of lenders and borrowers doubtless have a fundamental bearing on the tendency for the interest rate to be adjusted to broad changes in the price level, among other things, the explanations usually given along these lines are defective in not properly emphasizing the fact that the widest movements in the commodity price level have always been due to financing under war conditions, and under such conditions there is an independent factor deriving directly from the political atmosphere.   During a war, when the banks are meeting heavy demand for loans, there also tends to be unwillingness to purchase bonds other than Government bonds.   The Government may, of course, utilize the central banks to purchase Government bonds and thus sustain their value and to some degree the value of all prime bonds.   In addition to these factors, there may be an important imponderable factor, partly psychological, arising from doubt as to the ultimate outcome of war and its effect upon the solvency of a particular government.   Furthermore, there is likely to be shrinkage of accumulated income through the fact that prices may rise so rapidly that the customary investment by individuals, corporations, insurance companies, and savings banks are not capable of absorbing bond issues sufficiently to enable the market to finance all requirements.   Hence some part of this apparent correlation between bond prices and purchasing power of money has had its ultimate origin in the mechanics of war conditions.

BOND PRICES AND THE PURCHASING POWER OF MONEY

The relationship between the bond prices and the purchasing power of money is actually by no means as close as has usually been thought. In the early years 1835–1863, as shown in Chart 39a, the correlation between bond prices and the purchasing power of money was virtually nil.   In the later period, after 1875, there were several important inverse movements.   The relationships between 1895 and 1900, between 1915 and 1920, and particularly after 1932 are none too satisfactory.   At the same time it is obvious that important changes in commodity prices do affect the reserve-loan ratio *through* the fact that a very extensive rise in commodity prices has frequently been unfavorable to gold supplies, whereas falling prices have had the reverse effect.   Naturally, when prices are rising in the commodity market, the loans demanded of the banks by businessmen and even by security speculators will be written in higher figures, and vice versa.   Hence bank loans and bank reserves are themselves directly affected by changes in prices, and it is through these channels that the bond market appears to be primarily motivated.[1]

We may now proceed to still another method of stating the relationship of the banking position to changes in bond prices.   Let us consider somewhat more intensively the period from 1915 to date, as shown in Chart 40.   At the top of the chart the bond price index is shown in monthly form, with the use of the same basic data as before.   Next below is shown the course of the adjusted excess reserves of the member banks of the Federal Reserve System, and below that is a measure of the amount of gold added to, or subtracted from, the monetary stocks of the country.[2]   Excess reserves are a factor somewhat similar to the ratio of reserve to loans, although they represent differences between actual reserves and the reserves required in view of deposit liabilities, which, in turn, vary mainly with loans and discounts of the commercial

[1] An extended analysis of the interest rate in terms of changes in commodity prices will be found in Irving Fisher, "The Theory of Interest," New York, 1930. Fisher's general theory, as first stated in his "Purchasing Power of Money," New York, 1911, that the interest rate adjusts itself to changes in money (M) only after money supply has *first* brought about a change in the price level seems to the present writer erroneous.   What actually happens is that increase in bank reserves will usually depress the interest rate, which may or may not be followed by a rise in business activity or a change in the price level.   During a war situation, the matter is of course different, in that there will be heavy financing by the Government and rapid issue of means of payment by expansion of bank credit, which raises prices, but in this case the rise in prices and the rise in interest rates tend to be concurrent.

Another school of thought revolves about the original theories of Wicksell, that changes in the supply of money affect prices *through the interest rate*.   The reasoning, however, is not in accord with the facts of American experience and represents one of those plausible syllogisms that do not stand the test of statistical examination.   In fact, the present writer is skeptical of any theory that gives to the rate of interest or to commodity prices a causal role in the origination of business cycles.   There are times when this type of theory corresponds with the facts to some extent, and there are many other times when it does not.

[2] See Appendix 7 for further description of the data.   With regard to the measure of excess bank reserves, this is mainly in monthly form, but in the early years it has been necessary to estimate these excess reserves in a rather indirect manner, and the intervals are longer than monthly periods until 1925.

banks. It should be added that the excess reserves are here further adjusted by deducting the amount of rediscounting at the Reserve Banks in order to reveal the *actual* excess or deficit reserve position of the member banks (considered as typical of all commercial banks) apart from supplementary credit sources. We may refer to the adjusted data as "net" excess reserves.

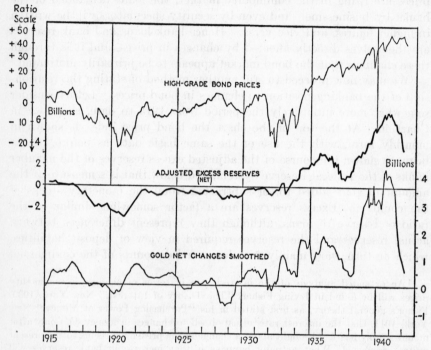

CHART 40.—Gold movements, adjusted excess reserves, and bond prices, 1915–1941 Net gold movement, operating through adjusted excess reserves, has an important influence upon the bond market. Excess reserves are here shown adjusted for member bank discounting. See also Appendix 7 Sec. 2.

As net excess reserves declined during the period of World War I, it will be noted that the bond prices tended to decline, although with numerous minor fluctuations. After 1920 a recovery occurred, followed by a long, slightly rising table ending in 1931, which is closely paralleled by the pattern of net excess reserves. Bond prices were affected by the shock of the 1931 crisis to an extent that suggests the emergence of psychological and solvency factors as well as credit factors. The ensuing recovery, however, shows a parallel movement until 1936, when the somewhat more sensitive excess reserve position was suddenly reduced by political action and bond prices did not reflect this condition for another year or so. From 1938 on, however, the movements have been fairly close in the two series.[1]

We turn now to the lower curve, which represents a smoothed series of the plus and minus changes in the monetary gold supply that controls bank reserves insofar as no deliberate political action or control policy intervenes, and we find that the changes in excess reserves can be fairly well anticipated. We find that the explanation of most of the changes in net excess reserves during the past generation can be attributed to the gold movements. Bond prices have been primarily subject to changes in the gold-reserve position of the United States, and during this period the effect of variations in the loan factor has been subordinate, although somewhat in the same direction. If we trace the record back, with such partial figures as are available prior to 1915, we find that in the earlier years it was not changes in gold reserves but rather the variations in loans arising from the various promotional excesses and liquidations connected with land speculation that usually affected excess reserve.

As a by-product of the analysis illustrated in Chart 40, we have a convenient instrument for the forecasting of the bond market insofar as its movements arise from the position of the banks. The reserve position must, of course, also be appraised in terms of potential or prospective changes, not only in demand for loans but also in those administrative rulings originating in the Treasury or in the Federal Reserve management that have the effect of varying excess reserves directly by changing the requirements in accordance with the provisions of the Banking Act of 1935. If we take the group of exhibits just discussed in conjunction with each other, it can be said fairly definitely that the course of the bond market is subject to statistical analysis and fairly successful forecasting. There is at any rate no mystery about it. Neither is it necessary to resort to the theory of capital demand and supply in the fundamental sense, relating to the "long run" of classical economists and the convenient world of imaginary equilibriums in order to make

[1] In the latter part of 1936 and early 1937, "the many 'country' member banks that carry most of their surplus funds with their city correspondent banks, rather than with their respective Federal Reserve Banks, withdrew funds from the city banks and deposited them in the Reserve Banks to cover the increases in their required reserves. Thus the large city banks sustained withdrawals of funds, as well as increases in their own reserve requirements. In the case of the New York City banks this pincer action absorbed practically all of their excess reserves, and caused them to liquidate some of their assets. The result was an abrupt tightening of money market conditions and an exaggerated influence upon the Government security market, even though aggregate reserve funds of all member banks continued ample." (*Annual Report for* 1940, Federal Reserve Bank of New York, p. 17.)

successful appraisals of the prospective changes in the significant expression of the interest rate.

We refer to the yield on high-grade bonds as a most important measure of the rate of return on capital, not because this rate or this type of bond represents a preponderance of the fixed-interest securities in the capital market or because the longer term indebtedness represented by bonds is to be considered as the most important part of all long-term indebtedness in existence. The importance of the return on high-grade bonds and the variations attributable to the factors that we have analyzed lies in the fact that by using interest rates or prices of obligations of very high grade, we derive a convenient basis from which the risk factor in its varying gradations may be measured and the effect of it discerned in individual bonds or groups of bonds. When we consider the capital market as a mechanism through which borrowed surplus is mobilized, we have the advantage of carefully recorded prices, convenient index numbers of yields and prices, capable of serving as precise recorders of the changes taking place. These, in turn, have important effects upon the investment flow insofar as it concerns funds obtained by bond issues. We shall also examine in the following chapter the extent to which changes in the interest rate appear to have a bearing upon the equity capital movement or issues of stocks.

When we refer to bond prices or interest rates, it should be kept in mind that index numbers or averages can be deceptive. One must know exactly what grade of bonds is represented in a composite measure before drawing conclusions with respect to interest rates in the sense to which the foregoing analysis has been confined. There are various indexes or averages of bond prices that contain numerous low-grade or medium-grade issues, whose movements may be not only much more violent than those of the highest grade bonds but occasionally even inverse to the changes in the highest grade bonds. The very highest grade naturally applies in the United States to obligations of the Federal Government; below these come a great many of the outstanding obligations of local governments, followed, in turn, by prime corporation issues. All these groups, including even the very best governmental bonds, will from time to time be affected by psychological conditions of a temporary nature. Quite apart from the technical factors, there are passing events that affect the state of the public mind and thereby the prices and yields of the very highest grade obligations.

The British departure from the gold standard in 1931 was such an event. Prior to the fateful month of September, 1931, the high-grade bond market had been surprisingly firm because of the technical conditions relating to bank reserves and loans, despite the fact that common stocks and speculative bonds declined. The coming of this great shock to confidence throughout the world carried all types of bonds sharply lower in the autumn. The writer is convinced that had this event not occurred and had it been possible to arrange a speedy and effective solution of the European financial tangle, the bond market in the United States would have continued on a very firm basis, despite some continuing weakness in the more speculative securites reflecting the continued impairment of the mortgage market and the final stage of the long spiral of foreclosure. Yet even this great break in world markets for securities and commodities did not suffice to interrupt the rising *drift* of high-grade bond prices much longer than a year. By the end of 1932 many of the highest grade bonds had regained levels at which they stood in the summer of 1931. From that point forward there was an almost steady rise in bond prices, even though marked fluctuations took place in the speculative, and particularly the railroad, bonds.

Another illustration of the effect of temporary disturbances of general confidence is found in the behavior of the bond market in September, 1939, upon the outbreak of war in Europe. This temporarily affected even the highest grade bonds, but the effect did not last long. Still another case occurred in the following year, when the Germans invaded France. In all these cases, the conditions that had been established above as contributing to an upward general drift of bond prices or downward drift in interest yield could be expected to serve as a very helpful guide to the *underlying trend*.

SAVINGS AS A FACTOR IN THE CAPITAL MARKET

We have good grounds for believing that the total supply of surplus funds destined for permanent or long-term investment came into the capital market (mainly through the investment institutions) in a relatively steady flow. This at least seems to be true of the United States. Complete statistical data for measuring over a long period the amount of total savings coming into the market each year do not exist, but from the fairly comprehensive data available on the deposits in savings banks, the amount of life-insurance assets, etc., the opinion seems justified that this flow is not susceptible to wide fluctuations from year to year. It does not even seem to respond appreciably to booms and depressions, and the long trend of growth in the aggregate is impressively persistent.

Saving, therefore, takes place, not in response to the going rates of interest or other conditions in what may be termed the capital market; rather, it proceeds systematically, almost unconsciously, motivated by social traditions of long standing and the innate tendency of all intelligent individuals to provide for the future. The life-insurance institutions, through their highly effective sales organization and emphasis upon family protection, have done much to systematize individual saving habits and thus to divert into the capital market an enormous and surprisingly steady flow of savings capable of being invested at long term. Although there is no certainty, of course, that the aggregate flow of savings will maintain necessarily precisely the rapid rate of increase of the past century or that the steady growth may not be affected by exceptionally adverse social or political conditions, there is a reasonable presumption that the surplus becoming available from individual savings will continue to be substantial. It will be maintained by the gradual extension of social insurance, such as that now sponsored by the Federal Government, and also by the new incentives toward individual saving created by the growing importance of consumer durable goods as a form of private capital.

If, then, the part of these annual savings actually put to work in the long-term bond market undergoes temporary interruption, the presumption is that the interruption is not in the saving incentives but in some interference with the operations of middlemen who mobilize these funds, particularly the investment policy of the banks. Even insurance companies, which usually purchase investment securities with the object of holding them to maturity, may for short periods reduce their use of available funds if they see prices weakening. Conversely, they are encouraged to accelerate their investing as the bond market resumes a firm tone. As between the banks and the insurance companies and other primarily long-term investors, there is the distinction that the banks do not vary their bond buying in accordance with prices or yields but rather with a view to meeting the demand of their customers for loans. Hence the commercial banks rarely make any considerable profit from their investment portfolios, which accomplish the purpose of keeping otherwise idle funds at work with a very modest net return that helps to cover overhead. The large investing institutions, on the other hand, employ the services of bond experts who study the timing problem closely, and the investment policy is thus more or less adapted to conditions in the bond market. Thus changes in the bond market initiated by the varying relation of bank reserves to the demand for loans are capable of spreading over a wide area and involving something of a cumulative tendency.

The connecting links between the important bond buyers and the borrowers are, of course, the investment bankers—the bond houses and bond brokers. The large distributing houses in New York have for many years been able to exercise powerful influence in originating and placing issues of securities. The ultimate savers, in a majority of cases, excluding very wealthy capitalists, have been remarkably insulated from the debt-capital mechanism. To a surprising degree in the past, although less evident in the past decade, there has been a "community of interest" among bond distributors, borrowing corporations, local government bodies, and the institutional investing middlemen.

The forceful persuasion of the bond distributors has had its effect upon local government administrators in much the same manner as upon the boards of directors of corporations in initiating a larger amount of borrowing than actual circumstances or financial conservatism justified. It has been proved over and over that the average municipality or county would have done far better to raise a larger proportion of its funds for public works and educational facilities through taxation rather than by an endless series of loans involving the payment of substantial fixed charges for extended periods, often far beyond the useful life of the property acquired. Corporations have again and again succumbed to the pressure emanating from the highly organized distributor organizations to issue bonds when they should have been financing themselves to a larger degree by more rational dividend policies, accumulation of surplus, or the sale of stock. There is increasing evidence that, although the bond distributing group on the whole have preserved a reasonably high standard of ethics with respect to the type of securities that they have undertaken to float, they have sought, on the other hand, to involve corporate enterprise in the practice of *continuous borrowing* and, as a result, the dependence year after year upon certain distributing houses, with the result of placing the corporations in a position of perpetual reliance upon debt expansion for the benefit of the distributors. This kind of arrangement has been furthered through interlocking boards of directors, reaching into such corporations as the holding companies in electric power and railroads and into insurance companies and even banks. In some important instances this has meant that a large corporation has been able, through its connection with a distributing group, to place very large bond issues with insurance companies or banks with virtually automatic certainty; vice versa, an insurance company desiring bonds of a certain type for its portfolio might cast about to initiate some new borrowing operation to accommodate its needs.

This has had the unfortunate effect of initiating too large a proportion of the capital of corporations and local governments in the form of rigid fixed-charge obligations and of keeping these debts in existence long after they have served their purpose and the tangible capital has become obsolescent or nonexistent. It has propagated a tradition that bonds need not be paid off—they are merely to be extended by new bonds. This goes far to explain the unfortunate financial experience of our railroads, and there are signs that such a condition gained remarkable headway through the holding-company exploitation of the electric-power industry until that was ended by legislation. Among *industrial* corporations, by and large, the raising of capital through creation of debt has become less and less prevalent, partly as the result of the favorable condition for equity financing created by the stock market boom in the late 1920's. This permitted many corporations to retire debt through stock issues or from earnings. The applied science of business management is becoming well understood among the manufacturing corporations, and the temptation to borrow when borrowing is not necessary is resisted.

Another unfortunate element in the prevalence of interrelated corporate management, bond distributors, and investing institutions has been the development of the philosophy that an industry with reasonably steady earning power can be "safely" saddled with large *fixed* indebtedness. This superficial dogma arose primarily from considering the financing problem from the standpoint of the immediate expansion of profit from bond distribution rather than that of the long-term solvency of the companies or other borrowing agencies. Whether a company should borrow capital or raise it in some other way is usually not so much a question of stability of earnings but a question to be decided on other grounds. No business enterprise should properly be considered to have the form of its financing dictated merely by the insistence on the part of investing institutions or the distributors of the securities upon past stability of earnings. The history of financial procedures plainly tells us that if this "stable-earnings" doctrine is followed through, as, for example, in the case of the railroads and, more recently, electric-power enterprises, the financial result is anything but stability. Once the amount of debt has been carried beyond a certain point, access to financing by means other than expansion of debt, fixed charges, and high leverage becomes less and less easy. In these ultimate consequences the distributors of bonds have usually been not at all interested. This concern with short-run underwriting gains and lack of reasonable concern for the longer future of corporate solvency has been particularly evident in the case of mergers.

The work of Arthur Stone Dewing and others has abundantly demonstrated that many of the important mergers in American business have been engineered not by industrialists but by financial middlemen. The great holding-company mania, which blossomed forth in the 1920's and became a conspicuous factor in the stock-market inflation of 1928 and 1929, also had its roots in a security-distribution system that furnished convenient devices for the flotation of enormous amounts of debt placed upon operating units whose assets were written up for the purpose, sometimes beyond all reason.

The vast holding-company empire of Samuel Insull was typical of many such fantastic pyramids of control, whose evil effect was not in vast profits accruing to the few owners controlling through the parent companies but in the enormous amount of debt placed upon operating units and created through the writing up of assets and attempted maintenance of rates to fit the debt rather than capital structures to fit operating trends. From these same sources, too, came the even more fantastic performance of some of the investment trusts that were set up with outstanding bonded debt and hence enormous profit (and

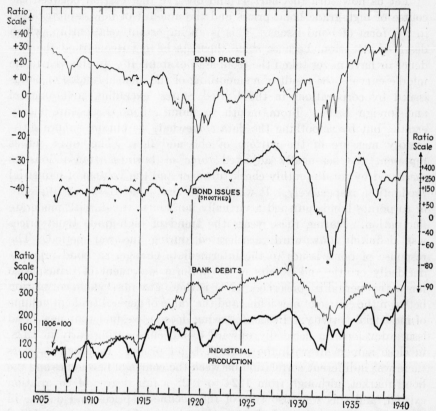

CHART 41.—Corporate bond issues, and business, 1906–1940. The small arrows indicate the months of cyclical extremes, high or low, in the actual figures of new corporate-bond financing, the curve shown being a 12-month centered smoothing of the data. The index of bank debits, adjuted for seasonal variation, is based at 1906 with the index of industrial production to enable comparison of business volume and value during the entire period. The ratio scales are not identical for the three sections of the chart.

loss) leverage. The bond-distributing system, therefore, has had much to answer for, and it is the opinion of the writer that although the machinery has functioned efficiently in a technical sense, it has functioned far too recklessly in bringing about rigid structures of indebtedness in certain basic fields of business, particularly transportation and power production, which have contributed to the excessive *sensitizing* of net earnings and solvency factors to cyclical influences. These practices and the loose superficial theorems underlying them did much to make the last great depression so severe, as these overcapitalized properties added their difficulties to those of the mortgages on jerry-built houses, the frozen debts of the railroads, the impaired solvency of local governments, and the abrupt extinction of investment return from many foreign obligations.

Let us now turn to Chart 41 and observe the relation between the course of high-grade bond prices and the amount of new capital raised in the form of bond issues. This is an important relationship, which deserves attention, because some theorists have misconstrued the evidence or have never taken the trouble to examine it. In this chart, the middle curve is the result of a smoothing of the monthly value of bonds issued by corporations in the United States, excluding governmental and foreign issues. From month to month, bond issues are highly erratic, but by smoothing the data somewhat, we obtain a more satisfactory measure of the pattern of ebb and flow. The lower curves represent the seasonally adjusted *value* of business transactions as measured by total monthly check turnover and the volume of industrial production, respectively. It will be seen that from 1906 to 1919 issues of corporate bonds pursued a virtually horizontal trend, with moderate fluctuation. During these years the trend of high-grade bond prices was definitely downward, accelerated during the war period. The response of bond issues to the intermediate changes in bond prices is decidedly erratic and admits of no uniform statement of principle so far as this period is concerned. Nor is there any observable correlation between the course of new issues and the value of general trade or volume of industrial activity. In the following decade, we find that new bond issues developed a decidedly upward trend, culminating early in 1928, in close agreement with the peak of bond prices. In previous years there was indifferent correlation between the course of new issues and the bond market, although from 1924 to 1928 a fair degree of covariation existed, and this was also true of the decline in prices and decline in issues from 1928 to the end of 1929. New issues of corporate bonds failed to accompany the rise in bond prices in 1930 and part of 1931; general business conditions during those years seem to have been the predominant influence in restraining new financing. This restraint turned to drastic restriction of new financing following the British abandonment of gold. Intensification of the depression continued to reduce new bond issues until, in 1933, there were several months when no issues appeared, in spite of the fact that bond prices were already moving irregularly higher. During the period 1935–1940, bond issues tended to decline well before the break in the bond market in 1937, and resumption of financing through bonds since 1938 has by no means paralleled the continued buoyancy of bond prices, accomplished mainly by governmental exploitation of the gold stock and progressive restriction of private credit uses.[1]

The conclusion appears justified by the foregoing evidence that corporate-bond issues tend to follow the general drift of bond prices in some degree, particularly in a rising bond market. There are, however, exceptions, and it would be more accurate to say that cyclical variations in bond issues have been the *joint effect* of business conditions and bond prices, as can be seen by relating the bond-issue curve to the combined results of the other variables. To maintain that changes in the interest rate on high-grade bonds (or the course of their prices) "automatically" regulates the flow of capital through even this segment of the loan market is erroneous. Over short periods, however, it is more frequently true that sharp cyclical advances and declines in bond prices result in the temporary acceleration or retarding of investing incentive, as previously explained.

A careful examination of the actual dynamics of the capital market in terms of bond issues, interest rates, and business conditions is a wholesome corrective to the tendency, so prevalent in recent years, to theorize about these processes and to draw conclusions concerning what is "normal" and what is "abnormal." Much has been written by way of hypothesis about the relation of bond yields to the rate of return on capital *generally* or what we may term the "over-all net operating-profit rate." Before drawing final conclusions or developing public policy on the basis of such arguments, it is well to recognize what limitations may surround the stating of such relationships in the discussion of capital.

INTEREST RATES NOT NECESSARILY A CONTROLLING FORCE IN CYCLICAL MOVEMENTS

Let us take, for example, the relation of interest rates (in terms of bond yields) and the average over-all rate of net profit to ownership derived from production, trade, and transportation. The relation between interest and profit rates, as thus defined, has no fixed "normal" level in the United States and probably has none in any other country. The long-term level for such a ratio will vary in ways that are not taken fully into account by the prevailing theorizing on the subject. Much depends upon the nature of the profits entering into the average at one time or another. They may or may not emphasize profit return emanat-

---

[1] It must be kept in mind that Chart 41 exaggerates the extent of change in bond prices as compared with bond issues, because the ratio scales are not uniform. The range of fluctuation appears to be about the same, but the range of the smoothed data of bond issues actually averages about seven times as great as that of the bond prices.

ing from promotional or speculative uses of capital or exceptional elements of capital gain; or, on the other hand, they may heavily weight the return from capital invested in well-managed mature productive enterprise. A rise or fall in the interest-profit *ratio* as such may easily be misinterpreted, because interest rates may seem high in relation to profits when, in fact, it is the profit denominator of the ratio that may have declined, or vice versa. To manipulate interest rates artificially in order to produce an effect on business net return or profits or to manipulate and regulate profits in order to have some effect upon interest involves the assumption that gross revenues or net profit rates must "normally" move in harmony with interest rates. Interest rates must be interpreted in the light of the extent to which debt is permanent or amortized and from the standpoint of lenders as well as borrowers; profit rates must be considered from the standpoint of the extent to which cyclical aberrations distort their average level. *It is doubtful whether artificial devices to force interest rates down accomplish anything that cannot be accomplished by making each individual loan soundly amortized.*

Since it is apparent that the incentive to seek capital in the bond market is influenced by other factors than merely the interest rate, it follows that cyclical changes in the relation of short- and long-term interest rates have no special significance from the standpoint of policy. Some writers have insisted that when short rates get "out of line" with the "normal" relation to long rates, something must be done about it. Actually, cyclical movements do express themselves in oscillations of the ratio between these rates, as was seen in Chart 38; during boom conditions the more volatile short rate rises farther above its trend than the long rate, and its direct ratio to the long rate also rises. The converse occurs during depression. Recently, however, the years of active trade conditions have made this oscillation much less pronounced as both rates have pursued declining trends with a minimum of minor fluctuation.

It is clear from our preceding analysis that a raising of banking rates may have *some* effect on speculation and trade activity, and it will extend an influence also to the bond market and to new bond issues. To work in the reverse direction, open-market selling of bonds by the Federal Reserve will usually reduce balances in commercial banks and, if carried far enough, will force higher short-term credit rates. But there is no particular point in endeavoring by control policy to "equilibrate" the various rates; their relative position at a given time is but one of several indications of the course of the general business cycle, and we have already seen that effective control of the cycle calls for much more than manipulation of the money market. There are times when putting the brakes on speculative credit may bring about a wholly unnecessary restriction of bond flotations; there are times when the latter may serve little purpose in preventing excesses in other directions; and there are times when commodity or security prices are indifferent to interest-rate changes. The emphasis, therefore, that is sometimes placed upon the relative position of short and long rates is part of a doctrine assigning too much importance to interest rates as *the* controlling forces in cyclical movements.

In conclusion, let us return to the recent emphatic and unprecedented decline in the trend of interest rates and consider some of the special factors contributing to this tendency and some of its effects thus far. Underlying the declining rate we can discern several distinct forces. The enlargement of monetary gold holdings and banking reserves has represented the combined effect of a broad shift in the international creditor position of the United States, a devaluation of the old gold dollar, a flight of liquid capital here seeking protection from foreign war hazards, and probably, too, a continuing advantage to gold producers in selling new gold to this country. But since the decline in interest rates is not limited to the United States and has, indeed, become almost a world-wide tendency, it is apparent that governmental policy has been an outstanding influence, quite apart from gold reserves. The governments of the world, either for military or for other reasons, have sought to enlarge financial reserves, either through gold acquisition or in the absence of this possibility, through various paper substitutes for gold. And to prevent these expansions of the bank-credit base from developing into indefinite enlargement of the monetary *circulation* and hence continuous price inflation, *supplementary policies* have been employed. These have taken the form of restrictions upon foreign financing and all speculative uses of credit and capital, more rigorous scrutiny and limitation of security issues, and (since the outbreak of World War II) direct regimentation of business operations, prices, corporate capital, and consumer credit. This goes far to explain why devaluations of currency have not produced the unlimited inflationary results that were so confidently predicted in the 1930's. Through political measures contracting the private use of capital and credit, *the magnifying of monetary resources* (*in gold or paper*) *has had its major effect in forcing down interest rates*. It follows that as further expansion of monetary stocks or reserves occurs, probably through war-financing operations, it will require still more stringent public regimenting of private financing if low interest rates are to be maintained.

Supplementing this explanation of the phenomenon, some observers see a tendency for business "need" for capital and credit to falter and even decline. This may have been a partial explanation of demand conditions during the last depression, and it does pertain to the use of commercial financing through bank credits; but to make this the major factor, as some pessimists about the future trend of our economic system imply, does not serve to explain why interest rates have declined even in countries where industrial progress in the past twenty years has gone forward much more rapidly than in the United States. The main reason is found in the policies of government and the ambitions of bureaucracy.

A number of apparent objectives are sought by political action to depress the rate of interest. Foremost has been the awareness of a new international struggle and the need for enormous public financing to prepare for, and prosecute, the present War. Borrowing has been resorted to by all governments considerably in excess of revenue, and it is expedient to keep current charges on this fast-growing debt as low as possible. Under war conditions regulation of production and the use of capital and credit can be carried, and is being carried, to extreme limits in all major countries. Hence demand for financing is virtually being restricted to government as the outstanding borrower. By resorting to the prerogative powers of government, it is possible to amplify the source of borrowed funds by direct resort to bank credit and thus far (in 1942) the inflation of prices that has begun to appear in all countries has been kept within limits by resort to more and more drastic taxation than ever before attempted. Furthermore, governments, having established a low interest-rate policy, can perpetuate this policy by direct appeal to lenders and financial institutions to accept public bonds on the desired interest-yield basis. In these various ways we arrive at the principal explanation of the seeming paradox of rampant public borrowing at low interest rates almost the world over. There is here an obvious and ominous implication for the future of private-capital survival, which is further discussed in the concluding chapter.

Apart from war financing, the Federal Government of the United States has sought lower interest rates as a means of accomplishing belated readjustments of frozen debt and reorganization of insolvent financial structures. Low interest rates have undoubtedly been helpful to the refinancing of farm obligations, rural irrigation projects, and the huge mass of urban mortgage debt. It has been possible in many instances to effect debt adjustment by agreement that would be more difficult to accomplish at high rates. It has also been a deliberate objective to lower the interest-rate costs in home building, particularly to extend a building-mortgage system involving long-term amortized loans that are feasible only under conditions of moderate capital costs. In this objective, however, and indeed in all cases where improved methods of financing have been developed and encouraged, the lowering of rates has been in part a phase of the effort to enhance solvency, a factor quite apart from capital supply and demand. The same influence is seen in the efforts made, prior to World War II, to improve the mechanism of consumer installment credit by making this essentially sound method of financing still more efficient at a lower cost to the average user.

On the other hand, apart from immediate war conditions, there are also unsatisfactory aspects of low interest rates with regard to corporate financing. Granting that such financing should predominately be through the medium of equity or surplus to provide flexibility and prevent financial domination of management policy, there are cases in which properly arranged borrowing operations can be helpful to industry. But investors, conscious of risk elements in all such situations, find that the cost of bonds is high, and the Government bond without appreciable risk affords almost the same return as the best corporate obligation. The investor is not yet sure that the prevailing interest-yield level is permanent or can be maintained in view of the more or less "artificial" factors that have created it. If it reverses its trend presently, high-cost bonds may involve paper losses years ahead of maturity and to the individual investor, in contrast to the investing institution, this is a deterrent. And, too (apart from war), if low interest rates are accomplished primarily for the benefit of political adventures in collectivism and by devices that more and more threaten, circumscribe, or tax away the fruits of private enterprise, it seems that the innovation is by no means an unmixed blessing. When solid corporations prefer to stay out of debt, even though money costs but 2½ per cent, but find that equity yields average 7 per cent and equity financing is therefore difficult and furthermore (as we shall later discover) find even surplus accumulation politically frowned upon and subtly discouraged, we may need to reconsider the alleged universal benefits of low interest if we are to continue to expand industrial productivity under private control and management.

CHAPTER 17

STOCK PRICES, SPECULATION, AND STOCK FINANCING

We now turn to the dynamics of the capital market as it concerns stock prices and the raising of equity capital. We shall not examine the case of preferred stocks specifically, but the reader will understand that they are included in what is to be said about issues of new capital in the form of stock. So far as stock prices are concerned, preferred stocks of the highest grade tend to follow the price patterns of bonds just below the highest grade. Most preferred stocks, however, develop patterns rather more similar to those of the higher grade common stocks.

The common stocks in which we are here interested represent shares of ownership in business enterprises under private control. Such ownership shares in the final profits through dividends that are dependent upon earnings. In a few cases, corporations have managed to pay dividends on common stock at a steady rate for extended periods of time, but in the great majority of cases it is a familiar fact that dividend disbursements rise and fall and may be omitted altogether. Since the net earnings of enterprises having outstanding common stock emerge only after allowance for operating costs and overhead charges, the degree of variability in the net available for dividends will be principally determined by the amount of annual variation in gross revenue and the size of the various fixed charges relative to operating income. This gives an indication of the amount of "leverage" (or, as the British say, "gearing") in any given situation. The resulting patterns of change in final earnings available for dividends tend to vary with the fluctuations of the business cycle, but this will be strictly true only for those companies whose operations ordinarily correlate fairly closely with business conditions or, more specifically, with the index of industrial production and trade. Given two companies whose revenue accrues from sales having a time pattern fairly similar to that of the general industrial cycle, the behavior of their common stocks will be similar except for such differences as may exist in the policy of management as to debt and other fixed charges, the proportion of annual surplus distributed in dividends, and, of course, the amount of stock outstanding and the breadth of its distribution and market activity.

These are all factors that will vary the pattern of change or the amplitude of variation in the price movement of the respective common stocks.

If, however, one of the companies is engaged in a business whose activity (or gross revenue) follows a pattern entirely different from that of the typical industrial cycle or is strongly influenced by price or other factors that do not correlate closely with the cyclical pattern, the earnings, dividend payments, and the prices of the shares will develop peculiar patterns, possibly not related in any significant degree to that of the general business cycle.   This general principle is important—the prices of stocks representing companies whose business tends to vary closely with the business cycle will tend to have similar movements.   If the movements of such "cyclical" stocks are combined in an average or index number, there will therefore be a reiteration of typical patterns in the composition of this index, and the final result will be little affected by the inclusion of more than a limited number of such stocks.   The "market-wise" pattern, in other words, is capable of being represented by careful selection from among a dozen or twenty or thirty companies whose business is known to move in close unison with the general cycle.

This is of some practical importance, because an investor who desires to make his stock purchases at reasonable price levels may protect himself by favoring the market-wise stocks whose movements will correlate fairly closely with general business and all the indicators that pertain thereto.   A decidedly non-market-wise common stock will at times move in response to earnings and dividends or expectations that reflect not only peculiarities in the nature of the business but possibly also factors at variance with the long-term *trend* of industrial growth, through circumstances relating to the industry or the company.   The significant movements of stock prices can be delineated for practical purposes by any of the numerous "averages" or index numbers now available.[1]

What has been said of close relationship of the pattern of stock prices, considered broadly, and the pattern of the business cycle in terms of industrial production and trade is not intended to imply that these patterns in terms of monthly or annual data are exactly similar.   We are dealing with *prices* of stocks, whereas the index of business is usually

---

[1] Probably the most accurate of the available measures of prices, in terms of general common stocks and group indexes for the United States, are the index numbers computed by the Cowles Commission for Research in Economics.   Their general index numbers, as well as several of the group indexes, extend back on a monthly basis to 1871.   They are carefully weighted in accordance with outstanding capital stock and are adjusted, where necessary, for stock dividends, split-ups, etc.   These indexes tie in with the somewhat similar indexes of the Standard Statistics Company at 1918 and are thus conveniently available to date.   The Cowles Commission has likewise computed careful indexes of both earnings and dividend rates.   (See Alfred Cowles 3d and Associates, "Common Stock Indexes," 2d ed., Bloomington, Ind., 1939, and Supplements.   See also the *Survey of Current Business*, February, 1942.)

expressed in terms of *volume*. If we chose to express the business cycle in terms of national income or the total value of transactions, we should find that the occasional inflationary and deflationary movements in commodity prices would prevent such a measure from showing as close a comparison with the movements of the stock market as is found in its relationship to business volume. The latter pattern is transmitted to stock prices through the earnings of corporations, particularly their dividends. The variations in earnings tend to be more violent in amplitude than dividend payments or dividend rates per share. In terms of both pattern and amplitude, the average annual dividend rate, or the rates expressed as an index number of changes, reveals the closest agreement with the general movement of stock prices. The disbursement of dividends in the case of most corporations does not, of course, exactly parallel changes in earning power. Dividends are maintained for a while in the face of declining trade activity or commodity prices. Dividends, once omitted, may not be restored until some time after improvement is registered in earnings. The fairly large number of cases in which there is pronounced stability in dividend rates, despite fluctuation in earnings, gives any dividend-rate index considerable stability.

The index of dividend rates on common stocks naturally differs in many respects from the interest-rate pattern. A dividend is not a contractually fixed rate of payment. There is much more variability in average dividends than in average bond yields. In the case of stocks there is no concept comparable with "yield to maturity," as in the case of bonds; there is merely a more or less supposititious "current rate of return" derived by dividing the ruling price of the stock into the annual rate of dividend or the closest estimate of it that can be had. Since both yields on bonds and dividend rates represent forms of return on capital, there must, of course, be some degree of relationship between them, although, as previously stated, the existence of any fixed normal level of relationship is doubtful because of shifting risk and other qualitative factors. When an investor considers the alternative of investing through the purchase of bonds or of stocks, he represents one of the forces that in the long run keep these markets in a semblance of equilibrium but that cause divergence over short periods.[1]

Within short periods of time and through the cyclical movements, there is an alternating tendency in the yield on stocks above and again below the yields on bonds, and this has considerable similarity to the changing relation of over-all business profit rates to interest rates. But we must not overlook the fact that the interest rate has an influence upon

[1] See in this connection the measurements by Leonard P. Ayres in terms of average bond prices as multiples of coupon rates, average stock prices as multiples of current dividends, in issues of the *Cleveland Trust Company Bulletin*.

the price of a stock and hence on stock prices in general. This is because the prevailing rate of interest will represent in some approximate degree the rate at which a given income will be capitalized to obtain the value. Although, of course, the strict "capitalization" formula implies a constant income or fixed rate of return stretching into the future to maturity (or indefinitely in some cases), this cannot be applied to common-stock dividend rates or dividend expectations with the hope of

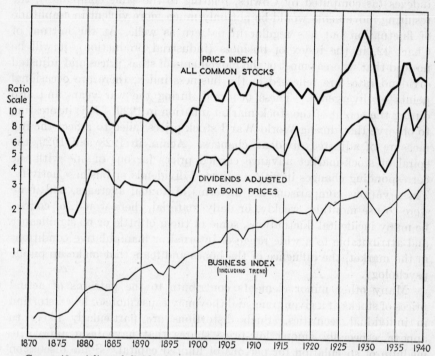

CHART 42.—Adjusted dividends and common-stock prices, 1871–1940. Except in war periods, or when speculative credit is extraordinarily inflated, common-stock average prices move closely in unison with average dividend rates multiplied by an index of high-grade bond prices, which is equivalent to capitalizing the dividends according to the current yield on high-grade corporate bonds.

results that agree exactly with actual quotations. But there is enough applicability of the general principle of capitalization to the case of common stocks to warrant an experiment, and we find that when broad averages of dividend rates are translated into measures of change in average stock prices, the rate of interest *does* contribute to improve the result when compared with the actual price pattern. To put this in another way, if we adjust an index number of dividend rates for a large group of common stocks by an index number of bond yields as a rough measure of changes in capitalization rate, we obtain a pattern that approximates the pattern of average stock prices more perfectly than dividend rates alone.

These results are illustrated in Chart 42, with the use of annual data. The movement of the comprehensive index of stock prices at the top of the chart parallels with surprising consistency the course of the middle curve of dividend rates adjusted by bond yields (with the use of the same data as previously employed). If, instead of dividends, we used earnings indexes (as computed by Cowles, relating to the same companies), the resulting movements would be not only much more violent in amplitude of fluctuation but less regular in pattern as well. At the bottom of Chart 42, in the index of business (industrial production), it will be noticed that whereas most of the movements of stock prices and adjusted dividend rates are reflected in the business index, there are occasional points of divergence. These occurred during the war years and also during the height of the stock-market inflation in 1929. It is interesting to observe that during World War I stock prices failed to reflect the full measure of adjusted dividend changes. Again, in 1928 and 1929, the spiral of stock-market advance carried prices far out of line with the corresponding changes in either adjusted dividends or business activity. These various comparisons are in terms of annual averages, and if we were to use monthly, weekly, or daily material, there would, of course, be many incidental fluctuations, some of them of little or no significance and attributable to a wide range of internal or manipulative conditions in the market, the influence of the hopes and fears that make up public psychology.

Many other minor elements contribute to the patterns of actual prices of stocks at a given time, and they may cause more or less distortion in individual securities. Such distortions are particularly likely to appear, especially among low-price shares that have been a favorite medium of speculation for persons of limited capital. Some discussion of the special factors entering into these fluctuations that are not attributable to fundamental factors or the rate of interest will be of advantage, if for no other reason than that so much mystery and so many dubious hypotheses and trading superstitions have been built up around these phenomena. When we say that stock prices are primarily responsive to adjusted dividends, we recognize that buyers of common stocks do not merely perform an abbreviated mental operation of computing the discounted future value of a known and definite rate of return; rather, they roughly take into consideration what seem to be the probable future industrial trends and the prospective dividends. F. R. Macaulay cites the case of a Wall Street economist who satisfied himself in 1929 that there was really no ceiling to stock prices, because the prospects for annual growth in industrial production and dividends of at least 3 per cent indicated possibilities of a continuing upward trend in dividends that he thought might be logically discounted at 3 per cent per annum.[1]

Although such fantastic long-range prognostication of future dividends is seldom encountered, there is a persistent tendency on the part of those who wish to make quick capital gains from the purchase or short-selling of equities to exaggerate the possibilities both of increases in dividends over relatively short periods or, in the converse case, of declines in dividends and, therefore, prices. These estimates may have no sound basis in the facts of the situation. In the case of a market in which prices fluctuate considerably, there is always a tendency to attract a speculative following. The speculative group may be further divided into two main segments: those who trade the market with relatively moderate financial means (a group frequently referred to in the language of the Street as "the public") and, on the other hand, the much smaller group of professionals and semiprofessionals, which includes also those managers and officers of corporations who are disposed to exploit their positions of responsibility and command of inside information to derive capital gains by frequent purchase and sale of the securities of their companies or (what is still more reprehensible) by affiliation from time to time with pool manipulators of their own stocks.

STOCK MANIPULATION A FACTOR IN CAPITAL FINANCING

In the past there has been considerable deliberate manipulation of stock prices with the assistance or connivance of officers and directors. During the 1920's all these operations were facilitated by the liberal credit facilities made available to speculative groups by a friendly banking system, but financial reform has now virtually eliminated these activities as factors in greatly intensifying market vibrations. Today the amount of deliberate manipulation of stock prices is very greatly restrained, if not, indeed, negligible. The availability of bank credit to speculators in the stock market has become circumscribed in various ways.[2] Stock prices today probably reflect fairly well the combined effects of dividend possibilities, the interest rate as a rough measure of the current capitalizing factor, and the state of general opinion shaped by the current news. But since there may be some who still hark back to the late 1920's to form an opinion of what constitutes a "healthy" or "normally active" stock market and since the reforms that have been made to create a more conservative and more honest market were so persistently denounced in Wall Street and in brokerage circles, we may devote some brief attention to the tricks of the trade to demonstrate why it would be unwise to

[1] Macaulay, *op. cit.*, p. 132.

[2] In 1941 the average amount of outstanding brokerage loans in New York was less than 5 per cent of the volume in the autumn of 1929.

abandon these reforms. In what follows, the reader will imagine himself once again in the atmosphere of the 1920's.

At the outset, let us consider why the average representative of the "public," operating as a trader or speculative investor, in a stock market subject to little effective regulation, was so often led to appraise the current value of common shares at prices so widely at variance with the trend of values as determined mainly by earning power and dividends. First, the average person among the vast throng that crowded the brokerage offices not many years ago was rarely able to secure adequate information regarding earnings. Publicity in corporate affairs has made gratifying progress but the publication of earnings statements at quarterly intervals is a surprisingly recent innovation. It was not until 1910 that the New York Stock Exchange was able to induce corporations listing shares to make quarterly reports. Fifteen years later, the Stock Exchange was still exerting its efforts to encourage companies to make available interim earnings figures, but unfortunately this was still a matter of moral suasion and not a definite prerequisite to the listing of shares on the Exchange. Although practically all companies that have listed shares on the New York Exchange are under agreement to publish annual reports, as late as 1926 only 25 per cent of the active listed domestic companies were under agreement with the New York Stock Exchange to publish earnings at quarterly intervals. A fair degree of progress has been made in this direction, so that by 1931 over 60 per cent of all listed companies were publishing quarterly statements of earnings, and 17 per cent were issuing semiannual statements.[1] At present all newly listed companies must meet requirements with respect to releasing quarterly earnings statements, but the Exchange still adopts a lenient policy toward already listed companies, which, on one pretext or another, refuse to issue such statements or even estimates. Although from an accounting standpoint, quarterly earnings figures can seldom be made completely accurate, particularly in view of various costs which pertain to a full year's operations, the long delay in making public reasonably careful preliminary estimates of earnings has had no fundamental justification. On the other hand, the progress already made in this direction is highly commendable and it has removed one of the great difficulties facing our man in the street who wishes to engage in stock-market dealings.

Our typical speculative investor, however, has encountered another obstacle to realistic appraisal of values, because many officers and directors traded in their own shares or participated in pool manipulation. This whole matter of manipulation continues to be more or less shrouded in mystery, because it has been a practice requiring secrecy. Manipulation of stock prices has been of several types, ranging from small amateur

[1] *New York Stock Exchange Bulletin*, August, 1939.

pools, operating largely on borrowed funds, perhaps without connivance of insiders, to large and wealthy pools having expert managers and operating with option agreements in collusion with company officials. In many corporations, including some of the largest, such collusion has been rare or nonexistent, but for many years there was enough of it to create conditions capable of exaggerating the ups and downs of particular stocks and, occasionally and temporarily, the entire market. This has been particularly true of inside manipulation of the shares of companies with small capitalization or high leverage due to heavy fixed charges in proportion to revenue. It was true also of the shares of companies in the durable-goods industries, where the swings of the business cycle are ordinarily violent and opportunities for tremendous speculative gains on the rise alternate with the risks of enormous losses on the decline when production falls off and earnings collapse.

The primary objective of pool operation was to accumulate quietly a substantial block of stock during a period of business depression or in the very early stages of apparent recovery, to acquire more stock through purchase or exercise of options as prices rose, and at the proper time to attract the "public" into the stock on a more rapidly rising market, so that pool holdings could be "distributed" to speculative investors and probably to some actual investors also at the highest prices possible. In some cases manipulation was intended to "make a market" for new capital issues in the form of stock (and bonds also) or to create a price situation favorable to splitting up shares when those inside the company wished to create a larger potential market at a lower price range either for legitimate financing or for unloading purposes.[1] But the latter price-pegging operations are not the type of manipulative activity to which we are now directing our attention. Temporary price pegging has usually been undertaken by security distributors; outright manipulation has originated principally among the officers and their friends and occasionally among brokerage houses desiring to increase activity in their trading accounts. The manipulative pool usually had access to information regarding existing buying and selling orders of the stock from the books of the so-called "specialists" on the Exchange. These individuals still operate both as brokers and on their own account and in this curious fashion have been able to participate advantageously in pool operations or to provide valuable data. There are also "floor traders," having seats

---

[1] When shares are split in a rising and very active market, the price thereafter may fall not merely because of the proportionate dilution of the stock but because of less favorable factors in the corporation's prospects, which were anticipated when the split-up was arranged. This, however, is not invariably true; some companies have split their stock for legitimate reasons as they reached prices so high that a reasonably broad and continuous market in them was difficult to sustain.

on the Exchange and access to trading information, and these also are to be considered among the groups that have participated in manipulation.[1]

In the typical manipulative operation for the rise, the pool operator might secure options for certain amounts of stock at prices above the current market but well below the level to which the pool would attempt to advance the stock. In this option agreement, frequently made with large holders of the stock, particularly insiders, it was usually stipulated that these holders would not dispose of the stock except as the pool specified. Thus the pool was well protected during its operations for the rise against sudden heavy sales and possibly heavy loss. The pool would also protect itself against any sudden avalanche of selling from the general public by seeing to it that the rise was maintained at an orderly pace in the early stages of operations. Pool managers would occasionally sell shares to depress the market temporarily and discourage the public from enlarging its purchases and potential selling prematurely. As these temporary declines occurred, amateur short sellers would enter the market and depress the price somewhat further than the pool liquidation alone justified, and thus a further reason for market instability developed. Short covering aided the pool in the later stages and helped form the final distribution level.

When we consider the stock market as a whole, much of the price instability emanating from pool activity in individual stocks tended to be washed out, but in sustained bull markets, pool objectives tended to reinforce the general upward sweep of prices. In the late 1920's a great convergence of pool activity drove the market higher than could possibly be explained by any other influences. These pool activities naturally presupposed the ability of numerous small traders to secure liberal brokerage (essentially bank) credit to finance extensive lines of securities on relatively small margins of equity. This thin-equity-margin system has, indeed, been one of the flagrant abuses of both banking and stock trading in the United States. In Great Britain, where speculation of all kinds has long flourished actively, a small group of relatively well-informed professionals and capitalists make up the bulk of such buyers and sellers. But unfortunately, in the United States, long accustomed to a banking system having all sails set to catch the breezes of speculation, the public interest in stock trading grew to tremendous proportions. It was propagated, too, by numerous publications and trading services and the systematic dramatizing of the market's tantalizing glamor.

A curious aspect of this public participation in common-stock dealings has been the manner in which holdings were divided as between investors,

---

[1] Among the activities of pools, the gaining of profits through short selling are by no means unknown, but such objectives were not so common as to distribute a substantial amount of shares from a few hands to many hands on the rise.

insiders, and pools, on the one hand, and the in-and-out speculative holders on the other. Naturally, precise information upon this distribution of ownership is not available, but we do have evidence for a very limited number of individual stocks and for several groups of stocks pointing to the fact that the number of individual holders has varied inversely with the movement of prices. This is perhaps the most important feature to observe in connection with manipulation. Although this phenomenon is not necessarily related to manipulation, it obviously suggests that when prices of stocks are relatively high they tend to be in relatively few hands; and when the prices are low, the public interest in them has usually reached a maximum. This reveals, not that all officers and directors have systematically engaged pools to distribute their shares at high prices or that they have entered into option agreements with pools to assure themselves various levels of possible profit but that there has been a transfer of huge amounts of stock from officers to the public as prices reached high levels and from the public back to the insiders after prices touched bottom. In these operations pools have probably not been the predominant factor, but they have frequently rendered the process much easier.

Another closely related aspect of public participation in the stock market is the striking tendency for the volume of sales (both of individual stocks and on the market as a whole) to vary closely with the movements of prices. The peaks of the price swings almost invariably are also high peaks in the turnover, and the lowest prices mark periods of desultory transactions. If we analyze the dealings in greater detail over a long period, we find ground for the conclusion that when prices generally are at or near peak levels (in relation to their broad underlying trend), the proportion of transactions contributed by the lower grade stocks—the "cats and dogs"—is almost always relatively high, whereas in the price troughs, when total volume of sales is usually small, the activity is concentrated much more heavily in the investment grade stocks and the so-called "market leaders." This is another way of expressing the general principle that the crowd buys not only much more stock but also more of the *mediocre* stocks as the upward price wave reaches its crest. When prices subside, the more discriminating investors do their purchasing of prime equities. In so doing, they occasionally take advantage of the fact that victims of the pool operators, who purchased stocks on thin margins in the previously glorified atmosphere of rosy press releases, are having their holdings sold out by the brokers as margins threaten to be impaired. During such a periodic housecleaning of brokerage accounts the speculative holders are thinned out rapidly, and sales of stock may be temporarily heavy and indicative of rapid liquidation.

One of the most accurate "internal" tests of the market's position, that is, the extent to which holdings are on a cash or a liberal margin basis, as compared with a thinly margined mass of holdings, is found in the tendency of the turnover to dwindle as intervals of liquidation dry up and the market finally comes into a position that is regarded as a strong "technical" situation. At this point prices are usually lower than a strict appraisal of earnings and adjusted dividends would warrant, but such a quiet period of apparent solidity, followed by some recuperation in values, may again be followed by still further and more serious liquidations if the intermediate trend of business is becoming impaired and a recession in industrial activity is broadening into a major decline of several years. Thus these internal indications of the market strength after prices have declined may be deceptive unless supplemented by study and interpretation of the external factors relating to production and earning power.

There is no exact way of *currently* distinguishing between the minor fluctuations and the major cycles in stock prices, but for our present purpose we may roughly distinguish the two types of movements by saying that the minor changes occur over periods of several months, and the major changes are those that might irregularly trace over several years the pattern of the industrial cycle to which the stock market will always more or less conform. If we confine our attention to the very short fluctuations, such as those that occur from day to day or week to week, we encounter confusing and essentially meaningless vibrations that may run counter to both the minor and the major drifts, some of them incapable of rational explanation. The place of pool manipulation in these patterns has probably been more important in the framework of the minor movements, although the major pattern itself was occasionally reinforced and exaggerated by concurrent pool manipulation in a given direction in numerous stocks.

There is a powerful psychological influence in the rising prices of stocks that has been given prominence by adroit publicity and expert dramatization, combined with an expanding volume of transactions. It is the kind of stimulus that creates irrational propensity on the part of amateurs in finance. Although common sense would always dictate the purchase of any securities subject to market fluctuations when they are relatively cheap in relation to the broad trend of business activity, or in terms of the relation of prices to the earnings and dividends, there is the temptation to join the crowd and make purchases of stock under the impulse of the buzzing board-room atmosphere, the lure of future profit from anticipated advances, and the invitations to buy coming from tipsters and "market betters." Hence, when the stock market in the past was exceptionally active, prices were rising, and the manipulators were preparing to unload, a situation was created that favored the operations of still other groups, such as investment trusts.

Many of the investment trusts that were hastily put together in the late 1920's sought to distribute large blocks of stock, not through the usual pool channels but through trust shares. These were ostensibly for the purpose of enabling the small investor to spread his holdings over numerous equities held in trust, including the blocks to be distributed. The year 1929 provided an admirable opportunity for such operations, and it fostered the distribution of a vast amount of stock, particularly of the holding companies being engineered in the public-utility field and to some extent in railroads. The stupendous rise in the market in that year cannot be understood without awareness of this systematic distributive mechanism that floated buoyantly on an ocean of bank credit.

COMMENTS ON THE DOW THEORY

The mind of the individual stock purchaser in the midst of such a swirl of dazzling activity becomes subject to peculiar aberrations. He comes to believe that the usually accepted rules limiting prices to some rational relation to earnings no longer hold true. Times are now different. Stock prices seem to rise so much faster than business activity would justify that certainly there must be some powerful new factor in the situation, known perhaps to the omniscient insiders, which will put the market very much higher in the future. One should purchase before the news is out and it is too late! At this juncture it is pointed out that in accordance with the so-called "Dow-theory,"[1] industrial-stock average and railroad-stock average are "confirming each other" on the rise; both averages have passed preceding peaks so that there is prospective strength in the price advance. This idea of one group of stock prices being used to confirm another has some basis in logic, but usually it is difficult, if not impossible, to determine whether the confirmation of movement signifies something for merely a few weeks or for a major cycle.

The Dow theory of market behavior so widely referred to by traders emphasizes the supposition that those who "make" the market know all the facts and are able to look far ahead into the future to give the market

---

[1] Developed originally by Charles H. Dow, one of the founders of the Dow-Jones Company, publishers of financial papers and news reports and ticker service. The original principles were elaborated and somewhat revised by W. P. Hamilton in "The Stock Market Barometer," published in 1922. Many other commentators and elaborators of the Dow principle have since appeared and disappeared with the passing years. Today the Dow theory is held in various forms by a wide variety of commentators and market observers, whose principal contribution to the subject is that they disagree with one another at every stage of the market and are always able to diagnose the trend of prices after it has revealed itself.

its proper price position at all times.   Here again there is undoubtedly an element of truth in the Dow principle.   Those who were active in making prices in the heyday of stock trading through organized manipulative efforts or through their internal knowledge of corporate affairs were perhaps the ones who really did do much to establish market trends in leading equities.   But at the top and bottom levels of the market swings, prices have revealed the true pattern of the coming phase of the business cycle only in an uncertain, confusing way.   Even insiders can rarely look ahead with respect to industrial trends more than a few weeks or months.   The supposition by accurately informed persons that stock prices are always in close conformity with these trends and prospects has proved to be a common source of popular misconception and investment error.   It has created the impression that however fantastic prices might seem, they were always "justified."

As a means of guiding either investment or speculation, the underlying principle has the great defect of encouraging action in the wrong direction.   The Dow principle interprets the ability of both the industrial and the railroad groups to advance definitely above some previous peak as a bullish signal.   This means that the purchaser of stocks following this principle too closely will accustom himself to purchasing *on the rise* rather than on the decline.   He must reverse himself frequently, for the turns indicated by Dow may be very short.   When the railroad and industrial stocks have both confirmed a declining "trend," purchases will be delayed in accordance with this principle, and this may be helpful; but, on the other hand, the fact that there may be no confirmation of an impending decline for weeks or months may prevent a holder of stocks from selling when he should sell.   He acts *with* the market and *with* the crowd, not *against* it.

There are scores of other devices that have been used by traders, all resting upon the mere surface phenomenon of price movements.   The trading element that seeks to exploit short turns usually disregards the factors in the industrial or credit situation, and the temptation is strong to rely upon wishful thinking rather than on economic analysis. For this reason it is extremely difficult to discover a person who over any extended period of time has actually made substantial capital gains by trading in the stock market.   Almost all the gains have been eventually in the hands of the brokers, insiders, and participants in successful pool performances.   Both the banks and the brokers have usually (and quite legitimately) protected themselves against losses on collateral loans because of the margins of safety agreed upon and strictly maintained. The sudden impairment of this margin protection has usually been possible by the prompt sale of the collateral and the wiping out of thousands of small speculators overnight.

ELEMENTS HELPFUL IN MARKET APPRAISAL

The technical position of the market, therefore, has to do primarily with the extent to which, broadly speaking, common stocks are in strong hands or in weak hands. A vast army of traders and speculative investors who have accumulated shares at high prices make the market "technically weak," because it requires little in the way of unfavorable business or political news to start a spiral of liquidation, particularly if these holdings are poorly protected by thin margins. The market is said to be "technically strong" when there is no appreciable overhang of potential selling in prospect and when the holding of shares is firmly in the hands of long-term investors, who will hold so long as the status of business or politics is broadly favorable, and in the hands of corporation managers who view the future in a favorable, even though dim, light and are not inclined to entertain the thought of selling out. When the market is thus in a strong position and prices are perhaps below the level that will ultimately be revealed as the underlying drift, unfavorable news will have little effect upon prices, and at times this is demonstrated to a remarkable degree that puzzles the layman. This, in fact, is one way of testing the solidity of market prices. On the other hand, a weak technical position will respond very sensitively to unfavorable news, but it is not the news or the unfavorable developments somewhere that weaken the market. These merely precipitate what would inevitably happen as the result of a topheavy situation.[1]

In view of the fact that there is such extensive reliance, even today, among traders and some investors on the half truth that the underlying market trend can be deduced from *price behavior alone*, it is well to emphasize that correct interpretation of changes in the volume of turnover are probably more important than price changes and should not be ignored. To read the ticker tape or merely watch price quotations through charts and deceptive imaginary "trend lines" is all part of the superficial snap judgments of the rarely successful trader. Even the conservative investor, who desires to purchase stock at reasonable levels and to protect himself when exceptional declines are in the offing, should not overlook the fact that rational study of the technical position of the market can be helpful. It is capable of tolerably accurate appraisal *if the volume of trading and the price movements are correlated in the proper*

---

[1] The reader will find further detail relating to the stock market and its functioning in the following sources: "The Security Market, Findings and Recommendations of a Special Staff of the Twentieth Century Fund," directed by A. L. Bernheim, New York, 1935; J. A. Ross, Jr., "Speculation, Stock Prices, and Industrial Fluctuations," New York, 1938; W. F. Hickernell, "What Makes Stock Market Prices?", New York, 1932; J. T. Flynn, "Security Speculation," New York, 1934; Kemper Simpson, "The Margin Trader," New York, 1938.

fashion. The following propositions may be helpful in the application of this principle.

1. If we disregard the fluctuations from day to day, a rise in average stock-market prices, accompanied by a perceptible rising tendency in the volume of turnover of shares, is evidence of strength in the market that will probably continue at least somewhat further. The higher the total turnover of shares rises the more likely it becomes that an important turning point and reversal in prices is imminent.

2. Near the top of almost every substantial rally in stock prices extending over several months or even several years, there will come one or more periods of temporary reversal, irregularity, or hesitation, at which time the volume of turnover will decline sharply. If prices then continue to advance but the volume of transactions no longer has the momentum previously established, it is an almost conclusive indication that the top of the principal movement has been established.

3. As prices decline rather broadly and persistently, the lowest point of the movement prior to the reversal into another rising cycle will probably not be established until there has been a period of relatively heavy liquidation. The amount of this liquidation will depend upon the degree of speculation supported by margined stock, but the selling by frightened or discouraged investors usually contributes considerably to these waves of liquidation. An investor is not warranted in purchasing broadly in common stocks until there is clear evidence that price declines following a wave of liquidation no longer call forth sales of stocks *and also* that thereafter any significant rallies are not followed by declines involving a rising momentum in the volume of turnover. Once this has been observed, the basis for renewed advance is usually well established. It is desirable to observe the price and volume momentum (rate of change) in both weekly and monthly form.

4. The activity can be measured in terms of the *breadth* of the market, that is, the percentage of the listed shares that appears on the market for purchase or sale during any given period. So long as a rise in prices is accompanied by an increasing breadth in the number of issues that appear among the transactions, the market may be regarded as reasonably firm. If, however, the breadth index rises while prices droop, or vice versa, it is an indication that manipulation is taking place somewhere and that the market lacks balance. If, on the other hand, prices are declining but the breadth index is moving contrary to prices, it may indicate the beginnings of a liquidating movement that may not yet be registered in the volume of transactions.

5. In the transactions there may also be found an important clue to the *quality* of the securities that are being bought and sold. This may be conveniently tested by observing, during weekly or monthly intervals,

to what extent the current transactions are concentrated in stocks that are obviously of low investment caliber as compared with the substantial market leaders.

Ratios developed from this principle, after small fluctuations have been smoothed out, will indicate when the general market has reached a stage at which the quality of the transactions has deteriorated into cats and dogs (the sign of an approaching rally top) and the periods at which activity in this class of security is at a minimum and when the better securities are being quietly accumulated by the discriminating and those fully conversant with the industrial fundamentals.

In view of the fact that so much of the fundamental and basic information regarding industrial conditions, corporate earnings, and political policies reaches the observer or investor more or less tardily, the writer considers that it is entirely legitimate and helpful to utilize sound statistical evidence of the technical and internal condition of the stock market as an auxiliary guide supplementing the more basic analysis of the industrial drift, the commodity price-level prospects, effects of legislation, etc.

THE INFLUENCE OF CORPORATE CAPITAL ON THE BUSINESS CYCLE

We are now in a position to observe the relationship between the broader fluctuations in the prices of common stocks and the major cyclical movements in the value of new issues of capital in the form of equities. Chart 43 illustrates this in much the same fashion as for the bond market. The index of stock prices at the top of the chart is the comprehensive Cowles-Standard Statistics index, in monthly form, beginning at 1906. The middle curve represents a smoothing (as in the case of the bond issues) of the monthly totals of reported new capital issues in the form of common and preferred stock, insofar as these can be obtained from the estimates of the financial journals.[1] Although the smoothing of the data to iron out the violent and erratic month-to-month situations introduces some very minor distortions, in the sense that it is difficult to locate the exact month of peak or bottom of a movement, this curve does record clearly the pulse of the stock issue cycles. It is apparent that there is a high degree of concurrent movement in the stock issues and the major cyclical fluctuations in prices. The relationship is indeed much closer than in

---

[1] Beginning at 1906 and through 1917, the data represent *New York Journal of Commerce* estimates; thereafter, the data of the *Commercial and Financial Chronicle*. Prior to 1906 both stock and bond issues in monthly form may be roughly approximated by L. P. Ayres statistics of listings of these issues on the Exchange. Ayres' figures for stocks go back as far as 1884; the bond listings go back to 1863. There is some question as to how far the listings are equivalent to new issues, inasmuch as some listings occur long after the date of issue and numerous securities are issued that are never listed (*cf.* Ayres, "Turning Points of Business Cycles").

the case of bond prices and bond issues.   The lower section of the chart
again shows the index of business in terms of both the money value of
trade and the physical index of industrial production.   The much closer
relation of stock prices and new stock issues to the index of business
volume as compared with the index of trade value is, of course, to be
expected.

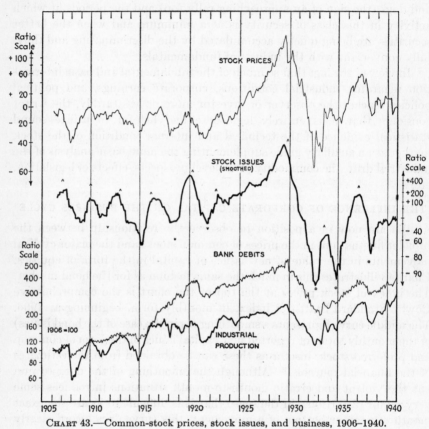

CHART 43.—Common-stock prices, stock issues, and business, 1906–1940.

It is apparent, then, that stock issues tend to be relatively large on
rising markets, whereas falling markets are probably the cause of equally
emphatic decline in new stock offered.   The exact timing relation between
stock prices and new issues to stock is rather difficult to define; there
appears to be no uniform tendency for cyclical turning points in new issues
to precede by any significant interval the corresponding turns in stock
prices.   If we bring new issues of stock (smoothed out) into comparison
with new issues of bonds, as in the preceding chart, we find occasional
cases in which the turning point of a cyclical movement in bond issues

precedes the similar turning point in stock issues; but this is not a uniform tendency. There are cases in which the drift of offerings of new capital in bonds indicates no clear tendency matching that of the stock market. Since it has frequently happened that the cyclical turns in bond prices precede those in stock prices and since the new issues of bonds are influenced to some extent by prices, the activities of the bond distributors have at times begun to fall off ahead of the distributing operations in new stocks. But the sensitiveness of the bond market is more consistently apparent in prices than in issues.

Since new issues of both bonds and stocks have frequently preceded the corresponding cycles in business activity,[1] the view has become widely accepted that the course of the business cycle itself is powerfully influenced, in a causal sense, by the ebb and flow of corporate capital in the form of bonds and shares. Foremost among the protagonists of this opinion is Leonard P. Ayres, whose study "Turning Points in Business Cycles" (1939) is largely devoted to statistical illustration of the opinion. Ayres has sought to establish the further belief that it is the motivation arising from decisions of business managers rather than the changing rate of income flow or capital formation on the part of consumers that brings about the undulations of the business cycle. We have already furnished evidence that this view is not wholly in accord with the facts and overstates the case. Not only has the value of capital that has passed through the mortgage market in the sweeping ebb and flow of the building cycle been far greater than the total funds moving into new corporate securities but the ebb and flow in creation of mortgages for home building alone has ordinarily preceded the cycles of business activity by longer intervals than in the case of new issues of corporate securities. There is fairly broad evidence that the dominating forces of cyclical disturbance have usually reached the industrial corporations through the financing of consumer durables, and *this* has created the main cyclical incentive to expand plant. This does not necessarily mean that there is always a close correlation of cycles in consumer income with such financing or that the income moves first and the financing follows; we have already pointed out that it is not so much consumer *income* as the

---

[1] The reader is again cautioned regarding this principle, since we have already seen that in 1930 and 1931 interest rates and bond prices did not furnish an accurate clue to the direction of the business cycle. It is also apparent that in recent years the stock market has failed to precede in its decisive turning points the corresponding cyclical changes in the business index, probably because the market is now more responsive to the retarding influence of widely distributed stock ownership and the operations of investment trusts that change positions rather less promptly than is possible on the part of individuals, and because manipulation is much less prevalent than formerly. This situation is further discussed in Chapter 22 in connection with business forecasting.

movement of *people* and the retarding of construction by wars that have been the basis of many of the great business-cycle movements.   But it should be added that the promotion of new forms of major capital equipment, such as transportation facilities, has also contributed to the pattern of the business cycle, and security issues associated with these innovations in the development stage are to be considered among the causal elements. Ayres is correct, also, to the extent that we may consider very rapid expansion in stock financing as an accelerating factor in the rising phase of industrial activity and an abrupt, sustained decline in corporate bond issues as a possible factor precipitating the collapse of overextended positions in stocks, commodities, and the downturn of the cycles of relatively moderate intensity, in which such speculation formed the main stimulus.

Chart 43 clearly shows that a great deal of the new stock is launched on the high tide of prices.   It appears rather consistently to have required a glamorous atmosphere and bullish psychology of a strong market to induce or enable corporations to float additional stocks.   In this way the stock market appears more sensitive as an accelerating element in boom conditions than in the case of the bond market.   It is unfortunate that so much of our equity financing has been apparently a product of stock-market inflations, intensified by credit manipulation and market manipulation, although from the standpoint of the issuing corporations this has meant ability to sell new shares at higher prices than would otherwise be obtained, and the capital has therefore been obtained on favorable terms.   It was the ability to sell enormous quantities of new stock in the late 1920's that enabled industrial corporations to reduce debt, repay bank loans, and develop strong working-capital positions.   From the standpoint of investors, however, the ultimate result was to create suspicion and hostility toward common stocks as mediums of investment, since markets crowded at high levels with new issues will fall farther than if new capital in stock could be issued in a steadier flow.   The historical picture presents much food for thought on questions that are basic in our economic system.   How can the flow of capital into productive use be divorced from unessential market gyrations?   How can legitimate, constructive, expansion or initiation of worth-while new enterprise obtain equity financing without the false stimuli to the price structure that forces investors to pay exorbitant prices for securities that may be thoroughly sound and desirable but that soon decline in value?

In the case of corporate borrowing, we find reason to believe that the tendency of bond prices to decline from cyclical peaks ahead of stocks results in the fact that corporations seeking new capital in the bond market find it difficult to obtain the optimum advantages of low interest rates, since it has usually been only in the very early period of cyclical expansion that there existed both low yields and a rising bond market. Once bond prices start to decline (usually long before the peak in business), even though yields are low, the borrowing company finds it increasingly difficult to float large issues at low cost, and it is remarkable that so large a proportion of bond financing has been done on an interest basis highly unfavorable to the borrowers. All this shows the incidental undesirable effects of marked cyclical instability in both the bond and stock markets, even though we do not regard either as the prime movers of the general cycle.

As in the case of other aspects of American finance already noted, reform legislation has introduced important changes in security speculation and flotation, and we should regard the foregoing description of manipulative practice and other chicanery that have existed in connection with securities sold to the public as having historical rather than current significance. It is important to understand the steps already taken to rationalize these markets.

SECURITIES AND EXCHANGE COMMISSION AS REGULATOR IN SECURITY MARKETS

The important legislative steps taken by the Federal Government in the interest of sounder and more honest security finance may be considered as having originated in the Securities Act of 1933. This was followed by the National Securities Exchange Act of 1934, having to do with the mechanism of the securities markets. In 1935 came legislation regulating public-utility holding companies. Still further legislation was passed in 1940, bringing within the scope of Federal scrutiny the operations of investment companies and investment advisers. We shall first summarize the changes that have come about in the operations of organized security markets. The regulatory functions were placed in the hands of a new agency known as the Securities and Exchange Commission. Although the functions of this Commission relating to trading and operating practices are but a segment of its far-reaching responsibilities, we may observe these first as they bear upon the moderating of speculative fluctuations. We shall then turn our attention to the broader matters of security issue and regulation of the agencies that have played a prominent part in bond and stock financing and investing.

The Securities and Exchange Commission acquired authority to regulate stock-exchange practices through the requirement that all stock exchanges be licensed by the Federal Government.[1] The licensing of the exchanges was a step in the direction of affording greater publicity, not

---

[1] Even over-the-counter trading in securities has been brought within the authority of the Commission in the interest of thwarting fraudulent promotions.

only as to character of transactions but also as to the affairs of the corporations whose securities are listed. No securities may now be listed on exchanges unless they are registered with the Commission. This requires disclosure of detailed facts regarding the financial structure of the company, the technical characteristics of their securities, and the identity of all officers and directors and those owners of the securities holding 10 per cent or more of the equity. Corporations must disclose whether officers enter into options with regard to the stock of their companies. Each officer, director, or holder of 10 per cent or more of the registered stock must file a monthly statement with the Commission showing all transactions and the amount of securities held. This information is made public after some delay.

Obviously this is a far-reaching and effective restraint upon stock manipulation by pools, since the cooperation with insiders that most pools have relied upon in conducting their operations is no longer readily accomplished. Manipulative operations are further discouraged through the provision that officers, directors, and owners of 10 per cent or more of the shares who realize profit from purchases or sales within periods of six months or less must turn over such profits to the corporation. The Commission maintains a close watch of the ticker tape, and its experts have from time to time detected peculiarities in the behavior of prices or the volume of transactions in various stocks leading to the prosecution of manipulative operators. Even the milder and perhaps legitimate forms of manipulation associated with "preparing a market" for new issues or stabilizing the price of rather inactive stocks are brought within the purview of Commission observation and possible discipline. The practice of short selling, which was given exaggerated importance during the collapsing market of the 1930's, has been circumscribed by the requirement that short sales may not be made except at prices slightly higher than the last recorded sale on a registered exchange.[1]

[1] The Commission publishes daily releases showing, among other data, the short sales and regular sales and purchases in terms of number of shares on the New York Stock Exchange. This information, although somewhat tardy, is nevertheless useful in showing the expert analyst of the market the nature of the transactions.

The original Securities and Exchange Act provided for a clear-cut division of functions as between dealers or underwriters in securities and members of a stock exchange. This would have abolished the existence of "specialists" on the floor of an exchange, who have acted both as brokers and as buyers and sellers on their own account. Much of the criticism of the exchange mechanism, particularly as it relates to the New York Stock Exchange, has centered upon the long-established permission given under Exchange rules to members who combined the functions of acting as brokers and also trading for their own account. Many of these floor traders acted as specialists in particularly active stocks, keeping records of the various orders "off the market," and there has long been a suspicion that at times specialists have used their confidential information to their own advantage, perhaps at the expense of price

MARGINAL REQUIREMENTS REVISED BY FEDERAL RESERVE BOARD

Still another important adjunct of security speculation has been brought under control in authority given the Federal Reserve Board to supervise the minimum margins permitted in speculative transactions. The rules of the New York Stock Exchange in the past were unduly liberal as to the margins that brokers require for their protection in extending credit to customers. In setting minimum requirements prior to 1933, the Exchange did so by suggestion rather than definite edict, and when, in 1933, definite rules were laid down, the percentage of margin was expressed as a ratio to the *debit balance* of the customer rather than as a ratio to the *market value* of the securities involved. This had the effect of allowing brokers to extend credit on margins as low as 25 or even 20 per cent of market value. The Reserve Board began in 1934 with the requirement of 25 per cent minimum margin, expressed in terms of market value and applying to all registered securities.[1]   It was further

---

stability. On the other hand, it has been contended that they provide a useful function in preserving continuity of market quotations and thus avoiding wide gaps between successive recorded prices. The Act as passed, however, provided merely for a study of the matter by the Commission, and thus far policy has not been definitely crystallized. The Commission found from a study of combined broker-dealer functions that nearly one-fourth of the total volume of all trading on the large exchanges was done by exchange members for their own accounts, presumably on margin. At present the Commission is working out under the broad authority delegated to it certain rules intended to prevent undue influence upon prices of the various types of exchange members, so that without specific legislative enactment, these matters are probably now well within the control of the Commission.

These features of American Stock Exchange mechanism differ from what is found in the London securities market, where dealers and brokers have long been strictly separated with regard to the type of business performed. But the greater decorum and freedom from mass hysteria that has long characterized the London Stock Exchange does not arise from this separation as much as it arises from more fundamental characteristics of British finance generally. The lay public does not figure appreciably in London security transactions. Brokers do not advertise or solicit business and do not have branch offices. Short-term trading is decidedly limited and, indeed, is discouraged by a tax upon transfers of all securities. The operations are primarily of an investment nature, although speculation does sometimes become rampant in particular situations and among more or less professional operators.

[1] In 1909, the investigating committee, of which Charles Evans Hughes was chairman, suggested that a minimum equity margin for brokerage loans be set at 20 per cent of the *value* of the securities. But the New York Stock Exchange did not adopt this suggestion and contented itself with efforts to influence members through moral suasion to adopt more conservative margin practice. When, in August, 1933, the Exchange finally made effective a rule that the minimum margin in case of a debit balance of more than five thousand dollars was to be 30 per cent (or 50 per cent for balances owing to the broker under five thousand dollars), the actual margin percentages of market value were to be, respectively, only 23 per cent and 33⅓ per cent. These percentages were, in fact, not far above the prevailing rates during the 1920's

provided, however, that if stock purchased on margin rose, a broker's customer was not to be allowed to "pyramid" his credit, a practice that had undoubtedly created badly overextended positions and periods of stress when weakly margined accounts were sold out. This was done by providing that additional credit could not be available until a substantial rise in market value occurred.

Early in 1936 the Reserve Board, observing a vigorous upward movement in the stock market, ruled that pyramiding would not be permitted until the margin of equity had reached 55 per cent of market value, and soon thereafter a flat requirement of 55 per cent margin in all cases was provided. When the market reversed in the autumn of 1937, the Federal Reserve minimum margin requirement was revised to 40 per cent. The new margin requirements have tended to reduce the amount of public participation in stock-market trading by restricting what has undoubtedly been one of the worst features of capitalism—overtrading on thin equity. This is bad enough in legitimate business, but the practice has been a source of unnecessary fluctuation in security values and destruction of personal savings when applied to speculative operations guided by inadequate information and subject always to the vagaries of mass psychology and the hidden tricks of manipulation.[1]

The general result of the Federal Reserve control of margin practices thus far seems to have been to hold the range of stock prices within a narrower compass, to reduce the volume of speculative turnover, and to create a "thinner" condition of the market under ordinary conditions.

and early 1930's, but during the earlier history of stock-market trading in the United States, equity margins as low as 10 per cent are said to have been fairly prevalent in New York.

[1] An additional feature of the Federal Reserve supervision of margin practice extends to modification of the selling out of security collateral by brokers to protect their positions when prices decline. At present, when the debit balance of the customer to his broker exceeds the allowable 60 per cent of current market value of the securities, the customer is allowed three days to make up the deficiency as protection to the broker. Previously the broker used his discretion in selling margin collateral and frequently did so on such short notice that the customer was powerless to prevent action. As a result, there were excessive waves of selling in a weak market, which reinforced the downward movement as further margins became endangered. This was probably a more important factor in the cumulative momentum of declining markets than the total amount of influence contributed by short selling. In selling short there is automatically an accumulated necessity for purchase, but in the selling out of margin stock there is no such accumulation of buying orders. The higher margin requirements also extend to the activities of floor traders and specialists who previously had enjoyed very liberal treatment in the matter of permissible debit balances. This is probably in the direction of introducing greater stability in prices, although it does at times restrict the continuity of the market insofar as this may depend upon the ability or willingness of floor traders to operate for their own account and thereby create conditions bringing bids and offers closer together.

Although frequently of some disadvantage to the investor in making his purchases or sales, a more stable condition has been introduced for the benefit of the conservative investor who is primarily interested in preserving capital and obtaining a reasonable rate of return.   From the standpoint of the banks, the prevailing rules have very definitely reduced the volume of credit used in speculation.   Although some bankers have regretted this shrinkage in what formerly was a highly lucrative and essentially safe form of bank-credit extension,[1] the fact remains that one of the most flagrant temptations for banks to use the funds of their customers plus their own credit potentialities in unstable and speculative ways has been considerably restricted.

Space does not permit discussion of Federal regulation of speculation in the commodity "futures" markets, but it should be added that somewhat similar limitations have been imposed in those directions.   The more important short-term advances and declines in such favorite items of speculation as wheat, cotton, sugar, etc., are now principally produced by announcements from Washington having to do with production or other quota revisions.   As World War II approached, all these forms of speculation were subject to progressive Federal restrictions.

SECURITIES ACT OF 1933

We now turn to regulation of the issue of securities.   We previously observed a tendency for the momentum of new stock financing to correlate with stock-price movements.   If the recent regulation of stock trading may be considered as infusing greater stability in the market, we might conclude that this in itself would place some restraint upon wide fluctuations in the flow of new stock issues.   Similarly, it might be expected that the "stabilization" of interest rates at a very low level through political policy and large gold supplies would in some degree tend to eliminate a part of the bond issues that might otherwise have been offered, through unwillingness of investors to pay persistently high prices for securities of this type.   But these particular factors cannot easily be separated from other, and probably more potent, influences that have been brought to bear upon all new capital financing in the United States. Foremost among these factors is the far more stringent control exercised by the Securities and Exchange Commission over new issues of securities by virtue of the Securities Act of 1933.   We shall outline very briefly the manner in which the Commission is now empowered to scrutinize and control the flow of new corporate capital.

The Securities Act of 1933 was the outgrowth of elaborate investigations directed by Ferdinand Pecora, acting under the chairmanship of Senator Fletcher of the Committee on Banking and Currency.   The

---

[1] That is, safe for the banks and the brokers but not for the customers.

investigators were impressed by evidence that the marketing of new securities was usually dominated by the pressure to sell rather than by any propensity to investigate or to base decisions upon complete information. The bill that resulted from these studies of the creation and merchandising of securities emphasized the thesis that the security buying public was entitled to all the facts concerning a security and the corporation it represented, and it was also entitled to information about the interest of underwriters and distributors. There was an expressed desire (possibly somewhat exaggerated) to eliminate fraudulent and dangerously unsound securities from the market. It was apparently supposed that by making all new capital offerings adhere to a procedure providing for full disclosure of all pertinent facts, the degree of risk might be more readily ascertained, and the process of raising capital funds would be divested of its more speculative and reckless features. This was doubtless suggested by the tremendous abuses that had attended the flood of holding-company financing in the late 1920's and by the study of the British Companies' Act, under which the raising of capital in the London market had for many years been accomplished with less chicanery and loss to investors than had been evident in the United States.

The Securities Act provides that any person or corporation proposing to offer a new issue of securities for sale publicly in interstate commerce must first place before the Securities and Exchange Commission[1] a statement regarding the securities known as a "registration statement." This procedure departs from previous precedent mainly in the elaborate detail that the statement must contain and the equally elaborate summarization that must be incorporated in the prospectus, through which alone any such security offering is formally made. The procedure is enforced with drastic penalties in the nature of civil liabilities and criminal liabilities, as well, if material omissions or misstatements are found in the registration statement or the prospectus. It requires that in all cases the registration statement must remain on file with the Commission during a "waiting period" of several days before the actual sale can be undertaken.[2] The form of the registration statement is prescribed by the Commission and must be strictly adhered to. In the statement there must appear a description of the business of the issuer, its history and organization; description of its plants, properties, and capital structure to the last detail; full information regarding the management, remuneration of officers and directors, and identity of

---

[1] As first administered, the Federal Trade Commission was the agency charged with the execution of the Act.

[2] The Securities Act does not apply to the offerings of governmental bodies in the United States. Issues of railroad securities are also exempt from the provisions of the Securities Act; the Interstate Commerce Commission supervises such issues.

principal stockholders; descriptions, terms, provisions of the securities to be offered for sale; underwriting terms, the names of the underwriters and the nature of any options that may be granted to them. There are also required balance sheets, profit-and-loss statements, and other financial statements covering a period of years sufficient to disclose the picture of the financial position of the issuer, together with the consents of experts to the use of their reports in the registration statement.[1] Among the exhibits are included copies of all indentures, contracts, guarantees, agreements, and patents.

The prospectus, filed along with the registration statement, must be given to every person to whom the security is formally offered for sale and to every purchaser of the security at or before the time of sale. Since so large a proportion of the corporate securities are offered for sale in a market that is interstate in character, these various requirements may be considered as covering a very high proportion of all the new business capital that is sought through security issues. In the event that the process of registration discloses irregularities or deficiencies that are not corrected, the Commission may prevent the sale of the securities through a stop order, and public hearings may be held to determine if the deficiencies actually exist. These powers to obstruct the issue of any securities involving deficiencies or omissions in the filing of information place with the Commission far greater powers than have ever been exercised by any of the state commissions. In order to be listed on any registered stock exchange, securities must in all cases pass through the process of formal registration with the Commission.[2]

One of the motives in this legislation was to effect a change in a practice of long standing whereby an investment banking house would attach itself to a corporation and become virtually a permanent financial medium for raising capital, especially loan capital. It has been felt that such a relationship has involved, in many cases, the virtual domination of

[1] See the "Handbook to the Registration Record," issued by the Securities and Exchange Commission, May 22, 1937, and later amendments.

[2] Some idea of the detail required to be filed in a registration statement for a new or unseasoned enterprise may be gathered from the following questions, contained in the general form for such issues: How frequent and how complete are its reports to stockholders? Who are the accountants, and what is the scope of their audit? What has been the dividend history? Are any lawsuits pending? Can substitutions be made in properties that are securities for funded debt? What options exist with regard to the proposed issue? *In detail*, what are the purposes for which the funds to be obtained will be used? Who are the principal stockholders of the issuing company? What underwriters, if any, control or are controlled by the issuing company? Are any securities being offered to anyone at special prices? What payments have been or are to be made to promoters? What amounts are to be paid for property to be acquired with the proceeds from this issue? From whom are these properties to be purchased? What interest have the "insiders" in property to be acquired?

a company's financial and even operating policies by an investment house or banking group.   Such relationships may also have resulted in a higher cost of financing to the corporation through the power of the financing house to set what it considered a fair level as the purchase price and the selling price of a particular issue.   This matter of middleman spread was given considerable attention, both in the Congressional hearings leading up to the Securities Act of 1933 and in the deliberations of the Securities and Exchange Commission since that time.   From these observations there has developed a further regulatory principle introducing into corporate financing the type of competitive bidding that has long been used in municipal financing.

It was during the period when the present Justice William O. Douglas was Chairman of the SEC that his strong views on this subject became a matter of wide discussion and controversy in the financial centers.   It was his conviction that all new corporate issues require competitive bidding, whereby bankers would not so easily be able to maintain continuing and exclusive relationship with an issuing company.   When this idea was actually subjected to experiment in 1941, it had the rather curious result of bringing about such keen competition between large insurance companies, on the one hand, and the investment bankers, on the other, in bidding for several important corporate issues, that the insurance companies acquired huge blocks of the offerings for themselves, and the individual investors and other institutions found themselves frozen out of the market.   It is therefore possible that this type of merchandising may favor the very large investing institutions at the expense of the rest of the public.   The insurance companies, which ordinarily retain their investments until maturity, are in position to accept a smaller net return than would be true of many of the other kinds of investing institutions and certainly individuals.   Carried to the limits conceived by Justice Douglas, it is quite possible that this competitive bidding system might even throw onto the smaller investors the unfortunate alternative of being content with inferior securities that the largest institutions do not want.   This entire matter, however, is still within the range of experiment, and it remains one of the unsolved problems of the marketing process.

The strict requirements of the Securities Act and the decidedly (and perhaps even excessively) meticulous administration by the SEC have had another curious effect in virtually short-circuiting the security distribution mechanism.   Long before the competitive bidding issue developed, there began to be attempts to circumvent the new issue requirements by not placing a security issue on sale to the general public at all, so that the necessity of preparing a registration statement and all the rest would be obviated.   The corporation raising capital would merely arrange a direct sale of the entire issue to some large financial institution, and in this way again the larger life-insurance companies played a very important role in absorbing choice issues.   Of all the corporate bond and note financing accomplished in 1936, the private placements are estimated to have amounted to about 7 per cent, but this proportion rapidly mounted in the succeeding years to 17, 39, 43.7, and, in 1940, about 56 per cent.[1]   As in the case of competitive bidding, the large issues of important and presumably strongly entrenched corporations went into the hands of the largest investing institutions to the extent that these direct placements were feasible; individuals were practically denied an opportunity to replace bonds being called or matured with the new issues of comparable caliber.

INTRICACIES OF HOLDING COMPANIES

In addition to the reforms having as a general objective the enhanced safety of the capital-raising process for the individual investor and apparently the end result of leaving him with fewer good securities to invest in (other than Government securities), recent legislation has also sought to "democratize" the entire mechanism by removing, so far as possible, the holding-company device and its undoubted tendencies toward undue concentration of financial power.   The great holding-company movement, which particularly dominated the electric-power industry and occasioned such terrific losses to investors in holding-company securities, was responsible for much of the excessive speculative fervor and public misapprehension as to the real trend of American business and earning power in the 1920's.   It seems obvious that whatever degree of minute information is placed on file concerning a company or the underwriters of its securities or the purposes of an issue, it is fundamentally the soundness of the corporation and its ultimate control that justifies confidence in the securities that it may issue.   Hence the Public Utility Holding Company Act of 1935, placing all holding companies in this field under the regulation of the SEC, may be regarded as a further extension of the power to limit the undue control over an operating company by an external financial interest.   Since every holding company's financial structure naturally gravitates toward a condition involving tremendous leverage effect of fluctuating earnings on the balance for common shares, the purpose of this Act in gradually eliminating interstate holding-company structures is in the direction of removing from the security market the highly volatile holding-company issues that excite bullish speculation when earnings are rising and tremendous liquidation when the leverage works the other way. Since most of the flagrant cases of holding-company abuses have represented enterprises of an interstate character, regulatory practice within

[1] Temporary National Economic Committee, *Monograph* 37, p. 63.

the individual states proved entirely inadequate to keep the movement within reasonable limits.   The Securities and Exchange Commission is now given authority to scrutinize all security issues of such companies in the public-utility field and to do so in the light of the existing financial structures and probable ability of the securities to provide continuing dividends or interest.   It may withhold permission to issue additional securities if outstanding securities appear to represent progressive impairment of the enterprise.   Beyond this there is a still more important responsibility to supervise the simplification of corporate structures, which is likely to be a slow and difficult process.

Inasmuch as the holding-company movement resulted in such reckless expansion of indebtedness imposed upon the underlying properties, with attendant write-ups of assets, etc., the "death sentence" imposed upon interstate holding companies having no real purpose means that in the future there will be less bond financing and preferred stock issue designed merely as watered capital.   To anyone who will take the time to examine the intricate maze of such fantastic financial pyramids as Middle West Utilities or Associated Gas and Electric, it must be abundantly clear that the removal and prevention of such useless and dangerously unsound "financing" is probably one of the greatest achievements in economic reform ever accomplished.

The various registered holding companies have now placed with the SEC tentative plans for integration and reorganization, and the process of simplification is under way, but it will take time.   No registered holding company will eventually be allowed to operate more than a single integrated public-utilities system unless subsidiaries now operated cannot be dispensed with without loss of substantial economy or are comprised within one state or the immediately adjoining area of such a state or the combination of the various systems under the holding company is of such a nature that all the advantages of localized management, efficient operation, and effectiveness of regulation may be maintained.   As for the rest, a great unscrambling and intricate readjustment process is inevitable. The SEC will go even further, delving into such technical matters as depreciation in all these systems, and marked changes in depreciation and maintenance practice may result from these investigations.   Even the matter of dividend payments is brought into focus, since the SEC will restrict dividend payments in all cases in which impairment of earned surplus or other deficiencies are discovered.   Eventually it is entirely possible that many of the overcapitalized and heavily indebted companies producing electric power will have more rational capital structures, such as will permit their rates to be lowered.[1]

[1] The SEC has no legal authority over rates but may affect the rate structures indirectly through bringing about financial reorganization in the case of all holding

In the light of British experience (which really is no perfect model), it was long considered that one of the solutions to the problem of providing a sound flow of investment capital into corporate securities, particularly equities, might be furnished by investment trusts. But unfortunately, most of the investment trusts that were formed in the United States during the decade of the 1920's proved to be financial disappointments. There was not the background of experience in the mobilization of capital from the middle and lower income groups and its satisfactory investment in equity securities. The financial machinery of institutional investment had become so thoroughly imbued with the principle that only bonds are sound investments that this attempt to institutionalize stock investment was in the nature of a radical experiment. It appealed to those who were endowed with recklessness and salesmanship rather than with judgment and conservatism.

The investment-trust movement paralleled the orgy of holding-company expansion in the power industries. The two movements were coordinated at various points so that the one assisted the other. Numerous trusts themselves embodied high profit leverage through issue of debentures and preferred stock. Numerous trusts were formed for the deliberate purpose of distributing large blocks of particular securities. A fundamental weakness of the trust movement was the concentration of its most rapid development in a period when the stock market was already greatly inflated. Trusts of the "fixed type," whose portfolios were more or less rigidly defined by indenture, were unable to adjust themselves to the radically changed market conditions following 1929. The so-called "management" trusts either tended to be mainly speculative in their objective or were so poorly equipped with timing technique that they misjudged market positions and failed to observe the principle that cash is an excellent security under certain conditions. The trust movement in a few rare cases of exceptional management showed itself capable of becoming eventually a useful part of the financial mechanism, but the volatility of our markets and the factors contributing to rampant inflation and deflation rendered this type of institution a poor medium for the investment of savings by those who had no right to speculate and no desire to lose their capital. Too much of the operation of these trusts was predicated upon the hope of an indefinite rise in market values. If we consider the large average amount of loading charge representing management and sales expenses, the matter of average yield from the trust securities would

companies. In 1939 the SEC reported that its Public Utilities Division had found that at least 20 holding companies with consolidated assets of about 6.5 billion dollars would have to be recapitalized. Some of the operating companies, as well as many holding companies, had arrearages so great in relation to the earnings available for preferred stock dividends that recapitalization was inevitable.

not in itself have justified purchase of most trust shares on a yield basis when compared with the yield on reasonably good bonds.

Investment-trust promotion, therefore, has also received governmental attention through the Investment Company Act of 1940, which gave the SEC additional work.[1] Investment trusts formed in certain instances by security distributors were found to be a useful means of distributing nonmarketable issues by having them incorporated or "sandwiched" in the portfolios of investment companies and utilizing their sales force as a means of distributing.   Bankers also found the trust organizations advantageous as a means of placing blocks of securities in which their capital had been too heavily involved.   During the latter 1920's, the community of interest between investment bankers and trust managers became painfully obvious.   No less than 265 new investment companies were created in 1929.   In that same year the outstanding securities of all types of investment trusts amounted to over three billion dollars.   It is safe to say that most of this represented the purchase of existing securities rather than new capital destined for productive industry.[2]

[1] The study of the investment-trust problem that led to this legislation was pursuant to Sec. 30 of the Public Utility Holding Company Act of 1935.   The SEC not only studied investment trusts in the United States but also engaged experts to make studies of foreign institutions.   See the report of the SEC entitled "Investment Trusts and Investment Companies," 1939.

[2] The SEC, as a result of its studies, made the following interesting observation: "Influenced by leverage, extensive trading in these securities and other factors, the junior securities of a great majority of closed-end management investment companies, in particular, experienced rises in market prices exceeding the rise in their asset values. Whether these premiums resulted from rising market prices, public speculative fever, leverage, trading accounts and pools, misleading accounting or fictitious valuations, pyramided systems or other causes, the net result was to provide a further incentive to the formation of investment companies and the sale of their securities.   Furthermore, these conditions encouraged the creation of investment company systems with one investment company pyramided upon another, or with cross-holdings of different investment companies.   As a consequence asset values were further inflated through intercompany holdings and intersystem transactions on the basis of securities already selling at substantial premiums."

Following 1929 the trust movement disintegrated along with the stock market. The Commission found that "during the period after the stock market collapse in October, 1929, many of these dominant persons who were in financial straits immediately turned to the large liquid resources of their investment companies to obtain assistance.   These insiders often sold unmarketable securities or other properties, many of which were of doubtful value to their investment companies or caused these companies to take over dubious and illiquid investments in which they were interested; compelled these organizations to assume large and onerous commitments on which they were obligated, such as participations in underwritings, trading accounts, loans, and other commitments; required these companies to relieve them of existing liabilities and obligations to their investment companies; caused these organizations to

The investigation record discloses that in this hastily developed phase of American finance, there was, as in other phases, ample opportunity for conditions to develop that were inimical to financial stability and sound capital formation, and thus regulation was inevitable. In accordance with the Investment Company Act of 1940, therefore, investment companies are now required to register with the SEC, and in the light of the complete information required to be furnished to the Commission, this body is now in a position to eliminate most, if not all, of the types of abuse that unquestionably existed prior to the great collapse.

Somewhat parallel to this Act has been the still more recent extension of SEC authority over investment advisers and investment counselors who are also now required to register with the Commission if they are supervising more than a specified number of accounts. In this connection, they must furnish to the Commission fairly detailed information regarding the nature of their organization, their operations, and other pertinent details.

It is unfortunate that the profession of investment counsel was merely in its infancy and was represented by but a handful of practitioners prior to 1929. Had there been in these years a more intimate contact between economists and the world of practical affairs and had there been also more available information and easier access to the necessary statistical information regarding corporations, the development of this profession in the safeguarding of investment in securities by individuals lacking the necessary facilities would probably have been accelerated. The rapid development of disinterested counsel work in recent years, under the helpful supervision of the SEC in developing a code of sound practice and standards of conduct, promises much for the future of investing procedure in this country.

---

finance their clients and companies in which they were interested; and induced the making of direct loans to them often without any collateral or upon inadequate security." (*Release* 1520, Holding Company Act, May 3, 1939.)

CHAPTER 18

CORPORATE EARNINGS, SAVINGS, AND CAPITAL INVESTMENT

It is clear that the process of corporate capital issue and the operation of the security markets could not suddenly be brought under drastic regulation without some effect upon the amount of financing undertaken. The reform movement discussed in the previous chapter has indeed exerted a restraining influence upon almost every phase of security market activity, but it has not been the only, or even most important, moderating or retarding influence.

A glance at Chart 44 will provide a general perspective of new corporate capital flotations in recent years. The chart reveals that a tremendously large proportion of the new bond and stock issues by domestic corporations during the latter years of the 1920's represented merely the financing of investment companies and other miscellaneous nonproductive purposes. A relatively small but significant segment of the securities issued were for the purpose of refunding securities previously issued. The really *productive* (new capital) portion of the total issues of stocks and bonds, as estimated by Moody's Investors Service, is surprisingly small. It is also interesting to notice that this portion remained fairly steady from 1924 to 1930.[1] The sharp decline in productive capital following 1930 coincided with the general market collapse, so that by 1934 only about 63 millions of domestic corporate productive capital issues were distributed. During the next several years—in fact, continuing to 1940—there occurred a heavy volume of refunding, as corporations took advantage of low interest rates to refinance outstanding securities or bank loans. The issue of trust shares by investment trusts and for other purely financial or nonproductive purposes increased, but the volume was infinitesimal compared with the stupendous totals of the late 1920's.

The strictly productive issues reached over 600 millions in 1937, the generally active year, compared with almost 2 billions of productive issues in 1930. But the *proportion* of productive uses even in 1929 amounted to only 22 per cent, and this portion actually increased during the depression,

[1] The data used by Moody were derived from the *Commercial and Financial Chronicle*. A summary of the results may be found in Moulton, Edwards, and others. "Capital Expansion, Employment and Economic Stability," Brookings Institution, Washington, D.C., 1940.

428

for we find that it was about 66 per cent in 1933 and about 64 per cent in 1924, prior to the years of reckless excesses.   It must be kept in mind that of the total corporate issues from 1925 to 1930, by far the largest part represented financing by electric-power enterprises and holding companies whose expansion during these years was one of the major economic developments of the period.   There is reason to believe that public-utility expansion of plant was considerably overdone, and the relatively drastic shrinkage of such financing after 1930 was a natural consequence.   During 1930 there were efforts by the Federal Government to check declining

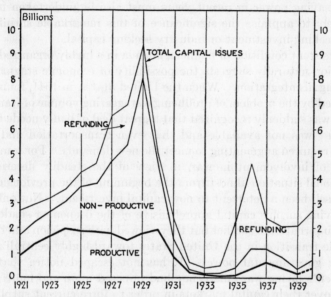

CHART 44.—Corporate-capital issues and estimates of productive portion, 1921–1940. (*Data from the Commercial and Financial Chronicle.   The segregation of the totals into refunding and other nonproductive and productive issues capable of representing new investments in plant and equipment, are estimates of Moody's Investors' Service.*)

industrial production by exhortations to continue all possible construction work and to maintain employment so far as practicable.   This probably contributed some further plant and equipment financing, even after the main current of business had begun to contract.

The failure of capital financing to revive in the past few years has often been attributed to the restrictions imposed upon security financing and speculation by Federal legislation and the extremely exacting requirements of the SEC.   It is probably true that the curbing of speculative excesses has decidedly tempered the psychological atmosphere favorable to expansive and ill-considered promotion.   Now there are no holding companies being formed to whip up public enthusiasm for propositions promising high-leverage "appreciation"; the promotion of investment trusts has virtually ceased; even the attempt of corporations to window-dress their shares in contemplation of new stock or bond issues is likely to attract sharp scrutiny in Washington.   Full disclosure of facts and drastic penalties for failure to meet the new tests of financial honesty have certainly deprived the securities market of millions of capital that might otherwise have flowed through its channels—most of it into the sea of liquidated ventures whence no dollars ever return.   *But this is not all.* An analysis of the financial status of American corporations in several major groups and also of the financial status of individuals with respect to their saving power in recent years must also be undertaken in order adequately to appraise the significance of this remarkable shrinkage in capital seeking investment or industry seeking capital.

A persistent condition of financial anemia in a highly organized industrial nation naturally suggests the possibility of economic stagnation or impending disintegration.   When the United States, in 1941, found itself confronted by the problem of producing a staggering volume of war equipment, it was suddenly recognized that a great deal of badly needed industrial plant was not available and that even transportation and power facilities required augmenting to meet the new demands.   For some years the fear of involvement in war, in view of the steadily deteriorating international situation almost from the beginning of the previous decade, had in itself been a deterrent to new capital investment.   Not only were those having surplus capital apprehensive of the deepening shadow of a gigantic international conflict but they viewed with suspicion and distrust the subtle transition in the United States toward highly centralized and arbitrary governmental power.   It has not escaped notice that other governments facing war emergency had imposed more and more drastic controls over their capital markets in order to force current surplus into governmental securities and the public treasury.   This world-wide tendency received a sharp impetus after 1934.

Hand in hand with these tendencies inspired by world events there has developed a peculiar new philosophy of national policy that has insisted upon diverting income and capital from those having efficiency and productivity to the underprivileged and the shiftless.   Capital investment does not easily flow into enterprise in the face of political effort to equalize wealth by fiat rather than by increasing the productivity all along the line.   Despite a decade of constructive reforms and the reconstruction and salvage efforts undertaken by our Federal Government, it must be acknowledged that private capitalism has not been able to function adequately and with assurance that its place in the scheme of things was fairly appreciated and respected.   Ingenious devices have been invented in Washington to siphon off the mobilized capital resources of the nation and fritter them away in the attempt to "create mass buying power." Among these devices, the imposing of punitive taxes and virtually capital levies on corporations and individuals has perhaps been an outstanding feature. It is highly probable that the steadily increased Federal rates upon the higher levels of personal income prior to the present War progressively reduced the type of surplus that, as potential capital, has usually made up the bulk of the investment in equity securities and hence the financing of projects involving the hazards of innovation. This is but one of several aspects of a progressive, deliberate public appropriation of surplus income to provide for subsidizing the farmers, building workers, the industrially unemployed, and a thriving and costly bureaucracy. In examining the financial records of important groups of corporations, we shall seek still other factors that may contribute to our understanding of the recent decline in new financing through security issues.

PROVISION FOR DEPRECIATION AND MAINTENANCE

To anyone familiar with corporation finance, it is apparent that to a considerable extent provision for new plant and equipment may require no borrowing, flotation of stock, or resort to bank credit. One of the fundamental requirements of accounting practice is that there be segregated among the costs of doing business allowances for depreciation of plant and equipment.[1] These depreciation allowances are primarily designed to maintain in good working order a given aggregate of production facilities. The setting up of depreciation accounts may in actual practice involve explicit allowances for obsolescence or potential *qualitative* changes, but these are not always included and frequently are overlooked entirely. Another form of deduction having much the same objective as depreciation is known as "maintenance," which again expresses the objective of maintaining in working order an organization's plant and equipment. The essential difference between the two concepts is that depreciation allowances are usually set up on a basis that allocates evenly distributed sums from year to year corresponding to the roughly estimated annual loss in efficiency or value of the physical assets. In the case of maintenance accounting, the sums allocated in a given period usually vary according to earnings or revenue; or they may simply be considered

---

[1] In the case of industries that control natural resources, it is customary also to provide for depletion allowances. These provide the means whereby a business enterprise may hope to remain in business, despite the using up of a particular source of raw material, by developing new sources or purchasing them. Depletion allowances differ from depreciation in that they may provide for exploratory operations and other necessary activities not specifically involving the acquisition of durable equipment or structures. In the charts that follow, the references to depreciation will be understood to refer to figures that include a minor element of depletion, but for convenience the term "depreciation" alone will be employed.

the cost of replacing what wears out when replacement becomes necessary. The distinction is essentially one between a systematic and regular prearranged schedule of amortization and a more or less opportunistic policy of recording renewals as they occur.

Opinions differ as to whether depreciation charges in American industry are generally in excess of the precise ratio of physical capital deterioration or whether they are deficient. According to Stuart Chase, no accountant ever underdepreciates physical assets in practice, "It simply isn't done. The records must gallop ahead of moth and rust—far ahead. This is sound, conservative, universal accounting practice."[1] Chase goes on to assert that excessive depreciation results in the fact that solvent concerns "do not often need to go, cap in hand, to Wall Street to borrow money for the expansion of their plants. They already have funds in their depreciation reserve accounts." He appears to assume that in the good old days business *borrowed* for depreciation purposes! On the other hand, it is familiar knowledge that the Securities and Exchange Commission has lately reaffirmed findings of the Federal Trade Commission in the opinion that the depreciation accounts of public-utility companies have been deficient. And it is by no means uncommon to find a corporation deciding to write down capital assets that had not been sufficiently depreciated in the regular course of past procedure.

There is no conclusive evidence that excessive allowances prevail. But there is reason to believe that very inadequate attention has been given in corporation accounting to the increasingly rapid pace of actual obsolescence in capital facilities, and hence too narrow and rigid a concept of depreciation has been employed by many corporations. Although the emergence of obsolescence is an essentially qualitative aspect of capital goods and something that requires judgment to estimate in practice, it cannot be omitted from the general consideration of physical depreciation if a company is *to maintain the most efficient possible producing apparatus.* As Fabricant has said,

In the world as we know it, all other things do not remain the same . . . Competing machines spring up through advances in the arts. Demand for the services of particular pieces of capital equipment waxes and wanes. Obsolescence is ubiquitous. The economic efficiency of a machine, and the economic life that rests upon it, is related to the rate of obsolescence. The economic life of a machine, as forecast on the basis of its economic as well as physical attributes and conditions of use, is the life over which capital consumption must logically be allocated.[2]

[1] Capital Not Wanted, *Harper's Magazine*, February, 1940, p. 228.
[2] Solomon Fabricant, "Capital Consumption and Adjustment," p. 13, National Bureau of Economic Research, New York, 1938.

The same principle, viewed over a longer term, holds true for plant structures. Businessmen probably do take into account this relatively intangible but potent factor of obsolescence, but the writer is inclined to believe that in most cases they greatly minimize obsolescence in setting up depreciation charges. One reason for this is the fact that the United States Treasury allows cost deductions for what is termed "normal" obsolescence only, and this constrains accounting practice toward underestimating rather than overestimating the amount that should be set aside to keep plant facilities not only at par but also in a condition *fully* adjusted to the progress of applied science and technique.

DESIRABILITY OF CORPORATE SAVING

Formal depreciation allowances in American industry have served to *maintain* but not to keep step with progress, and Stuart Chase's insistence that depreciation in the broad sense is a financial source of adequate plant expansion and improvement seems erroneous.

Apart from certain contingency and special reserves that may be set up to supplement formal depreciation, industrial corporations appear to have derived the major part of the resources to expand their demand for structures and equipment from two sources: the securities markets, and such additions to surplus as management finds it possible to accumulate after all charges and payment of dividends. Businesses, like individuals, can practice the art of saving and can express these savings in various ways, including the setting up of special reserves for various purposes, the maintenance of adequate cash position (including holding of securities), and the improvement and enlargement of operating facilities. Corporate saving has recently occasioned considerable discussion, and opinions are at variance as to the significance of this internal accumulation of capital and its possible relation to the reduced activity in the securities markets and the course of demand for durable equipment generally. Again we find Stuart Chase seeking to convince us that these savings have been so large that they take on the appearance of hoarding. This seems to be merely a phase of the old superstition, periodically revived in new forms, that business enterprises manage to take away funds that should be distributed and hold them inactive at the expense of the community.[1]

In *TNEC* Monograph 12 Martin Taitel, in discussing this subject, stated that despite the great depression, the cash funds held by the corporate system were actually greater in 1935 than in 1929; therefore, "in

---

[1] A considerable amount of attention was given by the Temporary National Economic Committee, 76th Congress, Third Session, to this matter of savings and investment in durable goods. See particularly O. L. Altman, *Monograph* 37, and Martin Taitel, *Monograph* 12. Alvin H. Hansen, in his evidence, stated: "In modern times you can have a perfectly enormous increase in productive capacity merely by expending depreciation allowances and not tapping a cent of (individual) savings."

spite of the huge money capital reduction, the corporate system has been able to hoard cash.   And, of course, cash accounts are the easiest *sources* of investment expenditures to tap."[1]   This cash-hoarding obsession seems to have become a characteristic feature of the economics of those who believe that the corporate capital market will progressively disintegrate and hence the Government should make up the resulting "vacuum of purchasing power" by vigorous expansion of public works and subsidization, as illustrated in Chapter 15.

There is also a sympathetic understanding between observers who are suspicious of all business finance and management practice and those who desire confiscatory Federal taxation to absorb corporate surplus and reserves entirely and thus reduce the power of "big business" in its competition with "small business."   What is usually overlooked is that the more taxes a corporation must provide for, the more cash balances must be maintained for this specific purpose.   Furthermore, contingency reserves are naturally augmented in the face of continuing acute uncertainties arising not only from disturbing world conditions but from a succession of Government experiments in all directions whose effects have been to increase the violence of cyclical disturbance.

Fortunately the Treasury Department for many years has compiled statistical information capable of throwing some light on aspects of this subject, and we shall now turn to the record of what nonfinancial corporations actually do with their revenues in order to see the tendency in recent years in the apparent ability to retain, obtain, and utilize capital resources. Chart 45 presents the earnings and net savings, 1922–1938, of all manufacturing corpotations reporting to the Treasury.[2]   We shall direct our attention to this highly important segment of our corporate system and later compare the results with those relating to the public-utility and transportation corporations.

The Treasury statistics afford a composite picture of how the vast majority of corporations engaged in manufacturing dispose of their revenue each calendar year.   The data prior to 1922 are less complete, and we therefore begin the record at that point.   The top of each bar in Chart 45 represents the amount of aggregate gross profit after deducting all purely operating expenses.   The height of the bars traces the familiar course of the business cycle during these years.   We proceed then to make

---

[1] Taitel, *op. cit.*, p. 80.   What Mr. Taitel did not clearly point out was that his figures related to *all* corporations, and that this alleged accumulation of cash was *exclusively* among the *financial* corporations, whereas those in manufacturing, transportation, and trade had actually 1.25 billions less cash in 1935 than in 1929, according to reports made to the Treasury.   Why financial corporations of various kinds should have had more cash in 1935 at their disposal than they had in the boom year of 1929 has already been explained.   See again Chart 9.

[2] The data for 1938 were the latest available at the time of writing.

a series of deductions from gross profits.   The largest deduction comprises various miscellaneous items, some of them in the nature of operating costs and others overhead charges, which have not been segregated here in order to avoid confusion.   We next observe the relative importance of the

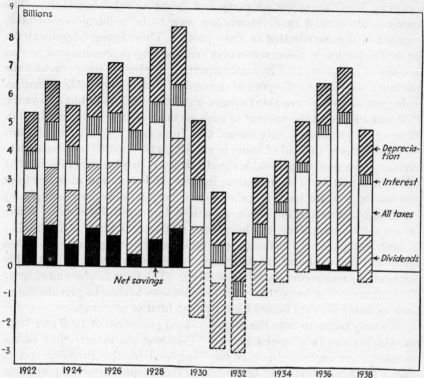

CHART 45.—Disposition of net revenue by manufacturing corporations, 1922–1938.   For description of data see Appendix 8.

deductions from gross revenue for depreciation, interest, taxes on income and profits, dividends, and whatever savings have not been distributed. The base line of the chart represents *zero saving,* and bars reaching below the base denote dis-saving or withdrawals from surplus or reserves.[1]

It will be noted that the depreciation allowances, as we might expect, have shown no marked variation over these years, despite great fluctua-

[1] It should be pointed out that these are aggregates of reported data that include the strong and the weak companies, some with profits in a given year and others with net losses.   If all the manufacturing corporations taken together indicate a certain result in a given year, such as a loss or negative saving, it does not mean that some (perhaps many) companies were able to show profit or positive saving.   Our interest, however, is in manufacturing enterprise taken as a whole, inasmuch as the later comparisons that we shall show between these financial results and capital expenditures are again in terms of totals reflecting the results of general experience.

tion in business conditions. The payment of interest on outstanding debt has become considerably smaller as the manufacturing corporations have reduced such obligations in recent years. Tax payments represent a segment that tends to vary with net income, other types of taxes, including local taxes on property not being shown separately. The amounts distributed in dividends are seen to be a fairly considerable segment of the distribution of gross profit. There is some tendency for marked reduction in disbursements in years of deep depression and revival in years of prosperity. The most important disclosure, however, and the one most pertinent to the present discussion, is that since 1929, manufacturing corporations were able to register positive savings in but two years, 1936 and 1937, and the amount of such saving was extremely small. For all practical purposes it may be said that from 1930 to 1938, manufacturing corporations, instead of being in a position to "hoard" or accumulate savings, have paid considerable dividends from surplus, whereas in 1931 and 1932 a portion of depreciation, interest, and taxes was also met from past saving. They have, in other words, been more generous in *paying out* than in providing for future growth or improved technique. There are numerous exceptions, but here is the picture as a whole. The ability of some companies to maintain positive savings and perhaps to invest these savings in productive facilities was offset by the fact that other corporations conspicuously failed to do so. The facts disclose an entirely different situation from that which economists hostile to private enterprise or dubious of its future have been so fond of painting.

We may pause to note the large dividend payments of 1936 and 1937, for which there is a special reason. This was the direct effect of the so-called "undistributed-profits tax" imposed by the Revenue Act of 1936, a further embodiment of the theory that corporations are pernicious hoarders and should not be permitted to accumulate wealth.[1] This attempt to force corporations to squander their savings in excessive dividends represented in part merely the political desire for more tax income, in part the theory that more money should be circulated via public agencies to provide *mass* "purchasing power," and beyond that a variety of sociological ideas as to who should control decisions involving capital use and expansion of production facilities. The gist of the idea became clear as early as 1932, when, amid the general clamor against financial abuses and the inability of corporate business to maintain

---

[1] One of the objectives of this Act was to reach personal holding companies and restrict the ability of wealthy individuals to utilize personal trusts in corporate form as a means of amassing capital enhancement through nondistribution of income from investments. The enthusiasm for the tax among those who hold to the rich-corporation theory amply demonstrates that it was actually one of the subtle means to restrict saving as indicated above.

employment, attention was being directed to all the real and imaginary shortcomings of top management. According to Robert Weiden-hammer,[1] the economic situation demanded not only revival of the capital and durable-goods activities but a more competent direction of expansion and investment. Large and semimonopolistic corporations should not be permitted to have undisputed control over such decisions or over the development of new projects, inventions, and ideas. Weiden-hammer therefore suggested the organization of a Federal board to "regulate" investment and capital flow (anticipating the SEC). But among these functions there would be provided close scrutiny of the reinvestment of corporate profits in order to prevent "overinvestment" as the result of unwise decisions by the corporations themselves.[2]

A few years later, Mordecai Ezekiel, economic adviser to the Secretary of Agriculture, who spends much of his time studying the sins of corporations, expressed the typical Keynesian view that business depressions are the result of the "oversaving" of capital. He pointed to the close relation between the annual savings of corporations and individuals and the annual expenditures on plant and equipment, both these factors exhibiting wide cyclical fluctuations, and concluded "that one way to defer recessions might be to reduce the extent of the changes in savings from year to year. Governmental policy in taxing and in other ways, might well aim toward increased stability in saving."[3] These are but examples

[1] Control of the Capital Market, *American Economic Review*, September, 1932.

[2] In a subsequent article (Causes and Repercussions of the Faulty Investment of Corporate Savings, *American Economic Review*, March, 1933, p. 36) Weidenhammer expressed the opinion that "the investment of corporate savings probably contributes a higher percentage of 'submarginal returns' than the stream of funds that passes through the regular channels of the capital market, namely the scrutinizing analysis [sic] of the investment house and of the ultimate investor." This is all part of a highly artificial theoretical viewpoint that emphasizes the interest rate as the great determinant of "equilibrium" in the capital market. By greatly exaggerating the role of steady dividend payments and concluding that this in itself renders the annual internal corporate savings highly cyclical, this writer entirely overlooks the much greater difficulties and instability resulting from the high cost of debt, created by the careful "scrutinizers" of the money market. He makes entirely misleading assertions implying that corporations of all types have failed to reduce debt by means of internal saving. These articles are, however, good examples of the kind of thinking that has become prevalent on this subject in recent years.

[3] *The Agricultural Situation*, June, 1937.

Former Secretary of Agriculture Wallace, in a series of lectures at the University of North Carolina, revealed his acceptance of the belief that corporations *promoted cyclical overproduction of capital goods as a result of large profits*. He implied that depressions might be prevented by taking most of these "profits" away. Reference should also be made to the remarks of G. C. Haas, of the Treasury, at the Senate Committee on Finance (1936) on the undistributed-profits-tax bill. Mr. Haas stated: "It has been argued by very respectable economic authority that among the causes for the depression was the starving of consumption through the withdrawal of a too

of a considerable body of the ramifying oversaving doctrine that formed the basis of this remarkable tax legislation of 1936.

As a result, a corporation distributing all its net earnings in dividends escaped paying a special tax. On net earnings that were not distributed, a progressive scale of taxes was set up, starting at a rate of 7 per cent on retention of 10 per cent of net income and rising to a maximum of 27 per cent on all earnings retained in excess of 60 per cent. Obviously corporations were forced to estimate in advance what their final net profits were likely to be and to pay more generous dividends on the basis of rough estimates in order to avoid a punitive tax. A more grotesque piece of tax experimentation could hardly be conceived. Curiously enough, in the same year, 1936, along with a great outpouring of forced dividends, there was also a most generous distribution by the Federal Government to the war veterans, adding nearly two billions of dollars, in a lump sum, to the total of potential mass spending.

Since 1936 business was also being greatly stimulated by war-goods orders coming from Europe and a resulting sharp rise in commodity prices, it may be said that the politicians did their level best to manufacture prosperity in that year. They created so much of it, in fact, that when these politically sponsored disbursements were suddenly cut off "to prevent inflation," one of the most severe recessions in our history naturally followed. The padding of dividends in 1936 and 1937 could not be kept up, and amid the ensuing chorus of complaints the Administration was forced to abandon this experiment, and the undistributed tax was repealed in 1938.[1]

ALLOCATION OF CAPITAL FUNDS

The question may be asked with regard to manufacturing corporations, whether their ability to accumulate surplus so consistently during

---

large proportion of our funds for corporate capital expenditure. Is it not quite possible that in many instances . . . overexpansion of plant capacity was stimulated by a desire of the controlling stockholders in corporations to reinvest earnings for the purpose of avoiding the taxes that they would have paid if earnings were distributed?" 74th Congress, Second Session on HR 12395, May 1, 1936, p. 59.

[1] In looking back upon this, one cannot fail to note another extraordinary case in which two political theories were working against each other. On the one hand, it was the desire of the Administration to discipline the leaders of our financial system, particularly the bankers, for their failure to keep the financing machinery free from speculative excesses and abuses. On the other hand, the proponents of this particular tax paid these very same bankers the compliment of recommending that they be given a greater share of responsibility for corporate investment decisions. There was repeated reference to the desirability of submitting such decisions to the "judgment of the capital market," rather than merely the directors of particular business units—certainly an expression of distrust in the soundness of the judgment of all managers of corporate enterprise.

the 1920's really contributed to sound prosperity and a wholesome degree of activity in the durable-goods industries, which so closely depends upon the financing of plant and equipment. Did these accumulations in the main merely add to idle cash? The Treasury figures indicate that this

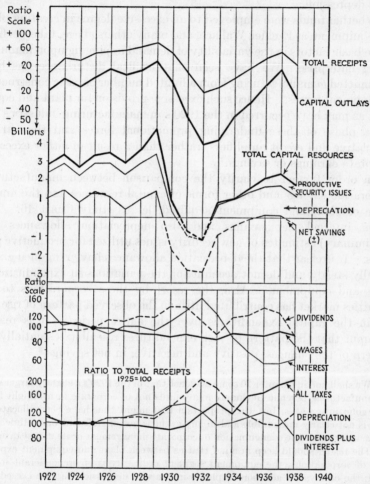

CHART 46.—Receipts, capital outlays, and capital resources of manufacturing corporations, 1922–1938 (preliminary estimates). The two top curves are drawn to uniform ratio scale. The middle curves, involving some negative values, are drawn to arithmetic scale. The ratios in the lower section all relate to 1925 as the base. For description of data see Appendix 8.

was not the case; cash was not so rapidly accumulated during the 1920's as to warrant the conclusion that accumulated surplus resulted in virtual hoarding. Without specific information derived from individual companies over a period of years, it is impossible to say just what form of assets were made possible by these internal additions to surplus. Presumably some of these funds were maintained in cash (and security investments), and to that extent accumulated surplus was available as a stabilizing factor and a protection to solvency in the early years of the great depression.

Whether funds were employed to an excessive degree in creating plant and equipment, as Ezekiel, Wallace, and many others allege, takes us back to the basic factors in the variability of demand impinging upon manufacturing enterprise. We have seen that cyclical disturbance has been transmitted *to* manufacturing from a limited number of basic construction development forces. Hence such excessive provision for plant and equipment as may have occurred in the 1920's in manufacturing industries was but a phase of these underlying promotional forces and the various speculative and credit amplifiers, rather than a result of either excessive corporate earnings or savings.[1]

In order further to clarify the comparison between manufacturing corporation savings and other forms of capital resources and the annual value of plant and equipment acquired, let us study Chart 46. This shows internal net savings and also depreciation allowances and (preliminary) estimates of new security issues utilized for productive purposes. It is clear that the depreciation allowances have remained exceptionally steady and do not account for the variations in expenditure for plant and equipment.[2] Also, the resort by these corporations to the securities market has contributed little to the observed pattern of rise and fall in the capital expenditures over the entire period. It is readily apparent that the pattern of such expenditures resembles essentially the pattern of the changes, positive and negative, in net savings.[3]

---

[1] We shall find in Chapter 20 some evidence that in the 1920's a slightly larger share of manufacturing revenue (including many firms not of corporate form) might fairly have gone into wages, but the proportion that might thus have been allocated to labor is not clearly measurable and in any event is not of sufficient magnitude to be the basis for wholesale condemnation of corporate management or its unjust taxation.

[2] The reader should keep in mind that as between plant and equipment expenditures of corporations, the equipment segment ordinarily is of preponderant importance; the outlays for addition to plants in years of depression become exceedingly small, absolutely and relatively to the total. The estimates for expenditure on plant and equipment are derived from other sources than the Treasury statistics.

[3] There are, of course, other elements that might be included among resources available for capital and plant expenditures. No account has been taken of bank loans, receivables, accounts payable, or various other minor sources of means to acquire capital goods. The reader will find interesting supplementary exhibits in the article by A. D. Hersey, Sources and Uses of Corporation Funds, *Journal of the American Statistical Association*, June, 1941. Mr. Hersey, of the Federal Reserve Board, has utilized the actual statements of a selected group of 58 large companies in the field of manufacturing and mining from 1930 to 1939. His results indicate that

In view of the fact that fluctuations from year to year in the volume, particularly in the value, of inventory are relatively important for manufacturing companies, it is necessary to consider the results shown in Chart 46 adjusted for inventory value fluctuations. The curve of plant plus equipment expenditures has therefore been adjusted (plus or minus) according to the annual changes in inventory values as reported by these corporations, and this adjustment appears on Chart 47. It is apparent that after making this adjustment, the correlation between the total of available funds primarily destined for capital use and the investment in plant and equipment adjusted for inventory changes becomes very much

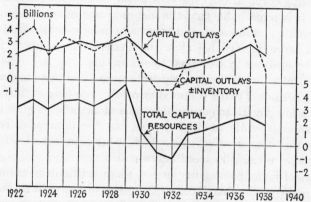

CHART 47.—Capital outlays of manufacturing corporations adjusted for inventory changes, 1922–1938. For description of data see Appendix 8.

closer. If the necessary adjustments were made in the original net earnings to remove the effect of inventory gains and losses, considering that these, after all, are not actually *realized* profits or losses, the degree of fluctuation in the curve representing means available for investment in plant plus equipment would be measurably reduced. The high cyclical instability thus turns out to involve an important inventory element as distinct from the financial element.

While we are referring to inventory values, we may parenthetically consider the manner in which accounting practice and Treasury regulations have introduced quite unnecessary fluctuations in the "declared

---

in addition to inventory value adjustments (which are discussed above), the various other means of obtaining facilities for plant and capital expenditures are relatively unimportant for these companies. See also the study by Ruth D. Mack, "The Flow of Business Funds and Consumer Purchasing Power," New York, 1941. In this book Mrs. Mack analyzes in considerable detail the sources and applications of corporate resources, based upon selected companies for a limited period, mainly 1932–1938.

Some corporations appear to have made charges directly against income for the purchase of capital assets, although the extent of this is difficult to appraise (*cf. TNEC Hearings*, Part 9, pp. 3687ff.).

profits" of corporations. There have recently been changes in the official regulations as to computation of inventory gains or loss that deserve careful attention. Until very recently it has been the practice of management to value inventories at the close of an accounting year on a replacement-cost basis. That is, it was possible to enter as profit the difference between a given physical inventory previously purchased at a low cost and now valued at a higher price and to enter as loss the difference between inventory items first acquired at a high price and now valued at a lower price. The inventory curve in Chart 47 involves not only price fluctuations but also changes in physical inventory; but (for manufacturing corporations) the wide swings are due principally to *price* changes. It is remarkable that the incorporation of such fluctuations in reported profits and losses should ever have become established practice. It is even more remarkable that the Federal Government for years required corporations to keep their books on this basis and to pay income taxes on "profits" resulting merely from unrealized inventory appreciation during periods of rising commodity prices. As long as thirty or forty years ago, a few American corporations abandoned the practice in reporting their annual results to stockholders, but the number of companies employing this conservative method of valuing inventories for actual policy purposes remained exceedingly small.

In years of rising commodity prices, these fictitious inventory profits naturally had considerable effect on the prices of shares of those corporations whose operations involved the carrying of raw-material inventory. This was an unstabilizing factor in the stock market, since among the corporations of this type are some of the leading enterprises, whose shares have an important public following. Inventory losses reported for years of declining prices of basic materials sometimes resulted in substantial readjustment of net earnings and by affecting dividend payments weakened share prices. In addition, the traditional valuation of inventory introduced a speculative element in purchasing-department policy, and the desire to obtain realized as well as unrealized profits from inventory gambling led to excessive fluctuation in the commercial loans of the banks. Here again we can establish the connection between commercial banking operations of the past with primarily speculative industrial procedures. Needless to say, the violent ups and downs in the shares of certain companies, whose earnings statements were continually affected in this fashion, were not infrequently an invitation to manipulation and pool activity that were likely to be successful for the insiders, in view of their greater knowledge of the commodity factors involved in these fictitious profits, or, in the words of Arundel Cotter, "Fools' Profits."[1]

---

[1] See Mr. Cotter's interesting popular discussion of this subject in his book "Fools' Profits," New York, 1940.

At long last a change was made in Federal tax provisions by the Revenue Act of 1939, which eliminates the necessity of including in reported profits for tax purposes these fictitious unrealized gains but at the same time requires that reported losses also exclude the unrealized element.[1] Manufacturing and mining industries are now able to operate more freely on a rational inventory-valuation method that unquestionably will introduce greater stability in income statements. In view of the wide advances occurring in some segments of the commodity markets as this is written and of the probable further instability that the War will yet bring forth, it is fortunate that political authority recognizes the wisdom of at least mitigating some portion of the result of price fluctuations.[2]

EXPANSION OF PLANT FACILITIES NOT SOUNDLY FINANCED

Returning again to Charts 45 and 46, we can conclude that with proper adjustment for inventory gains and losses or expansions and contractions in the physical inventory, the amounts spent by manufacturers for plant and equipment have been provided principally from depreciation allowances and from net additions to surplus out of earnings. The former have been relatively stable; the latter have fluctuated, even after inventory adjustments are allowed for. Resort to the capital markets to issue bonds or stocks, although highly spasmodic, has nevertheless been a minor factor. There was a fairly consistent rise in plant expenditures prior to 1929, but the trend has not been particularly steep *and certainly does not suggest that manufacturing enterprise was engaging in a wild and unjustified program of equipment and plant expansion.* The marked shrinkage after 1929 in the outlays for plant and equipment may be considered to have resulted from curtailment of demand for the products of manufacturing industries. This naturally resulted in suspension of plans for plant and equipment expansion and thus further reduced production, because capital equipment is itself a product of some of these companies.

We are justified in regarding manufacturing enterprise, broadly speaking, as a vast aggregate of producing resources and organizations that

[1] If a corporation once adopts a cost basis for inventory as a fixed starting point and employs the principle commonly referred to as "last-in first-out," it may result in the cost figure being either lower or higher than market values thereafter, but if reserves are set up to allow for declining prices since that starting point, they are not to be considered as deductible items for tax purposes.

[2] Since in previous years bankers frequently adjusted their commercial loan policies to the earnings statements of their borrowers, there was a direct temptation to exploit paper profits in order to secure larger bank loans than necessary for inventory accumulation. Under present conditions there is much less likely to be expansion of bank credit for this purpose, and as a result, despite war conditions, there will be that much less expansion of bank loans and also less reason for readjustments in bank secondary reserves.

respond in highly sensitive fashion to the demand for products emanating from consumers and other groups of industries, such as building construction, transportation, electric power, mining, and government, which, particularly under war conditions, forms a very important external demand factor.   If these external demands impinging upon the aggregate manufacturing system are expanding, there will necessarily be a cumulation of this expansion as manufacturing companies undertake to bring their plant facilities into better adjustment to new orders.   This proceeds to cumulate in various ways, not only as between one company and another but also through the fact that as the labor force is expanded and payrolls are augmented, a still further increase in demand for manufactured products, durable and nondurable, is likely to occur.   This process involves so much circular causation that it is exceedingly difficult to distinguish what is causal and what is resultant.   But in the light of our preceding analysis, particularly as it concerned the major cycles of the building industry and the promotion of major innovations in equipment, such as the automobile, electric power, and war equipment, it is not difficult to perceive that there were much more powerful forces prompting such capital expenditure as did take place among manufacturing industries than are represented merely by the magnitude of corporate savings or of productive security issues.   When we come to the years of depression, when net savings turned to net dis-saving, the ability of many companies to obtain access to the capital market was probably impaired by the wiping out of surplus.   Companies that are unable to disclose net savings find access to capital through the securities market difficult, and, in extreme cases, impossible.   Naturally, during years of tremendous shrinkage in general buying power and demand, there was little occasion to expand either plant or equipment, and such demand as did exist for these things was met almost entirely from depreciation allowances.   This continued to be true during the succeeding recovery period.   As we have already seen, the amount of actual net saving has been insignificant in recent years, at least as far as 1938 and probably 1939.   Hence the ability to secure such additional funds as might be helpful in developing plant improvement and innovation has been greatly restricted as compared to the period prior to 1929.   In addition, or as an alternative, to capital raised from securities, there was a considerable expansion after 1935 in bank loans that are not shown in the charts.   These partly explain why the expenditures for plant and equipment had risen so substantially by 1937 in spite of the persistent low level of the indicated available resources. To some degree, also, there may have been purchase of equipment charged directly to current expenses.

One may conclude that negative or very small positive corporate net savings represent impaired ability to finance, particularly through the use of stock.   The larger the surpluses the more management can resort to equity financing and avoid becoming involved in debt.   To the extent that saving power is low, there will be resort to borrowing but only for relatively necessitous short-term commitments in capital goods.   The incentive, as well as the ability, of these corporations as a whole to engage in long-term projects is not present when savings are low or negative. These conditions in recent years go far to explain the financial anemia that we have been exploring.   Although not the whole explanation, which, as we have stated, involves matters of taxation of personal capital and the security-market reform movement, they suggest one of the reasons why the demand for labor and the flow of income into the hands of wage earners in the durable-goods industries has been so disappointing since 1929.

If we turn to the lower portion of Chart 46, some further interesting features of the disbursement of manufacturing corporation receipts can be studied.   Taking 1925 as a base, index numbers were prepared to express various ratios to total receipts or gross revenue.   We find that wage and salary payments have represented a surprisingly stable ratio to receipts for these companies.[1]   By and large, the labor disbursements vary in proportion to total revenue.   On the other hand, the dividend-disbursement ratio shows a rise in depression years, as we might expect in view of the tardy reduction of dividends when business activity deteriorates and the delayed increase or resumption as business revives. There is no necessity for dividends to vary even more widely than manufacturing revenue.   Apparently the tendency has been to pay out to stockholders more in good years than would be consistent with Sound Practice and adequate reserves for all purposes, including obsolescence. Much of the excess should have been devoted to the financing of research, technological and economic.   Some of it, as we shall later indicate, should have been set aside for unemployment reserves.   But there has been a tendency on the part of management to be influenced by the enhanced availability of equity capital in a rising market, and dividend payments have often been expanded beyond wise limits to give an added attraction to a corporation's shares from the standpoint of seeking large sums in public financing.   It would have been better to build up by internal saving and keep dividends more in line with revenue and with the movement of wages.   Since our ratio indexes relate to 1925, no conclusion can be drawn as to the long-term relative movements or levels of wages and payments to capital.   As for interest payments, these have shown a

---

[1] As indicated in greater detail in Appendix 8, the wage-salary payments are not derived from the Treasury returns for *corporations* but are figures pertaining to manufacturing companies.   The salary element in the index is a relatively minor component.

rising ratio to revenue at the bottom of the depression but a definitely declining tendency since then. In the lower segment of the chart, the varying depreciation ratio illustrates the effect of stability in the *absolute* amount of these allowances. As for tax payments, there is a very significant rise after 1934 in the ratio to revenue, whereas the dividend plus-interest ratio has sharply declined to a new low level. This is one of the most interesting divergences revealed by the data. We find here one of the reasons for the persistent failure of manufacturing enterprises to maintain a substantial volume of saving from operations. Interest and dividend payments, as a result, have recently suffered more than disbursements to personnel.[1]

To take the evidence together, there seems no justification for the view, so far as manufacturing corporations are concerned, that ability to accumulate surplus from earnings and to use it in ways that management considers designed to accomplish improvement and development of operations has in itself been a major unstabilizing factor in the business system. In periods of depression, when it is desirable to maintain the flow of national income and activity in the durable-goods industries as much as possible, the stability of depreciation allowances is of great value, and those concerns that have been careful to maintain a reasonable portion of their surplus in liquid investment or in cash are able to go forward with their depreciation program with more assurance than would otherwise be possible. When recovery is under way after a depression and management should be taking the long view in planning capital expenditures, adequate surplus enables capital plans to be put in motion sooner and with less involvement in the distorting influences flowing from the securities markets. It has, of course, been argued that boards of directors do not necessarily utilize their surpluses wisely and that capital-expansion plans *rightfully* should be submitted always to the "impartial judgment of the free capital market."[2] In this way, it is supposed that officers of corporations and their sales departments would be less likely "to be overoptimistic in good times as to the future earnings possibilities." Such assertions presuppose that the financial markets are devoid of wide oscillations of excessive optimism and pessimism. The errors of judgment committed by investment banking through the years are monu-

[1] To refer again to the capital expenditures by manufacturing industry, these do not, of course, account for all the means available for capital purposes; they do not include utilization of funds for acquisition of existing plant and other facilities, patent rights, land, sources of raw materials, etc. These may indirectly serve to create the demand for labor and durable goods.

[2] J. D. Smith, The Undistributed Profits Tax, *American Economic Review*, June, 1938. Such arguments represent an extreme form of the idea that somewhere in the so-called "capital market" there are omniscience and wisdom in the use of corporate funds. To the writer this view seems quite unrealistic.

ments of financial folly compared with the misjudgments of managers and individuals using their own surplus in ways that they at least partially understand, and what is not understood is a matter for education in planning capital investment, not a matter for the free and easy capital market.

CORPORATE RESERVES SHOULD BE BUILT UP THROUGH ADEQUATE SYSTEMATIC SAVING

It must be frankly admitted that the propensity or ability to accumulate business savings from earnings does not throw forward into future years liquid resources capable of sustaining total wage outlay and hence capable of preventing occasional great washouts in demand for the products of manufacturing industry. If wide fluctuations in the demand for manufactured goods could be prevented from developing in the first instance, a good many of the cumulative boom and depression tendencies could be modified and vibration toned down. It is borrowed capital unwisely used rather than savings directly used that goes far to explain the underlying instability. We shall examine in Chapter 21 the possibility of using reserves or credit based on bank balances for stabilizing labor income in a systematic far-reaching manner, and at this point it is necessary only to refer to this as one example of use of surplus in the interest of stability that manufacturing industry had already explored to some extent before it received governmental sponsorship. It might further be suggested in this connection that corporations be encouraged by tax benefits or credits to accumulate productive net savings from current operations and to avoid excessive payment of dividends. The Treasury still insists upon a minimum of current dividend disbursement that in individual cases can definitely penalize the ability to build adequate surplus and is therefore directly contrary to sound principle. The rules might very well be revised to penalize companies paying all their earnings in dividends and then borrowing to build better plants. So far as investors are concerned, dividends are not the whole story. Maintenance of competitive position, ability to keep abreast of progress, and the growth of productive equity form part of the appreciation in value to which both lender and equity owner give serious consideration in making investment decisions. And by the same token inability of a management to show prudent disposition of earnings and accumulation of productive assets cancels out the payment of huge dividends or the offering of high-coupon bonds.

Let us now turn to Chart 48 in order to compared manufacturing corporations with regard to disbursement of revenue with similar results in the public-utility field. The bars shown on Chart 48 represent in their entire length the approximate net operating revenue of all transportation and other public-service corporations combined, based upon their reports to the Treasury Department. Although the railroads, on the one hand, and the electric power companies, on the other, show some contrasting features in some respects, they have been thrown together in this exhibit in order to exemplify a group of corporations characterized by heavy interest charges on funded debt and a tendency to pay relatively large amounts in dividends to equity holders at the expense of ultimate solvency. It must be explained also that whereas depreciation, as shown in this chart, has shown an increasingly large magnitude during the period, these charges are mainly by electric power and other nonrailroad corpora-

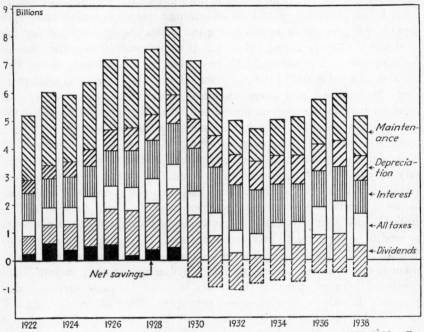

CHART 48.—Disposition of net revenue of public-utility corporations, 1922–1938. For description of data see Appendix 8.

tions; railroad allowances have been very largely on a maintenance or "replacement" basis and are not shown in this particular chart. In the general public-utility field there has also been a tendency for the tax payments to increase rapidly through the years, although these increases represent relatively minor payments, compared with interest and dividends. Perhaps the most interesting feature is the decisive transition from annual net savings (after dividends) prior to 1930 to a general condition of persistent and considerable "negative saving" down to 1938. This condition largely reflects the gravely impaired solvency of much of the railroad industry, but even among the much stronger corporations in the nonrailroad public-utility field, it will be found that persistent heavy interest charges and very liberal dividends on equities have been progressively impairing, and in some cases altogether eliminating, net savings. It is impossible to escape the conclusion that this group of corporations, taken as a whole, has for some time been in a position not only of impaired saving but of declining ability to secure equity capital—for this very reason.

As a result, either there are inadequate efforts to develop improvements and a tendency to drift along on a purely maintenance basis or the funds to be used in desirable capital improvements and extensions have had to come mainly from additional debt financing. This perhaps is the central point with regard to the ability of corporations to save. Without adequate systematic saving there comes sooner or later impairment of that basic test of solvency—the ready access on favorable terms to equity capital. Without such power to command equity capital in liberal amounts, an industry or company is driven to debt. The larger the debt the more likely is the further impairment of saving power and all that this means in terms of unwillingness on the part of those who take equity risks to place capital in enterprises where internal-growth possibilities through earned surplus have become dubious or have vanished. *Thus the vicious circle of debt feeds upon itself.* Let none of those superficial thinkers who regard so highly the benign advisory powers of the "free capital market" overlook this principle, written indelibly into the annals of business history.

Chart 49 presents again the relationships between savings, depreciation allowances, and capital raised by issue of securities and, on the other hand, the estimated expenditures by utility corporations for plant and equipment. It should be noted here that maintenance (primarily pertaining to the railroads) has been added to the depreciation. As we should expect, the maintenance allowances prove to be very large in prosperity and are decidedly reduced during depression. Depreciation, however, not only has been relatively steady but has even tended to expand through the rapid growth in most of this period of the power industry. We find also that the estimated totals of security flotation by these corporations, considering only those believed to be productive, were persistently large until 1930 and shrink thereafter to insignificant amounts. The general pattern of these features bears a fairly close relation to the well-sustained plant and equipment expenditures as late as 1930 and the decidedly subdued level (contrasting sharply with manufacturing corporations) in the later years.

In the field of transportation and other public utilities, then, there was a well-sustained contribution to demand and production and employment in the capital-goods industries until 1930 but thereafter a pronounced and sustained shrinkage. This greatly reduced contribution to the operations of capital-goods production represented (1) the approaching end of a major cycle of new development in the electric-power field and (2) severe contraction of maintenance outlays by the railroads. This calls for some further consideration. Here we have an example of depreciation prac-

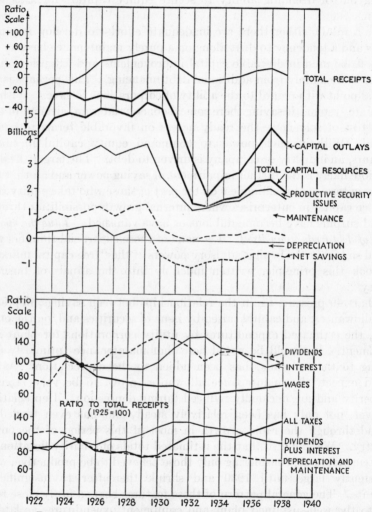

CHART 49.—Receipts, capital outlays, and capital resources of public-utility corporations, 1922–1938 (preliminary estimates).

tices that actually do intensify economic instability. Whereas manufacturing industry and some other kinds of business have systematically built up substantial depreciation allowances, thus affording some stabilizing effect to expenditures for equipment, the railroads, apart from depreciation of equipment, have not made systematic and evenly distributed depreciation allowances for structures or roadbed. When times are good and the high leverage in the capitalization of most railroads suddenly creates high net earnings, funds are liberally appropriated for maintenance, and, conversely, when earnings shrink, maintenance shrinks rapidly with it. There is here an example of pyramiding of booms and depressing of depressions, at least insofar as durable capital goods are concerned.

It has been maintained by some accounting theorists that all business should depreciate its plant in this fashion, the allowances being higher in times of prosperity and lower in times of recession.[1] This is supposed to accomplish the result of sterilizing or segregating some profits in good times and not reducing them as much in poor times. From this point of view depreciation is reckoned as a cost deduction that is to be increased in good times and lowered in poor times. This may be a sound idea in a strictly accounting sense or from the standpoint of stabilizing forces operating upon the prices of shares and the stock-market position of an enterprise, but it suggests a procedure in the wrong direction so far as stabilizing demand for durable goods and its fluctuations are concerned. Straight-line depreciation accounting may result in the introduction of what may be relatively large fixed outlays, tending to accentuate fluctuations in net earnings, but these are not of the same economic significance as interest charges or rent or salaries. If we assume that depreciation allowances are used for the purpose for which they are set up, which seems mainly to be true, funds are released into the stream of demand for durable goods and thus sustain, to a certain degree, at least, the operations of the related industries when other sources of demand for capital goods—let us say, from residential construction activity, agriculture, foreign sources, or from Government—may be temporarily impaired. Most other types of fixed charges represent merely the shifting of surplus funds in ways not immediately leading to production.

Although a policy of variable depreciation allowance might contribute in some degree to security-market stability, there are so many other ways in which this may be accomplished that this part of the proposal has little significance. What we must work toward in moderating the fluctuations of the business cycle is the elimination of unnecessary variation in capital and credit use capable of impinging upon the structural and fabricating industries, so that violently fluctuating demand is not permitted to cumulate through the entire system of enterprise.

Continuing the inspection of Chart 49, we may compare in the lower section the movements of outlays for wages and salaries with outlays to

[1] See, for example, John B. Canning, A Certain Erratic Tendency in Accountants' Income Procedure, *Econometrica*, Vol. I, January, 1933, pp. 52*ff.*

capital, again in terms of ratios to revenue.   In this group of industries there has been a significant declining tendency in payments to personnel while dividend and interest disbursements maintained a fairly stable ratio to total revenue until 1932.   Not only have these corporations failed to sustain their contributions to activity in the field of durable goods but they have been unable to maintain either employment or their contribution to wage income.   From the 1925 base we find that the depreciation and maintenance allowance ratio has declined slightly, confirming what was shown in the chart.   The taxation ratio has not risen so rapidly as in the case of manufacturing industries for the principal reason that aggregate income has not permitted large income-tax payments into the Treasury in recent years.   Since 1932 dividend and interest payments have declined more than revenue.   The entire picture, therefore, suggests a condition of impairment of solvency, inability to adjust to changing conditions, inadequate allowance for the maintenance of equipment and plant, and the possibility that adequate provision for obsolescence has not been made.   These deficiencies are most marked and can be readily confirmed by everyday observation of the physical assets in the case of the railroad system.

PROVISION FOR OBSOLESCENCE

Let us return for a moment to the general question of obsolescence and provision for improvements in structures, equipment, and technique. It is at this point that the magnitude of corporate savings is most significant.   The vitality of business organizations and their ability to maintain or expand employment, directly or indirectly, and to generate a rising trend of income through the years call for more than routine allowance for wear and tear on a *given* aggregate of capital facilities.   In a dynamic age, in which technology makes incessant forward strides, it is imperative that management should be increasingly alert to the adoption of new methods, new forms of productive assets, improved organization plans, and adequate financial resources as a defense against the stealthy encroachment of obsolescence.   The extent to which systematic provision against obsolescence in all its forms can be generalized throughout the system of private enterprise must depend in large measure on the degree to which sound financial provision for it is encouraged or discouraged by Government.   There must be definite assurance to business management that not all the gains or advantages that may be obtained as the result of improved processes will be ruthlessly appropriated by Government on the theory that all corporate enterprise is inherently unsound and essentially predatory.   There must then be assurance to those who are willing to pioneer and to keep their organizations productive to the maximum degree that their efforts will not be considered merely capricious ways of throwing labor out of work—one of the prevalent superstitions among labor leaders.

It so happens that of all the financial requirements of business, the one that is hardest to finance in the allegedly omniscient "free capital market" is this very provision for obsolescence and technological pioneering. No banker will make loans for such purposes. Corporations may float securities or obtain additional capital from their stockholders, but should these be earmarked for purposes of this character, the funds may not be easily obtained. To obtain capital or credit from outside sources, a business enterprise must *first* be able to demonstrate its ability to accumulate productive assets through systematic internal savings. The matter boils down to the proposition that to provide adequately for obsolescence, a business, whether it be a large corporation or a small firm, *must demonstrate saving ability*. This has been the general rule of progress for businesses and individuals alike. Capital aids those who know how to use capital. Corporate savings in the past have been directed toward numerous objectives other than the heading off of obsolescence or lowering the cost of operations through improvements affecting capital equipment, but there is no apparent reason why there should not be greater educational effort directed toward this end and a wider acceptance of the principal idea by top management. The code of Sound Practice should explicitly emphasize it. There are ways of improving management policy through educational processes rather than through the crude machinery of punitive taxation or the irresponsible denunciation of corporate business by the politicians. We have done a great deal in Washington to educate farmers but very little officially to educate business managers; this effort is still in its early stage.

There may be good reason to vary obsolescence allowances somewhat more flexibly with variations in revenue than is usually the case with straight depreciation. It may be possible to separate obsolescence policy into two phases—one having to do with those preparatory research and planning operations which are somewhat similar to what is called "development" work in the mineral industries. The second phase would be the putting of these plans into operation through building of structures or orders for new equipment. It is the writer's suggestion that these outlays might well be deliberately made in periods of business recession or depression, provided that some part of net saving has been previously allocated for such purposes. There might be incentive taxation designed to promote such a policy. This would tend to prevent what has so often happened in the past—the adoption of new devices and systems at or near the top of a business boom—and would tend to distribute or stagger innovations, thus building up compensatory support to national income. It takes time to develop the complex structures of business organization.

There is no adequate reason why all the effort and expense of building these structures and the communities built up around them should be sacrificed either to confiscatory taxation of saving or to the popular fear of corporate size, leaving management unable to provide fully adequate means of keeping abreast of progress, always ahead of the potential competition of new products and new ideas, in a condition always flexible and adjustable rather than financially frozen.

We have an excellent illustration of "frozen" industries in the case of many railroads, whose unfortunate financing, inadequate depreciation policies,[1] and indifference to research effort and the challenge of the internal-combustion motor have combined to restrict the contributions that might have been made to production and employment in durable goods. In the case of the electric-power companies these negative conditions have thus far been much less prevalent, but with a growing debt problem and a tendency to pay out excessive dividends and the restraining hand of political regulation and competition, there are signs of essentially similar possibilities in the future unless something is promptly done. Excessively long-term fixed charges arising from faulty capitalization are inherently inconsistent with adequate provision for obsolescence. Let there be some brilliant contribution by chemistry or physics permitting efficient utilization of the hidden powers of the atom, and our power industry, despite its existing high efficiency, would find itself financially unable to adapt itself to the change. The chapters of history are full of cases of business decadence and social deterioration, the result of inability to accept change and to adjust business methods, well in advance, to the inevitable dynamics of progress. Among such cases, perhaps the most impressive and persistent is that existing in our railroad system.

In view of the fact that something like one-third of our railroad industry is already bankrupt, another reason is apparent for the recent retarding of capital flow. The failure of an industry to provide through its own earnings for its future solvency may not *immediately* obstruct the channels through which it may gain access to new capital or, perhaps, capital for refunding old debt. But it is certain that no industry that is unable to save from its earnings can long continue to finance on favorable long-run terms and avert insolvency and reorganization. If we wish to know why long-term capital is not moving more briskly into productive uses, here is one of the major reasons and one conspicuously overlooked by the economic theorists who have been so exercised about

---

[1] The Interstate Commerce Commission, as far back as 1926, laid down accounting procedures for railroads involving the principle of depreciation allowance on an evenly distributed basis, but it was not until 1941 that the Commission really began in a serious way to require the railroads to adopt this procedure.

the metaphysical relations of savings, investment, and "interest rates." Loan capital is similar to money in the respect that it *must continue to circulate* in order to maintain its vitality. If it becomes stale or frozen in situations incapable of assuring its *return flow*, there is a break in the circulation that blocks capital use in still other directions. This implies that one of the effective means of maintaining the vigor of capital flow *out* of, as well as into enterprise, would be to hasten reorganization of capital structures that have already become permanently impaired.[1]

LEGAL ASPECTS OF REORGANIZATION OF CAPITAL STRUCTURES

But we here enter the domain of the law, and the wheels of the law grind with exceeding slowness. Here we find that Government has been negligent and inept in formulating by legislation such procedures as would result in prompt and equitable distribution of permanent capital losses and the preservation of going concerns with modified capitalization better adjusted to the realities of earning power.

The slow progress in the solution of these problems results partly from the fact that elaborate reorganization procedure is extremely lucrative to legal experts in this field, and it is expedient to prolong them as far as possible. Another reason is that reorganization of capital structures lacks the glamour to be found in other directions where the beneficent hand of Government may be more prominently revealed for the purpose of obtaining votes. Among the causes of delay must also be mentioned the fact that banking intermediaries frequently express an interest on behalf of those to whom bonds have been distributed, and through the formation of bondholders' committees under such sponsorship proceedings can be dragged through the courts for many years. This is another example of the possibility that such banking intermediaries have had excessive power, not only in decisions as to initial capital structures but in the attempt, not always successful, to readjust the structures when it is definitely recognized that earnings no longer suffice to service the claims of creditors. To be sure, there are various ways in which a business enterprise may avoid legal action by creditors or what may be termed the "regular course of reorganization" through court procedure. Capital may be written down and negotiation with creditors or preferred stockholders may result in agreements that do not require resort to legal contest. But in the case of large corporations such as the railroads or public utility holding companies, there is likely to be resort to the courts in order to obtain settlement of the claims upon asset values, and, in terms of revised capital structures, claims on earnings and control over voting rights.

[1] On the subject of obsolescence and its manifestations and results, see Mean and Grodinsky, "The Ebb and Flow of Investment Values," New York, 1939.

Although the failure of a corporation to discharge its liabilities to creditors may seem to be a definite factual proposition, the contentions among rival groups of creditors and between equity holders and creditors take place in an atmosphere not devoid of illusion. Some groups contend for drastic revision of capital structures and final claims upon earnings on the revised basis; others take the view that the misfortunes of the business are merely temporary and will shortly be corrected, and they press for adjustment on a much more optimistic interpretation of the facts. Since the alleged experts of the "free capital market," primarily trained in salesmanship, tend frequently to be influenced by the more optimistic future prospects, there is a tendency to resist thorough and drastic adjustment of capitalization to a realistic view of changed conditions, particularly in cases where the difficulties have been due to a cumulative effect of obsolescence and a definite downward trend in the competitive position of the industry or the particular unit. The long-drawn-out negotiation and argument may therefore turn upon reorganization proposals that, after all, will not be of practical benefit in the light of future events. Since individual bondholders are virtually helpless in these cases, they must entrust their solution to committees or take their chances as dissentients, with the result that the committees dominate the proceedings, and either large investing institutions or banking groups, through their lawyers, establish the final revisions.

In order to prevent very small minorities of creditors from blocking reorganization plans and to provide for more definite codification of procedure, legislation was finally passed in 1933 and 1934 and again in 1938 aiming, among other things, to revise the Bankruptcy Law to provide for the *rehabilitation* of companies in difficulties, as distinct from complete liquidation of their affairs, and to improve upon the procedure that had developed in the past under equity receivership. By virtue of these changes, dissentient investors were not to receive cash payment for claims, and the percentage of agreement necessary to constitute approval of reorganization plans was lowered. The 1938 revision of the Bankruptcy Act (Chandler Bill) introduced a further refinement, as the result of which the SEC, as well as District Court judges, were given authority to approve plans drawn up by an independent trustee. In the case of railroad companies, the Interstate Commerce Commission has an important role in granting or refusing approval and even in the drawing up of the plans themselves. This means, however, that corporations under reorganization as the result of insolvency still find the legal process slow and tedious, as Commission investigations and approval, *plus* judicial review and approval, may involve months or years. In the meantime, there may still be effective criticism of a recapitalization plan if a single creditor can show that the principle of absolute priority of claim has not been adhered to; or in other words, if the proposed plan gives the debtor or equity interest participation in the future of the company without satisfaction of all creditors' rights or claims.

In some instances, corporations, including several railroad companies, have been able to obtain the voluntary assent of security holders to make various adjustment plans, including extension of bond maturities or reduction of interest. But even with the assistance of the RFC in servicing the debts, little progress is to be expected in this manner in the task of railway recapitalization. Scores of railroad enterprises now in receivership or trusteeship must still go "through the wringer" before a substantial portion of capitalization in this field of enterprise is properly adjusted to earning power and provides regular amortization of debt and sinking funds. Only then will the railroads be in a position to attract new long-term capital readily or on an equity basis and, by reduction of fixed charges, assuming no confiscatory taxation, be able to develop adequate internal saving that can certainly be used in important modernization and service in present undertakings, such as should have been under way thirty years ago.[1]

In the case of industrial enterprises, the recapitalization problem, so far as large corporations are concerned, does not now appear to be a major one. As for public-utility companies, the SEC is now, and for many years will be, wrestling with the complex problems of unscrambling widely scattered holding-company organizations and revising capital structures of such integrated units as are likely to remain. This field again is likely to be one in which a ready flow of capital into needed plant expansion will be delayed by uncertainty as to the precise manner in which operating units will emerge from the unscrambling process. Although the elimination of unnecessary remote control by holding-company devices is fundamentally sound and desirable, the prevailing war emergency finds the country already facing acute shortages of generating capacity, partly due to the unavoidable delay in the process of financial housecleaning pursuant to the Holding Company Act of 1935 and the prospects of public absorption of the entire industry. The imponderables as to the financial status of electric-power holding companies are complicated by the fact that there has not yet been a thorough Supreme Court test of the constitutionality of the Holding Company Act, which was the basis for the so-called "death sentence" upon noncontinuous holding companies. Over these matters the SEC now has authority to establish rules, and in the long run these changes

[1] The reader will find a compact summary of the principles of reorganization law and procedures in Norman S. Buchanan, "Economics of Corporate Enterprise," Chapters 13 and 14, New York, 1941.

appear to be in the direction of facilitating equity financing and reducing the possibility of this industry being submerged in a flood of indebtedness, as were the railroads previously. These matters have been given attention in this discussion of capital and its uses in order to emphasize the complexity of the problem and the variety of factors that in recent years have contributed to slowing down both the *backflow* and the *inflow* of capital funds.

It is apparent that corporations in the fields referred to have spent less for plant and equipment in the past ten years than in the preceding ten years. In the latter period, manufacturing corporations, in particular, might conceivably have utilized much more long-term capital by increasing outstanding indebtedness, had they so desired. Their failure to do so implies no lack of loan capital available and certainly no absence of ability to develop reasonable earnings. One fundamental reason for the reluctance to obtain loan capital to improve or expand plants and appliances seems to have been unwillingness to execute long-range plans. Management has been constrained, broadly speaking, to limit new undertakings to those absolutely necessary and beyond this has sought merely to maintain existing facilities in good order. Behind this persistent hesitancy has been acute uncertainty created by foreign and domestic political policy as it has steadily converged upon the problems of total war. Management has also been aware of a growing spirit of animosity toward all private corporate enterprise, expressed or implied again and again in the statements of political leaders. Counteracting much of the thorough, courageous, and constructive financial reform accomplished by the New Deal Administration has been the persistent tone of disapproval among its advisors of the use of private capital in productive ways and the implied predilection for the use or supervision of all capital by Government. In other words, there appears to be a growing suspicion on the part of business leaders that a subtle and progressive expropriation of private capital, both corporate and individual, is being planned, on the ground that such capital is not wisely used, that it promotes "concentration of economic power," that it is not used by those who own it, that it deprives general "buying power" of full and active circulation, and that the great cyclical disturbances that have lately shaken the country cannot be controlled without a much greater command over all capital resources in the hands of the Federal Government.

It is difficult to establish a justification of these suspicions. We have indicated in Chapter 15 the manner in which they have been in a measure confirmed in the matter of investment in public works. The present war will create new opportunities to supplant private by public finance in many directions. As these apparent trends affect corporate financing and the flow of capital into productive tools and industrial plants, we may hazard some further tentative observations. Drawing upon statements and expressions of opinion that have clustered about, or contributed to, the more adventurous aspects of recent governmental policy, there stand out such implied propositions as these:

1. It is considered that too much of corporate earnings has flowed into the hands of a small group of wealthy capitalists who do not wish, or cannot find ways, to reinvest what they receive in dividends and interest to afford enlargement of production and employment in the capital-goods industries.

2. Corporations should not be permitted to accumulate surpluses from savings, or even liberal allowances for depreciation, since these provide opportunity for unwise investment decisions and the piling up of such internal savings amplifies the booms that, in turn, create depressions.

3. The accumulation of appreciable reserve to permit continuation of essential outlays despite periods of temporary or cyclical impairment of sales sterilizes funds that should be flowing through the channels of general trade and supplying the public with "buying power."

4. If private capital "goes on strike" whenever business conditions are depressed, the Government should borrow freely and build lavishly in order to provide demand for the products of industry that otherwise would not exist (the cycle "compensating" idea, which, as we have seen, has gradually dissolved into a progressive program of deficit spending, now vastly expanded by war requirements).

5. The more the community's savings can be "mopped up" through drastic taxation the more demand can be created by Government as these funds are spent (it is assumed always wisely), and private business can obtain all the capital equipment that it is entitled to by its depreciation allowances without further saving and without flotation of bonds or stocks. The soundness of business enterprise is, therefore, to be judged by the *absence* of new capital flotations rather than by their continuation or expansion. Since the general price level must be sustained at all costs by keeping in existence a given aggregate value of debt claims, these are properly to be created and manipulated *by Government* at very low interest rates. Thus private capital, insofar as it still exists after all "progressive" taxes have been collected, finds that it might as well invest in Government bonds at 2 per cent with safety as in corporate bonds at 4 per cent, with the prospect of ever-narrowing margins of profit and less and less protection against political harassment and competition.

6. When the Federal Government uses tax revenue or borrowed funds, it creates prosperity. When corporate boards of directors make

decisions as to utilization of saved capital, they only make mistakes. The introduction of machinery is bad. It displaces labor. Hence it is desirable to "freeze," temporarily at least, the whole nefarious process of mechanization and labor-displacing technology so that more labor can be kept employed.

Consider this implied political philosophy in the light of these further facts. The trend of events is moving steadily in a direction that suggests far-reaching new alignments of economic power. The control of capital is being appropriated by Government so that private management no longer has full control over its own savings. The individual owner of capital finds that after taxes are paid he has inadequate capital funds for new ventures requiring substantial pioneering outlays and inadequate net returns to compensate for risks already undertaken in the interest of enlarged or improved production. Even the farmer is no longer in control of his own acreage; he has become essentially a ward of the state; his operations are directed and his financing arranged in Washington. Instead of the business system being operated as a resultant of *many* decisions of *many* minds—fruitful ideas intermingled with mistakes— it is becoming subject to the dictates of a concentrated centralized authority whose decisions, though often wise, are subject to all the errors and misconceptions of a few minds that tend to run in identical channels. The subdued activity in long-range capital use basically implies that our corporate system may in the future revolve less and less upon the decisions of many managers of capital and productive organization, unless the current political drift is prevented from leading us all the way to permanent economic regimentation.[1]

[1] If the reader has doubts regarding the existence of such underlying ideological trends, let him consult *Monographs* 7, 12, 20, 25, and 27 of the Temporary National Economic Committee, Final Report and Recommendations of the Temporary National Economic Committee, 1941, *passim;* D. C. Coyle, "Uncommon Sense," Washington, 1936; and H. A. Wallace, "Technology, Corporations, and The General Welfare," University of North Carolina Press, 1937.

CHAPTER 19

CONSUMER INCOME USE AND MERCHANDISING CYCLES

Our discussion of the relation between net savings and other sources of capital funds to estimated capital expenditures for two important segments of business showed that plant and equipment expenditures are much more volatile than total receipts through the course of the business cycle. There is a still higher degree of variability in net savings available for capital use, which holds true even after depreciation, maintenance, and externally derived capital resources have been added to net savings. Our analysis of the net savings originating in these groups of corporations indicated that there have been several factors tending to restrict the amount of such net savings since 1929 and that this tendency has restrained recovery in capital expenditures, particularly in the public-service group. The pattern of net corporate savings, however, does not in itself contribute to an understanding of the basic causes of upswing and downswing in the cyclical pattern or in revenues.

Although some part of the instability in the demand for, and production of, plant and equipment arises *within* the industries that we have considered, it would not be correct to say that the forces of contraction and expansion in these industries are mainly generated internally, without regard to the basic factors discussed in Chapters 4, 9, and 10. We have emphasized the role played in the generation of cyclical movements in industry by major wars, by building waves and their relation to population growth and investments, and by outstanding innovations in transportation construction. The dynamics of residential building and transport equipment naturally involve many aspects of the economic behavior of individual consumers, whose earnings, savings, and spendings doubtless contribute a powerful influence on demand, which presumably derives some distinctive characteristics from the close relation of the average family to what happens in the housing cycle and the mass distribution of such durables as automobiles.

The average family is in a sense a business enterprise, in that it deals with gross revenue, direct costs, overhead costs, positive or negative savings, and investment in various directions. In the case of farm families, which at a later stage we shall discuss separately, the business aspect is more pronounced, but we are nevertheless dealing primarily with individuals as entrepreneurs. We shall seek to attain a better understanding of the extent to which the flow of income or revenue to individuals—or, as we may say, consumers—results from the operations of industry (using manufacturing as the principal type) and to what extent this flow appears to be more directly motivated by one or another of the basic cyclical factors summarized above. In Chart 50, let us first examine, in terms of seasonally adjusted monthly data, the cyclical relationships among a number of elements associated with the flow of

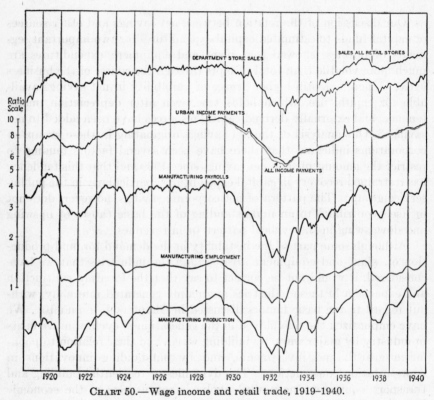

CHART 50.—Wage income and retail trade, 1919–1940.

income to individuals, in this case excluding farmers. We have already observed that the volume of manufacturing production establishes a cyclical pattern fairly typical of the pattern of the general volume of business, exclusive of agriculture. This pattern, with some diversity of amplitude, is also apparent in transportation, trade, the generation of power, and various service enterprises.[1]

The lowest curve in Chart 50 traces the course of the physical volume of production in manufacturing. Next above, and closely correlated, is employment in manufacturing. This index is somewhat smoother in

---

[1] See Appendix 9 for description of the data referred to in this chapter.

its course, and it does not appear to have so pronounced an upward trend as production, a point to which we shall return later.   The amplitude or range of fluctuation in employment, which covers a somewhat wider range of industries than the index of production, is slightly less than in production, but when we examine, next above, the index of payroll disbursements in manufacturing, we find that its amplitude is greater than that of the production index, since variations in wage rates and working time per man are introduced.   The cyclical ups and down, however, are faithfully reproduced.   It is notable that in 1929 there was some damping down of the movements; in 1922 the upturn came rather slowly, and some of the smaller movements between 1933 and 1936 suggest retarded impulses.   If we compare the payroll disbursements with the next curve above, we are again struck by the general similarity of pattern.   This (solid line) is an index, again seasonally adjusted, showing approximately the monthly income payments to nonagricultural employed workers.   The pattern of this index resembles the employment index, with an amplitude more in agreement with employment than with payroll disbursements.

If the nonagricultural labor income flow is closely observed, it will be seen that the principal turning points upward and downward are preceded by a few months by the payroll index.   The latter, in turn, is preceded by a several months' interval by the manufacturing production index.   It thus appears that the flow of funds into the hands of individuals (after allowance is made for seasonal variations) appears to be *derived* or governed by *prior* changes in manufacturing operations.   Is it possible, then, that the flow of labor income, so tardy in its cyclical adjustments, can be a *causal* factor in generating the cycles of activity in the manufacturing industry?   This question becomes all the more provocative if we observe the dotted line that closely follows and is almost identical with the solid line of nonfarm labor income from 1929 on. This dotted line represents the total of income payments to all individuals in the United States as computed by the U.S. Department of Commerce, including disbursements of wages, dividends, interest, and all the sources of income flow in terms of *individual recipients*.   It is remarkable that there should be so close a degree of resemblance in pattern between this general income flow and the payments to industrial workers.

The question that we have raised becomes even more interesting as we observe the upper curves in Chart 50.   The principal one is an index of the aggregate (seasonally adjusted) sales of representative department stores.   Apart from the fact that its trend is slightly less pronounced than in the case of income payments (probably because of competitive factors within the retail distribution system), there is again a striking resemblance to the general pattern.   The department-store sales show less smoothness of movement owing to the statistical imperfections of seasonal adjustment and the numerous factors that enter into the value of this trade from month to month, such as weather conditions, sales policies, credit factors, etc.   But if we should superimpose the respective indexes, we should find that after making some slight adjustments in trends or broadening the retail distribution represented, the income index would correlate almost exactly with the value of merchandise sales.   For several years an index representing the most recent attempt to measure general merchandise trade is added, and so far as it goes this confirms the foregoing principles.

At first glance Chart 50 would create the impression that the cyclical fluctuations in manufacturing output generally contribute *to* variations in national income and in the value of merchandise purchases by consumers.   This circumstance would be in harmony with much traditional thought about business cycles that finds the nucleus of the problem in the operations of "business" or "industrial" processes, dominated by the seeking for profit and the use of credit and capital.   Business management has been charged with the principal responsibility for bringing about wide variations in employment and payroll income.   From this kind of thinking emerge the highly critical policies and attitudes that were noted in the previous chapter.

Let us look a little more deeply into this matter of lead and lag.   First let us consider that when we translate physical production and employment into value terms, we introduce price elements.   It is well confirmed that most price movements have a tendency to move more slowly through the phases of the cycle than the physical changes.   We have already had occasion to consider the statistical difficulties confronting measurement of physical *volume* in various phases of economic performance.   In the case of industrial production, we have available excellent volume measures, but measurement is more difficult in the case of physical turnover of the thousands of articles of merchandise in retail trade or what may be termed the "real income" passing into the hands of individuals, especially if month-to-month changes are to be observed. We can, however, approximate the pattern of physical retail trade by using an appropriate index of prices as a deflating device applied to the available index of values.   We can also approximate such a physical measure indirectly by the use of an index of physical production comprising only nondurable goods or "consumer goods."   Naturally, there are nondurable goods that do not come into the hands of consumers; and in the course of retail merchandising, goods are sold to consumers that are durable or semidurable.   But in the main, retail trade is dominated by the sale of food products, apparel, textiles, shoes, and the less durable household appurtenances, so that it is reasonable to assume that the ebb and flow of nondurable-goods *production* would be closely associated with the physical volume of retail *turnover* if that could be comprehensively and accurately measured with respect to its dynamic pattern.

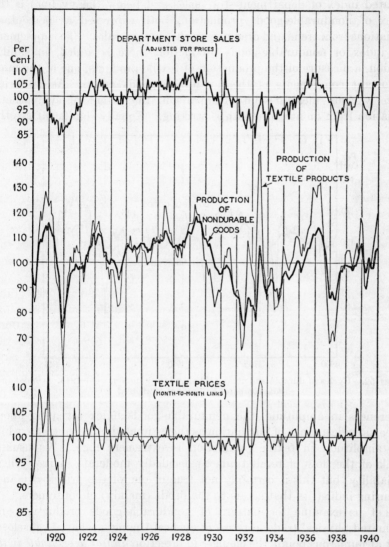

CHART 51.—Cycles of retail-sales volume, nondurable- and textile-goods production, and textile prices, 1919–1940. Production of textiles introduces most of the cyclical instability in nondurable goods. Retail-trade volume shares the cyclical sensitivity found in the nondurable-goods production.

Taking the best statistical materials available at this stage of progress in economic measurements, let us first observe the relationship between what we shall term "estimated physical retail trade" (based upon deflated department-store sales) and a monthly index of nondurable-goods production. This comparison is made in Chart 51. At the top is the deflated index of department-store sales and below (heavy line) is the index of nondurable-goods production, both expressed as percentage deviations from trend and drawn upon the similar scales. To supplement the index of nondurable-goods production there is added, in similar fashion, a measure of the production of textile products, one of the most important components of the nondurable-goods group. As we bring these various measures into comparison, the extent of sympathetic variation from month to month is striking. Equally significant are the

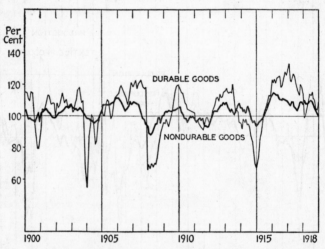

CHART 52.—Cycles of durable and nondurable-goods production, 1900–1918. (*Based upon data computed by Leonard P. Ayres.*)

differences in amplitude, the nondurable-goods index revealing about twice as wide a range of fluctuation as the estimated physical trade, while the amplitude in textile production is extremely high. We usually think of the flow of retail trade as decidedly moderate in its cyclical variability, but this is certainly not true of one of the principal manufacturing industries that caters to the needs (mainly) of consumers.

Let us examine the pattern of nondurable-goods production and estimated physical trade in terms of cyclical timing. Chart 51 discloses that at numerous points the changes in direction *appear to originate in the deflated retail sales rather than in the nondurable-goods production.* This would appear to suggest a causal influence running *from* the volume of actual consumer purchasing *to* the operations of textile mills, shoe factories, some types of food-processing enterprise, and other providers of things sold as retail merchandise. We can examine this further by reference to Charts 52 and 53, in which production of nondurable goods is brought into relation with the index of durable goods. In order to examine this relationship over a long period, the indexes have been extended back as far as 1900, Chart 52 being based upon data computed by Leonard P. Ayres.

One is at first struck by the fact that the deviations from trend for the more recent period in Chart 53 are more violent than those in the earlier period. What is still more striking is the further evidence presented in Charts 52 and 53 that the variation in production of nondurable goods not only is narrower in amplitude but tends usually to *precede* the cyclical movements of durable goods. Since the general index of manu-

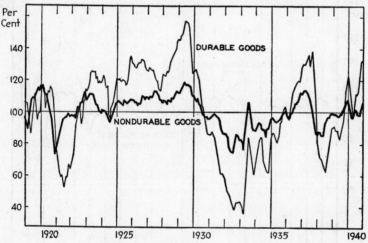

CHART 53.—Cycles of durable- and nondurable-goods production, 1919–1940. (*Based on data of the Federal Reserve Board.*)

facturing production comprises both these segments, it follows that the production of nondurable goods tends to precede by a considerable interval the *dollar value* of retail trade as shown on Chart 50. Referring again to Charts 52 and 53, observe particularly the sensitive nature and timing lead of the nondurable goods index in 1902–1903, 1905–1908, 1913, 1916–1917, 1920–1921, 1923, 1929, 1937, and 1938. In 1933 and 1934, the inflationary policies of the Federal Administration brought a sharp simultaneous stimulus into both durable and nondurable industries, and the usual sequence was not maintained. In 1932, however, there was a slight lead.

How are we to explain this tendency for producers of goods entering into retail merchandising to vary their operations, usually ahead of the changing phases of total manufacturing employment and still farther ahead of the monetary income flow into the hands of wage earners and, indeed, of the general population? Is it possible that consumers or large groups of consumers begin to reduce the volume of their retail purchases long before it becomes apparent in the dollar value of merchants' sales? Is it possible that a converse tendency develops in expanding demand after a trade recession? May there be changing phases of consumer propensity to spend or ability to acquire staple merchandise that originates highly sensitized cycles in certain branches of manufacturing before other branches are affected?   If this is true, it would be a reasonable inference that, in view of the highly volatile movements of such

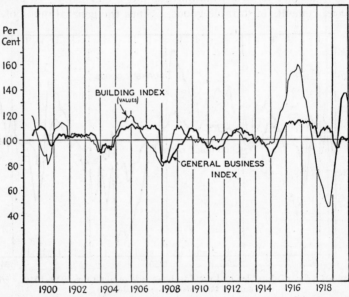

CHART 54a.—Monthly cycles of building construction and general business activity, 1900–1919.   Building index represents a 12 months' centered smoothing of the value of building permits in leading cities.   (*Compiled by Clarence D. Long, Jr., "Building Cycles and the Theory of Investment,*" 1940.)

industries as textiles, there would be abrupt changes in employment and therefore in payroll income, occasioned by these variations and that these might contribute to further changes in demand impinging upon still other products and ultimately upon many branches of manufacturing and hence upon the general course of payroll disbursements and national income.

In order to establish a reasonable hypothesis, let us connect these facts with what we have already established in our analysis of the prime movers in the business cycle. Our hypothesis would be that forces capable of generating, as well as amplifying, cyclical movements not only are transmitted *through* consumers to industry activity but may even originate in the economic behavior of consumers or consumer groups.

This is particularly to be expected in the case of housing, which, as we have seen, not only undergoes cyclical changes of tremendous range but has been correlated with population movements and with financial characteristics that tend to precede by a significant interval the turning points in general industrial activity. Referring to Chapter 9 and Charts 28 and 31, let us observe again the index of building in relation to general production and the timing of the mortgage solvency index. This is illustrated even more clearly with monthly data in Chart 54, in which the

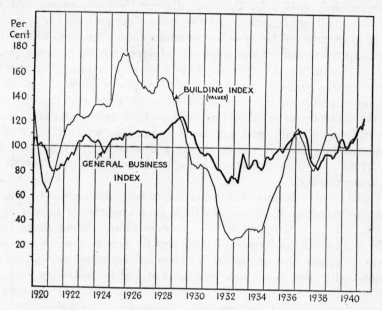

CHART 54b.—Monthly cycles of residential-building and general business activity, 1920–1940. Building figures are a 12 months' centered smoothing of the Federal Reserve index of residential contracts, 1920–1927, spliced to similar adjustment of Dodge residential-contract values in 36 states, 1927–1940. (*F. W. Dodge Corporation data.*)

deviations from growth trend in *residential* building (adjusted for seasonal variation) are brought into comparison with manufacturing production over a fairly long period. Not only does the building index have an enormous range of amplitude but its cyclical movements in almost all cases precede those of manufacturing by a considerable interval. This was not true in 1932–1933, when, as previously pointed out, political policies intervened to stimulate manufacturing operations but tended to delay construction revival.

RELATION OF FAMILY CAPITAL OPERATIONS TO BUSINESS CYCLES

What bearing does this problem have upon the relation of nondurable goods activity to manufacturing as a whole? The answer requires consideration of several aspects of consumer use of capital and of current funds for family maintenance. Let us first discuss what occurs during and following boom conditions in residential construction. As the building cycle has approached peak level, thousands of families have found (and may also find in the future) increasing difficulty in meeting capital changes related to home construction. The early phase of decline in the major construction cycles ushered in a period of more acute difficulties, which had the effect of curtailing, at first slowly and later more rapidly, outlays for the more dispensable merchandise, clothing, and the small semiluxuries. At the same time manufacturing output in the aggregate was being well sustained by the overhang of industrial-plant expansion and various other special developments and innovations associated with a generally expanding phase of promotional finance and rising security prices. Apart from the creeping financial involvement of many families in mortgage difficulties, we must consider the early decline in employment in building itself, and somewhat later in the many material, installation, and appliance industries, screened at first by continued buoyancy in numerous other directions but really the first important retarding influences brought to bear on the demand for consumer nondurables.

Consider also the fact that in the case of both housing and such major consumer durables as automobiles there is an important class of outlays, seldom wholly anticipated by the average family, which come inevitably in the wake of large capital outlays for new homes and new cars. There is a new and unfamiliar problem of depreciation allowance to contend with: new taxes, new purchases of fuel for operating purposes, new outlays for furniture and other household amenities, and a long list of appurtenances such as tires, etc., for transport. All these demands on family incomes that are no longer expanding rapidly or are already being reduced where income is affected by the building cycle are likely to converge upon less liberal expenditures for the nondurable goods that can be readily postponed or eliminated. Food, of course, is not much affected, but many other items of general retail merchandise begin to feel the effect of this competitive crowding carried over from the previous capital investing in durable enjoyable wealth. In business operations accounting practice and careful budgeting tend to obviate in large measure such conflicts of supplementary capital charges and provision for current expense and maintenance, but as is perfectly obvious, the average family does not run its financial affairs on a meticulous business basis. The funds it releases into the business stream in various directions carry along the influence of recurring difficulty in providing simultaneously for long-term investment in durables and for current spending on nondurables. The early cyclical decline in nondurable purchases (in volume) and hence in their production has been at least a significant part of its explanation.   The extension of a weakening influence to all manufacturing ultimately proceeds (in most instances) from this process. Many manufacturing concerns work on orders for industrial equipment and plant that were planned early in the course of the upswing in general conditions.   It may require months to complete work on these products, and hence actual production operations may continue in durable goods for a considerable time after there has been a perceptible slackening in consumer demand for nondurables.   The length of the production processes in the latter group is generally short, and in this difference in length of period we find a further answer to our problem.

Putting this in another way, we can say that the cyclical reversals in consumer durables lead the movements of total manufacture by a relatively wide interval, greater in the case of buildings and less marked in the case of household equipment, automobiles, etc.[1]   The pattern of consumer nondurables leads the general cycle also by a moderate but significant interval.   The production of a wide variety of business equipment and materials relating thereto has a sufficient weight in the production index to throw the timing of the cyclical downturns in the general index into a later phase than is found for the consumer goods. All this is rendered the more significant by the fact that from 1922 to 1940 the total estimated outlay for buildings and durable equipment used by consumers amounted to 183 billion dollars.   This was actually larger by over 60 billion dollars than the estimated expenditures by industrial producers for plant and equipment.   The consumer and his capital are thus in a pivotal position, not only to transmit but to originate cyclical disturbances in view of the lead in the business cycle of his expenditures and also the huge amounts involved in the durable expenditures alone.   It therefore appears that the contention of Leonard P. Ayres[2] that security financing in the capital markets is the prime mover and prime anticipator of general industrial or business cycles is incorrect. Ayres has sought to establish the fact that it is "business" financing, rather than the activities of consumers and the financing pertaining to family capital operations that primarily motivates the turns of the business cycles.   But he is considering financing that naturally accom-

---

[1] *Bulletin* 69 of the National Bureau of Economic Research, May 28, 1938, presents evidence that the cyclical revivals of passenger-automobile production since 1915 have preceded those of *total* factory employment by an average of six months and the physical volume of production by about four months.   In 1929 the motor industry and its auxiliary lines of production showed a tendency to decline well in advance of general industry and physical trade.   There was also a significant broad decline in automobile production from the end of 1925 to the end of 1927, which apparently was contributing *to* general manufacturing activity rather than resulting *from* it.

[2] "Turning Points in Business Cycles," New York, 1939, especially Chapter 17.

panies for the most part industrial equipment and plant that either turns simultaneously with industrial production or leads it by very short intervals; he has overlooked or misinterpreted the much more sensitive dynamics pervading consumer expenditures for both capital goods and nondurable goods.

The relatively sensitive behavior of consumer nondurable goods and the retail-trade volume associated therewith and their tendency to move in advance of general industry on the upturn of the cycle probably are explained mainly in the typical periods of production.   During the course of a depression, as consumers defer the purchase of dispensable merchandise and some items and quality classes of food, a potential of demand is accumulated.   Unlike business units that purchase materials only as orders for products appear, families cannot indefinitely postpone purchases of apparel and other merchandise to preserve decent living, health, education for children, efficiency of working members, and presentable appearance of those members seeking jobs.   A time arrives when wear and tear require some replenishment.   It usually arrives when merchants' stocks are low, when retail credit is again available at reasonable terms, and a flurry of retail demand gets under way.   The activity cumulates by at least temporary stimulus to employment in nondurable-goods factories, and these producers can usually meet the demand quickly, in fact, much more quickly than is true of most business equipment—hence the sharp turning points frequently (although not invariably) seen in nondurable-goods activity well in advance of general industrial revival.

Statistical estimates that have recently become available enable us to develop a preliminary and approximate measure of the annual income flow into the hands of all individuals, as potential consumers, and its disposition in various ways.   The results are shown in Chart 55.   This follows the type of procedure employed in the case of the two outstanding industrial groups previously shown.   There is clearly evident the same divergence in the amplitude of the income or total receipts and the estimated expenditures for all types of consumer durable equipment and plant.   In order to explain the pattern and relatively high amplitude of these outlays, there are presented separate indexes of expenditure upon capital goods and of saving and investment generally.   We first deduct from the total receipts the estimated outlays for those goods and services that constitute the typical "operating overhead" of families and single individuals.   These are mainly nondurable commodities, such as food, clothing, fuel, and a broad variety of service expenditures that consumers customarily provide in meeting the requirements of prevailing standards of living.   The typical consumer is reluctant to vary the amount spent for staple foodstuffs; he will vary only moderately the outlay for the commodities and services that are basic to comfort and essential to maintain health and efficiency and to meet the social standards of the income level in which he finds himself.

In the average household changes in gross receipts do not immediately produce as marked a change in spending associated with these types of

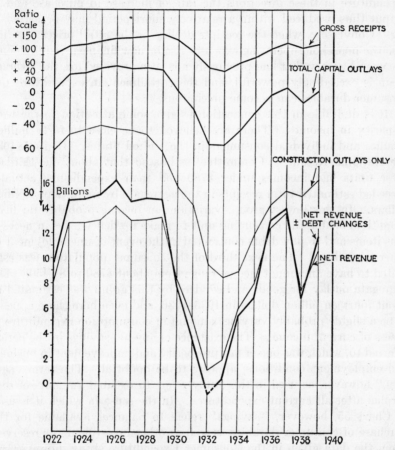

CHART 55.—Receipts, capital outlays, and net capital resources of individuals, 1922–1939 (preliminary estimates). The chart is drawn in a manner similar to that of Charts 46 and 49. For description of data, see Appendix 9.

goods and services as would be found in business operating costs, which comprise mostly labor and material outlays geared exceedingly close to gross receipts. The average household budget, therefore, appears to involve a relatively high proportion of what may be termed "fixed-charge" and "operating" overhead. Consequently variations in total receipts, after deduction of the rather narrowly fluctuating but relatively large amount of customary outlay, *produces a powerful "leverage,"* that is, wide variability in the amounts available and destined for expenditures on various kinds of durable capital, building, household equipment, automobiles, etc. These durable goods are postponable; their purchase can be deferred. On the other hand, many of them are keenly desired, and as income becomes available to permit at least some expenditure in these directions the rate of increase in purchase and in output thus produced within a relatively short period may be astonishing. Conversely, when the receipts decline or the retail prices entering into the household operating expenses rise or new financial requirements become necessary that had previously not been provided for, the leverage again is exceedingly powerful, and the curtailment in expenditures for consumer durables can become precipitous.

It is desirable in this connection to give some attention to the wide disparity in incomes. There are believed to be close to forty million families and individual consumers in the United States. In 1935–1936 the National Resources Committee[1] estimated that about one-third of these units had incomes under $780 and their expenditures actually exceeded estimated total receipts in the aggregate by more than a billion dollars. In this lowest group, variations in income probably do little more than enable the consuming unit to make up deficiencies in necessitous items and to pay debts contracted in the event of unemployment or other misfortune. The next third of the consumer population was estimated to have an annual income range from about $780 to $1,450. The aggregate outlay for goods and services by this group was estimated at about fourteen billion dollars in 1935–1936, and even here there appears to be a slight (probably varying) amount of consumption expenditure in excess of current income. The existence of any net savings in the period referred to, which was one of fair prosperity and improvement in business and employment conditions, appears to be doubtful. The term "savings," however, as used in this study refers to residual amounts of *cash* surplus after all current expenditures. In the sense in which it is used in Chart 55, however, "savings" refers to balances available for the purchase of consumer durables as well as other investments or reserves. From the data given in the Consumer Expenditure study, however, we may conclude that the margin of funds available even in a fairly good business year to the lower two-thirds of the consumer population represents not a negative amount but a relatively small part of total receipts. Beginning with the income group ranging from $1,450 to $2,000, there begins to be appreciable net cash saving, and as income levels rise still higher, the proportion of expenditure for durable goods and services of the luxury type becomes relatively high, and there remains over and above all current outlays a substantial amount of cash saving available

[1] "Consumer Expenditures in the United States," Washington, D.C., 1939.

for external investments.   In the study referred to, these net cash savings in the income range of $15,000 and over are actually slightly larger than the total current expenditures.

We do not know a great deal about the cyclical expansion and contraction of spending in various directions among these various income groups.   Some hypotheses, however, may be ventured.   Since the relatively high incomes provide apparently ample reserve, it would appear reasonable to expect that in the event of curtailed receipts or rising prices, the propensity to spend for both durables and nondurables continues much longer than among families in the lower groups.   The relatively wealthy groups, then, may be expected to continue fairly active spending and investment in durables and also in securities until investment income is sharply cut or there are signs of acute impairment in the business situation capable of producing grave apprehension.   Apart from the instances of losses in the securities market or curtailment of salaries or entrepreneurial income, the psychological factor in variation of expenditures probably plays a large part in these higher income groups.   When dividends are reduced, bonds no longer pay interest, rents cannot be collected, or banks fail, these groups do curtail for financial as well as psychological reasons, and in such curtailment the durable goods very likely suffer more than the nondurables and the customary services.

This propensity among the wealthy to continue ordinary expenditures even as the sky begins to darken and curtailment begins to occur in employment and industrial production probably explains in some degree the curious phenomenon of continuing retail sales in some departments at the same time that lower income groups may be rapidly restricting purchases.   When a business recession has been under way for some time, the families and individuals in the "comfortable" income brackets still have reserve and will be capable of spending and replenishing supplies and equipment and thus placing a brake upon indefinite business curtailment, *provided* that there is no acute psychological influence capable of spreading apprehension over the future and accentuating the propensity to hoard rather than to release income and savings in the markets.   But adverse psychology is certain to exist if there *are* signs of a cumulative extension of financial involvement such as exists if the building cycle enters a prolonged and catastrophic period of foreclosure; or when social unrest brings about pressures upon Government to resort to emergency relief expedients that raise doubts as to the future of the social order.   Our hypothesis then suggests that the wealthier income segment among our consuming units maintains spending actively in spite of *minor* interruptions in business activity, and even for some time after the main turning point of what proves to be a *major* collapse; on the other hand, they are *among the first* to enter the market for durable goods after a depression has occurred, particularly when they see that their surplus income can be used to advantage to acquire the things that they desire at advantageous prices. These incomes probably have led the way out of the bottom levels of the residential building cycle.

There is no necessary association between the *size* of income and its *stability*. Many high incomes are from equity investments and are unstable. And there is some evidence that throughout the *medium* brackets of income there are numerous cases of families and individuals

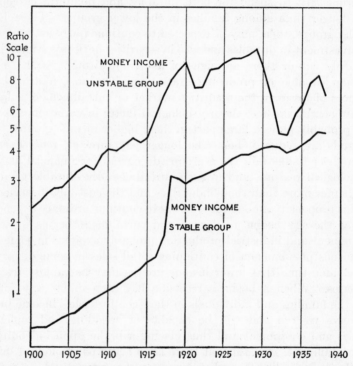

CHART 56a.—Money income of relatively most stable and least stable groups, 1900–1938 (classified according to origin). (Based upon national-income estimates of the National Industrial Conference Board, classified by the author.)

who enjoy remarkably stable money income. Just how many there are and what the precise components of this relatively stable income may be we do not know. In an attempt to illustrate the existence of contrasting income groups with respect to stability, two sets of data have been compiled and are shown in Chart 56a in terms of actual dollar income and in Chart 56b in terms of the income deflated to allow for changes in cost of living. The two income groups comprise a somewhat artificial aggregation of various income payments, mainly with respect to source and character of payment rather than in terms of receipt by particular individuals. Thus, for example, certain types of interest payments, entrepreneurial income, or wages appear to have remarkably little cyclical variation, although they may at times be subject to marked change in level through the existence of price inflation. Assembling these relatively stable income flows in a single group exaggerates the extent to which actual individuals or families rely for their *total* income upon these *particular types* of payment, but among the population there are many

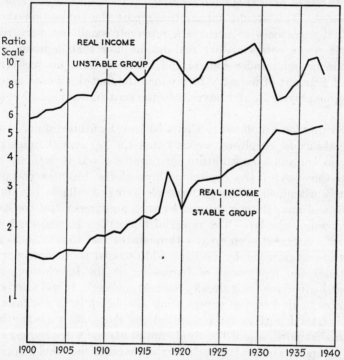

CHART 56*b*.—Real income of relatively most stable and least stable groups, 1900–1938 (classified according to origin). (Based upon national income estimates of the National Industrial Conference Board. Real income is derived by deflating money income, using the Conference Board and Bureau of Labor Statistics indexes of changes in the cost of living.

families who enjoy a stability of income essentially similar to that shown by these composites from relatively stable income sources. The unstable income group is more realistic in the fact that it is composed mainly of the wages and dividends flowing from industrial sources subject to the play of the business cycle.

In Chart 56*a* the contrast between the two groups of income as expressed in actual dollars is impressive. In Chart 56*b* the several segments of income have been adjusted for the changes in average living costs, and we again find remarkable results. Apart from the single instance of rapid change during World War I, the real income of the stable-income group pursues a fairly even course, and what is even more interesting, it maintains a rapidly rising general trend. On the other hand, the unstable group of real income not only suffers frequently from cyclical variation but appears to have made no important net progress in its general drift during the past generation. Most important from the standpoint of the present argument is the tendency of the stable real income *to rise in periods of business recession when the unstable real income is depressed.* This would appear to support the contention that it is through the existence of perhaps a relatively small but very resistant and, in a sense, compensatory real-income flow that depressions eventually are brought under control and a base is built for recovery in a sufficient segment of industry to produce the first significant support in activity, employment, and payrolls to the next upward spiral of general industry.

Returning for a moment to Chart 55 and the utilization of estimated individual-income surpluses, we find that the percentual range of fluctuation in consumer expenditure for durable goods is actually greater than in the case of the capital outlays of the business corporations previously examined. The patterns of savings available for consumer durables and annual expenditures for such equipment and construction are exceedingly similar. The range of fluctuation in consumer savings resources is rendered even greater through the fact that in some periods savings are augmented by positive additions to borrowings,[1] while at other times the repayment of borrowing or the foreclosure of loans represent deductions from already reduced savings. It will also be noted that the estimated capital expenditures are shown in two segments, the first being total outlays for residential construction, while the interval between that portion and the total capital expenditures represents outlays for durable equipment such as automobiles, household appliances, etc. Attention is again drawn to the fact that expenditure for building during the 1920's was the bellwether of all the durable plant investments in the nation, as the peak was reached in 1926 and the progressive impairment, gradual at first but violent later on, served as probably the fundamental restricting influence upon maintenance of employment, expansion of payroll income, and ultimately the solvency, not only of consumers but of institutions, railroads, and service corporations in a wide variety of fields.

Although it would be inaccurate to say that the manner in which the average family handles its capital financing and the nature of the financial

---

[1] These represent the total of estimated annual changes in capital derived from the mortgage market and credit obtained for the purchase of durable consumer goods on installment basis.

practices that have been associated with consumer capital goods are always, or always will be, the predominant forces in the business cycle, the evidence is clear and definite that these have been the basic underlying and generating factors in business cycles not produced by political action or major types of industrial innovation. It is the instability emanating from *consumer* capital goods representing large aggregate values and dominating the operations of a large segment of manufacturing industry that serves to explain over long periods of time much of the causation of cyclical vibration. A corollary from this analysis is that any forces that could be set in motion to preserve a greater degree of stability in consumer income and that would provide that stability on a progressive scale as the range of income narrows to the range comprising the great consuming body of the nation *would contribute powerfully to the maintenance of activity in productive industry itself.* To attack "business management" as being primarily responsible for the business cycle is, in the light of this evidence, clearly meaningless, despite the fact that business makes plenty of mistakes. There is, of course, much that management in all branches of business can do if it recognizes its responsibilities and the advantages all around that might flow from a greater stability in production resting, in turn, upon a greater degree of stability in the flow of funds into the hands of the mass of the population. Without overlooking the fact that real income is a matter of production and not merely the circulating of money, we can say that there is room for improvement in the technique of dividend disbursements, the reduction of all business indebtedness to reasonable proportions, and the deliberate setting up of reserve to provide for at least as much protection to the stability of two-thirds of the national income as is now provided for a very much smaller fraction. Once it is clearly recognized where the primary sources of cyclical instability really lie, great strides can be taken in crystallizing and formulating a code of Sound Management Practice with a challenge to business and to capital to provide for *their own* protection in the *long run* by taking greater pains to stabilize employment and payrolls in the *short run.* To these matters further attention will be given in Chapter 21.

In Chart 57 one further comparison of receipts, capital expenditures, and surplus available for capital uses is established for the agricultural "consumer" group. The procedure here is essentially the same. The index of estimated annual surplus is derived by deducting from cash income from sale of farm products all estimated items of farm expenditures, but without allowance for the outlays for farm family maintenance as such. Further adjustment is made for changes in the value of inventory on farms, which is important in the case of livestock raising. The final result is then further adjusted to allow for the estimated amount of annual change in mortgage financing. Here again the final results afford substantial verification of the principle that capital expenditures vary more than in proportion to receipts. The high variability in expenditures for plant and equipment is associated with the even more volatile behavior of available savings plus capital borrowed. Here we have marked instability in the demand for a wide variety of important manufactured products and materials created by changes in world conditions and markets, in weather conditions, and in political policies

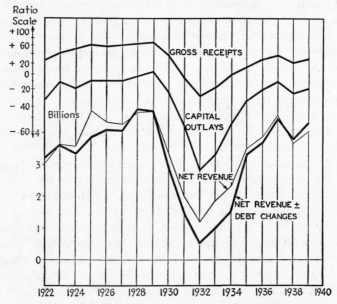

Chart 57.—Receipts, capital outlays, and net capital resources of farmers, 1922–1939 (preliminary estimates). The reader should bear in mind that the lower curves are on an arithmetic scale, while the upper curves are on a common ratio scale. The degree of fluctuation in adjusted net revenue or net capital resources far exceeds the fluctuation in capital outlays or gross receipts. For description of data, see Appendix 9.

affecting prices and production, all of which are transmitted to industry as highly variable demand factors.[1]

At this point we may devote some attention to the use of short-term credit by consumers. Broadly speaking, this kind of financing expands and contracts along with industrial payrolls. The amounts of such credit being extended represent a reinforcement of the rise in payroll (and other) income and later an accentuation of the decline in that income. With an extended increase in income disbursements, the volume of outstanding installment credit expands, and saving operations are

[1] The reader should keep in mind that in Chart 55 the exhibit pertaining to individual consumers *includes* (so far as possible) the agricultural group.

enlarged, and in the reverse case repayments so far outbalance new credit extension that the saving element is brought to its minimum level. As installment credit is utilized, it results in acceleration, particularly in the activities of durable-goods producers, and this is transmitted along the line as these industries, in turn, expand employment and payrolls.

The use of credit by consumers in retail purchases goes back a long way. A century ago it was manifested in the "book credit" extended by merchants to customers, usually in the upper income strata. What may

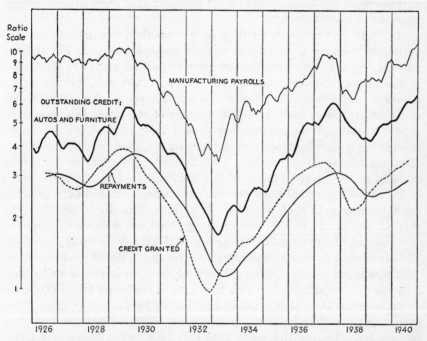

CHART 58.—Installment credit for automobiles and furniture, and industrial payroll income, 1926-1940. The data of repayments and credit granted have been smoothed by a 12 months' moving average, which accounts for their greater degree of continuity as compared with the amount of credit outstanding, which has been adjusted by a seasonal index, as has also the payroll income.

be termed "installment credit," involving the use of a formal contract and payments at stated intervals over a specified period, seems to have been used more than a century ago in the sale of furniture. Gradually this was extended to sewing machines, pianos, books, etc. The growth of the installment-credit system more or less paralleled the expansion of manufacturing activity and the development of large cities where rising living standards manifested themselves in a rapid expansion of consumer durable-goods industries. While the use of installment credit expanded with particular rapidity in the 1920's, along with the spectacular development of the automobile and numerous electrical devices, this was really a continuation of what had already been taking place over many years. We are now able to trace statistically, beginning in the middle 1920's, some of the important aspects in the extension of credit for consumer purchases of durable goods. In what follows we shall confine attention to installment credit granted to individuals for the purchase of durable commodities, without special reference to other forms of consumer credit, such as book credit, cash loans not representing acquisition of durable consumer assets, and distress loans used for miscellaneous urgent purposes or for refinancing.

In Chart 58 are shown monthly data (smoothed to eliminate seasonal variation) relating to installment credit granted to consumers and the amount repaid in financing the two most important groups of purchases, passenger automobiles and furniture.[1] The interval between the two curves indicates positive or negative changes in the total amount of such credit outstanding, and the actual amount of the latter is shown separately. Although the outstanding debt develops broad cyclical movements closely paralleling payroll disbursements, there is a significant lag after payrolls at many points. A much closer agreement in the timing is found in the (dotted) curve of the credit granted each month, which lacks many of the smaller movements[2] but agrees substantially with the main turning points of payrolls. It is important to notice that the cyclical amplitude of the new credit granted, as well as repayments, exceeds that of the payrolls for reasons that we have already indicated. The repayment cycles lag considerably after the cycles of credit granted.

There is not yet available sufficient information to enable us to state fully the precise manner in which the curve of consumer credit extension expands during the rising phase of a typical major business cycle. From partial evidence, however, we can venture a tentative statement of what takes place. During the years 1935 and 1936, when business activity and national income were expanding rapidly, it was estimated[3] that the lower income groups increased their installment indebtedness proportionally more (that is, in relation to income) than did the higher income

---

[1] The data are those of the National Bureau of Economic Research, as given by Holthausen, Merriam, and Nugent, "The Volume of Consumer Installment Credit, 1929–38," 1940. This study summarizes a series of studies of the National Bureau on this subject. See also in this connection Rolph Nugent, "Consumer Credit and Economic Stability," Russel Sage Foundation, New York, 1939, and Evans Clark, "Financing the Consumer," 20th Century Fund, Inc., New York, 1933.

[2] The two lower curves were smoothed by a 12 months' moving average, which eliminates many minor fluctuations present in the upper curves, adjusted by the use of indexes of average seasonality.

[3] R. A. Young and Blanche Bernstein, The Statistical Pattern of Installment Debt, National Bureau of Economic Research, *Bulletin* 76–77, Oct. 15, 1939.

families. For the groups having incomes below $1,000, the average increase in installment debt ranged from $71 to $100 during these years. We do not have such detailed estimates for other periods of business expansion, but it appears probable that in the course of such a period the demand for labor increases sufficiently to enable lower income groups to obtain, at least temporarily, some of the cheaper types of household equipment and low-priced or used cars, the purchase of which was impossible until that stage of industrial activity had been reached. The extension of consumer credit to these groups of low and unstable purchasing power involves a larger and larger measure of hazard to the financing institutions. In other words, the quality of the advances deteriorates, just as the quality of the long-term securities floated near the top of a business boom represent the marginal borrowers and the more speculative types of enterprise. At the upper end of the income structure the use of installment credit appears to be much more restrained, as cash reserves are ordinarily available. The financing as a whole essentially represents the advancing of funds from those who have considerable surpluses to those who, for the time being, at least, have a credit standing just within the limit of acceptability and who therefore are tempted to utilize this credit in the satisfaction of modest hopes long deferred. But as the structure of credit expands, a point is reached at which the additional stimulus thus given to the manufacturing industries brings still further numbers within reach of credit facilities of this type. Meanwhile, the repayments begin to be an appreciable factor in the family budget, particularly among families who had begun to utilize such credit on more substantial credit standing earlier in the prosperity period.

NEED FOR CONSUMER EDUCATION ON FINANCIAL COMMITMENTS

This process of repayment generates no particular difficulties within a considerable range of the borrowers, but it produces just enough strain (when we consider the inevitable consequences of overoptimism and the lack of full provision for all the auxiliary expenses connected with durable capital goods) to deprive the nondurable-goods markets of a portion of their expected demand. It is in these industries, such as apparel and textiles, that we find many of the workers near the bottom of the wage-income scale. As these industries are curtailed with the sudden, volatile action, we have noted, the possibilities of credit repayment by workers depending upon very modest payroll income are impaired. This introduces immediately a further restriction in the purchasing of nondurable goods by these same people. The spiral therefore appears to travel through the nondurable goods and to affect presently the demand for some of the durables. As the spiral proceeds, it becomes evident to those who are granting consumer credit that a situation is developing warranting somewhat more restricted terms and more careful scrutiny of those desiring to make new loans.   In 1937, this was clearly evident as the banks and many institutions in the installment-credit field took vigorous action in stiffening the terms and contracting outstanding lines of credit.   In part, this represented a response to governmental pressure, which was exerted as a part of the general policy of contracting credit in view of general inflationary prospects.

It has been the experience of consumer finance institutions that the repossession ratio, although rising considerably during a depression period, has never been of disturbing proportions or such as to impair the financial position of the better companies.   The consumer who enters into an installment contract and has made a number of payments in addition to his original cash payment (or surrender of a used asset) has a natural inclination to continue payments lest he lose his equity in the new asset.   This is a pressure capable of forcing many families to forego for as long as a year or two the purchases of unessential merchandise and nondurables.   Families assume most of these obligations during a prosperity period under the atmosphere of spirited sales promotion and advertising that emphasizes the long period of repayment and the moderate monthly installments.   But once committed, the tendency is very generally to complete the ownership.   Unfortunately, as conditions of business deteriorate, the failure to make payments has frequently occasioned a harsh attitude on the part of some lending agencies.   Something like 40 per cent of all consumer credit in the past few years has originated in loans made by commerical banks, either directly to consumers or to the financing companies.   The finance organizations using their own capital have in most cases been disposed to maintain a given set of terms, regardless of the general condition of business.   The banks, exposed to various external factors, with considerable variation in the funds available for lending, have been inclined to be more liberal in making installment loans or granting credit to finance companies in the early phase of a period of prosperity; in the later phases they have restricted credit, to the disadvantage of the borrowers.   Nugent states:

The banks themselves frequently exerted pressure upon consumer credit agencies to liquidate their loans in periods of depressions.   There were many examples during the depression of 1930–1933.   In some instances the depression impaired the liquidity or even the solvency of the consumer credit agencies and banks perhaps properly refused to renew their loans to such agencies.   In other instances banks were compelled to call the loans of consumer credit agencies because depositors were demanding their money and many other types of assets were frozen.   But in many instances, in 1931 and 1932, banks in good condition called the loans of eminently sound consumer credit agencies.   A few years later the same banks were aggressively soliciting the further expansion by the same customers of credit lines which already far exceeded the level at which they had previously been called.[1]

Here again we find evidence of the unstabilizing effect of commercial banking practices. It should be added that a good deal of the stimulus to induce consumers to avail themselves of term credit when times are good emanates from manufacturers of automobiles, radios, refrigerators, etc., who appear to be willing for competitive reasons to run the risks of overextending the current boom rather than forego the final small margin of business in the interest of preserving greater industrial stability.

If there are aspects of installment credit subject to criticism from the standpoint of being an unstabilizing factor, these probably can be regarded as problems in consumer education rather than fundamental defects in such credit as an institution. The consumer is gradually becoming in a sense a capitalist, and he is being gradually educated in the ways of handling his finances to preserve his solvency and avoid being trapped in overcommitments and unwise investments. Leaving aside such technicalities as excessive interest charges, unethical and unreasonable practices with respect to repossession, tricky contracts, and promotional pressures, all of which are being brought under the control of regulatory provisions, the underlying problem here is one of restricting the credit granted to a given borrower or family unit to such an amount as can be readily liquidated over the period contemplated.

This problem has not yet been solved, since it is difficult to carry personal investigations far enough to ensure that the borrowers do not overextend themselves in the simultaneous financing of too many kinds of durable goods at once as soon as some measure of surplus income becomes available. The commercial banks have been very slow to enter this field, which is certain to be of increasing extent and importance in the future, but they are now exerting a wholesome competitive influence. Attention must also be given to the fact that even after safeguards have been introduced, there will probably still be a tendency for consumers to misjudge the future outlays that durable goods bring in their train as auxiliaries and maintenance requirements, which, together with the repayment process (essentially a saving operation), serve to retard the rising drift of nondurable purchases following a period of unusual outlay for durables. On the other hand, a sound system of regularly amortized or installment credit, with all possible safeguards and regulations to eliminate abuses, is of outstanding importance as a means to provide for millions of people a means of systematic saving and a basis for enlargement of consumer acquisition of capital wealth as a source of demand

[1] *Op. cit.*, p. 142.

for industrial products.   This is of vast importance, because the field of consumer durables has *no observable expansion limits.*

It is another of the remarkable features of installment credit, as it has developed in the United States, that it represents very clearly the principle of *systematic amortization of debt.*   Regardless of all minor abuses and defects, there can be no doubt that so long as consumer saving can be encouraged by amortized borrowing, repayable on schedule, and utilization mainly for durable capital, no fundamental objection can be raised to the gradual expansion of such loans.   Now that we are approaching the point at which both residential construction capital and installment credit are being placed upon a systematically amortized basis, we may confidently expect, as soon as the world is restored to a peaceful basis, that capital growth, surging up from the demand of consumers, with a responding expansion in the capital facilities of industry and transportation may continue indefinitely.   Let the reader observe, however, that the provision for these durable appurtenances and production facilities all involve *saving* operations.   If individuals are to continue in the future to pursue such systematic programs of saving, there must be surplus income available for this purpose, and this must be assured not only to individuals but to business management and to the providers of business capital without fear of political expropriation.[1]

From the foregoing discussion one further important corollary may be fairly drawn.   This is that in the interest of stabilizing the operations of business, it is important that sudden and violent changes in the flow of income to consumers be avoided.   What we seek primarily is a rising *trend* of *real* income, not a succession of spurts and slumps in money revenue.   Political policy has frequently overlooked this point, because its attention has been directed by false economic thinking to the alleged necessity of disciplining business management rather than smoothing out the flow of those funds that, in the hands of consumers, tend to produce instability in demand for the products of business.   Inasmuch as the flow of funds in the hands of consumers, even neglecting the least

[1] In connection with the cost of consumer installment financing, the generally declining level of interest rates, as well as the reduction of risk, favors gradual reduction in the interest charges connected with such financing.   The old principle of "cash credits," which was explained by Adam Smith in "The Wealth of Nations," applies to this case.   The consumer is gradually learning that his credit standing on the average is excellent and that he is entitled to installment contracts in which not only is there provision for amortization of the principal sum but also there should be payment of interest *only on the outstanding balances.*   Much confusion has been created by promotional devices purporting to offer 6 per cent credit when, in fact, the charges were several times this if figured upon the average amount of outstanding balance.   As these matters become better understood, we may expect the results to become impressively favorable to the development of this aid to systematic saving.

efficient group at the poverty level, amounts to such enormous sums and in view of the tremendous leverage as the result of the high proportion of fixed charges in household operation, it is a grave mistake to attempt to stimulate business by suddenly pouring billions of dollars into the hands of consumers, as the New Deal Administration has frequently done. To reinforce a recovery movement already under way by capricious release of large subsidies or income supplements is a foolish policy. It would be far better to direct political policy toward the particular barriers that may stand in the way of a free flow of investment, a prompt reorganization of impaired financial structures, the liquidation of stale debt, and the ability of productive enterprise to accumulate and retain for productive-capital purposes a reasonable fraction of its revenue. We cannot lift ourselves by our bootstraps.

The provision of a gradually increasing volume of useful goods and services must be considered as a problem of properly organized productivity rather than merely a phase of the circulation of money that in itself is meaningless. Abrupt spurts in the circulation of money invariably produce maladjustments that later reduce the momentum of production, but a gradual rise in the variety and volume of useful wealth cannot fail to bring into existence as it expands an adequate volume of the means of payment. If the total volume of debt is brought under reasonable control, it is quite immaterial whether this expansion in physical volume is accompanied by a gradually changing price level. Stability over long periods in the price level is important only in an economy that tries to finance everything by means of unpayable debt. The best results can be accomplished by less attention to prices and by confining the use of amortized *debt* more and more to *consumer* interests and less and less to the *productive* interests, that is, business organizations. Let us divert our credit machinery to building up equipment demand where it can count most, but at the same time relieve productive enterprise of the unnecessary burdens of debt, whether public or private. There is no sound reason why productive enterprise cannot, by and large, develop itself and its capital resources primarily through its own accumulation of savings and through flexible equity financing. This concept of the broader aspects of finance contemplates a society in which the *loan* machinery is made increasingly available to consumers (including Government, insofar as this is unavoidable) while at the same time industry, trade, transportation, and corporate enterprise generally are put in a position to provide the resources for growth and development out of unhampered earning power and equity capital. This is the key to still higher living standards that mean, in the last analysis, merely the willingness to keep on producing more and better things, and not the equalitarian distribution of poverty.

APPAREL AND TEXTILE PRODUCTION A BAROMETER OF BUSINESS BOOMS AND DEPRESSIONS

Let us now examine the business cycle a little more closely in terms of merchandising. We have already seen that the typical amplitude of fluctuation during the course of the cycle in retail trade is relatively subdued, whether we consider it in terms of volume or money values. We have noticed the curious tendency of this phase of business, when considered in physical volume, to precede or anticipate the cyclical turning points of general production and income flow. There remains the puzzling question why it is that both the volume of turnover in representative general retail business and also the physical volume of production of nondurable merchandise (or textile products) tend to turn up and down so sensitively *before* the corresponding changes in the *money funds* flowing into the hands of consumers. How does the typical merchant know when to release orders to manufacturers or wholesale dealers or when to curtail his purchasing in the absence of what would appear to be the clear evidence in the form of purchasing power made available through his customers? Do these customers reduce their buying months before they experience actual reduction in their money income? Do they reassert their interest in purchasing goods months before they find their revenues recovering after a recession? These are puzzling aspects of the business cycle, for which we find no ready explanation.

The writer has submitted this problem to a number of prominent merchandising executives and specialists in retail economics throughout the United States. He asked a number of questions, to which the responses proved to be decidedly interesting. On the basis of this information, supplemented by dynamic observations of several branches of merchandising, production of textiles and wearing apparel and food and the behavior of prices in these lines, the following analysis is offered as a preliminary explanation of what takes place.

We shall consider primarily the case of retail stores, the major part of whose sales consist of wearing apparel, textile goods, and footwear, and we shall examine the relation of their business to consumers, on one hand, and to manufacturers of apparel and shoes and textiles, on the other. These activities constitute a relatively important segment of American industry. According to the Census of Manufactures, 1937, the production of all types of wearing apparel and textile goods represented a total value amounting to 7.7 billion dollars. The total wage disbursements were 1.75 billions and represented 2 million workers. In that same year the estimated total retail sales of apparel, department, and dry-goods stores was over 7 billion, nearly one-sixth of the total estimated sales of all retailers in the United States. The value of all food products consumed exceeds by perhaps as much as 50 per cent the value of the apparel and textile goods, but we shall not include foodstuffs in our comment because of the well-known fact that cyclical variation is of very minor proportions in the flow of foodstuffs to the consumer, while the production and processing phases reveal a diversity of cyclical movements that more or less offset in the aggregate. If we break down the total value of non-durable merchandise purchased by consumers into its various elements, we find that the foodstuffs have the least tendency to vary cyclically, and such items as gasoline sales, tobacco products, beverages, and some miscellaneous items also reveal relatively narrow fluctuation.

When we come, however, to wearing apparel and the closely related activities of the textile industry, we find, as shown on Chart 51, a surprising degree of cyclical instability, with movements that compare in intensity of rise and fall with those found in the durable-goods industries. It is these volatile movements that mainly give to the composite non-durable-goods sales and production indexes such cyclical variability as they do reveal. Were it not for this high degree of instability in the textile group, the flow of output catering immediately to consumer ephemeral and semidurable goods, as well as their sales at retail, would reveal almost negligible cyclical instability. Since we are analyzing the matter from the standpoint of causal dynamics, it is here that we must perhaps seek some clues to the nature of the mechanism. Incidentally, it is of interest to observe that the total estimated amount of nondurable goods purchased by consumers in 1937 amounted to over 36 billion dollars, more than twice the combined expenditures of producers *and* consumers on equipment and buildings. In that same year the durable goods purchased by consumers were less than 8 billions, and the amount going into housing for residential purposes was somewhat less than 2 billions. With this perspective as to the relative values here involved, let us proceed to examine the nature of those segments of retailing in which apparel and textile products are of primary importance in view of their cyclical pattern.

It is fairly well established that neither consumers nor retailers appear to be able to forecast very far ahead as to the probability that income or sales will expand or contract (apart from purely seasonal variations). Prior to World War I and as far as about 1920, merchants appear to have been frequently inclined to speculate in ordering merchandise from manufacturers and jobbers. This was particularly the case in periods when prices were advancing rapidly and the tendency was to anticipate consumer demand farther ahead than usual and to ensure against still higher prices later. In rural sections many local merchants appear still to operate in this fashion in view of the dependence of their sales upon farm price changes, which, in turn, affect the purchasing power of their customers. The swift collapse of commodity prices in 1920 produced such widespread havoc among merchants caught with large inventories that in the succeeding decade a marked change in practice spread through the merchandising field, and the inclination to purchase far ahead of requirements is now limited to a small minority of the large houses and a limited number of the very small and rural retail units. Today the typical department store or apparel shop does not endeavor to purchase more than two or three months ahead of the season, which means that the rate of turnover of the inventory is generally higher than it was twenty or thirty years ago. This change in purchasing habits has, however, placed somewhat more responsibility upon manufacturers to maintain reserve stocks to meet the demands of customers. These tendencies are rather general throughout the field of retail distribution.

The typical substantial urban department store or apparel house usually places orders for a given season on the basis of its sales in that same season of the previous year. This forms the "basis," amounting to perhaps 50 to 75 per cent of requirements, with the balance held in abeyance pending a study of consumer responses as the season gets under way. The general tendency for merchants in the lines that we are particularly considering is to consult consumer response rather than to attempt to anticipate it by any appreciable interval of time. A rising drift of prices, either of raw materials or of the merchandise itself, is apparently not generally regarded as a reason for increasing the orders over the level indicated by past experience unless it is believed that in the locality or areas served there will be considerably better response from consumers. A special reason for caution in ordering goods lies in the fact that the style element today is subject to much more rapid and perhaps capricious change than was true a generation ago. Yet the merchant or merchandising organization is intent upon having inventory in hand *at least adequate* to meet the rate of demand that materializes. If in a given period orders have been sent to mills or dealers on the basis of a previous season that happened to coincide with a business recession, and if the current season reflected improvement in conditions, it would soon be found that the orders were insufficient to maintain a satisfactory competitive position. One of the merchant's greatest fears is that he will have to turn customers away because his lines are not well filled out. An equally acute fear is that inventory will become too large so that price markdowns will be necessary, perhaps involving substantial loss, in order to clear the shelves for the next season. It is probably to *inventory*, either in terms of ratio to sales or on some other basis of record, that a merchant gives his most concentrated attention.

The type of merchandise that we are considering has a relatively short consumption life, and replenishment after any period of interruption occasioned by impaired buying power becomes virtually a necessity. The average cycle of replacement in the case of apparel seems to work out roughly at about two years, but there is some doubt as to whether this precise period is realistic.[1] Merchants appear to be fairly conservative as to inventory expansion as times improve. As soon as a relatively small rise in employment and income occurs, wage earners begin to spend for essential articles. Although the sustained spending by those having steady income from Government, annuities, pensions, educational services, etc., exerts some degree of stabilizing effect and modifies the extent of trade depression, the first sharp improvement appears to come in sales of various semiluxury goods in which style elements attract a portion of available surplus income. As merchants observe, for example, that furs and jewelry are having better than expected sale, they immediately revise their estimates and expand orders for other goods. These larger orders instantly cause similar revision in the policies of the manufacturers. Apparel and textile production represent the survival of relatively small-scale manufacturing and commercial units and intense competition, especially in the case of women's wear. So intense is the competitive situation that the moment orders begin to appear, a buzz of activity causes some firming of prices, and men and women are suddenly put back to work.

The curve of production of textiles in Chart 51 vividly illustrates the sharp reversals, well ahead of practically anything else in industry, from one phase of the cycle to the other. Merchants with whom the writer has discussed these matters have referred to the fact that the clever retailer is always on the alert to discern a change of attitude among his customers; a few days of better-than-expected business encourage the placing of orders beyond the basic inventory already ordered or in hand. Apparel retailers again represent in the main a highly competitive branch of business. They vie with each other through elaborate advertising, keenly watching the smallest signs of change in consumer attitudes and sales in the more sensitive lines of merchandise that from experience they have found to afford clues to the immediate future. Should there be some especially favorable news, the orders to mills and jobbers will expand overnight. As this takes place, the response in production is virtually instantaneous. In this regard it differs from the production response in most durable goods, building materials, and the like because of the

[1] G. F. Warren and F. A. Pearson claim to have found a sine function of 23-months period fitting the curve of textile production from 1919 to 1938. The tendency during these years was for textile production to be relatively high in the odd years and low in the even years. This is an interesting discovery, but there are many cases in which such regularities of fluctuation observed for a period of time prove to be more or less accidental and do not maintain themselves indefinitely. See *Farm Economics*, Cornell University, February, 1939.

length of time that is required in these lines to bring idle facilities into operation and to assemble working forces, etc. In the apparel and textile industries, the workers are close at hand, and the mills and work-shops find it possible to expand production enormously because of the ready resort to overtime work or use of several shifts. The textile industry can work on a 24-hour basis and repeatedly does so, alternating with periods of partial idleness.

Consider now the manner in which curtailment takes place and why it can occur so far ahead of statistical evidence of a downward turn in the general movement of industrial production, income, etc. Let us examine the dynamics first on the assumption that important changes in prices are taking place. Let us imagine that prices at wholesale are rising, merchants have already stocked up liberally with apparel and textile materials. The more alert merchants begin to be apprehensive that they may be overstocked and prices are closely watched. If at that juncture there is either an unusually sharp rise or a sudden decline in prices, the tendency will be *to cut orders abruptly*. Such a sharp further rise in prices, after a period of previous advances, suggests to the merchant that there are persistent forces at work to raise prices, and he may have to replace merchandise at a much higher cost. He sizes up his stock very closely in the light of consumer taking. The slightest hesitation on the part of consumers to buy affords additional warning that it would be unwise to enlarge inventory. The experienced merchant decides to begin to reduce inventory without delay, and the first step is to curtail orders. The estimates of adjusted sales of department stores (Chart 51) indicate the hesitating, initial decline in the *volume* of trade in 1919, transmitted to the operations of the textile mills near the close of 1919 and *well ahead* of the peak in the general business indexes that came in 1920. This decline in activity occurred as the combined result of consumer resistance to further advances in prices, especially after the spring of 1919, and the evidence that sales were not holding up sufficiently well to justify existing inventory. The larger merchants led the way to a curtailment that was as dramatic as it was disastrous to the majority of them, as well as to employment in the textile and apparel industries. Wanamakers, early in 1920, announced in national advertising that they would reduce prices horizontally at a given date. This set the precedent for others, and a spiral of contraction lasted for over a year.

It appears that the larger mercantile establishments in this field, as probably in others of a similar character, give attention to the possibility of price weakness in the basic markets such as cotton, wool, silk, rayon, leather, etc. In Chart 51, the wholesale prices of textiles are shown as month-to-month percentage changes, in order to emphasize the changing rates of advance and decline to which the keen retail buyer gives attention in trying to gauge the price outlook in the basic markets of greatest concern to his business. Accelerating advance and decline in prices quoted by mills and jobbers stimulate action quickly among the retail leaders. Actual wholesale prices, of course, move more slowly than the physical volume of business, and the turning points in the industrial cycle occur in most instances well ahead of corresponding changes in prices. It is the *exceptional* price advance during a rising trend that produces the first rush to safety.[1] After an extended decline in prices, a similar accentuation of decline would be expected also to instill additional apprehension rather than furnish a buying incentive, but an ability of prices to hold for a time or to taper in rate of decline would be observed as an encouraging sign. But these indications are probably used as a basis for policy by a small minority rather than the great majority of merchants.

Apart from price movements, merchants appear to have other ways of gauging the points at which to shorten sail. In agricultural areas they are able to observe directly the probable tendencies in farm income based upon crop prospects and farm prices. Very alert merchants pay particular attention to the movement of merchandise sold to men, whose purchases appear to be most volatile and sensitive to a change in the temper of business conditions. The writer finds that in the case of the higher priced women's apparel, turning points in sales appear usually to come relatively late. Among wage earners there seems to be a tendency for highly sensitive adjustment of their retail purchases of nondurables. Workers seem to gather from the atmosphere of their places of employment when the signs point to prospective curtailment that may affect them. This is particularly true of the clerical and salaried workers, who appear to adjust their affairs to these indications, thus affording a highly sensitive barometer that is soon transmitted to the volume of the apparel and department-store business. As previously stated, the revival of trade following a depression or recession is primarily a result of replacement demand, gathering momentum first as the result of purchases by those with stable or surplus income and producing the same quick response among merchants who find inventories too low to' meet the inquiries for goods and who, by placing orders, give the first sharp impetus to production revival.

More fundamentally important, there is at work in these merchandising cycles the effect of the systematic saving by the mass of consumers as the result of previous commitments for durable goods and construction. The consumer today uses a liberal amount of credit (either

---

[1] If an accentuation of price advance is associated with conditions likely to result in a marked reduction in available supplies (such as occurred in 1941 under war conditions), the tendency would be for merchants to increase inventory rapidly.

installment or simple book credit) in connection with his merchandise purchases, but the amount of borrowing involved in the purchase of durable goods is a much higher proportion of the values involved. A period of sustained recovery in general business will usually expand the consumer acquisition of automobiles, household equipment, and accessories of many kinds, and these expenditures precede, rather than follow, the saving operations involved. If a period of expanding business also coincides with the period of rapid momentum in building construction and financing, we can expect this situation to have a definite effect upon nondurable purchasing. In the event that housing, house accessories, and automobiles are being actively acquired by wage earners, there will be an accumulating amount of consumer credit outstanding. The expansion of the saving to make payments on capital advances *increases faster than income itself.* This follows from the fact that the rise in expenditures for these durable goods reflects the use of surplus income subject to powerful leverage (see again Chart 55). Many merchants have conveyed to the writer their opinion that this saving is not an imaginary element in bringing about gradual curtailment and ultimate reversal of the spending by consumers in such retail stores as we are considering. From about the middle of 1928 to the middle of 1929, the *volume* of department-store business appears to have expanded little. In 1936, the signs of impending curtailment in nondurable goods came sooner than in any other significant branch of business.

In the event that such a curtailment in retail business takes place as the result of consumers' attempting to carry too large a financing program in housing and household durables at the same time, the resulting curtailment in the textile and related industries may be the forerunner of an extended depression. In the past, *e.g.*, during the depression of 1929–1933, the unsound nature of the building-finance system created a cumulative spiral of contraction through foreclosure and widespread unemployment almost without parallel. In the course of that severe contraction, it is interesting to observe the nature of the cyclical movements of the textile industries. There was actually a minor textile and retail boom in 1931, short-lived but extremely emphatic, as Chart 51 indicates. In the textile industry there was a decided upturn in the autumn of 1930; this lasted until the middle of 1931, followed by a relapse. This indicates that there is some validity in the concept of a short consumer-goods replacement cycle, but if the *major* cycle movement is still deteriorating, it tends to prevent the improvement in the apparel group itself from proving effective in reversing the general current of conditions. We may, therefore, speak of the apparel-textile-retail short cycle as one that weaves in and out of the more comprehensive and usually more protracted industrial cycle.

The very sharp upturn in the textile industry in 1932 again characterizes the high degree of sensitivity in this field. At that juncture replacement demand apparently became urgent, and inventory having been progressively curtailed in retail business, the ordering of new goods in the autumn of 1932 appears to have been exceptionally active. The relapse in the spring of 1933 was relatively minor and brief, followed by an enormous uprush in production in the summer of 1933. An examination of orders indexes[1] further substantiates the anticipatory character of these movements, as well as their dramatic intensity. The extreme, almost explosive expansion in textile production was, of course, occasioned by a curious concentration of unusual political policies. There was the initial monetary program for price inflation, capable of raising abruptly the price structure in the sensitive textile material markets; there was the National Industrial Recovery Act, which foreshadowed sharp increases in wages and shortening of hours and therefore immediately instigated mills to anticipate trade requirements before production costs were increased; and, finally, there was the new agricultural program, with its processing taxes and objective of reducing supplies and raising prices of several raw materials. Similar excited movements may be noted in the imports of wool during 1932 and 1933. They reached a considerably higher point in the summer of 1933 than in 1929.

Following these extreme disturbances, reflected also in the volume of retail trade, a consistent recovery in the apparel industry did not get under way again until the end of 1934. The boom in 1936, which culminated in curtailment of textile orders at the end of that year and about six months before general industrial production began to decline, occurred under circumstances involving a considerable rise in commodity prices growing out of the world armament race. A decline in orders for textiles appeared as early as November, 1936, and we have already noted the inability of department-store *volume* to expand after the summer of 1936. By that time retail inventories were already becoming excessive, and as soon as the rise in wholesale prices in the textile field began to accelerate, the curtailment of orders to the mills followed immediately.

Naturally, these abrupt booms and depressions in the textile and apparel field bring in their train more or less corresponding movements in employment, although the latter are by no means as volatile in their movements because of the highly flexible productive capacity of the typical concern. But this anticipatory change in the tempo of the textile industry brings about a corresponding early change in the retail

[1] Such as that prepared by the Associated Industries of Massachusetts for textile products, available on a monthly basis since 1927.

buying of *these particular groups of workers,* and we have already noted that they amount to a substantial population. Since so much of the textile activity is still concentrated in New England and so much of the apparel industry centers in New York, this concentrated effect of abrupt variations in employment in these fields, well ahead of general conditions in industry, is itself a factor of no small consequence in initiating and extending trade decline or revival. Whenever the general cycle of business conditions affords some internal evidence of having reached close to a peak level of capacity operations, the business analyst should closely observe the conditions in retail merchandising and the course of apparel and textile orders to manufacturers for the first signs of a general business decline. On the other hand, if a prolonged downward movement in the general cycle appears to be reaching a level where it may stabilize, this relatively sensitive group of indicators will again serve as a useful means of anticipating the earliest developments in the direction of a broad recovery in general business.

CHAPTER 20

INDUSTRIAL LABOR PRODUCTIVITY, WAGE INCOME, AND EMPLOYMENT

In discussing industrial labor income, we must carefully distinguish between wage *income* and wage *rates*. In the course of a typical cyclical upswing in industrial production, there occurs an expansion of payroll disbursements, but this represents mainly a rise in number employed and to a lesser degree more average hours worked per man or higher wage rates per hour. Usually the increase in amount of employment is the principal factor in the expansion of aggregate wage income during this phase of the business cycle. Conversely, when the succeeding phase of recession occurs, the reduction in total wage income is principally a reflection that fewer workers are employed and that fewer of those employed are working overtime or even normal time. The wage rates per hour, in money, naturally are responsive to demand conditions, as well as to the extent of organized efforts among the workers to bargain with employers collectively or to introduce coercive measures in maintaining or establishing rates and hours.

During an upswing neither the total wage income nor the hourly rates rise uniformly in different occupations. We have already seen that the forces at work in creating an acceleration in production, following recession, are never combined in exactly the same fashion. The leading impetus will dominate some fields of production, and others may respond but little. This disparity is naturally translated into the patterns of employment and labor income, also. The bargaining power of labor groups is also by no means uniform. Hence it is possible that readjustments in wage *rates*, as production revives and expands, may presently bring about wide gains in aggregate labor income in some sections and no gains at all in others. It is this *uneven distribution* of the expansion, both in production and in the flow of income to labor, that prevents the rise from continuing indefinitely. Some large groups fail to participate; others are involved in operations that sooner or later lead to more final product than can be absorbed quickly at going prices by the entire population. Hence there results a period of curtailment, especially marked in the durable or capital-goods industries but involving non-durables also, as we have seen, with an accompanying reduction in labor income. This labor income being by a wide margin the most important segment of the national income (distributed to individuals), it follows that the final disposition of structures, equipment, and other goods whose creation for a *growing* demand characterized the boom is rendered all the more difficult while the interruption of activity curtails buying power and with it the credit advances to consumers.

If, instead of the usual business-cycle oscillation, we have a period of rapid advances in prices, such as occurs under war conditions, there is a definite tendency for wage *rates* (per hour) to adjust themselves to the rising cost of living. This will be true to a more limited extent during a business boom in which for special reasons prices are stimulated and sharply raise the average living costs. But once the inflation of prices gives way to deflation, the industrial wage-rate structure is strenuously supported by the action of the workers. In other words, "real" wage rates in industry tend at least to stabilize in periods of price inflation and tend actually to *rise* during the succeeding price deflation. But to translate this into changes in real wage *income*, we must observe whether in such periods there is an increase or decrease in numbers employed, in hours worked per week or per year, and in the average amount of product per man-hour. As we have already noted, periods of violent price inflation are usually marked by irregular or actually impaired industrial production. In such periods, although the hourly price of industrial labor may be promptly adjusted to the general price inflation, the *total real income* of the wage earners may actually fall, because of war disturbances, acute unbalance within the industrial system, partial employment, etc. When prices become readjusted after an inflationary rise and more normal production conditions return, the extent to which real wage *income* will be restored or be capable of advancing further will depend upon the resistance of labor to reduction in money wage rates and, in the longer view, the extent to which general production and employment are expanded. Unless productivity in terms of the product per man-hour expands and unless the total employable population is kept at work, there cannot be a rise both in real wages per hour or in real income in the aggregate.

We find statistical evidence that in the United States postwar periods have been times of rapid industrial recuperation despite the higher level of money wage rates and a growing spread between the "price" of labor in this sense and the irregularly falling prices of commodities. The reason is probably to be found in the fact that higher labor prices encourage the improvement in manufacturing processes and the use of more power mechanism, and thus total production is greatly enlarged (although again not uniformly throughout the system), *and on the average*, the cost of labor per unit of product actually declines. This implies, of course, the existence of alert business management, resourcefulness of invention, and the availability of capital to introduce innovations in process and product.

As a result, the wage earners as a group obtain higher real wage *rates* and per capita real *income* by receiving a more or less proportional part of this increase in real wealth. We have distinguished between the aspects of wage adjustment that occur during a typical cycle oscillation and during the longer periods of inflation and deflation in the price level. In the former case, wage rates and income rise and fall in a pulsating movement that leaves the situation little changed, except that when the cycle has again returned to the depression phase, the bottom level may still be higher than the previous bottom, and some net upward trend is evident in real income, notwithstanding the ebb and flow. The ebb and flow are in themselves an unfortunate interruption of progress, and to eliminate them requires some moderation of the forces of acceleration, including a less rapid and better balanced distribution of wage income to prevent the acceleration, along with consumer credit and savings leverage, of consumer demand, so that it cannot be evenly or continuously expanded.

It will be emphasized as we proceed that a considerable part of the cyclical expansion in wage income and some part, too, of the rise in wage rates during the business upswing merely serve to create stresses that produce eventual reaction. Were the process more stable, it is entirely probable that the underlying general trend of wealth production and enjoyment might be capable of rising somewhat faster by eliminating the vibration and the financial and social losses occurring during depression. The stresses come about through the fact that industrial efficiency, broadly speaking, is reduced rather than enhanced as a boom condition reaches a high level. The cost of services, including labor, rise more slowly than the prices of commodities, and profits accelerate much more rapidly in the early stage of the rise than in the later phase. As wage rates are raised through pressure of demand and ability of labor to secure adjustments, the profit differential tends to be reduced, and stiffer resistance to further wage advances comes about at the same time that plant capacity in many lines is approached. Meanwhile, however, demand for nondurable goods may already have been impaired by financial involvement of consumers and the powerful undertow of a decline in consumer capital-goods demand, while introduction of major innovations has run into the difficulties of temporary overdevelopment.

Among these forces reversing the boom there stand out prominently the results of too rapid an expansion in income, resulting from the existence in the preceding depression of considerable unemployment and hence greatly impaired income, which is suddenly amplified and which creates tremendous leverage as it grows. If this cumulative enlargement could be kept within limits, even such basic forces as population movement or major industrial or transport innovation could be rendered less disruptive in their ultimate cyclical effects. All the evidence points to the conclusion that most of the gains made by labor income during a boom are illusory and the changes made in wage rates in a boom atmosphere, under temporary pressures, have no sound basis. The proof is in the fact that these adjustments do not long endure.

It is in the longer periods of wage adjustment that we find the most remarkable positive gains made simultaneously in the real return to labor and in industrial productivity. We shall find surprising and indeed paradoxical evidence that it is in the long intervals of fairly stable *money* wage rates, after they have been adjusted to inflation, when prices are falling, that the upward *trend* of productivity is most pronounced. This raises an important question of principle that should be kept in mind as this subject is further illustrated. Has industrial labor been able to raise its real hourly wage to parallel a gradually rising trend of productivity per man-hour by the accidental circumstance of the adjustment of money wages during inflation of prices and the equally fortuitous effect of subsequent "high" wages upon technical improvements and efficiency of processes? Is there really no other scientific basis for current wage adjustment that can at all times assure labor of at least a proportionate share in the gains of productivity? And is advance in industrial efficiency *mainly* dependent upon the pressure and stimulus of higher and higher spreads between the price of labor and commodity prices? If industrial labor and management can formulate a method of keeping real wage rates always adjusted to efficiency in terms of rising output per man-hour, what is to prevent labor from seeking a more than proportionate share of this product and rates of return, which may impede the full employment of the available labor force? And what is to prevent industrial production from changing its component elements to the end that more or less of total output shall consist of consumable wealth, as distinct from productive plant or war goods or things that only the incomes in the highest brackets can purchase? Obviously, a parallel movement of production per man-hour and real wages received per man-hour does not serve as a wholly accurate guide to fundamental wage adjustment; we need long-term measures of production in terms of distribution or consumption categories. Although we must pursue our investigation in this chapter in terms of rather crude over-all industrial-output indexes from the analysis, we can perhaps still better visualize historical tendencies and the real nature and importance of the problem of wage-income rationalization.

In order to survey historically the extent to which various groups of wage earners have participated in economic expansion and improvements in the creative arts during the past century, we should require statistical data on wages far more complete than are now available. We can, however, trace fairly accurately the manner in which annual wages and income have changed in relation to product and productivity in the case of the manufacturing industry, over the past half century, and, as to general trend, as far back as 1859. It is in the field of manufacturing that technological progress has been most impressive. The manufacturing industries have consistently afforded employment to nearly 30 per cent of all those "gainfully employed" during the past century. The operations associated with manufacturing occupy a central and strategic place in our economic system. Although the personnel associated with trade, professional service, and clerical work has expanded relatively faster than in mechanical occupations, most of the work done in these service lines

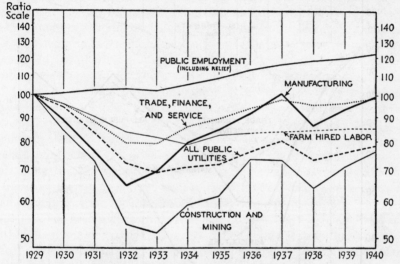

CHART 59.—Estimated annual employment by industrial segments, 1929–1940 (1929 equals 100). (*Based upon data compiled by the U.S. Bureau of Labor Statistics, with the exception of farm hired labor, which is from Works Progress Administration, National Research Project Report A-8, Trends in Employment in Agriculture, 1909–1936, and later data from U.S. Department of Agriculture, Farm Labor Reports.*)

directly contributes to coordinating, maintaining, financing, and distributing for manufacture.

Before we examine the broad historical trends, we may observe the manner in which changes since 1929 in numbers employed in manufacturing enterprise compare with those in a number of other segments of industry. In Chart 59 we can compare the annual changes in manufacturing employment with those in transportation and other public utilities, construction and mining, a broad service group including trade and finance, agriculture (estimates for hired labor only), and governmental service (including Army and Navy personnel). In these widely divergent movements we can detect the dominating influence of the Great Depression and also the presence of technological and political factors that have prevented the recovery since 1933 from being uniformly effective in the various groups. The construction and mining industries, for example, had by 1940 recovered only 75 per cent of the employment existing in 1929, but even this was a decided improvement over the extremely severe reduction in 1933 by nearly 50 per cent. In the transportation and public-utility industries, recovery has been relatively slow, and there is a suggestion of permanent impairment of total employment for a variety of reasons. Among farm hired labor there has been the influence of remarkable

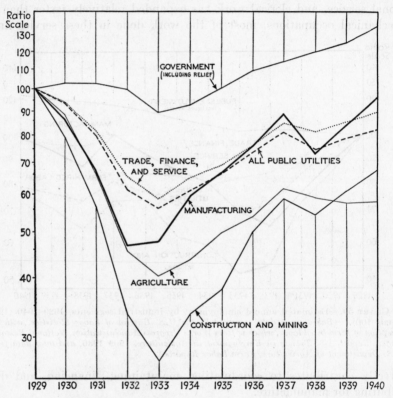

CHART 60.—Wage disbursements according to industrial origin, 1929–1940 (1929 equals 100). (*Based on indexes compiled by the U.S. Department of Commerce, Survey of Current Business, June, 1941.*)

improvements in mechanization, offset by limitation of product demand, which has retarded the reemployment of as large a labor force as existed in 1929. The trade, finance, and service groups, closely related to retail and consumer activities, suffered less during the Great Depression and by 1940 had, like manufacturing, substantially regained the employment level of 1929. Nevertheless, the total number of employable persons seeking work in these divisions had increased above the 1929 level. In the case of total governmental employment, there has been a remarkably consistent upward trend, which by 1940 had carried this group some 30 per cent above the 1929 level. The Government has absorbed in its employ a portion of the workers displaced elsewhere. With the exception of governmental employment, the manufacturing industries, by 1937, had restored employment more effectively than any of the other groups.

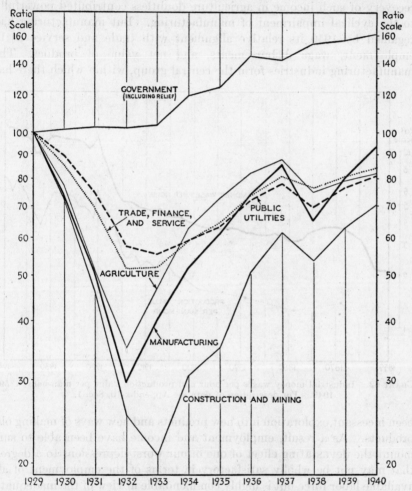

CHART 61.—Income payments by industrial origin, 1929–1940 (1929 equals 100). (*Based on data compiled by U.S. Department of Commerce.*)

In Charts 60 and 61 these changes since 1929 can be studied in terms of the money distributed to employers in the same groups of occupations and, again, in terms of the total value of income originated in the groups. As we pass from employment to these money payments and net values of product, we find the patterns much the same but the extent of variation progressively enlarged, as wage rates, prices, and the interplay of depression and revival forces are seen in their full pecuniary effect.   Throughout these exhibits it is clear that construction and its closely related mining activities suffered most acutely during the Great Depression, and the impairment of wage income in that segment and also the dragging recovery of such income in agriculture doubtless contributed powerfully to the cyclical impairment of manufacturing.   But manufacturing had regained by 1940 its relative alignment with trade and service as to employment, wage disbursements, and net value of product.   The manufacturing industries form the central group, within which there has

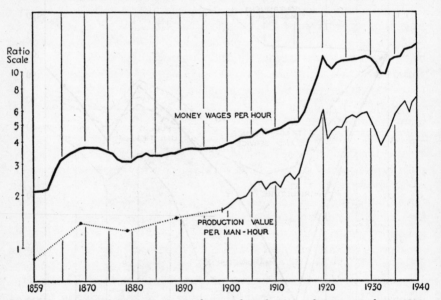

CHART 62.—Industrial money wages per hour and production value per man-hour, 1859–1940.   For description of data see Appendix 10, Sec. 1.

been incessant exploration into new products and new ways of making old products.   As a result, employment and income have been able to surmount the devastating effect of one of our worst depressions to a degree that may not be wholly satisfactory in terms of the employment of all available labor force but is highly commendable in view of the inadequate support given to demand for manufactured products by other industry groups struggling with obsolescence, excessive political domination and repression of initiative, or beset by the retarding influences of masses of stale debt and the heritage of unsound finance.

As the reader will find more fully explained in Appendix 10, we have for representative manufacturing industries sufficient data to provide, with considerable splicing and use of representative sampling, significant measurements of the trend of wage rates, labor productivity, and related aspects. We are to be concerned here primarily with wage earners (artisans), as distinct from clerical, service, or salaried employees of manufacturing enterprises. In Chart 62 we can compare annual average money wage rates per hour in manufacturing and the estimated money value (at wholesale) of production per man-hour, beginning at 1859. For the value of manufactures produced per man-hour of employed wage earners, we do not have complete annual information prior to 1899, but Census data enable us to interpolate at 10-year periods to establish the general drift.

In this comparison we are interested in the extent to which the money wage that the workers received per hour has kept pace with changes in the value of the products, reduced to a man-hour basis. It is apparent that there has been a parallel movement to a surprising degree. After about 1890 there was a slightly more rapid rise in value of product per man-hour than in average remuneration per hour of the artisans, but from the beginning of World War I, with a very prompt and rapid adjustment of hourly pay to the general price rise, the parallel drift was reasserted. The movement of the value of product per man-hour appears slightly more volatile than money wage rates per hour, possibly partly because of incomplete or not wholly suitable data. This close and consistent adjustment of hourly wage rates and value of product per man-hour may represent forces impinging upon wage rates through both prices and living costs and the amount of output, and, conversely, forces emanating from wage rates *to* both prices and output or efficiency.

During the last war period, inflation of the cost of living arising from wartime Government spending translated itself promptly into wage adjustment as the result of two somewhat related factors. One was the policy of the Federal Government, expressed in the Adamson Railway Wage Act of 1916 and in official admonitions to all employers to maintain wages as nearly as possible in line with the changes in living costs. The second was the powerful stimulus given to labor unionization during these years of emergency and inflation. The record of A. F. of L. membership from its beginning shows that periods of rapidly rising retail prices have always been periods of very active organization campaigns. From 1916 to 1920, A. F. of L. membership doubled. After 1921 union membership declined but held fairly steady between 1923 and 1930. During this period, with the cost of living relatively stable, there was less economic stimulus to unionization. The postwar boom in building activity and the major expansion in the automotive and electric-power industries afforded a continuously unfolding opportunity to find employment and to improve wage income. The upper curve on Chart 62 indicates, however, that there was but little improvement during these years in average hourly wage rates in manufacturing, which contrasts with the rapid rise from 1921 to 1929 in value of production per man-hour.

Following the reaction of the Great Depression, which created an emphatic shrinkage in union membership (to about where it stood before World War I) and in the power of organized labor to combat closing of factories and progressive weakening of solvency in all directions, there came the dramatic efforts of the new Federal Administration in 1933 to improve the situation. With a far more friendly Government attitude toward union labor than at any previous time, the natural result was an intensive drive for union organization, beginning in 1934. A new nucleus of union organization began in 1937 to supplement the American Federation of Labor when the Committee for Industrial Organization (now known as the Congress of Industrial Organizations) became a medium for rapid unionization of wage earners in important industries that previously had not been unionized. Important, also, in this postdepression period was the effect of the National Industrial Recovery Act (1933) and the so-called Codes of Fair Competition, aiming quickly to lower hours of work and raise wage rates per hour and thus provide for absorption of the unemployed. Although the NRA Codes suffered at the hands of the Supreme Court in May, 1935, a good deal of this abrupt revision of hours and wage rates persisted.

In July, 1935, there was also another important political effort to strengthen the hold of organized labor through the Wagner Act. This was aimed at counteracting the mushroom growth of many "company unions" that the coming of the NRA had stimulated. The Wagner Act provided that agreements between labor and management should be specific and that labor organizations were not to be sponsored or dominated by management. A National Labor Relations Board was given power to investigate controversies and to establish, as far as possible, the right of the employees to form and join labor organizations and bargain collectively through representatives of their own choosing. Although the work of the Board with respect to many details of this complex process of collective bargaining and the determination of the union having an actual majority in given situations were not wholly successful and not wholly fair to employers, the objectives of the Act in promoting unionization were abundantly attained. In addition, the last decade has witnessed several inflationary movements as the result of currency policy, the NRA experiment, the boom of 1935–1937, as the world began preparations for war, and the still more menacing initial inflation under actual war conditions. All this has afforded additional stimulus to a powerful industrial labor organizing movement. It is important to understand this close relation between unionization, as a means of fortifying labor bargaining power, and the ability of the wage earners to improve hourly earnings and income as measured in other ways. In Chart 62 the results may be seen in the sharp recovery in manufacturing wage rates per hour, particularly from 1934 on.

WAGE RATES AND PRODUCTIVITY PER MAN-HOUR

It might be expected that there would be a continuous tendency for hourly wage rates to adjust themselves to the value of product turned out per man-hour, but actually the wage adjustments, as previously stated, have accompanied periods of unusual distortion in the cost of living and accelerated activity in strengthening the bargaining solidarity of labor that always parallel these price movements. Responses in the improve-

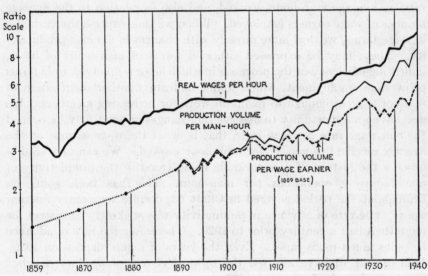

CHART 63.—Industrial real wages per hour and production volume, 1859–1940. For description of data see Appendix 10, Sec. 2.

ment of technique, mechanization, and the organization of processes have been generally much less prompt and emphatic than adjustment of money wage rates to living costs, but they have eventually been equally emphatic. When deflation of prices is under way, the effect of revised hourly rates of pay upon particular commodity prices depends largely upon the trend of productivity per man-hour. Prices can be lowered if the productivity of the processes rises rapidly in spite of high wage rates. But these adjustments are further complicated by the extent to which changes in price may, in turn, affect sales. Enlargement of sales by efficient mass production naturally is much more practicable in new industries than in industries becoming mature or obsolescent. In these latter cases, probably business mortality is hastened with attendant shifting of

working forces.   In a vigorous new industry whose products are of wide
and expanding appeal to consumers, there is a considerable range within
which prices may move regardless of wage rates.   In view of these diverse
conditions in various industries it is difficult to generalize on the point,
despite the fairly reassuring nature of the historical evidence.   So much
depends upon the vigor of innovation and the productive flow of capital
during these long periods of price readjustment.

Let us now consider the effect of reducing our measurements to a
"real" wage and physical-volume basis.   In Chart 63 we have the hourly
wage index adjusted for cost-of-living changes.   We wish to compare this
with the index of physical volume of manufacturing output, expressed as a
ratio to average man-hours worked, and also in relation to the average
number of wage earners employed.   When we thus express the variables
in these terms, we deal more directly with changes in average productivity.   These may be expressed either in terms of man-hours of labor,
indicating efficiency of the processes in which labor is involved, or in terms
of average employment, which would indicate whether distribution of
product is great enough to maintain work for increasing members.   We
also have an opportunity to observe the changes in what may be termed
the real wage rate per man-hour, that is, what the wage earners on the
average receive "in goods" for each hour worked.   We can now readily
observe the history of a remarkable rising trend in the productivity of
manufacturing operations per man-hour.   This has been going on
throughout the period covered in Chart 63, despite temporary fluctuations.   The rate of advance in productivity was strikingly consistent for
more than half a century prior to 1920.   Thereafter the rate of advance
becomes much more rapid.   Even the years of severe depression 1930–
1933 appear to have affected the upward course of productivity but
momentarily.   In fact, since 1932 the upward trend is even somewhat
steeper than during the decade of the 1920's.

Underlying this striking increase in output per man-hour (or, as we
might express it, reduction in man-hours required in the shop and at the
machine to produce average units of product), there are, of course, numerous influences.   There has been remarkably sustained technological
progress, expressing itself in the manifold application of power to mechanization and the development of apparatus that is virtually automatic.
There has been a tendency toward larger units of plant capacity, so that
increased production can be undertaken within a wide range without anything like proportionate enlargement of the number of operatives.   There
has also been rapid progress in the more effective organization of work
through the adoption of assembly lines and continuously operating mass-
production systems, reduction of lost time and motion in the handling of
materials, better standardization and improved workability of raw mate-

rials, and the integration of operations that previously had been performed in separate plants or in distant localities. The coming of the automotive industry did much to promote this new era of efficiency in production, but these technological advances have not been limited merely to manufacturing. In agriculture there are many examples of the introduction of mechanical devices that have made it possible to reduce the amount of hand labor in harvesting, cultivating, seeding, and final processing. Outstanding is the case of wheat production, in which American output per man-hour has actually been doubled in the past twenty years. We find similar tendencies in mining and service industries.[1]

Under conditions of persistent expansion in productivity such as has marked this modern industrial revolution, still in progress, the readjustments could be of several possible kinds. We must first distinguish between increase in productivity per man-hour and expansion in production. To bring out the principle, we shall assume two distinct cases: first, no increase in production but an increase in output per man-hour. To make our reasoning less complex and essentially realistic, we shall further assume that average prices over a trend period may be either constant or lower, but not higher; that no average net increase in hours of work occurs; and that no average net decrease in money wages per hour occurs. Let us examine the theoretical implications of higher productivity in industry before we proceed with the statistical record of what has happened.

First, assuming no change in industrial production or in employment, the fact of increased productivity would imply a lowering of hours per

---

[1] The problem of technological change and its bearing upon employment and unemployment has been intensively studied by the Work Projects Administration. A series of Monographs constituting a National Research Project, under the direction of David Weintraub, has been issued during the past several years. Among the studies in this series the reader may find it helpful to consult the following: "Unemployment and Increasing Productivity" (G 1); "Effect of Current and Prospective Technological Development upon Capital Formation" (G 4); "Industrial Research and Changing Technology" (N 4); "Production, Employment, and Productivity in Fifty-nine Manufacturing Industries, 1919–36" (F 1); "Trends in Employment in Agriculture, 1909–36" (A 8); "Survey of Economic Theory on Technological Change and Employment" (G 6). The study of the "Effect of Technology in Agriculture" has been revised and extended in a separate publication of the U.S. Department of Agriculture, May, 1941, as "Changing Technology and Employment in Agriculture," by John A. Hopkins. The general series of WPA studies includes also a considerable number of reports on individual industries. The significance of mechanical developments in connection with opportunities for employment was also discussed by Theodore J. Kreps in testimony before the Temporary National Economic Committee, Apr. 8, 1940. See also the study by Spurgeon Bell, "Productivity, Wages and National Income," prepared for the Brookings Institution, Washington, D.C., 1940, and criticism of it by Mordecai Ezekiel in the *American Economic Review*, September, 1940.

man-year. This would permit higher wages (this being in money per hour throughout), and if these were proportionate to the reduction in hours the payroll and total labor cost would remain constant. If prices of goods were constant this would balance out, leaving real income to all workers in industry constant so far as the products of industry are concerned, the only gain being in more leisure. If wages are increased to a still higher level, there is a rise in total labor cost that must reduce employers' profit. A moderate reduction of profit might be absorbed without difficulty; and there might be ways of economizing in purchase of raw materials, on salaries, financial charges, etc., but it would not be realistic to assume any reduction in taxes and other service charges. Hence, unless private management is to be deprived of sufficient net earnings to make saving and improvement in processes worth while, there are definite mathematical limits to the changes, under our assumptions, that could be made in wages, hours, and prices.

If we assume that more men are to be hired, without a change in total production, it follows immediately that a reduction in real annual labor income (from manufacturing) is unavoidable. Hours will still be reduced, but the more they are reduced the further will be the decline in real income. Prices cannot at the same time be reduced without serious deduction from profits. To avoid such a deduction, further improvements in the technology of industry and improvement in organization might be made, but these depend on the progress of invention and the arts of management and the extent to which business capital structures and the incentive to make investments in industry are not impaired by the prospect of progressively heavy losses. Unless production *is* increased faster than employment, no gain can be made in real wage income derived from commodities, and reduction in working time cannot proceed faster than is consistent with industrial solvency.

If production does not expand (and we are still speaking of *trend* intervals, not cyclical oscillations) and average prices fall, a constant working population could reduce hours and enjoy more leisure time, but it could *not*, at the same time, raise wages, either in money or in commodity income. If more workers were engaged, to avert unemployment, there would be a deep reduction in working time, a curtailment in real income, and no change in wage rate.

Assuming now that *production*, as well as productivity, is expanding, wage earners could have a gain in real income so long as product more than kept pace with numbers employed. A static working force would obtain the benefit of this progress by constant wages if prices were reduced or by a wage increase proportionate to the increase in commodity values, with prices steady. Put in another way, if a higher real income is sought, with higher money wage rates also, average prices cannot be reduced. If the working population is expanding and more men must be hired, real wage income will not be increased if the expansion in employment balances the expansion in total output; under these conditions there would simply be a reduction in hours and more leisure. If the numbers employed increased less rapidly than in proportion to total production (still assuming the same rise in *productivity* as before), there could be a limited reduction in hours and a limited rise in real income. Wage rates in money could not be raised unless prices were steady, and there would be strict limits to the extent that wage rates could be raised, hours shortened, or prices revised if the system was to remain solvent and production enterprise not impaired. A consistent, moderate, restrained pressure on management to increase efficiency and production per man-hour, through wage and hour adjustments, is not to be considered undesirable, but if management can bring about a prompt distribution among wage earners of the gain made on its own initiative this pressure would seldom be of any material consequence. But if labor lost all sense of the importance of technical efficiency and the vital part that capital, invention, and management play in promoting it and press for exorbitant gains in money wages that do not and cannot result in real income gains, the only possible result is industrial chaos and disintegration. What is sorely needed in wage bargaining is more accurate determination of the effective limits of wage and hour changes in the light of production, productivity, commodity prices, and the various other costs facing both workers and employers.

If prices were very drastically reduced so that payroll income were to rise faster than total commodity values, there would either be an enormous value of saving by wage earners, much of it going ultimately into the wages of those rendering services (and thus increasing business costs also), or a tendency to restore prices and the total value of products, including durable consumer goods. This might incidentally stimulate a further rise in productivity, but only if the savings flowed primarily in highly effective industrial uses and did not merely pad the pockets of private or public servants. If taxes usurp the differential to provide for the prosecution of war, it can be assumed that the production constituting real consumable income would be reduced. So far as services are concerned, under normal conditions they cannot be expanded far out of line with industrial production for the simple reason that those rendering service require physical commodities in return as the principal part of their real wage. To say that more service occupations are a remedy for unemployment is absurd; the only remedies for unemployment are either more production *by industry* (agriculture can be considered general to population) or a willingness on the part of those employed to forego some wage income rather than to pay out this much income in taxes for poor relief. Shorter hours are a solution only within the limits set forth above.

We thus see that any reasoning about the manner in which changes in productivity affect an industrial situation involves a number of variables, including number of workers employed, hours per worker per annum,[1] wage rates per hour, production volume, and price of the products. What seems most definitely clear from a study of the historical evidence, however, is that the broad trend changes are distributed among these factors so that there is a give and take. If average productivity in industry is doubled, there will probably be intermediate results with regard to the number of hours worked and money wage rates. But these tendencies will depend in large measure upon the strength of union organization and its contribution to bargaining power, the extent to which labor's demands are given additional support by public policy. Results will depend upon the attitude of employers or those who control the businesses that the managers manage. As industry does not move forward as a unit and many segments may not progress at all, there are many obstacles to a final adjustment in terms of real income that would represent the best result all round.

We are now in a position to examine the relationships shown in Chart 63. It will be noticed that the spread between the upper curve measuring the average change in real wage rate per man-hour and the second curve below, the change in volume of manufactured products per man-hour, has been *narrowing* throughout the period. In comparison, however, with the lower curve, volume of production per wage earner employed, the disparity is much less pronounced. This means that the rise in productivity has not brought about a wholly proportionate distribution of goods to the wage earners in manufacturing; rather, the gains in technological progress have been divided in such fashion that more men have been kept at work than would probably have been possible had real wage rates been elevated strictly in accord with productivity. Those workers who have had jobs have shared their remuneration with those who might otherwise have been deprived of jobs.

It is important to keep in mind that we are speaking of the return to *employed labor*, not employable labor. Our chart tells us that not only are fewer men needed per unit of manufactured product but that each one

---

[1] We have not considered the variation in intensity or difficulty of labor as a distinct element, in order not to complicate the discussion unduly. For many purposes an increase in intensity may be considered as offsetting a shortening of hours, since it creates fatigue, which neutralizes leisure time and may ultimately reduce the advantages of shorter hours by an abrupt shortening of working life. Much of the recent antagonism of labor to management practice appears to have grown out of unreasonable speeding up of processes in ways that gave the worker no means of adjustment.

of these fewer men works fewer hours. In order to keep our industrial wage earners employed over the period as a whole, we have been hiring fewer and fewer men in factory work and engaging fewer man-hours to obtain a unit of product. But the total units of product have been expanding fast enough, until recently, to ensure a rising or at least a stable trend in employment. We have already noticed in Chart 50 that the volume of employment during the 1920's, after allowance for the cyclical fluctuation, did not seem to make much progress. After 1929, the decline in employment was very much pronounced, as was shown in Chart 61. We shall presently discuss this emergence of persistent unemployment.[1]

Let us now examine more closely the index of real wages per man-hour in Chart 63. Observe that it has not risen continuously but by a series of broad steps. There was a marked gain after the Civil War, and then the purchasing power of an hour's work held fairly steady for more than a decade. The rise to 1893 was largely due to the decline in the cost of living, and this was followed by another very long plateau, lasting until 1919, more than a quarter of a century. The impressive rising trend that developed from 1920 exceeded anything in the preceding period, but much of this recent rise was accomplished in the abrupt advance in 1934, followed by a still further rapid advance after 1936, mainly the effects of the NIRA and the organizational drives previously discussed. Although productivity per wage earner employed made no such striking gains in these years, there was a widening of the disparity between productivity and production per worker that reflects the shortening of hours. But the average industrial wage earner not only increased his leisure time but made a significant gain in the real hourly rate of pay.

---

[1] In speaking of productivity per man-hour, we do not imply that there is a "specific" part of the man-hour product neatly attributable to labor's own contribution. We are tracing the *comparative change* in estimates of what a wage earner receives in real income with the change in *productivity of process expressed for this purpose* in terms of labor. Actually, the product is divided up among several claimants in ways that represent bargaining powers and competitive forces. We are assuming for the present purpose that a broad rise in productivity should result in *at least* as broad a rise in real labor income, but the shares of all product going to wages, to salaries, to capital, to enterpreneurs, and to Government will depend upon the proportionate participation by all these groups in the process of production. Furthermore, total wage-earner income may derive some enhancement from capital investment, and the return to capital and management may be modified to provide Government income. As pointed out below, the test of parallel progress in productivity per man or man-hour and production per man or man-hour is, after all, a rough approximation only; it does not allow for the fact that some services must expand to assist production (other than wage-earner services) and that wage-earner *income* actually includes changing elements of capital and property return that supplement the pay envelope.

COST-OF-LIVING INDEX

We cannot be wholly sure of the accuracy of this measure of real wages, whether in terms of hourly rate or the annual rate, since these involve conversion of money payment to real wages by an index of average change in the cost of living.   This adjustment is subject to numerous minor errors that it is impossible to verify or eradicate.   Cost-of-living measurement during most of the period covered by Chart 63 involves an attempt to estimate the average effect of changes in the retail prices of a fixed group of commodities and services upon which wage earners in manufacturing industries are believed to spend the major part of their income.   As indicated in Appendix 10, the farther back we go, the more we must depend upon rough and indirect statistical evidence rather than on specific retail-price data.   As we move toward recent years (let us say since about 1913), we can have more confidence in our data, but it is difficult to make full allowance for certain important tendencies in the manner in which wage-earning families spend their incomes.

We are still using the cost-of-living index prepared by the Bureau of Labor Statistics, whose list of basic commodities and services priced in the retail markets has not been materially altered for nearly a quarter of a century.   Actually, consumers have been shifting their spending constantly in new directions, and although we may have accurate retail prices paid for a complete list of items that constituted a typical budget many years ago, the drift of these prices so weighted would not afford an entirely accurate index of the real purchasing power of wages.   The more recent studies have not sufficed to show just what these changes have been, although we do know a great deal more about the manner in which consumers spend their funds today than was ever known before.   It is known also that the distribution of expenditures over different types of commodities and services always shows different results for each income bracket, and as the wage earning group has altered its general income position there has naturally been a resulting change in the distribution as well as the size of income.[1]   These statistical defects throw some doubt upon the complete accuracy of our measure of real wages.   Improved measures, however, will doubtless be made available in the near future.

There is a further point in connection with attempts to measure real income as distinct from money wage changes.   This is important in explaining the apparent lack of perfect adjustment of the real wage rate to productivity or even production per worker employed, in contrast to

---

[1] If we consider the matter in terms of the contribution of the principal wage earners to family income, we must also take into account the fact that supplementary family earnings probably make up somewhat more of the total income today than was true twenty or thirty years ago.

the much more perfect adjustment of money wage rates to the per man-hour value of manufactured products. The cost-of-living index used to derive real wages is not the same as the average of prices whereby we translate the output of manufactures (in physical units) into aggregate values. The cost-of-living index involves other than manufactured goods, and these other items involve price changes that do not agree with those in the commodity markets. If wages received were spent *entirely* on manufactured goods and if the retail prices of these goods were found to move exactly in unison with their wholesale prices, then, the purchasing power of the hourly wage would have moved along in almost complete parity with the value of the goods bought, as indicated on Chart 62. But retail prices include many service charges and prices involved in distribution and financing.

In recent years retail merchandising has entailed more and more refinement in the service demanded by consumers. The cost of distribution has probably been rising per unit of goods sold, although accurate measures of this are not yet available. It has probably been more difficult to expand the productivity of service labor in retail distribution to anything like the proportions achieved in manufacturing. Hence the consumer, in spending his money, encounters a certain friction or leakage in *the channels of distribution*. Even more important is the fact that in addition to commodities, consumer outlays include a wide range of utilities.[1] There are sales taxes, rent, and amortization of capital costs in connection with housing, etc., in comparison with these outlays the consumer's dollar has not been endowed with increasing purchasing power.

This disparity between changes in the cost of living and the movements of most industrial commodity prices is shown in Chart 64. It would appear at first glance that the cost of living has been virtually held in suspense between the very rapid rise of hourly wage rates and the relatively depressed position of raw material prices. Although, as we have seen, the industrial hourly wage has been fairly well correlated with rising productivity, it is nevertheless quite possible that in some degree the cost of living has failed to adjust itself to the trend of the wholesale prices of manufactured goods because of excessive elevation of wage rates in *some lines* where the rise is *not* compensated by higher productivity. There are certainly many instances in which demands for higher wage

---

[1] In an analysis of distribution costs by N. H. Engle, under the auspices of the U.S. Department of Commerce, September, 1937, it was found that for such items as tobacco products, confectionery, medicines, toilet articles, furniture, radio apparatus, and washing machines, the cost of distribution was a larger percentage of the "value added" by manufacture than was the percentage of cost of production to those values. See also the study of the Twentieth Century Fund, "Does Distribution Cost Too Much?" New York, 1939. The subject is also discussed by W. H. Lough in "High-level Consumption, Its Behavior and Its Consequences," New York, 1935.

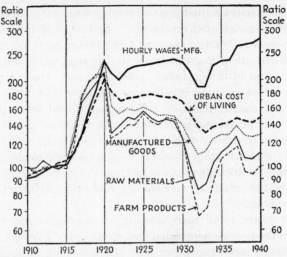

CHART 64.—Indexes of prices and wage rates, 1910–1940 (1913 equals 100).   (*The hourly wage rates represent the same data as used in Chart 62.   Cost of living is the Bureau of Labor Statistics index.   Price indexes for manufactured goods and raw materials are those of the National Bureau of Economic Research, compiled by F. C. Mills.   Index for farm products represents the prices paid to farmers, taken from Agricultural Statistics, U.S. Department of Agriculture.*)

CHART 65.—Annual industrial wage earnings and production, 1890–1940.   Based on data described in Appendix 10, Sec. 3.

rates have been carried over from highly productive operations to other fields of production, especially service, where, in the absence of any proportionate increase in productivity, the higher rates have been in part passed on to purchasers, either through higher prices or prices that have resisted the downward trend since 1920.

Thus far we have considered only the remuneration of the wage earner in manufacturing in terms of the hourly wage rate. We have attempted to compare the changes in this average rate with the measure of productivity most closely associated with it. But, of course, the hourly pay rate is no adequate measure of the *earnings* of labor. The drift in earnings should properly be measured in terms of the average *annual* remuneration per employed worker, since changes in hours may involve changes in the length of the working week, and there may be variations in the number of weeks of work during the year. In the last analysis the family bills of the wage earner must be paid on an annual basis. We may first compare in Chart 65 the changes in average annual earnings per employed wage earner in manufacturing with the estimated value of the manufactured products per employed worker (lower curve). These indexes cannot be carried back with any accuracy beyond 1890, but a comparison of the annual pay and the per man value of goods produced reveals the same tendency for closely parallel and proportional movement that was found in the case of the indexes in Chart 62. In other words, the annual average earnings have fully held their own in keeping pace with the value per worker of what was turned out of the factories.

To compare in volume terms, observing the upper curves that refer to the real annual earnings (income) and the volume of production per worker employed, we find the same gradual pinching out as before. There is the same lurking doubt as to the entire accuracy and validity of the cost-of-living adjustment applied to the money earnings. The cost-of-living index itself is shown in the chart in comparison with the actual money earnings (base at 1913). In the light of this evidence we can again say that the annual pay of these wage earners has sufficed to purchase *manufactured goods* (but not necessarily all other things) to an extent virtually keeping pace with the advance in productivity. It is important to keep always in mind that rising wages and rising real income necessarily require and involve expansion in productivity, whether measured in terms of production per man-hour or in the more general terms of production per employed wage earner. There has been some misuse and misunderstanding of these trends in order to make it appear that wage earners have been attempting to inflate the "price" of their labor beyond all reason and to the disadvantage of other social groups. A clear conception of the significance of the productivity measure is, therefore, necessary to maintain an intelligent viewpoint. On the other hand, the recent ascendency of mass-production labor and its rapid mobilization into aggressive union organizations bent upon dictatorial power over management and business policy make it important to refer to the measures of productivity as among the essential standards for testing the validity of the demands for higher pay or more leisure.   Although our indexes are in terms of average experience and the case of a particular labor group in a given industry does not necessarily permit the application of the production or productivity test, these elements must always be given consideration, as must also the general evolutionary development of the industry.

RATIO OF PAYROLLS TO GROSS PRODUCTION VALUE

Let us now examine the matter of wages and production from the standpoint of measuring changes in average labor costs.   These may be

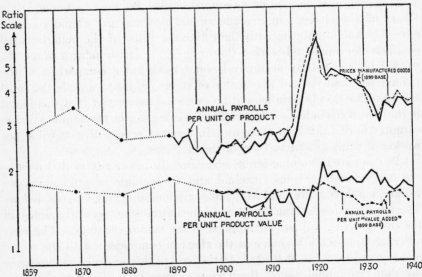

CHART 66.—Industrial payrolls per unit of product and product value, 1859–1940. For description of data see Appendix 10, Sec. 3.   The index of prices of manufactured goods (*Bureau of Labor Statistics*) and annual payroll disbursements per unit of value added by manufacturer (*Census of Manufactures*) are both shown relative to their 1899 levels to show their relationship to the other data through the following period.

shown by the ratio of hourly pay rate to hourly production per man or, more accurately, annual payroll disbursement to the annual volume of production.   The upper line in Chart 66 illustrates the changes in manufacturing labor cost, beginning at 1859, by decades, and annually from 1889.   This is given in terms of average annual payroll disbursement related to production volume.   Payroll data have been carefully adjusted to the comprehensive Census of Manufactures returns; the volume of manufacturing production is reasonably representative in the earlier years and increasingly so for the past twenty years. The labor-cost index naturally responds to the rise and fall in the cost of living and the efforts of organized labor to adjust earnings to these changes. But it also responds to productivity changes. The combined result of these factors develops a dynamic pattern that is remarkably close to that of the wholesale prices of manufactured goods, as shown by the upper dotted curve. Since the inflation interval of World War I and at least until 1933, one of the important reasons for the deflation of commodity prices has been the *ability of industry to reduce the manufacturing cost per unit so far as labor is concerned.* Of course, there is also to be considered the trend in cost of raw materials, which form a substantial portion of the total cost of manufacturing. As we have seen, there were independent factors bringing about enlarged supplies and some excessive surpluses of raw materials following the last War. Is it possible that these have been the main factors operating upon the price level and the reduction of average unit cost of manufactured products?

Some light is afforded if we turn to the lower set of curves in Chart 66, which illustrate, respectively, the interesting ratio of manufacturing payroll outlay per unit of product value and (from 1889) the ratio of total payroll outlay to the "value added" by manufacture, based upon Census data. Taking first the ratio of payroll to *value* of production, we have a measure of the share that wage earners have derived from the operating revenue of the employers. We cannot be sure of the precise pattern prior to 1900, since we have only the decade figures of the Census, but there has been a tendency toward oscillation about a *horizontal* trend ever since 1859. In other words, the industrial wage earners have been able to obtain (with some temporary variations) an almost constant percentage of total revenue. Periods of rising prices have temporarily disturbed this equilibrium, insofar as workers had not promptly adjusted annual earnings to prices and employers had diverted a somewhat larger fraction of revenue to the purchase of raw materials on rising markets. This was notably true in the early years of the last War. When prices began to collapse after 1920, there was a tendency in the opposite direction. From 1921 to 1940, the drift of the payroll-earnings ratio to the selling of products has been following a gradually declining course, but on a slightly higher plane than prevailed for many years before the War.

In the two decades prior to 1920, insofar as data are available, we find a fairly close alignment of this ratio of payrolls to gross production value and the second ratio of payrolls to the net value of manufacturers, deducting the value of raw materials. After 1920, however, this alignment no longer holds true. The ratio of total payroll to "value added" breaks away to a very significant degree. The wage earners in their payroll earnings averaged a less satisfactory share of net values from 1921 to 1933. This indicates that more of the revenues of manufacturing companies were disbursed in other directions than labor, presumably in payments for capital and provision for expansion of capital equipment, as we previously noted in Chart 46. Here we find one possible reason for criticism of industrial management during the years preceding the last Great Depression. We have seen that during these years there was not a particularly active labor-organization campaign comparable to what existed during the preceding War years or to what has recently been witnessed. In this rather neutral situation, labor appears to have been content to accept a somewhat lower share of the net product values, and it possibly also failed to obtain an entirely adequate adjustment of wage rates to average increase in productivity. Although these disparities are not large, they nevertheless are fairly clearly indicated in the data and should not be overlooked in conclusions as to the manner in which labor has shared in the result of industrial development.[1]

We may summarize by saying that labor costs to the employer in manufacturing industry cannot be understood apart from changes in commodity and raw-material prices or the general drift of prices. Since prices are now irregularly moving upward and have already been given sharply advancing impetus by the developments of World War II, manufacturing enterprises find themselves in a position in which they must contend with not only higher costs of materials but a rising drift of wage costs when expressed relative to other outlays and changes. This will certainly involve trenching upon the residual shares going to capital and to depreciation and maintenance if the highly significant ratio of wage earnings to value added continues to rise above the level that seems in the past to have been indicative of equilibrium. If inflation of the price level continues, in spite of drastic measures to limit prices and ration scarce goods, and increasing pressures from organized labor for shorter hours and higher rates of pay not justified by productivity are tolerated, the problem of maintaining capital and technological progress and expansion in the manufacturing field will become acute.

---

[1] The reader will notice that following the bottom of the Great Depression, some interesting changes in trend have occurred in several of these measurements. The average cost per unit of product has been rising irregularly rather than continuing the previous declining drift. Employers have had to pay somewhat more per unit for raw materials, but after allowance for this it is significant that after 1933, and as the result of the political dispensations in favor of labor, there was an abrupt rise in the share of payroll earnings in the *net* value of manufacturing product. Interrupted in 1939, this has since continued its reversal and has apparently brought about a ratio more nearly approximating that which prevailed fairly consistently during the decade prior to World War I.

Following the present War, these issues may become of paramount consequence if prices are not deflated. The problem may not be what the employed wage earners will derive as their share of the net values created but rather how many workers will be permanently deprived of jobs in order to establish the more favored and highly organized segment of industrial labor living on a plane of income out of balance with the real productivity of the processes. These are fundamental and basic issues that must be faced and minutely examined by the friends of labor as well as by those who fear or oppose the claims of labor. This analysis brings us back squarely to the question whether there should continue to be some approximate adjustment of reward to service or whether we are to be guided by new formulas, leading to a world in which rewards will be dispensed on a per capita basis, regardless of what the individual, or the process of which he is a part, can contribute to the real wealth and welfare of the nation. The current tendency, fostered by a decade of paternalistic crusading, is definitely toward pay for any and all, service or no service, and the eventual result may be a pronounced rise in *service* costs, borne by production and those who do produce something.

We have all along been speaking of wage payments in the manufacturing industries to those who *have jobs* and have seen that employment in manufacturing has not kept pace with the volume of production, even though the ratio of employed wage earners to volume has not declined as far as would be proportionate to the gains in productivity. As previously stated, the gains in progress have been split as between workers and hours. If the average hours of work had been more promptly shortened during the 1920's, it is quite possible that a larger number of workers could have been retained in industry. The chaotic NRA labor codes and hasty revision of the terms of hours and pay in the middle 'thirties might not have been necessary. To say that shorter hours would have prevented a deep depression does not necessarily follow, and the reasons will shortly appear. We have actually experienced, as a result of the depression, an unprecedented unemployment crisis, and not all the public policies so hastily thrown together, in an atmosphere of perpetual emergency, to deal with this condition have been entirely wise or helpful. But without doubt the unemployment crisis has been real and not imaginary. There may be legitimate doubt of the more fantastic figures arrived at by some who have estimated the total of unemployed persons during the depression.

PROBLEMS OF THE UNEMPLOYMENT CRISIS

At the peak of unemployment in March, 1933, fairly careful estimates placed the number of those seeking work as 17 million (Alexander Hamilton Institute); Robert R. Nathan's estimate (*International Labor*

Review) was about 15 million. The American Federation of Labor estimate and that of the National Industrial Conference Board were intermediate. Nathan's estimate for March, 1929, when employment was still close to its peak level, was nearly 3 million idle persons, agreeing closely with American Federation of Labor figures. There is apparently, therefore, some statistical basis for saying that from the prosperous year 1929 to the depths of the depression in 1933 roughly 10 million persons were added to the ranks of those unable to find jobs. After 1933, with irregular revival in production, there was not only a shifting of some unemployed persons to Government work or Government relief occupations but a gradual improvement in the number of workers absorbed by private industry and trade. By the end of 1936 there appears to have been a reduction in unemployed of roughly 5 million.[1] When the Federal Census was taken in 1940, efforts were made to secure a more accurate figure of the number of unemployed persons seeking work. The final results of this count at the time of writing are not yet available, but a 5 per cent sample indicated that at the end of March, 1940, about 5 million persons were seeking work, and about 2.4 million were engaged in various public emergency projects and activities. Independent private estimates of that date range from 9 to 11.6 million.[2] From the middle of 1940, aided by an accelerating pace of the National Defense effort and, later, the War Program, industrial employment rose rapidly, and an actual scarcity of some types of labor was apparent early in 1942.

We now return to the question of the relation between the unusually large and persistent volume of unemployment in the 1930's, notwithstanding substantial improvement in production after 1934, and at least some underlying progress in technology and productivity. Even though we cannot say precisely how many unemployed industrial workers there were prior to the rise of National Defense production in 1940, the number was sufficiently large to be a matter of great concern, and naturally many explanations have been offered. Particularly insistent has been the suggestion on the part of labor-union officials and social workers that it is the rapid progress in mechanization of industry that forms the principal reason for this stubborn problem. This is a plausible argument, and it is made doubly so when supplemented by illustrations drawn from particular

[1] See Selected Current Statistics, *Desk Bulletins*, Bureau of Research and Statistics of the Social Security Board, for charts of these various estimates since 1929. In November, 1937, after much public criticism of the unwillingness of the Federal Government to make an actual census of the unemployed, it was finally decided to take a "voluntary registration," which resulted in a figure of 7.8 million persons out of jobs, able and willing to work. But later checking revealed that this was inaccurate and below a "reasonable estimate," which was placed at 11 million.

[2] See Appendix 13 for further discussion of the problem of arriving at accurate estimates of the unemployed.

crafts, where it can be shown that a high proportion of the skilled workers have been replaced by mechanical devices within a limited period of time. A good deal of this reasoning has been in terms of specific cases that have been offered as the basis for broad and occasionally reckless generalization.

Phillip Murray, chairman of the Steel Workers Organizing Committee of the C.I.O., said in 1940:

The present program of industry, insofar as I am able to observe with relation to the introduction of new mechanical devices and other technological changes, follows this pattern: introduce a machine or a new method; increase productive efficiency fifteen, twenty-five, or fifty per cent; increase hourly wage rates a fraction of this percentage; lower the number of man-hours per year considerably; lay off such other men as may not be required where the new machine or new methods for increasing productivity have been introduced; and gobble up most of the benefits of greater productivity into profits. There is the situation in American industry today.

This, indeed, may be considered the basic gospel of the C.I.O. The American Federation of Labor in its various organs of publicity has not been slow to emphasize that mechanization is one of the principal sources of unemployment,[1] but A. F. of L. spokesmen, in recent years, have emphasized the desirability of expanding industrial production and increasing productivity of wage earners, so long as management would promptly translate this progress into shorter hours and higher rates of pay and so long as prices were not advanced on the pretext that higher wages made this necessary. Yet even among the more experienced leaders of the A. F. of L. unions, a tendency to imply that every increase in productivity must necessarily mean that *all* the gain must at once be obtained by labor without any consideration of the participation of management and capital and special circumstances that they might be facing. Among those associated with the Roosevelt Administration, opinion has shown considerable divergence, there being those who went almost as far as Mr. Murray, whereas others held to the view that the progress of mechanization is by no means the most important factor in our unemployment problem. A fairly representative cross section of the views of Government research workers and public officials can be gained by the testimony given to the Temporary National Economic Committee in the spring of 1940 during the discussion of technology and its effect on employment. Among the employers present were those who admitted the technological unemployment problem and the displacement of some workers, at least temporarily, as the result of machine processes. On the other hand, some labor representatives were willing to admit in their statements that in the

---

[1] In the *Monthly Survey of Business* of the A. F. of L., January, 1939, it is stated that labor-saving machinery probably eliminated about two million jobs since 1929.

long run technology may be the means of creating additional employment through a lengthening of the roundabout process whereby capital serves to aid the human hand.[1]   These discussions further developed an interesting distinction between advances in technology that represent the introduction of major new products or services, which can rapidly enlarge the sphere of employment, and the mere introduction of labor-saving devices in established industries, including some that are essentially obsolescent or are following a declining trend for reasons beyond the control of management or due to financial involvement.

In December, 1935, a WPA Research Project was initiated to study the general subject of reemployment opportunities and changes in productivity and industrial technique.   Since this program developed statistical findings and theoretical conclusions bearing on our discussion, we shall summarize briefly some of the results and observe the general tenor of the interpretation placed upon them.   Although these studies ranged beyond manufacturing into agriculture, the mineral industries, and others, we shall confine our remarks to manufacturing, of which 59 distinct segments, comprising about one-half of all manufacturing enterprise employees, were analyzed with respect to employment, productivity, production, and output per wage earner, from 1919 to 1936.[2]   The results entirely dispel and possible impression that there has been a uniform or general tendency in productivity, production, or employment during this period.   We may distinguish a number of contrasting tendencies.   First, we have industries that have had relatively pronounced growth in production during the past few decades and have also utilized increasingly elaborate mechanical equipment, resulting in more productivity per man-hour.   In these lines the effect upon employment has depended upon the extent to which the industry has shown cyclical instability.   The automobile industry, for example, has rapidly expanded output per man-hour, but employment has not consistently advanced because of the wide cyclical swings in produc-

---

[1] The late Samuel Gompers had argued (1923) that it is "absolutely futile for workmen to protest against or go on strike against the introduction of a new machine, a new device, or a new tool."   And William Green, speaking in 1929, said "the American labor movement *welcomes* the installation and extension of the use of machinery in industry."   Matthew Woll, also of the A. F. of L., has stated: "It is not a function of the labor movement to resist the machine.   It is the function of the labor movement to turn the installation of machinery to the good of the worker."   These quotations are taken from Sumner Slichter, "Union Policies and Industrial Management," pp. 205–206, Brookings Institution, Washington, D.C., 1941.   Slichter points out that the impact of the depression caused labor leaders to be increasingly concerned over leaders taking generally the attitude that it was the responsibility of management to prevent undue hardship as the result of mechanization, but individual unions in particular cases still encourage resistance to mechanization in some industries.

[2] "Production, Employment, and Productivity in 59 Manufacturing Industries," *National Research Project*, WPA S 1, especially Part 1.

tion.   On the other hand, the more stable chemical industries, insofar as this study covers them (about 50 per cent), have shown a remarkable increase in both employment and productivity.

LABOR'S ATTITUDE TOWARD MECHANIZATION

Apart from the case of widely cyclical industries, it is fairly generally established that employment has more than held its own, or has increased substantially, in industries that have been in the stage of growth favoring development of new types of products and new customers, at the same time increasing man-hour productivity either by mechanization or by other ways of facilitating the flow of production, improving organization, and adopting better raw materials.   Next we have the case of industries in which there has been an exceptional and rather sudden increase in productivity per man-hour due to quite revolutionary inventions that have displaced numerous workers and produced a declining tendency in the numbers employed.   In this group there are industries that are gradually expanding and others pursuing a relatively slow production trend or already at the stage of "saturation."   The tire industry is an example of the latter; mechanical innovation in recent years has probably sought to economize labor and reduce costs in an effort to avoid insolvency and offset the terrific competitive pressures within the industry.   On the other hand, the rayon industry has shown a spectacular advance as to both production and productivity, and its employment has been increasing consistently, although at a slower rate than production.   The case of cigarette production is again somewhat different, the trend being consistently upward, but at a slow pace, while the extraordinary improvements in mechanical and automatic devices have reduced labor demand emphatically.   Other instances of conspicuous labor displacement owing to machinery occur in the manufacturing fields of electric lamps, window glass, cigars, manufactured gas, and blast furnaces.   There are a number of curious contrasts in the food group, employment having risen in bread baking, where output per man-hour has remained little changed; in confectionery there has been a moderately rising productivity, but employment has declined.[1]

Still another curious contrast is between cane-sugar refining, with rising productivity and declining employment, and the canning industries, where employment has increased in spite of rising productivity.   In the food and nondurable consumer-goods industries generally it appears that wherever the trend of production has been horizontal or very moderately

---

[1] These references to change are made in such fashion as to give the reader an impression of the general movement, so far as possible distinct from merely cyclical effects of the depression.

upward, the introduction of technological improvements reducing man-hours per unit of product has brought decline in the trend of workers employed. Such lines of industry are rather better represented in the National Research Project Study, but there is unfortunately complete omission of such important growing industries as household electrical appliances, motion-picture and film production, air-conditioning equipment, cosmetics, the dairy industry, metal containers, plastics and resins, distilling and brewing, all of which, had they been included, would have altered the impression of a generally dropping *trend* of employment created by the Study. This Study also included an inadequate coverage of total wage earners in the printing and publishing, chemical, nonferrous metal, machinery, and textile industries.

There is a much more significant result of this Study in the evidence afforded that much of the recent decline in employment has been associated with what has happened in construction and cannot be adequately explained without reference to the existence, since about 1925, of a *major* cyclical collapse of the building industry. It is most important to observe that this building depression has no historical parallel in recent history; to find conditions at all comparable *we must go back to the* 1870's *or the* 1850's. The present generation of economists, statisticians, and public administrators has had no personal recollection of such a major construction debacle, and it has, therefore, given very inadequate attention to the possibility that when such a cataclysm takes place it is capable of creating exceedingly adverse conditions in manufacturing, mining, and other industries and destroying a sufficient amount of purchasing power for manufactured products to force many millions out of work. *A major building collapse represents more than the usual business-cycle recession;* it has the characteristics of a tidal wave whose tremendous power is not generally recognized during its occurrence.[1]

There is, then, no mystery as to the reason for a marked decline in employment in such industries as lumber, planing-mill products, cement (with qualifications), clay products, furniture, and the smelting of non-ferrous metals. If the reader will again glance at Charts 59, 60, and 61 and observe the extraordinary deflation of employment, of wages, and of income produced in the construction and mining industries,[2] he will

---

[1] Estimates made by the writer, on the basis of information collected by the Employment Service of the U.S. Department of Labor, indicate that in 1935 *at least* 40 per cent of the unemployed were connected with construction and transportation industries and production of materials relating directly thereto.

[2] With regard to the mining industry, we must distinguish three distinct tendencies, a fairly satisfactory trend in production and employment in petroleum refining, a decidedly downward trend in employment in the obsolescent coal industry, and highly cyclical depression factors among the nonferrous metals, which are important contributors to the raw material of the building industry.

recognize that the progress of mechanization is by no means the only, or even the most important, factor that has militated during the past fifteen years against full employment. Here is the outcome of the unsound financial background of the building industry, particularly that segment of it concerned with residential and real-estate promotion. We can understand, but not condone, the attitude of organized labor in the building trades, setting up crude and unintelligent defenses against the ruthless impact of depression and opposing labor-saving devices and at the same time keeping wage rates high and out of line with productivity per man-hour on the job. We can see the reason for the same tactics among producers of building materials and installation equipment; it is the same desire for protection against the long years of shrinking demand and resort to all manner of devices to sustain prices, restrict improvements, and limit competitive trade. These practices are borne of acute depression, and they doubtless help to create just that. Had the building industry been solvent, progressive, and on the ascendant in these latter years, the entire picture of manufacturing employment, as well as industrial production, would have been radically different.[1]

Firms engaged in the building-materials field not only have been unable to secure the benefits of consistently rising productivity by reason of the cycle impact but also have been motivated in their high-price and price-boosting proclivities by pressures from building labor unions and leaders, especially in the larger cities. All this has been given very inadequate consideration in studies of production, productivity, and employment. Deep depression has its own tendency to stimulate the adoption of cost-reducing techniques in industries already in the forefront of progress, but it cannot be said that it has had that effect among the industries most conspicuously involved in the creation of depression.

---

[1] Assistant Attorney General Thurman Arnold has found that Chicago hod carriers absolutely refuse to allow the use of truck mixers; in Houston, Tex., plumbers insist that pipe made for a particular job will not be installed unless the thread is cut off and a new thread made for the job; plumbers and electricians in many cities insist that pipe cutting and wiring must be done on the job, where it is more expensive than in the factory; painters' unions in many areas will not tolerate the use of spray guns; in Washington, D.C., machinery may not be used to cut or thread pipe; there are many union limitations against the use of frames and sash manufactured, painted, or glazed in a factory; contractors who wish to use prefabricated materials or economical methods in Cleveland dare not do so for fear of union antagonism; in Chicago the Building Trades Council will not permit use of stone cut in Indiana; in Pittsburgh and San Francisco and doubtless in many other places, carpenter unions prohibit the use of millwork made out of town; in New York, metal lathers will not use lath fabricated outside the city. And so it goes all along the line in this great industry where, *instead of mechanization being the cause of unemployment, there is neither mechanization nor adequate employment.* (Thurman W. Arnold, Labor's Hidden Holdup Men, *Readers Digest*, June, 1941.)

The Research Project Study summarized its findings in the following points: "There is little doubt that depression stimulates efforts to reduce unit labor requirements, particularly by speeding up operations and introducing technical and managerial improvements which require little capital outlay." But during a period of declining output, productivity in some industries may decline, despite efforts to decrease unit labor requirements, depending upon maintenance requirements and overhead labor, particularly in industries of the durable-goods group. It is emphasized that although average productivity increased less rapidly after 1929[1] there continued to be persistent efforts to reduce costs by mechanization, and many workers were displaced by changes that did not actually increase production. It is this aspect, probably exaggerated, that prompted such defeatist conclusions as the following:

The probability for the future seems to be that there will be less, rather than more, employment in manufacturing industries. Should manufacturing industries reach and sustain the 1929 level of output within the next few years, the average number of wage earners required will not far exceed, if at all, the average number employed in 1929, despite the 20 per cent reduction in the average number of hours worked per week that occurred between 1929 and 1936. In the long run, since output per man-hour seems certain to increase further, manufacturing employment will probably be below that of 1929. Only a great increase in production or a marked decline in hours worked per week could bring manufacturing employment to levels appreciably higher than 1929.

It happens, however, that in 1936 and again in 1940 and *prior* to the great increase in employment occurring thereafter as a result of the Defense Program and the War, employment in manufacturing industry *did* exceed the highest level of 1929 (after seasonal correction).

Let the reader closely observe in the quoted concluding statement the subtle implication that *the structure of our manufacturing industries must necessarily remain virtually static in the future.* Although some account was taken of the actual changing complexion of our industries, this Study did not adequately take into account actual shifts and innovations that have occurred during the period covered. In much of the reasoning presented in other related documents and in the writings of other research workers associated recently with the Federal Government, there are to be found this same assumption of a *static economy* and an attempt to estimate future labor requirements in terms of the *same identical industries* that happened to be operating in some particular year. The argument is put in such terms as to imply that future production must necessarily be merely an extension of the operations of a given set of industries, but we

---

[1] A conclusion not borne out by the writer's measurements, which are based upon somewhat different data.

have already referred to several very important cases of expanding industries that were entirely omitted by the WPA Study. A similar interpretation of the matter of labor displacement during prosperity is to be found in the earlier conclusions of Frederick C. Mills,[1] who had found that, between 1923 and 1929, 49 out of every 1,000 employees separated themselves from the industry group in which they were working, as compared with only 21 per 1,000 during the period 1899 to 1914. He then concluded that workers were being "forced" to an increasing extent out of their original jobs into new industries or into nonmanufacturing occupations. But to say that people are *forced* to make changes in their occupational status in the course of a period of active industrial development suggests a static point of view and may imply that all change and opportunity for improvement of individual status is something objectionable, dictated by the hard necessities of a failing economic system.

The fact that machines required fewer workers in the shop did not imply that fewer employees were necessary in the many interweaving processes and operations extending far beyond the lathes and assembly lines. Without attempting to minimize the difficulties of displacement for individual workers who did find it necessary to change their place of abode, as well as the direction of acquired skill and experience, it is obvious that this has been true from the very beginnings of the industrial revolution, centuries ago. The wider use of power, capital, and mechanism is a never-ending struggle against poverty and scarcity. Labor unions did not fully recognize the necessity of looking ahead and assisting their members to train themselves along new lines to facilitate inevitable changes. Management, too, has been remiss in the same unwillingness to assist workers to make necessary changes, to acquire new skills, to avoid being caught in the toils of technological advance. And even Government has been far behind in the task of assisting the individual workers least able to make these changes rapidly. Public Administration has mainly concerned itself with relief disbursements and other emergency devices whose purpose is to replace private industry by public works.

"PATTERNS OF RESOURCE USE"

The philosophy of the WPA is well expressed by Corrington Gill, who has repeatedly asserted or implied that industry *deliberately* resorts to labor saving to the disadvantage of the workers and can do so without appreciable added expenditure of capital; hence corporate saving is unnecessary. He says:

Until private capital outlays increase substantially, government must continue to assume large responsibilities to meet the need for expanding purchasing

[1] "Economic Tendencies in the United States," pp. 419–423, National Bureau of Economic Research, New York, 1932.

power and to provide for the necessary expansion of investment.   This expansion of investment can take the form of direct public capital expenditures which meet such pressing needs as low-cost housing and the development of capital facilities which tend to stimulate business enterprise, for instance, airports, roads, streets, and sewage systems.   As long as we are faced with the existence of a large number of unemployed or of groups unemployed for long periods of time, the government must care for these jobless.[1]

Thus the argument is brought around to the justification of public borrowing and spending for the building up of a vast "relief" bureaucracy. Since capital is no longer "needed" by business, it should be put in public hands to hire workers for the State.

[1] "Summary of Findings to Date," WPA National Research Project, March, 1938, Letter of Transmittal by Assistant Administrator Corrington Gill.

The prevailing tendency to contemplate a static future, in terms of *a given framework* of industrial enterprise, is conspicuous in an elaborate technical report entitled "Patterns of Resource Use," submitted to the National Resources Committee by its Industrial Section, under the direction of Gardiner C. Means (Washington, D.C., 1938).

In this report an attempt was made to estimate the future utilization of materials, types of equipment, and manpower, on the assumption of various levels of general production.   "Under prevailing technical conditions, what is the level of economic activity which would absorb practically all of the great army of unemployed?   What would be the market for commodities and services, industry by industry, at such a level?"   In carrying this through, the factor of manpower, or employment, was estimated on the basis of its relationship to production over a period of years.   Production itself and future estimates thereof were imagined to be causally affected by the amount of change in consumer income and "purchasing power" but apparently by nothing else.   If the dollars in circulation were to establish a level of "consumer income" of 100 billion dollars, there would be expected on the basis of past relationships, a *fixed* industrial structure, a total level of production 95 per cent higher than in the average 1923 to 1925.   On this assumption, carrying through the various estimates for over 80 industries and occupations step by step, the conclusion was arrived at that this would represent for all employment a total of 60 million workers, with jobs, as compared with 46.6 million in 1929 and 41.4 million in 1935.   There is the further implication that were income limited to 70 billion, as compared with 65 billion in 1929, jobs could be found for only 47.2 million workers, as compared with 46.6 in 1929.

The sheer artificiality of this laborious piece of statistical extrapolation is obvious; in fact, just as obvious as the delicately insinuated implication that consumer income alone *causes* employment rather than that capital expansion, sound industrial management, and *sound government* may equally well contribute.   Although, of course, we must develop estimates of future progress in the light of past trends and upon the principle of *continuity* of development, the attempt to deduce employment estimates from money-income levels or even general production levels without regard to time intervals and with inadequate attention to possible changes in productivity and the potentials of invention and innovation is a serious qualification of the results and conclusions.

The War has already torn these patterns to shreds, and it will doubtless also demonstrate by the time it is over that a political system dedicated to the proposition

By thus developing emergency relief into a projected program for replacing private- by public-capital "investment" and placing most of the blame for unemployment on management in the manufacturing industries a condition was created that naturally retarded the investment of private capital in production and contributed to perpetuate under-employment despite the sickly war boom of the late 'thirties. Capital became hesitant not only because of the turn of domestic political exploitation of the depression but because of a growing uneasiness about the general world drift toward a new international conflict of unlimited scope and unpredictable consequences. Chart 59 serves to remind us that there have been unfavorable world forces impinging on American agriculture, quite apart from technology, mechanization, or more rapid transportation of farm products. These conditions, until 1941, contributed to impair farm income from wheat, cotton, and meat animals. If one observes the relatively unsatisfactory trend of employment since 1929 and wage payments in the public-utility industries, it is apparent

---

that the standard of living and the level of production depend upon the rapidity of circulation of money will have generated so vast an expansion of the public debt that the employment created per dollar of "national income" during the next few decades will certainly not be in line with Means' correlations. The unpredictability of special factors affecting given industries is further well illustrated in the case of the iron and steel industries for whose capital requirements further estimates were prepared in 1939 by Means and Paradiso. War requirements by 1940 had made the pattern of steel-industry-plant requirements quite remote from that estimated by these statisticians.

The reader will find an interesting commentary upon the methods and conclusions in the "Patterns of Resource Use" in a paper read before the Cowles Commission for Economic Research, July, 1939, by John W. Scoville, of the Chrysler Corporation, reprinted in a pamphlet entitled "The Government Looks at Our Economic Past and Future." After showing the absurdity of mere correlation analysis as a means of deducing cause and effect, Scoville says, "The fundamental fallacy in patterns is the assumption that the kind and number of articles bought when the national income temporarily reaches a high figure would continue if the national income remained at the high figure. The result is that the table in Patterns which shows what would be produced at the income level of 100 billions overestimates the production of durable goods and underestimates the output of perishable goods and services." Scoville clearly discerns the implications of a "planned economy" and totalitarian governmental control of industry that are so neatly imbedded in the study that we have considered. He quotes a significant phrase from "The Modern Economy in Action" (a popular version of the New Order) by Means and Ware: "We have already seen how disastrous to the economy the exercise of unchecked power by corporate control is likely to be. And the only body that might be strong enough to meet the economic strength of the corporations is government," p. 210. He refers also to Mordecai Ezekiel, a member of the Industrial Committee responsible for the Patterns Report, who, in his book "Jobs for All," advocates "a regimentation of industry corresponding to the regimentation of agriculture now in effect, except that in industry he would have the government reward the entrepreneur for producing more instead of rewarding him for producing less, as in agriculture."

that in spite of the continuing prosperity of the electric-power industry, the semi-insolvent condition of the railroads was without doubt another major factor in paralyzing the buying power of a large segment of workers and in obstructing progress in adopting new forms of equipment, especially for faster and cheaper freight movement.

The shrinkage, as well as the technical retardation, of railway transport and its contribution to total productivity and buying power were well summarized by Weintraub and Kaplan in the WPA Research Project (March, 1938). They pointed to the contrast between the shrinking capital expenditure by railways and the vigorous expansion of outlays for roads, bridges, and tunnels by the Federal and State Governments to facilitate automobile travel and truck transportation. But they did not go to the root of the matter and clearly define the financial and legal reasons for the failure of the railroad industry to keep itself abreast of technological progress.[1]

Apart from technology and the cyclical forces associated with some basic industries, it is entirely possible that the somewhat belated adjustment and, indeed, accelerated adjustment in hourly wage rates in manufacturing may have had an effect upon employment. A point is doubtless reached, as has been demonstrated by Paul H. Douglas, at which advances in the wage rate become so rapid that the process of displacement is forced ahead faster than is desirable. Also, this has an effect in retarding new business enterprise. There is, under prevailing tendencies in organized labor policy, a relatively prompt extension of wage advances from the shop to the distributive services and other types of work where efficiency in no wise compensates for the higher cost. There may then be tendencies to replace men by women and some duplication in the unemployment figures as more members of wage-earner families list themselves as seeking work.

[1] In testimony before the Temporary National Economic Committee, T. J. Kreps really did place his finger upon the nature of the railroad factor in retarding progress. "Outstanding is the rapid increase in [railway] dividends and interest from 1919 to 1927, at a time when payrolls were declining, and production was barely holding even. Also outstanding is the fact that in the years 1930 and 1931, dividends and interest tended to maintain themselves at a high level. . . . Extraordinary efforts have been made by railway management to continue making interest payments. Too small a percentage of the dollars which they collected from the public were made available for the improvement and betterment necessary to maintain competitive position. In short, instead of writing obsolete capital off the books—capital made obsolete, it should be said, by the development of newer methods of transportation—the industry has written employment and payrolls off the books but handicapped itself in its competitive struggle by heavy fixed charges." ("Measurement of the Social Performance of Business," *Monograph* 7, Temporary National Economic Committee, Washington, D.C., 1940, p. 41.)

In a human sense we adapt ourselves to change, whether it be technological, financial, political, or sociological, with a lingering reluctance.
There probably always will be those who resist progress because old ways
are more congenial and we fit into them more easily, with less exertion.
A few are alert and look ahead, but the great majority are looking backward to the "good old days" or denouncing the disconcerting novelties
crowding the present. It is these human propensities that doubtless
explain a great many of these attempts in our day to rationalize the
destructiveness of machinery, just as it was done a century ago, when
steam power formed the basis of concern, rather than internal-combustion
engines, electric generators, or the magic of chemistry. We tend to
reason plausibly from the particular to the general, failing to recognize
that this may exaggerate as to the general what we see taking place at a
particular point. This is the commonest source of error in economics.
It is so with respect to machinery and employment. We see particular
cases of displacement due to mechanization; and we jump to the conclusion that the future of labor working with tools and power apparatus is
doomed. Hence the financial mechanism supplying the tools and
developing the labor-using innovations is also doomed, if not already
obsolete. Let us go back to the blissful days of *simplicity*. That
pervasive skepticism toward mechanical contrivance and the lock step
of factory routine which appealed so strongly to Ruskin and the neo-
medievalists is ever with us. Roy Helton[1] expresses it well in saying:

Against the benefits of machinery, or rather of industrialism, I am thus forced
to set two harms, both very serious and both of growing dimensions: first, that
the machine impersonalizes and sanctifies power and the use of power, and makes
power the dominant factor in human life. There can be no international peace
while that process continues unchecked. Second, I charge machinery of divest-
ing, by its very nature, any important motive from production but that of profit
to laborer or manufacturer. While that process continues there can be no
internal peace in any industrial nation.

These are powerful words, and they may contain a modicum of truth.
They go far to explain why it is so easy to find conveniently simple
explanations for complicated economic problems in a convulsive age.
    The writer prefers to believe that opportunities for all willing and
competent workers to obtain jobs in the future involve not the restricting
of mechanization, the regimentation of industry by public action, or
irrational limitations upon saving and capital investment. Basically,
there is required an improvement in financial solvency in some directions; the willingness on the part of organized labor to recognize the

[1] The Anti-industrial Revolution, *Harper's Magazine*, December, 1941.

ultimate social gains involved in improved methods of production; a better understanding on the part of management of the necessity for going part way with labor in assisting in the training of skilled labor for new types of work; the willingness of capital and management to pioneer in new fields and new products; and a reasonable degree of cooperation on the part of Government in encouraging corporations to occupy a more prominent place in the initiation of major new advances in technique and products. Education and research are required. Rationalization of those financial processes that have in the past contributed to disastrous breakdowns in the construction industry and awareness of the loss of momentum in particular segments of industrial innovation and the adjustments here and there that this demands are required.

What shall we do about purely *cyclical* unemployment, which so closely correlates with the vibrations of production in manufacturing operations? Why should it be necessary for business to forego the demand for its products by resorting every so often to the temporary discharge of workers who much prefer work to idleness? Many employers have come to appreciate the stupidity of all this, but thus far there has been no really effective attack upon this problem in industries where cyclical fluctuation is violent. We shall discuss this problem further, along with related problems of price relationships and capital investment policy in the following chapters.

CHAPTER 21

CYCLICAL STABILIZATION OF WAGE INCOME

It has been shown in previous chapters that public policy to restore and maintain employment can be led astray by confusing monetary disbursements of *public charity* with *real* income. This must necessarily flow from productional work, from well-organized, efficient, and smoothly functioning industries. The true objective of expanding real income and productive effort simultaneously can be utterly defeated if the economic system becomes a battleground of contention between Government seeking to wrest control of job-creating capital and privately owned industry, which loses its incentive to invest in production if the investment return is progressively extinguished. Assuming that such warfare is an interlude rather than a path toward ultimate totalitarian rule (and the United States will not find it easy to resist the trend of a world already in the grip of dictators), there are aspects of short-term cyclical instability that call for further study of wage income. If business continues predominantly under the control and ownership of citizens rather than commissars, there will doubtless continue to be vibrations arising from the mistakes, the occasional exaggerated hopes, the exploring and innovation that are inseparable from industrial progress. But surely the severity of depression and the excesses of booms *can* be restrained by wise and coordinated action. Anything that can be done in this direction helps to avert the recurring "emergencies" that so readily invite political exploitation for the aggrandizement of political power, with the fateful consequences of global conflict.

Is it feasible to develop ways of keeping the flow of wage income moving more steadily in trade and consumer capital channels so that industrial capital can flow more steadily into plant production? A continually rising *trend* of total production per capita is the ultimate objective. We might make the course smoother, with less friction, if the violent cyclical swings in business-plant investment were reduced by toning down the high variability of consumer demand for durable goods and, vice versa, if the violent swings in consumer capital-goods demand were reduced by toning down vibrations in plant construction and employment. We must work from both ends to accomplish the main objective. To say that enhanced consumer income flow can serve to stimulate business-capital creation and plant development has validity *in the long-run sense*, but during the shorter periods of the typical business cycle,

535

spasmodic raising of that income can be nothing more than a temporary stimulant, accompanied by inflation and followed by deflation of both wages and income. To say that productive plant investment must be expanded as a means of promoting employment and hence wage income is also valid in the long-run sense, but excessive commitments within a short period in erecting factories, office buildings, ships, or railroads lead to the inevitable reaction and to unnecessary interruption of consumer income and demand.

Much thinking on this subject has revealed a double error. It has exaggerated the role of one or the other of these motivating factors, and it has lost sight of the fact that although expansion or stimulus is good in the *trend sense* of gradual and orderly continuity, there are definite limits within which the total amount of business increase arising either from consumer income and business capital development can occur per annum, without involving the internal stresses and leverage in net incomes and psychological observations that produce violent readjustment. Since these readjustments, recessions, or depressions are not conducive to maintaining the optimum over-all rate of progress and expose the entire society to a political menace, it is essential to work constantly toward maintaining economic balance along a *gradually* rising gradient by placing governors on the speed of the engine. Let us first consider how such a governor might avert undue cyclical inflation of wage income and its consequent magnified inflation in demand for consumer durables.

The instability of industrial production is not created by variations in the money flow of wage income. The variability of the latter arises out of variability in production, ultimately created by a few basic factors, capable of being independently brought under control. But as wage income rises with boom and collapses with depression, we have seen that it has its own features of flexibility, which form important accelerating influences on the momentum of rise and decline. During the typical business upturn, wage income rises faster than production and by the use of borrowed funds expands demand at a faster pace than can be long sustained. This represents an acceleration of already stimulated activity, which leads presently to a retarding and a decelerating that interrupts many useful projects, temporarily curtails money income and real income, and creates capital losses among rich and poor alike. Our problem now is to determine, on the assumption that some cyclical instability will continue to accompany industrial progress, whether wage income cannot somehow be better maintained during periods when unemployment occurs. Certainly something can be done to avert the *total* stoppage of income for millions of persons when the business system must pause to permit *a few* readjustments in finance or production.

We face a complex problem in determining how to trim down the cyclical rise in labor income as a brake upon the general boom through moderating in some degree consumer spending on durable goods. It is complex because it is the *number* of workers, not changes in wage *rates* per week or per hour, that mainly explains the abrupt departure of national income from the long-term trend to the point where a vulnerable economic condition is created, subject to a reaction, and both capital and income losses. This problem is rendered still more complex if it is regarded as primarily a matter to be adjusted by private enterprise, industry by industry, plant by plant, with responsibility resting primarily upon employers and employer groups. There are employers and corporation boards of directors who see the problem clearly, are quite willing to set up measures for its solution, and have actually done something about it. These are clearly in the minority, and so long as this is true the net result cannot be very important. On the other hand, if we regard it to be the function of Government to apply some broad, uniform income-compensatory policy throughout industry, trade, agriculture, and transportation, in order to avoid the full effects of unemployment, we encounter other disadvantages. We must then be content with less equitable distribution of burden and benefit, because of the wide diversity in cyclical patterns, among the various industries. In a sense we are on the horns of dilemma. Left entirely in the hands of industrial management, the carrying out of ever so sound a compensating or reserve plan involves either microscopic supervision or inadequate cooperation and coverage. Placed in the hands of Government and applied over a broad front, the results might represent unequal burdens on the community. In addition to management and Government, the *workers themselves* might cooperate to avoid unnecessary wage-income instability. But this is difficult to achieve and to mobilize without Government action.

UNEMPLOYMENT BENEFITS

The provision of compensatory income to unemployed wage earners may be considered from several standpoints. It may be outright public charity; it may assume the form of a system of reserves, accumulated during prosperity and paid out during recession; or it may be viewed as something analogous to insurance. In the sense of a relief or charity plan, the payment of benefits would represent nothing more than an opportunistic makeshift, likely in the long run to be as demoralizing to the workers as it was disruptive of sound finance. Huge public doles for the idle, nonworkers and workers alike, almost inevitably culminate in attempts to enlarge the scope of governmental competition with private business, impair financial confidence, and result in padding of the public payroll as new bureaus are set up to *absorb* as well as *assist* the jobless.

To regard unemployment benefits as analogous to insurance is not wholly incorrect, for there is a probability of loss, and it is desired to pool contributions to minimize the loss or hardship. The extent of hazard over a given future period, however, is not closely calculable according to past experience, since we are dealing with the pattern of a *time* process that repeats itself through the years in no exactly uniform or inevitable pattern. We cannot tell in advance how long or severe will be the next depression, and insurance must contribute toward *prevention* as well as *protection*. There are possible ways of reducing the severity and duration of depression, and "insurance" measures to deal with the cycle more nearly resemble insurance against accidents or fires, which are amenable to control and preventive effort. It is difficult to judge in advance the adequacy or fairness of cyclical insurance premiums. It is difficult to take account of new conditions that presently may alter the effect of depression in a particular industry.

If, finally, we look upon these benefit plans as primarily similar to reserves, such as are set up by business firms, we see again an imperfect analogy. If we set up reserves by a system of premium payments, there is the tendency to follow both insurance and business-reserve precedent by having these reserves "invested" until funds are needed for distribution. This raises complex questions, because we are dealing with equalization of buying power *over time*, and if reserve funds are used in one way while not being used in another, the general result of distributing purchasing power along a different kind of time pattern may not be accomplished. This view has the merit, however, of recognizing that an element of holding something in reserve is an essential feature of the problem and recognizing, too, that in much of the practice hitherto, the reserve-fund idea has been more typical than either the charity or the actuarial principles. We shall presently state some reasons for believing that none of the foregoing analogies is valid and that a successful plan can best be developed along the analogy to the processes of commercial or consumer credit. We must observe also that not all unemployment is of a strictly cyclical character. Some of it is due to personal deficiencies, some of it to excessively rapid technological change. These cases must receive distinctive treatment.[1]

Historically, much experimenting has been done with various forms of reserves to provide supplementary wage income in depression. If the

[1] Special types of policy must also apply to other cases, such as those in which it is difficult to define unemployment or difficult to handle the complex details of accumulating premiums and distributing benefits because the workers are widely scattered or much of the work done is for individual employers. Compensation plans, therefore, rather generally except workers in agriculture, domestic service, hotels, restaurants, and shipping.

plan is administered within an individual business unit, it is commonly referred to as a "plant-reserve" system. Both employees and employer contribute according to some schedule of regular payments into a trusteed reserve, from which benefits according to a specified proportion of normal earnings are paid to those workers who are regarded as involuntarily unemployed. There are many degrees of limitation in the various plans with respect to length of prior service with the employer, the inclusion or exclusion of clerical and salaried workers, or the qualifications as to skill. If such a plan is carefully worked out, the size of the "premium" payments to the reserve fund might be expected to have some rough relationship to the very rough estimate of the unemployment risk peculiar to a given industry. If such plans were generally in operation, we might expect the more cyclically stable lines of business to set up payment schedules involving smaller monthly contributions than industries such as steel, automobiles, building materials, etc. The more stable industries would not contribute directly to reserves for the more highly cyclical industries. This would be similar to fire insurance on a localized basis and more concentrated risks in terms of extent of possible loss rather than expectation of frequency of hazard. But if benefit payments are to be adequate, rather high premiums will be necessary for some groups.[1]

Such plans might give recognition to the degree of income-loss risk in particular industries, in view of the historic pattern of their cycle behavior. There might, therefore, be an inducement to management to adopt more careful advance planning of operations in order to reduce the possibility of extended unemployment and therefore high premium costs. On this last point a good deal has been said that probably exaggerates the extent to which an individual management *can* combat business depression. There are some things that managements can and should do (or be permitted to do) to enable policy to rest more solidly on facts and statistical information and less on guesswork. But since the business cycle does not have its roots in the operations of manufacturing or commercial business, we must frankly recognize that reserve plans set up within those industries on the expectation that they automatically provide inducement to modify the general cycle will not suffice. To make

[1] A further possible disadvantage of the plant-reserve system is that if the contributions to reserve are set at a given percentage of payroll in a given firm on the basis of the estimated future unemployment probabilities of the industry, these payments might not take fully into account the momentum of expansion in payroll income. In order to accumulate a really effective reserve in highly unstable industries that happen to be in the stage of rapid growth but subject to the relapse that usually occurs when the maturity or saturation level is reached, arrangements would have to be not constant percentages of total payroll but gradually *rising* percentages of payroll. But this would involve very complicated administrative problems that might make the system impracticable.

these plans more effective, a particular firm operating its own insurance reserve plan might be penalized by very high premium rates, which, in the last analysis, do not contribute toward the elimination of the cyclical risk impinging on that firm from sources beyond control.

VARIOUS UNEMPLOYMENT-COMPENSATION PLANS

Systematic provision of unemployment benefits was very slow to develop in the United States. As long ago as 1911, Great Britain took steps to provide reserve and benefit plans in a limited number of industries, and the British system has since developed, through severe trial and grievous error. France made beginnings in this direction in 1905, Denmark in 1907, Belgium in 1908, and Holland in 1916. Some form of voluntary or compulsory wage-income insurance or reserve plan was in effect in most of Europe when World War II broke out. In the United States the only progress, as late as 1932, toward unemployment compensation through legislation was the passage of the Wisconsin Law of 1932. The American Federation of Labor steadfastly opposed the idea in principle. For the rest, there were a number of reserve plans, differing considerably in character and scope, under the auspices of individual managements. Few of these had their beginnings prior to 1920. Despite the fact that such plans are of limited general effect, they are a credit to the intelligence and fairness of the companies willing to encourage them and contribute financially to their support. Their adoption attracted the attention of top executives during the beginning of the last Great Depression, and in the succeeding years several plans were introduced along with considerable discussion of merits and accomplishments. In 1930 the General Electric Company, for example, introduced into some of its plants a plan whereby qualified employees and the corporation each contributed 1 per cent of normal payroll to a trusteed reserve fund, from which, in the event of unemployment, benefit payments up to $20 a week per worker were to be provided. The Geometric Tool Company, in 1931, developed a somewhat similar plan, limited, however, to the "stable" workers as distinct from the temporary and occasional employees.[1]

---

[1] A summary of a number of these private plans may be found in a pamphlet entitled "Unemployment: Industry Seeks a Solution," prepared by the U.S. Department of Commerce (1931) under the auspices of President Hoover's Emergency Committee for Employment; also, in a pamphlet "Employment Regularization," compiled by the National Association of Manufacturers, New York, 1940. It is noteworthy, in connection with the General Electric plan and many other of these private reserve plans, that normal contributions to the reserve fund ceased as soon as payments from the fund were approximately equal to the receipts and an unemployment emergency existed. This characteristic distinguishes most of these plans from the Federal Social Security plan, described subsequently, in which payments into the fund continue regardless of business conditions.

As early as 1915 the Dennison Manufacturing Company, upon the initiative of its farsighted president, Henry S. Dennison, set up a reserve in the hands of trustees to alleviate unemployment among the workers. Although the fund proved inadequate in the Great Depression, it was used for many years and in the brief depression of 1921, operated fairly successfully. In the plan developed by Leeds & Northrup, in 1923, it was provided that wage benefits during unemployment were to be at the rate of 75 per cent of normal wages to the workers with dependents and 50 per cent to those without dependents. The period of benefit distribution was to run for a period proportionate to the length of service of individual employees. As in the case of the Dennison plan, the Leeds & Northrup fund was contributed by the company.[1] Another variant is found in the making of loans to employees in lieu of unemployment benefits during depressions. Such a plan was that of General Motors, which, in 1938, provided that all employees who had served for five years or more would be assured of at least 60 per cent of standard weekly earnings through the year. If this involved payment to the workers of the necessary amount during idleness and an "indebtedness" was incurred by the employees, the debt was to be repaid later when employment was resumed, but without interest. This differs from most reserve plans in the sense that the contributions serve to extinguish a previous draft upon corporation reserves. The International Harvester Company, early in the Great Depression, developed a somewhat similar plan of loans without interest to employees of a minimum length of service.

It was the hope of Gerard Swope, of the General Electric Company, that the plant-reserves plan would be considerably expanded through trade associations to be formed among the various industries.[2] In 1930 the American Association for Labor Legislation developed the so-called "American Plan," whereby reserves were to be accumulated on an *industry* basis, with each fund managed separately by representatives of the industry, but under the supervision of the State Governments. Under this plan employers would make contributions, and employees would be permitted to do so if they chose. The interesting feature of

[1] There have been interesting variants of these plans. One is the guarantee by management to the workers (or a specified number of them) that a minimum number of hours of work per year will be assured or that a certain minimum of pay per week, per month, or even per year will be guaranteed. The Sears Roebuck plan (1936), for example, guaranteed 40 hours of pay a week for all those regularly employed, with the understanding that the workers would redeem in overtime any overpayment to care for slack periods. A limited number of companies having fairly stable sales and operations have been able to carry through for a considerable period of time guarantees of a minimum amount of work or of wages per annum.

[2] See his address before the Academy of Political Science, New York City, Nov. 13, 1931, on Stabilization of Industry.

this plan, which was not adopted, was its emphasis upon the industry as a unit and supervision by State authorities. The plan thus recognized that even a large business unit is too narrow a base for adequate benefit payments in a major depression; yet it took account of the unequal degree of income-curtailment risk among the various industries and pointed the way toward public-agency supervision such as ultimately became the basis for the Federal plan of 1935.

The Wisconsin Unemployment Insurance Law of 1932 was based primarily upon the assumption of plant reserves rather than industry-pooled funds. Each fund was built up by the individual employer and maintained for his individual account, the contributions being 2 per cent of payroll, with benefits provided up to 50 per cent of the normal wage earnings but not over $10 per week per worker. The State agency, as trustee, invested the separate reserves. This plan was clearly predicated upon the assumption that all employers have it within their power to reduce or eliminate unemployment, and hence a payroll tax is an incentive toward that end. But unfortunately, the weakness of all such narrow base plans was revealed when, by the spring of 1938, Wisconsin had more than eighty funds in the system insolvent.[1]

Although the Wisconsin Unemployment Insurance Plan and a limited number of private-reserve arrangements still had adherents and defenders in 1935, the preponderance of opinion was rapidly swinging toward plans of broader scope, involving Federal Government action. This was delayed by uncertainty as to how far the Constitution, or decisions of the Supreme Court, would permit the Government to impose a general plan of contributions and benefits, which might require state organization and machinery to administer. Hence Federal legislation proceeded cautiously in the direction of joint Federal and State action of a rather complex, but legally impregnable, character. The idea of "insurance" and its related concept of "social security" were integral features of the

---

[1] The Wisconsin plan began operations in 1934, and the first payments to unemployed beneficiaries were made in July, 1935. The author of the Unemployment Insurance Act was Harold M. Groves, of the University of Wisconsin, who had the earnest support of Governor La Follette. At the time that the Wisconsin Act was put in operation, closely observed by those interested in labor problems, the idea of company reserve funds was still receiving wide support. Elizabeth Brandeis wrote in the *New Republic* (Dec. 5, 1934): "Even if unemployment should prove (or were known to be) largely unpreventable, there would still be a definite advantage in allocating its cost insofar as possible to the industries and concerns that are its proximate cause. This can best be done through company-reserve funds. The pooled insurance schemes in operation in Europe virtually treat unemployment as an over-head cost of the entire community. Similar proposals are being urged in this country. Thus to treat all unemployment as a generalized overhead cost of society cannot be defended as economic wisdom when the effects of such a policy are analyzed."

new political philosophy, and "unemployment insurance" was fitted into a comprehensive new Administration, providing for old-age pensions, assistance to the blind, to the crippled, to dependent children, etc., as well as unemployment income benefits. In order to surmount the legal problems of "states' rights," it was provided that unemployment reserves would be primarily under state administration and that each state would develop its own legislation, subject to final approval of a Federal Board. Contributions, on a state basis, would be provided by employers only, through premiums amounting (upon full operation of the plan) to 3 per cent of the payroll of workers covered by the plan.[1]

The funds thus accumulated in the various states, all of which had their plans in operation by the middle of 1937, are placed in the hands of the Secretary of the Treasury and "invested" in Federal obligations. This trusteed fund is credited to the agencies of the individual states and is subject to requisition as benefit disbursements may be required. Of the total gainful workers in the United States, roughly 40 per cent are excluded from the operation of the plan because their occupations are not yet covered (as of 1940) by the Social Security Act.[2] The premiums are flat rates, in the form of a percentage of the payroll of those workers who qualify; there is no provision for variation according to probable intensity of unemployment of the several industries. The reserve is technically pooled, state by state, which obviously provides a very unsatisfactory demarcation of risk and in some instances (particularly the smaller industrial states) results in undue concentration of cyclical risk upon a narrow premium base. The benefit payments made to wage earners are considered, as far as possible, to be proportionate to the contributions, which results in an excessively elaborate system of record

---

[1] The contributions were to be paid technically in the form of a tax paid *to* the Federal Government, but with the provision that nine-tenths of the tax would be remitted if the employer made his payments to an approved state unemployment-insurance authority; thus the plan was kept actually on a state basis. The 10 per cent differential is contributed to the Federal Government to provide funds allocated to the states for administrative purposes only.

[2] Among the more important exclusions are workers in agriculture, miscellaneous hand trades, all Government employees, workers in professional and other lines of direct service and in forestry and fishing. The various state laws were largely patterned upon a suggested or model plan that exempts employers of less than eight persons from contribution. As a result, some 20 per cent or more of the total gainful workers are excluded.

The program in 1941 covered almost thirty million workers. The 3 per cent payroll tax on employers has yielded about four and one-quarter billion, of which one and three-quarter billion has been paid out in benefits to the end of 1941. During the year 1940, about five and one-half million persons drew unemployment compensation at one time or another, but in some cases these payments were as low as two or three dollars per week.

keeping and high administrative costs, which have run in some instances more than double the anticipated 10 per cent. Instead of payments being according to *needs*, they are in accordance with the amount of *earnings* of the employee. The plan is therefore far removed from the insurance principle of pooling resources to meet specific incidence. Benefits are limited to one-half of regular earnings in practically all the state laws, and the maximum amounts of benefit per week are in the neighborhood of fifteen dollars. In the event of severe depression, it is to be expected that in the highly industrialized areas these very inadequate payments will require large supplementary financing in the form of direct relief so long as this arrangement stands. In contrast to most European plans, the American system of unemployment income benefits is undoubtedly much too complex and topheavy with detailed paper work. There are cases of long delay in making payments, much dispute as to the amount of benefit accruing to given individuals, and the payments during unemployment are likely to be periodically inadequate.[1]

The pooling of funds by states affords very inadequate reserves in many instances, because of the concentration of industrial volatility risks in certain limited geographical areas. There is good reason to believe that despite previous doubts as to the constitutionality of Federal action in such matters, unemployment compensation will presently be integrated on a national basis, with considerable gain in efficiency and economy. Were the entire fund handled as a single reserve, the paying of adequate

---

[1] The actual results of unemployment compensation benefits in a typical industrial area were studied by the Social Security Board in the case of Detroit during the 1938 recession. (See *Employment Security Memorandum*, 1914, January, 1941.) Although the Michigan Unemployment Compensation Law provided benefit rights among the most liberal of any state system, it was found that 44 per cent of the men and 59 per cent of the women in this area exhausted their benefits in six months, and the period of unemployment for most of them was longer than a year. This analysis took into account, not the actual benefits but those that would have been available had the plan been in operation from the very beginning of the sharp recession that began in 1937. The study therefore concludes that the system did not provide adequate protection to eligible unemployed workers during a sharp business recession of relatively short duration.

In New York State the recession of 1938 produced embarrassing difficulties in administration. In November, 1938, 11 months after benefits began, 68 per cent of the payments were overdue. There were 378,680 claims pending settlement on Dec. 31, 1938. In addition, 230,000 claims of persons who filed more than once during the year were being held up until their eligibility could be determined. Much of this inefficiency was the result of inexperience and administrative complexity. (Abraham Epstein, letter to *The New York Times*, Mar. 10, 1939.)

See also the paper by William Haber, member of the Advisory Council to the Social Security Board, "Some Current Problems in Social Security," published by the Bureau of Industrial Relations, University of Michigan, 1938.

benefits might be measurably strengthened.[1] It is also apparent that much of the excessive bookkeeping now necessary to ensure that benefits exactly offset individual payments on a payroll basis could be eliminated by making distribution according to a number of wage classifications and other similar departures from the meticulous. But this does not yet reach the central difficulty.

Not only must we look forward to broader pooling of reserves and inclusion of a larger fraction of the working population but there is grave doubt as to the manner in which the accumulated reserve is "invested" and as to the need for a strict "reserve" system at all. For investment purposes, the Secretary of the Treasury, as trustee of the (state) funds, treats the reserves as a single fund; he must place the fund in securities that are direct obligations of the United States or that are guaranteed as to principal and interest by the National Government. These investments must be made to yield a "return" equal to the current average rate of interest on all interest-bearing obligations of the United States. This idea is obviously carried over from insurance practice. But there is no sense in one department of the Government being concerned about "interest return" on obligations issued by some other Federal agency. If the funds are invested in Government securities at all, they may be considered as used either to purchase outstanding Federal bonds to be retired or to purchase new bonds issued for the purpose. In the former case payment with Federal Reserve funds means adding to bank reserves somewhere and adding to credit potential. The latter case is equivalent to the beneficiaries loaning new money to the Government and helping to defray the general costs and outlays of the Government. In fact, they are *forced loans* to pay current public bills! Actually, the Social Security funds *have* been "invested" in new debt and not in the retirement of outstanding debt. Thus, instead of there being any *reserves*, there are merely *claims upon future income*, to be realized by *additional* taxation or borrowing when the need arises!

Reasons might perhaps be brought forward to justify this remarkable procedure in the case of the old-age or other insurance funds, but there is absolutely no justification for this process in the case of the unemployment income reserve. It is of the very essence of cyclical stabilization that a reserve not be used in any way likely to result in additional general purchasing power being created, *directly or indirectly*, during a period of

---

[1] Such a step is the more likely in view of passage in 1938 of an Unemployment Insurance Act covering railway employees, which provides for a nation-wide system considerably simpler and more direct in all its features than the cumbersome Social Security machinery. It is understood that President Roosevelt has approved proposals for an all-inclusive Federal system of social insurance.

better than average business conditions. For the Federal Treasury to be permitted to throw these accumulating reserves, as they become available, into the general expenditures of the Government is economically unsound and politically reprehensible. Since there is presumably no reduction in total purchasing power such as would be dictated by any strictly reserve operation, there must be additional funds raised to afford the support to purchasing power when it is needed under depression conditions, unless, by the merest chance, the Government happens to have cash balances to use for this purpose.

Since our Unemployment Insurance Reserve represents neither sound insurance nor actual reserve, what can be done to provide a more straightforward Federal plan that might actually work? Let us look at the problem from a somewhat different angle. Let us regard the wage-earning group as continually facing a zero income risk that *probably* will be (for the vast majority) a hazard of temporary duration. Why build a reserve and involve all the subterfuge of investing it when that group of workers in the mass has as sound a credit rating as any corporation? Let us forget about reserve funds and insurance and charity and put the problem on a straight bank-credit basis, reversing the order of premium and benefit. Why cannot our commercial banks supply a volume of loans to meet a conservative proportion of depression payroll loss if the inevitable recovery is thus made more certain, less distant, and can quickly serve to amortize the loan? In this plan the premiums accumulated in the rising phase of business and employment cycle would systematically extinguish a debt, the interest cost of which could be borne by the whole nation. We should accomplish with almost perfect timing and no indirect, roundabout money-market juggling what has long been sought—a prompt cyclical support to purchasing power to prevent its utter demoralization in recession periods and an effective restraint upon excessive momentum in spending and in bank-credit expansion in periods of boom. The mechanics of this would not be complicated.

A PROPOSED FEDERAL PLAN TO OVERCOME DISTURBANCES CREATED BY UNEMPLOYMENT

Without entering into minute detail, the writer offers the following outlines of a Federal plan to modify the effect of occasional unemployment upon income, trade continuity, and capital flow. We cannot reach all individual cases and not even all types of work. We can avoid the narrow limits of state authority and yet secure the advantages of flexible adjustment to conditions in various areas and industry types by having the system supervised by a central board, as at present, but with the administration by regional agencies somewhat similar to those of the Railroad

Retirement Board. Federal Reserve districts might serve as a preliminary guide. The data being accumulated by the Social Security Board and the Bureau of Labor Statistics will presently provide a basis for estimating fairly accurately the cycles of wage-earner employment, both generally and according to industries, in relation to the employable and eligible working population. This will serve as a guide to the proper timing of mass premium payments, while actual, complete unemployment of individual workers, after a suitable "waiting period" and the usual certifications, would constitute the occasion for benefits.

Regardless of all the other ways that may be found to modify the business cycle, it is essential to be prepared for real depression. Benefits, instead of being approved for a few months, should be adequate, at least, in principle, to *any* emergency. But since this in itself would assure quicker business recuperation, less destruction of trade continuity, financial confidence, and industrial solvency, it could be considered virtually certain that what was paid out to sustain decent family life among employees would be repaid in due course. The procedure would be as follows. As soon as the proper measures of the extent of unemployment indicated the need for payment of benefits, the Social Security Board would discount at the commercial banks Federally guaranteed notes, not subject to rediscount, and repayable after six months, with discount at an appropriate rate. The resulting proceeds would be raised as needed and disbursed through the regional units directly to strictly accredited unemployed workers. Benefits would be inversely proportionate to normal employee earnings, ranging from six-tenths for the lowest to three-tenths for the highest paid groups. Benefits would continue as long as unemployment existed, provided that beyond a set period idleness possibly resulting from chronic difficulties in an industry or conditions peculiar to an individual would be investigated, possibly with the result of bringing obsolescence and other problems involving chronic unemployment within the range of effective study much more promptly than at present.

In order to simplify the repayment of these advances (which, it will be noted, resemble in principle the General Motors' and other loan plans), contributions would begin as soon as the general employment ratio advanced to a designated point close to or above the long-term average. The "premiums," instead of being taxes paid to and insured by the Treasury, would be specifically designated for the discharge of this total of loans. From its general revenue, the Federal Government would contribute all payment of interest. From the wage earners, quarterly contributions might be made in several classes, corresponding to the relative severity of the previous unemployment and hence the degree of income salvaged, but not less than 1 per cent of payroll. These amounts would be deducted from payroll and remitted to the Board by employers. The employers or employing firms would also contribute similar percentages, but these would be applied to the total payroll, plus executive salaries, plus all executive bonuses.   In the event that premiums did not meet previous outlays and cancel the notes within a specified period, a Federal grant (derived exclusively from tax revenue) might on very rare occasions be necessary.   But anticipation of such a modest grant is far better than the waste of many billions by the Roosevelt Administration, tinkering with the problem and getting nowhere.

Here is a plan that fits into our present banking machinery, which has long been seeking to keep alive the business of extending sound self-liquidating loans.   In the preceding plan such loans would be essentially similar to mercantile credit or consumer installment credit, except that they would be intended to restore, in part, the topheavy inclinations of the usual credit extension during recovery periods.   They would prove an invaluable help in securing a more even distribution of all business *through time*, and no sound credit process ever did anything but that.   There is no occasion to bring Federal Reserve credit into the picture, with the difficulties of ramifying leverage inhering in Reserve deposits, or other matters on money-market policy with which we are not at all concerned.   By such an arrangement the money market could actually be given considerable internal stability apart from central-banking policy.   It should be possible in this way to dispense with many of the WPA, PWA, and other clumsy relief schemes.   The writer is fully aware, however, that no plan of unemployment compensation can ever do more than serve as one of several kinds of brakes on business excess and as a shock absorber for business depression.   All that we intend to set forth is the necessity of making whatever plan we adopt at least prompt in action, tolerably effective, and thoroughly honest.[1]

In the words of a British observer, "Once an unemployment insurance scheme is adopted, it should not be permitted to become the only, or even the major, reliance of the struggle against unemployment.   There must be a framework of protection that influences management and individual establishments and entire industries and that also affects governmental policy."[2]   We should therefore give some consideration to those features of the process of bargaining between workers and employers that appear to have special significance for problems of cyclical stabilization.   Let us hope, first of all, that these processes of bargaining and negotiation will in the future continue to develop in the atmosphere

---

[1] See the article by Sumner Slichter, Making Booms Bear the Burden of Relief, *Harvard Business Review*, April, 1933, for earlier suggestions somewhat along this line.

[2] Mary Barnett Gibson, "Unemployment Insurance in Great Britain," p. 388, 1931.

of a growing confidence of each party with respect to the other, without resorting to regimentation, crude force, or chicanery.

Management has still much to learn about the art of personnel administration and sound labor relations. It has been preoccupied with the technical complexities of production and the difficulties of finance; it has lost sight of the connection between total wages and total sales. And on the other hand, labor, both organized and unorganized, has (perhaps of necessity) restricted its viewpoint to the short-run and immediate gains. This attitude has been vulnerable because it has been based upon inadequate factual measurement and not enough of the spirit of give and take. Labor leadership in recent years has achieved astonishing success in the rapid organization of workers in the mass-production industries, but that same leadership has been sadly lacking in economic statesmanship. It has insisted upon bargaining processes that instead of developing productivity have frequently nullified it. By losing sight of the importance of *annual real earnings*, it has encouraged large groups of wage earners merely to insist upon the inflation of the price of an hour's work when times are good, leaving to others the problem of the deflation of *employment* after the boom. The basic problem of wages is the problem of keeping the annual real wage *continuously* in approximate adjustment to the productivity of the processes in which labor participates.

This problem also involves maintenance of employment, so far as possible, by avoiding unreasonable and *sporadic* demands for wage-rate advances whenever a pretext appears, likewise, the needlessly sudden and abrupt reductions in working time or wage rates by employers on the slightest pretext. In the past these bargaining processes have been crude, harsh, and not particularly effective as to the ultimate objectives. This has been due in large measure to the fact that labor has had wholly inadequate reserves against the future, whereas management, more often than not, has been forced by creditors, competitors, tax collectors, and sheer ignorance from taking the long view and the broad view of what is really involved in setting wage rates.

As Dean Wallace B. Donham has said with candor, "We build great industrial corporations which introduce amazing novelties into life. Their executives behave first, last, and nearly all the time as if their companies had no function except to manufacture and sell. They have a fine understanding of their own business, too little grasp of their industries as a whole, almost none of the relation between their particular interest and our general social and economic structure, and far too little grip on the social consequences of their activities."[1] Hence we find the setting of wages a matter of spasmodic conflicts accomplished through

[1] *Harvard Business Review*, July, 1933.

the use of threats and force and even in the milder cases, through the wasteful and costly procedures of the lawsuit, usually referred to euphemistically as "arbitration." What is required, and what will undoubtedly be of supreme importance in the years to come, is a procedure to permit parties charged with high responsibility for the maintenance of something that we can still call a free economic order to replace futile argument and palaver and work according to factual evidence *continuously* and earnestly. The fundamental of this procedure is the requirement that adjustments should be made as part of a continuing effort, not merely in spasms. The broad changes that affect wages, labor costs, and productivity should be *anticipated before they become critical* and subject to exploitation and distortion, just as tax payments, orders, and mechanical requirements are regularly anticipated as a guide to financial policy. Business executives have planned ahead, or sought to do so, in every phase of their businesses except relationships with labor. Labor was not considered *part* of the business. It is time that this studious avoidance of facts, advance study, and willingness to discuss and receive suggestions be ended.

By stressing *continuing* adjustment of wage rates through frequent small changes, to preserve some degree of parity of annual real-wage income with production per worker, we can promote the establishment of principle opposed to the half-conscious, ill-conceived, and irresponsible demands on the part of labor groups not yet sobered by responsibility. There are many humanitarians and charity workers, not concerned with long-term consequences, who wish to see low incomes and poverty abolished overnight by redistribution of wealth or income, or both. But this kind of abrupt change is the very negation of intelligent planning and flexible adjustment that is essential to the continued existence of a democracy. What organized workers should recognize as among their worst enemies is the impulsive, hasty, and shallow reformer who insists upon instantaneous, *quick* results. The "quickie" strike, the ill-considered "sitdown" are aspects of the willingness to resort to violent coercion and the picketing of plants by hired thugs to enforce demands. The quick-action spirit exposes all intelligent adjustment of wages, hours, and the very right to work to the machinations of the kind of subversive leadership that was gaining power in this country until temporarily thwarted by World War II. To maintain civilization, we must outlaw all such tactics of haste, surprise attack, and vindictive spirit.

As a means toward this end, the organization of wage earners into cohesive union groups *can* be made a powerful means of accomplishing by continuous negotiation the delicate adjustments to keep wage income in proper balance with the value of production and real income in balance with the productivity of the nation's effort. But the avoidance of income interruption by acts of sabotage and internal warfare requires understanding by both labor and management of the importance of putting the cards upon the table and being willing to discuss frankly and openly. This further means that union organization must develop responsibility in its leadership and the same disclosure of financial position that is expected of any business firm. Management, too, must drop its traditional aloofness; it must be, far more than in the past, *willing to talk face to face at any time* with those who, in the last analysis, are the very customers that produce the sales. Personnel management in the future will be a vital and indispensable adjunct to executive functions. Democracies today are fighting for their existence and for the right to continue to develop and refine types of productive organization and creative uses of capital that, despite all their historic defects, have contributed more to human life in the past century than can be readily appreciated. But continuation of this progress demands that when the present world effort to eliminate surprise aggression in international affairs has succeeded, we make the basis of all human relations willingness to change but to change gradually, intelligently, with conscious foresight.

Our emphasis upon the necessity of a *continuing* effort by employers and wage earners to adjust basic wage rates to the trend of general productivity does not mean that every minor incident or flurry in prices must immediately be translated into wages. This is particularly important to consider in the cases of minor, temporary fluctuations in the cost of living. Apart from price inflations produced by war or long-term changes arising from monetary causes, the attempt to establish a meticulous "parity" between the incidental fluctuations in retail cost of living diverts attention from the main objective and creates a series of adjustments that prevent *both prices and wage rates* from being properly adjusted to efficiency in the long run. The adjustment of wages must be continuous, with an eye to the underlying drift, not the month-to-month oscillations. If wages are tied too closely to small oscillations in the cost of living, usually arising from agricultural conditions, the result is merely to *generalize* this passing instability through a wider segment of society than is necessary, rather than bringing that instability itself under greater control. To tie wages to farm prices is just as unsound as to tie farm prices to wage rates.[1]

With respect to hours of work, we have seen definite evidence that during the decade of the 1920's there was very inadequate recognition of the fairness and economic desirability of shortening average hours of work. The result was some intensification of the unemployment problem in the 'thirties. In this matter again there is need for understanding and factual measurement to create a proper atmosphere in which adjust-

[1] See John D. Black, "Parity, Parity, Parity," 1942.

ments can be made, not in spasmodic jerks but in orderly procedure and in terms of recognized principle. Wage earners cannot expect to achieve prosperity if they insist upon a total number of working hours far out of line with the prevailing requirements of productive technique. Employers are shortsighted and incompetent if they fail to recognize that the setting of hours of work in each operation is just as much a part of the wage equation and as important a determinant eventually of the demand for their products as are the wage rates themselves.

DEFECTS IN PROFIT-SHARING SCHEMES

There was a time when profit-sharing schemes were popular, and some of these plans still are in operation. Profit sharing is a device that is difficult to reconcile with the basic principles here presented. The wage earner has a right to an adequate wage when tested always against the trend of productivity; he has a right to share equitably in the gains of progress. He has a right to expect that management will be increasingly able, as the result of a more adequate conception of its responsibilities and a wider use of specialized research, to open up new avenues of employment and counteract obsolescence so that labor demand and employment can be well maintained without violent interruptions. To consider that the worker must have his earnings eked out or augmented by something in the nature of profits or bonuses or other embellishments reminds one of the merchants who give presents to their customers. If what is sold is worth its price, it needs no such subsidies, and the same is true of labor. Profit sharing, although sometimes sincere in intent, smacks of that form of paternalism that in the past expressed itself too often in company-controlled unions and in incidental "welfare" concessions that were subtle ways of screening an obstinate unwillingness by the employer to recognize labor as a permanent cooperating factor or to talk with labor face to face. All such plans are inconsistent with the stabilization principles that we have outlined. To disburse occasional bonuses is equivalent to raising income suddenly and temporarily, usually in a good year, when total income is accelerating. The effect upon labor expenditures of many such disbursements would merely be to broaden and intensify the overexpansion of production already occurring in the capital goods and consumer durables. During depression the disappearance of these handouts would merely serve to emphasize the general reduction in income and employment. Profit sharing is essentially unstabilizing and inimical to the placing of labor remuneration on a secure foundation, on its merits.

This brings us to the problem of wage rates in a period of depressed business conditions. There has been much controversy as to whether wage rates should not be reduced as a means of cutting costs and readjusting the relationship between costs and prices to a basis at which the incentive to resume full production could be restored. If wage rates during prosperity in a given case are pushed suddenly and coercively beyond a workable relationship to productivity, the chances are that when the depression begins they are entirely out of line with the possibility of maintaining employment. This is another way of expressing the unsatisfactory results of irrational wage adjustments in boom periods. If management were more willing to make *moderate* adjustments in accordance with all pertinent facts and data during such periods and labor leadership was rid of its gangster elements, wage earners would accept these changes as the facts revealed them to be fair and adequate. But if wages are forced out of line in trades lacking the saving grace of rising efficiency, equitable readjustment becomes a baffling problem. Organized labor naturally resists any readjustment, and the more it resists the more inevitable is the eliminating of workers on a wholesale scale. If a union overplays its hand in raising scales, the employer will sooner or later overplay his hand in cutting jobs.

In a society that strives to avoid undue regimentation of the individual, we should not too harshly criticize the tendency of wage rates to resist adjustment during periods of depression. If we resort, in a spirit of panic, to drastic cuts all along the line in wage rates, it is inevitable that we shall merely contribute to the spiral of deflation, leading to prolongation of the difficulties. Again, we insist, price parity is an illusion. To slash wage rates in depression presupposes that there is no other alternative way to solve the problem, and we know that there are such alternatives. Even on its merits, wage cutting does not keep labor employed in lines where production has outrun sound market limits and curtailment is necessary. It is a crude way of maintaining business solvency at the expense of labor solvency, and in the end depression is lengthened and deepened by the workings of a vicious spiral. To slash prices, on the other hand, may serve the purpose of moving existing stocks of more or less perishable and seasonal goods off the shelves in the face of impaired income of the usual buyers. Some price cutting may be a belated recognition that prices were out of line while conditions were still prosperous, but adjustments should be made in prosperity, not in depression. Many price cuts, as we shall observe in a later discussion of the price stability problem in Chapter 24, fail to do anything more than postpone buying, and in a wide segment of distribution the effect of shrinking demand cannot be in any discernible measure counteracted by lower prices. Thus, in the absence of better ways of coordinated action and the exercise of simple foresight, price and wage cutting are harsh, costly, desperate ways of maintaining solvency for some at the expense of others and, except in retail trade, serve to prolong the reactionary spirit rather than to neutralize it. The presumption, when general demand begins to falter and shift backwards and depression reveals unbalance somewhere, to cut prices or wages ruthlessly implies that these will probably be *raised again*, and with abandon, when times get better. And this is merely a way of saying that it is sound policy to accentuate business instability rather than to counteract it.

GENERAL ELECTRIC PLAN FOR EMPLOYMENT STABILIZATION

With respect to general operating policy as to labor and employment we cannot better conclude than by quoting the words of Gerard Swope in describing the procedure of the General Electric Company as it stood in 1930:

When business is increasing and optimistic conditions prevail, additions to the working force are made as slowly as possible and only when there is no other help available within the plant itself. If one department needs any additional workers, this need is met by a transfer from other departments. Overtime will be resorted to both in individual departments and throughout the plant generally before the working force is increased. When production is at a height, then plant renewal and maintenance work is kept at a low ebb, so that the maintenance staff may be kept at work on production.

These measures are the first important step toward employment stabilization for, by following them, it will be possible to postpone and, it is hoped, to eliminate entirely, the chance of becoming so excessively overstaffed that it will be impossible to absorb the residue by transfer to other types of work when this becomes necessary.

When production begins to fall off, no new employees are to be taken on, and time in all departments will be brought down to the normal week. Workers in departments where the work is temporarily slack are to be transferred to busier departments. Additional sales effort will be made to secure cooperation from customers and to get orders for future delivery. Production for stock will be inaugurated upon the basis prescribed by the research department, the estimate being derived from an average of the last three years' sales adjusted to the sales expectation of the next two years. Stocks at factory and district warehouses are brought up to the maximum permitted by this budget.

As many workers as possible are to be absorbed on maintenance and repair work, bringing the plant and equipment up to a high standard. Plant construction work is so planned that, when work is slack, it is possible to proceed with the development of new plant facilities, using General Electric employees for such work wherever possible.

If it becomes necessary to cut down the normal week, this will be done as generally and as gradually as possible.[1]

Management policies, looking toward stabilization of employment conditions so far as this can be attained within a given plant or firm, may

---

[1] *Executives' Service Bulletin*, November, 1930.

be facilitated by the statistical data now becoming available for many individual lines of manufacturing industry to measure various aspects of labor turnover. The U.S. Bureau of Labor Statistics regularly publishes index numbers[1] showing changes in the rate of termination of employment and the constituent factors. These include the quit rate (termination of employment initiated by the worker), discharge rate, and layoff rate (temporary interruption of work at the will of the employer but without prejudice to the worker). Through these measures, which should also be maintained by every personnel department and every employer, a very clear picture is presented of the forces at work in the labor market and the kinds of change occurring in the tenure of jobs. Figures reveal that there is a surprisingly high degree of industrial labor mobility. In good times the separation rate rises because of the desire of workers to improve their positions as they shift from one job to another. This frequently has the disadvantage of leaving workers stranded in unstable situations and without continuity of income at critical periods in the business cycle. When business conditions begin to deteriorate, the rise in layoffs can be precisely observed and its significance studied with respect to management policy. In general, a relatively high rate of labor turnover in a plant is a source of unnecessary expense and loss of efficiency. It costs money to train workers and to fit them into a smooth-running organization. A company having a persistently high turnover rate is virtually operating a training school for other employers, and as a result thorough training facilities are not developed. These data assist in determining critical points in the business cycle for a large number of industries and thus may be considered among the sources to be consulted in judging near-term probable changes in demand for products. Their use by management and labor organizations should be encouraged. They form an eloquent argument for such compensatory income plans as were previously discussed.

PROVISION AGAINST OBSOLESCENCE A RESPONSIBILITY OF BOTH LABOR AND MANAGEMENT

We come finally to the special problem of unemployment clearly arising from rapid technological improvement or the drag of industry obsolescence. As for technical progress, the answer is mainly found in the provision of dismissal wages and a willingness on the part of management to assist through training or otherwise in relocating the displaced workers. If the spirit of initiative endures in many industries it is certain that such changes will be enlarging labor demand in some lines while reducing it in

---

[1] Developed out of pioneer studies of the subject by William A. Berridge, now economist of the Metropolitan Life Insurance Company.

others. It is a problem of relocation. As for obsolescence problems, these are to be met by the conscious effort of both management and labor policy to combat obsolescence by maintaining a continuing awareness of the competitive potential in product or process, by active research and experiment designed to evolve new products, to improve existing products, and broaden service before the opportunities are lost. Once an industry has begun to disintegrate, leaving blighted areas and a helpless working population, the problem becomes one of public relief and mass migration. Conspicuous in the list of obsolescent industries that have left their workers stranded have been those made up of too many small, weak firms unable to mobilize and too ignorant to value facilities for looking ahead and adapting themselves to changing conditions. There have been industries in which financial and capital burdens proved to be insuperable obstacles to flexible policy, competent and alert management, and the exercise of a reasonable degree of foresight.

Provision against obsolescence is a responsibility to be actively shared by both labor and management. More particularly, it involves the problem of how new products and processes may be most advantageously introduced into the business system in an orderly fashion, without violent and disruptive effects, so that repercussions upon *existing uses* of labor and capital may be smoothly absorbed. Here we are face to face with the much-agitated question, whether the average business unit must necessarily be small and limited in order to satisfy the legalistic hypotheses of those who believe in "free" competition or whether it should be permitted to assume a size and form capable of fully rendering *all* the services we expect from it and capable of rendering them with continuity and foresight. Of late years the wealth redistributors, whose zeal often outweighs their common sense, have attempted to persuade us that all large corporations are a great social menace since they are tinged with the aspect of monopoly. They are supposed to accentuate the alternation of booms and depressions because they make "large" profits. Some of these zealots have endeavored to prove that the business cycle is essentially a joint product of the maldistribution of wealth and the existence of monopolistic corporations. The *size* of business units is associated in many minds with subtle collusion, price fixing, the browbeating of labor, gentlemen's agreements, control of legislation, and undue restriction of the circulation of purchasing power. In fact, however, the size of the business unit is not the prime test of its ability to promote or maintain economic stability and progressive efficiency. There are large corporations whose management has been less progressive, less farsighted, and less competent to handle labor relations than many a small or medium-sized plant.

In some fields of enterprise, corporations have failed to contribute to either stability or progress because the job to be done was beyond the range of a private undertaking. But in commerce and manufacturing, the core of our business system, a fair-minded survey would disclose many managements and indeed an increasing number that accept the responsibility to practice sound finance, to promote continuity of operations, and to see that relations with labor require conscious study and trained executives. Small business has its virtues in that the problems of mass personnel are absent, but in the majority of cases the small shop and its employees suffer the consequences of limited financial resources, speculative or chiseling managers, ruthless competitive tactics, and all the shortcomings of amateurism in control. Obsolescence closes in on the small unit, not because it is small but because the mass of managers lack education or the qualifications for executive ability. Those who would atomize all industry into managerial units on the farmer's level, with blind adherence to a production routine, uncoordinated with demand conditions, are urging steps that run counter to all our modern efforts to develop expert management through systematic training and to develop new ways of providing labor with new jobs. When we consider that systematic training for executive responsibility has existed in the United States for but a small fraction of the time that legal, medical, or even engineering training has existed, the problem of extending Sound Practice on the part of top management is plainly a matter of education, not repression. No one would deny that the managers of some large corporations have been indifferent to these problems; the mere enlargement of corporate *size* has of itself no bearing upon efficiency, alertness, or willingness to develop new techniques. What we are here concerned with is the matter of principle in recognizing the possibility of utilizing all the potentialities of free enterprise and initiative by mobilizing its support to assist wage earners in adjusting themselves to the course of progress. Like other requirements of modern business, this becomes a matter of recognizing what is Sound Practice and constantly encouraging it.

Specifically, this means the adroit timing of new mechanisms to minimize labor displacement. It means the cultivation of research as an essential and continuous, not a spasmodic, activity. It means the retention of workers beyond the years of their most productive efforts to assist in training and research activities where experience and skill count. It means, above all, willingness to set aside ample research funds and to mobilize against obsolescence all the power that can be marshaled. This requires organizations having sufficient command of capital and ability to incorporate these efforts into regular routine. The time is not far distant, assuming that our system of private capitalistic enterprise endures, when the powerful influence of demand for consumer durable goods as a vitalizing element in all production in the postwar period cannot fail to impress itself upon the responsible management of American business. Everything possible should therefore be done to avoid disruption of employment and wage income, at the same time that ever larger efforts in discovery and technical improvements are provided for. Business amateurs and weak companies cannot be expected to make any material contribution to these ends.

CHAPTER 22

BUSINESS FORECASTING

Our analysis has brought to light a number of basic factors in the economic system that have contributed to the vibrations of the business cycle. We have noted the powerful unstabilizing influences transmitted into the stream of income and the flow of production as the result of population changes and unsound financing in construction, the impact of war financing upon the extractive industries, particularly agriculture, the unfortunate structure of farm finance, and a weak banking system, incapable of standing strain and subservient to the demands of speculation. We have seen how these basic factors of instability have been reinforced by major technical innovations, and we have seen the effect of leverage in magnifying the ebb and flow of income in the acquisition of durable equipment.

In developing sound policy for modifying cyclical disturbance, there is still much to be done by business management, within the scope of the individual business enterprise. We are working toward Principles of Sound Practice in handling the dynamic aspects of policy. In this chapter, we shall discuss some essential features of the problem of adapting business policy to the ever-changing rhythm of general conditions through intelligent use of dynamic measurement capable of throwing some light on the course ahead. Business management, like legal and even much of financial practice, still pays overwhelming respect to precedent and past performance, the worship of static rules and rule-of-thumb precepts, instead of boldly accepting the challenge of change and recognizing the continuity of events. So, also, Government has approached many regulatory problems from a static legalistic standpoint, insisting upon restrictive and punitive discipline while entirely overlooking unbalanced acceleration, dynamic consequences in terms of future growth, or the ways of reconciling future planning with the incentives of immediate return. It is indeed strange that the dynamic phases of business have been so long subordinated to the aspects that are structural or the matters of day-to-day routine. Of course, until a few decades ago it was not easy to obtain continuous statistical records or to observe the patterns of time relationships within the economic system capable of affording something better than mere guesswork as a basis for planning ahead. We cannot plan for what we cannot formulate; and we cannot formulate beyond what we can measure.

It is here that we find the distinction between economic forecasting, as primarily a statistical technique, and prophecy. A prophecy is an assertion concerning some future event, possibly specifying the date of its occurrence. Most prophecies relate to isolated occurrences that the soothsayer or prophet discovers through powers known only to himself. Scientific prophecy is based on knowledge of physical forces, cosmic relationships, or mathematical formulas, also to be recognized. To prophesy the date and character of an expected eclipse or the future exact position of a heavenly body illustrates the rational application of the laws of physical dynamics. But these are not strictly prophecies so much as they are extrapolations of a known sequence of forces or movements. In this sense they are essentially similar to the forecasts or predictions that we seek to obtain from the study of the continuity of economic processes. We endeavor to establish some degree of uniformity in the business behavior and time relationships of one factor to others and estimate from this the most probable future direction. In the realm of human events the strictly uniform behavior of physical forces and mechanical sequence is not to be expected. Any recurrent tendencies that our historical analysis or business processes reveal over an extended period cannot safely be used as a basis for forecasting unless qualified by continuous reappraisal of the entire economic, financial, political, international, and technological background. We must be constantly aware of institutional change and the fact that the apparently simple oscillations in production or prices that our measurements reveal may actually involve the combination of multiple factors. The combined pattern that we see may never repeat itself in exactly that form at any future time. However thorough and well-verified our purely statistical measurements of sequence may be and however long the period through which observations have been carried, in the last analysis the task of arriving at a reliable forecast as to aspects of business conditions will always involve the exercise of judgment and the proviso that the probable error of the forecast is high enough to make humility appropriate.

Business forecasting, through quantitative measurement, is concerned with ways of projecting observed continuity of movement into a future period whose distance ahead is limited by judgment and the nature of the various sequences discovered in the past. In general, it is never safe to project independently merely one isolated series representing economic performance, whether production, wage rates, income, prices, or anything else. In the case of physical quantities, such as the production of steel or the composite index of industrial production, our efforts to extrapolate the existing phase of the cycle into a future period is facilitated by what we can learn about the underlying trend of that particular variable. Since trends of growth usually alter that slope and rate of change gradually, it is much safer to extend a *trend* pattern a year or two than to estimate a probable future *cyclical* oscillation about the trend by as much as six months.   There is likely to be doubt as to the precise trend level that the distant future will finally demonstrate to have been correct at the present date, and we can easily go astray in estimating the *current* phase of the cycle here and now, with respect to its real intensity when measured against the (ultimate) trend.   Hence, in projecting ahead, our error will be still further increased.   This difficulty arises mainly from the fact that the recurring waves of the business cycle or the cyclical movements pertaining to a particular industry or enterprise are not precisely *periodic* in their timing or uniform in the amplitude of rise or fall from their trend. Some cyclical movements tend to be low in amplitude and of considerable length; others are violent in extent and brief in duration.   We shall presently comment upon this fact as it bears upon particular forecasting methods.   In the case of prices we have already seen that the long-term trends are not growth processes and hence are difficult to gauge in advance.   Hence the possibility of forecasting the direction of such a series presents a much more difficult problem than volume data.   Production has usually a fairly consistent long-term drift.   The case of value series is intermediate.

The problem of developing a reasonably reliable economic forecast becomes much more manageable if we are able to secure two types of information.   It is of great assistance if we know that certain particular disturbing factors in the past have repeatedly accounted for a substantial measure of the general cyclical pattern that reveals itself in the particular data that we are considering.   Thus, if we have reason to believe that the status of the building industry has much to do with the cycles of business activity and if we not only can measure the building cycle but also can find that financial or other factors logically influence building momentum, we have valuable information for predicting the outcome of current tendencies among these factors.   Second, we may observe from historical evidence that two or more factors tend to describe cyclical movements that repeatedly establish a consistent lead-and-lag relationship, that is, a regularity of sequence.   For many years a more or less regular timing sequence characterized the relation of money rates to industrial production and the relation of the stock market to industrial activity, but these cases incidentally demonstrate that we must be fully conscious of the underlying changes in the general structure that may render such sequences less useful than they were half a century ago.

SUNSPOTS AND THE BUSINESS CYCLE

Through the years the opinion has again and again been stated, in varying forms, that business cycles are the result of forces that originate outside the earth and are traceable to meteorological dynamics. We do not propose to examine in detail these theories or the statistical demonstrations pertaining to them, because no proof has yet been adduced that they have any practical validity. There are, in fact, so many different versions of the cyclical pattern or period in which these cosmic forces are imagined to oscillate that the doctrine of meteorological influence is usually smothered in a welter of controversy. Perhaps the

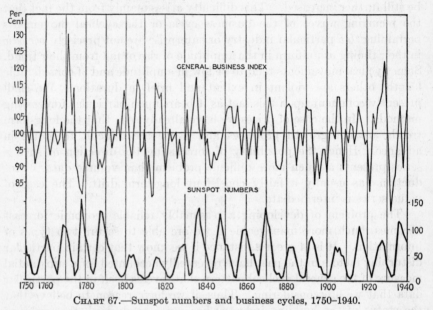

CHART 67.—Sunspot numbers and business cycles, 1750–1940.

most popular form of the idea is found in the alleged correlation between the pulse of business activity and cyclical variability in the radiations from the sun. This has been measured for several hundred years in terms of what are known as "sunspot numbers." Almost periodically the surface of the sun is observed to be clouded over, and this phenomenon, in turn, is suspected to be the cause of additional radiation reaching the earth.[1] In Chart 67 the sunspot numbers are shown over a long period. The reasoning, as expressed by Sir John Herschel, early in the nineteenth century, and later by W. Stanley Jevons, is that variation

[1] The sunspot numbers recorded in Chart 67 are technically index numbers in which 100 equals sunspot coverage of one five hundredths of the visible solar disk. The data in Chart 67 were taken from the table appearing in H. T. Stetson's "Sunspots and Their Effects," New York and London, 1937. His figures are those of Wolf and Wolfer, representing readings for various observatories. Stetson's table is supplemented beyond 1937 by provisional data given in the *Monthly Weather Review* of the United States Government and based upon data supplied by the observatory at Zurich, Switzerland.

in the radiation or heat from the sun influences the yields of important farm crops and hence farm prices and income; these, in turn, affect the state of general trade and industry. Among others who have given attention to this line of thought in recent years was Henry L. Moore, an American economist who sought to demonstrate recurring relationships between weather conditions, the rainfall in certain crop areas, and the occurrence of business cycles in the United States.[1] This was carried further to somewhat puzzling and intricate conclusions as to the changing phases of various astronomical bodies and forces, into which we need not enter in this connection. Still more recent has been the attempt to read a new meaning into the roughly cyclical pattern of sunspots by suggesting that it is not the effect of sunspots, or alternations in physical radiation from the sun, upon rainfall or temperature or crop production, but rather their direct effect upon human psychology that accounts for the ups and downs in economic motivation. Briefly, the theory is that the sun transmits varying amounts of ultraviolet-ray emanations, and these, in turn, have a physiological or neurological effect upon animal organisms that might conceivably be capable of bringing about alternation in moods, attitudes, and promotional energy.[2]

The actual relations between sunspot numbers and the cycles of trade and industrial production in the United States do, in fact, appear to be more or less correlated during the past half century, but a close examination of the data over a much longer period, as in Chart 67, serves to dispel the assumption of a high degree of correlation. Curiously enough, a direct correlation does seem to persist for several decades at a time, but unfortunately it is inverse at other periods and irregular enough on the whole to render any causal deductions whatsoever highly questionable. The reader can judge this for himself by a careful study of this chart.[3]

---

[1] "Economic Cycles: Their Law and Cause," New York, 1914. See the review of this by P. G. Wright, *Quarterly Journal of Economics*, August, 1922; also, the references cited in Chapter 8.

[2] See the article by C. G. Garcia-Mata and F. I. Schaffner, Solar and Economic Relationships, *Quarterly Journal of Economics*, November, 1934. The deductions of these writers have been challenged by the eminent astronomer Dr. Harlow Shapley, director of the Harvard College Observatory (*The New York Times*, Mar. 15, 1938), who claims that the factual material does not support the contention of any regular connection between sunspots and human pessimism or optimism. The theory, however, is accepted as plausible by W. I. King in his "Causes of Economic Fluctuations," p. 147, New York, 1938. King appears disposed to accept the sunspot-psychology thesis mainly because he has been unable to find other explanations of the business cycle that are more satisfactory.

[3] An interesting popular version of the sunspot-psychology view is also found in Stetson's "Sunspots and Their Effects." Stetson appears to be fairly well convinced of the validity of the hypothesis that abundant ultraviolet rays reaching the earth make people optimistic, whereas a shortage makes them pessimistic.

Although it is not impossible that further research along these lines may yet develop relationships that are fairly consistent, as well as rational, it cannot be said that our present knowledge of the sun and its possible complex effects upon mundane attitudes and business transactions is capable of being a safe basis for predicting the future course of events or for guiding business policy.

Somewhat akin to the meterological theory, in that it emphasizes the supposed existence of regularly periodic waves in business and economic processes, is the theory of F. A. Pearson and his associates at Cornell

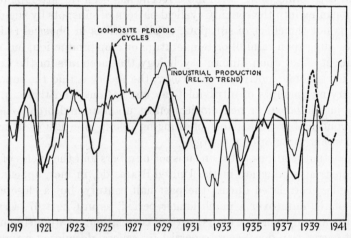

CHART 68.—Composite index of periodic cycles and industrial production cycles 1919–1941. The composite index of periodic cycles (*F. A. Pearson, W. I. Myers, and G. E. Brandow, Cornell University*) is a weighted average of periodic sine curves for automobile production, textile production, and the major and minor cycles of residential building. It is charted 7 months ahead of the actual timing, and is compared with the Federal Reserve index of industrial production.

University.[1] The production cycle is broken down into distinct elements, each of which, on the basis of long-term measurements from monthly data, is found capable of being "fitted" by a sine curve of appropriate period. Among the factors used are a major building cycle (period of related sine function 18 years), a minor residential-building cycle (period 33 months), a textile-production cycle (period 23 months), an automobile-production cycle (period 40 months). When these dissimilar, but in each case strictly periodic, curves are averaged together, with appropriate weights, they generate an irregular cyclical pattern that

[1] F. A. Pearson, W. I. Myers, and G. D. Brandow, Industrial Cycles and Business Activity, *Farm Economics* New York State College of Agriculture, Cornell University, February, 1939. The industrial production series shown in Chart 68 is not the same as the index used in the original.

gives a fairly close degree of correlation when compared with *later* business experience, as in Chart 68, from 1931 to 1936. This latter disparity is remedied by introducing a further factor in the composite, based upon the purchasing power of farm income. When this is included, the correlation with a series reflecting industrial production is improved.

Unfortunately, the projection of the average (prepared as of 1939) into 1941 produces a result that the actual facts show to be entirely erroneous, although possibly because of new conditions introduced by the War. This approach to the problem is ingenious, and this particular contribution to forecasting possibilities does not necessarily insist upon a meteorological explanation. It is a reasonable view to the extent that we know that the major building cycle has tended, at least in the past, to describe a fairly regular cycle pattern and perhaps the most regularly periodic in its long sweep of any known economic series. The short-term (approximately 2-year) cycle of the textile industry is likewise not wholly lacking in plausibility. The existence of a 40-month cycle in the automobile industry, however, is rather dubious, and the adjustment of the final sine-curve results by means of farm purchasing power introduces a factor that does not admit of accurate projection by itself, since it does not follow a sine function.[1]

By far the best results in predicting from six months to a year in advance the course of business conditions, as represented by the index of industrial production, have been obtained through the study of historical sequences involving financial data. As was pointed out in earlier chapters, there was a long period during which our banking processes and security markets moved in a fairly systematic relation to changes in the tone of business activity. It became a well-recognized principle that as money rates in New York began to rise from a relatively low cyclical level, under the influence of expanding business and rising security speculation, they foreshadowed a weakening of the stock market and somewhat later a downturn of production and trade (relative to their trends). Conversely, after the peak of money rates or bond yields appeared to have passed, it was considered an indication that financial strain would soon give way to conditions favoring resumption of borrowing, especially for speculative operations, and shortly thereafter for any reasonable business requirements. So long as bank loans played so large a part in trade activity and even in manufacturing and construction and so long as the banking system was so closely involved with specu-

---

[1] The reader may also consult sine curves developed by other workers, *e.g.*, the attempt of C. H. Whelden, Jr., to fit a periodic curve to the pattern of American stock prices, *The Annalist*, Jan. 1, 1937. The present writer suspects that any such methods of forecasting the stock market are likely to result rather badly for the operator who relies too much upon them.

lation and hence reflected the sensitive temper and anticipatory tendency of the speculative markets, the use of these relationships in forecasting cyclical changes had a sound, even though not entirely consistent, basis. Naturally, such statistical devices gained considerably in effectiveness if supplemented by internal analysis of industrial conditions and capital use.

DISCUSSION OF PROFESSIONAL FORECASTING SERVICES

The principles just described in brief summary were the basis upon which professional forecasting services released their systems and prognostications to businessmen, investors, and speculators. Without attempting a complete catalogue of the various business barometers developed in the United States, we may note a few of the best known that embody the financial-sequence principle. At the beginning of this century James H. Brookmire began to issue a systematic barometer, employing an index of the business cycle, measure of stock prices, and an index recording banking resources or ability of the commercial banks to extend loans. A reproduction of his original Brookmire Barometer, extending from 1900 to 1914, is reproduced in Chart 69.[1] It will be noticed in the Brookmire chart that when banking resources were becoming severely depleted (relative to the normal line), there soon developed a recovery that was almost immediately transmitted to a firmer tone in the stock market and, still later, a reversal of the declining tendency in the business cycle. Conversely, after banking resources had declined from their peak level and approached the normal line, there was consistently an extended position both in the stock market and in general business which called for correction. The reaction developed first in the stock market, at about the time when banking resources declined across

---

[1] This chart was made available to the writer through the kindness of Fred Messner, of the Brookmire Corporation in New York City, and has been reproduced by permission. A very similar type of graphic presentation has been used by the Alexander Hamilton Institute, also of New York City.

In the case of the Babson Statistical Organization more emphasis was placed upon what was known as the *Babsonchart*, presenting the result of a composite index of business and financial fluctuations around a line of trend, which was termed the X-Y Line. In the early form of this exhibit it was intended that the areas of excess or deficiency above and below the estimated trend level would necessarily be equal, but it was found in practice that the *current* position of the index with respect to the X-Y Line was rarely determinable with accuracy. Hence repeated readjustments of trend level became necessary, and the principle of equal (+) and (−) areas lost much of its supposed effectiveness. There was always doubt as to how much readjustment would probably follow from a given current situation and when the high point or low point of a particular cycle would probably be reached. On the whole, this method, in recent years considerably augmented by other types of analysis and greatly improved statistical indexes, may be considered as mainly of historical interest.

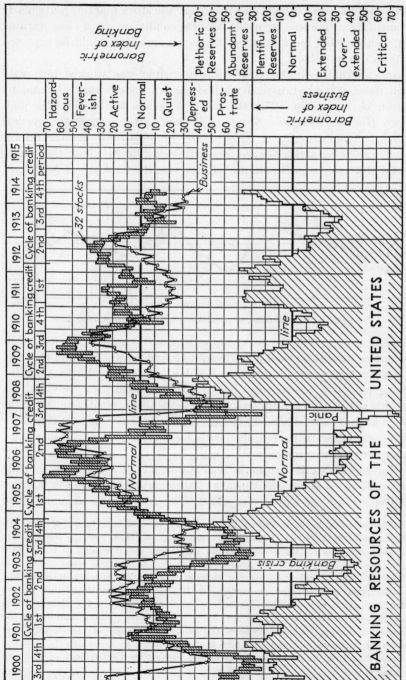

CHART 69.—Early business barometer of the Brookmire service, 1900–1914. (Courtesy of the Brookmire Corporation.)

the normal line, and usually this decline in the stock market, particularly if coinciding with a less favorable banking condition, was a clear warning that a substantial impairment of business conditions could be expected within a few months.

An essentially similar forecasting principle was worked out, with much more refined statistical methods and a wider range of data, by Warren M. Persons in 1917–1919, and this became the basis for the well-known *Harvard Economic Service*.[1] Persons, after testing the cyclical behavior of many series of business and financial data for the prewar period, produced a three-curve forecasting system in which the fundamental principle, as in Brookmire's Index, was the tendency of New York

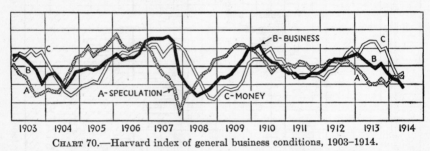

1903   1904   1905   1906   1907   1908   1909   1910   1911   1912   1913   1914

CHART 70.—Harvard index of general business conditions, 1903–1914.

speculation to precede the cycles in business and commodity prices, while the money market showed a tendency to move from a position of strain to ease or from ease to strain with a lag of several months after the turning points of the business index. This is illustrated by Chart 70. The only distinctive feature, apart from more accurate adjustment of the data, was that instead of using bank resources, whose movements more or less synchronized with business with an advance lead, Persons used money rates that correlated with a lag. In the accompanying example of the Harvard Index as it stood in 1923 (Chart 71), it can be seen that the method afforded an excellent means of anticipating the break in business conditions after the summer of 1920. The speculative barometer had

[1] Persons' basic experiments are described in Vol. 1 of the *Review of Economic Statistics*, published by the Harvard Economic Service, 1919, and the immediately succeeding volumes of this review contain additional contributions to the subject by Persons and other statistical economists. While the methods employed in presenting the Harvard Index and forecast underwent continuing changes in the ensuing years, the reference to the results shown above in the text is intended to illustrate the principal characteristics of the Harvard system. Subsequently the Harvard Economic Service became the Harvard Economic Society, Incorporated, and during the depression following 1929 the scope of the forecasting phases of the Society were considerably reduced, although the Index is still published by the quarterly *Review of Economic Statistics*, under the auspices of the Economics Department of Harvard University.

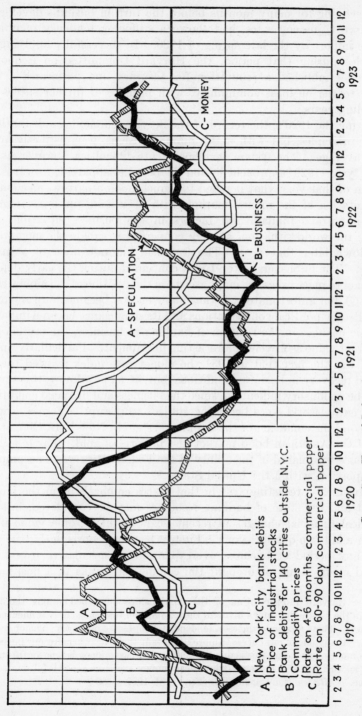

A {New York City bank debits
  {Price of industrial stocks
B {Bank debits for 140 cities outside N.Y.C.
  {Commodity prices
C {Rate on 4-6 months commercial paper
  {Rate on 60-90 day commercial paper

CHART 71.—Harvard Index of general business conditions, 1919–1923.

been declining for many months before the turn in business developed; and curve *C*, money rates, had shown a stiffening tendency of unmistakable import by the late spring of 1920.   In successfully applying its principles during that period, the Harvard Committee on Economic Research established a reputation for accuracy and performed a real service to the business community, with promise of further success in succeeding years.

During the 1920's, the record of the Service, employing substantially similar principles, but with many minor revisions, was distinctly good, on the average.   The system developed acute difficulties, however, as the fateful year 1929 approached, and it became apparent, toward the autumn of that year, that it relied too much upon a narrow, mechanical interpretation of the money market, with very inadequate coverage of other important fundamental factors in the business situation and, indeed, the world situation, as they converged to create the memorable breakdown later that year.   The forecasts did not warn of a major decline.   The publishers of the Index continued during the early depression years to place excessive emphasis upon the position of the money rates (curve *C*), but unfortunately, as the money market became more and more controlled by political considerations and its significance became impaired by basic changes in the relation of banking to business, the system had indifferent value as a cyclical forecasting instrument.   Particularly unfortunate was the fact that in 1931 the money-rate index pointed toward marked recovery in business conditions, but, as we now know, this turned out to be an illusory indication, since the business and financial conditions of the entire world were becoming subject to disruptive forces ranging far beyond the condition of the banking system in New York City or the tone of the American bond market and imports of gold.   Far too much confidence was placed in the ability of the Federal Reserve to accomplish the impossible within the United States.[1]

A business-forecasting system that places emphasis upon the money market and the state of banking resources may be considered, in spite of radical financial changes in recent years, to have some value if we bear in mind two qualifications.   First, it has been consistently true that when any period of business overexpansion or speculative excess has created credit strain or brought the commercial banks to a position in

---

[1] The Harvard interpretation of the relationships developed among the three curves in the forecasting Index involves the assumption that each curve influences the other two.   There was nevertheless a tendency to emphasize primarily the money-rate curve.   "If any one of our curves is more important than the others for our purposes, it is the money curve; and this is due to the fact that easy money is a powerful stimulant to speculation and business, while dear money exercises a powerful depressing influence."   (*Review of Economic Statistics*, April, 1927, p. 80.)

which they find it increasingly difficult to accommodate all those who seek loans, there has been created an influence adverse to further extension of the boom. Similar unfavorable conditions would arise from Federal Reserve action to reduce excess reserves, sterilize gold imports, sell bonds, or otherwise tighten the money market. This tightening of credit is reflected in the high-grade bond market; it tends to sober the speculative attitude toward stocks, and it also may have some effect upon mercantile houses that use considerable commercial credit. If this tightening tendency occurs following an extensive or long-continued boom condition and manifests itself in a drastic change in financial conditions, it may confidently be expected to serve not only as a damper upon the further rise in production and trade but as a definite factor in reversing the cycle.

But the rise of credit rates is not the *only* factor in these reversals. A forecast of the extent of the correction about to occur in business activity would be inadequate if it did not extend well beyond banking conditions or the state of the security markets and into such fundamental factors as the building cycle, international conditions, the state of agriculture, and raw-material inventories on hand in various positions. Even political factors would have to be considered, and under war conditions these naturally would become the most important, particularly as to financial appropriations and commodity supplies and controls. The difficulty encountered by most forecasters in 1929 was the tendency to anticipate a relatively minor readjustment in the situation; the background factors either were not sufficiently under observation or at that time were incapable of adequate measurement to indicate clearly how tremendous a reversal lay ahead.

A second qualification of this line of approach to business forecasting is logically associated with the first. The method almost invariably has some value in preparing for a *downturn* in business activity, but in forecasting an *upturn* it may become positively misleading, as it did in 1931. The major depressions, as we have seen in earlier chapters, have usually been associated with changing phases of the major cycle of construction, and when the building cycle is in the course of one of its long-term declining phases, it requires much more than a mere temporary improvement in banking conditions, interest rates, or fitful rallies in the stock market to turn the tide consistently in the other direction.

One further difficulty has confronted not only the Harvard Index but most other more or less mechanical or purely statistical barometers. This is the lack of smooth continuity in the movement of the index curves. Despite seasonal and other corrections, there are too many small fluctuations that at any given time cannot be safely regarded as significant turning points, up or down; and the Harvard Index has always been notably difficult to interpret for this reason.

DIFFICULTIES IN INTERPRETING BAROMETERS

Granting that statistical barometers of the Harvard or Brookmire type, which have been the basic foundation for numerous other attempts along these lines, have rested upon sound theoretical assumptions, as applied under certain conditions, there remains the question of interpretation.   Should the reading of the forecasting index or barometer be purely mechanical, with a conscious effort to exclude *all* other logical, psychological, political, or judgment factors?   Or should the observer attempt merely to draw a purely mechanical interpretation from the sequences shown by his index, as something to be judiciously combined with or balanced off against other possibly qualitative observations? The position of the Harvard authorities was never clearly defined on this point.   Their view, as stated in 1932, was that "under existing conditions in cases where the reading of the Index gives a different result from that obtained by economic analysis, we shall follow the former and present such a forecast as a mechanical reading of the Index gives."[1]   Yet the actual forecasts presented by the Service during its career do not support this wholly mechanical procedure.   Apparently what was done, and probably what should be done in the case of a mechanical statistical sequence barometer, is to interpret that index mechanically but then to combine the results with such *other* factors as historical evidence or common sense indicate may be important.   This is sometimes referred to as cross-cut analysis, and there are as many ways of doing this as there are forecasters.

In order to translate financial factors, such as we have been referring to, into a somewhat simpler form as a monthly business barometer, the following series were used by LeRoy Steele, under the direction of the writer, to make up a weighted composite index, beginning at 1881: an index of high-grade bond prices, an index of common-stock prices, an index of New York commercial-paper rates (inverted).   Each of these monthly series was expressed in terms of percentages of a long-term moving average serving as a trend.   The results were combined with appropriate weights that had the effect of increasing the amplitude of the bond-price index and reducing the amplitude of the other two series.[2] After combining the results the final composite was smoothed to remove virtually all the meaningless minor fluctuations.   After some further minor adjustments, the barometer assumed the form shown in Chart 72.   Since the barometer was prepared long after the period when this

---

[1] *Review of Economic Statistics*, Aug. 15, 1932, p. 143.

[2] A more complete explanation of the barometer will be found in Appendix 11. Mr. Steele's results were presented in an unpublished paper entitled "The Financial Market as a Business Barometer," March, 1940.

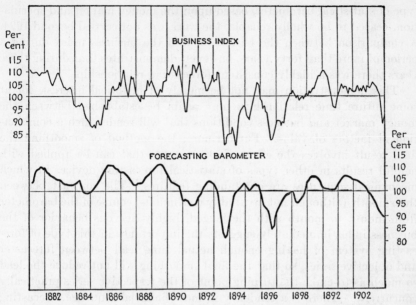

CHART 72a.—Composite barometer of business activity, 1881–1903. For description of data see Appendix 11, Sec. 1.

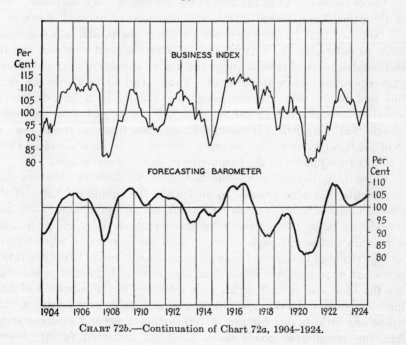

CHART 72b.—Continuation of Chart 72a, 1904–1924.

type of statistical barometer, based upon the money market and speculation, ceased to be wholly reliable, the work was not carried beyond 1924. A comparison between the barometer and the business index during a period of more than forty years, however, demonstrates that during these years there was a highly consistent forecasting relationship.

This demonstration may not be merely of historical interest, for at some future time relationships may again be established between the money market and business conditions that will render such a combination of factors of value. Furthermore, the method of smoothing the final result involves the effect of experiments that can be applied with helpful results in other types of statistical forecasting devices in which mechanical sequences are outstanding features. The contrast between the smooth (although not invariably continuous) course of the barometer from month to month with the jagged, highly nervous behavior of the business index immediately suggests the importance in this type of forecasting system of having enough actual time lead between forecaster and objective series, so that the final smoothing will not reduce the lead so much as to make the turning point of the respective series practically concurrent. There is a tendency in most financial sequence forecasting series to show a time lead well ahead of the business or trade index at the top of the cycle, while the lead at the bottom is much narrower. But on the other hand, except in major depressions of unusual duration, it will be noted that business declines are fairly sharp, and it is somewhat easier to determine the bottom limit of a pronounced recession and the likelihood of reversal than to judge the degree of vulnerability of business when operating above trend level. There tend to be numerous small dips and rallies that are confusing, particularly in a long-drawn-out period of exceptionally good business. It is in just such confusing periods that a statistical barometer based upon financial conditions can be of practical value to the manager who wishes to plan ahead and who is willing to supplement the barometer by other observations.

If we look beyond money-market data to discover other cyclical movements that tend usually to anticipate the significant turns of the general business index, we can find a number of useful series. We now have data relating to the value of new orders received by a large number of manufacturers. If such monthly data are seasonally adjusted and perhaps deflated to remove the price element, it is found that they reveal somewhat more sensitive action than the index of industrial production. But the time lead in such series with reference to the subgroup of non-durable-goods-production cycles is not consistent or very broad, so that orders are little better for use in forecasting a general business index than the nondurable goods index itself, as indicated further below. There is no series of new orders or, as far as the writer's experiments have extended, no combination of such data that will consistently lead the business index by a useful interval after smoothing to eliminate the erratic fluctuations. The time lead is usually limited to one or two months; after the necessary smoothing, this is eliminated, and the final result is of little more value than the business index itself. But a careful examination of a composite-orders index may furnish some help in appraising the general production position. This is particularly true if that index is observed in relation to other variables such as indexes of industrial inventories and shipments of goods. In a period of exceptional boom (or the feverish stimulus associated with war preparations), new orders received by manufacturers tend to describe much more acceleration than the slower moving processes of production. Contrarily, the relapse in such placing of orders may be so *emphatic* that it serves as a warning of impending reversal in production operations, at least for a limited time. But on the whole, as stated above, an index of orders or the cycle pattern of orders in a particular line of industry occasionally registers minor fluctuations and thus false moves that are confusing when the observer wishes to gauge the outlook for production operations or shipment more than a few months ahead.[1]

We saw in Chapter 19 (Charts 52 and 53) that the cyclical movements of the index of production of nondurable goods tended to be more sensitive than the index of durable-goods production. Although this has not been invariably true, it may be said that this relationship affords a helpful aid, or at least an auxiliary barometer, for anticipating the course of the general cycle. In this case again there are occasional periods in which the formation of a critical peak or a depression bottom may come almost simultaneously in forecast and general index. Some observers have employed the relationship between two aspects of production in terms of the ratio of one index to the other, that is, the ratio of a durable-goods-production index and a nondurable-goods production. Since this method of computation, however, places undue emphasis upon the consistent relationship in the long-term trends of the two such data, the emergence of a marked positive or negative spread between the series may be expected sooner or later to fail to appear at the right moment.[2]

Some statisticians have turned to the prices of commodities in their search for relationships having forecasting value. It has been found

[1] The National Industrial Conference Board and, more recently, the U.S. Department of Commerce have undertaken interesting and important work in preparing monthly measures of orders, inventories, and shipments in various lines of manufacturing, seasonally adjusted, extending back for several years. These may be found in the *Economic Record* of the Conference Board and in the *Survey of Current Business* of the U.S. Department of Commerce.

[2] Mordecai Ezekiel has used this device and has presented the results in various issues of *The Agricultural Situation*.

that the wholesale prices of some raw materials tend to be highly sensitive to the movements of the business cycle. This has been found true of hides and leather, cottonseed oil, zinc, steel scrap, and a number of other commodities, particularly those in which speculative activity is present. The attempt, however, to use "sensitive" prices, either individually or in a composite index, repeatedly develops difficulties because of erratic movements occasioned by particular market situations. There is also considerable uncertainty in estimating the long-term trend from which to derive percentage deviations. If such commodity data are used in the form of link relatives, or similar measures of relative momentum (*cf.* Chart 51), it will be found from time to time that the resulting index will develop misleading movements, although emphatic changes in direction are usually significant and useful. The use of sensitive commodity prices in terms of rate of change has been found by the writer of greater value in anticipating the turns in the general commodity-price index than those of the industrial production cycle. The price of cotton textiles shown in Chart 51 may be found of some practical use for this particular purpose.

Various observers have found import-trade statistics of interest in forecasting the general cycle direction. The imports of such commodities as wool, rubber, tin, and, indeed, the total value of raw-material imports do have some tendency to anticipate the corresponding cyclical movements of business activity. Here again we find, however, a limiting factor that impairs the value of the result in the lack of consistency and frequent influence of disturbing external or political elements. The import trade of the United States is dominated by a very few basic commodities, and unusual conditions in one or two of these markets may vitiate the entire result if the observer relies too much upon this method.[1]

The search for a satisfactory statistical forecasting index or series therefore narrows down to relatively few possibilities. Since it was found that money rates, interest rates, high-grade bond yields or prices, and even stock prices now have had less consistent value than in earlier years in forecasting the industrial cycle, it occurred to the writer that it might still be possible to employ a financial series that combined in its movement the most valuable elements of all the foregoing series. It was found that this could be accomplished reasonably well by an index of speculative industrial bond prices, first available in 1924. Speculative bonds have many of the characteristics of common stocks, being highly

---

[1] The reader is referred to an interesting summary of the statistical results of comparing cycle movements of a considerable number of economic series with the general business-cycle pattern, some of the observations being extended over long periods of time, in W. C. Mitchell and A. F. Burns, Statistical Indicators of Cyclical Revival, *National Bureau of Economic Research Bulletin* 69, May 28, 1938.

sensitive to changes in corporate earnings; they are also promptly influenced by money-market conditions and interest rates, certainly to a larger extent than stock prices. It was found that when business conditions steadily deteriorated after 1929, the behavior of bonds of this type gave an extremely consistent interpretation of the deepening of the depression without the false moves shown by interest rates. At the same time the series was found to be very sensitive to the major turning point in 1929, and in foreshadowing the depression there was a well-spaced time lead, usually characteristic of the bond-market action at such periods of reversal in the past. It was, therefore, decided to employ the index of sensitive industrial bond prices, adjusted for trend, with further adjustments described in Appendix 11. This was used to continue the original Steele barometer from 1924 to 1934.

With the radical changes beginning to occur in political action since the middle 1930's and the direct impact upon business of variations in Government spending, the importance of the money market is likely to be still further impaired from a forecasting standpoint. Interest rates in the future will be subject to more deliberate control and may reflect less and less accurately, through the various related financial variables, impending changes in the direction of industrial cycles. Furthermore, the amount of public contributions to general purchasing power through work-creating projects, direct relief, and subsidy will very probably have an increasing tendency to amplify, and possibly even dominate, the ebb and flow of aggregate monetary circulation and capital investment; hence the variability of total industrial output. Fortunately, data in monthly form have recently been prepared (although not for general release) measuring the *net* contributions to national income or spending power by the Federal Government after allowance for absorption of private funds through taxation. With suitable adjustments, these data were averaged with adjusted monthly data of residential building contracts, which, as seen in Chart 54, have had definite forecasting value, and this combination carries forward the barometer from January, 1934, to date. There is a sufficient time lead when these are combined into a single index to permit fairly powerful smoothing, so that the turning points are likely to assume definite significance even though some very slight fluctuation remains as a problem for future experiment and revision. The results are shown in Chart 73. Naturally, no barometer of this nature can be rigorously and indefinitely confined to a given set of components. It can be regarded as reliable and useful as a guide to business policy to the extent that the nature of the factors used is continually reappraised and logically tested to determine whether they truly represent cyclical factors capable of impinging later upon business operations.

It will be noticed that there is an auxiliary indicator in the lower section of Chart 73, which calls for further explanation. Within the band extending across the chart is drawn the index of urban mortgage solvency, on a very reduced scale, after the minor fluctuations have been smoothed out. This serves as an indicator of the probable intensity and duration of an impending cyclical change. The value of such a measure of the underlying financial position in the building field is familiar to the reader, and its use to assist in distinguishing relatively minor, short

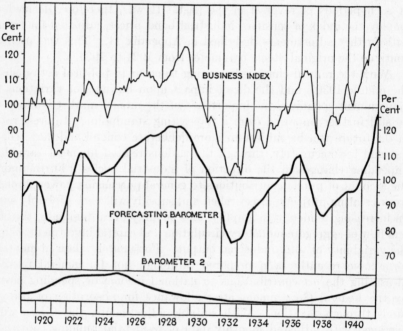

CHART 73.—Forecasting barometers of business activity, 1919–1941. For description of data see Appendix 11, Sec. 2.

oscillations in the business cycle from the more severe and prolonged readjustments appears to be logical as well as verified by historical evidence. In using this auxiliary indicator, the observor will expect to find in the future that so long as the mortgage-solvency indicator is rising, any interruption of business prosperity will be relatively brief, as, for example, the recession of 1921. When this indicator is steadily declining there is an ominous warning, to be closely observed by the alert business executive or investor, that the coming reversal of the business cycle will be relatively severe and long-extended, since there will not be the broadly sustaining influence always contributed by a rising phase of the building (and especially the residential building) cycle. Even granting that such cyclical waves in the future may be less pronounced, or even less regular in their periodic timing, than in the past, the existence of a tendency for gradual ebb and flow in the capital flowing into construction will have a powerful influence on industrial activity. If governmental activity in the planning of basic developments in the social-utility field continues, a barometer of this general type should form one of the indispensable guides to the timing of any projects developed out of that survey program.

Still another type of measurement may be employed as a forecasting device, perhaps as a check upon the others, since it is not always highly sensitive or turning from one phase to the other with a significant time lead ahead of the business index. We have referred to the use of statistics relating to industrial new orders, inventories, and shipments. These may be put in a form having some value. We may, for example, smooth out month-to-month *ratios* of sales to inventories. This can be done for a number of individual branches of industry, such as textiles, paper products, chemicals, steel, electrical machinery, etc., by the use of U.S. Department of Commerce data. The ratios of sales to inventory (both expressed in dollar values) represent essentially the relation between a concurrent series and a lagging series. Inventories pile up as orders decline and shipments reach their maximum level. The ratio of sales to inventories thus develops a more sensitive series, in the cyclical sense, than the use of the sales alone. If the ratio is smoothed, there still remains some degree of time lead at the significant turns of the cycle, if one may judge from the results of a decade or so during which data of this type can be checked.[1] Even though meticulously adjusted ratios from data of this type are not used, it is well for the business forecaster to have a picture of the current changes in orders, shipments, and inventory as they stand in relation to the index of business itself. It is particularly valuable if data of this type may be obtained for the industry in which a particular firm is represented and for such industries as general analysis indicates are in peculiarly strategic positions with respect to the cycle of production as a whole.

The attempt to test a given position of the business cycle to discern the most probable direction of movement over the next year or so is never adequate without a systematic survey of the leading industries, one by one.[2] Industry analysis is a relatively new, but important, field

[1] Measurements of this type have also been developed by the consulting firm of Bernstein-Macaulay, Inc., New York City.

[2] This is facilitated by the availability of production, employment, payroll, price, and other pertinent data for a considerable number of industry groups. For summary forecasts of commodity prices relating to various branches of agriculture the monthly bulletins of the U.S. Department of Agriculture, *Demand and Price Situation*, are of special value.

of study, involving familiarity with the structure, the geographic aspects, and the political environment of each industrial field, as well as its dynamic pattern in terms of production, prices, labor costs, etc. Such study must be reasonably continuous and be carried on with close observation of all pertinent statistical measurements. Naturally, among the various industries, those are of special significance in forecasting work which reveal new developments in product, major changes in location, the effect of changing political controls or taxation. During a period of war, such analysis, with special attention to governmental policy and the course of prices, taxes, and technological change, affords probably the only means of developing useful indications to guide the operations of a business firm or investment decisions. In peacetime it is possible to develop from continuous statistical records of the performance of individual industries a number of tentative projections into the near future, which can be combined with suitable weights into a composite projection as a forecasting barometer. Much the same use can be made of estimated projections of individual commodity prices, which can be combined to approximate a general-commodity-index forecast with weights proportional to those used by the U.S. Bureau of Labor Statistics in its general wholesale-price index. These procedures are laborious but in skilled hands can be made valuable business tools.

Attention must always, of course, be given to probable or imminent changes in governmental policy, since they are likely to affect industries, prices, financial factors, public regulation, and the undulating flow of national income that determines the rise and fall in sales of the great majority of business firms. In keeping closely in touch with developments in Washington, there are several specialized service letters available. There are numerous publications and bulletins of governmental bureaus containing information bearing on public policy, as well as providing valuable statistical data. The *Survey of Current Business*, *The Federal Reserve Bulletin*, and *Domestic Commerce* are examples. The Whaley-Eaton and International Statistical Bureau *Foreign Letters* are of value for their analysis of international developments and prospects.

PRACTICAL APPLICATION OF FORECASTING

Since there are various ways of anticipating the approximate direction of the general cyclical movement, it follows that these methods can be applied to the sales of an individual concern to forecast ahead from six months to a year. This will be possible for all lines of business that have a broad market, subject to the full effect of the national business cycle as it reveals itself in income, demand, and sales. Although this is true of the majority of industries and commercial lines, there are many cases in which we find the time pattern of sales, production, and employment quite different from the general pattern. This can be easily detected without elaborate statistical treatment of the data. It may be due to the vagaries of style and fashion, to the unusual influence of erratic weather conditions, to the effect of price variables having exceptional effect upon values and even the volume of output from time to time. There may be irregularities due to foreign conditions or political policies. The cases of new industries, or new firms in an old industry, are also likely to present difficulties as the data are inadequate and the performance of a particular firm may be dominated by rapid initial growth to such a degree that the purely cyclical element is not capable of being separated out. But as development proceeds, a time comes when the exceptionally fast expansion begins to slacken, and it is at that point that close attention must be given to the problem of gearing the activity into reasonable relationship to the general economic trend and to avoid being caught by the difficult competitive problems that accumulate as an industry approaches the maturity stage.

Incidentally, the keen observer of industrial conditions, with an eye to the future, must not fail to observe the evidence of approaching maturity in important newly developed lines of enterprise. The retarding of growth may have serious repercussions upon business as a whole, as was clearly illustrated in the late 1920's, when the coming of age of the vast automotive industry, selling more and more for replacement, less and less to new buyers, held forth vitally significant indications of a more severe readjustment than usual when the cycle finally did enter its declining phase. By that time enough statistical data were available to have given a fairly clear idea of the cyclical as well as the trend elements in the various segments of the automotive field and their relation to the general pattern, which, as we have seen, was considerably affected by that group.

To apply the general cyclical forecasts to the records and policies of a particular firm, we must first establish from as long a record as possible how its performance "ties in" with the general index. Since the long-term trend gradient for a single enterprise will usually differ from the approximately 3.5 per cent per annum growth in general industry and trade, in terms of volume, there are advantages in making comparison, if possible, between the physical volume of sales or product of the firm and the general index, with the trend eliminated in each series. This is not essential for preliminary work, but for close examination of monthly or quarterly results, especially the timing of significant turning points, the use of the deviations from trend is very helpful. This also brings out clearly the extent to which cyclical swings in the individual business tend to be more or less pronounced than in the general index.

If monthly or quarterly data are available it is, of course, necessary to eliminate purely seasonal movements, since these would have been eliminated from any general index of business and we seek to bring out the *cyclical* patterns as distinct from all other fluctuations or changes. If the available data happen to be *values* of sales, orders, billings, or production, either these may be deflated by a suitable composite index of prices (occasionally a single significant price is sufficient) or the dollar values may be adjusted for comparison with either the volume index of general business or a general index in terms of adjusted figures of national income, total check payments, or other similar data. Unless the price elements in the firm's transactions are very pronounced or erractic, the comparison of adjusted monthly values with the general (volume) index will usually afford quite significant results for practical purposes. It may, however, prove to be somewhat more difficult to estimate the underlying growth trend in the case of values than in the case of physical units. In some cases the most useful and reliable results can be obtained by constructing a composite index of the physical volume of sales or production for the particular business unit, using the same basic procedure as is used in the Federal Reserve indexes of that type. It is, of course, desirable in any case to use several sets of company records, if they are available, in order to test the patterns and timing relationships of orders, sales, output, and employment. The latter, as shown in Chapter 21, can be further explored by analyzing the various turnover rates. In addition to this a complete systematic and *continuing* effort to measure and forecast the dynamic elements in a business must include prices and wage rates in their relation to whatever general movements and trends in these aspects may be most logical and pertinent.

Forecasts of the direction of general business, in terms of any of the measures of it, can be applied, first, to the *cyclical* pattern of sales, etc., of the individual firm. In order to translate the estimate in that form into actual units or values, the cycle estimate deviations are multiplied by the estimates of trend, as tentatively projected a year or so ahead, and, if desired, the seasonal fluctuation factor (usually fairly regular) can be reapplied to provide the final estimates in monthly or quarterly units.

In developing future estimates for a particular establishment, the problem of underlying trend is always present. For sales and production forecasts of limited range, let us say a year ahead, the trends can be projected with fair assurance, but there remains the question of their *current* accuracy. As was pointed out in Chapter 3, the current position and direction of the long-term growth trend are always a tentative estimate; if this is projected a short distance it merely represents the extension *of an estimate*. The practical statistician should endeavor always to distinguish between *secular* growth trend and the intermediate drift. The latter, as we have seen with respect to the general production and trade index, will usually be somewhat flexible and undulating, although within five- or ten-year periods not widely variant from a straight line. It is the intermediate trend that balances the give and take of cyclical oscillation that it is important to estimate as closely as possible in practical forecasting work. Its current position can often be judged by careful graphic inspection, if we observe the tendency to equalize approximately the plus and minus deviations. More rigidly determined mathematical functions may be used to carry forward a long secular gradient if the business in question has had an extended life and good records of its performance are available.

In planning capital structures or other expansion of facilities looking toward the distant future, attention must be given to the most probable slope and position of both intermediate and secular trends, as they may develop in the national economy as a whole and in the area within which a business derives its major income. To adapt these more general trend patterns to the future course of the individual firm and its plant and equipment needs, attention must be given to the following points: (1) Where does the industry itself appear to stand in its development and what evidence of retardation of growth is apparent? (2) Has the trend of expansion of the particular unit in the past been in fairly close alignment with that of the industry? (3) Are there in this business elements of product diversification, of innovation along new lines, such as would modify the expectation that its future long-term course might deviate considerably from the course of any particular industrial segment? (4) Is every precaution being taken to avoid confusing purely *cyclical* performance of the firm during the recent past with the underlying *trend*, so that an excessive future growth rate is not made the basis for over-borrowing or overinvestment? (5) Is there statistical evidence of enough future expansion to warrant immediate action in undertaking necessary financing or construction operations before competitors get the jump?

It is clear that statistical research along the lines discussed in this chapter is one of the essential specialized functions in business management. In an organization of any size successful management must increasingly rely upon two sets of quantitative measurement and analysis —those provided by accounting and by dynamic statistics. Said Leonard P. Ayres:

The job of the business statistician is to look into the future. He is employed to furnish those in positions of top control in his firm with a fact-basis for their thinking and acting. If he can do this successfully he becomes one of the most valuable men in the organization. His is a difficult and an exacting job, for it involves a most unusual combination of theoretical knowledge with the ability to transform his theory into recommendations for practical action.

The university economist and the governmental statistician are seldom called upon to submit their conclusions to the immediate and drastic test of application. The successful business man is usually innocent of any thorough understanding of the economic laws affecting his operations, or of the statistical technique by which the lessons of previous transactions may be interpreted.   It is the business statistician who is called upon to bridge the gap between knowing and doing. . . .

The work of the business statistician in the industrial establishment is closely related to the three great divisions of the firm's own activities.   The first of these relates to the purchase of raw materials, the second to production, and the third to the sale of the output.   In each case the task of business research is to study the figures of the past and the present, and from them to draw just inferences as to the probable future.   The terms in which this work is done are those of time and money.   The importance of business research depends on the degree to which it can increase money returns. . . .

. . . the activities of the business statistician call for thorough training, a wide range of knowledge, and a considerable amount of resourceful ingenuity, combined with an unfailing ability to turn out results of practical usefulness.   They are not merely economics, although a good grasp of economics is involved.   They are not entirely statistics, although they require a high grade of statistical ability. They are not exclusively research, although they include real research of an exceptionally applied sort.

More and more work of this sort is going to be done.   The need for it is almost without limit.   The materials and methods for carrying it forward are at hand in a profusion entirely beyond anything that existed or could be foreseen even five years ago.   Persons with the requisite training and ability to carry it forward are beginning to appear.   Probably it constitutes a new profession, included within statistics, but sufficiently specialized to demand individual recognition. . . .

Two conditions are necessary if the work of the business statistician is to be carried forward on productive scientific lines.   The first is that his office shall be one of interpretation and presentation, rather than one charged with the duty of compiling primary records.   His job is to sort out the essential facts from the great mass of merely incidental ones, and to interpret their significance.   He must have time to study, combine, and compare his figures, and to point out their meaning.   If he is mostly concerned in tabulating, or in supervising a force of clerks that are doing it, he will not have much time or opportunity for his real job.

The second requisite condition is that he shall personally present his results to those who must base actions and policies upon them, and he must participate in the discussions concerning them.   By no other method can the value of his work be fully utilized, and there is no other process that is equally effective in improving its quality. . . .

It may fairly be asked of the statistician that if he aspires to such a position in business as the truly competent man should be able to secure, he give evidence of his capacity through technical preparation, and by contributing to the published literature of his profession articles on statistics and business research that can successfully bear the critical scrutiny of his professional co-workers. In proportion as business firms demand such standards and reward them, and statisticians equip themselves to meet them, business research will move forward to its rightful place among the professions. That place will be a high one.[1]

[1] L. P. Ayres, The Nature and Status of Business Research, *Journal American Satistical Association*, March, 1922, pp. 33*ff.*

CHAPTER 23

DYNAMIC BUSINESS POLICY

We have still to consider the ways in which forecasts of the course of general business may be applied to the operations of a particular establishment. Suppose that we have statistical and economic reasons to expect at a given time that the business conditions, national income, and demand generally are likely to improve following a recession. Let us further assume that this improvement can be confidently translated into a more or less proportionate degree of expansion in sales value or volume. Possibly this can be further translated into advance estimates for various groups of products. What are the practical implications of such an observation? Can management do anything about it? Should anything be done about it? If those in charge do nothing, what will happen? Should speculative commitments be attempted, such as buying raw materials or merchandise far ahead or taking options on equipment, plant, or other property? What should be the employment and personnel policy at such time?

The extent to which these and other questions can be answered depends in large measure upon the degree to which there has been a *continuing awareness* of cyclical change as it affects the organization and the extent to which policy aims to precede contingencies or merely follow them. Executives who find themselves in what appears to be the trough of a depression, after having made no *previous* preparations with respect to reserves and cash, intelligent inventory procedure and personnel matters, are obviously in a different position with respect to *future* policies than those who exercised some forethought while times were better. Let us assume in what follows that it is the latter type of management that is under consideration.

Since a business enterprise of any size is an organic entity, an upward revision in the estimate of sales for a period of six months to a year ahead may involve many adjustments. These may involve changes in purchasing policy, the employment of workers, problems of equipment, repairs, and renovation, and a host of altered relationships among the functions and departments, which must be maintained in efficient coordination. This is perhaps the fundamental idea in every kind of planning and budgeting; it applies to keeping expenses within income, obtaining resources to meet expenditures, and holding operations in balance so that over-all control is steadily maintained. The essential differentiation between budgeting, in the strictly accounting sense, and applied forecasting, in the managerial sense, is that in the latter we are projecting all our operations well ahead of the present moment and seeking to arrive at estimates of results in terms of physical units of output, number and distribution of personnel, and amount of inventory, as well as financial position. We expect that operations will be kept sufficiently in balance as between departments to exclude the possibility of deficiencies here, excesses there, and anomalies everywhere. As compared with budgeting in the governmental sense, dynamic business budgets tend primarily to stress the wise utilization of expected income rather than to provide income to meet assumed expenditures or known future appropriations. But, as we shall see, there often arises in business planning the problem of obtaining additional capital apart from what may become available through sales, and all such calculations turn upon the extent to which estimated revenues resulting from expanded capital facilities are likely to meet all financial obligations and otherwise justify the capital outlay.

Let us first consider some aspects of business planning with respect to cyclical changes, which do not necessarily raise questions of long-term capital revision. In order to bring into convenient focus the essential factors that must be considered from a policy standpoint, and in the light of sales and related estimates, we may list the following phases:

1. Anticipated demand for principal products or groups of products (or services)
   a. In terms of volume
   b. In terms of value
   c. Expectations as to prices or rates
2. Operating levels to meet expected demand conditions
   a. Available plant and equipment capacity; analysis by divisions or departments; storage capacity
   b. Available personnel, analyzed according to functions and departments and possibly regionally
   c. Inventories of materials, merchandise
   d. Availability of fuel, power, and incidental purchased service
3. Estimated revenue on the basis of existing capacity, but allowing for probable increase in demand
   a. Before provision for internal policy
   b. After allowance for probable effect of internal policy
4. Estimates of material or merchandise costs to meet demand conditions
   a. Unit costs (major groups)
   b. Totals
5. Estimate of wage adjustments and total payroll requirements by departments
6. Miscellaneous operating costs and gross profit
7. Indirect operating expenses
8. Nonoperating revenue, if any
9. Overhead cost and taxes
10. Total income, total cost, and net profit

11. Estmate of balance-sheet position at end of budget period, under varying assumptions as to dividend disbursements and reserves
12. Working capital and cash position

These various headings may be imagined spread (horizontally) across a work sheet of liberal proportions to permit an over-all view of all the aspects of the business for which specific estimates are to be made in accordance with both *external* factors and *internal* policy directed toward dealing with those factors. Upon the work sheet we can next classify (vertically) the distinct elements that are likely to influence the preliminary, intermediate, and final estimates that are desired. The following are the principal items:

1. External factors
    a. External economic conditions (originating outside the particular organization or industry)
    b. Conditions primarily affecting the industry group
    c. Political factors, insofar as they can be reasonably anticipated for the budget period
    d. Regional economic or political factors that may impinge upon the activities of the concern and the market for its product or service
2. Internal changes
    a. Passive, that is, translating the effect of external estimates upon internal results without allowance for policies
    b. Active, that is, allowing for probable compensatory effect of internal policy changes to compensate indicated cyclical effects on the business
3. Estimates, combining all anticipated changes, external and internal
4. Policy decisions as to plant expansion during or following the budget period
5. Adjustment of balance-sheet estimates to provide for capital plans and possible revision of dividend disbursements

Within each of these headings further details may be added to assure that no contingencies, or changes in policy to meet them, are overlooked. It is difficult to bring these details into this general discussion, for they will differ among the various lines of business. What has been outlined aims to suggest the advantage of a *systematic procedure* in clearly defining the fundamental elements and distinguishing between the *aspects of operation* and *types of factors* likely to affect *each one* of the operating and policy items. This breakdown does not necessarily narrow the work merely to preparation of a financial budget; it provides an over-all view of the organization as an organic whole, adapting itself to external probabilities and at the same time preserving internal structural balance and the maximum degree of solvency. A continuing analysis, carrying through the dynamic factors into each nook and cranny of an organization, is certain to reveal weak spots, waste, bottleneck situations, and the need for better control here and there. Business annals are accumulating remarkable records of actual results of such work in achieving greater economy and efficiency, frequently to a degree that pays several times over the cost of the effort of forecasting and budget analysis. Cases are on record pointing to the advantages of foresight and advance planning keyed in with statistical forecasts of business conditions in compensating increased labor costs at the same time improving the competitive position of the establishment.

FORECASTING APPLIED TO SALES POLICIES

Having now in mind the main divisions of our subject, we may comment briefly upon typical matters of executive policy considered in the light of the (passive) forecast position, as we originally stated. Let us consider first the matter of the demand and the sales estimate. We have provided for segregation of the external factors into several distinct categories in building up future estimate of sales. At this point it is important to stress that the sales estimate for a concern that is operating over an extended territory or on a national scale should be developed from two sets of observations, one having to do with the general direction of the business and another independent approach building up estimates from each sales division or other locality, depending upon the manner in which the sales are handled. In this fashion more allowance can be given to shifting tendencies and regional divergence from the general pattern. Special adjustments, for example, may be made for unusual prospective conditions in a region influenced by agricultural buying power. New construction activities or shifts of population can be given their proper emphasis as they bear upon the sale of the products of this particular firm, and these may have significance for the trend as well as the cyclical forecasts.

It is rarely desirable to base individual territory estimates or quotas as objectives for sales managers merely upon the general forecast *broken down* or porportioned for total estimates. A judicious combination of the over-all estimate broken down and estimates *built up* from separate regional analyses is desirable. The over-all sales budget may also in certain cases be built up from different types of products in the event that a concern is engaged in the sale of various products rather than concentrating upon a very few. In this analysis, the effort would be made to draw reasonable expectations for the future period for each one of the most important commodities and for a group or groups of the less important, with proper allowance for the diverse ways in which these various items tend to correlate with the movements of general production and their probable responses to special regional, political, sociological, or other influences.

What are some typical problems of executive policy with regard to sales? Naturally, we cannot discuss sales policy and its budget aspects as they might apply to many distinct types of enterprise. Only the outstandingly important phases will be considered, and the only distinction that we shall make will be between industrial and mercantile concerns and between durable capital goods and nondurable consumer goods. We shall discuss procedure on the assumption of peacetime rather than abnormal wartime conditions.[1]

Let us first consider the case of a sales budget prepared during the closing stage of a period of marked business prosperity, with the future estimates indicating the early stage of a general reversal toward depression and reduced buying power. Our sales forecast, extended as far ahead as a year and broken into quarterly or monthly estimates, will be studied in terms of volume, price, and money values, the latter analysis starting with the gross operating revenue. The extent to which management can hope to avoid the full impact of contraction of buying by internal policies for accelerated sales stimulus and promotion will largely depend upon the extent to which the products are destined for individual consumers or for the capital-goods market. Demand in the durable capital-goods field tends to be more or less dependent upon conditions in the financial markets and upon construction plans prepared a considerable time previously. The latter can be made available through specialized service sources. If curtailment is already under way in new orders for producer goods and structural equipment, there is unlikely to be any advantage in the attempt to stimulate such activity through advertising or other devices calculated to develop customer interest. The soundest long-term policy in such fields of business is to avoid excessive strain upon productive facilities as the prosperity period extends to what appears to be an unsound level and then to endeavor to arrange delivery dates as far ahead as possible. In highly competitive lines, this, of course, involves some difficulty, but too little attention has been given by executives to the advantage of inducing buyers of capital products to refrain from exerting pressure for unreasonably quick delivery in boom times, even to the extent of paying premiums for immediate shipment.

[1] The complex problems of adapting business policy to a war regimen cannot be readily codified, for each war situation has its peculiar aspects and emergencies. Modern war being so largely a matter of mechanized equipment, the most pertinent broad generalizations that can be made as to business policy under war conditions are (1) that conversion in whole or in part to war products should be promptly undertaken by every industrial concern, with statistical research effort mobilized toward assisting the military branches of the Government in developing statistical controls as to materials, transport routes, and personnel needs; (2) that normal competitive strategy be laid aside to permit coordinated industry-wide effort and speed in output; and (3) that as conditions permit, plans be prepared for conversion of operations to a normal basis after the emergency period in as orderly and financially sound a manner as possible.

This fever stage of the business cycle (if it has come about despite the control forces that someday will prove effective in the direction of more stability) is one in which the durable-goods industries should make every possible effort to begin a "stretching-out" process so that the inevitable recession in volume of activity may be met by a gradual rather than a sudden curtailment of operations. In such basic industries a gratifying expansion of orders may be obtained in a few boom years without much selling effort on the part of the manufacturers or mining companies, but there is still a considerable amount of promotional work done at a time when it not only does little to produce revenue but tends to overstimulate buyers. They need restraint rather than encouragement in the interest of maintaining the general situation sufficiently stable to keep solvent their own new structural investment.

There tends to be a curious follow-the-leader tendency in placing orders for plant and equipment items. Producers of capital equipment of various kinds could accomplish a great deal toward eliminating some of the excessive booms and troughs in their sales if they would undertake the responsibility of counseling and cautioning their customers, *in the light of specific statistical forecasts of the business cycle and the major construction cycle*, when they see the probability of their customers being misled by promotional enthusiasm to undertake expansion at an unfavorable moment. This is particularly true of those lines of business whose products are essentially made to order and cannot readily be turned out far in advance for the stock bins. These are the highly sensitive and volatile industries that do little to stay the winds of boom and depression, but they can at least do *something* toward moderating excessive momentum of demand in order that the business on the books can be made to fill in some of the gapping void that has usually marked the reaction from overbuilding. In some cases it is practicable and advantageous in the boom period and prior to an indicated recession to plan the development of new products or new types of products suitable for introduction, not at once, but at some time during the forthcoming period of temporarily reduced buying power and readjustment. Concerning this more will be said later in the discussion of production policy.

In the durable and capital-goods industries there is very little to be gained from price slashing with the hope of stimulating or reversing a probable shrinking tendency in demand. This problem has complex aspects, some of which will be further discussed in the next chapter. The machinery for leveling out, or at least moderating, the range of variability in the flow of general income can be controlled to a limited degree only by business management. The problem demands the exercise of such financial controls and wage-income compensating plans as only Government can effectively coordinate and administer. It is the function of the first-class business manager to do all in his power to reduce unnecessary speed, to avoid entering the doldrums of idleness, and to see that his own ship is kept safely afloat during a storm.   If this requires curtailment of his production, such a course must be followed, although, as previously stated, something can be done to avoid abrupt or complete stoppage and ruthless dismissal of workers.   In many cases alternatives present themselves whereby total production in the plant can be maintained through the exercise of foresight plus ingenuity, despite unfavorable general conditions.

The practical use of sound forecasting rests upon willingness to combat external forces with skill and diversified strategy rather than merely to take them lying down.   Industrial management must avoid the needless demoralization of its market that might result from reckless slashing of prices at the same time that production itself is being curtailed.   But it is most important to add that when the barometers point to a storm ahead, the price structure of an industry or a firm calls for closer scrutiny, lest conditions presently reveal that prices *have been out of line* with the broad general drift or with the actual trend of revenue or of income of those who mainly utilize the products, structures, or equipment.   These discrepancies in industrial-goods prices are not always recognized in good business years, and frequently it is not until conditions have greatly deteriorated that the managements of mills and factories begin to recognize that although it is advantageous to maintain fairly stable prices, they have not been *gradually* adjusted in accord with the actual general drift of values or with the price behavior of special groups of products or services that logically are closely related.   Thus the door is likely to be suddenly opened, with dislocating results, to intense competition from alternative materials and designs.   Periods of depression always challenge the ingenuity of inventors; these are times when old-established products made in old-established ways and sold at old-established prices suffer their worst blows.   Prices of raw materials, for example, may be already undergoing revision through the pressure of new sources of supply or new methods of production that no longer justify old quotations.   While business generally remains active, this may not be obvious except to the alert and well advised.   Sooner or later it will be necessary to revise the pricing of manufactures utilizing such materials.   If, in accordance with sound policy, these changes have been accomplished gradually, it is not necessary to accentuate recession by drastic price adjustments when all markets are becoming thin and vulnerable and the revisions tend to spread in all directions.   Drastic price cutting is, therefore, a policy adapted to the kind of business policy that fails to practice sound foresight.

It is desirable for the research staff to maintain charts of pertinent price movements and of the *ratio* of the specific prices of a given industry or firm (after all necessary allowances) to (1) general commodity prices, (2) the general price level, (3) cost of living, (4) special groups of prices such as those received by farmers, the prices of durable goods, nondurable goods, and manufactured goods, and various raw materials. In endeavoring to anticipate changes in these various prices or groups of prices, as they may be important to an individual enterprise, it is desirable to have statistical information upon stocks, production, export and import data, and, in the case of products having an agricultural bearing, information as to acreage, plantings, carry-overs, etc., in the principal producing areas. The relative position of prices should be especially observed *before* drastic and abrupt modification is forced by the sheer weight of depression upon an organization. Costs may have to be tailored to fit prices if they are far out of line with the general trend of things. On the other hand, mere quixotic and random slashing of prices to lure buyers is no sound solution for the business-cycle problem.

FORECASTING APPLIED TO ADVERTISING POLICIES

If our company is engaged in the manufacture of commodities destined for individual consumers, the problems of advertising policy and the granting of consumer credit become important. There has been considerable discussion as to whether it is advantageous in such lines to base advertising appropriations upon the course of sales, thus making appropriations a function of the business cycle, or whether to regard advertising to some degree as a *compensating* device. The exceedingly close correlation between the index of general business conditions and the cyclical patterns of advertising expenditures, so far as these are available, proves that businessmen rather generally permit their advertising to rise and fall *with* the business cycle, rather than utilizing it deliberately and strategically as a corrective device. This may have resulted from the slow acceptance by executives of statistical methods capable of showing how much of the additional business obtained during a prosperity period can actually be fairly attributed to sales promotion as distinct merely from greater ability and willingness of consumers to make purchases! Even in the types of business that we are now considering, in which appeals to the consumer through dealers or through advertising of the manufacturers are of importance, the question may be asked whether managers have not exaggerated the value of their own selling appeals during periods of cyclical expansion.

This entire subject needs much more study, and analysis may lead to considerable alteration in practice. We must follow out the general fundamental principle that business should not encourage excessive momentum in any direction when it is evident that the general cycle has reached dangerously high ground.   Naturally, we must not overlook competition and the many pressures brought upon every management to keep step with the field and not lose customers by leaning over backward to heed a purely logical challenge to conservatism.   To the extent that any segment of trade or industry is dominated by shortsighted and wolfish competition we can expect no restraint anywhere.   Everyone will try to get all there is to be had while the getting is good.   But to the extent that business is run on something like scientific lines, in the interest of promoting sanity and stability *for its own good*, it is appropriate to consider whether sales-promotion effort and outlay should not be varied *inversely*, or nearly so, to the business-cycle tendency.   When general buying power begins to fade, following an unusual rise, the time has already passed when advertising addressed to consumers will do much good other than as a good-will or institutional reminder.   It serves to drag in customers who will not buy much or often because they are the *marginal fragment* of potential demand.   Why should it be necessary to force in this deceptive business at a cost far in excess of what it is usually worth?   And along this line, why should it be necessary to browbeat dealers, overencourage salesmen, or permit sales managers to run wild in goading their staffs to superhuman efforts when some part of this activity and enthusiasm should be released at another and more strategic phase of the cycle?   That stage would be somewhat later on, when the statistical evidence points toward the bottom of the recession being formed and recovery of more or less substantial degree may already be in prospect.   Of course, strategic timing of policy depends on *measurement*.   The tendency merely to do what everyone is doing implies the absence of facilities to get the facts or a trustful indulgence in ignorance.

The matter of credit terms to customers also calls for careful consideration in the light of the various phases of the cycle.   On this subject there has been encouraging evidence that businessmen are becoming more willing to coordinate their efforts to the end of being cautious in extension of credit when there are signs of excessive business momentum. The extension of credit to customers may be beyond the range of a manufacturer's control, but some manufacturing enterprises are in a position to control credit or have affiliations with organizations extending credit to consumers.   Even when this is not the case, however, the larger manufacturer may have it within his power to urge upon his dealers or retail distributors the need for some restriction of credit terms or possibly, also, increase in interest rates when it becomes important to refrain from overstimulating purchases by families whose incomes during a business recession will not suffice to repay borrowings on schedule and who thus will leave behind them additions to physical inventory that must be sold before production can be revived. It is desirable in such a period to scrutinize not merely the current condition of business and what it may portend but the manner in which various major industries are likely to respond to an indicated change in the direction of general industrial activity, exposing many wage earners to unemployment. The Federal Reserve System has undertaken on its part to revise installment credit terms generally in the light of conditions, but not yet with the precision of timing that is desirable.

FORECASTING APPLIED TO INVENTORY AND PRICE POLICIES

What has been said above relates in a general way to several groups of industries. When we come to merchandising organizations, we can emphasize even more strongly such policies as relate to offset variation in advertising and conservative administration of the terms of consumer credit. The merchant, however, has further problems to consider. Like the farmer, in some degree, a merchant expects to move his inventory to make room for new supplies. He cannot close down and leave goods on his shelf when buyers are few. His fate as a businessman rests very largely on his skill in handling and pricing inventory. His business turns upon his inventory. This suggests that during the upswing of the cycle, caution is necessary in avoiding excessive inventory and in curtailing the temptation to purchase *too far ahead*. Prices are usually thought of in terms of "markup," usually expressed as the percentage of profit expected on the sale value. The merchandising concern that refrains from buying long ahead or, rather, that refrains from adding to the "basic" inventory excessive additions for uncertain future sale, will be able to adjust the markups to the average replacement value of the merchandise.

Although prices do not always rise substantially during a period of general expansion, there are occasional cases in which commodity prices are the prominent or even the leading factors. At such times it is particularly important for a merchant to avoid being caught near the crisis period, just before prosperity weakens and prices begin to decline, with large amounts of merchandise on his shelves which cannot quickly be disposed of and in which markups were set too high. Since the goods *must* be moved, once they are bought, the sound policy at such a time is to make price concession *promptly*, even though not necessarily drastically. By having a sound forecast of business and supplementary estimates of the drift of basic prices, an alert house can begin a policy of price readjustment *before* conditions actually deteriorate. Thus markups can be pared into line with the indicated trend of prices rather than pyramided on the deceptive crest of the wave. The volume of merchandise may thus be moved along a little faster, avoiding unnecessary holding costs and, in particular, sudden and drastic markdowns later. Revision in markup under such conditions should be more substantial in the case of style goods than in the case of staples. But careful buying during the preceding prosperity period will obviate most of this problem of excess stocks.

In general, price policy will depend upon the skill with which a merchant has previously gauged and adjusted his inventory to reality rather than to hopes and speculation. Since it has become the tendency of merchants rather generally to make purchases at shorter intervals and to avoid long-term gambles, it follows that manufacturers have been forced to assume more of the responsibility of holding inventories ready for shipment. Today they are assuming more responsibility than in the past for correctly judging the proper timing of their own production schedules. This does not necessarily imply that manufacturers should accumulate unreasonably large stocks to fill dealers' orders on short notice. It does mean that well-controlled and budgeted manufacturing operations involve the function of anticipating the cyclical element in volume of orders from mercantile customers and, beyond that, foreseeing those changes in the economic situation that are likely to alter *ultimate consumer* buying power and retail demand. The merchant who has been able to gear his purchasing policy fairly accurately to the ebb and flow of consumer demand will rarely be caught with unwieldy inventory or excessive markups, should general buying power relapse. Merchants, like farmers, must move their supplies somehow to make way for new supplies and the continuous seasonal schedule of operations. Both *must* accept lower prices if maladjustment of supply to probable demand has occurred and it is necessary to move supplies.[1]

In view of the growing proportion of retail purchases financed by consumer installment credit (except in wartime), the retail merchant is in a strategic position to assist in the cyclical control of the consumer buying of nondurables and some types of durable equipment also the flexible adjustment of credit policy. In this he may be influenced by the credit policy of the larger installment houses and the banks with which he should cooperate. The retailer, in his own credit department, can apply this flexibility effectively as the cycle approaches its upper limits by taking account of the varying degree of risk relative to various lines of merchandise according to their durability, their selling prices, and

---

[1] Leslie Aczel has suggested that measure of merchandising efficiency should involve the factors of both profit markup and rate of turnover of capital; he suggests that these might be combined by multiplying the annual rate of capital turnover by the average *net retained* markup to secure an efficiency index. This could be used for departments as well as for total sales. (*The New York Times*, May 5, 1940, p. 8.)

the extent to which a more or less temporary style element enters into their purchase. The adaptation of credit policy all along the line to the probable cyclical drift of buying power can someday be developed to a fine art, capable of contributing in no small measure to the stabilization of marketing and many advantages to merchandising. This implies that the merchandising unit cannot exercise control intelligently unless it is financially sound and is operated by well-trained and alert executives with adequate facilities for well-coordinated planning. The terrific failure rate among small retail stores clearly demonstrates that much more education in this field of business is essential in the interest of solvency and general trade stability. Merchandising probably will never be carried on predominantly by large units, despite the growth of great chain systems in the selling of groceries, shoes, drugs, apparel, and in the department-store field in the last few decades. The point that is worthy of repeated emphasis is that Sound Business Practice, contributing to solvency and greater stability, yet allowing for maximum growth in total distribution, means essentially an attitude of mind, not size or scope of operations. The exceptionally capable merchant, though he have a small establishment, can exercise the functions of foresight and planning, and he has done so in conspicuous cases.

In the foregoing discussion, the problem of business policy in the upper range of a business upsurge has been particularly emphasized, because if serious mistakes are avoided *at that stage*, the exercise of sound policy in the ensuing stage of decline and depression becomes much easier. Business obtains whatever means it may have to offset depressions from the resources, accumulated from the period of high activity, conservatively administered. To be sure, business as well as consumers can borrow in a depression, through bank loans or the sales of bonds and notes, but it is sounder practice in the long run to develop the means of preparing for revival after depression from internal strength and conservative policy during the boom years. If business used *less* borrowed funds, the banking system could do that much *more* to place economical credit at the disposal of consumers, where it can do most good in smoothing out cycles. We should have fewer financial and mercantile *speculators* wasting credit and more *consumers* using it thriftily and constructively. This involves clear ideas, derived from actual study, not offhand guesses, of the distinction between the longer trend of growth in sales, as distinct from the shorter movements, which sometimes last for years at a time but which are cyclical in nature. The ignorant manager makes mistakes because he confuses trend growth and cycle rise when times are good. The thoroughly competent businessman has a fair idea of the rate of expansion (allowing for location) that can be counted upon to prevail in sales over a decade or more as a *reasonable* expectation. If actual progress at any time greatly exceeds that rate, the longer such a condition lasts the more intent must he be on conservatism to prepare for the inevitable reaction.

FORECASTING APPLIED TO MERCHANDISING

We can now survey some of the major policy problems during prosperity periods as they pertain to *production*. As we have seen, manufacturers are confronted by the problem of meeting more frequent orders from distributors than was usual a few decades ago. They must estimate output requirements months ahead rather than proceed on the basis of large forward orders already on the books. In these days of hand-to-mouth retail buying (and this holds for consumers also), difficult policy problems emerge in the case of products having style or seasonal features. Style, fashion, design, color, and novelty have become dominant factors in the sale of consumer goods. Even in industrial equipment a style factor is expressing itself in the frequent changes of design accomplished by the swift pace of technical progress and the insistent demand for improvements in mechanical apparatus and office appliances. As a result, it is more and more difficult for most manufacturers to "produce for stock"; they must either gear their operations to incoming orders as they are received, or anticipate those orders as well as possible over relatively limited periods and to the extent that abrupt changes or competitive elements associated with design and style appeal are not likely to create stocks of obsolete products on hand. This places a limitation on efforts to steady the mass production of even low-priced finished consumer goods.

Some important industries, among them the automobile industry, have sought to meet this problem by providing products of several price classes, corresponding to the degree of refinement and range of accessories. But design is constantly in flux, and the annual change-over to "new models" has probably intensified rather than stabilized its effect on the time pattern of the output. Here we are dealing with the double problem of the buying-power cycle and the strong appeal of improved design that reflects continuing improvements in the product. But something may be accomplished, even in the face of this style problem, by observing the cyclical probabilities and indications.

A period of unusual general prosperity is a time for consideration of designs or models of consumer durables that can best accommodate not the existing fleeting upsurge of buying power but the recoil that will surely follow. Greater simplicity and economy, linked with maximum performance in the hands of users, should characterize industrial offerings to the public as the cycle turns toward a less favorable phase. Management should constantly scrutinize its products and new offerings to see whether some wholly new *type* of product might be made the means of sustaining production during a lull.   This is a way of exploring more fully the possibilities of regularly reaching into the great mass of potential consumers in the lower income groups.   Naturally, such plans must take account of the used-product markets in the case of some durables.   The principal reason why the motor industry has not been able to do more to perpetuate the original idea of Henry Ford of a low price consistent with large-scale output, usability, no frills and gadgets has been the reservoir of used cars sold cheap.   But for most of the electrical equipment designed for household use, this is not the case, and that industry appears to have missed many opportunities to explore the market for plain goods at rock-bottom prices.

If we are thinking rather of productive equipment and capital goods, the foregoing considerations are less applicable.   There may be an occasional opportunity to dovetail into volatile operations some relatively stable items at the proper stage of the cycle to reduce wide fluctuation in revenue.   Such an offset has been found by some companies in the practice of leasing equipment to customers on terms that provide a relatively stable income, capable of tempering the wide oscillations in orders typical of producer goods.   But a firm that must depend primarily upon sales of such products as the chief source of revenue has restricted opportunity to avoid the wide swings in demand, as long as this is subject to cyclical leverage, as explained in Chapter 18.   The more specialized the products the greater is the exposure to wide alternations in demand.   If little can be done to stabilize operations, the safest course is adoption of conservative methods in the disposition of revenue and the accumulation in active periods of substantial reserves.   If management is alert and willing to engage in the necessary research and study of its problem, there is always the possibility of *diversifying products* and endeavoring to reach some relatively stable markets in industrial lines not marked by excessive cyclical vibration.

Production policy during a period of prosperity may then involve several further aspects.   First, some production to stock can be undertaken of semifinished but easily adaptable basic parts and repair and replacement items, with continuous regard, of course, to the business-cycle forecast.   In this way some portion of total output can be held back in peak periods and allocated to periods of probable slack demand in order to sustain operations.   Second, during a period of unusually high level of orders and probably the receipt of some orders that represent speculation and overextension somewhere, there should be a deliberate policy of *extending delivery*, or what may be termed "stringing out," as a means of bringing more operating activity into a period of clearly indicated recession rather than feverishly speeding up operations to meet "boom" orders, which usually turn out to be associated with fantastic expectations of continued exceptional prosperity.   The wise manufacturer of durable equipment, who has a firm statistical grip upon the business-cycle position and knows the extent to which operating results beyond reasonable expectations can last, can well afford, even in his limited way, to exert some braking influence upon the overenthusiastic contractors or expansion-minded promoters oblivious to the general course of business and intent upon doing too much of tomorrow's business today.   Here again one may well weigh carefully whether it pays to accept for immediate delivery all the orders that present themselves at a time when exceptional momentum is evident and it is increasingly probable that a reversal of the business tide portends.   The pursuit of such an ultraconservative attitude cannot, of course, be considered practicable if the ultimate demand emanates from Government under conditions of emergency or if the field is so highly competitive that such policy would involve undue sacrifice of business.[1]

We turn now to comment upon purchasing policy and the business cycle.   Something has already been implied as to purchasing procedure in our discussion of merchandising, as well as in Chapter 19.   In the case of manufacturing operations, it is clear that sound purchasing policy is a corollary of sound selling and production policies.   The outstanding merit of applied forecasting and budgeting is that it coordinates the activities of all responsible executives.   Without such planning of operations, there is usually a tendency to go off at tangents and to work in opposing directions, with the result that purchases are made without regard to production schedules, and production operations are planned ahead with no sane relationship to probable sales.   It is incumbent upon industrial management not to copy the practices of the farmer, who produces and then tries to sell; the correct policy is to produce as much as the market will stand, at prices that will extend sales to the widest possible market, horizontally and vertically.   There must be continued awareness of probable variations in the strength of the market structure, and purchases of materials, the hiring of labor, and financing must be appropriate to the volume of sales afforded by external conditions, modified by reasonably effective internal policy.   This means a balancing of operations and a coordination of functions, which are already attempted by many companies, and it marks one of the great achievements of modern business. In terms of the purchasing function, it should be noted that the purchas-

---

[1] Thomas W. Mitchell, in his study, Competitive Illusion as a Cause of Business Cycles, *Quarterly Journal of Economics*, August, 1924, deals in an interesting way with the advantages of production to stock under certain conditions and the cumulative instability developing from undue restriction of such production.   His analysis is still worthy of attention from serious-minded executives.

ing agent deserves a higher status in the executive realm than he has ordinarily been accorded. His functions are vitally important, and the proper exercise of them involves as much study, statistical research, and careful judgment as any other aspect of management.

If industrial purchasing operations are rationally budgeted ahead, the resulting advantage is not expected to be one of deriving speculative profits through buying supplies at bottom prices. Rather, it is found in having available *adequate* supplies under one set of business conditions and *not excessive* supplies, tying up capital or requiring extraordinary borrowing, when requirements are below average. When conditions are nearer the top of the cycle and indications begin to point downward, further commitments can be tapered off gradually rather than with a sudden jolt, and a schedule of requirements should be carefully worked out in terms of stock on hand, stock ordered, stock en route, and material in process. As the decline in business gets under way, purchases may be somewhat scattered as to sources, rather than concentrated, if thereby more reasonable pricing can be promptly obtained. If the plan for production during impaired business conditions calls for development of some new type of product or a major innovation under unit-cost conditions that are favorable to initial operations, the purchase of the necessary supplies to take care of these requirements also becomes a part of the purchasing budget as laid out while conditions are still favorable.

FORECASTING APPLIED TO PERSONNEL

We come now to the problems of personnel and labor force, which again must be worked out in terms of sales expectation and plans for production rates. Much has been written in recent years regarding the steps taken by management to stabilize employment during subnormal business conditions, and something has already been said in Chapter 21 of employment policy. The sum and substance of actual plant experience is that most of the successful results have been in consumer-goods lines having a minimum average of cyclical fluctuation. As already indicated, there is no generally applicable policy of stabilization in manufacturing operations that is typically subject to wide oscillations in demand and cannot resort to stock production. The problem cannot be solved without the kind of comprehensive wage-income compensation plans already discussed; it is not primarily a problem within the control of management. But business management does have the responsibility of doing what it can to sustain employment through stabilizing of production, development of auxiliary products, and similar devices that have been mentioned. Sound policy requires that the addition of many new workers to the force at the top of a boom is unwise, unless there is a fair presumption of retaining a substantial part of their services during at least moderate recession.

We should have less firing of workers during depression and unnecessary cutting down of the demand for *all* goods if we did less reckless hiring under the spur of the heedless "optimism" of a boom atmosphere. Plans for absorbing more labor to be carried along into the future must necessarily be part of that integrated program of development that devises new ideas, new products, new territorial expansion, new sales effort, not for release at the top of the boom but at the time when these can get the best start and derive the full benefit of the upswing in conditions (assuming that alternations will continue to occur). To accomplish a steady expansion of the employed labor force and to absorb all who are willing and able to work demands industries that can provide a *continual proliferation of new products and services*. This is not to be confused with the usual tendency to crowd all possible help into the factories when conditions are already overextended, only to release them within a few months to walk the streets. Management should appreciate how utterly silly this really is. Not every plant can be fruitful in developing new ways of using labor, but a conscious effort to minimize unnecessary hiring and firing will make any general system of compensatory income that much more practical and effective.

FORECASTING APPLIED TO CAPITAL FINANCING

As we translate future expectations as to operations into financial data, they become estimates of such items as total revenue, operating costs, semioverhead costs, overhead costs, and indicated profits. These preliminary estimates may be carried forward, as previously suggested, first, as a purely "passive" resultant of the various external factors that can be expected to influence the business of the firm during a future period and then carried out again in terms of the probable effect of external plus *internal* factors to ascertain the final probabilities and their expression in the income statement and balance sheet a year ahead. If changes in financing, taxes, cash, or capital payments are indicated, preparations for them can and should be made well in advance, rather than, as so often happens, on the spur of the moment. When we come to financial policy having to do with the provision of new plant and equipment over and above the routine provisions for depreciation and maintenance, we come upon momentous and complex aspects of policy during the changing phases of the business cycle. Whatever error executives make in forecasting sales or planning production, purchases, or personnel, there is little doubt that the most serious mistakes are usually made at the point of initiating capital expansion and its financing. If such plans reflect merely the spell of contagious prosperity sentiment and the prospect of orders that existing capacity cannot handle, there is the typical result of inadequate measurement of all aspects of the trend and cycle pertinent to the case.

New capital frequently is borrowed at the very time that its embodiment in new structures and equipment is the prelude to a shrinkage in business that no one expected. The enlarged capacity must then be operated for months or even years at a low percentage of its potential and at high unit cost.[1]

It must be acknowledged that even if management has tolerably well gauged the outlook for sales and planned all dependent aspects of operation intelligently with respect to the general outlook, mistakes cannot be wholly avoided in judging the amount and character and location of capital development. In other words, the plant budget and the capital expansion plans do not flow mechanically or automatically from mere expectations as to business conditions. This is particularly true if these plans call for changes in type of product or cultivation of a large new domestic or foreign market. We must also distinguish between policy developed in anticipation of a relatively mild, temporary setback in general business and anticipation of a major depression. In the former case, plans for capital expansion, if they are clearly in line with the trend of market requirements, may go forward with no material modification, but if the basic measurements of general conditions, not only in the market for the product but in the construction industry and capital finance generally are facing substantial impairment, the planning of structural development should be such as to direct appropriations and the letting of contracts, not at the top but nearer the bottom of the cycle. In prosperity it is essential that finances be planned year by year so that funds secured from revenue will be available as far as possible. Additional funds, if necessary, may usually be obtained much more readily through the sale of stock at the prosperity phase than they are obtainable during a major depression. If it is desired to supplement resources with borrowed funds, it will usually be found that the terms upon which long-term capital is available for a conservative and sound enterprise will be more satisfactory in the very early phase of recovery than at the height of prosperity. But this does not necessarily mean that borrowing is more advantageous in the long run than securing equity capital, if the latter can be *utilized* at the proper stage of the cycle.

[1] The writer has had occasion to observe the cyclical timing of some of the important business-plant constructions undertaken in parts of the Pacific Coast and has found striking instances illustrating these tendencies.

A better timing of major plant expansion can be achieved not only by closer attention to the various advance indications of significant turning points in the business cycle but also by more carefully and realistically estimating how far the cyclical movement already developed, at the time when capital decisions are made, has carried the general current of trade and production above its long-term apparent trend. The mortgage-solvency index and the relationship of durable-goods production to that of nondurable goods are useful auxiliary measures for this purpose.

The decision to expand or improve plant facilities or to develop new locations during quiet times is one that demands not only a factual sense and good judgment but backbone and moral fiber. The builder must ever rely upon the trend of the nation to justify his effort in the long run. If, in plotting the course ahead, the occurrence of depression is interpreted with undue pessimism as a permanent decline or breakdown in the vitality of the economy, there will naturally be no incentive to make new capital investment. This, broadly speaking, was the unfortunate state of mind of too many American businessmen and also of many of our political leaders during the decade of the 1930's. It was feared that at last the basic trend of the nation's economic growth had begun to sag and might soon actually decline. The future no longer existed. The great frontiers had gone. Growth was an illusion; so why risk preparing for it? Of course, the long-term future trend of production and living standards is as much a matter of judgment as it is of measurement, but until it is actually demonstrated beyond question that future growth in total wealth or in new forms of wealth is impossible, forward-looking executives can continue to consider themselves intelligent as well as courageous if they make plans for enlargement of capacity or improvement of facilities for future use when times are dull, prices are low, men are eager to work, and the planning can be done deliberately with sound judgment. The creation of the Rockefeller Center group of buildings in New York City was a fine demonstration of this faith and strategic timing. If more business plants were built on such principles, we should hear much less of the alleged impelling need for public works as a depression cure-all. Even though a new plant is not being considered from the standpoint of the peak level of probable future production, there is the continuing necessity of developing better methods and fighting obsolescence. By timing such expenditure off-peak, a stabilizing element is contributed to the capital and the raw-material industries; it may be feeble in the individual instance but can be of impressive aid to general stability if Sound Practice becomes more generally understood. There is no reason why the continued development of sound planning along these lines cannot carry forward in new directions what the stable depreciation allowance has already accomplished with respect to minor replacements.

In this matter of plant provision, the command of financial resources is of the utmost importance. If a concern depends upon external financing whenever there is occasion to develop new plant facilities, it must accept that financing on the terms that market conditions dictate. This means in simple language that usually the terms will be easier when it is not the "right" time to make these commitments. Bankers do not find conditions favorable to large financing undertaken in deep depression, since securities are difficult to sell. That is one reason for unemployment cycles. But that is the very time when the concern that has been conservative in its financing and has accumulated resources for future use, when the time is right, can take action and be independent of capital market pressures.   This is one major reason why the theorists who would squeeze down all corporate surplus and saving ability to the bare minimum or to zero are *really arguing against the whole philosophy of stabilization within the framework of a system of private property*.   They imply, consciously or unconsciously, that business management is inherently stupid or incompetent and cannot or should not plan *capital* as it plans ahead for sales or other functions.   Again we face the issue—is this a matter of creating, through education, research, and helpful provision of factual data, a better managerial use of private capital, or must we accept the dictum, unsupported by factual evidence, that *all* use (and accumulation) of productive capital is properly a function of the State?   Business management should not fail to recognize and face this issue squarely and handle capital planning problems with the fullest sense of its responsibility, with a long view and a broad view.   It is in the handling of these major capital problems that its competence, skill and foresight will be judged and weighed, as never before, in the years ahead.   The results will go far to determine whether management in private or in bureaucratic hands will be the pattern of the future.

FORECASTING APPLIED TO LEVELING OF SEASONAL PEAKS

American industry has given more attention to the problem of stabilizing operations from month to month, that is, seasonal stabilizing, than to the broader and more difficult problem of leveling booms and depressions. Seasonal concentration of sales and production in a few months of the year, leaving a vacuum at other points, calls for careful study of the seasonal characteristics of each business, and an exploration of policy adapted to these problems would carry us beyond the scope of this discussion.   However, one aspect of seasonality bears directly upon the planning of capital expenditures.   Plant capacity must be designed so that it is adequate to meet the demands of peak seasons, and in some fields there is a wide variation from seasonal trough to peak.   It is not generally practicable for a business concern to utilize outside plant capacity for production or to "farm out" orders among other suppliers at the peak season of a highly prosperous year.   This is particularly true of industrial products of the made-to-order type and the goods that have style features. If we are dealing with such staples as soap, electric-light bulbs, or shoes, the meeting of peak seasons of demand can usually be effectively accomplished by intelligent forecasting of the cyclical movement and adjustment of month-to-month operation in such fashion that inventories can be built up during part of the year and deliveries made in excess of production during other parts of the year.

This is how such concerns as Procter and Gamble have been able to achieve excellent results in evening out their production schedule and stabilizing employment. But their success by no means implies that the problem is capable of solution in the case of many establishments, particularly in the public-service industries, where the accumulation of supplies to meet peak seasons involves undue risk or where the service must be rendered when and as needed and there is no possibility of physical accumulation of supply. When capital facilities and expenditures are being planned, however, a management should endeavor to determine whether some means can be found to reduce, even moderately, the typical seasonal peaks in operations so that a given amount of capacity can be utilized more evenly through the year. This would permit some reduction in average overhead cost per unit. All this implies, of course, that accounting analysis is being carried to the point at which accurate schedules of unit costs at varying percentages of capacity are obtainable. Accounting practice has developed far ahead of scientific future planning of operations, and it is fortunate that the technique of cost analysis, if carried far enough and subjected to thorough analysis by a research assistant or staff, can be made an important element in the planning of plant layout. In some cases, a diversification of operations can be worked out to permit the use of facilities to fill in seasonal valleys, while at the same time leveling out seasonal peaks. Careful study of this would avoid excessive plant designed for exaggerated guesses as to future cyclical plus seasonal maxima of demand.

In order that ample funds be available in dull times, when they can go so far to provide facilities for more efficient, more abundant, and more economical production later, it is vitally important that *financial conservatism* dominate all policy at that critical stage of overextended general conditions that we have thus far been considering. One of the most serious mistakes made by responsible executives has been the reckless disbursement of net earnings at the upper level of the cycle, with the result that resources are not available at the time when they can best be used to take advantage of opportunities and provide for future development. Just as it is essential that the funds disbursed to labor should be in some measure conserved when the flow of purchasing power has achieved a momentum in excess of the underlying trend, so that provision can be made for maintaining purchasing power when capacities and other limits are being reached, so in the case of business resources, ample funds should be set aside when conditions provide exceptional revenue. This is another way of saying that the heart of conservative and sound management consists in a higher degree of stable continuity in disbursement of dividends or compensation to individual entrepreneurs. The typically reckless management pays out most of its earnings when times are good and then runs to the bankers in distress when orders evaporate. This has been the manner in which American railroads (and some other businesses closely allied with the railroads in financial control) have been operated, and it is certainly not a model to be followed by other business.

The hand of politics is also apparent in this matter, since there is a traditional suspicion that undue conservatism in the distribution of earnings is a form of "hoarding" and may somehow be a means of padding salaries and achieving growth in corporate opulence that is imagined to be synonymous with monopoly.

Human nature, among businessmen as among politicians, is not perfect. There have no doubt been abuses on the part of irresponsible promoters and boards of directors in withholding a fair return to the providers of their capital in order to accomplish objectives not in the interest of efficiency or honest wealth creation. But exceptional cases aside, the funds that are held back and *prevented from overaccelerating an already overextended business situation* can be utilized to hire labor and construct plant facilities at the proper time if Sound Practice and foresight are management objectives. There is no reason why they cannot be made objectives in a far greater number of cases, but repressive public policy is not going to accomplish this. There is no justification whatsoever for the continuance of political policies that place flat and arbitrary limitations upon the amount that a corporation or any other business unit may withhold for its own legitimate capital uses as distinct from the amount that it distributes to ownership. The prevailing practice of the Treasury Department in discouraging the setting aside of annual surplus in excess of about 30 per cent of net earnings is nothing more than a phase of the current ideology of "share the wealth" in order to create more *immediate* buying power. This shortsighted, arbitrary rule of thumb is as contrary to the basic principle of stabilization of income flow as the philosophy of labor-union leaders who demand that wage rates be increased by leaps and bounds at the very top of every cycle, so that the already accelerated flow of income is rendered still more vulnerable to cyclical readjustment as wage earnings are used to buy tomorrow's capital goods today.

All this represents *confusion between trend and cycle;* it is insistence upon focusing all possible *current income* to build the booms higher rather than distributing income rationally *through time.* It fastens fanatically upon the rich-poor complex, ignoring the manner in which needless cyclical vibration is the most potent single factor in bringing about undue concentration of wealth at the top and inadequate income at the bottom of the social structure. If we wish to have more stability and yet preserve vigorous growth in production and real income, it is apparent that the translation of improved business earnings into wages and remuneration to capital must be accomplished always with a factual sense of the trend limits of sound growth and not on spur-of-the-moment impulses, which, in a complex economy, drive the cycles higher and higher and the succeeding slumps deeper and deeper.   Putting it bluntly, in a few words, unless we save our money when we have it so that it may be used at those times when otherwise uncontrolled cyclical forces retard the flow of demand, we have no private resources to utilize in filling up the vacuum. We can adopt income compensation en masse, as suggested in Chapter 21, but even that cannot wholly eliminate vibration or the need for management efforts in the same direction.   There is no reason why business cannot be given, within reasonable limits, an incentive to *build up* the depressed areas of the cycle from its own resources.   There is no sense in jumping to the conclusion that business is utterly helpless or unwilling to adopt principles of Sound Practice that can contribute something to the general purpose.   There is no reason why there should not be a specific tax incentive to aid far-seeing management in setting aside funds from good earnings in order to develop innovation when that may be done to advantage.   We shall need innovation more and more in the future, not less and less, as the static minds would have us believe.[1]

IMPORTANCE OF LONG-RANGE PLANNING

The high years of a period of unusual prosperity are the time to get out of debt or to reduce indebtedness involved in expansion undertaken in the low years.   There are periods in every business where consideration must be given to the possible advantages of borrowing some portion of needed capital.   One of these periods is in the early stage of operations, when some tangible assets have been accumulated and the firm has begun to command some measure of confidence among investors.   The raising of funds through bond issues or bank loans, when other channels of capital supply are not available, is justified as long as certain basic safeguards are observed.   There are times when emergencies arise that cannot be foreseen and when funds must be obtained quickly through borrowing.   But the conservative management that is endeavoring to stand on its own feet and work out its destiny through its own resourcefulness will avoid borrowing as far as possible.   It will also safeguard itself by avoiding, in any event, the borrowing of funds at very long maturity on terms that make it difficult to retire the obligations within a reasonable period, as

---

[1] The notion frequently expressed that business in some mysterious fashion can develop expanding production without providing any capital itself has been propagated by referring to specific cases in which the balance sheets of various corporations indicate (superficially at least) a very much less marked expansion in "plant valuation" than in the value of sales or production.   This overlooks the fact that in many cases plant values on the balance sheet represent nothing more than the write-off of past investments to a nominal figure.   The only information of any value in throwing light on the capital required to provide a certain volume of production must be derived from a complete inventory of investment or capital input and a study of the particular type of capital apparatus and structures utilized during the period covered.

resources may permit. Unless debt can be written down or retired during good years, the chances are that it will become larger and larger, more and more onerous, *until finally it is impossible to secure capital in any other way than by continued borrowing*, at the expense of flexibility all along the line and with the ultimate prospect of permanent impairment. A debt-ridden enterprise cannot fight obsolescence; it cannot fight the cycle; it cannot carry its share of the task of promoting economic progress. Any political regime that is ambitious to "take over" business functions will give its hand away by the steps that it takes to fasten debts upon private industry. The present War may reveal that such a tendency is already beginning to develop.

This is an old story, verified over and over again, but the underlying principles have been overlooked in theoretical treatises on finance. Too much attention has been given to the formal rights and legal prerogatives of lenders of capital, rather than to the proper business use of borrowed funds designed to keep productive enterprise continuously solvent and adaptable to change. If, therefore, it is necessary to borrow and if the plans represent the considered judgment of management rather than merely the effectiveness of salesmanship of investment bankers, every effort should be made to make the debt callable, of reasonable maturity, and otherwise designed to provide for retirement in accordance with earnings and cyclical opportunity. To borrow at long term with the thought that the debt is to be permanent and then to pay out dividends recklessly in good years is an invitation to disaster that can be historically verified to the letter. No one can complain fairly of the criticism that a labor union or a political administration might make of such a management. Lenders, in the past, when capital was scarce, had things too much their way as to the terms of business loans. Those times and conditions are past. Lenders must face the choice of lower interest, safeguarded by enhanced protection to the solvency of the borrowing enterprise, or, on the other hand, the disappearance of their function in the business process altogether. They, as well as management, must make their choice and face facts rather than lean on the law or on precedent.

The adequate provision for future conditions in the matter of plant capacity naturally carries us, in many industries, beyond the range of merely cyclical movements. In the case of such service industries as the telephone or electric-power production, which are still in the state of a rising trend of growth, much attention has been given by management to the provision of plant facilities to take care of requirements, not merely a year or two ahead, but ten, fifteen, or thirty years in advance. Much of this long-range planning is concerned with the provision of service having naturally a close relation to population and the number of family units. Hence the analysis of the population trends, both in general and in specific localities and areas, becomes the central feature of the forecasting research.   This carries us back to the technique of population estimation, which was discussed in Chapter 2.   There is also involved in such future projection[1] a study of the probable trends, either of expansion or decline, in such industries as dominate the general income prospects of a particular area, for the service of which plant capacity needs are to be estimated. Unfortunately, all such long-range planning is likely to be confronted by the exigency of war conditions, with their distorting effects upon population movements and industry location.   There is an inescapable conflict between the planning ahead done by private business, on the assumption of continuation of peaceful and orderly progress, and such planning as may be done by governments, which involves strategic considerations necessarily shrouded in more or less secrecy.   So long as wars are the means of settling essentially economic world problems, there is the grave hazard, seldom fully appreciated by the majority, that the assurance of national security will throw *all* future planning in the hands of political groups, since they alone, in a world perpetually at war, can command the statistical and strategic information affording the basis for permanent capital planning.

Looked at from this angle, the prospect for continuation of privately worked out capital and plant provision, especially of the long-range type, is none too well assured.   The nature of the peace that follows the present conflict will be of supreme importance in this matter.   Until that is known, we remain in doubt as to how much of the responsibility for capital operations in the postwar world will be in the hands of private management in any country.   All that we can do at the moment is to suggest the ways in which such private management can continue to function productively and efficiently, in the interest of all concerned, on the one basic premise that the foundations of private property, private initiative, and management working toward the principles of Sound Practice will substantially survive and that we can go forward once again in the process of raising standards of living and per capita wealth through the only kind of industrial system that has been able to combine high productivity and the adaptation of that productivity primarily to the interests of peaceful living.[2]

[1] The reader is referred to the files of the *Bell Telephone Quarterly*, which from time to time has contained interesting articles on the general nature of the trend forecasting and capital planning developed by the Bell Telephone commercial engineers.   It is difficult to find in print any detailed descriptions of such techniques.   See also the monograph of the National Resources Committee, "Technological Trends and National Policy," 1937.

[2] Some writers have expressed amazement at the production results that can be obtained under war conditions when the economy is mobilized and centrally controlled by Government with emergency powers.   There is nothing really surprising about the speed with which an enormous increase in war production can be achieved

We have now surveyed some of the fundamental problems of management in planning ahead during prosperity. We have seen that the problem of sound policy during depression *is a corollary to what is done, or not done, during prosperity*. Let us finally summarize some aspects of business planning in depression, looking toward the probable revival of business conditions. At the depression stage, sales-promotion efforts should be expanded actively as soon as there are indications that the turning point has been passed and the general situation is preparing to move in the direction of improvement. This is the time when advertising and other efforts to promote and develop new business should be liberally expanded, rather than at the *top* level. This is the strategic phase when new products, services, and locations should be initiated so that their development can be firmly supported by such general expansion in income and demand as the next phase of the cycle affords. This is the time when credit terms should be adjusted to the most liberal basis possible consistent with due conservatism. This is the time to direct sales effort toward those localities, or industry segments, which analysis shows to be favored by the impending revival of buying power. Attention must be given to all indicators capable of throwing light on the probable extent of such a revival and the likelihood of its carrying through over a period of years. The state of the construction cycle and the status of basic commodity inventories on a national or international basis may

---

under these conditions. A concerted effort is made to attain a military objective, in which time is of the essence and without regard to what may be the ultimate effect of regimenting management and curtailing ownership of productive property after the emergency is over. It is always possible to step up production effort to capacity under emergency conditions, but the fact that this is possible does not imply that such operations, if continued indefinitely, would be equally efficient or tolerable, except in a society where the individual was willing to become a serf. The citizens of any nation are willing to undergo hardships and the severest discipline by public authority in order to survive and preserve their national integrity; but arguments as to industrial operation or control derived from such emergency conditions have no direct bearing on the kind of economy that will afford the best results in the long run in a rationally regulated world or a society of free men.

Mordecai Ezekiel, in his provocative tract "Jobs for All through Industrial Expansion," New York and London, 1939, undertakes to develop a "plan" for politically regimented high-level production, frankly predicated upon the efficiency of wartime planning and productivity. Ezekiel gives some credit to the general idea of industrial budgeting and forward planning, so far as they have been employed, but finds that their effectiveness is limited by the inability of concerns to cooperate with one another in developing sound decisions and by the unwillingness of some managements to keep abreast of progress. He therefore proposes that planning be done by management on an industry basis but with the Government tolerating a close approach to cartelization and standing willing to purchase at a price discount any portion of the planned production that cannot be sold. Thus management would be "protected" from its mistakes in estimates of demand, but it would be presumably encouraged to continue development of future forecasts and to adjust operations thereto. Thus

afford valuable indications with regard to sales policy at this stage of the cycle.   Sales quotas should be established to afford reasonable incentive to the efficiency of those concerned with distribution, but always within the limits suggested by the basic statistical information.

Production policies in manufacturing industries can, at this stage of conditions, provide for the gradual shifting from forward production (to stock) of staple goods, materials, and equipment parts to the output of a larger proportion of style goods and finished articles incorporating specialized features and forms adapted to rising demand.   Production for stock should be relatively important *in* depression but less important proportionately as the drift of the cycle begins to carry the general momentum upward.

The depression period is one in which purchasing budgets as to staple commodities can be extended, within reason, to take advantage of price concessions likely to exist at that stage of the cycle.   This is a means of providing a margin of safety for the future rather than merely indulging in speculation in these markets.   This is a strategic time to provide for more control over essential raw-material resources by lease or ownership if reliance on purchased supplies has been found to involve needless costs or risks and a greater degree of integration is found, on the whole, to be sound policy.   At this stage, just prior to the upswing, there may be

---

production would not only be stabilized but expanded to a higher average level than at present.

This, however, would obviously involve the participation of Government in making the advance estimates and allocating to various concerns their quotas of production to fill the expected orders.   The Government, in fact, would force all concerns to participate eventually in this program.   It is analogous to regimenting agricultural production through the AAA, but looking primarily toward *expansion* under compulsion.   Ezekiel's Industrial Expansion Administration would subsidize expansion in industry, just as the AAA has subsidized contraction, under certain conditions, in agriculture.   Ezekiel finds himself confronted by a dilemma in visualizing the planning some time ahead for production of goods and services *of a given type*. But just who will provide, and how, for the *new goods* and the introduction of improvements and *innovations* is exceedingly vague.

This is another example of projecting ahead a *static system* comparable to the future statistical estimating that we had occasion to refer to in Chapter 20, in discussing the rigid statistical projections of Gardiner Means.   So long as we are content with Government regimentation of the productive system and are concerned merely with existing commodities and existing methods and techniques, this may be a solution of the planning problem.   But it is predicated upon the assumption that it is more important to spread *existing* wealth over a wider area than to make provision adequately for the development of *new* wealth.   It rests upon a passing phase of social philosophy that fears that we can no longer expect new investment to produce buying power and instead proposes artificially to equalize buying power to form the basis for investment.   It involves the hypothesis that the growth of capital in the past was merely a function of population growth, a view that overlooks the fact that population growth itself does not necessarily provide for capital development.

advantages in concentrating sizable orders for material in order to obtain, over as long a period as possible, the advantages of minimum cost attainable through fairly continuous operation on the part of the suppliers. Caution, however, should be exercised against overbuying; this is particularly true in industries where technical changes are introducing new types of goods and materials.

In personnel policy, one of the important aspects to be given attention at this stage is the adequate training of new workers and the prompt reengagement of such employees as it was necessary, in spite of all efforts to conserve staff, to disemploy during the previous declining phase. We are assuming that under even the most efficient general unemployment income compensation plan, there will be occasional reduction of working forces for cyclical reasons. If average working time has been somewhat shortened during the first stage of depression or recession, it is important to maintain the shorter hours as long as possible as an incentive to individual efficiency and a means of reestablishing as promptly as possible as many workers as possible. Individual planning must do its part in avoiding a chronic condition of high unemployment. There are, naturally, limits surrounding the extent to which such personnel policies can be carried out in the individual firm, but there is considerable indirect benefit to be derived from careful personnel adjustments through the contributions that can make harmonious and sound relations between management and employees. The concern that, through careful handling of its finances, is able to introduce new products, or extensions of service during periods of subnormal business and thus offer to workers new openings for employment provides just that much more evidence of the ability of private capitalism to carry on successfully and in the interest of the national welfare.[1]

[1] A study was recently published by Paul E. Holden, of the Stanford Graduate School of Business, assisted by Lounsberry S. Fish and Hubert L. Smith, of the form of organization and functional responsibility at the top management level in 31 leading industrial corporations. ("Top-management Organization and Control: A Research Study of the Management Policies and Practices of 31 Leading Industrial Corporations," Stanford University Press, 1941.) The authors carefully sifted the forms of management structure in the light of industry characteristics in order to throw into relief the best practice with respect to delegation of authority, definition of functions, and setting of responsibility among the higher executives. We need more of this searching analysis of current practice to determine by actual test what are the soundest possible ways in which executive control can and should function in the formulation of policy, and the extension of such analysis to dynamic functions and policies is urgently needed. In this way, Sound Practice in applying forecasting to planning for the future can provide standards for dealing with the problems of time and change, representing the best results of actual experience, as well as deductions from theoretical analysis.

CHAPTER 24

PRICE DISPARITY AND CYCLICAL INSTABILITY

We found in Chapter 20 (Chart 64) that since 1920, following a fairly uniform inflationary movement of prices in World War I, there has been a marked tendency for groups of prices to move in a fanlike way, with a growing disparity. The average urban cost of living has been conspicuously resistant to deflation influences and has followed a course midway between hourly wage rates and wholesale prices. The wholesale prices of manufactures have been somewhat better sustained than prices of raw materials, while the average movement of prices at the farm suffered a very marked deflation, followed by recovery after 1932. If we were to add indexes relating to stock prices, rents, building costs, the price of electric power, etc., the divergent price patterns would be all the more emphasized.

There has grown up in recent years a body of economic doctrine that emphasizes these disparities and holds up to criticism the apparent rigid and insensitive character of some groups of prices (or rates). These contrast strikingly with the extreme volatility and cyclical instability of other prices, some of which, as we have previously seen in the case of the agricultural and mineral industries, virtually determine the changes in income received by millions of people. These features of rigidity and disparity have important significance with regard to the business cycle and economic policy, particularly since there are those who assign great importance to the maladjustment of prices as among the factors tending to generate or intensify depressions and booms in general business. What are the elements of price rigidity, monopolistic dictation or administration of prices, and the problems presented by prices that are continually in vibration and frequently reach levels far out of line with less variable prices? Are these disparities an important source of general instability in the economic system? Do they form obstacles to the steady flow of income or to progress of real income? What are the essential objectives of a sound price policy, public and private? Should our efforts be directed toward introducing more stability in the variable prices or primarily toward effecting greater flexibility of adjustment in the prices that seem to be so artificially steady? And should these possible policies be primarily directed toward the *trend* of prices or toward their *cyclical* manifestations during shorter periods?

There is certainly nothing new in the phenomena that in periods of pronounced business depression a relatively wide spread develops between the more sensitive prices of commodities and those that are more stable. Adam Smith referred to this tendency more than a century and a half ago in stating that "the price of linen and woolen cloth is liable neither to such frequent, nor to such great, variations as the price of corn." In the depressions of the 1830's, 1870's, 1890's, and 1930's, we find the same tendency for prices to "disperse," with conspicuous weakness in the more highly competitive markets.[1] Despite this long-continued characteristic of prices, there has recently come about a belief that in the "old days," when competitive conditions in business were much more wholesome and flexible and large corporations did not exist, the behavior of prices was much more "orderly." In recent years much opportunity has been given to business executives to discard the old rules of competition and to set prices deliberately and arbitrarily. Some have argued that although the price-disparity phenomenon has a long history, a larger proportion of business during the past generation has taken the form of semimonopolistic organization and has permitted more markets to become "administered" rather than left to the mercies of competition. What is most important for our present interest is the view that by virtue of these disparities depressions and booms not only are rendered more severe but are actually generated. In fact, the Honorable Henry A. Wallace has asserted that "corporation policies not only intensified the severity of the depression once it began, but they also helped create the fundamental maladjustment that made the depression inevitable. The most serious of these policies was their eagerness to hold back too much of their profits for their owners and to distribute too little of the increased efficiency in lower prices or higher pay."[2] Although this statement is typical in its exaggeration, it is not wholly untrue, since we have seen that during the 1920's manufacturing companies (not all of them corporations) appear to have raised hourly pay rates somewhat less than they might have done, with the possible result that the inadequate lowering of prices may have prevented the ideally perfect adjustment of mass purchasing power. Such ideally perfect adjustments are hard to find either in business or in politics. But our previous statistical analysis indicated that this degree of maladjustment was not important, because there are other elements than commodities in the purchases made by wage earners, and the prices of some of these things are beyond the control of manufacturers. Mr. Wallace goes on to say: "corporation policies having to do with production, employment, prices, and savings are dominating factors in the

---

[1] See the interesting chart presented by Rufus S. Tucker in the article Essential Historical Facts about "Sensitive" and "Administered" Prices, *The Annalist*, Feb. 4, 1938.

[2] "Technology, Corporations, and the General Welfare," pp. 35–36, University of North Carolina Press, 1937.

business cycle. . . . To nearly everyone, the big corporations have been in a position to say, 'take it or leave it,' and the public had to take it even when it meant millions of men walking the streets, even when it meant 3-cent wheat, even when it meant prices for manufactured products which had been cut very little."[1] With regard to the causation of business depressions, the statistical evidence is against Mr. Wallace's sweeping conclusions. But inasmuch as the placing of responsibility for all booms and depressions upon corporate *price* policy has become an important phase of political and economic propaganda in recent years, it is necessary to examine it rather carefully.

STUDIES ON PRICE DISPARITY

The basic source of much recent emphasis on price disparity is to be found in a number of studies by Gardiner C. Means, particularly a memorandum on "Industrial Prices and Their Relative Inflexibility," undertaken for the Secretary of Agriculture, pursuant to a Senate resolution in 1935.[2] In this monograph Means dramatized the depression experience of a number of commodities. He classified degrees of price "sensitiveness," based upon frequency of change and upon the extent of decline to the low point and of rise to 1934. It was demonstrated that in agriculture, production remained almost rigid while prices melted away swiftly after 1929. In the production of agricultural equipment, on the other hand, prices remained rigid while the production of implements declined even more than farm prices. This suggested the general thesis that old-fashioned *laissez faire* now operates in only the rural segments of our economy, whereas the larger industrial segment administers its prices as it pleases and adjusts its volume of production with enormous flexibility to maintain those prices. Means did not imply that the alleged ability of industry to regulate prices at rigid levels was evidence of any willful intent to gain unfair advantage; it was rather a natural and unavoidable corollary of the manner in which markets dominated by a small number of sellers may be expected to function.

The basic cause for the failure of a *laissez faire* policy is to be found in the very same forces which have made possible a high standard of living for all, namely, the gradual, century-long shift from market to administrative coordination of economic activity which has resulted in modern industrial organization and modern technology. This shift to administration has brought a new type of competition and inflexible administered prices which disrupt the workings of the market.[3]

[1] *Ibid.*, pp. 41–42.
[2] *Senate Document* 13, 74th Congress, First Session, 1935. Senate Resolution 17 had requested a report relating to the subject of industrial prices and their relative inflexibility.
[3] *Op. cit.*, p. 9.

From this it was deduced that markets are no longer capable of equating supply and demand through a flexible price mechanism, which is a way of saying that farmers, for example, being subject to extreme price movements, find it utterly impossible to make adequate purchases of "high-priced" equipment, house furnishing, and other administered products when their prices and incomes decline. There is a further implication here either that farmers should be subsidized and their prices not permitted to fall so low, or that industrial price policy must be revolutionized and replaced by keener competition and presumably a much larger number of sellers than prevail in many industries today.

Gardiner Means did not draw this precise implication but rather pointed out that as an alternative to atomizing the administrative units in industry in order to "restore" the freely competitive market, there might be some way to supplement the market organization by institutional arrangements worked out with Government assistance and supervision along the lines of the NRA industrial plan and the AAA farm program. Under the NRA (as originally proposed), there would be a measure of sanction granted to trade associations to establish within a given industry a fair price level and to prevent that level from being broken down by unfair tactics. To balance this there would be further expansion of trade unionism and agreements taking the form of industry "codes" for the wage rates and other labor terms, to be similarly placed on a fair and presumably stable basis. We now know that the latter has been accomplished to a considerable extent, although the former objective was entirely eliminated by the Supreme Court decision abolishing the NRA in 1935. The Agricultural Adjustment Administration still continues to function along lines slightly different from the original plan, which was also held unconstitutional, but there are now sufficient "administration" of agricultural production and sufficient subsidization of farmers under the present workings of the farm program that we may say that this phase of Mr. Means' alternative has actually been put into practice in principle. The Means Memorandum, therefore, was intended to show the reasonableness and necessity for NRA and AAA, and to this extent his analysis had considerable validity. He appears to have been unwilling to accept the alternative of breaking down industrial units into small fry, as he explicitly stated with regard to industrial policy: "In order to make a *laissez faire* policy truly effective, productive efficiency would have to be greatly impaired and a lower standard of living accepted than is made possible by modern industrial organization."[1]

In his conviction that governmentally supervised agencies could, if they continued to function, be made to reach correct decisions at critical points, Means demonstrated his faith in the continuance of a large meas-

[1] *Ibid.*, p. 13.

ure of private initiative and hence the continuance of a high degree of productive expansion in corporate enterprise and a fairer level of prices and income for the extractive industries. Unfortunately, however, the interesting NRA experiment to rationalize the planning of industrial policy, as an alternative to a cutthroat competitive state of affairs, had to be laid aside for legal rather than economic reasons, and with this impairment of the twin controls much of the force of Means' general policy program was lost. There has been a tendency on the part of some economists and publicists to carry forward the argument as to price disparity as essentially an attack upon all corporate management and a demand that corporations be *required* to observe the old and healthy rules of competition, even though many farmers and most organized labor no longer observe any such rules.[1]

PRICE DISPARITY IN EXTRACTIVE INDUSTRIES

In an important sense, the problem of price disparity is a depression problem. It raises the question what can best be done, if depressions cannot otherwise be avoided, to preserve the flow of income of the extractive industries. It *is* important to prevent a wide shrinkage in extractive industry purchasing power from becoming an added source of weakness in the national demand for industrial products. But it is just as important to refrain from misguided efforts to create chaos in the manufacturing and processing industries or a spiral of insolvency that might react in disastrous fashion upon the demand for farm products and other extractive materials whenever business conditions temporarily falter. Public policy and individual policy in this matter call for the most careful theoretical analysis, the exercise of calm judgment, and the avoidance of emotional bias. The results of our long-term measurements of agricultural income have clearly demonstrated that the postwar readjustments

---

[1] In an article entitled Price Inflexibility and the Requirements of a Stabilizing Monetary Policy, *Journal of the American Statistical Association*, June, 1935, Gardiner C. Means again stated his views on the alternative policies describing as unwise the attempt to atomize corporations and restore the utmost flexibility in the prices of manufactured goods. But in contemplating the acceptance of the modern industrial organization and its rigid administered prices as an alternative, he develops ideas regarding general monetary policy without giving adequate attention to the much more important specific policies for proper control of production or other internal problems in the fields of agriculture, forestry, mineral, and petroleum production. This represents another instance in which the rationalization of production is subordinated to an over-all monetary policy that, in the nature of things, cannot be expected to be directed toward problems of *disparity*, as distinct from problems of the general *trend* of prices. Both the Senate Document and this article were prepared by Means a few weeks before the Supreme Court invalidated the NRA. The adverse decisions in the matter of the original AAA plan was in January, 1936, but this was quickly revamped.

tend to take the form of unusually severe and long-continued periods of subnormal income for farmers, but such periods should be clearly distinguished from the shorter and less severe business disturbances occasioned by financial or promotional excesses in various directions, such as basic construction.

The United States has been passing through a long period of agricultural readjustment since World War I, and it was the peculiar combination of rural maladjustments arising from overstimulation of world food production during and immediately after World War I that gave the problem of price disparity its prominent place in a search for remedies that appear to have since ranged far afield from the specific problem. If inflation during war could be avoided, much of the price-disparity problem would probably vanish. We are presently again to be confronted by the problems of a postwar readjustment period, and more effective control as a means of making that period less productive of price and income injustice will be considered later in this chapter. But since extractive raw-material prices probably will always be more vulnerable to business depression than most manufactures, let us first consider just how far industry can go or should go in adopting price flexibility as one of its working principles.

In the United States we must recognize that our legal framework may need substantial revision before an economically sound solution of the disparity problem is reached. We still proceed in our legal thinking on the simple and possibly antiquated assumption that all business should be competitive and that "competition is the life of trade." Accordingly, any action on the part of industrial management seeking to stabilize market conditions and to *adjust promotion constantly to the actual strength of demand* is immediately viewed with suspicion. The Federal Government already has a variety of legal weapons to discourage such an attempt. The Sherman Antitrust Act of 1890, at first without much power, was effectively implemented by the establishment of the Federal Trade Commission in 1914. The Roosevelt Administration has made this body, as well as the Department of Justice, a means of leveling a steady fire of prosecution against all business practices that are found in the slightest degree incompatible with "free competition," which is supposed to have been so beneficent in maintaining economic justice and freedom of opportunity in some vaguely defined Golden Age.[1]

[1] According to one observer's cogent statement: "Any arrangement among competitors whereby they achieve a power to affect prices is condemned, regardless of the fact that their primary object is to correct an unfortunate situation in the business world, regardless of the fact that similar plans have been initiated and favored by Government authorities, and regardless of all question of reasonableness." (Nathan Isaacs, Price Control by Law, *Harvard Business Review*, Summer, 1940.) This well

Let us examine this idea of competition and what it implies.   Essentially it implies the offer of goods by many sellers acting independently with respect to price and production.   The buyers also act independently of each other but may have information concerning the supply available. No one of the sellers can appreciably affect the ruling price by enlarging his own supply or by withdrawing entirely from the market.   Under perfect competitive conditions it is assumed that he can make no decisions capable of affecting the great market.[1]   If sellers wish to dispose of what they have—and this is true of farmers raising food crops—each one must accept what the market affords.   This may be defined as an average price, a ratio of all the money that buyers are willing and able to spend to the size of the supply offered for sale.   If the price falls because supply is temporarily larger than usual—and this, again, is a frequent occurrence in industries exposed to the weather or to international unbalance as to supplies—the excess will be drawn into less important uses, and a larger carry-over may be avoided.   A lowering of price thus enlarges the amount disposed of.   In such a competitive market there is thus a tendency toward automatic readjustment of supply, it being assumed that excess (or at other times deficiency) arises from conditions *in production* rather than from conditions associated with a strengthening or weakening of the aggregate demand.   As we have already noted in Chapter 8 (Chart 21), there is a tendency for the aggregate demand for food products to strengthen or weaken within a relatively small range.   The automatic process of competition works out its adjustment in a more or less "static" demand situation.   It is this static kind of market and the static assumptions made in the analysis of the typical competitive price that have long dominated the theory of economists with respect to supply and demand generally.   The doctrine of the unlimited virtues of free competition is, in fact, rooted in this kind of market and may be valid insofar as these assumptions hold true.   This point deserves emphasis, inasmuch as it is the key to the entire problem of unrestrained competition versus some degree or type of supply control.

The so-called "classical" economists imagined that free competition was a beneficent adjunct of the natural economic order, because they made various other assumptions that may or may not have been realistic in past centuries.   One such assumption was that in the supposed area of

---

expresses the manner in which the legal mind divorces itself entirely from economic consideration and practical issues and focuses upon "minute statutory interpretation" of the *concept* of free competition, laid down apparently with no concern for the varied conditions found in actual production and no regard for the consequences if the so-called "free competition" were extended universally throughout the business system under modern technological conditions.

[1] In a narrowly defined market this might not be true.

perfect competitors, the costs of production, although not necessarily equal for all the sellers, are fairly *rigidly determined*. Second, the early economists, in laying down their propositions regarding supply and demand, gave little attention to the demand situation or the possibility of the variations in the structure of the demand. They did not fully recognize the possible tendency of demand, even for such staple necessities as foodstuffs, to *shift* position, either toward strengthening or toward weakening, toward more or less *aggregate money offer* for the total supply (see again Chart 8). The workings of free competition were also imagined to be aided by the fact that in most of the extractive types of production, expansion of operations involves higher and higher necessary costs (the word "cost" being used by economists to include not only necessary outlays but such net profits as are necessary in the long run to assure productive effort). This expectation rested upon the hypothesis that these lines of industry are closely dependent upon natural resources, which are unequal in their productiveness, so that there is a natural "resistance" to expansion. There followed the comfortable conclusion that there were automatic brakes on overproduction. This applied to "the long run," but it was usually applied to existing conditions also, and hence it was held that the ruling price at a given time could be imagined to hold everything in a proper balance and that there would always be a tendency for price normally to seek an equilibrium or stable level. It is this self-balancing equilibrium, established by the potent "unseen hand" of free competition, which captivated the minds of generations of economists and which today, in spite of great changes in the economic structure, is still imagined to be the cardinal principle of all trade. The reason for the plausibility of this doctrine lies in the subtle concept of "long-term equilibrium." Cyclical stability is confused with a long-term average of normal equilibrium. "Sea level" becomes so well defined that the storm-raised waves no longer need be considered!

In recent years more and more attention has been given to the manner in which the so-called "schedules of demand" (expressing at a given time the relation of price offers to quantity potentials) have considerable *cyclical instability* and the effect that this may have in creating a series of disturbances before a new position of equilibrium or stability is achieved. We have already had occasion to observe the manner in which major wars bring about wide shifts in the position of the demand pattern in the case of products of the extractive industries. Such shifts are in the nature of a more or less *vertical* elevation of demand schedules under the pressure of inflationary public spending and, also, *horizontal* shifting in response to the urgent need for essential supplies. As these forces cease to operate, the reverse demand movement, downward and horizontally contracting, take place, and it is this weakening of the entire demand structure that forms the central problem that we are now discussing in terms of depression price disparity, particularly as it affects highly competitive producers.

EFFECTS OF COMPETITIVE MARKETS

Let us consider how a weakening of total demand for a basic farm product is thought to work out its effects under what is loosely termed a "completely competitive set of conditions." There is a prevalent tendency to argue in some such fashion as this: As demand weakens and the schedule of price-quantity relationship shifts to the left or downward, the price at which *all* the quantity available can be sold naturally declines. This is imagined to impinge upon the costs of producers, so that there *is a fairly prompt response* in the reduction of supply by limitation of future production. This is expected, since the cost situation is presumed to be fixed; it cannot be materially revised. The various producers have unequal costs, largely associated with the relative advantages of their *natural* resources and location, and the pattern or array of individual costs, each weighted according to the portion of total product associated with that cost, tends to rise rather steeply as we pass from the lowest to the highest. Unfortunately, statistical measurements of such cost arrays are conspicuous blind spots in our economic knowledge; it can be stated with some assurance that in the extractive industries the disparity between the lowest and the highest cost tends to be considerably greater than in the case of modern industrial products in which relatively few large concerns account for a high proportion of the total supply. Now, since a weakening of demand is imagined to bring severe pressure upon the most exposed (high-cost) farmers, if we may continue the agricultural illustration, the corollary is that these are soon driven out of the market; they cease production, and supply naturally rebalances itself in relation to the new position of demand, and price is again stabilized near its "normal equilibrium" level. The readjustment does not greatly affect the more favored, low-cost producers; to be sure, they accept lower profit,[1] but the adjustment is essentially one in the "marginal" area, and competitive markets are imagined to have these critical marginal fringes, which absorb the shocks and protect the industry as a whole from serious or cumulative maladjustments. It is usually assumed, without further examination of the facts, that with every important shift, as demand conditions weaken in a depression, there is an *elimination* of supply, if not immediately, at any rate over the "near term." The marginal producers cannot lower their costs any further, because they are *already* supposed to be operating at or near the very minimum of return in all the factors that must be compensated to sustain production at all.

---

[1] Technical economists break this down into cultivator's profit and land rent accruing to the ownership of superior holdings.

This is a very significant assumption, and there are doubts as to whether it is commonly true. There are doubts whether these markets *do* readjust themselves so neatly. First of all, the marginal area in real life does not necessarily involve costs that are inflexibly minimal. There is seldom, in fact, a tendency for the supply of any important farm product to accommodate itself to shifting of demand with anything like the alacrity that theory calls for. We have good evidence that in many of these competitive markets, during a prolonged shift of demand in the wrong direction, supply not only is held remarkably steady but *may even expand for a considerable time against the current*. This may be because, first, cost (per unit of product) of the less efficient producers is not at any time rigidly determined. There is always the possibility that these less fortunate contributors to supply will grind down wages and lower their own standards of family living to almost inconceivable levels in order to hold their position. This is especially true if they can support themselves after a fashion with produce from their land. Finally, in many extractive industries, inferior or poorly situated land, instead of being put *out* of production in times of impaired demand, may merely be shifted to other hands as the result of insolvency, and instead of being removed from production or diverted to other products, it may remain indefinitely in production on a somewhat better scale of cultivation.

Hence the comfortable assumption that competitive markets always adjust themselves flexibly, to the advantage of all concerned, in proportion to their free competitiveness and regardless of changes in demand or supply conditions, is fallacious. The adjustments actually may not affect the quantity at all, and the failure of quantity to adjust itself to change in demand may result in prices that are merely passed along by reducing the standard of living throughout a large segment of a particular industry or nation. The flexibility in competitive markets *is more than price flexibility; it* extends to flexibility in *living standards*. This tends to perpetuate itself as long as hundreds of thousands of sellers cannot coordinate their efforts to adapt supply to demand conditions, if these are subject to cyclical instability, and thus fortify their own buying power for the products of industry. This is as important for enlarging supply, as promptly as technical factors permit, to accommodate enhanced demand, as for such limitation of supply as is necessary when demand shrinks, since slow expansion may produce the familiar result of added income, that ultimately overstimulates production.

We can now attempt a more precise statement of the relation of price change to basic change in demand. If there is no material change in the structure of demand in a perfectly competitive market, a reduction in price does not alter the demand situation but may accompany a somewhat larger amount of product sold. If, on the other hand, demand conditions deteriorate and the demand schedule alters its position, price must be lowered considerably in order to sell, within the normal period, the usual quantity, and it must be lowered even further in order to dispose of any additional quantity. The weakening of demand primarily registers unwillingness or inability of the buyers, *as a group*, to purchase. If quantity is promptly reduced in order to maintain price, it may be reduced mainly in the "marginal" (high-cost) range of production, as expected by traditional theory; or it may be a reduction allocated all along the line, so that every producer shares in the adjustment without substantial impairment of living standards anywhere. The latter is not a result of free competition, however, but rather the result of some coordinated action that goes beyond the range of what we may regard as *perfectly competitive conditions*. The alternative is usually between acceptance by a segment of the industry of lower living standards in order to continue the usual routine production or coordinated action to accomplish reduction along lines that are more or less fair and equitable.

The program of the Agricultural Adjustment Administration in the prevailing revised form (made necessary by the Supreme Court action in 1936) represents the actual use of the latter alternative. It is a realistic recognition of the ruinous effect of competitive conditions in world markets subject to occasional shrinkage of demand in depressions or post-war periods. In a sense, it is a civilized answer to the facile reasonings of rugged individualists. By setting the desired production objectives for a few designated key crops (*e.g.*, wheat, cotton, tobacco) each year and by offering incentives to producers to restrict acreage and agree upon marketing restrictions, the agricultural program aims at stabilization of price and income. It thus contributes an element of stabilization to general economic activity, insofar as farm purchasing power is an influence in industrial demand. Obviously it has imperfections, not only in administration but in principle. It contemplates a more or less insulated national farm economy. It disregards (perhaps necessarily) the possibility that some degree of artificiality in setting annual production quotas may tend to hamper the flow of exports and even to encourage production in other parts of the world outside the range of this system. This implies that such control machinery must be on a broader geographical basis in order to be completely successful in the long run, as there are indications that it is being adopted by other countries.[1] Furthermore, there is the obstinate difficulty that proportionate or "quota" adjustment of production may afford advantages to the high-cost producers and enlarge unduly

---

[1] See the file of *Foreign Agriculture*, published by the U.S. Department of Agriculture, Office of Foreign Agricultural Relations, for summary studies of the control of systems of other countries. The resemblance in principle of many of these programs, even before World War II, to our own farm program is striking.

the profits of the relatively efficient ones.   In dealing with a major or world-wide problem of excess supply, this policy has directness and an element of fairness.   But it should always be supplemented by other measures to lower marginal costs and provide for larger returns to the more efficient producers by reducing the proportion of total supply representing high cost and permitting more volume at low cost for the benefit of consumers.   Only in this way can competitive supply or indirect competition with a given product be prevented from becoming a menace. In any event, "administration" of basic farm prices has already proceeded, with Government sanction a long way and promises to continue in the future.   Yet this great change and its implied repudiation of the virtues of perfect competition (that is, complete helplessness of individual producers to adjust themselves to market changes) have not yet served to alter the persistent criticism of the very same policies, when adopted by industrial management.

The foregoing analysis points toward the conclusion that price is *not* the primary controlling factor when market conditions alter dynamically. To give exclusive attention to price as the controlling element in the automatic equilibrating of markets is to cherish illusion.   The illusion is concealed by overlooking the abjectly depressed human conditions associated in fact and in history with highly competitive extractive industry the world over.   The great peasant populations of the world, including our own sharecroppers in the cotton belt and the field-crop cultivators in the Dust Bowl, all represent examples of the tenacious maintenance of routine production at the cost of progressive or intermittent lowering of standards of human life.   There is no firm resistance offered by alleged "minimum costs" when expressed in terms of the maintenance of serfdom.   When we are told by political economists that it is among industrial companies that price rigidity and overcapitalization are typical, we must remember the lessons of American agriculture between 1915 and 1932 and the solution found for these results of competition.[1]

[1] The details of the present program of Agricultural Adjustment are complex. It may suffice to point out that following the Supreme Court invalidation of the original Agricultural Adjustment Act of 1933, a new plan was developed in 1936, known as the Soil Conservation and Domestic Allotment Plan.   This involved no specific contracts with benefits payable through processing taxes, which had been opposed by the Supreme Court in its previous decision.   Rather, it provided for understandings between growers of designated crops and the Secretary of Agriculture for the payment of conditional benefits financed by Congressional appropriations and directed toward adjustment of planted acreage, with the emphasis upon soil conservation rather than possible restriction of production.   This plan, in turn, was replaced in 1938 by a new Agricultural Adjustment Act, which developed the arrangement into more refined detail, supplementing the plan with marketing agreements under certain conditions and continuing the original 1933 plan for "parity-price payments" to farmers, in

We have thus far briefly considered agriculture as one field in which adjustment of supply conspicuously fails to take place promptly and in accordance with the expectation of the "free-competition" economists. Here it is difficult to enlarge sales, even though prices are cut sharply, and likewise difficult to contract production when demand shifts bodily downward.   But agriculture is not the only field in which large numbers of producers and sellers, with virtually no individual control over markets, find themselves from time to time or chronically in this predicament. The competitive dilemma presents itself in many of the extractive industries.   Producers of minerals and forest products, for example, in the face of marked demand instability, find it relatively difficult to avoid incessant wide variations in prices and disorganization produced by cutthroat competition and blind production that may become chronic.   There are many types of complicating factors in special cases, such as the attempt to exploit natural resources with an unwise use of capital which congeals into

---

addition to the benefits afforded for crop restriction or soil conservation.   There was also involved a plan for crop insurance, applied to a limited number of field crops, in order to establish reserve supplies in the event of unusual scarcity, and a plan for Federal crop loans to enable farmers to borrow on the growing crop and to contribute to Government-held surpluses in the event that they wished to avoid repayment of the loan.

The principal change in emphasis in the recent farm legislation and control administration has been away from the attempt to establish a parity as between farm prices and other prices, but a greater degree of adjustment, or parity, as between total farm income and nonfarm income.   We saw in Chart 14 that in recent years there has been a persistent downward drift in the ratio of farm gross income to total national income.   This has occurred in spite of the fact that the broad drift of farm prices relative to nonagricultural (or general) prices has been upward for many years. There are good reasons for placing the emphasis of crop control and adjustment on *income* relationships rather than on *price* relationships.   The U.S. Department of Agriculture itself has pointed out that price parity "is not always a reliable index of disparity between agriculture and industry.   It assumes that over a period of time prices of all agricultural products will continue to bear the same relations to one another that they bore during the period selected as a base.   In many instances the attainment of parity prices will bring undesirable results, such as impeding the normal consumption of farm products and even reducing the net income of producers below a fair level."   (The Development of Agricultural Policies since the End of the World War *The Agriculture Yearbook*, 1940, p. 320.)

It might be added that a price-parity principle really assumes a cost parity, also, and, indeed, a fixed distribution or the array of costs within the industry.   Nothing could be further from the fact in a dynamic agriculture, experiencing technological changes in rapid succession.   To establish price parity under these conditions in which a fairly large segment of the growers of the crop enjoying the full benefits of improved methods of production and reduction in cost are virtually prevented from attaining a volume that can reduce the cost of food and clothing to the urban population is really tantamount to subsidizing the inefficient.   The writer has actually been in correspondence with representatives of the U.S. Department of Agriculture who

excessive and rigid fixed charges and high profit-loss leverage. Obsolescence may emerge, as in certain phases of the coal industry, where a rigid ceiling extends over the further expansion and where utter demoralization of market conditions can exist if there are many producers.[1] Again, in the oil industry, there is the absurd "law of capture," which requires that every operator actively compete with every other operator to get all the crude oil to the surface as rapidly as possible, since it belongs to him who captures it, regardless of how far underground he may be drawing out petroleum from other people's property. This directly contributes to excessively competitive and reckless development and to price wars in the sale of the products. Competitive overexpansion under favorable demand conditions or the accident of new resource discoveries and, on the other hand, difficulty in contracting supply, once it has been developed, both contribute toward instability, waste, and overexpansion of production capacity in the hands of those who do not put these assets to the best use or draw from them returns that are adequate to maintain satisfactory standards for labor or the maintenance of sound capital structures. It is most unfortunate that the law in the United States, as it now stands, virtually dictates that once we cross the line separating agriculture from other types of production, it is no longer considered important that prices have some semblance of rational stability and that markets be orderly and

---

insist that this practice does no harm so long as the urban wage earner is able to buy *as much* food and clothing with his wages at one period as in a previous period. But technological improvements in agriculture should pass on these benefits to the population as a whole through more efficient agriculture and less subsidized aid to marginal growers.

Although production control seems important and indispensable in the last analysis, neither price parity nor income parity alone afford the *sole* bases for control. Curiously enough, Congress is still appropriating many millions of dollars to pay price-parity benefits, simply because the original concept of price parity is retained in the law. Although the U.S. Department of Agriculture, with its thousands of employees and huge appropriations, collects numerous statistics and studies many aspects of the agricultural problem, it has never contributed much that is useful in the way of estimates capable of affording a view of the actual *cost array* for any important American crop or agricultural product. Regardless of the vagueness that characterizes agricultural "costs" and the flexibility of definition arising from the fact that the farm is also a home and many farmers keep no books, there is nonetheless a challenging problem of ascertaining (even within wide limits) what are the expenses of production at a given time pertaining to the various portions of the total production. If we could have estimates of this character, it would be possible to determine how far the subsidization of the marginal growers is placing an unnecessary burden on an already overexpanded expenditure of public funds and perhaps on the urban consumers and the processing industries.

[1] In the case of bituminous coal, one of the country's most chaotic and unsuccessful industries, the machinery of the NRA has been perpetuated in a Federal Board that regulates prices and market conditions in the industry.

waste of resources be avoided by foresight and sound policy.   Let there be
in any of these nonagricultural industries the slightest attempt by
management to rationalize operations by agreement or understanding
among the firms involved and the policies immediately are subject to legal
attack as being contrary to the Sherman Act and inimical to that great
dogma, or legal fiction, known as "free competition."

DIFFICULTIES CONFRONTING PROCESSORS

Agriculture is closely related to a distinct group of processing industries.   When farmers or livestock raisers release a certain quantity of their
products for sale, it is the responsibility of the processing industries to
accept *all* of what is offered and immediately prepare it for the market.
The farmer usually does not ship his products subject to conditions or
terms, but he sells for what they will bring rather than transport them
back to the farm.   In the typical case the processor is in a position where
he must and will accept what is destined for marketing, and the result is
that he does his best to judge on the basis of experience and in the light of
probable demand conditions and arrives at a price to the farmer that
closely correlates with the ratio of total demand to supply being offered.[1]

In processing industries such as canning, dairy products, flour milling,
meat packing, or tobacco manufactures, there is the characteristic low
cyclical amplitude of demand, that is, the absence of wide swings except
under very abnormal conditions or war emergencies.   The processing
establishment cannot hope to obtain a substantial increase in sales merely
by cutting prices.   It usually has a large investment in plant and characteristically works on a narrow profit margin.   These processing industries differ among themselves as to the degree to which competition prevails among many units.   In the meat industry there are a few dominant
large firms, and the same is true of tobacco manufacture.   The textile
industry, on the other hand, has characteristically been a field of relatively
small enterprise, as we pointed out in Chapter 19.   But regardless of the
average size of the processing firms, there has arisen a feeling in agricultural
circles and among farm politicians that processors always tend to
"exploit" the farmer, because the latter has so little to say as to the
destination or the price of his products (unless they are fresh fruits and
vegetables consigned through cooperative channels direct to the most
promising consuming markets).   When the farmer deals with the meat
packer, the cigarette manufacturer, or the dairy-products company, it is
alleged that he always sells "cheap," while the processor passes the

[1] Or, more precisely, the *rate* at which supplies are being offered as it may vary
from what experience and analysis indicate to be the rate consistent with ready
absorption, without abnormal carry-over, by the expected demand, with seasonal
factors allowed for.

finished product on to consumers at "high" prices. The price spread is considered wide and unreasonable, and some even contend that it is becoming ever wider. In the particular case of milk, farmers have found it desirable to organize cooperative associations that seek to stabilize prices in their bargaining with the dairy firms. In most of the important urban distribution areas, the number of distributing units is relatively small, and they have conspicuously maintained stability in prices of their processed products at retail. But the fact that many milk producers sell through a few processors does not in itself establish the existence of monopoly price control by the latter group. They have an interest in price stability, accomplished by keeping demand and supply in rational relation to each other the year round and from year to year, and, like industry generally, they have an interest in financial solvency, the businesslike handling of capital and technical operating problems, and the constant pressure for higher wages and better living standards on the part of their service men. To brand these objections as monopolistic may be effective rural politics, but it is not necessarily sound economics.

Recently the Federal Government has sought to augment the bargaining strength of the dairy cooperatives in the interest of keeping the prices of fluid milk to the farmer *as high as possible*.[1] Control boards in various states cooperate with the U.S. Department of Agriculture and seek to define *minimum prices* for producers of fluid milk. These apparently are based (at least in some cases) upon the principle of affording to the producer a "satisfactory" price covering cost of production and a "fair profit." When it comes to the processing industries, however, the Government appears to be entirely uninterested in either costs or fair average profits. Although the objective of maintaining stable and high prices for farmers is defended and promoted, any such tendencies in industry are regarded as unfair, contributory to depressions, something to be rooted out by legal inquisition. The implication, although not self-evident, might be construed as leaning toward the ultimate objective of declaring all essential processing industries "public utilities," whose prices would be set by Commissions and whose profits would be regulated as for the electric-power companies or the railroads at present. There has indeed been much discussion of public-utility status being imposed

---

[1] This has been done under the terms of the Agricultural Marketing Agreement Act of 1937, which empowers the Secretary of Agriculture to adjust parity prices upward if he finds that they are unreasonable *in comparison with costs or other conditions* that affect the supply and demand as to milk and its products. See the discussion of this complicated situation in "Economic Standards of Government Price Control," *Monograph* 32, Part 2, Temporary National Economic Committee, Washington, D.C., 1941. With regard to other processing industries, brief comments will be found in A. R. Burns, "The Decline of Competition: A Study of the Evolution of American Industry," Chapter 5, New York and London, 1936.

broadly upon such industries as dairy products, bread, and also petroleum products. This trend of thought, or implied thought, among political economists emphasizes the supposed inability of industrial management to arrive at satisfactory and rational prices and the all-seeing wisdom of public Commissions in imposing such rates or prices as will protect consumers and also the capital structures of the respective industries.[1]

The meat packing industry has been repeatedly criticized by Government agencies seeking to enforce the letter of the Sherman Act. It has been found that in the most important livestock markets the large packing concerns have exercised considerable control over stockyard facilities and over allocation of animal supplies among a few large buyers instead of leaving this to competitive dogfights. But, of course, if the function of the packing industry is to do the best job possible in transforming a perishable moving supply into finished products of high and dependable quality, with the least possible loss of time or material, there seems little from an economic standpoint to complain of if the supply *is* allocated more or less equitably in some proportion among these firms. But it is contended that this violates "free competition," under whose auspices no one shall plan but may only produce and take what comes.[2]

The continued emphasis upon price ratios, price parities, and price spreads has led the U.S. Department of Agriculture to prepare index

[1] In *TNEC Monograph* 32, referred to in the previous footnote, there is some discussion of the experience of Commissions in regulating rates for public utilities in the electric-power field. It is interesting to note that even public-utility regulations have not apparently been too successful in attaining properly adjusted rates, despite the long experience with such regulation in the United States, under both state and Federal authority. There is, in fact, considerable evidence that instead of public-utility rates being set or stabilized to protect consumers, they are actually merely a way of perpetuating capital structures and debt charges translated into "necessary costs" of capital, which, from an economic standpoint, may or may not have any justification. They tend to perpetuate costs that the precepts of Sound Business Practice would not indefinitely tolerate, and the consumers pay the bill.

[2] Arthur Burns comments on the Federal Trade Commission's attitude toward the metal industry and its objection to the agreement for dividing purchases by allocation among the packers, as follows: "According to the commission, the meat packers aimed at a monopoly policy; in order to calculate these prices they estimated the demand for each of the meat products at different prices and the supply of livestock that could be expected at each price offered for it. In fact, however, the calculation of a monopolistic policy would be extremely difficult in this industry; the range of products sold by the packers is so very wide that it would be very difficult to estimate the condition of demand for all products; both the supply and the demand of many of these products are mutually dependent; the supply of livestock over long periods of time is difficult to calculate. The monopoly policy would also be limited by the probability that any success which the large packers might have in widening the margin between costs of production and selling prices would induce the establishment of local packers and the expansion of those already existing." ("The Decline of Competition," New York, p. 179.)

numbers measuring the changes in the average price spread, farmer to consumer, for a group of 58 food products.   This is based on prices paid

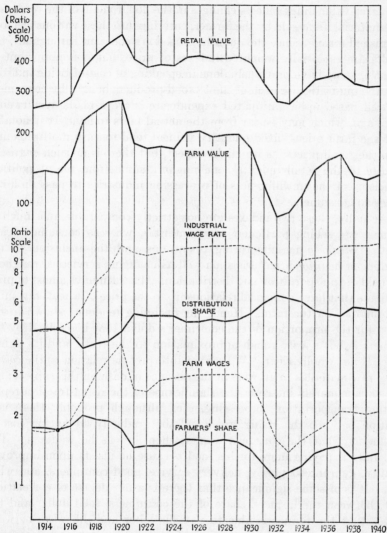

CHART 74.—Farm- and retail price spreads and distribution of shares compared with wage rates, 1913–1940.   The two upper curves are dollar values of a constant group of farm commodities.   The lower curves are relative to 1915, and show the respective distribution shares compared with industrial wage rates and farm wage rates.

to farmers and final retail prices paid by consumers, which include the costs of transportation, processing, marketing, and distribution.   Chart 74 shows the results from 1913 to 1940.   The retail and farm "values" at the top of the chart actually are based on the dollar amounts that typical wage-earner families are estimated to spend, at current prices, for a fixed quantity of various meat products, cereal products, canned goods, etc. The farm-value index reflects changes in the dollar value of the *equivalent* raw-material items sold by the farmer, entering into these various 58 foods in finished form.　Since the quantities used are constant throughout, the results are essentially weighted indexes of price, but it is important to observe, as we have previously done in speaking of cost-of-living indexes, that the quantities for each of the 58 food products bought by consumers are still based upon antiquated expenditure surveys made over twenty years ago, which may be far from the actual facts today.　It is notable that the farm prices (fixed quantity values) tend to vary more violently than the retail prices, as we might expect, but there is no such degree of *rigidity* in the retail index as one might assume from recent political criticisms of the unwillingness of processing industries to pass on lower prices to consumers.

Actually, these two indexes are not strictly comparable, inasmuch as farmers are selling particular raw materials, whereas consumer prices involve *changing* manufacturing operations and the inclusion in the product of *additional* materials, as well as changing services throughout the field of transportation and distribution.　These involve a host of price elements that have no logical relationship to the price of wheat, raw milk, or tomatoes on the farm.　Hence the declining tendency shown in the chart for the proportion of the consumer's dollar that is received by the farmers is but a very rough approximation to the truth, and its significance is not wholly clear.　We cannot interpret its relation to the *cost* of these raw materials to growers in the absence of data on this subject; nor can we adequately interpret the significance of the rising fraction representing transportation, processing, etc., although probably there is a relation between this rising trend and the gradually advancing cost of producing what the consumer wants when and as he wants it.　The consumer is paying more for his food because he insists upon improved quality, guaranteed purity, delivery service, good containers, and what not.　It is of some significance that there is a fair degree of correlation, first, between the farmers' share of the consumers' food dollar and the wages that the farmer is able to pay his labor and, likewise, between industrial wage rates, fairly typical of the distribution and processing fields, and the marketing differential.[1]　But in the hands of those who are particularly sympathetic with the farmers' problems or antipathetic to

[1] The indexes of price spreads are explained in a bulletin of the U.S. Department of Agriculture, Bureau of Agricultural Economics, Division of Marketing Research, entitled "Price Spreads between the Farmer and the Consumer," by R. O. Been, Jr., and F. V. Waugh, Washington, D.C., July, 1936.　Supplementary issues of the data

business enterprise in any form, these tendencies can be effectively used in emotional appeals, as illustrated by the remark that the changes in retail values "are passed back to the farmer in the form of extremely violent fluctuations in farm value" or in implications that the farmer is not being given justice by consumers or the processing-distribution system. If these figures demonstrate anything, they clearly demonstrate that labor standards are far better maintained by the manner in which industry and processing do their work than the way in which good, bad, and indifferent farmers do their work in spite of Government assistance. What is actually important in the food business is the demand by consumers for an increasingly complex aggregate of utilities superimposed upon farm raw materials, and all these cost money.

With respect to at least a number of the basic agricultural products, we may here repeat what was said in an earlier chapter concerning several characteristics of agriculture that have been inherently contributory to lack of farm prosperity and stability of income. There has been far too much dependence upon a fickle, highly variable, foreign market. We have now learned a hard lesson concerning the advisability of serving such markets and exposing farm operators to these unnecessary hazards. And we have learned the lesson of overconcentration by farmers in a

---

may be found for more recent periods, particularly the issue of February, 1940. See also the data given in U.S. Department of Agriculture *Agricultural Statistics*, 1941, p. 582.

An index of the monthly average cost of distribution of food in the United States has been prepared by the New York State College of Agriculture, Cornell University, published regularly in *Farm Economics*. It is of interest to note in this connection the remarks by F. A. Harper, *Farm Economics*, September, 1941, in summarizing the results of a study of the profits realized by large food-processing and marketing corporations in 1940. The data assembled for 18 corporations, averaging in that year 270 million dollars of sales per company, led to the conclusion that "the net income for all corporations combined was 1.9 per cent of sales. This allows no deduction as return to those who invested the capital fund, and so this figure overstates what should be considered excessive profits. Some return to investors is allowable, the same as interest to bondholders or salaries and wages to employees. A business cannot operate without the investment of such funds or its equivalent. A return on these capital funds serves the necessary purpose of inducement to save and invest. . . . If 5 per cent on net equity is allowed, the remaining profits were only 0.7 per cent of sales, varying from 0.1 per cent to 1.6 per cent for different types of business. Three of the 18 corporations suffered loss even on this basis. . . .

"As a group, they do not seem to have large profits relative to their size of business, if a fair return is allowed for invested capital. Possibly, much of the profits that do exist are due to basic efficiencies that are possible because of their large size. We should be careful not to destroy any such efficiencies, or the result would be to widen the marketing spread rather than to narrow it. Any grievances against the large-sized marketing corporations other than the accusation of excessive profits should be treated as separate and distinct problems." P. 3170.

single crop involving the focusing of risk, both natural and economic. Fortunately this tendency is now giving way to more rapid progress in diversification of products and the inclusion of more animal raising, which enjoys an expanding urban market. If farm experts will work along the lines of enlarging the scope of diversification, particularly the possibilities for wide industrial uses for farm products, we can perhaps successfully bury many of these traditional illusions regarding "just prices," which, if applied too rigorously and narrowly, threaten to place handicaps on processing efficiency out of all relation to the benefits achieved for producers.

MONOPOLISTIC TENDENCIES IN DURABLE-GOODS INDUSTRIES

Let us examine a little more carefully the case of manufactured products, particularly durable goods, in which markets it is alleged in some quarters that unfair and cyclically disturbing price-making practices flourish along with excessive variations in production. Let it be said at the outset that there is an abundance of price records to show clearly that the manufactured goods as a group have preserved more stability in their prices, as paid by final buyers, than have the raw materials used. This is true of these industries abroad as well as in this country. It is also true that there has been remarkable progress in the direction of conscious control of production and price through the possession of patents good for many years or through enlargement of the scale of enterprise in corporate form, bringing a progressive reduction in the number of independent units serving a particular market. "The decline of competition" has indeed been an accompaniment of this trend. But observe that by competition we emphasize usually the existence of a large multitude of sellers, their independence of each other, and their inability individually to affect market conditions within a given product. It has escaped the attention of many of those who lament the passing of what they regard as the great institution of price competition that these trends have brought with them a new form of competition arising from the ever-widening latitude of choice among a bewildering variety of products that exposes each one of them to more severe competition *for the consumer's dollar*. It is true that large business enterprise may encompass groups of these commodities within the scope of quasi-monopolistic operations; even so, the variety of things that modern civilization and a progressive technology make available creates *product* competition of an entirely different order from that which has ever before confronted the average consumer.

It is a familiar fact that throughout modern industry the scale of managerial operations has enlarged through internal expansion and that this affords a peculiar degree of latitude for management to determine the potential effect of price upon sales. Similarly, deliberate control is possible as to the rate of output. In a few cases there is so close an approach to control of supply that the few small competitors are unimportant. The popular conception of "monopoly" is that it naturally exacts the highest possible prices and severely restricts production to maintain those prices so that monopolistic profits, over and above the average rate of profit in competitive lines, may be maintained. What the popular view ignores is that the number of cases in which a given product is entirely protected from the competition of actual or potential substitutes is negligible. We no longer live in the simple rural civilization in which commodities were few and transportation facilities were primitive. In the phrase of Edward H. Chamberlin,[1] we have today very few, if any, cases of complete monopoly, but many cases of "monopolistic competition," where sellers are few. As the variety of products multiplies, it naturally follows that each is represented by fewer makers, even though some producers engage in making more than one article. It is possible for a given firm to "monopolize" a style, a design, or, for a short time, a grade or price class, but the profusion of types and the vast proliferation of new things smothers any possibility of long-enduring complete monopolization in the sense of exorbitant price and fractional supply. Cases may be found, but they turn out to be gadgets, not fundamental goods.

The important questions to consider are (1) whether it is reasonable to assume that the price determined by individual sellers, who are few in number and who make some agreement among themselves, must be assumed to be "high" price and (2) whether general economic interest in terms of the cyclical stability of trade conditions and enhancement of real national income are antagonized if the prices in such fields are so determined that they appear stable or inflexible over relatively long periods or over cyclical periods. Since a stable price maintained through the entire course of a typical business cycle may sooner or later be contrasted with the violent decline in certain raw materials, that price always invites the criticism that it is "too high." It is perfectly natural that it should be assailed as unfairly rigid. The price should accommodate itself to permit an impaired demand to continue to absorb the commodity and thus expand, or at least maintain, production and sale.

Let us consider this situation from the long-term standpoint. We are all familiar with cases of important commodities showing a progressively declining tendency in price along with increasing volume and a broadening of sales, even though during the process there has also been a rapid reduction in number of business units. On the other hand, there are cases in which certain commodities have somehow been held at a steady price for

---

[1] See his "Theory of Monopolistic Competition," *Harvard Economic Studies*, Vol. 38, Cambridge, 1933.

a decade or more, under conditions that appear to be "monopolistic competition" or total monopoly. In truth, the economic record reveals a wide disparity in results as to both prices and the degree of enlargement of production and sales. There is a tendency to argue that *unless* prices are permitted to decline continuously, the small group that controls production is unfair to the public and consumers. But each case must be examined *on its merits* and with a view to the peculiarities of the industry, the product, and the degree to which it represents an innovation or a fully mature or even obsolescent industry.

In the familiar case of the automobile, we know that prices have been reduced and quality steadily improved as production has expanded. The gradual decline in price has represented a process of interaction whereby rapid enlargement of the scale of operations permitted lower unit costs, which, in turn, made possible still lower prices and expansion of sales to the income strata that could not be reached at the beginning of the new industry. Consumers gradually allocated more of their income to the new market and, indeed, were able to expand their total income as a result of the very growth of a giant industry. Such conspicuous cases have led to serious misconceptions as to the nature of a demand pattern as it appears at a given time. It is commonly assumed that since motorcar production increased with prices falling, there is a notably "elastic" type of demand for cars and similar things. But what actually has occurred in this and similar cases is an *expansion* of demand that involved a shifting, along the axis of production, of a typically inelastic schedule. After the period of dynamic growth has ended and a market becomes essentially one of replacements, the possibility of further expansion is limited, and further price reduction (relative to general prices) can be attained only by unusual technical improvements. The practical significance of this is that historical trends of price involving marked reduction in unit costs are not to be regarded as proving that at any given moment, or for any and every manufactured product, a lowering of price, regardless of demand and cost conditions *at that time*, will *automatically* sell more goods. In the particular case of producer goods, industrial equipment, etc., such an expectation would be still less realistic, since in these markets demand patterns are extremely inelastic over short periods and price cannot readily be lowered by expanded volume. In fact, so far as concerns elasticity of demand pattern, most manufactures, including both consumer and producer goods, have highly inelastic patterns, and for this reason relatively drastic price reduction is necessary if any appreciable gain in sales is to be accomplished *within limited time periods* and even if no impairment in the demand position is taking place.

As a product becomes well worked into the economic system, it becomes increasingly difficult to obtain more distribution, whether conditions are purely competitive or highly monopolistic. Price may decline as the result of improved production methods, but this decline also has limits. In some of these cases prices cannot easily be lowered with increasing volume, because there is a high proportion of direct cost, and the unit cost fails to decline over a wide range of added volume. What is needed here is specific analysis, industry by industry,[1] with full appreciation of all surrounding and pertinent factors.

Manufacturing enterprise has translated technological initiative and progress into higher wage rates and real income per worker and in the typical case has lowered price *relative to raw-material prices*. Obviously, if it is important that these gains be translated largely into labor income, we cannot expect progress to take the form of still more emphatically lower prices. If farmers insist on higher prices to attain parity with urban wages and industrial labor demands adequate wages, price can be reduced only by marked gains in efficiency, and this requires both ample capital and a reasonable profit incentive. This raises questions of cost and the legitimacy of cost calculations. It raises the question of how much profit incentive should be properly included in economic cost and how much provision for capital development, maintenance, and reserves should be allowed for in accounting costs. We are sometimes told that business costs are inventions of the accountants and can be manipulated as managerial accountancy may desire. It is claimed that they include much fictitious padding and hence are not a fair basis for determining the degree of impairment that drastic price reduction might actually cause. Of course, in complex modern industrial organization, the establishment of certain costs pertaining to capital provision and reserves *for the future* involves human judgment; there are no hard-and-fast rules for cost allowances that are not cash expense items. Just what "cost of production," in the accounting sense, must necessarily be recovered from revenue to get definite solvency limits? And in the economic sense, how much profit is a "necessary" allowance in total cost to assure continued existence of a business unit and the incentive to fully efficient operation? And how many years of fluctuation in net profit should constitute a fair average of good and bad?

The answer to these questions is that under modern market conditions, if costs are inadequate, efficiency lapses; if they are set extravagantly high to pad profits, *product competition* becomes merciless. "The man

---

[1] Attention is called to the important pioneering studies to Joel Dean, of the University of Chicago, directed toward determining statistically, from actual business records, what changes in unit cost (both average and differential) result from varying combinations of factors in a given establishment and under different conditions of volume of output. See his study "Statistical Determination of Cost, with Special Reference to Marginal Cost," University of Chicago Press, Chicago, 1936.

who today tries to fence in an industrial highway and exact an exorbitant toll from those who would travel this road to consumer satisfaction is in danger of defeating himself. Under modern conditions of technology, applied science is likely to find other methods of progress. The chemist will build a detour around him, the physicist will drive a tunnel under him, or a biological overpass will be devised."[1] Furthermore, direct costs tend to be more nearly uniform among the limited suppliers in industry than among very numerous competitors. At any given time the spread between lowest and highest "necessary" costs in most types of agriculture is very wide; an abrupt lowering of price can completely eliminate all profit and force down wage income in the higher cost range, but it would have to be tremendously severe to impair profits much in the lower cost range. Conversely, a marked raising of price can enormously increase profits of a substantial proportion of the producers. But in the typical case of large-scale concentrated manufacturing, the array of necessary costs is more uniform (although never equalized). Hence severe lowering of price not only can wipe out profit for almost all units but can cut deeply into revenue needed for *direct outlays*. Hence a slash of prices tends to be a *direct attack on solvency all along the line*. Even failure to discharge overhead obligations can be ruinous to modern business organization.[2]

In modern industry, accounting practices have been brought to a high degree of scientific development. They are under the scrutiny of bankers, investors and customers, organized labor, and such Federal agencies as the Treasury Department and the SEC. Cost allowances in a given case may represent excessive padding, guesswork, or concealment of business savings; but this does not mean that the modern management unit, small or large, lacks integrity or can, by and large, set its prices according to cost schedules that can be easily rigged. In the setting up of costs to guide production and price, even under conditions of "monopolistic competition," management may perhaps rightfully expect that its estimates may serve as legitimately for its objectives as the farm costs that are usually so vaguely conceived that prices for years at a time may have no relation whatsoever to any specific cost data and subsidies are sought on the basis of price in relation to *other prices* but not to *actual outlays*. In some instances it is well recognized that manufacturing enterprise has failed to see the practical advantages of large-scale output of a type of product designed for simplicity and severe economy and

[1] E. G. Nourse and H. B. Drury, "Industrial Price Policies and Economic Progress," p. 221, Brookings Institution, Washington, D.C., 1938.

[2] The classical economists, looking always at their will-o'-the-wisp the "long run" and ignoring intermediate consequences, comforted themselves by supposing that a firm could always struggle on so long as its *direct* costs were met. Overhead and capital charges could somehow always be postponed until the storm was over.

capable of low-price mass distribution. In many kinds of specialized industrial equipment for which the market is narrow, mass production and low price are virtually impossible of attainment, although methods of production can and should be continually improved to secure lower unit costs. But none of these cases has any necessary correlation with size, control of supply, patent privilege, or even the corporate form of organization. They are not features of the *price problem* that can legitimately be exploited as pointing to inherent defects in "big business" or "modern management" as an institution.

PROBLEMS OF PRICE STABILIZATION

A substantial shrinkage in demand associated with cyclical decline in national income represents new conditions under which it is impossible to maintain *constant* sales or production *unless price were reduced to an extreme degree*. This is the important point. A reduction of price of mild, intermediate degree would still involve contraction of sales. But apart from this, there is a psychological factor to consider that will bring about cumulative tendencies. If there is an initial price cut, many buyers will simply wait for further cuts, and if these are made they will expect still further concessions. Instead of the market stabilizing, with sales being actively resumed at the lower price, there probably would be utter demoralization through the reluctance of consumers to buy at all. These psychological spirals are important, even though the classical price-competition economists have ignored them. The businessman knows that they occur and that they can be of vast effectiveness in the wrecking of a market or, under the converse conditions in an inflationary situation, in precipitating an unhealthy boom condition.

Reduction in sales is inevitable under the conditions that we have indicated, unless price is reduced so much that it threatens further demoralization by anticipation of further cuts, and such a policy may not merely wipe out profits and surplus but force equally drastic reductions in wage rates and impairment of the ability of labor to hold its wage gains during cyclical fluctuations. Of course, capital integrity means little to those who take modern business organizations for granted, but elaborate industrial organization is not a thing to be taken for granted, and no management can afford to overlook the hazards of bankruptcy any more than wage earner consumers as a group will overlook the pounding down of wage rates that price chiselers usually achieve. Under these conditions the investor is usually called upon to expect a lower return in dividends or omission of return. Corporate management, however, is actually encouraged by our political policies to maintain dividends at too high a level when revenues are temporarily expanding. It is at precisely this point that we must be reminded of the supreme importance of stabilizing income flow so far as possible without throwing all the burden on this or that group. These matters cannot be left to mere revision of *price* quotations; that is no answer. To expect price changes to right the situation is to reveal confusion of thought, since anyone who places his faith in price juggling to overcome *income distortion* is plainly directing his attention to *static* demand schedules rather than the dynamic shifting of demand that is the manifestation of cyclical disturbance.

It is essential to cut price to move a standing surplus of what has been already created. Price is a means of rectifying fortuitous scarcity and unplanned excess. It is a crude means of correcting accidents and mistakes *after* they have occurred. But where rational planning is possible, the adjustment of production to the optimum level consistent with ready sale and coverage of *all* legitimate economic costs is not merely a price problem. To be sure, curtailing the production of X when consumer income, following overproduction of Y, is declining, is unfortunate, since it means more unemployment *added* to what has already occurred. But this is an inevitable result of forces over which any one management, regardless of its size, has little if any control. The business cycle impinges upon manufacturing almost entirely from *specific* excesses and maladjustments, usually *outside manufacturing enterprise itself*. Ignoring this simple fact accounts for much erroneous and shallow thinking on this subject. When promotional enterprise affecting building, transport, power, military activity, or other basic "prime movers" release their demands upon industrial fabrication, they affect a highly sensitized mechanism. It is geared to respond flexibly to these stimuli; its response sets up additional stimuli that create the typical cumulative spiral of new orders, production, employment, payrolls. Naturally, when the basic forces that start the process fade out or collapse of their own weight, the ramifying spirals of activity begin to reverse and contract. The question then becomes one of alternatives. Should industrial goods produced currently at a faster rate than change in income, which is *now impaired by contraction in the prime movers*, be put on the bargain counter to fit the shrinking income?

So far as concerns *existing stocks* in the hands of dealers, producers, or bankers, certainly *yes, and as quickly as possible*. Ordinarily, the shrinkage in income, instead of being restricted to the few important segments where basic forces are moving in reverse (*e.g.*, house building), tends to spread about as weakness in one part affects the whole. This involves a spreading of the very forces of contraction by curtailing production and payrolls far beyond the segments of original disturbance. But the alternative of drastic price readjustment would be even more disastrous, since it would not prevent considerable production curtailment, and it would either force down wage scales or destroy solvency. Even large surplus and access of manufacturers to borrowed capital could not be counted upon to continue the direct outlays necessary to keep employment constant. Labor would be forced to accept either drastic wage cuts or temporary unemployment. Since experience has amply proved that wage scales, once cut, are difficult to restore, organized labor will not tolerate wage readjustment, which rules out that alternative for all practical purposes. The result is that production is restricted until the original disturbing situations are brought under control and readjustment. Unfortunately, total production is curtailed far more than would have been necessary, because there was no way to isolate the disturbing factors or segments and quarantine them.

This is the heart of the cyclical problem. We must develop ways of protecting the sensitized industrial mechanism from these intrusions of speculative, promotional, or political aberration that initiate the spirals of the cycle, or we must provide compensatory income devices to cancel their cyclical effect, as described in Chapter 21. If we are seeking such a positive solution to achieve more stability of real income, why must we waste time and effort with false and deceptive precepts that glorify *price* instability and are capable, if pushed far enough by uncompromising legalists, of creating permanent impairment of capital structure in the vain hope of gaining temporary maintenance of buying power? To the fanatical Marxist, concern for capital, management, and solvency, of course, counts for nothing, and the problem cannot be argued with those who conceive it in terms of totalitarian collectivism. Although such a system may have merit, its advantages should not be predicated upon fallacious analysis of why our system of private initiative and capitalism has occasionally suffered breakdowns. And if we seek a solution, we should not be confused by the advice of those who are in reality advising a change of system, not a remedy for cyclical instability.[1]

[1] The response of industrial management to weakening demand through reducing output affords a convenient pretext for the accusation that "business always and deliberately restricts full production." This becomes easily mixed up with discussion of patent abuses, international cartels, monopoly privilege, etc., and results in allegations of sweeping character or subtle innuendo of disparagement of all industrial organization of any substantial character. To insist that all industry must keep on producing without making provision for either income compensation, unemployment reserves, or prompt liquidation of basic excesses is merely to argue that insolvency of business itself is of no concern.

There is a further technical point involved here in connection with industrial management in the early stages of depression. To apply the principle of "flexible" price in a mechanical way would require that upon every incipient wavering of demand, or the effect of a weak situation in one important commodity, prices should be immediately revised. Such a requirement could not possibly be fulfilled, in view of the necessity of quoting prices well in advance of delivery in the case of many industrial goods and materials.

Consider now the dynamic short-term aspects of markets in which the sellers are few. Should price policy, as a general rule, be in the direction of *cyclical* variability? Does the effort to maintain price stability create or accentuate major booms and depressions? Can price policy in industrial markets counteract the shifting movements of total demand? If prices are cut to counter depression, should they be raised again when conditions improve? If so, how do the "long-run" *average* results differ from stable prices? May they not turn out to be actually higher? Consider the case of an incipient depression. Should those who "administer" the prices of automobiles begin to reduce prices, or should they maintain prices with little or no change? It is important to understand clearly the nature of *demand* under these conditions. Notice that it is a matter not of selling more goods at lower prices but of attempting to use price policy *as a weapon to stem a general contraction in income and expenditure.* What would probably be the result of a drastic reduction in price in the face of an unfavorable shift in demand? Knowing that the demand pattern in the case of durable consumer goods tends to be relatively inelastic at a given time (even though its dynamic changes of *position* may be elastic in the sense of shifting over a wide range under varying conditions of trend or cycle), it is difficult to discover what useful result would be accomplished.

Conversely, let us examine the case of price policy in periods of excessive business expansion and too fast a pace in creation of income and the purchase of durable goods. Is it the function of *price raising* to put brakes upon such income flow? Can we stop a building boom by price boosting? We have tried it in the case of interest rates, wage rates, and other prices, but these have all failed to bring adequate results within any reasonable time. Here again we must emphasize that the raising of prices during boom times is not at all an effective means of putting a brake upon the expansion as it usually arises from the superior driving force of innovation, the need for housing, the movements of population, or, most imperious of all, the demands of military emergency. *None of these forces will bow to price*, and raising price merely adds fuel to the explosive forces. Hence the writer doubts the legitimacy of the assertion that elastic prices limit booms any more than they stop depressions. Considering the cumulative spirals of anticipation, booms are invariably carried to greater heights under the stimulus of price, just as depressions are deepened by well-meaning but stupid attempts to match dwindling incomes by bankruptcy prices. We cannot stimulate buyers by low prices when they have no money, nor can we place barriers in the way of blind competitive promotion when its effects in various major directions distend national money income. It is often overlooked that a reasonable degree of price stability is a check upon the cumulative and speculative tendency in a boom condition, just as it is a check upon a destructive spiral of excessive deflation when recession occurs. The alleged virtues of "flexible" prices are usually extolled to convince the ignorant that they *reduce* living costs, but not much is said of the reverse action in accelerating boom conditions and creating a fictitious level of general money income that soon becomes vulnerable to collapse. We cannot hope to stabilize the trend of real income by unstabilizing the trend of prices, but we *can* stabilize *both* if we analyze our dynamic forces thoroughly and in a scientific spirit.   To be sure, depression reveals plenty of situations in which price was held too high in the previous boom, and readjustment through product competition comes about abruptly rather than gradually.   But this merely means that such competition does work, however prices are set.

It seems unlikely that we shall find any simple or uniform test to establish within short periods the true significance of price relationships. Stability of price may be sound in one case and not in another.   We may compare the trend of prices with the trend of wages or with the trend of dividends and interest; we may relate total cost or variable cost or overhead cost to various other factors.   There are many possible combinations and comparisons; but no one set of these relationships, *based merely upon price*, is likely to be a fair and logical test of balance for all industries.   Business units are organisms; they form distinct groups and subgroups, but their character and vitality are not readily measurable merely with a foot rule or a pair of scales.   Willard Thorp established the following very significant conclusions from an examination of the performance between 1929 and 1933 of 117 industries and 1807 products.[1] The price and production policies for some products resulted in stable prices, but the contention that these "price and production policies were more widely characteristic of products manufactured under conditions of high concentration [of control] is definitely not tenable.   The determination by a concern of a price and production policy which manifests itself in rigid prices accompanied by curtailed output would appear from this material to be conditioned by some circumstances other than the potential or actual control over the supply of the product."   For the period 1933–1937, the same general conclusion was derived.   To quote further, "Most important is the demonstration, with better evidence than has ever before been available, that the degree of concentration in production is not a significant factor in determining price-quantity behavior of manu-

---

[1] In *Monograph* 27; see also his summary, under the title Price Policy and Business Behavior, *American Economic Review*, February, 1941, Supplement, pp. 390*ff.*

factured products with reference to the business cycle. . . . It does imply that so-called 'price rigidity' is not in any considerable degree a function of the extent of concentration.   Rather, the price-quantity patterns as well as the degree of concentration appear to be directly related to the economic characteristics of the commodities involved."

This conclusion of an experienced and discriminating observer of business should be kept before us as we study particular situations and cases, noting the importance of specific features of the structure of an industry or of a business unit, apart from mere size or the proportion of total output that it accounts for.   There may be an unsound financial structure that interferes with a correct price policy.   Excessive fixed charges cannot be reconciled with sound prices, whether these are steady or variable.   They will in that case be stable at an excessively high level or violently competitive and unstable.   There may be abnormalities, such as the attempt of individual financial groups to magnify their power through unnecessary holding-company devices.   There may be mergers of company with company, having no observable economic justification other than to furnish securities for bankers to distribute.   There may be such stupid or poorly administered public regulation of price, as in the case of public utility corporations, that there is a peculiarly dangerous correlation between price level and increasingly frozen financial structures and perhaps the withering hand of obsolescence lurking in the background.   Price stability and capital flexibility are sound, but frozen-debt burdens as an excuse for frozen prices are unsound.

We must observe whether, in those industries that feel (or have felt) the baneful effect of the major cycles of construction, prices are kept at high levels as a defensive device to counteract the extreme length and depth of the depressions.   This has apparently occurred in many cases and has been intensified by labor pressure arising from the same desire to cash in when times are good in despair of any income at all when times are bad.   The answer to all these situations is not variable prices but a reasonable level of stable prices, once these basic factors can be effectively stabilized for more continuous activity.   In examining business structures and price policies, we must know how far the industry or company has been exposed to the distorting effects of war.   We must know approximately the stage of maturity at which an industry or firm has arrived before we can compare its performance with respect to prices, costs, payrolls, or any other test of efficiency with something else.   We must also distinguish the durable goods from the nondurables, producer goods from consumer goods.   Among the latter are those that promise little room for further growth in per capita volume and that can fight against obsolescence and meet product competition only through better organization, better coordination, and a greater use of capital for enhanced efficiency. Low price can result from these, but low price artificially dictated will not necessarily produce it.[1]

To maintain the sensitive prices of agricultural products on a more stable basis and to minimize the antagonism of rural politicians to corporate enterprise, it is necessary to guard against war inflation. The requirements for this are (1) to prevent wartime agrarian inflation of prices, (2) to prevent unnecessary increase in rural debt, and (3) to devise ways of readjusting the usual heavy war production of foods in orderly fashion when abnormal supplies are no longer needed. Preventive action in all phases of economic stabilization is the only effective action.

As for inflation control, the basic requirement is that superfluous income, released by the public expenditure for arms and other war essentials, should be promptly recaptured to restrict its circulation and pyramiding through credit devices in the channels of voluntary civilian purchase or investment. Like so many other aspects of stabilization, it is an *income problem.* By taxation directed squarely at expanding incomes, the borrowing away of much of that income promptly before it becomes invested otherwise, and by removing entirely from the markets

---

[1] The "Final Report and Recommendations" of the Temporary National Economic Committee contains some sound and instructive comment on the need for scrutiny and regulation to prevent undesirable financial features in corporate enterprise as a means of preventing frozen prices. But there is inadequate attention given to the fact that *manufacturing industry* has not revealed such defects on a scale at all comparable with several other segments of our economy.

The monographs of the TNEC at several points contain references to tests of the efficiency or satisfactory performance of industries and companies. In *Monograph* 13 there is an elaborate attempt to measure efficiency in terms of cost of production correlated with size of unit. Relative efficiency of large, medium-sized, and small business was compared by the Federal Trade Commission for the Committee. W. J. Ballinger studied companies in 18 industries from the standpoint of cost-of-production arrays. Both cost of production and rate of return on invested capital were investigated. The data used do not refer to identical dates; in fact, some are taken from records 30 years old. This greatly qualifies the general conclusion to the effect that "the results of the total test reveal that the largest companies made, on the whole, a very poor showing. This should not be taken to mean that in every test all medium-sized or small companies have lower costs or better rates of return on invested capital than the largest company. . . . Certain efficient, medium-sized units—and in some industries certain efficient small units—generally made the best showing." (P. 10.) The very nature of the data used and the obvious bias revealed in the text commentary throw doubt upon the significance of these conclusions. Not until we have proper statistics and know the nature of the industry and a great deal more about the setting can we use costs or rates of return as measures of efficiency.

More ambitious and involved have been the statistical tests of the "social performance" of business devised by Theodore J. Kreps. In *Monograph* 7 of the series, Kreps presents data for 22 industries that are measured according to a *uniform* scheme comprising the following elements: trend of production, employment, payroll, ratio of employment to production, ratio of payrolls to net value of product, ratio of produc-

the opportunity to acquire various nonmilitary goods, the national income can be directed into channels capable of supplying the needed war goods and equipment. Price-fixing is not, in itself, the answer. In order to hold prices down, it is necessary to hold private incomes down and to restrict to the limit the use of consumer credit and the access of purely civilian business to bank credit or the long-term capital markets. These policies have been effectively applied in the present War effort. In a democracy prompt action along the proper lines is difficult to achieve, but the action taken in 1941–1942 to control inflation in the United States has promise of being much more effective than in World War I. It is highly probable that agriculture will not expand its indebtedness with the reckless abandon witnessed in the earlier conflict and the postwar situation will not be one of such wide disparity between price-income levels and debt-tax changes. Since so much of the farm tirade against urban prices has really arisen from inflated farm debts in postwar periods, this particular prospect can be considered a favorable one. Whether it will be possible to avoid war overexpansion of farm production, capable of

---

tion to deflated net value of product, and the ratio of payrolls to dividend and interest payment.

Unfortunately, the data begin in most cases at 1919, and in exhibiting these elements of measurement in terms of index numbers, with bases 1923–1925, or 1927, there is possible a considerable distortion due to arbitrary selection of base. This is particularly true of the comparisons between dividend and interest payments in the various industries and the patterns of their payrolls or production. In order to show these relationships in true perspective, it would be desirable to carry the measurements back through World War I, inasmuch as there were distortions during that period affecting relative production and financial payments. By selecting a base for the graphic exhibits (which form an important part of the presentation) in the postwar period and prior to 1929, the result naturally suggests an exorbitant rise in 1929 in payments to capital, as compared with labor income or net value of product (essentially "value added" by manufacture). If we consult Robert F. Martin's "National Income in the United States" (1939) and note the estimates of income payments to labor, on the one hand, and payments of dividends and interest, on the other, at 1910 and 1929, we find that instead of capital payments having far outrun labor payments, they both advanced during this period about equally. And the decline from 1929 in total dividend and interest payments to the bottom of the depression (1933) was again almost exactly proportionate in the two groups; Kreps' charts make it appear that capital selection of base for the graphs in many of the industries covered was relatively far better off than labor in 1933.

This also has some effect on the final "ratings" in the industries which rest upon *average rates of change,* and there are doubts as to the significance of the final results, because they are applied in a *uniform* manner to every industry without regard to the organic or dynamic characteristics of the industry. Furthermore, the interest and dividend payment trend is distorted because of the undistributed profits tax of 1936 and 1937, which had the object of pumping dividends into circulation at a rate far greater than the decline in interest payments due to fall in interest rates. Kreps does not even refer to the real reason for this seeming overpayment to capital at that

creating acute price weakness after the War, is problematical. The result of this unavoidable expansion in some lines of production will depend upon postwar export possibilities and the extent to which urban industry can continuously sustain employment and payrolls.

Control of price inflation was slow to take shape in the United States in the preparatory period from the autumn of 1939 to the close of 1941. During 1938 and 1939 wholesale prices had reached a level well below the previous speculative peak of December, 1936. The outbreak of war caused a sharp rise, followed by partial relapse until the late summer of 1940, when a rapid and fairly general rise began. This accelerated in the spring of 1941, after passage of the Lease-lend Act, which provided for huge shipments of supplies to friendly powers at war. By December, 1941, farm prices had risen no less than 40 per cent from their prewar (1939) level, and this contributed materially to a rise of 11 per cent in urban retail costs of family maintenance. Average wholesale prices had advanced but 22 per cent, clearly indicating that farmers, as usual, were the leading beneficiaries of the early phase of the wartime demand and price situation. But urban wage earners were not far behind, and the

---

time or its effect upon the trend that enters into the index. Again, the labor income is merely that of wage earners and cannot be compared with other phases of an industry performance without clearly defining the possible error of omitting payrolls or employment of nonwage earners or, for that matter, of the auxiliary workers whose income and employment may be conditioned upon the development of an industry during a decade or more.

If any one of Kreps' tests has special significance, it is probably the ratio of payrolls to the net value of products. This is an important test of industry performance, because the numerator of this ratio provides for the element of wage rates, employment and production; the denominator measures the extent to which the industry is able to achieve a price tendency relatively favorable to consumers. But unfortunately, the results of *this* test do not all agree with Kreps' *composite* tests.

Although this effort is highly commendable as one of the pioneer attempts to give statistical expression to the rating of an industry's caliber, and the place of price factors in that rating, the inadequacy of the data and the method certainly do not justify reference to these particular results as anything in the nature of an "acid test" of performance. In particular, the writer doubts that these results in any way demonstrate that there is anything peculiar in the "present day business world" that necessarily constrains those having managerial responsibility to direct funds into channels that "cause" major business depressions or booms. Nor is it adequately established that "in that range of enterprise dominated by large aggregates, although prices may behave uniformly and be set with certainty, risks and losses are shoved over on laborers, consumers, farmers, and the public. The tendencies of monopolies and corporate bureaucracies to destroy competition emphasizes one characteristic or arrangement of the American people which is of supreme importance for the preservation of free competitive enterprise." The evidence justifies no such assertion. "Laborers, consumers, farmers, and the public" have certainly been far more victimized by cutthroat price competition than by anything that large-scale industry has ever done.

increase in wage rates more than kept pace with average living costs. Thus a cumulative spiral was already imminent when this country actually became involved in the War with Japan, Germany, and Italy, following the Japanese attack upon Pearl Harbor on Dec. 7. From that point to mid-1942, retail price advances were continuing at about the same rate, although key farm products were beginning to approach levels at which they would be fully at statutory parity and hence subject to some indirect retarding influences such as the crop loan rates. When the Emergency Price Control Act passed Congress early in 1942, the farm group effectually opposed efforts to impose ceilings on farm products in accordance with the strict parity relationship to farm outlay prices; instead of 100 per cent of parity, Congress gave the Secretary of Agriculture authority to set limits not below 110 per cent of parity.[1]

At the time that this initial legislative action on the inflation problem was taken, there was already in effect an elaborate system of priorities and informal Administrative price-limit orders pertaining to materials needed by the war-production industries. The wholesale prices of "strategic and critical" metals (listed in Chapter 4) were exceedingly well controlled months before the general Price Control Law. The priority rulings of the Office of Production Management served to avoid simultaneous concentration of civilian and war demands upon limited material supplies. As the country entered the War, the OPM became a still more effective administrative body, and priority assignments were developed into a full-fledged system of material rationing and allocation in order to move supplies quickly to those needing them for the most urgent war production. This was continued by the succeeding War Production Board. Entire industries, such as those producing passenger automobiles, radios, refrigerators, and other civilian goods, were forced to convert plants and equipment for manufacture of war equipment. A tremendous plant-conversion operation was performed in remarkably short time. In May the Office of Price Administration took action to "freeze" retail, wholesale, and manufacturer prices all along the line, at levels not higher than the highest prices charged by any individual firm in March. Rents in important defense-production areas were frozen somewhat later. Wage rates in industry were not specifically limited, but it was expected that the stabilizing of living costs would go a long

---

[1] Despite the clear admonitions and forceful warnings of the President and other Administration leaders that inflation of farm prices could not be tolerated, Senator O'Mahoney, of Wyoming, insisted that the upper limit should be raised to 120 *per cent of parity!* Since some important farm product prices were still 15 or 20 per cent below strict parity, this would have permitted a considerable further advance in retail food costs. This, incidentally, was the very same Senator O'Mahoney who served as Chairman of the Temporary National Economic Committee to Study the *Concentration of Economic Power.*

way to prevent demands for wage increases, and public opinion and War Labor Board action would do the rest. This program, it must be recognized, involved far more than mere price fixing; it was implemented by direct control over industrial production and sale and the rationing of basic consumer goods such as sugar, gasoline, and tires which became scarce. This averted competitive bidding and all the usual speculative price-kiting activities that otherwise can drive the price level cumulatively upward.

There still remained, however, the problem of the expanding income payments to individuals throughout the nation in excess of the value of production of the things that consumers were free to buy. The necessity of turning out huge quantities of armament, planes, ships, and supplies of all kinds for Britain, Russia, China, and other Allies, as well as for the American war effort, had created, in the spring of 1942, an estimated spread of more than 15 billion dollars between available personal income and total retail-goods values. The fiscal problem was already acute, inasmuch as Federal tax revenue was able to defray less than half of the current war expenditures, approaching the rate of 3 billion dollars a month. The problem of securing more taxes under such conditions has always been difficult, and it is certain to be beset by all manner of political and social pressures. The principal difficulty has arisen from the limitations characteristic of taxation imposed on income. Ordinarily, the Federal income tax has secured almost equal sums from corporations and from individuals in the middle and upper income groups. Under war conditions corporate revenue in industries serving the war effort rise rapidly, and the excess fairly attributable to war business can be readily appropriated. As in British procedure, the normal earnings base was set at a prewar period, but in addition, an alternate was afforded to companies desiring to use a percentage of computed invested capital as the base from which war excess profits were measured. As long as such an alternative is granted, the result represents an essentially reasonable levy on corporations while extraordinary revenues arising from war expenditure continue. There is no need, however, for any tax on *corporate* income to be graduated or progressive. Large corporations may be more efficient and more in need of conserving resources for productive requirements than others, and there is no sound reason why the size of an establishment should be a barrier to adequate provision for such purposes. In view of the pressing need for reserves and plant purposes it is very easy to exaggerate corporate earnings as "potentially inflationary." Actually, what is added to corporate profits would go mainly into surplus invested in War Bonds, affording a stabilizing factor for postwar contingencies and adjustments, or into the hands of stockholders who, in turn, pay it back in taxes that can legitimately be scaled progressively, within reason. Under conditions that make industrial equipment and productivity the very key to national survival, errors may be made in corporate fiscal policy, under the guise of "inflation control," by making total levies so high that working capital is impaired and borrowing from the banks is necessary, virtually, to pay taxes. This is a wholly undesirable result that is actually inflationary. No tax at any time is sound that trenches upon capital destined for essential war purposes, but justice as between war industries and others is difficult to achieve.

In a vast war of production the greatest increase in income is in neither corporate nor capitalist groups; it is among the working personnel of the factories and the farms. But prepossessions and solicitude for the "low-income groups" is difficult to set aside in a war emergency, particularly when a Federal Administration dedicates itself to the equalizing of wealth distribution instead of promoting the maximum of industrial productivity. But the issue was at last being faced in 1942, and income taxes were imposed upon incomes at the wage-earner level. With more workers per family busy in war-industry occupations, the *family* earnings of hundreds of thousands rose enormously, and it was essential and socially sound policy to tax them. It is desirable that taxation of war-created individual income should be accomplished promptly by direct withholding at the source. The usual income-tax collection procedure is too slow. Probably, too, the levying of reasonably adjusted general sales taxes is sound under such conditions, especially as a means of raising revenue from families and petty transients. Although usually regarded as "repressive" in taking more than proportionate purchasing power from the lower income groups, they serve to accomplish exactly that purpose in wartime when the wage-earning groups unquestionably secure by far the widest gains, along with farmers, in *family* revenue. A sales tax, properly balanced, is an effective brake on unnecessary spending.

As for Federal borrowing, the program pursued a well-considered plan. In selling War Bonds, the Government wisely stressed individuals and business firms, but sales to banks could not be avoided altogether. If forced saving can be avoided during war, so much the better. Direct appeals and voluntary purchases should be sufficient if tax policy is sound.

The problems of inflation control, maximum war output, and sound fiscal policy are interrelated. They are not beyond solution. Properly and courageously handled, they can go far to avert acute postwar price disruption and the kind of disparity between raw materials and manufactured goods that in the past has created not only social problems but social attitudes inimical to the accomplishment of economic stability by sound and constructive policies.

CHAPTER 25

THE FUTURE OF PRODUCTION AND CAPITAL

It is true that the discovery of new processes of manufacture will undoubtedly continue . . . but it will not leave room for marked extension, such as has been witnessed during the last fifty years, or afford remunerative employment of the vast amount of capital which has been created during that period. . . .

There may be room for further intensive, but not extensive, development of industry in the present area of civilization. . . .
—CARROLL D. WRIGHT, U.S. Commissioner of Labor, 1886.

There is one great danger: the fear, the apathy, the give-up spirit that comes in all periods of depression, the product, perhaps sheerly, of economic and historic ignorance, and the inevitable myopia, lack of wide perspective, that invariably moves with it. So easy to lose the sense of time, to see only the immediate difficulties, which often loom so portentuously. Always a waning faith in progress, in invention, in energy and initiative. Always the same supine superstition that somehow the great advance of mankind has come to a tragic end.
—CARL SNYDER, 1940.

The great depression of the 1930's was a profound economic readjustment after a postwar boom, during which unsound financial practices in construction, inherited from our past, continued to flourish. It was entirely natural that the inevitable reaction was very severe. Its intensity was aggravated by other circumstances. One was the virtual ending of a major phase of our transportation development, as the automotive industry approached its culminating replacement stage at the end of the 1920's. Another, and more important, was the international financial breakdown, an outcome of insolvent war claims that abruptly checked the resumption of capital investment and the recuperation of trade that was already beginning to appear in 1931. Added to all this was a highly vulnerable banking system subject to these combined shocks, as well as psychological and international forces impinging on gold reserves and credit solvency.

The weaknesses in American finance intensified a world-wide reaction and gave rise to a social-political movement, as important in Europe as it was in the United States, dedicated to the urgent task of reemployment and the restoration of production and income. Out of this came some significant and long-deferred financial reforms, but along with these, a tendency to exploit the facts of depression to justify policies resting upon the hypothesis that a basic change had been revealed in the nation's growth opportunities and that it was time to readjust the economic and political structure to this change. There crept into the remarks of leading

651

publicists and political economists increasing reference to "maturity" and "stagnation." It began to be pointed out, as we have already noted at several points, that the amount of annual growth in population was now declining; the old frontier and its opportunities to the individual were gone.[1] It has come to be widely accepted that the opportunity for capital investment under private auspices has passed, it being imagined that capital is a frontier phenomenon. Attention is called to the apparently superabundant volume of capital available for investment, heretofore considered a symptom of depression rather than decadence. Low interest rates, accentuated deliberately by Government policy, become a means of "proving" the existence of excessive saving. This, in turn, has been rendered plausible by such statistical compilations as those of Brookings Institution in 1934 and 1935, purporting to prove that American productive facilities, even in 1929, were far more than ample to meet peak demand. This was supposed to be one aspect of a persistent tendency toward an excess of savings, which in the pioneer days would surely have found ample outlets in all directions.[2]

Millions of workers in industry, according to widely held views, are unable to find employment because modern mechanism is alleged to displace so many men, while greedy monopolies, "hoarding" reserve funds and charging "high" prices, obstruct the sale of products to the major part of the population. The conclusion is supposed to follow that economic stagnation will continue unless the Government steps in to equalize wealth and income to fortify purchasing power and directly to perform the services that private capitalism has failed to accomplish. From all this there follows the now familiar justification by political economists of fantastic public spending, elaborate and progressively larger programs of "public works," a stupendous and permanent public debt, and the transfer of all saving and surplus capital to the control of a bureaucracy. Since this bears upon the longer term outlook for the American economy and its possibilities of further progress, we shall

---

[1] "The so-called 'New Deal' . . . laid the foundation for the awakening by the American people to the realization of a new national outlook that had to be faced. Our political and economic policy had, from the beginning, been based upon an ever-expanding Western frontier and an ever-increasing population, much of which came directly from immigration. Slowly but surely both of these doors had been closing, but it took the violent crisis of 1929 to 1933 to make the American people demand that something be done about it!" (James Roosevelt, press interview, Feb. 12, 1939.)

[2] See Harold G. Moulton and associates, "America's Capacity to Produce," 1934, "America's Capacity to Consume," 1934, "The Formation of Capital," 1935, and "Income and Economic Progress," 1935, Brookings Institution, Washington, D.C. See also the criticism by Henry H. Villard, *American Economic Review*, September, 1937.

examine these contentions and test them against the facts, so far as they are available, and determine whether this philosophy of stagnation and its corollary of bureaucratic capitalism have really been deduced from a correct interpretation of the last depression and of the forces involved in the trend of our economic growth in the past.

ECONOMIC SIGNIFICANCE OF POPULATION CHANGE AS EXPRESSED

In much of the thinking that underlies recent public policy in the United States, it is possible to discern the influence of J. M. Keynes, the British economist, who has elaborately rationalized the general theory of disintegrating private capitalism and algebraically established the need for bureaucratic capitalism. In the United States, Alvin H. Hansen, a follower of Keynes' general views, has repeatedly stated that the volume of employment-creating construction during the nineteenth century was predicated upon a rapidly growing population. Since the increment of growth will soon disappear, the opportunities for full employment in durable capital formation will progressively diminish. Hence the supposed need for some revolutionary method, breaking away entirely from accepted financial principles, whereby the Government may be required to provide the employment and the "income" that can no longer be expected to originate in the efforts of more business enterprises to satisfy the demands of more people. Hansen says:

The enormous capital outlays of the nineteenth century were, of course, in the first instance conditioned by new technological developments, but they were determined also by the vast growth of population. It seems not unreasonable to suppose—and some rough estimates lead to this conclusion—that approximately one-half of the capital outlays of the past century were due to the growth of population and its expansion into new territory. . . . It is my growing conviction that the combined effect of the declining population growth, together with the failure of any really important innovations of a magnitude sufficient to absorb large capital outlays, weigh very heavily as an explanation of the failure of the recent recovery to reach full employment.[1]

In support of this thesis, Hansen refers to figures showing the amount of increment in population each decade from 1800 to 1940 and estimates for later decades. These figures, as shown in our Charts 1 and 5, indicate that the maximum number of people *added* to our population occurred in the decade ending at 1910, with a slightly lower peak in the decade ending at 1930. After 1950 the anticipated per decade decline is marked. We have already established (Chart 5) that in terms of 10-year averages of the total production index, the volume of our business has shown no close long-term correlation with the pattern of population increments.

[1] Hearings before the Temporary National Economic Committee, Part 9, "Savings and Investments," pp. 3504 and 3514.

In Chapter 3 attention was called to the fact that there was some evidence of sympathetic relationship within periods of a decade, but the longer movements are decidedly in contrast. We are reminded also of the fact that our population has been advancing at a slower and slower *rate* of change ever since the Civil War, while the smoothed rate of change of total production and trade has shown very little variation, although there have been several periods of interrupted progress in the past. To be sure, the long-term trend fitted to the business index during a period of nearly two and a half centuries may ultimately require readjustment to a lower rate of advance, perhaps retroactive for several decades, should the next half century fail to maintain the momentum to which we have been accustomed. But we can be fairly sure that as far as 1930 the long-term trend of our economic growth, as shown in Chart 4, is a reasonably accurate measure of the trend from the beginning of the eighteenth century to that date. Since there is this wide contrast in the behavior of the rates of business and population growth since the Civil War period, there is doubt as to the correctness of Hansen's analysis. It is important to have an accurate appraisal of the significance of population growth as we peer into the more distant future and seek to form a reasonable expectation as to production development in the next half century. The attempt to extrapolate the future trend of our economic growth with excessive emphasis on population is likely to mislead us.[1]

In some particular directions there is no doubt that a future declining increment of population growth has definite economic significance. This is true, for example, of the domestic demand for agricultural products. We have seen in Chapter 7 that there is a very close correspondence between the long-term trend of agricultural production and the trend of population, further modified by an index of export demand. Had our population been expanding during the past decade as vigorously as it was a hundred years ago, and farm exports likewise, probably the rural income collapse of the 1930's would have been considerably less serious. But behind that collapse we have seen that there were unnecessary and clearly excessive fixed charges arising from indebtedness incurred during the War and rapid expansion of rural local government expenditures that forced farmers to pay much heavier taxes when their export markets were shrinking. The latter condition was due to the War, not to population factors. In the opinion of the writer, this aftermath of extravagant war prosperity and financial recklessness was a much more important factor

[1] Hansen in some degree recognizes this, saying that the exceptional unemployment problem of the last depression was not wholly due to population retardation but other factors such as "our failure to grapple effectively with certain specific situations, such as those presented by the railroads or the public utilities, or building construction." (*Op. cit.*, p. 3514.)

in the farmers' distress of the last decade than factors involving the rate of growth in population. American agriculture borrowed itself into a situation wherein solvency required a *faster* expansion of demand than in previous decades, and the result was widespread difficulty, soon carried over into determined and embittered attacks upon industrial enterprise, as in all previous periods of agrarian unrest. In terms of the total number of persons occupied in agricultural pursuits, it is important to remember, as we peer ahead into the future, that while about half of our working population were in agriculture in 1880, less than 20 per cent are now so engaged. The declining *percentage* of the population increment has kept step with a declining proportion of effort in that field, and this will doubtless be true in the future also. To that extent we must expect that investment opportunities and the demand for equipment and housing will become proportionately less active in the rural areas than in the rest of the country. But industrial demands for farm products, as distinct from family needs, may yet expand particular segments of farming against the general drift.

Among the technological factors that for several centuries have served to maintain our economic growth trend with such remarkable consistency, after allowance for the long-term cyclical fluctuations, the application of new forms of power to productive operations is of special importance. As the development and use of the steam engine served in the nineteenth century to create an ever-expanding volume of production and demand for raw materials from all corners of the world, so the application of electricity served to create new products and stimulate new industries after about 1890. World War I served as a developing ground for still another source of economical power capable of wide and flexible use, in the form of the internal-combustion motor, the applications of which have by no means reached their limit. As we look ahead, it is reasonably certain that still other sources of power will be developed capable of application to the wheels of industry and to transportation. One of the probable results of the present War will be to stimulate active research in the development of power sources independent of petroleum and coal. Should these efforts be successful, one of the geographical reasons for war may be rendered less potent. The successful application of power sources not dependent upon erratically concentrated deposits of oil or coal might, indeed, be considered one of the prerequisites for an enduring peace. At any rate, there is no reason to believe that the succession of major developments with respect to power capable of being applied to prime movers that has been so dramatically spread over the pages of past history will fail to materialize in the future.

We have illustrated in earlier chapters the dramatic cyclical movements in the history of transportation development. Certainly one of the basic causal factors in the cyclical movements of business generally lies in the field of transportation innovation.   The railroad-building era, it is true, was also one of rather rapidly expanding population, although the actual increments throughout the latter half of that era were at a progressively lower rate of growth.   It was, after all, population movement that motivated the railroad builders.   But neither railroad nor automobile development has had any necessary relation to population growth or migration.   In fact, many demographic events of past centuries produced no railroads and no motorcars.   In a country whose political policies were for so many years shaped by farmers and dominated by the Jacksonian principle of avoiding all governmental planning and coordination of large scale basic-utility enterprise, competitive railroad building by amateur promoters resulted in boom after boom, crash after crash.   These recurring financial crashes became so disastrous that comprehensive reorganizations were undertaken in the 1890's, but in such fashion that capital structures became rigidly determined and stale debt eventually proved to be far out of proportion to the trend of revenue.

We referred in Chapter 10 to the consequences of this procedure, particularly the inability of the railroads to keep themselves fully abreast of technological progress in transportation and to retire obsolete loan capital in order to use new capital in effective ways to make railroad service fully modern and more economical to the users thereof.   The utter collapse of railroad solvency in the 1930's, granting business depression, was a direct corollary, not of a tapering growth in population or even of the growing competition from other forms of transport service; the collapse was due to improper financial policy and the mediocre management and bad reorganization practice that followed therefrom.   Had sound policies been adopted during the 1830's in railroad planning and financing, there would surely have been less reduction in the output of several major industries during the 1930's.   As we pointed out in Chapter 18, the flow of new capital into railroad transportation awaits further action in bringing capital structures in line with realities.   While the courts leisurely discuss meticulous procedures for harmonizing the claims of bondholders and equity holders, economic progress in this field must wait, population growth or no population growth.   Even though mileage has not expanded for several decades, railroad facilities need billions of fresh capital to give the United States twentieth-century service.   In his later writings, Alvin Hansen himself acknowledges that in terms of transportation progress, extensive growth in numbers is not essential; the changes pertaining to automobiles and electricity "involving vast investment of capital, can take place without extensive growth, and under the progress of technology we shall doubtless experience again far-reaching revolutionary innovations of this sort."[1]

[1] A. H. Hansen, "Fiscal Policy and Business Cycles," pp. 45–46, New York, 1941.

POPULATION TRENDS AS THEY AFFECT THE BUILDING INDUSTRY

In analyzing the causes of business fluctuations, we have had occasion to observe the major cycles of building activity through many years. The collapse of building construction in the last depression and its conspicuous contribution to unemployment have been considered by some observers as primarily due to slowing down of our general growth and population. This misconception underlies the program of unlimited Government spending on public works and the virtual recognition today that this is a *trend project*, not merely a *cycle* stabilizer. Again it might be said that had population been advancing as rapidly as in the 1850's, there would have been a better sustained demand for urban real-estate and housing accommodation in the decade of the 1930's. We must remember, however, several important points before jumping to the conclusion that there is any close relation between the last major building slump and changes in total population.

First of all, we have taken pains to demonstrate statistically that the building booms over a long period of our history have been the result primarily of *movements* of population rather than the trend of its total growth. Building cycles have come and gone for well over a century, regardless of changes in population. The shifts of population have in some degree been motivated by the development of new industries, such as the transportation industries. Building and realty booms have also, in some measure, been motivated by the interruption of housing construction during war, so that the succeeding building activity to make up these deficiencies in housing units has tended to develop quite unnecessary speculative momentum resulting in physical as well as financial excess. But this point has been frequently exaggerated with respect to the building boom of the 1920's. The war did interrupt housing, but this had been declining since 1909 as a phase of the major cycle. Furthermore, it is the local changes in the number of *families*, not *people*, that dominates housing construction.[1]

It was actually the unsound financial practices of urban building promotion in the 1920's, inherited from our reckless past, that made the downward spiral of insolvency and foreclosures so disastrous. It was our financial laws that encouraged mortgage conditions such as those in Michigan and Illinois and brought the spiraling impact of foreclosure

---

[1] All these matters are crudely stated in the "Economic Program for American Democracy," by seven Harvard and Tufts economists (New York, 1938), in which it is asserted: "Houses were built to fill the gap occasioned by a still growing population and the cessation of construction during the war. . . . When the limits of expansion had been reached, when the rate of population growth slowed down, building for the future became an increasingly hazardous adventure. . . . The severity of the great depression of 1929–1933 was due to the fact that upon a basic change in trend there was superimposed a violent cyclical downswing." (Pp. 20–22.)

into the banking system so that it was transmitted in all directions. We had failed to learn the lessons of earlier periods of building booms and their financial aftermath. We had failed, indeed, to heed the most elementary principles of capital investment as applied to mortgages and mortgage bonds. We failed to comprehend that the banking system was mainly serving speculation rather than production. We failed to observe that it is impossible to continue substantial investment in construction when so much of the old investment was already insolvent. Perhaps at this late date we should dismiss some of these foggy misconceptions as to population trends and the loss of frontiers and come face to face with the primary facts of capital investment and its retirement in such fashion that the *circulation* of long-term loan capital can be maintained. Let it be remembered that there is clear statistical evidence that the collapse of construction in the autumn of 1931 was intensified by an international financial debacle of political origin. Had it not been for this spreading of insolvency, we should have been able to clear away the debris of urban mortgage foreclosure by 1934 or 1935, and recovery of building expansion and employment would probably have followed.

The problems of introducing more rational financing methods into the public-service industries, such as railroad transportation, and also into urban housing construction are admittedly difficult. Broadly speaking, progress has lately been made in this direction, partly as a direct result of the depression experience. The manufacturing industries, which depend so much upon these basic lines of utility development, cannot secure adequate orders or hire labor if their customers are in financial difficulties and thus cannot provide a steadily and gradually expanding demand for the products of those industries. Since manufacturing industries, through their payroll disbursements, contribute the most important element to national income, it is apparent that failure of these disbursements to reach satisfactory levels during the decade of the 1930's has a direct relationship to historic financial practices in *certain particular phases of our economy.* Yet political reformers insist on placing all the blame upon manufacturers and condemn *them* as monopolists. Is it not time that we recognize the basic reasons for the industrial unemployment that continued to 1941? For the duration of the present War we may have many other more pressing and urgent problems of public policy to consider in order to assure our survival, but it is certain that the post-war period will again bring these matters to the fore in a most challenging way. There is certain to be a brief period of readjustment in employment and production following the war-created stimulus to production. There will be a new wave of urban building because of the shiftings of population created by the War. There will be a new transportation boom in automobiles and air transport. We may expect, following a brief period of transition lacking the sharp price deflation of 1920–1921, another "secondary" war boom that may conceivably extend to 1950 or beyond. Then will come the possibility of a secondary collapse, its extent depending upon how the postwar reconstruction has been controlled and how much further progress is made in ensuring sound methods of long-term financing, particularly in reorganization of basic-utility enterprises whose capital structures now impede the free flow of capital in those directions and hence the flow of demand to equipment-making industry.

If the Federal Government finds it necessary or politically expedient to embark upon enormous peacetime expenditures to continue the scale of financial outlay of the War, the expectation will be for simultaneous expansion of Federal and private investment in durable goods and structures. If the Federal program for highways, buildings, power, etc., is developed with restraint and a considerable portion of the planned expenditure is deferred until civilian construction has reached a temporary halt, the results will, in the end, be much more satisfactory. Probably, in avoiding the usual duplication of public and private construction stimulus, the extent of boom conditions in urban construction after this War will be less pronounced than in the 1920's. It is entirely possible to restrain both public and private financial excesses and overinvestment during the future. Government effort can be exceedingly helpful in long-range planning and the processes of survey and research involved in broad-scale coordination of utility facilities; private capital can do most of the legitimate development. But for Government to plan ahead without placing existing private-capital structures in the utility field on a much sounder basis is merely to build on sand.

At this point we may indulge in a few rough calculations designed to show what might be our future pattern of economic growth, based upon a number of assumptions. We shall sketch projections of the secular trend of total production on both a per capita and an aggregate basis and then consider to what degree they seem realistic and how far they may be affected by the general policy of Government. Since we have seen that the long-term trend of total production and trade, as far as 1930 and possibly 1940, has continued at a virtually constant rate (slightly above 3.5 per cent per annum), while the rate of increase in population has continued to decline for nearly eighty years, it follows that production per capita has been rising (until the present time, at least) *at an increasing rate*. The stagnation experts have not been particularly attentive to this fact. They have been observing essentially cyclical aberrations and have been insisting that the last cyclical depression was a wholly unique experience, unlike any previous depression, and hence the beginning of a new era of retardation. In proof, they point out that unemployment has already become "chronic" (that is, it seemed so in 1940), and we must change our economic and political system to create work and income.[1]

Chart 75 shows two groups of trends. The curves at the top indicate secular trends of per capita production; those below are the indexes of trend as such. The topmost curve projects the per capita secular trend of production and trade to 1980 by the use of the population estimates of Whelpton and Thompson (estimate 2 of Chart 1). This projection continues the general pattern of rates of increase from the past, so that during the final five-year period the rate of per capita change coincides with that of the actual production index, since population by that time is expected to reach virtually a stationary level. Prior to that period the rate of increase in the per capita production continues to proceed at a rate that is less than the rate of actual production but that tends to accelerate *faster* and to continue this acceleration *until* the period of population reaches its expected maximum. In other words, our average living standard has been advancing faster and faster, and on the basis of our first assumption this rate of acceleration would be expected to continue until, by 1980, the per capita index would have risen 300 per cent higher than it stood in 1930 (in terms of trend units). Since this assumption involves the expectation that population will continue to rise with about the same degree of tapering per decade as in the past, the resulting projection of production itself (shown below) results in a continuation of a constant *rate* of increase until the end.

The second assumption (*B*) shown among the upper group of curves is that the per capita secular trend until 1980 will be a point-to-point *logarithmic* projection, 1880–1930–1980. When translated into the production trend below, this results in a departure from the first assumption as the trend gradually tapers with some degree of curvature. The actual course of production and the intermediate trend would, of course,

---

[1] The fact that the expansion in production arising from the War turned unemployment into a labor shortage in two years might imply several distinct things. First, to the collectivist, it would suggest confirmation of the thesis that once all economic affairs are placed in the hands of Government the problem of unemployment is automatically solved. On the other hand, the believer in individual freedom and the right to private productive effort and property might say that were our reforms of long-term financial investment carried further along lines that have already been shown to be rational and beneficial, it might be expected, with entire confidence, that the opening of new jobs to serve peacetime demand as stale debt is lifted from great segments of industry will serve to revivify the entire economy and create ample expansion of industrial activity and jobs in private plants. Let us develop an equitable reorganization formula that can work with military precision and speed so that capitalists are not induced to cultivate false hopes of salvaging long-frozen debt that has ceased to represent fully productive assets. We shall then be able to release capital and activity in *new* phases of *old* enterprise, to say nothing of new enterprise.

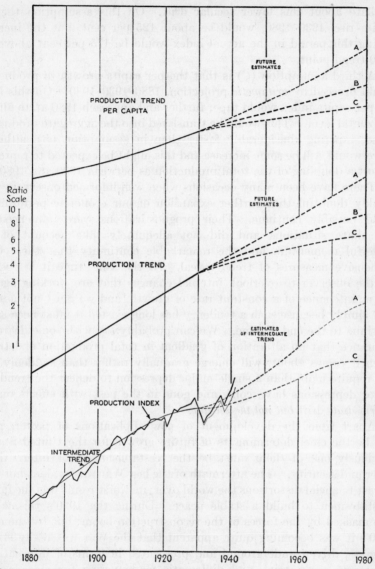

CHART 75.—Production trend and projections, 1880–1980. The future estimates are based upon assumptions explained in the text. The projections of intermediate trend in the lower section (A) (C), represent possible possible directions of the wavelike intermediate trend about the respective long-term trend projections, assuming that these wave movements would approximately resemble in pattern and amplitude those of past centuries.

oscillate about this lower secular drift. On this assumption the per capita rise, 1930–1980, would be about 125 per cent, but the increase during this period in the actual index would be 175 per cent above the 1930 trend point.

A third assumption (*C*) is that the per capita growth in production would proceed by *arithmetic* projection, 1880–1930–1980. On this basis the per capita index would taper further and approach 1980 at an almost horizontal level. This would be translated into the aggregate production trend, tapering considerably faster than in assumption (*B*), although there would still be some increase and this might be expected to represent almost a doubling of the total production as between 1930 and 1980.

There have been many occasions when well-informed observers were frankly doubtful that further expansion of our economic performance could possibly continue. Their prognostications were influenced by immediate situations and did not adequately take account of the powerful momentum and the remarkable continuity that these comprehensive measures of trend reveal. At the same time it is possible for the observer to overlook internal changes that are working against the maintenance of a constant rate of growth, and we must not assume that simply because such a tendency has long existed it must necessarily continue to the end of time. We can probably say with some degree of assurance that an alteration of gradient in total production and trade, when it comes about, will emerge gradually rather than suddenly. It will require more than a single major depression to deflect the trend, for major depressions have come and gone in the past with effects on the *intermediate* drift *but not the secular*.

Apart from the development of new applications of power, what will be the chief determinants of future growth for the United States? Obviously one of them must be the reestablishment of international order and security. The aftermath of the last War was evident not only in vast financial distortions the world over; its worst result was the failure of statesmen to build a stable peace. During the 1920's this failure was masked by the forces of the reconstruction boom; but by the early 1930's it was becoming quite apparent that the War was really still in progress, driven underground and prosecuted in terms of international monetary, commercial, and diplomatic maneuvering for more war to follow. It has been commonly overlooked that one important reason for lagging business initiative and inadequate employment, in Europe as in America, during most of the 1930's was the darkening cloud of a new conflict. This certainly restrained capital investment and gave governments a potent pretext for unsurping more of the function of private financial enterprise. There cannot be a strong incentive to hazard capital, time, and energy in the face of world-wide political movements working toward objectives that imply the use of unprincipled force, complete disregard of simple integrity, deception and intrigue carried to the point of applied science, cunning undermining of confidence in all free initiative, and a designed contempt for privately conducted enterprise. These rapidly gathering clouds darkened the sky for many months before they issued as a final challenge to arms. The future of industry cannot be better than the extent to which all such forces are rooted out, to end once and for all their menace to peaceful development predicated upon basic human rights.

Perhaps we can express the fundamental issue of the stupendous global conflict in terms of concentration and diffusion of productive assets. During all periods of tranquil industrial expansion there is a profound, even though gradual, tendency toward diffusion of income and wealth. Industrial output can go forward rapidly for short periods under the lash of dictatorship or the emergency of war; but wars are fought in the last analysis to resist or break down concentrations of political power or to overcome the extraordinary advantages accruing to this or that segment of the world's people from possession of an unduly large proportion of vital raw materials. War is not the only avenue of solution of these problems. It can be the instrument whereby political groups in the end merely build up *new* concentrations of power and possession, and in the course of this process the diffusion of economic assets, instead of being broadened, may become all the more restricted.

Wars, in fact, have been the great designers of wealth concentration, looked at from the point of view of either political entities or groups within nations. Through warfare, imperialism can obstruct equitable access to the world's material wealth, and the losers in these great campaigns have no alternatives and must remain relatively impoverished. To assert that "trade" can create liberal access to basic material assets against the guns of armies and navies or the chicanery of diplomacy is an error of shallow thinking. Trade is created by, and can exist only to the extent of, a widening of the availability of tangible essentials that enter into the fabricated products of modern industry. As for internal concentrations, it is obvious that war accentuates the age-old tendency toward an asymmetrical distribution of income and assets. The normal peaceful tendency is for diffusion of product and return to broaden the *middle groups* of an industrial society, somewhat reducing concentration at the top and raising the average of living standards at the bottom. We shall not argue as to the reasons why, in all centuries and all nations, there is found a large and persistent concentration in the low-income strata; certainly the evidence clearly points to the existence of noneconomic as well as economic factors in this phenomenon. But the point of immediate interest is that warfare is the most potent of all forces in obstructing potential diffusion of wealth and accentuating the degree of property concentration at the top and poverty-ridden numbers at the bottom. It comes about through the destruction of middle-class income by inflation, war taxes, the direct casualties of war, which usually affect the middle groups most severely, and the destruction of small and medium-sized business units in the course of major war emergencies. Farmers are whipsawed into poverty by postwar deflation. The waging of war to rectify maldistribution of basic assets among nations merely produces further unfortunate results of the same order—the setting up of new concentrations of political control, and the displacement of international rules and principles of conduct by the kind of ruthless aggression typified by German and Japanese freebooters, masquerading as governments.

The nature of our economic trend in the next half century will be profoundly affected by the present contest to determine how more diffusion of wealth, in its larger aspects, shall be accomplished—by the creation of a new regimented serfdom or the slower and surer processes of economic enterprise, negotiation, and *preservation of the rights of the individual*. If it requires half a century to settle this issue, and well it might, the trend of our economy may project itself along a gradient no higher than estimate C, if, indeed, it does as well. If the issue can be fought out once and for all, and quickly, then estimate A is not too optimistic. Any estimate, indeed, must now be in terms of the world environment.

THE ATLANTIC CHARTER AND ITS IMPLICATIONS IN THE POSTWAR WORLD

In the momentous Atlantic Charter, drawn up by Roosevelt and Churchill in August, 1941, the basic war objectives of the democratic nations were set forth. Among them we find the following: "The United States and Britain . . . will endeavor, with due respect for their existing obligations, to further the enjoyment by all states, great or small, victor or vanquished, of access, on equal terms, to the trade and to the raw materials of the world which are needed for their economic prosperity. . . . They desire to bring about the fullest collaboration between all nations in the economic field with the object of securing, for all, improved labor standards, economic advancement, and social security."

These are profound and unprecedented declarations. They well express the prerequisites of a world resuming at some future time the industrial arts and peaceful trade to achieve broader economic welfare and security for the individual, rather than new concentrations in the hands of dictators or imperialists. But since we must include Russia and perhaps China in these professions of policy, is there not involved a hopeless and insoluble contradiction? The Soviet system is acknowledged to be a highly concentrated structure, operated to distribute "income," such as it is, but with no diffusion of property rights among the hundreds of millions of virtual serfs. There is no evidence that this represents the actual preference of the masses of these people. If that is the form of social order we are fighting to defend or establish in the name of social security, may we not actually be going back to the system of feudal lordship of medieval times rather than toward the broadening of economic security *arising from unquestioned individual rights* that in recent centuries supplanted feudal "security" and its counterpart of servile obligations? It will do no good in the long run to eradicate militaristic aggression as a means of acquiring national wealth if in its place there is to be set up an aggregation of dictatorships policing a world of individual slaves.

More realistic than this is the probability that we have overlooked the fundamental power of industrialism to accomplish the very purposes set forth in the Roosevelt-Churchill declaration. If we can see a definite and complete destruction of the fascist pretensions of infallible dictators and lawless piracy, it is entirely possible that a period of extended peace may release once again, as it surely has done in the past, the full energies of creative industry that, unobstructed by war dislocations, remain the world's greatest agency toward wealth diffusion. The Russian system as it develops will, in all probability, become more capitalistic for the reason that industrialization, once divorced from war objectives, cannot survive without private property. A concentrated bureaucracy can exploit the early stages of industrialization, as has been done in Germany and Japan as well as Russia; but such exploiting in the end merely accomplishes its own frustration. So also does the attempt of certain groups to exploit the Soviet example as a means of acquiring economic and political power in other nations, by endeavoring thereby to weaken popular confidence in the merits of private industry and the individual property tradition. That is merely a subtle effort to disparage a system making for gradual diffusion of wealth in order to concentrate it again in other hands, without any net advantage.

Fundamentally, we are in agreement with the collectivists in having arrived at the point of recognizing that at least wider diffusion of *income* is a basic condition of all future progress. Whether that is to be achieved by equally progressive diffusion of *ownership* may, after all, turn out to be a question of *means* rather than *ends*. We can be absolutely sure that so far as the people of all countries are concerned, they are now insistent, and will grow increasingly insistent, upon more adequate income, more stability of employment, and a widening of the opportunities for education and leisure. If we start from this basic and inescapable premise, we can see possibilities of progress, so long as we stand firm in our own economic convictions. Our traditional philosophy of personal initiative, the search for profit, and the guarantees of property rights must be tinged with concern for the maintenance of full productivity and the avoidance of *internal* political or financial concentrations.   Our Allies must likewise come to see that forever to deny individual equity rights is not consistent with the status of free men; the equalization of "income" distributed among slaves may be a way of introducing an industrial economy upon the groundwork of an ignorant peasantry long subjugated by landlordism and usury; to keep either the products or the property of an *expanding industry* forever out of the hands of individual people is impossible.   In the long run, and perhaps well within the next half century, we may expect to see a harmonizing of two apparently contradictory social philosophies.   Our own system may become more conscious of the importance of the basic planning of certain types of enterprise, such as we failed to accomplish in our early days, and extreme collectivism may yet recognize the impelling necessity of individual integrity and the impossibility of sustaining full production and a high standard of life unless property rights, as well as income distribution, are respected.

This War may, therefore, produce astonishing results in unexpected directions.   Perhaps only in this way does the world learn that continued warfare to achieve a better distribution of equity defeats its very purpose.   By the same token, internal warfare between the bureaucratic ambition to dominate wealth and production and the natural individual instinct to resist such domination leads in the end to further concentration, either in bureaucracy or in financial aggregations that are able to survive after the smaller units have been crushed by the struggle. These stupid internal wars are in the end as disastrous to human progress as the wars between nations.   A century and a half ago we learned from Adam Smith that trade was a means of diffusing rather than concentrating the world's goods.   Today we need to be reminded that industry has, under favorable political conditions, the same power and that that power can only be fully developed by recognizing individual equity in principle.   We must see more clearly through the haze of propaganda and half-baked sociology that a bureaucracy that assures its citizens of equalized income while it takes away their *property rights* is destroying the very source from which real income comes.   Once start this nefarious course and the spiral of confiscation travels faster in destroying production than the bureaucracy can move in redistributing the flow of goods. In the end there is again warfare to regain lost equity and perhaps warfare between one bureaucracy and another to determine which shall rule the entire world.   Whether we continue international or domestic contests to concentrate economic assets in few hands, the result is the same old spiral, ultimately reducing the masses to the status of serfdom, albeit "secure" serfdom.

If the Atlantic Charter means anything at all, it must mean that the only safe future course is one of increasing diffusion of equity both within and among sovereign states. It is the internal aspect that especially challenges attention in the present context. Our problem is to make our well-tried and successful economic system work better, more smoothly, and more efficiently. This cannot be done by destroying the middle class in order to give political dictatorship permanent power through domination and subsidization of the lowest segments. The only sound objective is to widen constantly the scope of the middle income group so that it can place its dynamic energies, large capital assets, and high technical and professional intelligence at the service of maximum productivity. It is the middle group in our own economic order that supplies most of the productive capital, almost all the competent management, the research effort, and the savings that sustain a standard of living without parallel in the world. Its efforts give the lower income ranks their opportunities to acquire increasing wealth if they have the human qualities capable of sustaining an interest in such acquisition. Its efforts are enhanced to the extent that wealth is not excessively concentrated either at the top of the income scale or in the hands of political administrators. But to the extent that the latter become ambitious and overreaching, they have the power, by taxation, to restrict these middle groups and frustrate them. They may seek to do this with the noblest motives of turning more "income" over to the poor or by dramatizing the effort to eliminate the very rich; but the plain fact of the matter is that we are already unconsciously wiping out by a stupid tax system the very group that holds in its hands the key to future expansion in productivity capable of wider diffusion. This is as serious a problem as the War itself.

To be sure, as our democratic economic system has worked out, it has revealed the tendency toward excessive vibrations and cyclical aberrations that it has been our task to analyze. These elements of vulnerability have arisen basically from the very restlessness of a free people and the wide latitude given to initiative and technological innovation. It has not been sufficiently recognized, possibly because of the rapidity of our growth, that capital use requires special safeguards to keep cyclical tendencies within reasonable limits and thus to prevent undue concentration of power. The heart of the problem is the lag between our progress in physical production, productive organization, and distribution, on the one hand, and that of the capital-finance mechanism on the other. The collectivists may be correct in placing great emphasis upon a wide distribution of products and services as the ultimate objective of an economic system; it is their means to this end that raise serious doubts. They solve the capital and finance problems crudely and

arbitrarily by doing away with private productive property and eliminating capital from the price system.   The democratic system, striving
to maintain a high degree of private initiative in capital formation, is
embarrassed by the historical evidence that our use of capital has not been
wholly sound or even clearly understood.   There is, therefore, the need
for a searching reappraisal of the capital mechanism in our own economic
order.   Instead of wasting time inventing wealth-sharing schemes inconsistent with capitalism, let us try to make capitalism really work as it
should work.

What is the basic defect?   In the opinion of the writer, it lies in the
fact that *loan* capital has too often insisted upon the right to a return
beyond the point at which its specific economic service stopped.   Loan
capital, like money, necessarily has a *circulating* function.   It is the
primary function of such capital, in a dynamic economy, to assist in
initiating and developing useful production and facilitating the ownership of durable wealth.   In order to keep these operations on the highest
plane of effectiveness, the owners and potential owners of durable wealth
and those who manage productive property as trustees or agents must
necessarily preserve solvency.   Solvency is not merely a matter of a
differential between revenues and costs; it is a matter of ability to
accumulate from revenue enough surplus to discharge all necessary
borrowing in a reasonable course of time and, *in addition to that*, to
accumulate funds to maintain operations at the highest possible efficiency.
Only in this way can ever-encroaching obsolescence be minimized and
employment maximized.   The full costs of research and the introduction
of improvements include provision of reserves for labor training and
displacement, and a constant adjustment of real wages to productivity.
These costs in fact, are much higher than usually imagined.   Business
management has been too much under the pressure of the age-old human
temptation to trade upon its equity, and capital has again and again
been used in the atmosphere of boom conditions in ways that have led
to concentration rather than diffusion and to impairment of the benefits
of technological advance.

NECESSITY FOR CHANGE IN GOVERNMENT POLICY
TO PERMIT BROADER USE OF CAPITAL

In attempting to correct these financial shortcomings, Government
has contributed some of its own.   It has in various ways attempted to
take away from business enterprise and from the reservoir of middle-
class surpluses still more of actual or incipient capital and to distribute
it, not only in useful, humane, and productive ways but also in large
subsidies to the shiftless and incompetent.   It has sought to compensate
the poorest from the resources of the richest without in the process

actually expanding the output of wealth or preserving the integrity of middle-class capital investment. What is urgently needed, therefore, is a new philosophy of capital and a new philosophy of Government policy with respect to capital, including the taxation affecting it. If these problems, so closely related to business cycles and the long-term trend of total production, can be thoroughly understood and solved with some degree of success, we shall probably find ourselves in the next forty years moving closer to the ideal of a more active circulation of both capital and income and a progressive extension of the intermediate grouping of income and wealth. This is the only safeguard that we have against the strong pressures to turn the other way, back to feudalism, in which the middle class is telescoped and the lowest strata assume the position of servile ministration to concentrated power at the top.

Since the stoutest bulwark against paternalistic feudalism is a continuing system of broadly distributed private ownership of property, with exceptions clearly defined, our first problem is one of deciding the proper course and scope of Government action with respect to the difficult border-line cases, such as are presented by the unit or utility industries, those foundational public-service networks that must be operated as a unit for the general good and that require closely coordinated operation so that they may function at all. These industries cannot have sound structures or efficient functioning unless Government exercises its proper functions to avoid bad planning, duplication of facilities, and inadequate financing which ultimately tends to encourage excessive proportions of loan capital. In the public-service field, of which rail transportation is a good example, monopoly characteristics are unavoidable, but effective coordinating, even at this late date, can render monopoly position relatively innocuous so long as capital financing is sound. That in itself requires the competent management that does not seek high profits from "high" prices or rates, as is often supposed; it seeks enlargement of earnings through extension of sales and expansion of service, which, in turn, create new production and demand in the business system. The popular fear of monopoly is a fear of high or discriminatory price. But these evils are not peculiar to monopoly; they are the attributes of unprofessional and improperly trained management. Had we trained our utility-industry executive personnel in sound finance and efficient sales development, we should hear less of price setting and rate making by Government. All that this has done is to adjust service rates not at the levels permitting maximum output but rather at levels capable of producing arbitrary returns on arbitrary aggregates of capital with inadequate provision for amortization of the fixed capital charges. The problem is as much one of capital as of price making. Durable-goods manufacture depends mainly for its markets upon the stability, solvency, and continued vitality of the great service industries and the ability of families to accumulate equity in housing and consumer durables.   To the extent that these are solvent, and loan capital is used to enhance rather than destroy their purchasing power, we can move forward continuously in industrial activity and employment.

The present problem in the case of the railroads, our most serious casualty, is whether to pull them out of their difficulties by public ownership or to hasten the day when reorganized finance can open the way to sounder management, new and better equipment, and lower rates.   The tendencies of population growth, the Great Depression and unemployment, the present War—all are irrelevant.   They do not of themselves justify a trend to public ownership.   That represents, not a solution, but merely a means of exploiting past political mistakes to carry forward a program of bureaucratic concentration.   If sound private capital and proficient management cannot be made to function in this field of our economy, then it has lost its case *in all sectors*.   That is why the issue has bearings on our future trend and on our attitude toward those nations united with us in the postwar world which may challenge our traditions of a democratic economy.   If we are to continue as a democracy and develop new growth in industry, we must meet the new world with our best, not with our mistakes.

Much current discussion of capital conceives it as a quantity of something homogeneous and of uniform consistency.   This has carried over from monetary theory.   However, once we separate the stream of investment into loan capital and ownership capital, it becomes misleading to continue the analogy to something that is homogeneous.   The streams diverge, not in their immediate function of providing present plant and labor for future production but rather in their ultimate disposition.   *Loan* capital, if legitimate at all, is sought to build up the useful potentialities of what is *owned*.   As this process develops, the need for continuing the use of loan capital should logically diminish.   If equity values cannot be created to provide for further expansion and adaptation to new situations and opportunities, it follows that *additional* capital can be had only under conditions that render impairment of equity inevitable—barring exceptional cases of sheer luck in acquiring new income sources.   Hence it is not merely the *amount* of capital available or invested; it is not the size of the loan fund or its effect on interest rates; it is the proportions existing between loan and equity investment and the extent to which loan capital is circulating or stagnant and equity capital can attract more equity capital to build and "share" its ownership.   Capital has thus complex organic characteristics that make simple Keynesian equations applied to more or less saving, more or less investment, misleading and valueless.

LOAN AND EQUITY CAPITAL JEOPARDIZED BY EXCESSIVE USE OF CREDIT

Loan capital has been to a high degree institutionalized; equity capital, much less so. Loan capital accumulated by saving fuses with bank-created credit and can be temporarily vastly inflated by factors affecting bank reserves, as we have seen. This can suggest the superficial appearance of excess of saving when there is no such excess. During the speculative 1920's, enormous amounts of credit were used to facilitate reckless inflation of equity values in all kinds of property. This was not evidence of superabundant capital; it was merely an evidence that banking, especially political central banking, was in the hands of the incompetent, who permitted inflation to occur for years on end. Loan capital has the one and only function of providing a means of building or accumulating equity in property, and only insofar as repayment is practicable and definitely provided for. This was true of but a fraction of the loan capital-plus-credit utilized in the decade of the 1920's. Instead of creating abundant equity, the process attracted equity capital into industries whose customers were living on loans; hence the excess of frozen loan capital impaired not only the equity of its users—in home building, stock speculation, railroads, power companies, large urban building projects, hotels, etc., but the equity in steel companies, building-material companies, equipment companies of all types. *Equity capital cannot be soundly used anywhere unless the system as a whole has a reasonable degree of equity balance.* (We are now speaking of the business system and shall consider loan capital pertaining to Government presently.)

Put in another way, excessive use of credit perils both loan capital and equity capital. Excessive use of loan capital leads to congestion and impairs its flow from old uses to new situations requiring its use. This renders equity or shares in ownership of productive property vulnerable to tremendous shrinkage, which, in turn, blocks new investment of any kind and in the extreme case shuts off the opportunities for employment and closes the door to the accumulation of equity capital among the families of wage earners and clerical workers. The result is a slackening of flow due to congestion at this or that point; the savings accumulate but cannot be used. This is called an "excess" of savings, and Government is called upon to confiscate and put to work, to end the "strike" of reluctant capitalists. Thus we see as the end result of such situations an invitation to Government to increase its power over capital funds, to use taxation as a weapon to concentrate rather than diffuse ownership, and a weakening of the over-all productive effort while all this goes on. It can become conceivably a powerful spiral. As industry finds orders from the impaired segments below the level needed for full employment, it is criticized for inability to provide jobs. To raise the money, business is taxed, which ultimately depletes its potential surplus. The result is still less incentive to invest in new production or even in ways to lower costs in old-established lines. The process can go on until concentration in political hands becomes enormous. And it all starts from a naïve "quantity theory of capital" and a failure to distinguish congestion of the flow of *loan* capital from "excessive" accumulation of *all* capital.

There can be no such thing as an excess of equity capital. It can be misused, but *if loan capital is not abused or credit facilities recklessly exploited*, it is very difficult to see how a nation can go wrong in encouraging the use of equity capital to the fullest possible extent. This in itself opens up a constant succession of new jobs for loan capital (and credit), so long as it circulates *in and out*. It is the growth of investment and capital development in equity form that not only launches new things but provides the possibility of continuing full employment, or even expanding employment, *after* an industry or firm has passed its most rapid stage of growth. It is the use of loan capital in unbalanced ways that shuts off these avenues of job-creating innovation. Hence, from the long-term standpoint, the trend of progress, under a private-property system, depends not alone on *how much* capital is used but on *how* it is used to build the kind of proprietorship that does not stagnate.

Returning once again to the problem of monopoly, it is clear that monopolistic tendencies in modern business derive much of their impetus from the failure of ownership capital to hold its own. As debt financing becomes institutionalized, there is concentration of control over its uses. This concentration tends to bring about the persistent congestion of loan capital by keeping alive large masses of semifrozen debt, because the system does not enlarge its viewpoint to provide for any other kind of capital. Investment banking and life insurance and the legal traditions dictating trustee investment all combine to keep great masses of debt in existence long after such investment should have been shifted to new issues. This creates pressures to induce established businesses to refund rather than repay debt, and less and less attention is given to the problems of capital in *new* and *small* business. This encourages promoters to merge small and medium units as a means of issuing new debt rather than strengthening the individual equity structures and operating capacity of these units. Thus is "big business" developed while at the same time the potential product competition that can best prevent extremes of monopoly concentration is denied financing and is impaired. The holding-company excrescences of the 1920's form still another illustration. It was relatively easy to mobilize savings destined exclusively for debt financing for the acquisition of small operating companies by inflating their asset value and issuing unnecessary new debt on the basis of these fictitious values. The equity shares, meantime, were given alluring leverage that in due course turns inflated profits into disastrous losses.

These and other aspects of the institutional channeling of savings so largely into debt capital have produced unwieldy corporate entities in which equity, instead of being developed, is progressively weakened, as anyone can prove by noting the prices of public-service shares on the Stock Exchange during the past fifteen years. Businesses that are sound in management and financing are not interested in mergers, holding devices, or unnecessary financing engineered by the money market. But a situation can arise in which the capital machinery, traditionally developed along a unilateral and legalistic pattern, does not bring new savings to business in the form that business considers sound. Manufacturing has largely rid itself of stale debt. What it needs for full activity is reduction of topheavy debt among its customers. It needs also that accumulated demand for goods and equipment that comes into existence when small capitalists place their funds hopefully, with confidence in the future and in the integrity of their Government, in new businesses that have always been the real source of our industrial vitality. But institutional investing must adhere to the precepts of "liquidity." More and more it confines itself to debt creation (or continuation) for established business and in the interest of the largest units of such business. *This runs counter to the most elementary principle of sound capital use.* As such situations and opportunities contract, it appears on the surface that savings are "excessive." Actually, capital is offered in the wrong package and does not go to work where it is most needed. While Aaa corporate bonds now yield 3 per cent, the equities of leading corporations yield 7 per cent.

There has been much discussion in political circles of special banks or loan corporations for small and medium-sized business units.[1] What these discussions signify and what most of the loan schemes proposed usually overlook is that equity capital is not readily available for any enterprise large or small, new or old, if its capital is unbalanced and, still more important, that new and struggling industrial firms are being

[1] See, for example, the bills S1482 and S2343 to provide Federal insurance of loans to business enterprises described and discussed in Hearings before a Subcommittee of the Senate Committee on Banking and Currency, 76th Congress, First Session, May–June, 1939; the report to the Secretary of the Treasury on "Availability of Bank Credit in the Seventh Federal Reserve District," by C. O. Hardy and Jacob Viner, 1935, in which a new intermediate credit system for industrial working-capital loans was suggested, extending in effect the operations of the Reconstruction Finance Corporation; the memorandum entitled "A Banking System for Capital and Capital Credit," submitted by A. A. Berle, Jr., to the Temporary National Economic Committee, May, 1939; also, "Credit Requirements of Small Industry for Recovery," U.S. Department of Commerce, October, 1934.

deprived of capital because of our tax laws. This deserves special consideration.

A very large and solvent industrial corporation, at least until World War II, could finance through its surplus accumulation and resort to its shareholders. Although heavily taxed, it could, by exceptional management, survive in sound condition, although we shall presently consider whether this will continue to be so. But the medium-sized firm or the small unit in the development stage has found it increasingly difficult to accumulate the surplus necessary to make either equity financing available or its loan risk acceptable to institutional lenders. This type of business in the past has found its most dependable source of capital financing among the upper middle-class savers. Loans cannot be made by any kind of private agency to those who have inadequate equity. But it is precisely this original—and originating—equity capital that is deficient. It is so because for more than twenty years we have been taxing it away and setting up one political deterrent after another to obstruct and discourage its use in business, especially in new business. As our Federal tax system has operated ever since about 1916, there has been a steady dissipation of saving power in this important class of individual savers as well as in the medium range of business enterprise. As the results have materialized gradually, there has not been general recognition of the creeping impairment of business capital. Its steady shrinkage has not been made up in other ways. While unrestrained borrowing and credit inflation in the 1920's and governmental efforts at price inflation and other temporary stimulants in the 1930's were taking place this problem was concealed. The Government attempted, in its taxing policies, to "equalize" wealth by progressive rates of income levies, ostensibly aimed at the very rich, and increasing appropriation of capital left in estates. It was overlooked that this progressive principle, although having some sound aspects, exposed medium-sized business and the potential capital of the upper middle class to attrition out of all proportion to the fiscal results.[1]

---

[1] In 1913 the normal Federal tax on individual income (we assume throughout rates applying to married persons with no dependents) was 1 per cent. Individual surtax began with the surtax income range $20,000 to $50,000, the highest rate being 6 per cent applicable above $500,000. The corporate tax rate was raised during the War to 6 per cent, plus graduated excess-profits taxes on amounts exceeding 15 per cent of the value of invested capital. There were also some minor levies. Individual tax rates were raised, particularly as to surtax, which by 1918 became 1 per cent on incomes as low as $5,000 and 65 per cent on incomes above one million. After 1919 there were reductions in individual rates, but little change was made in corporate normal rates. Corporate excess-profits taxes were abolished, but the corporation normal rate never again fell below 10 per cent. In 1934 mild excess-profits taxes (tied in with the capital-stock tax) were revived for corporations, together with graduated

FEDERAL CORPORATE INCOME TAXES

With minor and occasional qualifications, the Federal corporate income taxes were not graduated or progressive until 1935, when a very mild progressive feature was introduced. The medium-sized corporate business has had virtually no tax advantage in this respect. As for individual income, the graduation has in recent years become very steep, but the important feature is that the scale of rates, plus surtax, on intermediate incomes in the range from $10,000 to $50,000 (characteristic of medium-sized entrepreneurs in partnerships, family businesses, and new ventures) had risen by 1940 to roughly 10 to 40 per cent. This scale, together with the mild graduation of the corporation taxes, must be viewed in our present discussion from the standpoint of other conditions that surround medium-sized business generally. Such enterprise has actually derived little, if any, net benefit, because as taxes have risen various profit obstacles and hazards have been placed in its path. Instead of "favoring" small entrepreneurs and enlarging the incentive of middle-class capitalists to enter or participate in business, there has been progressively a lessening of incentive. Business units in the early-development stage are always subject to many uncertainties; surplus is not yet adequate to meet the contingencies of the business cycle; and it is difficult to secure outside capital. Securities can be much more readily and advantageously sold by large corporations than by small firms or corporations, particularly since SEC supervision was established. The failure of Federal taxes, prior to 1939, to permit any "carry-over" for net losses, even from one year to the next, has resulted in a heavy disadvantage to the small, struggling, new enterprise encountering the shocks of depression. Even at present these taxes allow but a two-year offset of loss and profits (not sufficient interval to bridge a cycle), and it can still be said that the Government takes liberally from the profits, while

---

normal income taxes, reaching a maximum of 15 per cent as applying to net income over $40,000. Undistributed profits became taxable between 1936 and 1938 at graduated rates. The rise in the maximum *normal* rates on corporate net profits thereafter rose to 24 per cent at 1940, accompanied by heavy excess-profits levies. By 1941 the normal maximum rate had become 40 per cent. "Excess" (war) profits after 1941 were virtually confiscated.

In 1934 the individual surtax rates were again raised to 4 per cent, beginning at $4,000, with the maximum of 59 per cent over one million (by 1936, 75 per cent). The War has since introduced further surtax increases and has sharply raised the normal individual rates. As the entire tax system becomes almost fantastically complicated, it becomes impossible to describe it accurately in summary figures. If we include rising taxes on estates (difficult to state succinctly), Federal taxes on "capital gains," which are essentially direct capital levies, Federal and local excise taxes, and local Government taxes of other types, which have also been rising, the picture represents a startling trend that appears to have no limiting factors.

the losses belong to the business.   The undistributed-profits tax (1936–1938) also bore very harshly on enterprises of medium size.

In the light of these and other handicaps facing the entrepreneur, the tax burden has been very real and clearly a factor discouraging initiative.   The apparent objective to reach high-income brackets has been very productive of revenue, but the manner of graduation has failed to compensate for the special (and perhaps inherent) difficulties facing middle-class business investment through ownership.   When the further heavy estate and capital-gains taxes are considered, the lack of incentive to direct, moderate-scale investment is readily apparent; the purchase of tax-free bonds has been the natural alternative.   As a corrective against monopoly and a means of developing more employment by building up new production, our tax system has been worse than ineffective.

When it is contended that the expanding scope of governmental activity *requires* these larger and larger seizures of what is virtually potential private capital, let the actual facts be considered.   In recent years nearly two-thirds of Federal expenditures went for relief and welfare work, war, and interest!   The social advancement of our people certainly does not depend in the long run on that kind of outlay; it does depend, however, on more jobs in private industry.   It is not to be denied that by scooping up large revenues from corporations[1] and diverting most of these funds to the need of the "lower third" and other political wards, some enlargement of "income" has been achieved, and this has perhaps stimulated demand for goods.   We are not criticizing the necessary cost of fine public buildings, highways, drainage and soil conservation, forest service and other useful works that are essentially public projects.   But in much of the current enthusiasm for more and more and more "social spending," it is overlooked that only one blade of the economic scissors is working; capital that might have created new jobs is turned into alms, not wages.   As the charity flow is enlarged, the chances for survival of the great middle class diminish.   As more production is absorbed by the mammoth corporation, the more readily can it be taken over *in toto* someday by an all-encompassing and ambitious bureaucracy.   Thus did the European revolutions of the past few decades come about, and thus did the stage become set for a new world conflict. If our production trend should continue to rise to 1980, but in the course of it we lose our economical social heritage, *cui bono?*   Let us devote much more attention to the fact that *income* is not necessarily *capital*. To appropriate capital accumulation and scatter it as income does not of itself provide the tools for translating that money income into real new wealth.

[1] Over 80 per cent of the corporate income-tax revenue came from companies with net income above $100,000 prior to 1941.

In Chart 76, the reader will observe some of the startling trends of the past fifteen years in the matter of the shift of economic effort and income from individuals to Government. Observe the rise from 1925 of over 200 per cent in the proportion of national-income payments flowing from all governmental sources. Observe the rise of nearly 200 per cent in the ratio of Federal and local Government tax receipts to the national income. Notice that the number of new businesses organized (according to Dun & Bradstreet), although it had risen somewhat from

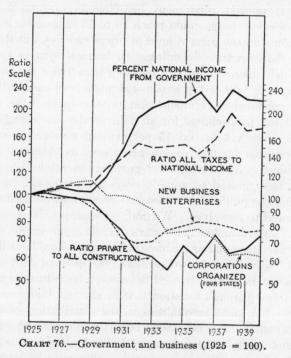

CHART 76.—Government and business (1925 = 100).

the very low point of 1932, had entirely failed, as late as 1940, to recuperate to the 1925 level, to say nothing of the 1929 level. The number of new corporations organized in four leading states has maintained a consistent downward trend ever since 1929. The ratio of private to total construction in the United States remained, even in 1940, more than 20 per cent below the level of 1925. These are disconcerting trends to anyone who conceives a democratic economic system as necessarily involving private-capital initiative and the integrity of equity ownership in productive and personal wealth.[1]

[1] In connection with this chart, consider the statement of Charles C. Abbott: "It seems probable that a series of studies would show that in view of the present tax structure a new promotion must promise, quickly, an annual return of 15 or 20 per

The possible trend to bureaucracy and unlimited public debt will be greatly accelerated by the present War. We entered it with public finances already gravely unbalanced. We have proceeded to raise tax rates and the scale of graduation and lowered tax exemptions, while conspicuously "protecting" the huge segment of national income represented by wages from more than nominal taxation. The Federal debt, already far too high in 1939, may soon exceed 200 billions. Without any repayments, the annual charge for interest alone can reach 6 or 8 billions. If modest repayment installments are made, the total annual-debt service charge could reach 10 to 15 billions for many years. National income on the present level of prices can rise, but it rises much less rapidly than wartime spending. *So long as inflation is controlled,* the Federal debt alone could still be more than twice the total income payments, and *the total cost of servicing it* might well exceed 10 per cent. Since there are local government and private (net) debts of at least 130 billions,[1] the total charge for all debt service, including reasonable amortization, may yet exceed 15 per cent of national income! This makes no provision for new requirements such as veterans' and social-security pensions, which involve fast-growing potential claims.

Hence it is suggested by some observers that we comfort ourselves by considering the public debt at least as *permanent;* no need to pay it— for it is all owed to ourselves. We find, for example, Hansen and Greer stating that "a government debt *internally held* is so completely different from an ordinary personal or business debt that it should hardly be called a debt at all." We are told further that "the internal debt of a government need never be paid. It need never even be reduced, except (1) to prevent inflation (through taxation that produces a budgetary surplus); (2) to correct too great inequalities in the distribution of wealth and income; or (3) when it has become so large that taxation to service it disrupts the functioning of the economy. Individual lenders to the government (bondholders) are, of course, repaid. They must be, whenever their bonds fall due. But always there are others ready to take their places; if not individuals, then banks. This is true in modern nations no matter what happens."[2] Taken in conjunction with the Keynesian notion that repayment of part of the war taxes is not only permissible but very desir-

cent in order to be attractive to persons of moderate wealth." (*American Economic Review*, March, 1941, Supplement, p. 135. See also C. C. Abbott and E. M. Zuckert, *Venture Capital and Taxation, Quarterly Journal of Economics*, August, 1941.)

[1] *Survey of Current Business*, November, 1941, p. 21. This appears to be a conservative estimate, made by the U.S. Department of Commerce.

[2] Alvin H. Hansen and Guy Greer, The Federal Debt and the Future, *Harper's Magazine*, April, 1942, pp. 491–492. Mr. Greer, it may be added, proposed in a previous *Harper's* article that the Government invest in the equities of large utility and other industries, borrowing funds from the public and thus becoming virtually a

able, this is indeed a bold declaration of the sanctity of permanent debt. Despite the superficial appeal to the historical record of nations (bankrupt or ruined) that have maintained enormous national debts, the central fallacy in this argument lies in ignoring the *stagnation of capital* as concentrated stale-debt charges mount. This view illustrates pointedly the present-day confusion of ideas as to income and capital. An enormous permanent national debt, like any other sudden mass of indebtedness, requires constant collection of taxes upon potential private *capital*, denying it an opportunity to mobilize for industrial uses, and the proceeds are continually scattered as *income* to public bondholders. True, they are all in the national family; but if the head of a family prevents its members from accumulating reserves by a continuous breaking up of savings, we can well imagine why they will not finance business. Whoever considers the size of internal-debt costs immaterial, by implication considers the continuance of private capitalism and private property immaterial. Government, by continually turning private surpluses into income, rather than useful capital, obstructs capital formation, especially among the intermediate groups. The three conditions named by Hansen and Greer as occasion (and the only occasion) for national-debt reduction fail to include the most important of all—preservation of private equity in the economic system. No government that has embarked on a course of permanent heavy debt ever worries about inflation, the concentration of (*its own*) economic power, or the economic system it seeks to supplant. These are all tangent points. The *real* reason for keeping down an internal debt, and reducing it whenever possible, is the same as the reasons applying to private debt or international debt—the avoidance of excessive leverage on equity ownership and the preservation of an individual-property system.

Much current opinion has not faced the simple political fact that there is no such thing as a "static" national debt. Once a nation assumes that there is no harm in a fixed debt, or in confusing income and capital, and goes merrily on continually breaking up capital accumulation by heavy taxes to pay debt charges, the result is that more and more loan capital fails to "circulate," and equity wealth is scattered centrifugally into smaller and smaller bits that eventually may become mere doles of "income" from the State. National debts are all spirals: either you pay off or you build up, as France, for example, did for decades, to her everlasting sorrow. To argue that there is no harm in standing still is merely an indirect way of intimating there is no harm in going the limit.

---

holding organization, with prospects of ultimately owning and managing the properties. The defense of a large public debt is usually found associated with some such collectivist preoccupation.

FINANCIAL PROBLEMS CREATED BY WORLD WAR II

Let us be realistic about the tremendous aggravation of our financial problems already created by World War II. A schedule of debt reduction must be initiated as soon as it is practicable. Such a procedure could go far to temper the very probable boom condition that will follow shortly after the peace. Large holdings of Federal obligations will be redeemed by individuals after this War. To meet these demands may require new Federal borrowing from the banks or the printing of new currency. There will probably be a spectacular increase in private spending to make up wartime deficiencies. Thus a part of our huge debt may be monetized—to the extent that redemptions are not accomplished by additional taxes or prompt reduction of nonessential spending. Since bond prices may decline during this period, new borrowings will further increase the fixed charges, and the conversion of short debt to long-term debt will be rendered difficult. We have merely deferred, not solved, our inflation problem of World War II. We also know that the great inflations produced by World War I came *after* the fighting was over.

It would appear desirable to utilize specifically all social-security[1] and all excise-tax (or sales-tax) revenue for several years following the War to redeem Federal obligations presented for payment. Any amounts accruing from foreign governments should also be so used. Voluntary retirement of the Federal debt can be accelerated in good business years and moderated in recession periods, but retirement must go on.

This implies that to launch large new public-work plans immediately after the War, by adding new billions of debt, would be exceedingly unwise. What is essential in promoting readjustment is not public spending but the use of the public planning agencies to assist manufacturers to resume normal production. This requires careful study to reduce confusion and lost motion. Concerns in the intermediate range must be given some protection against the technological advantages that very large units are certain to derive from their war-production experience and research efforts. There must be more attention to legitimate capital needs, far fewer to share-the-wealth panaceas. All industries will need the help of Government in reabsorbing labor and in overcoming the difficulties emerging from a temporary concentration of labor forces in certain geographic areas. These are a few among the many directions of helpful coordination that require intelligent and expert staff work, not the squandering of new billions to pump a postwar boom still higher.

If the huge Federal war debt can be reduced only gradually, it follows that private and local government debt must be drastically reduced.

---

[1] Assuming that the present system is continued and the rates are according to existing plans.

The low interest rates of recent years have already had some effect along this line, but beyond a certain point mere low rates of interest cease to accomplish anything worth while. There is an even greater need for a new set of legal procedures and formulas to speed the renovation of corporate capital structures.[1] There are many ways in which private production and service industries could be induced to cut down borrowing and increase the use of equity capital other than by hamstringing all business merely to create the appearance of a low "interest" rate. Let us keep interest rates on an even keel, but let the level be determined by the demand and supply of capital and the basic return from equity investment, not by money-market juggling and needless repression of new capital issue. Among the policies that could be helpful in rectifying an over-all debt congestion would be these:

1. Drastically reduce taxes on *business net income* (other than war excess profits) in order to restore and enhance solvency. The raising of "normal" taxes on corporate profits to the prevailing rates has already forced even large companies to borrow, virtually to pay taxes; this means that to that extent the war is being financed by bank credit and other borrowings, and the fiscal advantage of taxation is illusory.

2. If some taxes of this nature are to be continued, provide taxable income deductions for all debt repayment by business.

3. Impose any further business income taxes in such fashion that they do not penalize equity return. There is no sound reason why capital payments to creditors should be tax-free, while payment to equity capital bears all these taxes.[2]

[1] If Assistant Attorney General Thurman Arnold could be persuaded to divert the services of his many able lawyers to this problem rather than using their valuable talents merely to harass industrial corporations to make them fit the competitive theories of a past age, he would be performing an outstanding national service.

[2] The taxation study by C. J. Hynning, Gerhard Colm, and others submitted as *Monograph* 9 of the TNEC, points out (p. 92) that since 1918, the revenue laws have removed all the earlier restrictions upon deductibility of interest by corporations. Actual experience indicates that the income-tax burden is relatively heavier upon companies with a high proportion of equity capital, and vice versa. The Securities and Exchange Commission has already undertaken studies of this matter, with a view to introducing remedial action. Beyond this, the SEC has given considerable attention to the entire problem of reducing business debt and enlarging the proportion of equity financing.

Jerome Frank, while chairman of the Commission, several times expressed his views on this question. (See his address before the National Association of Securities Commissioners, Kansas City, Mo., Sept. 22, 1938.) He has stated: "The history of railroad financing goes to show that maybe, at least with respect to railroads, we need to take a new attitude concerning interest: that, while, in earlier periods, the condemnation of interest-taking—whether it purported to be based on theological, or moral, or economic grounds—was founded upon regard for the borrower, today we may perhaps need to put severe restrictions upon interest-taking out of regard for the

4. Eliminate, as general conditions become more nearly normal, existing legal restrictions upon institutional investment in equity securities (excepting commercial banks). There seems to be no valid reason why life-insurance companies should be forbidden by state legislation to invest their funds in accordance with simple prudence rather than narrow formulas. Present practice is calculated to enhance the very leverage and instability in share values that serves as the leading excuse for maintaining that practice.

5. Reduce State and local Government debt by eliminating tax-exemption features from such obligations in the future and reducing wasteful and unnecessary expenditures in these jurisdictions.

---

welfare of the investor. And if that should turn out to be true as to railroad financing, it may be that it would be equally applicable to the financing of our other great industries."

Mr. Frank has suggested that for small and medium-sized business organizations it might be possible to establish "frankly speculative" regional investment companies to encourage their development. (See *The New York Times*, Apr. 26, 1940.) These would be empowered to purchase stock of deserving and growing local businesses. It is in the range of companies having capital requirements from about fifty thousand up to a million dollars that have found the greatest difficulty in raising equity capital or even loan capital in the open market.

Another member of the SEC, Ganson Purcell, has made a number of addresses in which he has emphasized the importance of scaling down unnecessary funded debt of corporations rather than merely refunding that debt into new securities. He has stated the importance of this as a means of protecting the owners of corporations from the loss of their equity during the postwar readjustment period. He has pointed out that in readjusting ourselves after the War, it will be important for American industry to take advantage of its wartime earnings to set aside reserves. "Reserves not needed for defense activity must be carefully stored up against the day when they will be needed for this vital post-war purpose. This is a clear recognition of the need for corporate reserve as a protection not only to equity but to employment." (Some Future Aspects of the Financial Markets, Oct. 17, 1941.) In another connection, Purcell has stated, "The investment industry must be more than ever alert to its responsibility to encourage a type of corporate structure that will fit the needs of our productive economy, as that economy expands in some directions and contracts in others. We must have the type of financial structure that can weather the inevitable oscillations of the trade and business cycle. . . . Topheavy corporate debt must be replaced with more resilient forms of capitalization. . . . We cannot overlook the possibility that it may prove wise to require that corporations retain a substantial portion of their earnings as a further means of building up their reserves." (*National Defense and the American Investor*, Nov. 24, 1941.)

Such enlightened ideas with respect to the wisdom of permitting business units to accumulate adequate surplus are encouraging, for they indicate that at least some personalities among the membership of the Securities and Exchange Commission are aware of the importance of preserving that solvency in our productive system without which equity capital cannot function and without which we can easily drift gradually into a colossal, more or less frozen, debt structure that leads eventually to collectivism.

Beyond these steps we have also other possible opportunities to provide for continued financial integrity and postwar progress. Tax revenue must be obtained on a broader basis, not from the middle- and high-income segments alone. If we mainly confine income taxation, as we should, to individual income in the interest of well-sustained production incentive, we must develop a scientific, not a haphazard, fiscal procedure. We cannot indefinitely refrain from fair and reasonable demands upon employed wage earners for their contribution to the State; they must be regarded as *solvent citizens,* not the *charity clients* of bureaucracy. A modification of the unemployment-compensation taxes, as has been proposed, is highly important in this connection. The old-age-pension system may also come in for some overhauling to prevent its abuse as merely another debt-building device. The incidence of taxes on individual income might be modified in such fashion as to render graduation affecting the middle range less obstructive to capital use, at the same time reducing, throughout the scale, the estate taxes and other levies falling directly on capital. We must afford incentive to put savings to work and withdraw the incentives to preserve huge debts as a means of avoiding the kind of active investment that can contribute to full employment.

But over and above all these technical aspects of financial and fiscal policy, there must be emphasis upon production progress capable of validating the promises of payments to the holders of debt claims. If the national income is to be further expanded, with a minimum of price inflation, it must expand in terms of volume and therefore of *real* wealth. The great lesson to be learned from the past quarter century of war and international chaos is that economists and governments have failed to recognize the importance of production or the prerequisites of its existence. Through international claims, stagnant or frozen internal debt, and false theories of the uses of capital, the efforts of business and individual enterprise to develop full production and create full employment have been obstructed more than they have been encouraged. We have feared the consequences of full production because some segments of production had become unbalanced; we became suspicious of capital investment because it became confused with speculation or with money lending. But we must now choose our course as between full production and wise use of capital to build the equity of each and every citizen in a free civilization, or reversion, through war and wasted resources, to feudalism and serfdom.

APPENDIX 1

ANNUAL INDEX OF AMERICAN TRADE AND PRODUCTION, 1700–1940

The first statistical problem in constructing this index was to obtain data from which a reasonably homogeneous measure might be derived, reflecting closely the annual changes in physical magnitude, divorced from price and value fluctuations, and capable of affording a basis for determining not only the cyclical movements but also the gradient of long-term or secular trend.

It was decided that the foundation of the trade and production index would be an annual series taking the form of an "intermediate" trend that would adapt itself with some flexibility to such underlying long tidal movements as might be present. To accomplish this it was considered advisable to use a smoothing of the moving-average type. Five-year averages were computed from the intermediate trend, and with these as a basis, the technique of a least-square function for *secular* trend was applied to the five-year series, the annual data being calibrated later.

In order to express the year-to-year fluctuations of cyclical type, it was not practicable to use throughout the long period the same basic data as were employed for measuring intermediate trend. From 1700 to the early part of the nineteenth century —a period of extreme dearth of economic data—the annual cyclical index employed the same basic data, with adjustments, as were used in the intermediate trend computation. In the succeeding period it was found that better results could be obtained by superimposing upon the intermediate trend various series of cyclical deviation based upon such annual data as appeared best to describe these particular movements.

As stated in Chapter 3, a quantitative index of business cannot be merely a summation of physical quantities. It must be essentially an expression of either comprehensive production or trade values in terms of constant prices or aggregate money values of trade, national income, etc., adjusted to a "deflated" basis by an index number of prices of appropriate and comprehensive scope. Throughout the eighteenth century and first half of the nineteenth, production statistics pertaining to American economic life are extremely rare. For the early American Colonies there are no available Colonial records of *total* exports or imports for any Colony, save for occasional years, as preserved in the writings of contemporary chroniclers. It is exceedingly fortunate, however, that statistical data have been preserved of one very significant factor: the British exports to (and imports from) each of the American Colonies, beginning at 1697. These relate to essentially calendar years. The data were assembled with considerable care by the British authorities and include the trade from the standpoint first of England and Wales, and after 1752 from England, Wales, and Scotland, that is, Great Britain. It is of great importance, however, that these figures relating to the trade between Britain and the American Colonies permit the expression of variation in approximately the very physical (constant-price) terms that the problem demands.

Beginning at 1697, British foreign trade was officially recorded in terms, not of the prevailing prices of the goods but of the prices that prevailed in 1697. The resulting figures, therefore, may be converted to relative numbers, which are essentially weighted indexes of changes in the *volume* of imports or exports, substantially equivalent to those resulting from our more modern technique of the aggregative index number.   The trade records, it is interesting to note, were kept in this fashion until almost the middle of the nineteenth century, although prior to that time actual values at current prices were also introduced.

Tests were made of the data of British-Colonial trade in the form of imports into the Colonies, exports from the Colonies, and exports plus imports, over an extended period.   It appeared from these tests that the imports into the Colonies from England (or Great Britain) would serve quite as well as other alternatives as a basis for developing the intermediate and long-term trend indexes.

There was, furthermore, the consideration that imports into the Colonies from Britain (excluding other than British products) gave emphasis to the movement of manufactured articles such as the Colonies then obtained predominantly from the mother country.   British legislation and pioneer conditions in the Colonies during most of the eighteenth century contributed to the existence of an essentially agricultural economy, in which the production of ships, clothing, and buildings formed the principal tasks of the artisans in the few urban areas.   The Southern Colonies, with their production of tobacco and rice, provided export surpluses contributing in large measure to the means of payment for imports.   New England and the Middle Colonies provided timber and ships for Britain, but a larger part of their export trade was conducted with southern Europe, Africa, and the West Indies.   Yet imports of manufactured and processed goods from the British Isles found their way into the towns throughout the Colonial seaboard, and a part of this imported merchandise drifted into the interior and even frontier areas.   Fluctuations from year to year in the Colonial imports from Britain probably reflect with considerable accuracy the changing fortunes of the urban merchants and the numerous artisans of all kinds to whose support the merchant class contributed.   Agricultural surpluses, particularly in the Southern Colonies, largely provided the means for obtaining articles of British manufacture, but economic and financial conditions within the Colonies as a whole gave rise to changes in the importation of materials used in connection with Colonial industry and construction.   To this extent the imports from Britain would reflect the changing needs for such commodities, and this commodity flow would naturally reflect nonagricultural "business" activity.

A large part of the productive activity of the early Colonies represented self-supporting family enterprise and, in the great expanse of frontier area, virtually isolated, noncommercial existence.   There is no way accurately to measure just what part of the Colonial production was of this type, as compared with production entering in some measure into *trade*, either domestic or foreign, or into commercial fabrication or construction activity.   It could fairly be assumed, however, that changes in the relation of noncommercial to commercial enterprise came about gradually.   It can be further assumed that such production as occurred in the sparsely settled self-sufficing communities was predominantly of the agricultural type and that the changes occurring in this type of production through the years would closely correspond to the pattern of population growth.   According to the results stated in Chapter **7** (Chart 12), an index number constructed from annually interpolated population data almost perfectly approximates the long-term trend of total agricultural production. Therefore an index derived from available estimates of annual population was used to provide that portion of the total production index during the eighteenth and part of the nineteenth centuries, when agriculture of a largely self-sufficing character was decidedly important.

In 1869 agricultural gross income in the United States comprised about 40 per cent of total national income, on the basis of the income estimates described in Appendixes 4 and 5. This percentage was extrapolated back to 1800 by straight-line interpolation, bringing the proportion at 1800 to 50 per cent. The latter figure was maintained constant back to 1700, to provide an estimated relative weight for the *noncommercial* agricultural element in total economic activity. Since the gradient of import trade closely approximates that of population in the eighteenth century, errors in the foregoing weighting have very little significance. We are primarily concerned with a measure of the country's real income, divorced from price and value changes. We might express this either as an index of physical *trade* or an index of physical *production*. These are not exactly identical, because a certain part of commercial activity (in the broad sense) consists of direct personal service, not represented by the creation of physical commodities or structures. But in an index number for practical use this is not of material consequence, since the intangible service and trade elements in national real income tend to vary quite closely with, and, indeed, may be functionally correlated with, changes in that portion of the total activity resulting in creation of physical wealth. In other words, the vast preponderance of that mass of activities which we call "business," or the flow of useful goods and service into the control of individuals, proceeds along with changes in *physical production* and is largely conditioned thereby. Conversely, even in the early Colonial period, and certainly in the towns and cities, a substantial amount of fabrication and construction of all kinds was being undertaken for commercial ends and hence resulted in fluctuations and growth trends that a quantitative measure of imports from the world's great industrial center of that day reliably reflect.

We have, then, two sets of data from which, as far back as 1700, we can build at least a closely approximate statistical index of the significant changes in total production and physical trade. The intermediate trend series was, therefore, built up by combining, with variable weights, two constituents—one reflecting the agricultural factor, which correlates mainly with population growth, and a second industry and trade factor, which was represented throughout the eighteenth century by annual data of imports into the Colonies from the British Isles of British products, with the use of material that happened fortunately to be in a form appropriate to the problem.

At this point attention must be given to one special problem that arises in measuring the year-to-year *cyclical* fluctuations, as distinct from the *intermediate trend* or the long-term *secular* trend. Should the year-to-year changes be considered as including agricultural production, or are they to be considered exclusively a reflection of that part of the total activity which may be termed "industrial" and "commercial"? As stated in Chapters 7 and 8, the year-to-year changes in agricultural production do not necessarily reflect changes in the income, or purchasing power, of farm producers who sell their surpluses in the market. Over a *period* of years variation in the level of total farm production does have significance both for producers and for the general standard of living; but these changes, insofar as they depart from the pattern of population trend, do not appear to correlate statistically with what we know from the study of general industry, trade variations, or "business cycles" in more recent years. During the early Colonial period, when so much of the agriculture was localized and insulated from any "market," it appears wholly probable that year-to-year fluctuations in extractive production *in the aggregate* would probably have been relatively slight, since local variations of weather and harvest would to a large extent have canceled out. Also, the incentive to expansion or contraction of farm production resulting from general market conditions or prices would certainly have been of relatively minor net importance during at least the eighteenth century.

On the basis of these considerations, it was decided to advance the principle throughout this work that the *year-to-year* cyclical fluctuations should be divorced from purely agricultural factors as far as possible, in order to reflect specifically the rhythm or short-term vibrations having to do primarily with industry and physical trade and hence with what today is understood by the course of the "business" cycle.

Coming now to the specific data and statistical treatment, we begin at 1700 with the "official" sterling values (at the constant prices of 1697) of exports of English products to the American Colonies, taken from MacGregor, "Progress of America," Vol. II, Part 2, p. 916. At 1760 these are spliced to similar data from McPherson, "Annals of Commerce," Vol. III. The data make it possible to combine exports to the Colonies from England and Wales with data of exports to the various British Colonies in the West Indies. It is necessary to take into account that during the wars between the British Alliance and the French Alliance from 1793 to 1815, in which naval blockade was intermittently attempted, a considerable amount of the British exports destined for the American Colonies went surreptitiously through the various islands of the West Indies. American Colonial exports also utilized these entrepots. Prior to the War it was found that the West Indies trade with the British Isles fluctuated very closely with their trade with the American Colonies. By splicing these combined figures as far back as 1760, the resulting index takes into account the extent to which exports from England direct to the American Colonies were supplemented by the indirect and smuggling trade under the war conditions.

From 1799 to 1818, the index continues to include the British exports to the West Indies, but another splicing was necessary in order to permit a transition from McPherson's tables, which are based upon the trade originating in England and Wales, to the trade including Scotland. McPherson's tables end with the year 1800, and it is necessary to splice his data to a new series. The new series consists of exports from Great Britain to the American Colonies as given in MacGregor's table plus British exports to the British West Indies found in Marshall's "Digest of Accounts," Part II, pp. 71*ff*. These totals were spliced to the preceding series, using the 1793–1797 average for conversion and beginning the new series at 1799. These figures for the first time include Scotland as well as England and Wales as the source of the exports. The data continue to be expressed in constant "official" prices and pertain to virtually calendar years, as before.

Beginning at 1819 the British exports to the West Indies were omitted from the trade index, a splice being made on the basis of the ratio at 1818. Thereafter, the British data extend to 1833, beyond which year they become less useful, inasmuch as imports into the United States (total dollar values) become more representative of the flow of this country's trade and productive activity as a whole.

It would have been possible as early as 1790 to supplement the official values of British exports by the use of the total import figure of the United States. Prior to 1821, however, our import data were not completely recorded, although estimates were officially made (in 1835) covering the period 1790 to 1820 and the data from 1811 to 1820 were used for splicing purposes. Beginning at 1821, the values of total imports represent probably the most accurate business-activity figures relating to the United States, and this remains true until along in the 1860's, when some production and domestic transportation data begin to be available. Figures of the latter and more specific type were used at a later stage of these computations. But it was decided to utilize the total imports through a fairly extended period, first, because careful comparisons among all available materials indicated that at least for the purpose of establishing the *intermediate trend* of business activity the import data (as finally adjusted) represented a homogeneous measure, definitely correlating with general industrial and trade activity; and, second, these figures represent probably the most carefully recorded series capable of being used in this way.

Before describing the manner of splicing the United States import series to the British data, certain adjustments were found necessary. It was necessary first to translate the dollar values into a form roughly approximating an index of changes in physical trade volume. This was accomplished by "deflating" the dollar values by an index of wholesale-commodity prices, obtained by splicing several suitable series of import prices (Arthur Cole, "Wholesale Prices in the United States, 1700–1861," Smith and Cole, "Fluctuations in American Business, 1790–1860") and general wholesale prices (Warren and Pearson, "Prices").

The official import-trade figures are recorded for the period of greenbacks (1861–1879) in terms of gold. It was therefore necessary to apply a correction for the premium on gold in terms of paper currency and then apply the deflating index to the computed *currency* values.

Another adjustment was made in the trade series for the period 1861–1875, inclusive, by splicing on an index of United States imports *plus* exports. This was done in order to give due weight to the extraordinary effects of the Civil War upon *total* American trade and production. During that War and for a number of years thereafter, the great Southern export, cotton, suffered tremendous demoralization. By the late 1870's this regional impairment was becoming of minor importance for the country as a whole, and hence, beginning at 1876, the import series alone was again used and carried back to 1890. Beyond that date various tests indicated that import trade began to lose some of its significance as an indicator of the general course of American business.

A number of subsidiary tests were made with long-term series of data pertaining to shipping tonnage, coastal trade, various phases of internal commerce, etc., but it was found necessary to exclude all this material because of special characteristics that render these phases unsuitable as measures of either value or volume of trade and production as a whole.

We now return to the problem of tying together the index of general business activity based upon the British sterling figures to 1820 and the index based upon deflated United States imports. Both series were converted into relatives, with the average of 1811–1820 as a base. For this same period 1811–1820, the British index series and the United States import index were averaged; this was justified by the close degree of correlation between the changes of the two series, in terms of both trend and year-to-year movements. This also provided a means of interpolating a figure for 1813 for which the British data afforded no figures because of destruction by fire of the official records of that year. The index of deflated imports was then carried forward to 1890 and combined, as described below, with a total production index from 1871 to 1890.

The trade index down to this point is considered to reflect, with increasing accuracy through the years, those phases of American business which may be described as industrial, commercial, and not specifically related to agriculture or representative of the more or less isolated production processes. It is clear, however, that the total production or over-all real income of the American people experienced growth changes, which the index of trade, reflecting mainly industrial activity only, would not completely measure. It has been estimated that at the beginning of the eighteenth century, agriculture and activities of the self-supporting communities contributed to total production a component having a weighting of about one-half of the total and probably important as a *trend element* rather than a cyclical index. We employ the annual (interpolated) population figures as a means of approximating an index of that farm-frontier portion of the total economic activity. The over-all index, then, consists of two factors: (1) the volume index of trade (implying also industrial production), as described above, with the base at 1811–1820; and (2) an annual population-growth series, converted to the same index base. Population data were taken from the National Resources Committee's "Problems of a Changing Population," p. 21, 1938.

Beginning with the period shortly after the Civil War, several annual indexes of production or trade have already been developed. Some of these relate to industrial activity only; others relate to combined indusrial and agricultural and mineral production; still others combine industrial activity with indicators of commerce, transportation, etc. Among the best known of these various indexes are those prepared by G. F. Warren and F. A. Pearson, presented in *Memoir* 144 (1932) of the Cornell University Agricultural Experiment Station. These indexes relate to the production of *basic materials* and were prepared with several different systems of weighting, giving somewhat diverse results. This material was not used in the present work because all the indexes appeared to involve weights that vastly overemphasize the agricultural factors in basic production.

Another series of index numbers relating to total production was prepared by Dr. Warren M. Persons, to be found in his "Forecasting Business Cycles" (1932). His index begins at 1863 with industrial production only, but shortly thereafter an over-all index is presented, including agricultural production, but based upon a very narrow range of data. These annual index numbers were revised and extended, as of 1899 forward, in the *Review of Economic Statistics*, Aug. 15, 1933. Persons' index of total production is more carefully weighted than that of Warren and Pearson, since the relative weights assigned to agriculture and to industrial and mineral production were determined with considerable care from income estimates.

It was decided to construct a new index of *total* production utilizing Person's series for the *industrial* component as far as 1918 and the comprehensive index of farm production recently made available by Louis H. Bean and Frederick Strauss (see *U.S. Department of Agriculture Technical Bulletin* 703, December, 1940). The farm-production data begin at 1869. A wide variety of farm products, including animal products, is included, and the estimates for the earlier years appear to have been carefully made. This Bean-Strauss farm-production index was first converted to relatives of 1899, comparable to Persons' industrial-production base. These data were spliced at 1934 to the U.S. Department of Agriculture production indexes, as given down to 1940 in the *Agricultural Situation*, January, 1942.

The data of Persons' industrial production index, beginning at 1871, were taken from *Hearings before the Temporary National Economic Committee*, 75th Congress, Third Session, Vol. I, p. 200. In combining the two series, variable weights were used, derived by smooth interpolation of the ratio of total farm gross income to estimated total national private-production income. The latter data were the total of the estimates of the National Industrial Conference Board (Robert F. Martin, "National Income in the United States, 1799–1938," p. 58), excluding agriculture, and gross farm income prior to 1880, with the use of the data described in Appendix 5. A series of variable "weights" was derived, starting at 1869 with 40 per cent for agriculture and 60 per cent for industry. The agricultural factor diminishes gradually to 18 per cent after 1931.

Applying this weighting system to combine the farm-production index with the industrial-production index, beginning at 1871, a final index of total production was developed with the base year at 1899. A comparison of the general drift of this index from 1871 to 1890 with the index previously developed from the foreign trade statistics revealed virtually identical *trend* slopes.   Even the cyclical movements from year to year are clearly revealed in both of the series, although the patterns differ slightly in detail.

The production index was then used to carry forward the deflated-imports series with a conversion ratio based upon the average relation from 1871 to 1890.   The final index was obtained by averaging the import-trade series (1811–1820 base) and the total-production series (converted to the same base) over the period 1871–1890 and thereafter using the production index only, relating still to the 1811–1820 base and brought to 1940 in that form.

We now have a long annual series, extending from 1700 to 1940, which may be termed a "preliminary" index from which the *intermediate trend* of physical trade and production was computed.   In order to derive from these figures an intermediate trend having sufficient flexibility to adapt itself to such major cyclical or wavelike changes as might be encountered, it was decided to employ the principle of a long-term moving average.   A series of experiments indicated that good results were obtained by computing two sets of moving averages of varying length of period, one a 15-year centered moving average, the other a 21-year centered moving average. A final average of these two moving averages was, therefore, computed from the preliminary trade and production index.   It was found that this combination of moving averages tended to counteract the mild element of distortion inherent in any given moving average, and a much smoother final result was obtained than could have been had by using either average alone.

This intermediate-trend index (Chart 4) provided the statistical foundation for the final indexes of trade and production.   The further steps involved were, first, to relate to this trend the data of a year-to-year cyclical index and, finally, to fit a mathematical least-squares function to the *intermediate* trend to establish the overall *secular* trend of growth or rate of progress througout the entire period, 1700–1940.

During and somewhat beyond the period of the eighteenth century, there was found but one set of data capable of depicting general business change reliably, and this was used in the foregoing analysis to establish the *intermediate trend*.   By computing the percentages of the actual annual data to this moving trend, the year-to-year cyclical pattern is made clearly apparent.   But this pattern reveals an amplitude of fluctuation that is probably still an exaggerated reflection of the actual intensity of cyclical changes in the country's general business throughout those years.   The foreign-trade material that was used represents an aspect of business and a type of statistics known to have had then, and to have today, a much higher average amplitude of cyclical fluctuation than has been found in more comprehensive measures of business cycles.   If, for example, we compare the average cyclical amplitude of imports or exports today with the amplitude of the general production-trade cycle, as it has been measured by such indexes as Carl Snyder's Index of Total Trade and Production or Leonard P. Ayres' Index of Business Conditions, it is at once apparent that although the foreign-trade statistics still reflect fairly clearly the *pattern* of business conditions, they do so with exaggerated emphasis.   It was therefore decided to adjust the amplitude of the cyclical percentages of the index of trade by first comparing the cylical deviations, as obtained from the foregoing data from 1790 to 1855, with the similar cyclical deviations of the annual Business Index prepared by Ayres for the same period, inasmuch as Ayres had made careful adjustments for this amplitude factor.   Tests of his later data indicated that the amplitude of his index corresponds closely to what might be considered the average fluctuation range of physical trade and production (or real national income).   It was found that Ayres' data have a standard deviation of 7.98, whereas the cycles of the trade data have a standard deviation of 13.92 (ratio 0.573). Rounding out the ratio to 0.60 as an approximate cyclical correction, the deviations of the import-trade index were thereby readjusted to reduce the amplitude, and this correction was extended from 1800 back to 1700.

Coming to the nineteenth century, when the range of statistical data becomes wider, it was found possible to utilize for measuring the *cyclical* pattern of business changes various series not identical with those which entered into construction of the intermediate trends. From 1800 to 1833, the data used to obtain the *cyclical* deviations are of the same general character as for the intermediate series, but the cyclical index numbers, based upon British exports to the United States and the deflated imports into the United States, were averaged, and the import figures were converted to approximate calendar years by taking 2-year moving averages, entered as of the first year. From 1834 to 1854 the deflated United States imports alone were used with the same type of calendar-year adjustment. Throughout the period 1800–1854, an amplitude adjustment similar to that previously described was employed.

Beginning at 1855, there are available carefully prepared annual index numbers of the cyclical fluctuations of industrial production and physical-trade activity, prepared by Leonard P. Ayres. His figures, in terms of percentages of trend, were directly applied to the intermediate-trend series previously described, and this was continued down to 1884. Beginning at 1885, there are available the annual index numbers of Warren M. Persons relating (1) to *industrial* production and (2) from 1899 to 1918, a more comprehensive index of industrial production *and trade*. These segments were spliced together with the preceding data, and percentages of a 15- to 21-year moving average were computed as the basis for the *cyclical index*. No adjustment was made for amplitude, since the average amplitude of the series was found to be fairly close to that of Ayres' cyclical business index.

Beginning at 1919, Colonel Ayres had used the index of industrial production prepared by the Federal Reserve Board to continue his cyclical series. Most of the other well-known indexes of business conditions for this later period have utilized either the Federal Reserve index or data closely comparable with that index. The Federal Reserve index of industrial production, however, is responsive to the rather violent cyclical fluctuations in that segment comprising the durable-goods industries and therefore has a range of amplitude, as measured in terms of deviations from estimated trend over the past 20 years, considerably greater than the average amplitude of a comprehensive, over-all production and trade index. The Standard Statistics Company (now Standard and Poor's Corporation) has prepared an index of industrial production, using methods and data more or less comparable to those used by the Federal Reserve Board indexes. The Standard Statistics index extends back to 1884 and thus serves as a useful means of determining approximately how the Federal Reserve Board index would look if it had been worked back through those earlier years. During the period 1919–1940, the Standard Statistics index of production agrees very closely with the Federal Reserve index. The standard deviation for the Standard Statistics index from 1885 to 1918 is 16.73; Ayres' index shows a standard deviation of only 6.84.

Another set of comparisons of amplitude was worked out between the Federal Reserve index of industrial production (manufacturing and mining) and two other indexes, which were designed specifically to reflect the range of variability in over-all production and trade. One of these is the index of general production and trade prepared by the Federal Reserve Bank of New York under the direction of Carl Snyder. The average cyclical deviation of this index, 1919–1938, was found to be about 70 per cent of that of the Federal Reserve Board index, similarly adjusted for trend. The amplitude of the Federal Reserve Board index was also compared with that of the series prepared by the National Industrial Conference Board for total national-production income, deflated for cost of living. This series was found to have 67 per cent of the amplitude of the Federal Reserve index. These amplitude comparisons therefore agree in indicating that reduction of the amplitude of the Federal Reserve index cycles by about 30 per cent appears necessary to take fully into account those many production and commercial processes known to have a narrow range of cyclical variability. The Federal Reserve data, so adjusted, were used to continue the series of cyclical percentages relative to intermediate trend. It should be added that in comparing the Federal Reserve index in this adjusted form with other indexes of *general* production of trade or national (real) income, it was found that the range of cyclical movements from year to year was very consistent, and hence this reduction in amplitude of the Federal Reserve index cycles affords a result that, although involving a minor element of estimation, represents a reasonably faithful picture of the general trade and production cycles of the United States.

There remained, finally, the computation of an over-all *secular* growth trend for the general business index, covering the entire period of 240 years. The intermediate-trend index clearly indicated that the growth of the country's business activity in terms of volume has not been smoothly continuous but has rather proceeded in long waves, with almost no net upward drift during several periods of considerable length. It was then to be ascertained what had been the long-range average rate of growth, such as might be conceived as balancing the longer wavelike or tidal intermediate movements, indicating the extent to which the secular trend of growth may have been gradually modified through the decades.

A mathematically fitted secular trend was derived from data in the form of 5-year averages of the index of intermediate trend. This was fitted to the logarithms of the 5-year averages by the method of orthogonal polynomials (devised by R. A. Fisher). The result is equivalent to what would be obtained by the use of a third-degree least-squares equation in terms of logarithms of the data. The resulting trend series adjusts itself very slightly to long-term changes in the rate of growth, but these variations are so insignificant that for all practical purposes the secular trend line throughout almost its entire length approximates a *constant rate* of growth. The secular trend, as thus computed, was found to have an annual rate of increase of about 3.8 per cent during the 1870's and 1880's, then 3.75 per cent until about 1910, when the rate drops to 3.7, and thereafte· gradually approaches 3.6. This estimated rate of long-term growth is somewhat lower than has been established by previous studies, particularly those of Carl Snyder.

One of Snyder's series of long-term trend of the volume of trade was derived by the use of annual bank clearings, and from 1919 forward bank debits, all deflated by his specially prepared index of the general price level in order to translate the figures into an approximate measure of change in volume. This was carried back to the year 1866. A long-term, mathematically fitted trend applied to these deflated check transactions has much to commend it as an over-all business measure, but there are two difficulties involved that affect the accuracy of the results. First, there is much dependence upon the accuracy of the general price-level index as a deflating medium, not so much perhaps in the shorter cyclical movements but in the element of trend gradient. The second possible defect is more serious. During the past three-quarters of a century the circulation of checks drawn upon commercial bank deposits has expanded faster than has the physical volume of total trade transactions or the production activity underlying those transactions. Credit instruments have in some degree replaced the use of money in the making of payments, and this process was particularly significant in the period between the Civil War and World War I. Hence there is almost certainly an element of *upward bias* in the resulting trend measurement.

Snyder's second, and more ambitious, attempt to measure the long-term growth of production and trade extended back to 1830 and was based upon an ingenious method of chaining together the 5-year-interval rates of change found to be the central tendency in successive groups of production and trade data. The composition of the figures changes with each successive 5-year period, so that although the resulting splicing of the respective typical or median rates of increase seems to describe a fairly continuous series, there is an internal lack of homogeneity. Furthermore, the range between the lower and the higher percentages of increase for the constituent series in each period is rather wide, and therefore the inclusion or omission of series in successive periods is capable of affecting the final results, even though the median (or modified mean) method was used in securing the "typical" rates of increase for each time segment. Snyder's resulting long-term trend, fitted by the method of least squares to the logarithms of the index, reveals a rate of growth fairly constant until about 1900 and thereafter tending to taper gradually. The over-all average rate of expansion, however, is in excess of that found on the basis of the data and method described in this appendix.[1]

[1] For a brief description of Snyder's Chain Index of Production and Trade, 1830–1935, see Croxton and Cowden, "Applied General Statistics," pp. 616–623, New York, 1940.

APPENDIX 2

ANNUAL INDEX NUMBERS OF WHOLESALE COMMODITY PRICES, 1700–1940

The index numbers of commodity prices shown in Charts 6 and 7 represent several segments that have been spliced together. The index numbers, beginning at 1709 and as far as 1731, were compiled from Arthur H. Cole's tables in "Wholesale Commodity Prices in the United States, 1700–1861," by Roy W. Jastram and H. P. Woolley, of the Department of Economics at Stanford University. The quotations relate to Philadelphia. The writer is indebted to them for the privilege of using these unpublished figures. Their index was carried back to 1700 by the writer, using the same primary source; this part of the index represents a very limited number of quotations but serves to depict in a rough way the price drift during those years. At 1731 a splice was made with the index prepared by Anne Bezanson from wholesale-commodity prices at Philadelphia, also published in Cole's book, Table 50. These index numbers, in turn, were spliced at 1849 with those of Herman M. Stoker, representing price quotations in New York. Stoker's series of weighted index numbers was combined with the index numbers prepared for the nineteenth century by George F. Warren and Frank A. Pearson, of Cornell University. The Stoker-Warren-Pearson indexes were published in *Memoir* 142, Cornell University Agricultural Experiment Station, and are given also in Warren and Pearson, "Prices," pp. 11–13. The wholesale-price index of the U.S. Bureau of Labor Statistics was spliced at 1932 to the foregoing series.

The entire series of spliced-index numbers was finally reduced to the base period used by Warren and Pearson, namely, the average 1910–1914. For the purpose of charting, interpolations (in dash lines) were made to fill short gaps for the years 1782–1784, 1788, and 1792. The fact that the index numbers prior to 1750 represent unweighted results, as compared with the weighted indexes for the succeeding years, probably introduces no great error, in view of the fact that the relatively small number of commodities represented in the earlier years appear actually to include most of the basic essentials of trade and consumption at that time. The index of the general price level, shown in Charts 7a, 7b, and 11, is explained in Appendix 3.

APPENDIX 3

CONSTRUCTION OF AN ANNUAL INDEX OF CREDIT CURRENCY, 1811–1940

In order to derive an annual index of effective monetary circulation (that is, the means of payment capable of effective use in all trade transactions), it is necessary to exercise care in selecting and handling the available data. During the nineteenth century there were two periods of paper-money inflation resulting from war conditions: first, from 1814 to 1817 and, second, from 1861 to 1865. During this century the use of bank-credit instruments in making payments for goods and ordinary services was not so widespread as it has since become, especially in the last half century. It was decided to construct an index beginning early in the nineteenth century and including the best available estimates of legal-tender money in circulation, as well as the data of bank credit in use. The index based upon these two factors was carried down to 1878, just prior to resumption of specie payments following the Civil War greenback period.

From 1879 forward it is apparent that the use of credit instruments (or what might be termed informally "bank currency") expanded rapidly. Indeed, it expanded faster than the rate of growth of physical trade and production. The data clearly show that the preponderant changes in effective total currency are largely reflected in variations of bank credit. The lawful money circulation becomes a much less significant factor in general price-level changes; it appears to have adjusted itself *to* the changes in values produced by the growth of trade volume and the circulation of bank credit (or "use" of bank deposits) developed through loans and investments.

It is necessary, as will presently be explained, to make an adjustment in recent decades for the *trend* of bank-credit growth in order to allow for the fact that there has been a progressive displacement of lawful money by checks in the United States for the making of payments. With this adjustment accomplished, it was found that an adequate picture of the year-to-year changes in effective circulating currency is provided by the bank-credit data. If "lawful money in circulation" were to be included in the index during the latest years, it would introduce erratic movements, arising from the difficulty of estimating the actual commercial use of gold (prior to 1933) and the much more important disturbing factor of currency hoarding, especially since 1930, which cannot be disentangled from the "money-in-circulation" figures as officially reported.

Until the latter part of the nineteenth century, the available figures neither for monetary circulation nor for the volume of bank credit are statistically satisfactory. We must work with estimates and more or less fragmentary material, but significant and useful results are nonetheless possible if care is exercised in making the necessary computations. There are only two years during the nineteenth century for which no estimates are available—1812 and 1852—and these gaps have been interpolated. For 1811 we have what appears to be a fair estimate of the amount of money in circulation outside the Treasury. Following a gap in 1812, we have a continuous series of estimates of money in circulation, plus data of the circulating U.S. Treasury notes issued during the period of war with Great Britain and the years of fairly generally suspended specie payments down to 1817. These data, based on various previous estimates to be found in the Federal documents, are to be found in A. Barton Hepburn's "History of Currency in the United States" (1915; rev. ed., 1924). Hepburn gives the annual figures for money in circulation without deducting specie held in the Treasury. From 1830 forward, however, the actual amounts held in the Treasury are available from the *Reports of the Comptroller of the Currency*. These show relatively small sums held in the Treasury; round estimates could safely be made for the preceding years to adjust Hepburn's data to a comparable basis.

During the years 1813–1817, the money in circulation includes the issues of U.S. Treasury notes, which, with a huge volume of bank paper, made up the bulk of effective means of payment during these years. An interpolation was made at 1812, for which year no data whatever are available. At least as far as the 1870's, it is clear that the official estimates of "lawful money in circulation," as published in the *Statistical Abstract*, are inclusive of lawful money held in banks, since the specie as reported by the banks to the Comptroller repeatedly *exceeded* the amounts shown by the published tables of "money in circulation." The figures as used in the present index are therefore to be understood to include money in circulation and to *exclude* lawful money held in the Treasury and in the banks and also all bank-note circulation, state and national.[1]

Beginning at 1862, there is included the circulation of United States legal tender notes (greenbacks), and these data are continued as far as 1878, after which year the money series is dropped entirely from the index, the continuity being preserved by splicing.

Beginning at 1862, the monetary circulation as given in the *Statistical Abstract* includes the Civil War issues of United States legal tender notes, usually referred to as the "greenbacks." It includes also the fractional United States notes that were issued to replace subsidiary coin driven out of use by the paper-money depreciation, which remained in circulation until the resumption of specie payment in 1879. Still a third element, more or less in the nature of effective paper currency, was the certificate of indebtedness issued by the Federal Government, particularly to war contractors, and of a form making possible at least some circulation in commercial payment of large sums. (A description of these various forms of paper circulation will be found in "The History of the Greenbacks," by Wesley C. Mitchell, pp. 156–187.)

With the series of "monetary circulation," the next step was to obtain data indicative of the changes from year to year in effective bank credit. In A. B. Hepburn's "History of Currency," there are annual estimates of the note circulation of the banks, extending back to 1811 (1812 omitted). These figures were used to form an *index of variation* of commercial bank credit as far as 1834. In order to obtain a close estimate of effective bank credit, beginning at 1834, and to permit extrapolation backward by the previously described index of variation, the following procedure was employed. There are in the *Reports of the Treasury*, beginning at 1834 and extending until 1862, incomplete material for individual states, showing at the end or beginning of each year the cash position, "loans," note circulation, "specie," deposits, etc., of the reporting banks, and also the number of banks reporting.[2] An examination

---

[1] *Comptroller's Report*, 1920, Vol. II; for money in circulation, 1862–1878, *Report of the Secretary of the Treasury*, 1922, p. 624. Bank notes were excluded because their effect upon the price system is adequately represented by the bank-credit factors, as described below.

[2] By a Congressional resolution of 1832, the Secretary of the Treasury was directed to communicate to the House of Representatives such data regarding the position of

of this material disclosed that 1838 was a year for which a relatively large and representative sample was available, covering 29 states.[1]   For that year the total loans (and investments, so far as the latter were separately reported) were taken as a *base* figure to be extrapolated back to 1834 and forward to 1861 by an index of variation. It may be explained that in these years it was customary for banks in many parts of the country to report their investments as included among the "loans."   Banks holding State and Federal bonds, for example, appear to have considered these as loans to the Government.[2]   It was therefore considered that total loans (plus investments, where shown separately) provide a satisfactory indicator of variations in the credit made available by the banks through their total lending operations.

Beginning at 1834 and extending as far as 1861, a careful study was made of the figures, state by state.   For some years there were no reports from certain states. There was also a tendency for the number of banks reporting to vary from year to year, but this seems to have been due mainly to the reckless nature of commercial banking in these days of lax supervision, when both failures and promotions were abundant.   An attempt was made to obtain as complete a record as possible for 19 identical states, excluding returns from a few frontier states, which merely reported occasionally.   The states used include such important commercial areas as New York, Massachusetts, Pennsylvania, and New Jersey.   Estimates were made for individual states for a very few years to fill gaps and thus minimize the effect of nonreporting in the totals.   An index of variation extending the total loans and investments of reporting banks in the 19 selected states from 1838 back to 1834 and forward to 1860 was then applied to the over-all basic figure, representing the 29 states, as of 1838.

The bank-credit total obtained for 1834 was first extrapolated back to 1811 by means of Hepburn's series (*op. cit.*) of the note circulation, on the assumption that the variations from year to year in note circulation, as estimated by Hepburn, more or less approximated the changes in total loans and investments.   To the extrapolated data there were then *added* the loans and security investments of the Second Bank of the United States, beginning at 1817 and ending at 1834.   These figures also were taken from Hepburn.   Having now fairly complete estimates of bank credit, these, in turn, were reduced to the form of an index of variation, and this final set of interpolated estimates applied to the 1834 basic figure, provided the final bank-credit series (with the single omission of 1812, which was later interpolated in the final index). Using the same index of variation *forward*, from 1834 to 1861, a series of estimated annual totals of effective bank credit in terms of loans and investments was obtained. In this process only the year 1852 required special interpolation.

The Civil War period raises peculiar difficulties.   For 1862 and 1863, the bank data, as contained in *Reports of the Comptroller of Currency*, are definitely in error for the seceding Southern States.   The data for these are merely *repetitions* of 1860 *or* 1861!   In order to eliminate this repetition error and to obtain a consistent continuation of the preceding series at least as far as 1863, a special index of variation was

---

the banks as were reported to the legislatures, governors, or other officers of the several states, but there was no systematic or compulsory system for obtaining such information, even within most of the states.

[1] During a short period, including 1838, the preparation of the statistics of banking data was in charge of the well-known financial publicist, William Gouge, who was apparently a careful and conscientious compiler, as well as a keen observer of banking operations and problems of his time.

[2] This is known to have been the practice in Massachusetts.   In all cases, the term "loans" was, of course, used by the writer to include commercial "discounts."

constructed for the *Northern States* only and applied to the 1860 credit figure previously arrived at.

Omitting 1864 and 1865 for the moment, we come to 1866, when the new National Banking System had become well established, with an excellent reporting system for *these* institutions. The Comptroller of the Currency, from the beginning of his authority, received and published National Bank condition reports as of several "call dates" each year. But information relating to the State Banks was permitted to lapse, and their figures as recorded in the official tables are *entirely inadequate* until 1873 and not even reasonably comprehensive until 1887! There are only partial estimates extant for the period 1864–1873. It was therefore considered desirable to extrapolate backward from 1887, when comprehensive and fairly reliable State Bank figures again become available by means of an index of variation based upon the National Bank loans and investments. The figure used for 1887 thus consists of the total loans and investments of National Banks, averaged for the call dates, *plus* beginning-of-the-year loans and investments as reported for all commercial banks, excluding savings banks. The 1887 base figure was extrapolated backward by this variation index on the principle that the significant changes in *general* bank-credit extension would be approximately reflected in the operations of the important segment of National Banks only.

We now have data capable of approximating the changes in effective credit use on both sides of a short gap during 1864 and 1865, for which years there are no adequate banking statistics. The State Bank figures are essentially estimates inserted by later Comptrollers of the Currency on the basis of incomplete reports, and the National Banking data are not fully representative, since this was the organization period. An examination of the data, however, revealed that the annual percentage changes in the outstanding legal-tender money circulation just prior to 1864 and following 1865 had a consistent *proportionate* relation to the changes in the total bank credit as measured by the loan and investment data. There is a similar proportionate relation for these variables as between 1862 and 1866. The *amount* of annual percentual fluctuation in bank credit was about one-fifth of that in legal tender money (mainly paper) circulation. By using the adjusted change in money circulation as an approximate measure of change in bank credit (which doubtless accommodates itself closely to the wartime inflationary changes), the credit series for the years 1864 and 1865 was filled in.

From 1887 forward, the available data present no special difficulties as far as the bank credit factor is concerned. Figures were taken, as before, from National Bank reports made at call dates to the Comptroller of the Currency and for all other commercial banks from the data as obtained and published by the Comptroller once a year. Beginning at 1905, these are years ending June 30; for prior years the state commercial banks and trust companies reported at dates near the beginning of each year. In the case of investments of National Banks, the holdings of United States Government bonds to secure note circulation were excluded throughout. After 1934, the United States bonds used to secure note circulation were called, and the National Bank notes began to be replaced by Federal Reserve notes.

Beginning with the establishment of the Federal Reserve System and its own net contributions to total bank credit in use, there were added to the foregoing data, beginning at 1915, the annual average Federal Reserve Bank investments in United States Government securities and the bills bought in the open market. The credit released by the Federal Reserve Banks to member banks through the rediscounting of commercial paper is, of course, already represented in the loan-discount data for those commercial banks.

The foregoing data were converted to final index numbers, with 1878 as the base. The figures for bank credit plus legal-tender money in circulation extend back from 1878 to 1811; the index series consisting of bank credit in terms of bank loans and investments extends from 1878 to 1940.   For the years 1811–1862, the index number was further adjusted by averaging the data of successive pairs of years and entering the results as of the first year, in order to make an approximate centering adjustment for the fact that the data originally refer to the winter of each year.

Another adjustment was made in the index number from 1878 to 1939 to correct for the gradual displacement of coins and paper money by bank-credit instruments in general trade.   This correction factor was obtained by computing the ratio to total check transactions outside New York City[1] of an annual general index of the value of trade and production (volume index multiplied by general price index).[2] The long-term trend of this ratio, with base 100 at 1878, was then used as a correction factor to obtain the average long-term rate of advance in the aggregate credit in use, *apart from mere displacement* of other forms of currency.

Since the general level of prices, including services and property as well as commodities, varies mathematically as the ratio of change in total effective purchasing power in terms of money to change in the physical volume of all nonbarter transactions, we can now proceed to the statistical demonstration of this principle.   An index of the *general* price level for such a purpose, from 1860 to 1939, has been constructed by Carl Snyder.   This has been carried back to the close of the eighteenth century by R. S. Tucker (*Review of Economic Statistics*, Jan. 15 and Feb. 15, 1934).   The 1940 figure is a continuation by the writer of Snyder's series.   The continuous (spliced) index of the general level of prices is shown in Charts 7*a*, 7*b*, and 11.

Mathematically, it should be possible to develop synthetically an index that would correlate very closely with this index of the general price level by obtaining annual ratios of the credit-currency index, as previously described, to a measure of the long-term trend of total physical trade.   Carl Snyder had attempted this and has presented the graphic results in various of his writings.[3]   Snyder's series of bank credit extends from about 1865 and appears to have been mainly developed from the loans and investments of *National Banks*, with the addition of other commercial banks only since 1913.   He did not include at any point the element of money in circulation. For the trend of physical trade, Mr. Snyder used his long-term index of physical trade in terms of secular trend rather than annual data.   By relating the bank-credit index to the long-term trend of trade, a "computed" general price-level measure results, exhibiting a fairly consistent relation to his general price-level index itself.

It is to be noted that the ratio of money and/or credit in use to a long-term general trade-index trend takes no account of the velocity of circulation of the means of payment or of the cyclical movements in physical trade.   Snyder has shown that to a very large degree these are offsetting factors in the numerator and denominator of the ratios.   That is, changes from year to year in the velocity of credit circulation or the turnover of money correlate closely with the business cycles or, to be more exact,

---

[1] With the use of the clearings-debits index of the Federal Reserve Bank of New York.

[2] This index of *trade values* closely approximates the measure of national income prepared by Robert F. Martin and the staff of the National Conference Board, but the latter extends back annually only to 1899, thence decennially.

[3] See, for example, New Measures of the Relations of Credit and Trade, *Academy of Political Science*, 1930; Industrial Growth and Monetary Theory, *Economic Forum*, summer, 1933; also *Revue de l'Institut Internationale Statistique*, 1934, Vol. III; "Capitalism, the Creator," charts, p. 287, 1940.

with the *minor* business cycles. Instead, however, of using the long-term *secular* trend of physical trade, it was decided in the present study to use the *intermediate* business trend, since there is no evidence that the very long wave movements in the volume of business transactions are offset by similar types of change in the numerator of the ratio, that is, the credit-currency index.

By computing the ratio of the credit-currency index to the *intermediate trend* of physical trade and production (described in Chapter 3 and Appendix 3), a new computed or synthetic measure of the general price level was obtained (Chart 11).

The very close correlation observable between the actual and computed price-level measures not only is interesting in itself but serves to verify the essential accuracy of the three independently calculated statistical indexes that have been utilized. Here are three economic measures which, when placed in a relationship that has definite theoretical meaning in terms of the general equation of exchange, results in a surprisingly close check over a very long period of time. The close degree of correspondence between the variations in the computed and actual index of the general price level thus established does not, of course, dispose of the ulterior logical questions of *causation* or the direction in which the causation mainly runs, that is, whether *from* credit *to* prices or *from* prices *to* credit or *from* general trade conditions to *either* one. What has been obtained, however, is a long-term quantitative expression of relationship that may serve helpfully as a framework within which to develop further analysis of the causal forces that are at work and their predominant or shifting direction.

In the lower portion of Chart 11 there appears a further curve, which has been added as a means of illustrating one of the most potent single causal factors in the wide variations at certain periods in the volume of money and credit or of total bank credit as such. Almost every one of the major inflationary periods has been associated with war conditions and the sudden expansion of Federal Government expenditures. The data as charted in this exhibit are the sum of the Army and Navy expenditures, as presented in the *Statistical Abstract* and Treasury Bulletins. They are expressed as a ratio to the annual index of trade and production in order to eliminate the effect of national economic growth. In Chart 11, this series of relative Army and Navy expenditures has been plotted to a much smaller scale graduation than the other series, in view of the occasional extreme fluctuations.

APPENDIX 4

CONSTRUCTION OF MEASURES OF NATIONAL INCOME

The best available estimate of national-income payments in the United States during the nineteenth century is that of the National Industrial Conference Board, prepared under the direction of Robert F. Martin. Prior to 1899, these estimates are given only for 10-year intervals, inasmuch as Census material was mainly utilized in their preparation.

The Martin estimates for agriculture, not only in the nineteenth century but throughout the entire period, are probably not so accurate as the agricultural-income data prepared by the writer on the basis of production (represented in part by the trend of population) and farm-product prices, after allowances for deductions representing fertilizer, seed, and depreciation approximating Martin's estimates for these items. The new figures of adjusted farm income were therefore substituted in place of the old series used in Martin's original work, and revised totals from 1900 until 1928 were used as the final series of national income. Taking this adjusted figure for 1900 as a base for extrapolation backward, it was possible to derive annual estimates from an index of the value of total production and trade. This value index represents the product of the index of production and trade (Appendix 1) multiplied by the index of the general price level, as described in Appendix 3. When the revised Martin estimate for 1900 is carried back annually in this fashion, the resulting income figures come reasonably close to those of the revised Martin series at Census years. The closeness of this agreement is indeed remarkable, considering the fact that the methods of computation are radically different. The following table gives the comparison for these Census years, col. (1) being the revised Martin data, col. (2) those of the writer:

Year	Millions of dollars	
	(1)	(2)
1799	631	734
1809	912	841
1819	1,019	882
1829	1,044	1,034
1839	1,883	1,995
1849	2,441	2,435
1859	4,569	3,603
1869	8,172	7,194
1879	7,914	7,760
1889	11,833	12,235
1899	15,450	16,711
1900	16,537	16,537

It will be seen that the only important discrepancy is at 1859, where the Martin (revised) figure greatly exceeds that of the writer.

It was decided not to use the results of the product of the general price level by the business-volume index after 1899 because of the evidence that the trend of the general price-level index, although probably reasonably accurate for the measurement of general prices in connection with the equation of exchange, appears to become less reliable as a measure of comprehensive unit values adaptable to an income-payment series. Hence Martin's revised figures were continued as far as 1928. Beginning at 1929, the data of the U.S. Department of Commerce for income payments to individuals were used. The precise series employed represents the U.S. Department of Commerce income payments, not adjusted for payments into pension funds, payments from pension funds, or special disbursements. The source of the data was the *Survey of Current Business* June, 1941, page 17. It may be added that the revised Martin series of 1920–1928 agrees very closely indeed with the income-payment estimates of the National Bureau of Economic Research. The U.S. Department of Commerce figures also agree very closely with those of the National Bureau from 1929 to date. It can be expected, however, that there will be continuing revisions of all of these estimates as more complete and accurate data become available.

APPENDIX 5

1. INDEX OF TOTAL AGRICULTURAL INCOME, 1800–1940

Gross farm income, on an annual basis, may be considered as the total money received by farmers and raisers of livestock from the sale of their products, plus the estimated value of such products as are consumed on the farm, but with products used on the farm for seed or feed for animals deducted.

Prior to the Civil War period, when the U.S. Department of Agriculture first began systematically to collect data on agricultural production, the factual materials as to agricultural output are meager and unreliable. The earliest figures prepared by the U.S. Department of Agriculture on farm production extend as far back as 1862 but are only for the major field crops. Animals and animal products were not included until a much later period. The data for field-crop production were probably very inadequately reported prior to the Census of 1869, after which date increasingly reliable data began to exist. All the early figures, however, are to be considered rather as conscientious estimates than as closely exact records, in view of the fact that farm data, to be complete, must be gathered from many sources, and annual enumeration is virtually impossible.

In the case of the prices of farm products the available data are very much more complete and accurate—at least, in the wholesale markets. In many instances reliable data of prices received by farmers in various areas for a given crop or product can be found. Usually it is possible to substitute wholesale-price series for the farm-price series in order to obtain *indexes of variation*. In the absence of any more exact method of approaching the problem, the measurement of gross farm income or revenue becomes a matter of totaling the products of output (or sale) and price for as many types of farm commodities as possible. It was found from the official figures prepared in this manner that the principal changes and trends over periods of time in the more general estimates of income correspond closely to sample series built up from outstanding products in terms of value. Hence, although many minor products must necessarily be omitted from the totals and perhaps can never be wholly brought into the final estimate of farm income, we are reasonably sure that the broader fluctuations and trends developed from the data now available present a reliable picture of the essential facts.

The U.S. Department of Agriculture has for a considerable time estimated the value of total farm production for sale and family consumption on farms. These measurements, in terms of index numbers, extend back to 1909 by crop years. A study was recently undertaken by L. H. Bean and Frederick Strauss, as a joint investigation by the U.S. Department of Agriculture and the National Bureau of Economic Research, with the object of measuring gross farm income, farm production, and the course of agricultural prices over a much more extended period. It was found possible to obtain data or reasonable estimates for the production of a wide variety of farm products back to 1869. Farm-price data were used in conjunction with the production data to obtain annual values for each important commodity for the period 1869–1937. A new measure of annual aggregate farm production and an index of farm prices were obtained for both calendar and crop years of this period. The results appear in *U.S. Department of Agriculture Technical Bulletin* 703, December, 1940, entitled, Gross Farm Income and Indexes of Farm Production and Farm Prices in the United States, 1869–1937. The Bean-Strauss data served to establish a base, shortly after the Civil War, from which to extend back still further a series of estimated index numbers of farm income and, also, a recent base making it possible to splice in the latest U.S. Department of Agriculture data for farm income, bringing the entire measurement to 1940.

In order to obtain an approximate annual measure of the drift of farm income extending back as far as 1800, advantage was taken of a basic principle involving the relation of farm prices to short-term changes in the value of farm products. A rise of price is almost invariably correlated over short periods with a rise in the total value of the product sold.[1] This may be occasionally untrue of individual products, but it is certainly true generally of the entire mass of products raised on farms. This principle, of course, is primarily applicable to changes from year to year and would not necessarily afford a means of estimating farm values over longer periods of time, merely on the basis of price tendencies.

It has been shown, however, in Chapter 7 and in Appendix 1, that the longer term trend of total farm production tends to parallel exceedingly closely the trend of total population. This is eminently true of the experience of the United States, since farm-product exports have never been a large enough fraction of total production to modify the relationship, and the short-term disturbances involving foreign trade in farm products are usually well represented in the corresponding price behavior. We are safe in assuming that index numbers expressing the annual calibration of total population from the decennial Census data afford a reliable measure of the *drift* through the years of total farm production for sale and farm use as food. The more complete an index of farm production is made the more it tends to approximate the smooth growth pattern of total population.

By applying an index of average farm prices, based upon a wide variety of products, to an index based upon total population growth, selected as the best approximation to the over-all movement of farm production, we can derive a product index of the movements of total farm income. One feature of such an estimated income index is that excellent index numbers of farm prices are available that are probably more accurate and more comprehensive in coverage than even the best measure or estimates of production that will ever be available to us. The final estimate of income will be correct in pattern but will not always indicate the precise *degree* of change in rare cases when a few of the most important crops were extremely large or small at the same time. It must be remembered that even today there is a fairly considerable amount of farm production that does not enter the market in any way, and if this portion were to be completely recorded and represented in the production indexes, it would probably smooth these indexes even more than the Bean-Strauss results indicate.

Supplementing the foregoing principle as a basis for estimating annual farm-income values prior to 1869, it is fortunate that annual data for cotton alone can be directly utilized with respect to both price and production back to 1790. The data for production were taken from the *U.S. Department of Agriculture Bureau of Statistics Circular* 32, 1912. The data relate to periods comprising the major period of the crop movement, and for the present purpose this was regarded as equivalent to the corresponding calendar year. This circular also gives annual data of cotton prices and the total farm values of the crop. These farm values were used as far as 1839.

[1] See the chart of annual farm income and farm prices in *Agricultural Outlook Charts*, "Demand, Credit, and Prices," p. 2, U.S. Department of Agriculture, 1940.

Beginning at 1840, and as far as 1876, the value of the crop was computed from the production data of *Circular* 32 and the October average price of cotton given in the "Aldrich Report" (52d Congress, Second Session, Vol. III, 1893). The prices in this source are given in terms of gold during the years 1862–1876 and must be translated to a currency basis. From 1876 to 1880, data for average farm price of cotton were taken directly from the Yearbooks of the U.S. Department of Agriculture.

This series of the annual value of the cotton crop from 1790 to 1880 was then added to estimates of the gross farm value of *all other* crops, derived as follows. The index of total population, calibrated to calendar years, served as an approximate measure of the trend of general farm production, *excluding* the great export staple cotton. This partial "crop-production" index was multiplied by a special index of farm prices, also excluding cotton, derived mainly from the index numbers of Warren and Pearson from 1798 to 1880 relating to the subgroup "farm foods."[1] This covers a wide range of farm products other than cotton, and tobacco is the only important omission. In order to extend the range of agricultural prices, still excluding cotton, somewhat further, there was averaged with the Warren-Pearson farm-food index, beginning at 1816 and as far as 1860, another price index, prepared by Thomas S. Berry. This relates to annual wholesale prices of the chief products of agriculture in the Ohio River Valley. These figures are annual averages of monthly data contained in Arthur H. Cole's "Wholesale Commodity Prices in the United States, 1700–1861," Appendix 1. This weighted index includes some farm products not included in the index of Warren and Pearson and gives some weight also to tobacco, but it does not include cotton. The combined index represents a comprehensive group of wholesale farm prices that in the aggregate measures closely the changes in prices actually received on farms.

We have now a continuous index from 1790 to 1890 for the estimated total value of farm products produced, excluding cotton. This index was turned into the form of annual money values by extrapolating backward from the corresponding subtotal (that is, excluding cotton) farm values (in dollars) of Bean and Strauss. The average of the years 1881–1890 was used as the base. The resulting series in terms of annual dollar values was then combined with the estimated annual value of cotton to form a grand-total income value for each year back to 1800. This was then finally adjusted slightly to conform with the actual level of values as shown by Bean and Strauss. In order to effect a transition from the estimates, with the use of the preceding method and the series of Bean and Strauss, which begins at 1869, it was found possible to obtain a reasonable result by continuing the early series as far as 1877 and shifting to the Bean-Strauss series at 1878. This was then continued forward as far as 1910, when the income data, as prepared and currently reported in the regular reports of the U.S. Department of Agriculture, become available.

Since the Bean-Strauss series is not available beyond 1937 and since recent revisions of their data have been undertaken by the U.S. Department of Agriculture for recent years, it was decided to splice the U.S. Department of Agriculture farm gross-income figures with the Bean-Strauss series at 1910, with the use of the U.S. Department of Agriculture data, *Crops and Markets*, August, 1934, from 1910 to 1924; spliced at 1924 to revised data to 1940 obtained from U.S. Department of Agriculture "Material Bearing on Parity Prices," July, 1941, Sec. B, Table 8. Benefit payments are not included in Charts 13 and 14, for the object of the data there is to represent farm income from production. For Chart 57, however, benefit payments are included.

In order to convert the annual index of the dollar value of gross farm income to a form expressing the "purchasing power" of that income over commodities not of agricultural origin, particularly industrial products purchased by farmers, it was neces-

---

[1] Taken from Warren and Pearson, "Prices," pp. 25–26.

sary to obtain a price index suitable for deflation of the income series. The U.S. Department of Agriculture in recent years has computed several annual (and also monthly) indexes of prices paid by farmers for commodities purchased. In order to test the characteristics of available data that might be suitable for use as a deflater over a long period for which no direct data of prices paid by farmers are available, the U.S. Department of Agriculture series of prices paid by farmers, 1910 to 1940, was compared with a series of general wholesale prices of *nonagricultural* commodities. It was found that prices of nonagricultural products varied more violently from year to year than the cost of goods purchased by farmers, as computed by the U.S. Department of Agriculture. It was further discovered, however, that if the series of nonagricultural prices was expressed in the form of a 2-year moving average (used as of the second year), the results tended to approximate fairly closely the variations in the U.S. Department of Agriculture index of "prices paid" by farmers in recent years.

Probably the best long-term series for the purpose in hand is the index of nonagricultural prices extending from 1798, to be found in "Demand, Credit and Prices," *U.S. Department of Agriculture Outlook Charts.* This price index is based upon the materials of Warren and Pearson and later the group indexes of the Bureau of Labor Statistics. The index was converted to two-year moving averages and was used as far as 1912 as a means of adjusting estimated annual gross farm income to an index of deflated values. For the years 1913–1934, the U.S. Department of Agriculture index of retail prices paid by farmers for goods for "living and production" was used. These data were published in the series of monographs on "Income Parity for Agriculture," Part 3, Sec. 5, May, 1939. For 1935 to 1940, the data consist of a revised series, as published in the U.S. Department of Agriculture study of "Material Bearing on Parity Prices," Sec. C, Table 1, 1941.

To the estimates of real farm income thus obtained, 15-year and 21-year moving averages were computed and then averaged into a single long-term flexible trend. The data were then expressed as percentages of this intermediate trend, and the final results constitute the index of cyclical deviations from trend of the deflated farm income, as shown in Chart 19. The index in this form represents a measure from year to year of the movements of total farm purchasing power in a form comparable with the index of deviations from trend of general production and trade.

2. COMPUTATION OF PRICE PARITY FOR AGRICULTURE

As a supplement to the foregoing measure of real farm income, a special index, based upon prices only, expressing the ratio from year to year of *farm* prices to *nonagricultural* prices was obtained. The data were directly taken from the table given in "Demand, Credit, and Prices," *U.S. Department of Outlook Charts,* 1940, which contains both series, farm products and nonagricultural products, in terms of annual index numbers. The ratios were then smoothed by an average of 15–21-year moving averages, and percentages of this trend were computed. These appear in Chart 19 as the price-parity index, 1800–1940.

3. CYCLICAL MOVEMENTS OF AGRICULTURAL PRICES AND NONAGRICULTURAL PRICES

In order to compare the movements of commodity prices, expressed as cyclical deviations from trend—or drift—with the cycles of general business—deviations from intermediate trend (Chapter 8 and Chart 18)—it was considered important, to eliminate from consideration the periods of abrupt price inflation occasioned by war emergency and war finance. This is necessary in order to confine the study to periods in which price movements may be regarded as motivated primarily by circumstances arising from the play of economic conditions of boom and depression, exclusive of the occasional wide distortions of war finance.

It is not necessary entirely to eliminate the war periods but rather to consider that after the peak of abrupt war inflation has passed, prices tend to decline gradually over a long period and thus establish a gradual primary trend upon which the "cyclical" fluctuations are superimposed. Special precautions are necessary in deriving the "trend" or drift of commodity prices in years *preceding* the distortion occasioned by a war of major proportions and its inflationary accompaniments. If, as in the present study, some form of long-term moving average is employed, the war inflation must not be permitted to influence the values to the extent of introducing a depressed period in the relatives *prior* to the inflation. Such a depression in the relatives has no logical meaning, except to the extent that a major war might actually be preceded by depressed general business conditions, which reflect themselves also in the price cycles. Any degree of specific cyclical price weakness prior to major war inflation can, however, be approximately measured if the moving trend is projected *graphically*, with care and judgment, as far as the *beginning* of the advance in prices produced by the war conditions.

With these considerations as a guide, the two sets of price series were, in turn, adjusted for trend by means of the combination of two moving averages, one of 15 years and one of 21 years in term. Graphic interpolation or extension of the computed moving averages at either end was necessary, and the data were plotted on a ratio scale to facilitate these graphic estimates. In order to exclude the war periods as such, no attempt was made to obtain trend values or percentages of trend from 1812 to 1819, from 1862 to 1870, or from 1915 to 1922.

Taking first the farm-price index (from the *U.S. Department of Agriculture Outlook Charts* previously mentioned), a graphically determined trend was used from 1800 to 1811. A graphically estimated trend was also used from 1820 to 1829, spliced to the computed average of 15–21-year moving averages from that point until 1851. From 1852 until 1861, another graphic estimate was made. A graphic trend was used for the years 1870 and 1871 to extend back a computed trend beginning at 1872 and extending forward as far as 1903, after which point graphic estimates were again employed to extend the trend as far as 1916. During the period beginning 1922 to date, it was found necessary to estimate the trend graphically on the assumption that by 1922 the first impact of postwar deflation had carried prices to a level initiating a period of extended gradual deflation.

For the nonagricultural price series, a graphic trend was used in the first period, as before, from 1800 to 1811. Another graphic trend approximating the drift of the moving average was used from 1820 to 1828; thereafter the computed trend average was carried as far as 1851, followed, as before, by a graphic trend until 1861. In the period following the Civil War, beginning at 1871, the trend begins as a graphic estimate that extends as far as 1878, where it joins the computed moving average. This then extends as far as 1904, where it again joins a graphic estimate, carried to 1915. As in the farm-price series, the graphic trend was necessary in the postwar periods to date. Great care was used in making these graphic estimates to see that the cyclical deviations were approximately balanced and that the general sweep or drift of the data closely approximates that which might reasonably have been expected if the cyclical variations had continued without the distortion produced by war inflation.

APPENDIX 6

1. INDEXES OF TRANSPORTATION CONSTRUCTION AND BUILDING CONSTRUCTION, 1800–1940

a. INDEX OF TRANSPORTATION CONSTRUCTION

The objective is an annual index, in terms of physical volume, of the cyclical changes in production associated with the development of transportation facilities. We are considering this as a specialized phase of construction. It is desired to include those phases of transportation development that were of outstanding importance since 1800 as contributing to industrial employment and demand for the products of manufacturing and extractive industries.

Prior to the railway era, which began in the early 1830's, shipbuilding was unquestionably the predominant transport equipment industry of the United States and, indeed, of the American Colonies. Beginning early in the nineteenth century, there were, of course, occasional ventures in the construction of canals and in improvement of river routes and harbors. The intensive canal-promotion period, which began about 1817 with the Erie Canal and which extended in time for more than a generation thereafter, appears not to have exerted any consistent or powerful effects upon the employment of artisans or the activity of the fabricating industries, since most of this work was done by hand labor on the site, with the use of local stone, wood, and other crude materials. An attempt was made to secure a rough index of the funds utilized in the various canal projects of this period, but annual data for this purpose were found to be very meager, and such statistics as were suitable for use indicated no close or consistent relation to the measures of general trade activity.

Fortunately, fairly good statistics are available of the number of sailing and of steam vessels built in the United States in each year, beginning at 1797. These figures may be found in the *Census of* 1880, Vol. VIII, and also in *House Executive Documents*, 50th Congress, First Session, 1887–1888, Vol. XX, p. 962. After 1812, the figures are available classified according to various types of vessels constructed, but graphic tests showed that the total of all vessels constructed each year appeared to be the best series for use as an index of transportation-equipment construction. The total tonnage of sailing- and steam-vessel construction each year, beginning at 1797 and ending at 1850, was then expressed in percentages of the average of a 15-year and a 21-year moving average in order to measure the cyclical fluctuations. (The moving averages were extended back to the beginning of the data graphically.)

This series of cyclical deviations was used from 1800 to 1831 as the final index of transportation construction. From 1832 to 1849, the series was averaged with an index of cyclical variations based upon the annual mileage of railway track constructed, which is the first part of the railway-construction index to be described in the next following section. This average was computed with equal weight assigned to each series, and the average thus accomplishes a transition from the era in which shipbuilding was predominant as a representation of this field of capital-formation activity to the great era of railway construction that followed.

For several decades prior to the building of the railroads, there was considerable activity in many states in the construction of roads and turnpikes. This phase of transport, like that of the canals, furnished a fair amount of employment for hand labor, but it did not itself result in much industrial or fabricating activity. There are no records of annual data from which any kind of index of such activity of comprehensive scope can be derived. Nor is there any useful information on construction of road vehicles. Beginning with 1830, therefore, use was made of the miles of railroad track laid down, concerning which there are from the very beginning reliable statistics. The annual track mileage implies more than merely the labor on construction, for this work required an increasing tonnage of iron and steel and the production of locomotives, cars, accessories, etc., which soon reached enormous proportions and represented substantial additions to industrial operations and a major contribution to cyclical fluctuation in a widening range of contributing industries.

Annual data concerning the miles of railroad constructed were obtained from the *Statistical Abstract*, supplemented by Poor's *Annual of Railroads*, and annual reports of the American Iron and Steel Association. A parabolic trend was fitted to the data from 1831 to 1912 and annual percentages of this trend derived. These percentages, averaged with those previously obtained from the series of shipbuilding, were combined, as stated above, as far as 1849.

Beginning at 1850, the percentages of trend of the miles of railroad constructed were averaged with similarly derived cyclical percentages of the total reported consumption of rails, and this average was continued to 1864 as the final index of construction activity. Beginning at 1865, still another component was averaged with the foregoing, consisting of an index of orders placed annually for locomotives and for freight and passenger cars. This railroad-equipment-orders index was derived from the percentages of trend for locomotives, weighted two, and a composite of the freight-car and passenger-car orders, also expressed in percentage of their respective trends, weighted one. The combined index of mileage of track, consumption of rails, and orders for equipment was carried forward as far as 1899.

At 1900, when the construction of new mileage begins to give definite evidence of having passed the peak of expansion, a new combination of data was spliced to the foregoing. This begins the period of a new and vastly important form of transportation construction—the automobile. The problem was now to introduce this new factor while in the index certain significant phases of railway construction were retained, so that the result might give the new motor-industry production a gradually increasing "weight," in terms of relative product values. In effecting this transition, the railroad-construction factor, in terms of new mileage, was dropped, and the railroad index from 1900 to 1940 consists of a revised set of data relative to production of rails and orders for operating equipment. This component was combined with a new index based upon production of automobiles, including both passenger cars and commercial cars, from the data presented in the annual reports of the Automobile Chamber of Commerce.

In making this combination, the railway-equipment-construction index was revised in order to provide for more accurate weights for each of the component parts, based upon values corresponding with the data of the *Census of Manufactures*. For rails, the data refer to the production each year in long tons; for cars, they are the total new orders, in units, for freight cars and passenger cars, combined to form one component, and new orders for locomotives in units, second component. Since both these components are stated in number of units, it was thought desirable to apply a further correction to take account of changes since 1900 in the size (or industrial importance) of these units. For the railway-car composite, an index was constructed on the basis of the average annual capacity of freight cars in use as reported by the Bureau of Railway Economics. This series, although derived from data for freight cars only, is an approximate means of adjusting the combined series, including passenger cars, the latter of which have also tended to increase in weight and size through the years. In the case of locomotives, a correction index reflects the changes in average tractive power per locomotive, as given in Moody's "Railway Manuals."

By applying these respective adjustment indexes to the data of orders, a final series for effective equipment construction activity was derived. These series of rail-production and adjusted-equipment orders were then reduced to a base at 1900 and combined with constant weights in the proportion of 45 for rail production, 40 for adjusted car orders, and 15 for adjusted locomotive orders, these weights having been derived from the value of product data given in the *Census of Manufactures* for equipment and from price and production data for rails. The weights were derived by averaging the value of production of railway cars from the *Census of Manufactures*, with the use of the data for 1899 as an approximation of the values for 1900. These figures of the *Census of Manufactures* omit that part of the car production undertaken in railroad shops. Similar value weights were derived for locomotive production, also excluding railroad shops. For the value of rails, the annual tonnage of production was multiplied by average rail prices each year, as given by *Iron Age*. The estimated annual value of rails was then multiplied by three to give a rough estimate of the total value of track construction, taking account of ties, plates, switches, ballast, and other materials involved in this work. The resulting (constant) weights were 45 per cent for rails (and trade), 40 per cent for railroad cars, and 15 per cent for locomotives.

The next step was the combination of the physical index of automobile production with the physical index of production of railroad equipment (new orders used to represent production of rolling stock). It was decided to use an aggregative index, in which the volume would be expressed in units proportionate to the annual production data and in which the price weights would represent average unit values computed from the *Census of Manufactures* for 1899, 1904, 1909, 1914, 1921, 1923, 1927, 1929, 1931, 1933, 1935, 1937, 1939. The data for 1919 were omitted because of the postwar inflation at that time. The average unit value of automobiles was found to have gradually declined during these years; that of railroad equipment had risen, partly because of the increase in size and weight of the various equipment units. In this way the new automobile-production series was merged with the railroad-equipment series to form a composite transportation-equipment index with base at 1900, and this was spliced with the preceding index, as previously described.

A least-squares trend was computed for the new segment beginning at 1900; this trend was graphically adjusted, and percentages of this trend were obtained. These percentages constitute the final cyclical deviations shown in Chart 30. In connection with this index, it should be further added that experiments were made to determine the advisability of adding to the transportation-equipment index such factors as construction of highways or electric-power generating facilities, which might be considered as supplementary or related lines of major capital development having to do with transportation, communication, and power. It was found, however, that the available data relating to these phases of construction, had they also been incorporated in the index, would not have altered the general pattern to any material degree.

b. Building-construction Index

Beginning at 1830, there is available a physical index of the cyclical movements of building construction in the United States, prepared by John R. Riggleman. The preliminary results of Riggleman's work, covering the years 1875–1932, were presented, together with a brief description of the methods employed, in the *Journal of the American Statistical Association*, June, 1933. Riggleman subsequently carried back his index to 1830. The index consists of percentage deviations of per capita data, adjusted for building costs, from long-term trend. The data used are understood to be primarily building permits from various cities, supplemented by other data closely indicative of building-construction volume. Three cities afforded data in 1830; by 1875, 20 cities were represented; 65 by 1900; and this number was continued to 1939. From the description of the index given to the writer personally by Dr. Riggleman and from such tests as the writer could make on the basis of the early data of lumber production, volume of transportation of building materials over the Erie Canal, etc., it was concluded that the Riggleman index, although representing approximations in the earlier years, is a sufficiently reliable series to be used for the present purpose. The revised and extended final data were made available by Dr. Riggleman as a personal courtesy; they have not been published in their present form.

The Riggleman series appears to be largely influenced by urban housing construction, but in recent years the value of relating permits from the larger cities has apparently sufficiently recorded the housing developments in the suburban areas for which there are approximate estimates in the U.S. Department of Commerce data. For the years 1938 and 1939 it was decided to use, instead of the Riggleman series, estimates of deviation from trend based upon the number of family units of residential construction as reported by the U.S. Department of Commerce.

In the period 1800–1829, no data were found from which an index of building as such could be constructed. As a rough indicator of activity in the closely related field of land subdivision and speculation, emphasizing mainly the rapidly growing pioneer sections of the country, use was made of the official data of annual sales of the public lands. The purchase of public lands, for speculation or investment, was greatly facilitated in the early years of the nineteenth century by the rise of mushroom banks, especially in the frontier areas. It is probable that the record of sales of Government land portrays approximately the pattern of these broad cyclical movements from year to year.

The data of sales of public lands are found in official documents in terms of both value and acres. The annual data from 1800 to 1840, in units of acres per capita, were taken from Arthur H. Cole, "Fluctuations in American Business, 1790–1860," p. 185. These appear to be in terms of calendar years. To this series a moving average trend was computed and finally smoothed. The percentages of the final line of trend were then logarithmically reduced by 50 per cent, in view of the fact that the cyclical movements were extremely violent, and this degree of correction was found to bring the range of fluctuation approximately within limits closely comparable to those of the building-cycles index.

The finally adjusted percentage deviations after this correction were then averaged with the Riggleman series to form a composite index during the period 1833–1839. The final building index, therefore, consists of adjusted data relating to public lands from 1800 to 1832, the average of this series with the Riggleman building series from 1833 to 1839, and the Riggleman series alone from 1840 to 1920.

Beginning at 1921, Riggleman's index was spliced with an index prepared by the author, based upon total value of permits as compiled by U.S. Bureau of Labor Statistics (*Bulletin* 693), deflated by a specially constructed building-cost index based on a weighted combination of wholesale prices of building materials and union construction labor wages. This series was finally adjusted for estimated trend.

2. MULTIPLE CORRELATION OF THE INDEX OF BUSINESS ACTIVITY WITH TRANSPORTATION-CONSTRUCTION AND BUILDING INDEXES

The object is to study the relationship between the transportation and building indexes and the general business index, having in mind that these major forms of capital development may be considered as causal factors in producing many of the important cyclical variations in general business activity. It was first necessary to eliminate those periods in which business activity was obviously affected primarily by circumstances of war. Business in the years from 1800 to 1814, although not continuously dominated by conditions arising from the Napoleonic Wars, was frequently so influenced, and these Wars, involving for a time the direct involvement of the United States, contributed to marked irregularity in industry and trade. Hence the first period during which the relation of building and transportation development and business conditions was examined statistically begins at 1814 and ends at 1861, when the Civil War becomes a disturbing external factor. The second period, following the Civil War, begins at 1865 and ends at 1914, the beginning of World War I. The third period begins at 1919 and extends to 1938. The writer is indebted to Mrs. Frances E. McIntyre for her assistance in assembling data and computing these correlations.

a. PERIOD 1814–1861

For this first period, the coefficient of multiple correlation, expressing the over-all association between the cyclical fluctuations of the business index and the building and transportation-construction indexes, on the one hand, and the business index, on the other, together, was found to be .774. This is a highly significant degree of covariation, and hence by combining the two independent variables, construction and transportation indexes, with proper weighting derived from the correlation computations, a *derived index* may be obtained that closely approximates that of the observed dependent variable, the business index (see Chart 31).

During the disturbed years of the Civil War, as in the preceding Napoleonic War period, industrial and trade changes were brought about by the direct influence of political factors, and it would not be logical, therefore, to extend the correlations through such a period.

b. PERIOD 1865–1914

In this period the association between the indexes of building and transportation construction and the business index is expressed by the multiple coefficient .816. During this period there is evidence (from the square of the multiple coefficient .665) that somewhat more of the fluctuations in the business index may be explained (assuming there is a logical relationship in the facts) by reference to the two widely fluctuating independent variables. In this period it is interesting to observe that the transportation-construction factor appears to be much more important than the building-activity factor. As explained in Chapter 10, there is reason to believe that the correlation device does not fully measure the role of building activity as a major stimulating or depressing factor in the industrial system as a whole. But in terms of the year-to-year cyclical movements, it appears to be a fact that the cycles in transportation construction begin to be more closely associated with those of the business index than the longer, more widely spaced cycles of building activity.

c. Period 1919–1940

After World War I, the automobile became the major factor in the transportation-equipment situation, and it introduces a new logical element into interpretation of the results. Production of motor cars is not associated primarily with what may be termed "productive initiative," and the promotion impulses relating to so-called "producers'goods"; it is rather associated with those forces which motivate investment by *individuals* as consumers in durable equipment. There is close similarity, of course, between the type of cycle movements that characterize the development of the railroad system and its equipment and the cycles of automobile production. Both these phases of activity disclose violent cyclical movements. Another feature of considerable interest is disclosed in the correlation itself during the postwar period down to 1940. The coefficient of determination (or square of .894) is .799, indicating a higher degree of combined association of the two independent variables of the business index than in either of the preceding periods. But in this case the transportation-construction factor is overwhelmingly important from the standpoint of its apparent statistical influence upon the changes in the business index.

APPENDIX 7

1. CONSTRUCTION OF THE RESERVE-LOAN RATIO AS AN INDICATOR OF HIGH-GRADE BOND PRICES

A number of experiments were conducted to ascertain whether use might be made of data pertaining to business conditions, commodity prices, the money supply, etc., in order to develop a measure of the forces immediately affecting the high-grade bond market and interest rates. The first step in these experiments was to obtain a reliable annual index of bond prices (or yields) in the United States, extending over a very long period. For this purpose, the carefully prepared indexes of bond yields prepared by Frederick R. Macaulay afforded the best means of measuring changes in average bond prices beginning at 1867.

Macaulay's index numbers are based upon the yields of specially selected railroad bonds, and the method of computation involves an ingenious correction to adjust for the drift in yield arising from the gradually changing caliber of individual bonds over periods of time. Macaulay's yield index was converted into an index of bond prices by Leonard P. Ayres, who also extended the bond-price series backward from 1857 to 1831 by the use of data relating principally to municipal bonds. Ayres' index, in terms of variations in prices, as published by the Cleveland Trust Company in 1939, was therefore used during the period 1831–1924. Beginning at 1925, a proportionate splice was made to Moody's Aaa corporate-bond-yield index, expressed in terms of reciprocals, and continued to 1940.

An examination of the various available data relating to money in circulation, gold in monetary form, etc., led to the conclusions that the best results could probably be obtained by using data of *total bank reserves*. Banks, particularly those of commercial type, hold securities primarily as secondary reserve. Important variations in bank holdings of securities (mainly bonds) from year to year appear to be mainly occasioned by the intensity of demand for business loans as these alter the relation of credit-created deposits to available reserves, or the legal reserve-ratio requirements. Data were therefore assembled to form as nearly a *homogeneous* series as possible relating to bank reserves and bank loans in comprehensive form.

Prior to the organization of the National Banking System, banking organizations in the various states submitted to the Treasury Department voluntarily, without close inspection or audit, statistics of the principal items in their accounts. The reports were not rendered as of identical dates, and the number of reporting banks varied from period to period. The files of the Treasury Department, however, contain records of these early reports extending back as far as 1834. From *U.S. Executive Documents*, 52d Congress, Second Session, 1893, Vol. V, were taken the annual data of bank loans and discounts from 1834 to 1863. From the *Report of the Comptroller of the Currency*, 1893, p. 1023, statistics were transcribed for the same period, covering investments and the aggregate cash of reporting banks. These figures relate to dates close to the turn of each year. The "aggregate cash" included specie, specie funds, and notes of other banks. Interpolations were necessary for 1852 and 1853 from other volumes. Reports by the National Banks to the Comptroller of the Currency were first made as of the year 1863, and these banks continued thereafter to make several reports a year of the principal items of their condition.   For a considerable period, however, after the beginning of the National Banking System, imperfect records were kept of the condition of the numerous banks outside the National System.   So imperfect were these records that little use can be made of the data prior to 1865 for the purpose in hand.   Beginning at 1865, there are statistics in the reports of the Comptroller of the Currency for all banks reporting to the Comptroller.   These figures include cash, loans and discounts, securities, etc.   During the years 1886–1895, a splice was made to restrict the data to National Banks only, because during that period, reports of cash reserve included items for State Banks not comparable with the preceding data, and it was considered more accurate to use the National Bank figures only as a representative index for continuing the "cash" series.

Beginning with the Federal Reserve System in 1915, some difficulty was encountered in obtaining the necessary equivalent data to continue the record of bank loans and security holdings.   Throughout, the figures of the Comptroller of the Currency were used relating to all banks reporting to that official, including commercial banks, private banks, and savings banks.

In utilizing the recent data relating to reserves, a complex problem was presented, in view of the fact that the Federal Reserve System created a new cleavage as between the member banks and the nonmember banks, the latter including the savings banks.   This system also introduced changes in the reserve concept, especially as the result of the development of the system of legal reserve requirements.   Instead of using the Comptroller's figures of bank "cash" after 1914, it was necessary to utilize other data that were finally spliced to the earlier series of cash reserves as reported by the Comptroller.   In order to obtain a reasonably consistent series reflecting the general reserve position of all banking institutions within the Federal Reserve System, it was decided to use the gold-reserve holdings of the Federal Reserve Banks, inasmuch as they began in 1917 to hold all the legal reserves of the member banks capable of supporting credit extension.   During the years 1915 and 1916, comparable estimates were made, taking account of the fact that there was a gradual transfer of reserves by the banks becoming members to the vaults of the Reserve banks.   During this period part of the legal reserve was still in possession of member banks and appears in the reports as "vault cash."   From the total gold reserves (gold certificates beginning at 1934), it was necessary to deduct the amount of reserve held by the Federal Reserve agent against outstanding Federal Reserve notes in accordance with the 40 per cent legal minimum required.   These figures relating to the banking reserves were used in the form of monthly averages for each year.

Still other deductions from the reserves were necessary to take account of the fact (1) that the Federal Reserve Banks hold certain deposits that are not credited to the *member banks* and hence are not equivalent to reserve accounts; (2) that the Treasury has certain deposits in the Federal Reserve Banks that have no member bank-credit significance.   After these deductions are made, there is a resulting series of *adjusted effective reserves* pertaining to the credit-generating operations of the Federal Reserve System.   For the nonmember-bank cash reserves, the June figures from the *Reports of the Comptroller of the Currency* relating to nonmember (vault) cash were used.

But these figures still call for adjustment in order to translate the member-bank reserves into a form having a consistent meaning through the years in terms of the amount of credit-supporting effectiveness, or "valency," of each dollar of reserves, in view of the changes in legal reserve requirements.   In order to take account of these changes in reserve effectiveness, a "valency" index applying to member-bank reserves was developed.   Beginning at June, 1914, with the National Banks, figures were obtained for the required reserves of all National Banks.   These were expressed as a ratio to the total gross deposits of all National Banks. This percentage was expressed as 100, in terms of the 1914 ratio as a base, and the ratio data were continued from this base as index numbers. Beginning at 1919, these apply to the member banks of the Federal Reserve System. These index numbers were then converted to reciprocals in order to express the changing *significance* of member-bank reserves, from the standpoint of their effectiveness in supporting or conditioning credit expansion. The index numbers in this form were averaged with the constant figure 100, representing a rough approximation of the apparently stable valency of reserves held by nonmember banks, and the two index series were finally averaged, with weights based upon the respective annual proportion of all bank loans reported by member banks and by nonmember banks. This *weighted valency index*, expressing reciprocals of reserve requirements and giving preponderant weight to the changes in reserve requirements for member banks of the Reserve System, was then applied to member-bank reserves, adjusted as previously described, plus the (vault) cash of the nonmember banks, as given in the *Reports of the Comptroller of the Currency*.

The above computations were carried as far as 1939, but it was noted that beginning with the years of the Great Depression, the capital and surplus of reporting banks, as given by the Comptroller of the Currency, showed a marked decline, with little tendency to recover after 1933. A closer examination of this bank-capital situation, together with a perusal of remarks contained in the annual reports of the Federal Deposit Insurance Corporation, disclosed that there was beginning to be a rather indirect but yet perceptible limitation over bank-credit expansion, or increase in banking-earning assets, by reason of the average capital position. Inasmuch as we are seeking not merely a series of bank reserves in an accounting sense or a statistical inventory but an index of reserve power, consistently expressing the variations over a long period of years in *effective* banking reserve, it seemed necessary to take into account banking capital as a limiting factor coming into the situation and requiring to be expressed in the formula.

In analyzing the data of total capital (that is, capital, surplus, and undivided profits of all reporting banks), in relation to total earning assets, from 1915 to 1934, prior to the latest gold deluge, it was found that there was a tendency for capital multiplied by seven, to approximate the range of fluctuation of earning assets. Beginning at 1934, the reserve index was therefore further adjusted by reducing it in the proportion of seven times capital to a comparable annual multiple m applied to actual reserves. The latter is the reciprocal of the ratio of required reserves to earning assets, that is, the amount by which the reserves are multiplied to indicate, according to existing legal requirements, how far earning assets can be expanded before acute financial strain or rediscounting develop. Whenever the latter product mR clearly exceeds $7C$, there is the probability that earning assets will be expanded to the limit of $7C$ rather than mR, and the special adjustment for the reserve index becomes necessary to provide a continuous series of *effective reserves*, which, in relation to loans, determine the interest rate. In other words, the ability of banks to expand earning assets as their reserves increased abnormally was found to be limited by the much less flexible capital position. It was assumed that because of banking practice, recognizing the necessity of preserving sound capital ratios, plus the efforts of the FDIC to build up bank capital to a more adequate proportion of earning assets, the earning assets would be unable, without financial strain or significant changes in interest rates, to move much beyond a level of variation roughly seven times the total capital (as previously defined).

The final reserves index clearly indicates that the enormous additions to gold reserves in very recent years, particularly since 1937, have had but limited effect in increasing total earning assets of reporting banks.   If, in the future, banks increase their capital substantially, at the same time retaining large reserves, it will probably provide leeway for simultaneous expansion of loans and investments.   On the other hand, should there be a reduction in the actual gold reserves of the country, as expressed in the adjusted reserve index previously described, it would tend to force some banks having a narrow capital margin against existing earning assets to sell bonds.   This might become a cumulative tendency if the reduction in reserves, or reduction in effectiveness per dollar of reserves, continued rapidly.

Coming now to the relation between the adjusted reserve index and the loan index, the two series were charted on a ratio scale, from which it appeared that when related to each other at some constant multiple there was a consistent tendency to vary within a similar range.   Taking advantage of this, the reserve index was expressed as a percentage of the loan index, first for the period 1835–1861 and separately for the period 1875–1939.   During the first period, the average reserve-loan ratio works out at 19.2 per cent; during the second period, it averages 12.6 per cent for 1875–1932 (the later years of abnormal gold inflow being omitted).   The annual deviations of the data from these respective average ratios were then computed and summated algebraically, that is, *cumulated*.   By thus cumulating the deviations of the reserve-loan ratio about the long-term average, a series results that very closely approximates the pattern of high-grade bond prices.   This final cumulative index, or barometer, tends to rise as long as there is a succession of positive deviations; and it tends to decline as long as there is a succession of negative deviations below the mean level.

The cumulative index appears to express a basic principle in the formation of high-grade bond prices.   As long as there is a relatively ample banking reserve position or as long as loans, which form the primary business of banks generally, are relatively low in relation to their average tendency, just so long there will be a rising *tendency* in bond prices.   This rising tendency is presumably due to the gradual diffusion throughout the banks of decisions to increase earning assets in the form of securities, and this serves to raise the prices of these securities.   Conversely, a restriction of reserves or a relatively rapid increase in loans produces a tendency, which is not immediately fully effective but gradually tends to pervade the system as a whole, for banks to sell some of their investments, and the prices fall.   There is therefore an element of *lag* in the time relation between the effective factors at work and the ultimate result, expressed in bond prices or the rate of interest on bonds.   This type of bond-price "barometer" becomes very effective, since the relation of the reserve-loan ratio to its estimated average level can be made clearly apparent and the amount of *leeway* above the average level, or the amount of decline below it, indicates not only the bank-credit position underlying the bond market but its probable tendency over the near future.

A number of other factors were also compared with the index of bond prices, but none of them afforded a series having anything approaching the close similarity of the pattern of bond prices that was found in the "barometer" just described.   An index of the general changes in wholesale-commodity prices, which have frequently been considered the main controlling factor in the bond market, was one of the factors tested.   With the use of the Warren-Pearson index of wholesale prices, extended for recent years by the Bureau of Labor Statistics index, and converting the whole into reciprocals to express it as an index of the purchasing power of money, a comparison with the bond index revealed some degree of covariation, but in several periods there is marked divergence in pattern.   It appears that although commodity prices do have an effect upon the bond market, this effect is probably exerted through its influence upon the value of commercial bank loans.   Or, to express the matter more completely, those commercial impulses, waxing and waning in the system of business, which tend to expand or contract the use of bank credits, simultaneously raise or lower the denominator of the "barometer" ratio at the same time that they raise or lower the level of commodity prices. It is the effect of this expansion and contraction of prices upon demand for commercial credit, or in credit extended to the financial markets via collateral loans, and not the mere variations in the level of commodity prices *in themselves*, that basically produce the corresponding movements in the bond market.

2. COMPARISON OF MONTHLY DATA OF CHANGES IN GOLD POSITION, MEMBER-BANK EXCESS RESERVES, AND AVERAGE BOND PRICES

Referring to Chart 40, the lower curve indicates the course of the principal factors entering into total bank reserves. This is shown as a 12-month moving average (centered at the end of each period) of the net additions to United States gold stock plus the monthly net addition to Federal Reserve holdings of United States Government securities, the latter beginning at June, 1925. This computation excludes the so-called "inactive gold account" between December, 1936, and April, 1938. The effect of net changes in holdings of United States Government securities by the Federal Reserve is of importance only in the years 1932 and 1933, and it would make very little difference if this feature were entirely omitted.

In the middle section of Chart 40 are shown the actual monthly data of a specially adjusted series of "excess reserves" of the member banks in the Federal Reserve System. As far back as the beginning of 1919 and extending to the end of 1936, this series was first presented (to the writer's knowledge) on a chart on page 8 of the *Twenty-second Annual Report* of the Federal Reserve Bank of New York, covering the year 1936. In this chart the excess reserves were shown after deduction of member-bank borrowings from the Federal Reserve, that is, to show the true reserve position prior to reserve expansion through resort to rediscounts. Until 1933 there was rather generally a deficit rather than an excess of member reserves in this sense. This series was carried to March, 1915, and beyond for occasional dates, by the use of data for excess reserves kindly supplied to the writer by H. V. Roelse, of the Federal Reserve Bank of New York. These figures are not entirely complete; they do not include State Bank and trust-company member banks between June, 1917, and June, 1919. Care was taken to eliminate balances due to banks from city correspondence over and above the allotted reserve that the former were legally permitted to carry as balances with city correspondence. From these figures the amount of member-bank borrowings was also deducted for the corresponding dates, and the result, although not so accurate as in the period beginning at 1919, gives a general idea of the movement of adjusted excess reserve in the banking system.

For the past few years the data of the Federal Reserve Bank of New York, as finally published in chart form, have been continued, following the same general procedure, although since borrowings by member banks have been exceedingly small in recent years, that particular adjustment becomes much less important, and the curve as shown in Chart 40, registers substantially the excess reserves in the form in which they are shown at monthly intervals in the Federal Reserve Bulletin.

APPENDIX 8

CORPORATE REVENUE AND ITS DISPOSITION, 1922–1938

1. MANUFACTURING CORPORATIONS

The data for Chart 45 pertain to calendar years and were obtained from the Treasury Department, Bureau of Internal Revenue, "Statistics of Income," Part 2. The first year for which reasonably satisfactory data of corporate disposition of revenue are available is 1922. From the total receipts or gross revenue of all manufacturing corporations reporting to the Treasury Department, operating-cost deductions were made in such fashion as to reveal balances destined for capital uses and taxes. These annual balances do not correspond exactly with the accounting distinction between fixed charges and operating outlays, but we wish to study particularly the annual charges for depreciation, interest payments, aggregate tax payments, or rather accruals, amount paid in dividends, and the net savings carried to surplus. In Chart 45 the bars are erected from a zero line from which is measured the total amount of net revenue, this term being applied to that residual which was obtained in the foregoing fashion. The negative values represent payments of dividends, taxes, interest, and in one year depreciation charges, which deducted from reported net revenue involve minus quantities. It should be pointed out that there is a lack of complete homogeneity in the character of the reported data beginning at 1935 as a result of the revocation in 1934 of the privilege of filing consolidated tax returns for all corporations except railroads. While this introduces some important limitations upon the comparability of the data for individual industry groups, it does not materially effect the significance of the figures shown in Chart 45 relating to all manufacturing companies. It does, however, introduce some complication to the extent that manufacturing enterprises have controlled, or have been subsidiaries of, other types of enterprise, but it is impossible to estimate exactly how much of a discrepancy is represented. Additional detailed statistics may be found in *Monograph* 15 of the Temporary National Economic Committee, "Financial Characteristics of American Manufacturing Corporations."

2. PUBLIC-UTILITY CORPORATIONS

In order to simplify the exhibit in Chart 48, it was decided to combine the data drawn from the source described above for railroad companies and all other public-utility enterprises. The accounts of railroads and of most other public-utility corporations are not prepared according to uniform classifications of items, and it was desired to approximate as closely as possible the concept of net revenue and its disposition as worked out for manufacturing corporations. The maintenance figures, including a minor portion pertaining to other public-utility corporations than railroads, were taken from Solomon Fabricant, "Capital Consumption and Adjustment," National Bureau of Economic Research, New York, 1938, for 1922 to 1935. The amounts for 1936–1938 were estimated on the basis of railroad plant and equipment maintenance, from Interstate Commerce Commission Reports and U.S. Department of Commerce estimates of maintenance outlays for other public utilities (*Survey of Current Business*, August, 1939). The total of maintenance and depreciation charges appearing in Chart 48 is roughly comparable, therefore, with the depreciation allowances of manufacturing corporations, as shown in Chart 45. There are various minor capital adjustments that could not be included in either the manufacturing or public-utility corporation exhibit.

In Chart 46, the total receipts of manufacturing corporations are compared on identical ratio scales with the estimated outlays for capital purposes, including plant and equipment, with the use of the data of George Terborgh, presented in the *Federal Reserve Bulletin*, September, 1939, p. 732, and February, 1941, p. 103. These figures include mining as well as manufacturing companies; some mining operations are included in manufacturing enterprise in the reports of financial operations to the Treasury Department. The series of capital expenditures agrees in its movements fairly closely with that prepared for manufacturing companies by the U.S. Department of Commerce, under the direction of L. J. Chawner, *Survey of Current Business*, March, 1941, p. 10.

The estimates of total capital resources in Chart 46 were built up from the net saving, depreciation charges, and that part of the issues of capital securities estimated to have been for primarily productive purposes. The data on capital issues are those of the *Commercial and Financial Chronicle;* adjustment for nonproductive capital was mainly applied to the period prior to 1932, based upon an analysis of individual issues and their apparent purpose. Exact adjustments of this nature are not available. The capital resources made up in this fashion do not include bank loans, which in some years were of considerable importance, nor do they include miscellaneous minor elements such as might be provided by various balance-sheet adjustments. It is not clear whether the reported data of security issues are entirely complete or include all issues of securities sold directly to large financial organizations. The omission of bank loans is perhaps the most important defect in the index of total capital resources as shown. It will be noted in Chart 46 that the total receipts and capital outlays are rendered comparable with respect to their proportionate movements by the ratio scale; since the building up of total capital resources involved some negative figures, these were placed on an arithmetic scale, so adjusted that it is roughly comparable with the index of capital outlays.

In the lower section of Chart 46 the various ratios to total receipts, or gross revenue, are shown as index numbers, with the base at 1925. All these factors were derived from the same data as was shown in Chart 45, with the exception of wage payments. The wage-disbursement index is based upon data of payrolls of manufacturing industries of the Bureau of Labor Statistics.

The essentially similar exhibit for transportation and public-utility corporations, Chart 49, was prepared in the same fashion as the foregoing. In this Chart also the capital resources are shown arithmetically, and total receipts and estimated capital expenditures are shown on identical ratio scales. The ratio of wage disbursements to total receipts of this group of corporations is based upon the data of wage payments in transportation and other public-utility enterprises, prepared by Simon Kuznets, "National Income and Capital Formation, 1919–1935," pp. 63 and 64. This series was continued by the use of U.S. Department of Commerce figures of wage disbursements in transportation and public-utility industries, as published in the *Survey of Current Business*, June, 1941, p. 18.

Chart 47, comparing total capital resources of manufacturing corporations with capital outlays adjusted for increase or decrease in inventory value, reproduces the index of total capital resources as shown in Chart 46. To the value of capital outlays as shown in Chart 46 were added or subtracted the annual differences in inventory values, with the use of inventory data prepared as follows. Beginning at 1926, the inventories are from the corporate capital-stock tax returns as reported by the Treasury Department. For prior years, back to 1922, estimates were made on the basis of the data of Simon Kuznets, Inventories of Manufacturing Corporations, as presented in "Commodity Flow and Capital Formation," Vol. I, p. 412. All curves in this chart were drawn on arithmetic scale.

APPENDIX 9

RECEIPTS, NET REVENUE, AND CAPITAL OUTLAYS OF INDIVIDUALS AND FARMERS

1. INDIVIDUALS AND ENTREPRENEURS (CHART 55)

The basis of the gross receipts or income figures is the series of Kuznets, National Bureau of Economic Research, 1922–1928, including individuals and entrepreneurs. From 1929 to 1939, a similar series, computed by the U.S. Department of Commerce, was used. In order to obtain net revenue, the estimates of Kuznets for consumer expenditures on nondurable goods and services (the latter somewhat smoothed) were deducted from the income-payment totals. Further deduction was made for payments of income and state taxes and, after 1935, social-security taxes. The remainder was considered to be an approximate figure of net revenue. To these figures was added each year the increase or decrease in the total of indebtedness consisting of mortgages and installment-credit balances. The mortgage data are a combination of urban- and farm-mortgage indebtedness. The urban-mortgage estimates were derived from the data of the Home Loan Bank Board for all outstanding urban mortgages on homes beginning at 1929 and, for preceding years, an extrapolation backward of the former series on the basis of annual changes in the assets of building-and-loan associations from these statistical abstractions. The agricultural mortgages used as a basis for the estimates of annual change in outstanding amounts were taken from the data of Norman J. Wall, of the U.S. Bureau of Agricultural Economics, and include total farm-mortgage debt deducting amounts owing to individuals. The total of installment credit as a basis for annual changes was taken from *Monograph* 37 of the Temporary National Economic Committee, p. 83. This series includes only consumer credit for capital financing. With these additions to net revenue of the positive or negative amounts of annual change for construction and other types of consumer capital financing, an index of adjusted net revenue was obtained, roughly comparable to the similar measure for corporations. This adjusted net revenue is a rough approximation of the annual amounts of disposable income and borrowed funds available to consumers as a whole, from which durable capital goods, savings and other forms of insurance, security purchases, and gifts could be provided for. The estimated annual outlays of a capital nature, as shown in Chart 55, were obtained from Terborgh's table, *Federal Reserve Bulletin*, September, 1939, p. 733, and also the *Federal Reserve Bulletin* for February, 1941. These comprise estimated individual expenditures for building, automobiles, household equipment, and agricultural outlays for plant and equipment.

2. FARMERS (CHART 5)

Agricultural Income and Its Disposition.—The series of gross receipts of agriculture shown in Chart 57 is based upon data presented by H. R. Tolley, U.S. Bureau of Agricultural Economics, "Materials Bearing on Parity Prices," July, 1941. The gross receipts as shown consist of cash value of farm sales plus estimated value of family consumption of products plus Government benefit payments. The estimates of net revenue were obtained from data in the foregoing source and represent deductions from gross receipts of total production expenses of farm operators and a further adjustment for the estimated annual change in inventory values (*op. cit.*, Sec. A, Table 2). The estimated net revenue was then adjusted for annual changes in farm indebtedness from the data given in the source previously referred to, Sec. B, Table 12. These are data of the *total* farm debt. In order to measure agricultural capital outlays, data were obtained from several U.S. Department of Agriculture Bulletins. Income Parity for Agriculture, Part 2, Expenses of Agricultural Production, Sec. 5, March, 1941, gives estimates of expenditure for permanent improvements on farms; Sec. 3, August, 1940, gives outlays for equipment used on farms. The sum of these two items is shown in Chart 57 as total estimated capital outlay. In this chart, again, the relative changes in gross receipts and capital outlays can be compared by the use of ratio scale; in the lower section the changes in net revenue and adjusted net revenue were plotted on arithmetic scale, it being apparent that the percentual fluctuations would be enormously greater than in the case of receipts and capital outlays. It was not found possible to make accurate estimates of what might be termed the essential day-to-day living cost of farm families, and these were not included in the net revenue data. Had they been included, it is probable that in 1932 the net revenue might have approached zero or even fallen below it. Until further data become available on this point, no adjustments for this factor can be made, but it is probable that their inclusion would not alter the general pattern disclosed.

APPENDIX 10

INDEXES OF LABOR INCOME AND PRODUCTIVITY IN MANUFACTURING INDUSTRIES

1. Average Money Wages per Hour in Manufacturing and Value of Manufactured Products per Man-hour

In preparing this exhibit and the succeeding exhibits, it was necessary to assemble the data from various sources and to splice them into continuous series. Wherever possible, selection was made from the several series after charting the data on ratio scales and making careful comparisons. Comparisons were also made wherever possible with the comprehensive occasional data of the Census of Manufactures. The final series in all cases were reduced to index numbers, with the base at 1925.

The index of money wages per hour in manufacturing (Chart 62) consists of the following segments. (1) From 1859 to 1890 the wage-rate index is that of Rufus S. Tucker, as presented in the *Review of Economic Statistics*, Feb. 15, 1934. This series was found to agree very closely with the weighted average of wage rates published by the Senate Committee on Wholesale Prices and Wages, 1893 (usually referred to as the *Aldrich Report*). The Tucker series agrees somewhat more closely with the Aldrich data than with the U.S. Bureau of Labor Statistics wage index, as presented in *Bulletin* 499, 1927. (2) At 1890 the Tucker series was spliced with the wage-rate index prepared by Paul H. Douglas ("Real Wages in the United States," p. 108), which extends as far as 1925. (3) At 1925 the series is spliced with the hourly wage-rate index relating to manufacturing industries of the U.S. Bureau of Labor Statistics, published in the *Monthly Labor Review*, September, 1940, in the article Wages, Hours, and Productivity of Industrial Labor by Witt Bowden, and supplemented by current data from this source.

The BLS series differs slightly from the Douglas series in its composition. The BLS index is developed as a ratio between total payrolls in manufacturing and total man-hours worked. This is equivalent to a weighted average in which the weights are man-hours rather than merely number of employees, as in the Douglas series. Although the BLS method takes account of the fact that shifts are continually occurring in the *proportion* of workers at different levels of pay and in the speed of piece workers, etc., it is believed that the entire composite series extending from 1859 to date adequately represents the general drift of hourly wage rates in manufacturing industry, with as good a system of weighting as the available statistics permit. With respect to the data taken from the various studies by Paul H. Douglas, it should be added that there is abundant evidence that his studies were very carefully conducted, and the writer has a high degree of confidence in the accuracy of his results, which, as will be noted below, have been used for various portions of the measures referred to in Chapter 20, particularly from about 1890 forward.

An index of the value of manufacturing production per man-hour of employment requires four series of data. Beginning with production, the index for manufacturing constructed by Warren M. Persons was used, beginning at 1869 and carried to 1918. Data were found in W. M. Persons, "Forecasting Business Cycles," p. 170, and the *Review of Economic Statistics*, Aug. 15, 1933, p. 155. Persons' data were carried back from 1869 to 1859 by the use of a series of "industrial" production (which closely approximates manufacturing for that period), computed by Leonard P. Ayres and obtained through his courtesy. At 1918, Persons' series is carried forward to 1920 by use of the Day-Thomas index of manufacturing production, which is probably more accurate than Persons' series for those years, inasmuch as the latter does not agree with any of the production indexes available for the period. Beginning at 1920 a further splice is made to carry the series forward by means of the revised index of manufacturing production prepared by the Board of Governors of the Federal Reserve System.

To convert the production index to values, several experiments were made. A comparison of the Census "value of products" with the index derived by the foregoing indexes of production multiplied by indexes of nonagricultural prices (based upon the index numbers of Warren and Pearson and prepared by the U.S. Department of Agriculture) showed that although there was close resemblance in the shorter movements, the *trends* were not the same. Therefore, it was decided to utilize the Census values directly as far as 1899 and not attempt annual data.

At 1899 the Census of Manufactures' value of product data were spliced to an index obtained by multiplying the manufacturing-production series by the price index of wholesale manufactured goods prepared by Frederick C. Mills for the National Bureau of Economic Research ("Economic Tendencies in the United States," p. 584). This was spliced at 1913 with the group index of wholesale prices of *finished* products of the U.S. Bureau of Labor Statistics and carried to date. It was found that the index of industrial-production values obtained in this fashion agrees reasonably well with the Census of Manufactures gross values.

In order to obtain the series of man-hours in manufacturing, the following series were first computed. The index of manufacturing-industry wage earners employed, in terms of the average number per annum, is based upon the Census of Manufactures for 1859, 1869, 1879, and 1889. In these early years the data were based upon reports from factories and also from handwork and neighborhood industries, which in those days contributed a fairly important proportion of our manufactured goods. At 1889 the annual series begins and is based upon the index of manufacturing employment prepared by Paul H. Douglas, as given in his "Real Wages in the United States," p. 440, for the period 1889–1899 and "The Theory of Wages," p. 125, for the period 1899–1920. The first set of Douglas' data represent careful estimates based upon the statistics furnished by the employment records of several typical industrial states that provide interpolation between Census years. The second series, down to 1920, is an index based upon essentially the same method, but with more adequate material and probably greater accuracy. At 1920 the Douglas series was spliced to the index of employment in manufacturing industries of the U.S. Bureau of Labor Statistics. These figures are adjusted to conform with the biennial data of the Census of Manufactures as far as 1937.

To obtain the man-hours index it is necessary to use a measure of the hours worked, considered as a representative average over a wide range of manufacturing industries, with due allowance for weighting. The only series of this type available for any but recent years relates to what may be termed "full-time" hours worked, that is, the hours that in each of the manufacturing industries constituted a "typical" or standard period of work, beyond which overtime would begin. For the years prior to 1890, the *Aldrich Report* furnishes an apparently reliable series representing a *weighted* average of full-time hours worked in various manufacturing industries, expressed as the hours worked *per day*. These figures, however, can be spliced to later figures after 1890, representing hours *per week*, inasmuch as the length of the working week in industry did not materially change prior to 1890. An index number, therefore, was prepared from the Aldrich series, ending at 1890 and extending back to 1859.

At 1890 this series was spliced to the parallel index of Paul H. Douglas, as given in his "Real Wages in the United States," p. 116, extending as far as 1926. At 1926 the series was extended by means of data prepared by the National Industrial Conference Board, as given in *Bulletin* 71 of the National Bureau of Economic Research, in the article by Leo Wolman entitled Hours of Work in American Industry. This latter series extends to 1932. For the years 1933 and 1934, estimates were made based upon standards for industrial labor set up by the NRA and monthly reports of the U.S. Bureau of Labor Statistics. For later years the estimates given by Leo Wolman in *Bulletin* 71 and various other sources were used to establish an approximation to the current prevailing average full-time-hours schedules in manufacturing industries. The latest figure obtained for 1940 is approximately 40 hours per week. It is impossible for the years prior to about 1899 to secure anything in the nature of a series measuring actual hours *worked*, as compared with the hours understood to be a standard typical full-time schedule; so it was decided to employ a homogeneous series approximating the full-time hours so that the man-hours series would be thoroughly consistent.

The final man-hours index was then obtained from the employment index and the index of full-time hours worked per week. This is the denominator of the ratio value of manufacturing product per man-hour. The same man-hour index was used for Chart 63. In the discussion in Chapter 20 of the relationships disclosed by Chart 62, it was pointed out that the index of value of product per man-hour has a slightly more pronounced upward trend than the rate of money wages per hour. Had *actual* hours worked been used, it is possible that the fluctuations from year to year in the value of product per man-hour might have been somewhat more emphatic, and the trend of that series would probably have been somewhat steeper during periods of business depression and less steep in prosperity periods, without any appreciable change in the long-term drift. The conclusions drawn from Chart 62 would not have been materially different had the measure of product per man-hour been stated in terms of hours actually worked rather than full-time hours.

2. REAL HOURLY WAGES IN MANUFACTURING AND VOLUME OF PRODUCTION PER MAN-HOUR (CHART 63)

This exhibit requires adjustment of money wage rates per hour by an index of the cost of living and the use of the manufacturing volume index (without modification) to obtain a ratio per man-hour.

To convert the measure of money wage per hour to real wage per hour, that is, to approximate a measure of physical purchasing power per hour of work comparable with the physical index of output per man-hour, several sets of data were spliced to make a continuous series. From 1859 to 1861, R. S. Tucker's series of the cost of living was taken from the *Review of Economic Statistics*, Feb. 15, 1934. Beginning at 1861, this series was averaged year by year with the cost-of-living index prepared by Carl Snyder at the Federal Reserve Bank of New York. This combined series was carried down to 1890, where it was spliced to the cost-of-living index of Paul H. Douglas, as given in his "Real Wages in the United States," p. 60, and extended as far as 1913. At this point it was spliced to the cost-of-living index of the U.S. Bureau of Labor Statistics, which continues as far as 1934. At that point the Bureau introduced certain revisions that are incorporated in the results for succeeding years. The index of real wages per hour in manufactufing was therefore obtained by dividing the index of money-wage rates by the index of the cost of living.

For the second series shown in Chart 63, the data are the same as those used for preceding exhibits, except that manufacturing production is in terms of a physical-volume index rather than a value index.

3. TOTAL ANNUAL LABOR OUTLAY PER EMPLOYED WAGE EARNER, PER PHYSICAL UNIT OF PRODUCTION IN MANUFACTURING AND PER UNIT OF VALUE OF MANUFACTURED OUTPUT (CHARTS 65 AND 66)

For the Census years 1859–1889, the Census of Manufactures data were used to obtain an index of manufacturing-industry payroll disbursements. This series forms a comprehensive indicator of gross labor outlay for manufacturing. When related to an index of production volume, the result establishes the approximate trend and the intermediate changes in total labor cost per unit of product, although it is impossible to obtain for early individual years an index of production having the extensive range and inclusiveness of the Census figures.

Beginning at 1889, an index of payroll disbursements in manufacturing is spliced to the Census series. This index is obtained by multiplying the index of manufacturing employment previously explained by an index of the average annual earnings per worker employed. For this purpose use was first made of data for wage earnings prepared by Paul H. Douglas and presented in "Real Wages in the United States," page 246. The Douglas series of average annual earnings per worker, converted to index numbers and multiplied by the index of employment in manufacturing industries, was carried as far as 1925. At that point it was spliced with the U.S. Bureau of Labor Statistics index of payrolls in manufacturing, and this series was extended to date. It was then related, in actual and deflated form, to the index of (gross) value of manufactures, with the use of the series previously explained, and also to the index of manufacturing production.

APPENDIX 11

1. COMPOSITE MONTHLY BAROMETER OF CYCLICAL MOVEMENTS IN GENERAL BUSINESS ACTIVITY, 1881-1924

For the business-activity index the monthly series prepared by Leonard P. Ayres was used from 1881 to 1918. This index has the advantage of having among the component data not only basic industrial production, such as is known to correlate closely with cyclical variations in manufacturing, but also measures of general trade derived from statistics of railway traffic. Prior to 1880 or thereabouts, it is difficult to obtain sufficient figures on a monthly basis to carry back the picture of physical production or trade cycles. The Ayres index has another advantage in that its average range of amplitude agrees closely with other measures for more limited periods, but reflecting average amplitude of cyclical variation in a comprehensive range of industrial and commercial operations.

Beginning at 1919, the Federal Reserve index of industrial production was used as the basis for monthly continuation of the Ayres index. Long-term moving averages, such as were used to obtain the annual cyclical deviations, were calibrated to monthly form and extended graphically for the last ten years as tentative estimates of the approximate position of the "center of gravity" of this series. Second, the percentage deviation of the Federal Reserve index from this trend level were reduced 30 per cent, following the procedure employed in the case of the annual index of business described in Appendix 1.

The development of the monthly forecasting barometer proceeded for the most part on the basis of principles that have long been familiar and that were used, in various forms, with a fair degree of success, at least until the late 1920's. It has been observed that short-term interest or discount rates in the New York money market described cyclical movements capable of indicating the approach of tension, credit restriction, and business insolvency and capable, also, of indicating the easing of credit conditions following a recession or panic, when the financial structure at least was again able to accommodate and encourage general trade recovery. It has also been observed that the cyclical fluctuations in the money market have been highly correlated (allowing for wide amplitude and some degree of lag) with cycles in the yield on high-grade bonds. The latter data, when translated to represent the reciprocal of bond yields, that is, bond *prices*, tend to correlate, over long periods of time, with the cyclical changes in average stock prices, with a fairly consistent lead. Although the stock market movements have not invariably preceded those of the business index, it has been found in the preponderance of cases, down as far as the late 1920's, that the movements of stock prices have had some forecasting value, although usually at short range. The stock-price component was found to correct a tendency in the interest rate and bond series to shift cyclical direction somewhat too far ahead of the corresponding changes in a business index.

It was decided to develop a composite barometer rather than to employ the original method of Warren M. Persons, used by the Harvard Economic Service, in which two factors, reflecting the stock-market and interest rates, serve as separate indicators. It was considered that the forecasting value of the type of data referred to might be brought into focus more effectively by combining the data into a single monthly index that would indicate in advance the critical turning points in the business cycle but would not be too sensitive to irregular fluctuations such as were a source of difficulty in most of the results previously obtained.

In view of the increasingly artificial and novel circumstances influencing interest rates and the money market in the past decade or more, it was decided to carry the calculation now to be described only as far as 1924. After that year other data become available that appear to be less susceptible to changing political controls and international conditions, and the extension of the forecasting barometer beyond 1924 is therefore described in a separate section below.

The data for short-term interest rates relate to the average monthly rates on commercial paper in New York, adjusted for seasonal variation, as given in the *Review of Economic Statistics*, January, 1925. The deviations were measured from a trend in the form of a long-term moving average. Since it was intended to bring this series into combination with data of the cyclical movements of stock prices, the final results were expressed as percentage deviations, with signs reversed. The average yields on high-grade long-term bonds are those computed by Frederick R. Macaulay and published in "Bond Yields, Interest Rates and Stock Prices," 1938, Table 10. This series is likewise converted into the form of inverted percentage deviation from trend, to translate the data to price cycles. The series of industrial stock prices is that of the Cowles' Commission for Economic Research, published in "Common Stocks Indexes," pp. 68–69, adjusted to deviations from trend.

It was found that the amplitude of the cyclical deviations differed considerably among the three series. The highest amplitude was found in the cycles of commercial paper rates, followed next in order by the cycles of bond prices and industrial stock prices. Some adjustment for amplitude was therefore necessary.

Careful graphic comparison of the three selected cyclical deviation series with the monthly index of business activity disclosed that although inverted money rates and bond prices tended to precede the cycles of business by fairly long intervals, sometimes well over a year, the amount of lead was not uniform. Good results were obtained, however, by averaging these two series. The monthly cycles of stock prices represent, in part, the effect of interest rates and credit factors that influence speculative operations. When the series were studied in combination, it appeared that a properly weighted average of the three would form a consistent forecasting index, and adjustment for amplitude could be accomplished at the same time. It was found that both these objectives could be approximated by the use of the following weights:

Bond prices... 2.0
Stock prices... 0.7
Inverted commercial paper rates........................... 0.5

The composite cycles still presented the problem of minor erratic fluctuations. It was found that the degree of forecasting lead in this preliminary composite, however, was sufficient to permit a smoothing of the monthly data, which was done by the use of a progressively weighted short-term moving average. The resulting barometer of money-market and stock-market conditions may be considered as reflecting the forthcoming major turns of the business cycle with a degree of reliability that would have been very useful during the period covered. Every important boom and depression in these years was intensified, as well as foreshadowed, by conditions in the financial markets that affected particularly commercial operations.

In order to bring into relation with the barometer in this form some indicator of conditions in the long-term capital market and the construction industries, a series of urban-real estate foreclosures was found to be of special value.   The writer obtained through the courtesy of Roy Wenzlick, a close student of real estate and building finance and director of the Real Estate Analyst Service, a monthly index of per capita foreclosures on urban property, extending back far enough to permit its use in this connection.   The figures were first smoothed by a progressive moving average and converted into percentages of long-term trend.   The resulting deviations were found to be extremely violent, and in order to bring these into closer relation to the movements of the foregoing barometer and to reduce the amplitude, the percentage deviation was logarithmically reduced to the extent of one-twentieth of those in the original data.   The percentage signs were also reversed to permit the result to be used as a measure of cycles in mortgage solvency.   This series of adjusted foreclosure cycles was found to have the interesting property of serving as an auxiliary indicator, supplementing the foregoing barometer.   The financial barometer appeared for several years at a time somewhat further below or further above the long-term trend level than the business activity index.   But when the composite barometer was superimposed upon the adjusted foreclosure index (whose cyclical movements are of much longer term), there was a tendency to rectify this particular movement. Although this indicator of mortgage solvency is not necessarily a predominating factor in current business conditions or industrial activity, it has been pointed out that a major upward swing in the building and real-estate cycle has contributed powerfully to better-than-average business conditions over an extended period of years; the reverse tendency has been associated with more or less impaired general activity.

The final business-forecasting barometer, therefore, is a financial composite developed from smoothed monthly cycles of the money market, the stock market, and from the best available measure of the financial conditions that have usually foreshadowed major construction booms and depressions.

The writer is indebted to LeRoy J. Steele for assistance in developing the portion of the foregoing work involving the money-market factors.

2. CONSTRUCTION OF THE BAROMETER OF GENERAL BUSINESS ACTIVITY, 1919–1940

The composite barometer described in the preceding section was used without alteration for the years 1919 to January, 1924.   At that point a splice was made to a new series of data in the form of cyclical deviations.   This was obtained by adjusting for trend, amplitude, and smoothing the Standard Statistics Company's (now Standard and Poor's Corporation) monthly indexes of average yield on Bl+ industrial bonds, the yield basis being translated into a price basis by inverting the cyclical deviations from trend.   This series was derived from a very comprehensive group of industrial and realty bonds of a speculative character.   It was found by careful tests that this series combined the forecasting characteristics of both the bond and stock markets in such a way as to precede the business cycle in the downward movements in a way resembling the typical money-market factors and also to anticipate the upward reversals of the business index in the manner of stock-market movements in the past.   So sensitive was this index based upon speculative bonds that after considerable smoothing it retains forecasting value.   This series, after adjustments, constitutes the barometer until January, 1934.   (The original data are no longer published.)

With the pronounced expansion of governmental control over the money market, the tempering of speculative activity in all directions, and large contributions to the capital market made directly by the Federal Government after 1933, a change was made in the composition of the barometer index.   This was done in order to take advantage of two series that have a more direct significance with respect to the flow of new capital into construction and other industrial uses, rather than relying upon the speculative tendencies in securities or in money-market conditions.   At January, 1934, therefore, a splice was made to a new series combining adjusted cycles of the value of residential-building contracts and adjusted cycles derived from the series prepared by the Federal Reserve Board of "net contributions to national purchasing power" by the Federal Government.   The use of cycles of residential-building contracts was justified by the highly consistent behavior of these figures from a forecasting standpoint, as disclosed by Charts 54a and 54b.   The data used were those of the F. W. Dodge Corporation for residential contracts in 36 states, seasonally adjusted by the Federal Reserve Board.   These were reduced to one-fourth average amplitude and further smoothed.   The data for net Federal contributions to purchasing power are essentially Federal expenditures adjusted for certain types of Federal revenue. They were adjusted for trend, the deviations reduced one-half, and a smoothing was applied.   The two series of adjusted cycles were then averaged with equal weight and the results spliced, as stated above, to the series previously used at January, 1934. The barometer continues in this form to date.   The writer acknowledges his indebtedness to Lauchlin Currie, formerly of the Federal Reserve System, for his kindness in making these confidential figures available.   In this form the barometer retains usefulness even in periods of war, since in such periods the large Federal spending is offset by shrinkage in private-capital use, which is usually most pronounced in the field of residential construction.   Under more normal conditions, assuming that there will continue to be large Federal outlays designed to stimulate the capital goods industries, this barometer should preserve forecasting value with respect to the cycles of industrial activity because of the observed high degree of sensitivity found in the two sets of data and the logical consideration that this barometer measures the forces directly and promptly that develop orders for durable materials and equipment in the capital-goods industries.

As indicated in Chart 73, a second or auxiliary barometer is added.   This consists of the continuation of the adjusted (inverted) cycles of urban mortgage foreclosures, as described in the preceding section.   Instead of being incorporated in the first barometer, this series is used as a separate auxiliary indicator of the long-term movements in the most significant single measure of financial conditions in the construction field.   So long as a rising drift is shown in this barometer 2, it may be considered as reflecting underlying conditions relating to construction that can be expected to modify the severity or duration of such business recessions as occur during that phase.   Contrariwise, during a downward movement in the long-term cycle of mortgage solvency, there is a warning, long in advance, that general trade recessions encountered during that phase will be relatively sharp and severe, and if extensive financial or speculative excesses have occurred during the boom preceding the downturn, the depression will prove of a major character and probably of rather long duration.   The barometer system, therefore, is designed to be of service in business planning, not only a few months but several years in advance.

APPENDIX 12

1. REAL-ESTATE FORECLOSURES; FAILURES IN COMMERCE, RAILROAD COMPANIES, AND BANKS; AND THE GENERAL COMMODITY PURCHASING POWER OF THE DOLLAR

The data shown in Chart 33 present the annual records since 1870 of financial involvement in relation to reciprocals of wholesale-commodity prices. At the top of the chart the Foreclosure Index was plotted from data kindly made available to the writer by Roy Wenzlick, president of Real Estate Analysts, Inc., St. Louis. They are the number of foreclosures per 100,000 families in various cities, the number of which increases from four in 1870 to a much larger number in recent years. Although pertaining to all types of urban property, the number is predominantly associated with residential foreclosure, and hence the data have been placed on a per-100,000 families basis throughout. At 1932 the data have been spliced to the more complete statistics of annual urban-mortgage foreclosures as published by the Federal Home Loan Bank Board.

In the middle section there are two series. The lower line represents the annual fluctuations of commercial failures, as reported in *Dun's Review*, and in more recent years by Dun & Bradstreet. These are the total liabilities in dollars, expressed on a per capita basis. The upper of the two curves, which begins at 1876, is composed of the foregoing plus two other related series. The first of these is a series of deposits of all banks placed in suspension, according to the reports of the Comptroller of the Currency. The figures are given in the original Reports for years ending June 30, and in order to convert to approximate calendar years, 2-year moving averages, centered on the first year, of each pair were computed, as far as 1920. Beginning at 1921, calendar-year figures are available in the *Statistical Abstract*. The figures for 1933 are very high, since they include many cases of temporary closure during the banking crisis of March. The second component is a series of the estimated amount of bonded debt of railroads placed in receivership. The original data are mainly those reported by *Railway Age*, and compiled in the *Statistical Abstract*. The figures as reported show the total bonds and stocks of the roads placed in receivership. There are also given in the same source data from which it is possible to compute the percentage of all railway capital in the form of funded debt. These proportions vary little through the years, and from these percentages a smoothed series of percentage of funded-debt total capital was applied to the total capital of the roads placed in receivership to show approximate amounts of funded debt involved. Beginning at 1909, the outstanding bonds of electric railways placed in receivership or trusteeship were added to the estimates of bonded debt of failed steam railways. The three component series were finally reduced to per capita basis.

The series representing the commodity purchasing power of the dollar was derived by computing reciprocals of the Warren-Pearson and U.S. Bureau of Labor Statistics wholesale-price indexes, the latter portion beginning at 1890. These reciprocals, multiplied by 100, represent the percentages of the index of purchasing power of the dollar over commodities at wholesale.

2. NEW BUSINESS ENTERPRISE AND
GOVERNMENTAL ACTIVITY

In Chart 76, the percentage of national income derived from Government represented the computations of the National Industrial Conference Board, as given in "Enterprise and Social Progress," New York, 1939, Part 6, supplemented by the data in the "Economic Almanac, 1941–42," of the Conference Board. The ratio of tax to national income was based upon the tax data from the foregoing sources and the data on national income as explained in Appendix 4. The ratio of private to total construction was based upon the data of George Terborgh, as given in the *Federal Reserve Bulletin*, September, 1939, and February, 1941. A number of new businesses organized each year, compiled by Dun & Bradstreet, is given in Part 1 of the *Temporary National Economic Committee Hearings*, p. 227, supplemented by the files of *Dun's Review*. These represent the total number of names added each year to Dun & Bradstreet's reference files of credit reports. These include changes in ownership and legal form of organization but do not include mere changes in name or location. They do not allow for withdrawal from business and thus are the gross rather than the net figures; they afford a rough measure of the incentives to organize enterprise. The number of business corporations organized in the states of Maine, Delaware, New York, and Illinois are available, beginning at 1925, in the *Survey of Current Business*, based upon the material compiled by the Corporation Trust Company. All the foregoing data were reduced to index numbers, with 1925 as 100. The reader should interpret the percentage or ratio curves as being index numbers to the 1925 base, rather than reading the ratios direct to the scale shown in Chart 76.

APPENDIX 13

NOTE ON UNEMPLOYMENT ESTIMATES

Private estimates of unemployment have usually been arrived at by subtracting the number considered to be employed in private or nonemergency governmental agencies from the total number of persons estimated as making up the total labor force. In the absence of official information, the labor force has been estimated in recent years by extrapolation from the 1930 Census data, with allowance for gradual increase in population growth. It happens that in the 1930 Census, "gainful workers" were enumerated according to a somewhat wider definition than was used in the 1940 Census, which excludes consideration of retired persons, some inmates of institutions, recently disabled persons, and inactive seasonal workers. On the other hand, the 1940 Census, unlike that of 1930, does include in the total working force, or list of employables, those *without* previous work experience, that is, *new* workers.[1]

It is not yet wholly clear just how far differences in definition of working force will affect the validity of the latest (1940) official unemployment estimates, but possibly the final editing of the 1940 returns will establish the total number of employable persons available for work at a somewhat higher figure than the preliminary estimates, and the official total of unemployment will probably be somewhere between eight and nine million as of 1940. Since June, 1940, when the National Defense Program was initiated, a fairly rapid reduction in the number of unemployed occurred because of the enormous expansion of Government expenditures for the purpose of producing armament and supplies for foreign countries. After the nation entered the War the rapid increase in employment continued to accelerate, with acute shortages of some types of skilled artisans appearing.

When we attempt to narrow the estimates of unemployed labor to exclude the agricultural group (which is very difficult to define and enumerate), there are many statistical problems. It is much more difficult, for example, to arrive at a satisfactory estimate of the number available for work or seeking work in specific occupations covering even so broad a group as manufacturing. We have fairly accurate figures of the *changes* in employment; the *numbers* of the employed are far less accurate, and the numbers of the unemployed are still more subject to inaccuracy. One of the reasons for this inaccuracy is the fact that it is difficult to enumerate the persons working in new and small industrial enterprises that do not report to the U.S. Bureau of Labor Statistics or any other agency. A considerable migration of industries from the larger urban areas occurred after 1925. The U.S. Bureau of Labor Statistics has been primarily concerned with wage earners (that is, factory artisans), so that the *clerical force*, both as to employed and unemployed, has not been taken adequately into account, and only recently partial estimates have been made for this group, which

[1] W. S. Woytinsky considers that the definition of labor force in 1940 is not far from what would have been actually reported, in terms of "gainful workers" in 1930 (*Review of Economic Statistics*, May, 1941). If those on the payrolls of Federal emergency agencies are considered to include NYA Student Work Program groups, the number of such emergency workers would be about a million greater than the 2,400,000 in the preliminary Federal estimate of 1940.

comprised about 8 per cent of all workers in 1920.[1]   More recently, since the establishment of the Social Security System, reports by employers on a quarterly basis provide a much more complete current census of those employed in the industries covered; but even with these more complete figures of employment, there is the difficulty of estimating the employables, not only as to totals but particularly as to subgroups and individual industries.   Attention should also be given to the fact that in periods of depression there is usually a tendency for members of a family other than the usual breadwinner to seek work in order to supplement the family income or avert going on the WPA.   These so-called "additional workers" naturally enter into the unemployment count of those "seeking" work.[2]   During a prolonged depression, therefore, the unemployment of the chief breadwinner is multiplied by the partial or complete unemployment of one or more other family members, male and female, who had previously not sought outside work.   This pyramiding tendency has not been sufficiently noted in discussions of the subject.

[1] Woytinsky, *op. cit.*, p. 675, shows that the BLS estimates of *employment* in manufacture and mining, transportation, trade and finance, in 1939, ran substantially below the totals based upon the reports to the Treasury established by the Social Security Board.   Thus there is a tendency for the current monthly data of the U.S. Bureau of Labor Statistics to underestimate employment, and if these estimates are used in calculating unemployment, there is likely to be an upward bias.

[2] John B. Parrish holds that a part of this number represents the tendency for members of families experiencing reduction in income to place in the labor market members who had not previously contemplated employment outside the home. Many women sought employment and appeared in the enumerations of the unemployed who were merely attempting to augment or replace male workers in the same family who could not find work.   (J. B. Parrish, The Nation's Labor Supply, *American Economic Review*, June, 1939.)

Woytinsky has stated reasons for believing that the inclusion of these additional workers in estimates of the total working force in 1930 may have rendered the total higher than technically it should have been.   He believes that the additional job figures over and above the usual workers unemployed may have varied from 10 to as much as 25 per cent.   See "Additional Workers and the Volume of Employment in the Depression," Pamphlet 1, Committee on Social Security, Social Science Research Council, Washington, D.C., January, 1940.

INDEX